Higher Mathematics

Michael Mackison

Published in 2021 by Zeta Maths Limited
Reprinted in 2022 by Bell & Bain Ltd. Glasgow

ISBN 978-1-8381410-3-5

Acknowledgements:

The author would like to acknowledge and thank Philip Moon and John Mowat for their invaluable contributions to the manuscript and editorial advice.

Also, special thanks to Alyson Bell, Erin Beveridge, Caitlin Ferrie, Peter Knak, Hannah McGeogh and Kirstin West for proofreading and checking the mathematical content.

Introduction

Some time ago now, while studying a class on the Greek language, the professor told us that what we were about to embark on would be like drinking water from a fire hose! He was trying to prepare for what we were about to study – and what he was really saying to us was that the Greek class was going to be difficult... really difficult! He wasn't wrong. Every day in class we covered a new topic and lots of new vocabulary, there was seldom any opportunity to review prior learning and, if you didn't keep up, it very quickly became overwhelming.

For many students of Higher Mathematics, the experience is very similar – you probably don't realise it yet, but you will fairly soon. There is so much new content to learn every day, in such a short time, that it can seem overwhelming – like trying to drink water from a fire hose.

This book was written to turn down the water pressure, so to speak, on the Higher Mathematics course, to make it more accessible to all learners so that the learning becomes a bit more like a water fountain than a fire hose. We have done this by breaking the course down into all the individual skills that are required, as well as including some of the more important skills from National 5. Each exercise practices one skill with increasing difficulty through the exercise. This allows learners to develop confidence in their learning, at a pace they can manage – one skill at a time.

We have kept the teaching content to a minimum and, in most cases, provided worked examples of varying difficulties at the beginning of each exercise. This means that, as a learner, there is no need to look far to find what you need. We also recognise that, more than ever, learners are using other sources of instruction to find out how to complete questions in mathematics.

With teaching content at a minimum, we have provided lots of worked examples, probably more than most learners will need, which allows teachers and learners the flexibility to choose a variety of questions from each exercise until they are confident enough to move on.

We have also included review sections of all the basic skills at the end of each chapter and at the end of the book.

Our belief is that learners learn best when they are confident about what they need to know and how to go about learning it. We hope that this resource, along with the **Zeta Maths Higher Checklist** and **Higher Homework Pack** will be a comprehensive set of learning and revision material to give every student confidence, and to equip them to achieve their very best.

Michael Mackison

Contents

How to use this book

Teaching Content

The methods and teaching that accompany each exercise are included as a guide when needed. We recognise that teachers will use their own preferred methods to teach much of the content of the course, which is one of the reasons we have kept teaching content to a minimum.

Colour Coding

Each chapter is colour-coded by the following skills: **Algebraic**, **Geometric**, **Trigonometric**, **Calculus** and **Revision**. The content may be completed in any order; however, it is recommended that Quadratic Functions is covered early on, as the skills included in this chapter are required for many other topics. We have also used colour throughout to aid understanding.

National 5 Skills

Many National 5 Skills that are important for Higher Mathematics are included in the book too. These skills are labelled in the contents pages at the beginning of each chapter and at the top of each exercise. It is *not* essential to cover these exercises – rather they are included for individuals or classes in need of review before progressing.

Calculators

All sections in which calculators may be used are marked with the calculator symbol. Some exercises may have the symbol part of the way through the exercise, which means that a calculator may be used from that point onwards.

Review Exercises

These exercises follow each chapter and allow learners to assess understanding of the basic skills for Higher and to prioritise areas for further consolidation. Please note that the **question numbers correspond to section numbers** in the chapter in the first review exercise of each chapter – though they may not be consecutive. Some chapters have a second review exercise, which develops more advanced skills.

Extra info

These sections are included in grey boxes. The information in these boxes is not necessary for Higher Mathematics, but may be useful for students looking to study beyond Higher Mathematics.

It is not necessary to cover every exercise in this book, but learners working towards Higher Mathematics should have confidence in most of the content. For further assistance, see **chapter 16** and download the **Zeta Maths Higher Checklist** to aid revision.

Chapter 1
The Straight Line

The Straight Line

A straight line on a coordinate diagram represents the relationship between two variables, usually $\boldsymbol{x}$ and $\boldsymbol{y}$. In a straight-line relationship, the rate at which one of the variables changes with respect to the other is constant, the **rate of change** is also known as the **gradient** (this will be considered more in chapters 9 and 10).

Gradient

We already know that gradient is a measure of the slope or steepness of a line and that the **gradient** of the line may be calculated by finding the vertical difference and dividing it by the horizontal difference between any two known points using the **gradient formula**:

$$m = \frac{y_2 - y_1}{x_2 - x_1}$$

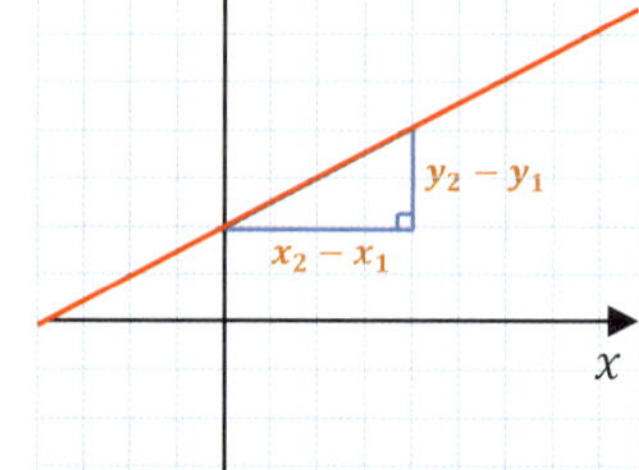

We also know that:

Parallel lines have the same gradient.

Vertical lines have an undefined gradient. These lines have the equation $x = a$, where a is a constant and is the value where the line crosses the x-axis.

Horizontal lines have zero gradient. These lines have the equation $y = c$, where c is a constant and is the value where the line crosses the y-axis.

Forms of the equation of a line

Gradient Point Form: $y - b = m(x - a)$

This is the form used to determine the equation of a line when a point (a, b) and gradient $\boldsymbol{m}$ is known. The equation should not be left in this form, but always expanded and simplified to one of the other two forms.

Gradient y-Intercept Form: $y = mx + c$

This is the most common and indeed the most useful form of the equation of a line, where $\boldsymbol{m}$ is the gradient and $\boldsymbol{c}$ is the y-intercept (**i.e.** the y-coordinate where the line crosses the y-axis). When a line is in this form, it is straightforward to determine the gradient, the y-intercept and the point of intersection between this line and another line. Where possible, it is helpful to leave the line in this form.

General Form: $ax + by + c = 0$

This is the least useful form of the equation. It can be used to write the equation of a line using whole numbers when the gradient is a fraction.

Key Fact

> To find the equation of any line, the most important thing to keep in mind is that two pieces of information are needed: **a point on the line** and the **gradient** of the line. This information can be substituted into the gradient point form of the equation of a line:
>
> $$y - b = m(x - a).$$

Exact Values

It will be extremely useful to memorise these at this stage in your learning (**see section 8.3**).

1.1 The Equation of a Line From Two Points

To determine the equation of a line, it is essential to know two pieces of information: **a point on the line** and the **gradient** of the line. If we have two coordinates, we can use these to calculate the gradient and then use either one of the coordinates to substitute into the equation of the line.

Worked Examples:

1. Find the equation of the line joining the points $(4, 1)$ and $(11, -20)$.

Points

$\overset{x_1\, y_1}{(4, 1)}$ $\overset{x_2\quad y_2}{(11, -20)}$
a b

Gradient

$$m = \frac{y_2 - y_1}{x_2 - x_1}$$
$$m = \frac{-20 - 1}{11 - 4}$$
$$m = \frac{-21}{7}$$
$$m = -3$$

Equation

$$y - b = m(x - a)$$
$$y - 1 = -3(x - 4)$$
$$y - 1 = -3x + 12$$
$$y = -3x + 13$$

2. Find the equation of the line passing through the points $(-2, 5)$ and $(6, 7)$.

Points

$\overset{x_1\, y_1}{(-2, 5)}$ $\overset{x_2\, y_2}{(6, 7)}$
a b

Gradient

$$m = \frac{y_2 - y_1}{x_2 - x_1}$$
$$m = \frac{7 - 5}{6 - (-2)}$$
$$m = \frac{2}{8}$$
$$m = \frac{1}{4}$$

Equation

$$y - b = m(x - a)$$
$$y - 5 = \frac{1}{4}(x - (-2))$$
$$4y - 20 = 1(x + 2)$$
$$4y - 20 = x + 2$$
$$x - 4y + 22 = 0$$

Exercise 1.1

1. Find the equation of the line passing through the points. Give your answer in the form $\boldsymbol{y = mx + c}$:

(a) $(4, 1)$ and $(3, -2)$
(b) $(5, 8)$ and $(3, 12)$
(c) $(7, -2)$ and $(5, 6)$
(d) $(-3, 2)$ and $(2, -8)$
(e) $(-7, 10)$ and $(-3, -6)$
(f) $(-1, -5)$ and $(-5, -17)$
(g) $(4, -7)$ and $(10, -4)$
(h) $(3, -9)$ and $(-5, 11)$
(i) $(-4, 7)$ and $(-4, 14)$

2. Find the equation of the line passing through the points.
Give your answer in the form $\boldsymbol{ax + by + c = 0}$:

(a) $(2, 2)$ and $(5, 14)$
(b) $(5, 2)$ and $(7, 10)$
(c) $(-2, 6)$ and $(5, 13)$
(d) $(-1, 1)$ and $(3, 3)$
(e) $(4, -5)$ and $(-11, -5)$
(f) $(10, -11)$ and $(-2, -2)$
(g) $(-6, 3)$ and $(1, 7)$
(h) $(-5, -10)$ and $(12, -7)$
(i) $(-3, 8)$ and $(3, -8)$

3. Find the equation of the line passing through the points. Give your answer in the form $y = mx + c$, or if the gradient is a fraction, $ay = bx + c$:

(a) $(5, 2)$ and $(-3, 18)$
(b) $(-6, 3)$ and $(10, -1)$
(c) $(1, 11)$ and $(-9, 8)$
(d) $(-4, 15)$ and $(2, -3)$
(e) $(4, -5)$ and $(-1, -6)$
(f) $(0, -8)$ and $(5, -2)$

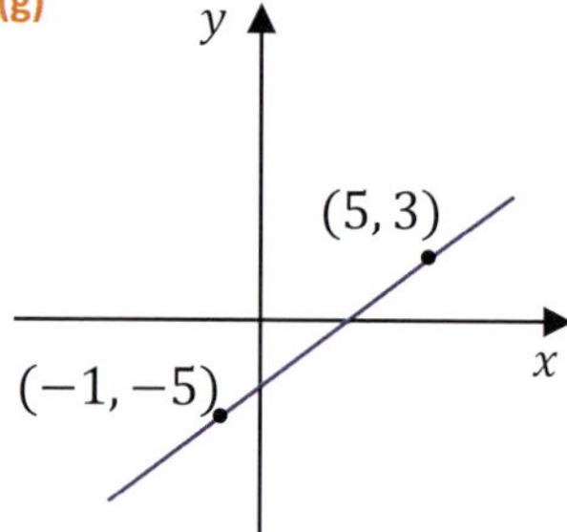

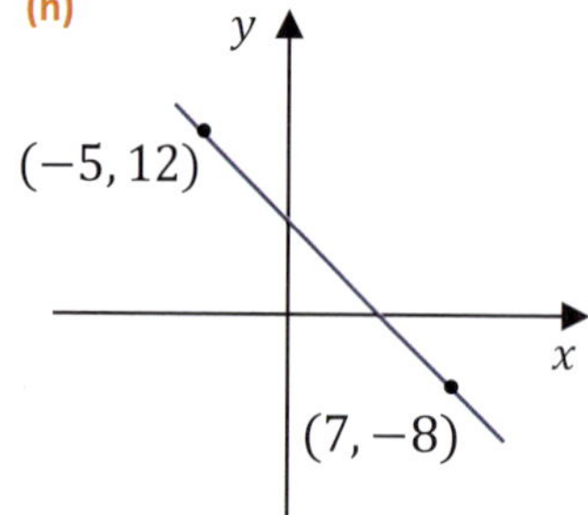

(i)

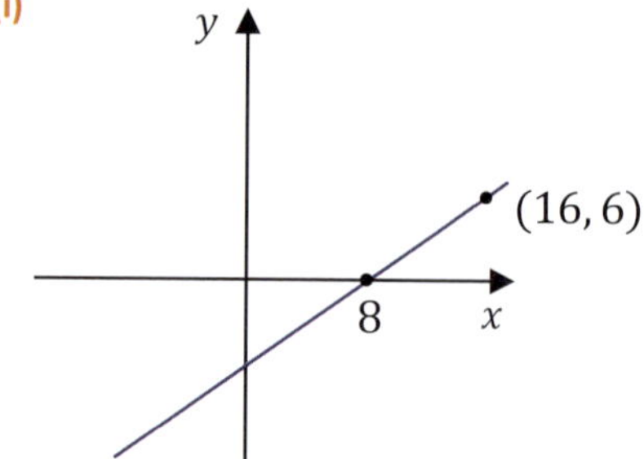

(j)

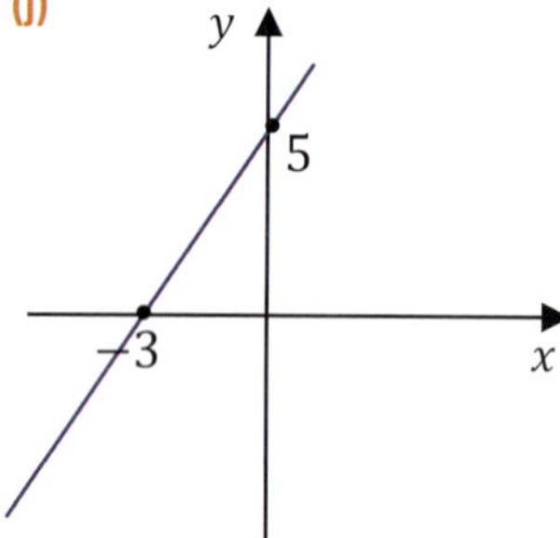

(k)

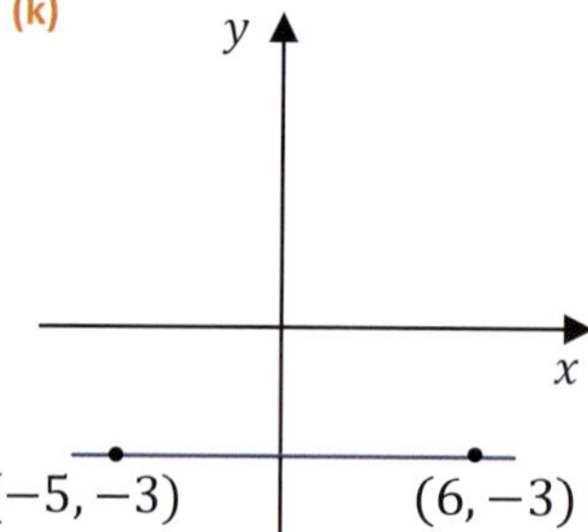

(l)

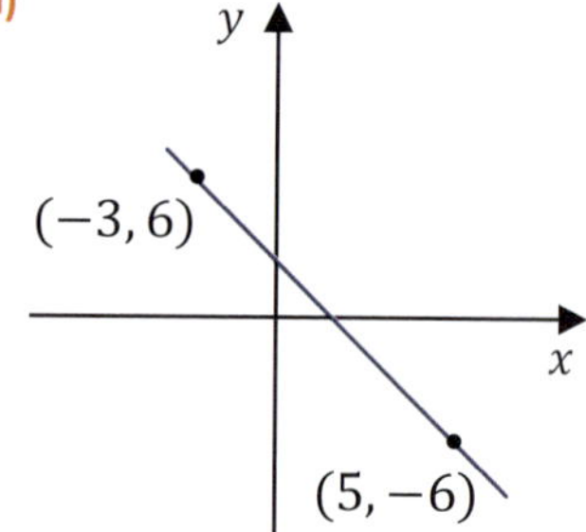

(m)

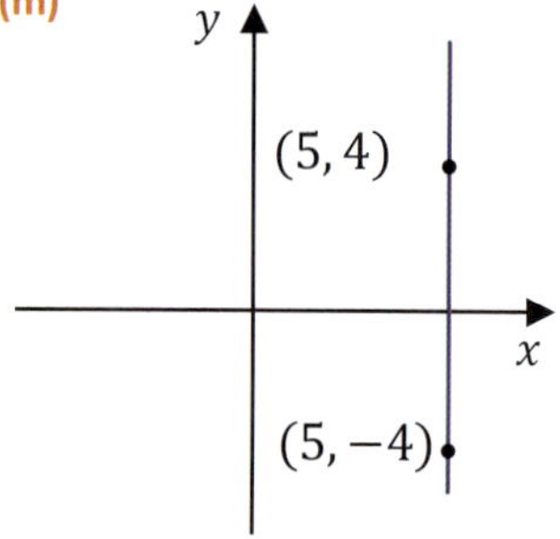

(n)

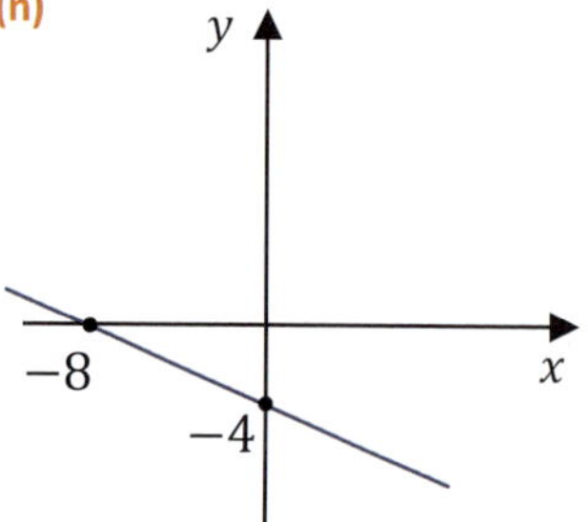

(o)

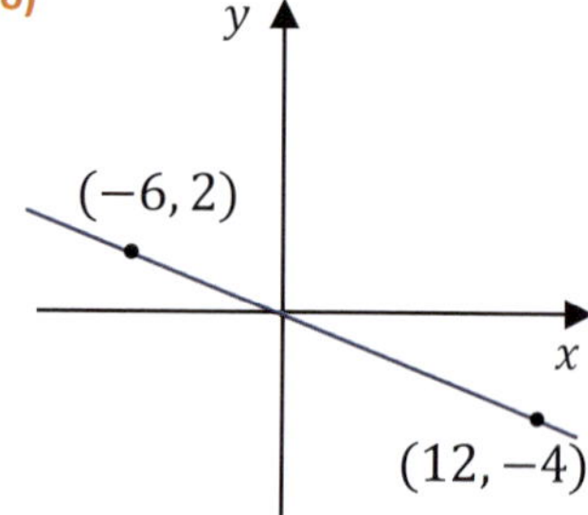

(p)

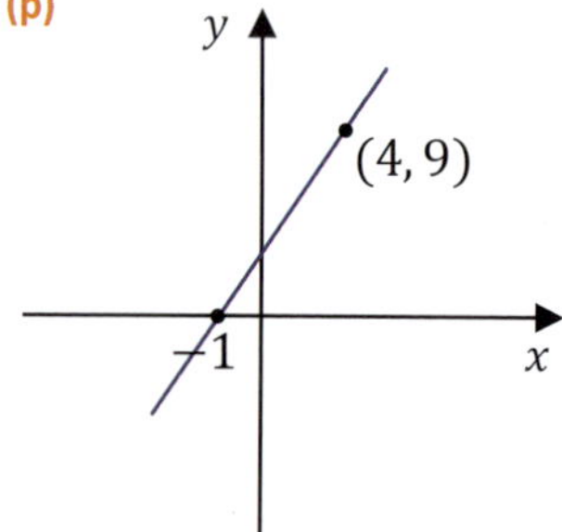

(q)

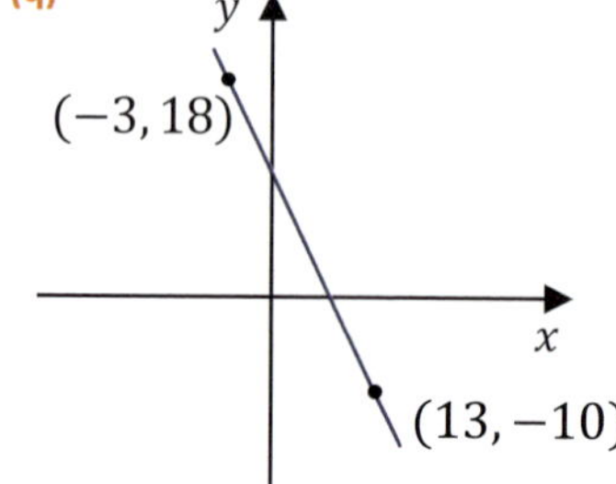

(r)

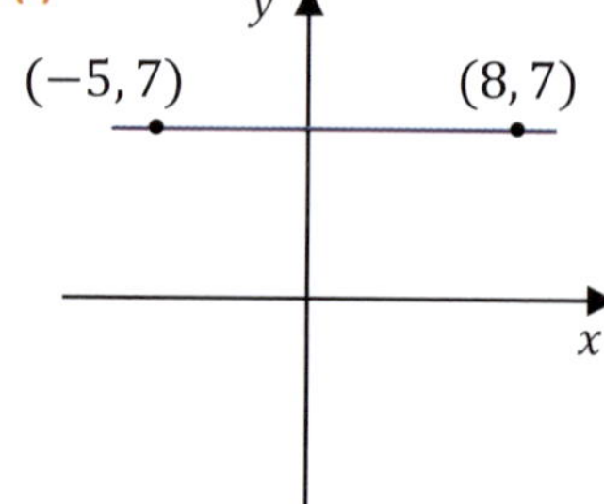

1.2 The Midpoint of a Line Segment

This is a useful skill in a number of mathematical applications. To find the midpoint of a line segment: add the x coordinates of the end points together and divide them by two, then repeat for the y coordinate.

$$\textbf{Midpoint} = \left(\frac{x_1 + x_2}{2}, \frac{y_1 + y_2}{2}\right)$$

Worked Example:

Find the midpoint of the line joining points $A(-11, 8)$ and $B(7, -14)$.

$$\text{Midpoint}_{\text{AB}} = \left(\frac{x_1 + x_2}{2}, \frac{y_1 + y_2}{2}\right)$$

$$\text{Midpoint}_{\text{AB}} = \left(\frac{-11 + 7}{2}, \frac{8 + (-14)}{2}\right)$$

$$\text{Midpoint}_{\text{AB}} = \left(\frac{-4}{2}, \frac{-6}{2}\right)$$

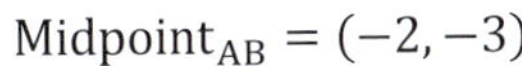

$$\text{Midpoint}_{\text{AB}} = (-2, -3)$$

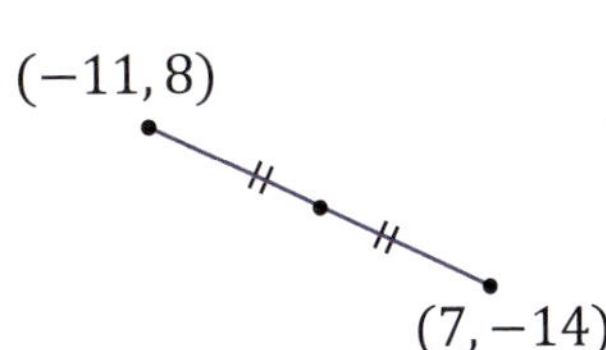

Exercise 1.2

1. Find the midpoint of the line joining the following points:

(a) A$(6, -2)$ and B$(8, 10)$ (b) C$(5, 4)$ and D$(-3, 10)$ (c) E$(1, 17)$ and F$(-11, -3)$

(d) G$(-8, 3)$ and H$(12, -9)$ (e) J$(5, -8)$ and K$(-13, 22)$ (f) L$(-12, 12)$ and M$(-2, 22)$

(g) N$(5, 9)$ and P$(-17, -11)$ (h) Q$(-7, 6)$ and R$(11, -10)$ (i) S$(-14, -17)$ and T$(16, 5)$

(j) U$(3, 2)$ and V$(15, -5)$ (k) W$(-5, -5)$ and X$(8, -8)$ (l) Y$(7, -18)$ and Z$(10, 9)$

2. A and B are points $(6, -3)$ and $(2, -9)$ respectively. M is the midpoint of AB and C is the point $(2, -4)$. Find the equation of MC.

3. D, E and F are points $(-1, 5)$, $(11, 7)$ and $(3, 10)$ respectively. Find the equation of the line joining the midpoint of DE to the point F$(3, 10)$.

4. Point N$(-5, 11)$ is the midpoint of the line joining points A$(-12, 15)$ and B(x, y). Find the coordinates of point B.

5. Point P$(7, -4)$ is the midpoint of the line segment joining points C$(15, y)$ and D$(x, -12)$. Find the coordinates of points C and D.

6. Point M is the midpoint of the line segment joining points A$(12, -3)$ and B$(-8, 15)$. Point R is the midpoint of the line segment joining points M and B. Find the coordinates of point R.

7. Point M is the midpoint of the line segment joining points $E(-15,9)$ and $F(9,-19)$. Point N is the midpoint of the line joining points E and M. Find the coordinates of point N.

8. Triangle PQR has points $P(-11,7)$, $Q(2,13)$ and $R(3,-5)$. Point M is the midpoint of the line joining points P and R. Find the equation of the line QM.

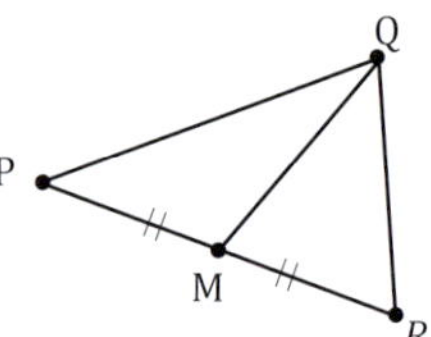

9. Triangle STU has points $S(-6,6)$, $T(8,7)$ and $U(6,-10)$. Point M is the midpoint of the line joining points S and U. Find the equation of the line TM.

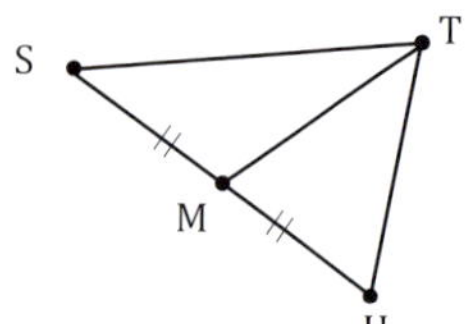

1.3 The Gradients of Perpendicular Lines

Perpendicular Lines are lines that intersect at $90°$. When lines are perpendicular, the product of their gradients is equal to -1. We write this as $\boldsymbol{m_1 \times m_2 = -1}$.

To calculate a perpendicular gradient we find the negative of the multiplicative inverse of the number. In simple terms, swap the numerator and the denominator and change the sign.

Worked Examples:

1. Find the gradient of the line perpendicular to the line joining A(−7, 2) and B(3, 7).

m_{AB}: $(3,1)$, $(9,13)$

$$m_{AB} = \frac{y_2 - y_1}{x_2 - x_1}$$

$$m_{AB} = \frac{7-2}{3-(-7)}$$

$$m_{AB} = \frac{5}{10}$$

$$m_{AB} = \frac{1}{2}$$

$$\therefore m_{\perp} = -\frac{2}{1} = -2 \qquad \text{as } m_{AB} \times m_{\perp} = -1$$

2. Find the gradient of the line perpendicular to the line with equation $3y + 2x - 4 = 0$.

$$3y + 2x - 4 = 0$$

$$3y = -2x + 4$$

$$y = -\frac{2}{3}x + \frac{4}{3}$$

$$m = -\frac{2}{3}$$

$$\therefore m_{\perp} = \frac{3}{2} \qquad \text{as m} \times m_{\perp} = -1$$

Exercise 1.3A

1. Find the gradient of a line perpendicular to the line joining each of the following points:

(a) $A(3,-2)$ and $B(5,4)$ (b) $C(-1,3)$ and $D(5,6)$ (c) $E(9,-11)$ and $F(5,9)$

(d) $G(-6,3)$ and $H(12,-6)$ (e) $J(5,-8)$ and $K(9,24)$ (f) $L(-6,0)$ and $M(1,14)$

(g) N$(6, 15)$ and P$(4, -3)$

(h) Q$(-5, 5)$ and R$(-2, -10)$

(i) S$(12, -2)$ and T$(16, 3)$

(j) U$(3, 2)$ and V$(7, -4)$

(k) W$(8, 9)$ and X$(5, 5)$

(l) Y$(2, -7)$ and Z$(-5, 9)$

Worked Examples:

1. Show that the line joining points A$(2, 3)$ and B$(5, 12)$ is perpendicular to the line joining points C$(2, -1)$ and D$(-13, 4)$.

m_{AB}: $\overset{x_1\ y_1}{(2,3)}, \overset{x_2\ y_2}{(5,12)}$

$$m_{AB} = \frac{y_2 - y_1}{x_2 - x_1}$$

$$m_{AB} = \frac{12 - 3}{5 - 2}$$

$$m_{AB} = \frac{9}{3}$$

$$m_{AB} = 3$$

m_{CD}: $\overset{x_1\ y_1}{(2,-1)}, \overset{x_2\ y_2}{(-13,4)}$

$$m_{CD} = \frac{y_2 - y_1}{x_2 - x_1}$$

$$m_{CD} = \frac{4 - (-1)}{-13 - 2}$$

$$m_{CD} = \frac{5}{-15}$$

$$m_{CD} = -\frac{1}{3}$$

$m_{AB} \times m_{CD} = -1$ $\therefore$ AB is perpendicular to CD.

2. The line joining points $(-4, -2)$ and $(8, a)$ is perpendicular to the line with gradient $m = 4$. Find the value of a.

$$m \times m_{\perp} = -1$$

$$m = 4$$

so

$$m_{\perp} = -\frac{1}{4}$$

$\overset{x_1\ y_1}{(-4,-2)}, \overset{x_2\ y_2}{(8,a)}$

$$m = \frac{y_2 - y_1}{x_2 - x_1}$$

$$-\frac{1}{4} = \frac{a - (-2)}{8 - (-4)}$$

$$-\frac{1}{4} = \frac{a + 2}{12}$$

$$-3 = a + 2$$

$$a = -5$$

Exercise 1.3B

1. Find the gradient of the line perpendicular to the line joining points A$(5, -6)$ and B$(4, 2)$.

2. Find the gradient of the line perpendicular to the line joining points C$(-6, 11)$ and D$(-2, 5)$.

3. Find the gradient of the line perpendicular to the line joining points E$(-1, 5)$ and F$(-1, 3)$.

4. Find the gradient of the line perpendicular to the line joining points G$(4, 15)$ and H$(-10, 7)$.

5. Find the gradient of the line perpendicular to the line joining points J$(8, -3)$ and K$(-15, -3)$.

6. Show that the line joining the points L$(2, 5)$ and M$(11, 2)$ is perpendicular to the line with gradient, $m = 3$.

7. Show that the line joining the points N$(-16, -1)$ and P$(14, 5)$ is perpendicular to the line with gradient, $m = -5$.

8. Show that the line joining the points Q$(-3, -3)$ and R$(3, 21)$ is perpendicular to the line joining the points S$(1, 3)$ and T$(9, 1)$.

9. Show that the line joining the points U$(15, -7)$ and V$(-15, 8)$ is perpendicular to the line joining the points W$(-4, -9)$ and X$(4, 7)$.

10. Determine whether the line joining the points $A(15, -8)$ and $B(11, 4)$ is perpendicular to the line joining the points $C(-6, -3)$ and $D(9, 2)$. Give a reason for your answer.

11. Determine whether the line joining the points $E(-9, -8)$ and $F(1, -3)$ is perpendicular to the line joining the points $G(-1, -3)$ and $H(-7, -6)$. Give a reason for your answer.

12. Determine whether the line joining the points $J(7, 2)$ and $K(15, -4)$ is perpendicular to the line joining the points $L(-5, -9)$ and $M(4, 3)$. Give a reason for your answer.

13. The line joining the points $(d, 3)$ and $(4, 9)$ is perpendicular to the line with gradient, $m = -3$. Find the value of d.

14. The line joining the points $(5, 5e)$ and (e, e^2) is perpendicular to the line with gradient, $m = -\frac{1}{6}$. Find the value of e.

15. The line joining the points $(4, 16)$ and (f, f^2) is perpendicular to the line with gradient, $m = -\frac{1}{2}$. Find the value of f.

1.4 The Gradient of a Line Using $m = \tan\theta$

There are several ways to calculate the gradient of a line. We already know that the gradient can be calculated by finding the vertical difference and dividing by the horizontal difference between two given points. We also know the gradient formula, which calculates the difference for us:

$$m = \frac{\text{Vertical difference}}{\text{horizontal difference}} \quad \text{or} \quad m = \frac{y_2 - y_1}{x_2 - x_1}$$

We can also find the gradient of a line using trigonometry. In the diagram opposite,

$$\tan\theta = \frac{\text{Opposite}}{\text{Adjacent}} = \frac{\text{Vertical difference}}{\text{horizontal difference}} = m$$

we can, therefore, use the angle that the line makes with **the positive direction of the x-axis**, namely θ, to calculate the gradient. To do this we use the property:

$$m = \tan\theta$$

When calculating θ, we are only interested in the two angles above the x-axis. If the gradient is positive, θ is acute. If the gradient is negative θ is obtuse, so we calculate the supplement of the acute angle.

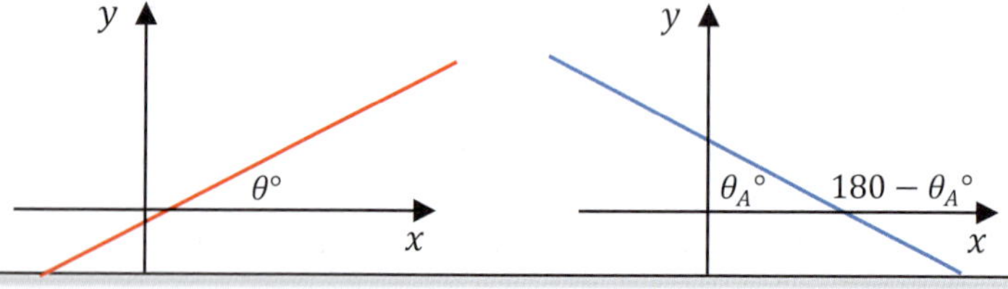

NB: When a straight line intersects the x-axis, there are always four angles.

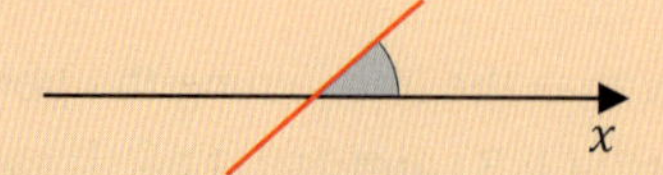

The positive direction of the x-axis is always the angle above the x-axis on the right-hand side.

Worked Examples:

1. The line, L_1, makes an angle of $30°$ with the positive direction of the x-axis. Find the gradient of the line.

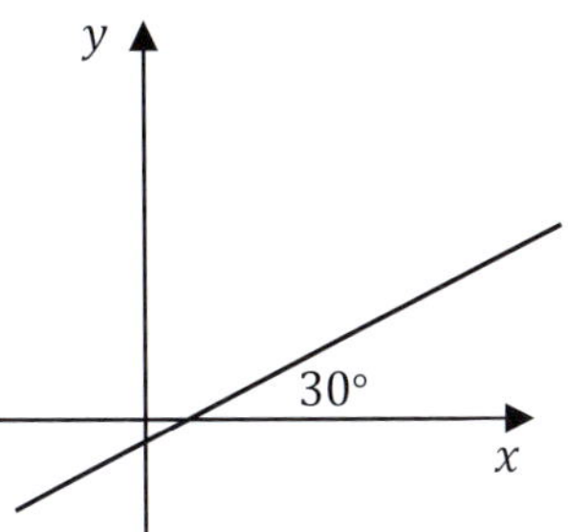

$m = \tan\theta$

$m = \tan 30°$

$m = \dfrac{1}{\sqrt{3}}$

NB: It is recommended that you learn the exact values if you do not yet know these (**see section 8.3**).

2. The line, L_2, makes an angle of $135°$ with the positive direction of the x-axis. Find the gradient of the line.

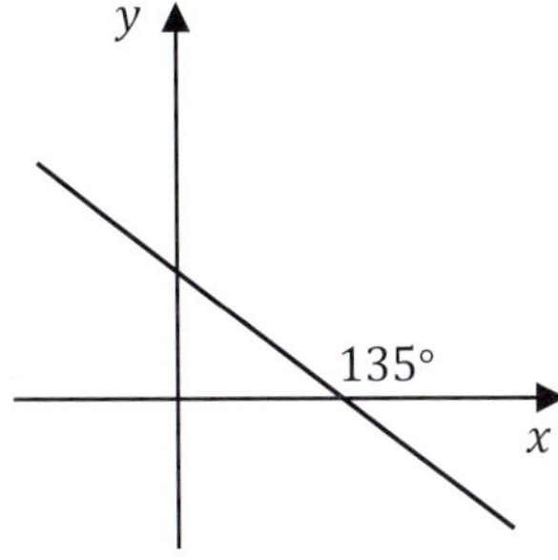

$m = \tan\theta$

$m = \tan 135° = -\tan 45°$

$m = -1$

NB: In non-calculator questions, consider the CAST diagram or another memory aid for solving trigonometric equations.

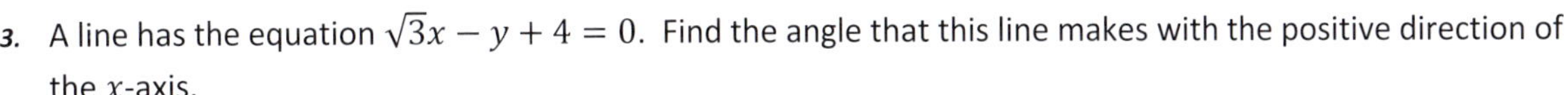

3. A line has the equation $\sqrt{3}x - y + 4 = 0$. Find the angle that this line makes with the positive direction of the x-axis.

$\sqrt{3}x - y + 4 = 0$

$y = \sqrt{3}x + 4$

$m = \sqrt{3}$

$m = \tan\theta$

$\tan\theta = \sqrt{3}$

$\theta = 60°$

4. A line has the equation $4x + 3y - 5 = 0$. Find the angle that this line makes with the positive direction of the x-axis.

$4x + 3y - 5 = 0$

$y = -\dfrac{4}{3}x + \dfrac{5}{3}$

$m = -\dfrac{4}{3}$

$m = \tan\theta$

$\tan\theta = -\dfrac{4}{3}$ (we know this is an obtuse angle as it is negative)

$\theta_A = \tan^{-1}\dfrac{4}{3} = 53.1°$

$\theta = 180° - 53.1°$

$\theta = 126.9°$

Exercise 1.4A

1. Find the gradient of a line that makes the following angle with the positive direction of the x-axis (these can all be found without a calculator using exact values):

(a) $45°$ (b) $60°$ (c) $30°$ (d) $150°$ (e) $120°$ (f) $135°$

2. A line, l, has the equation $x + y - 4 = 0$. Calculate the angle that the line makes with the positive direction of the x-axis.

3. A line, l, has the equation $x + \sqrt{3}y - 2 = 0$. Calculate the angle that the line makes with the positive direction of the x-axis.

4. A line, l, has the equation $\sqrt{3}x + y + 4 = 0$. Calculate the angle that the line makes with the positive direction of the x-axis.

5. A line, l, has the equation $3x - 3y + 8 = 0$. Calculate the angle that the line makes with the positive direction of the x-axis.

6. A line, l, has the equation $2y = \sqrt{12}x + 5$. Calculate the angle that the line makes with the positive direction of the x-axis.

7. A line, l, has the equation $5x + \sqrt{75}y - 2 = 0$. Calculate the angle that the line makes with the positive direction of the x-axis.

8. A line, l, has the equation $\sqrt{27}x + 3y + 10 = 0$. Calculate the angle that the line makes with the positive direction of the x-axis.

Exercise 1.4B

1. Find the gradient of a line that makes the following angle with the positive direction of the x-axis:

(a) $35°$ (b) $72°$ (c) $80°$ (d) $13°$ (e) $125°$ (f) $176°$

(g) $152°$ (h) $10°$ (i) $106°$ (j) $3°$ (k) $179°$ (l) $90°$

2. A line, l, has the equation $2x - y - 4 = 0$. Calculate the angle that the line makes with the positive direction of the x-axis.

3. A line, l, has the equation $4x - 3y + 6 = 0$. Calculate the angle that the line makes with the positive direction of the x-axis.

4. A line, l, has the equation $x + 3y + 7 = 0$. Calculate the angle that the line makes with the positive direction of the x-axis.

5. A line, l, has the equation $2x + 5y + 5 = 0$. Calculate the angle that the line makes with the positive direction of the x-axis.

6. A line, l, has the equation $6x - 5y - 12 = 0$. Calculate the angle that the line makes with the positive direction of the x-axis.

7. A line, l, has the equation $5x + 4y - 2 = 0$. Calculate the angle that the line makes with the positive direction of the x-axis.

1.5 Collinearity

The term **collinear** describes points or coordinates that are in line with one another, **i.e.** they lie on the same line. If two line segments share the same gradient, then the line segments are parallel, if both these line segments share a common point, then both line segments are in line and, therefore, the points are collinear.

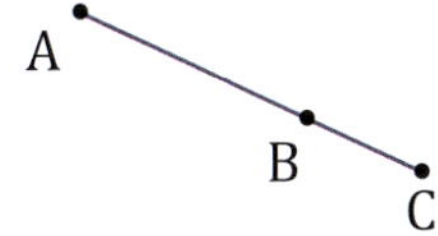

$m_{AB} = m_{BC}$ and point B is common, ∴ points A, B and C **are** collinear.

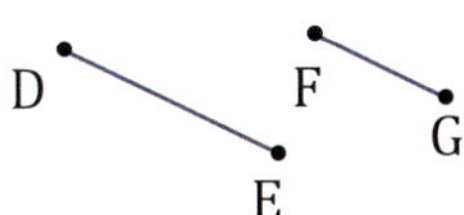

$m_{DE} = m_{FG}$ but these gradients do not share a common point, ∴ points D, E, F and G are **not** collinear.

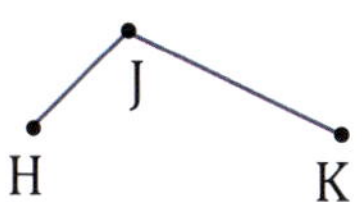

$m_{HJ} \neq m_{JK}$, ∴ points H, J and K are **not** collinear.

In order to show points are collinear, calculate the gradient of any two line segments joining two pairs of points. These segments must have the same gradient and one of the points must be common to both gradient calculations.

Worked Examples:

1. Show that the points $A(-5,3)$, $B(2,-11)$ and $C(4,-15)$ are collinear.

$\overset{x_1\ y_1}{A(-5,3)}, \overset{x_2\ y_2}{B(2,-11)}$

$$m_{AB} = \frac{y_2 - y_1}{x_2 - x_1}$$
$$m_{AB} = \frac{-11-3}{2-(-4)}$$
$$m_{AB} = \frac{-14}{7}$$
$$m_{AB} = -2$$

$\overset{x_1\ y_1}{B(2,-11)}, \overset{x_2\ y_2}{C(4,-15)}$

$$m_{BC} = \frac{y_2 - y_1}{x_2 - x_1}$$
$$m_{BC} = \frac{-15-(-11)}{4-2}$$
$$m_{BC} = \frac{-4}{2}$$
$$m_{BC} = -2$$

$m_{AB} = m_{BC}$ and point B is common, ∴ points A, B and C are collinear.

2. Determine whether the points $D(2,-8)$, $E(6,4)$ and $F(8,8)$ are collinear.

$\overset{x_1\ y_1}{D(2,-8)}, \overset{x_2\ y_2}{E(6,4)}$

$$m_{DE} = \frac{y_2 - y_1}{x_2 - x_1}$$
$$m_{DE} = \frac{4-(-8)}{6-2}$$
$$m_{DE} = \frac{12}{4}$$
$$m_{DE} = 3$$

$\overset{x_1\ y_1}{E(6,4)}, \overset{x_2\ y_2}{F(8,8)}$

$$m_{EF} = \frac{y_2 - y_1}{x_2 - x_1}$$
$$m_{EF} = \frac{8-4}{8-6}$$
$$m_{EF} = \frac{4}{2}$$
$$m_{EF} = 2$$

$m_{DE} \neq m_{EF}$, ∴ points D, E and F are not collinear.

Exercise 1.5

1. Show that the following sets of points are collinear:

(a) $A(-12,-10)$, $B(2,-3)$ and $C(10,1)$

(b) $D(-1,-8)$, $E(1,-2)$ and $F(5,10)$

(c) $G(-4,0)$, $H(8,3)$ and $J(20,6)$

(d) $K(-12,10)$, $L(-6,8)$ and $M(12,2)$

(e) $N(-8,14)$, $P(8,2)$ and $Q(20,-7)$

(f) $R(-12,-19)$, $S(12,13)$ and $T(15,17)$

(g) $U(-20,12)$, $V(-10,8)$ and $W(10,0)$

(h) $X(-21,-2)$, $Y(-7,0)$ and $Z(14,3)$

2. Determine whether the following sets of points are collinear:

(a) $A(2,2)$, $B(14,8)$ and $C(18,12)$

(b) $D(-8,6)$, $E(-4,0)$ and $F(12,-24)$

(c) $G(-6,-22)$, $H(2,2)$ and $J(4,10)$

(d) $K(-8,-11)$, $L(8,1)$ and $M(20,13)$

(e) $N(-12,22)$, $P(-4,12)$ and $Q(16,-13)$

(f) $R(-10,41)$, $S(-4,17)$ and $T(4,-11)$

(g) $U(-20,-15)$, $V(20,9)$ and $W(35,18)$

(h) $X(-54,9)$, $Y(-36,7)$ and $Z(90,-6)$

3. The points $A(-10,19)$, $B(14,-5)$ and $C(x,-11)$ are collinear. Calculate the value of x.

4. The points $D(-14,29)$, $E(x,9)$ and $F(26,-31)$ are collinear. Calculate the value of x.

5. The points $G(4,-10)$, $H(18,y)$ and $J(32,-4)$ are collinear. Calculate the value of y.

6. The points $K(-7,-43)$, $L(1,-7)$ and $M(3,y)$ are collinear. Calculate the value of y.

1.6 The Equation of a Line from a Point and a Gradient

National 5 Skills

To find the equation of any line, the most important thing to keep in mind is that two pieces of information are needed: **a point on the line** and the **gradient** of the line. This information can be substituted into the general form of the equation of a line $\boldsymbol{y - b = m(x - a)}$.

Worked Example:

Find the equation of the line which passes through $(3,2)$ and is parallel to the line with equation $3y + 2x = 3$.

Point	Gradient	Equation
$(3,2)$ $a\ b$	$3y + 2x = 3$	$y - b = m(x - a)$
	$3y = -2x + 3$	$y - 2 = -\frac{2}{3}(x - 3)$
	$y = -\frac{2}{3}x + 1$	$y - 2 = -\frac{2}{3}x + 2$
	$m = -\frac{2}{3}$	$y = -\frac{2}{3}x - 4$

Exercise 1.6

1. Find the equation of the line which passes through $(3, 5)$ and intersects the y-axis at $y = 1$.

2. Find the equation of the line which passes through $(6, 8)$ and is parallel to the line with equation $y = 2x + 5$.

3. Find the equation of the line which passes through $(4, 3)$ and is perpendicular to the line with equation $y = 3x - 2$.

4. Find the equation of the line which intersects the x-axis at $x = 8$ and is perpendicular to the line with equation $2x + 3y - 2 = 0$.

5. Find the equation of the line which intersects the y-axis at $y = -3$ and is perpendicular to the line with equation $3x - 2y - 1 = 0$.

6. Find the equation of the line which passes through $(-7, 11)$ and the midpoint of the line joining points $\mathrm{A}(4, 7)$ and $\mathrm{B}(15, -6)$.

7. Find the equation of the line which passes through $(9, 1)$ and the midpoint of the line joining points $\mathrm{C}(-3, 10)$ and $\mathrm{B}(5, 8)$.

8. Find the equation of each line in the following diagrams:

(a)

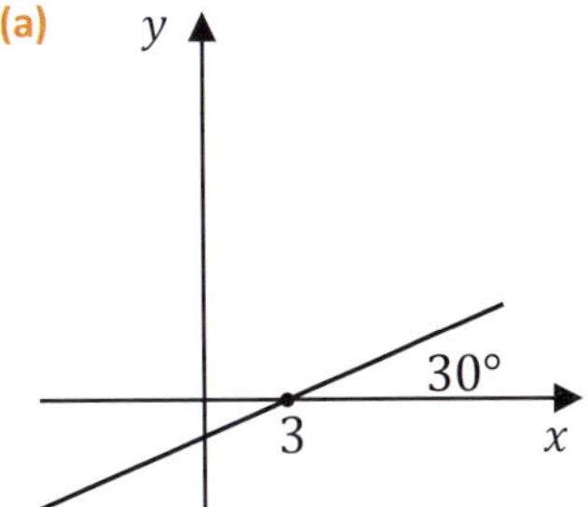

(b)

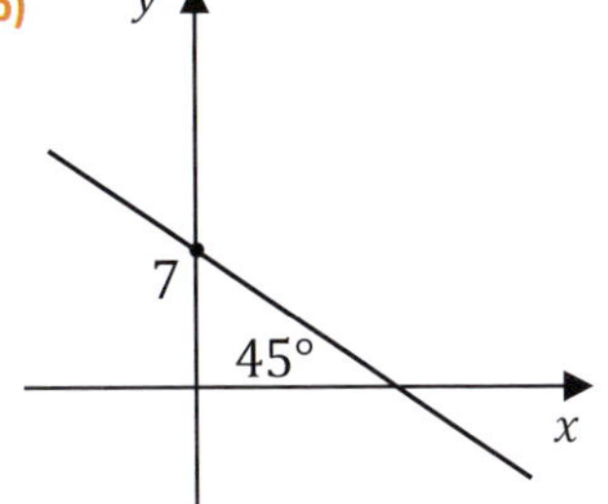

(c)

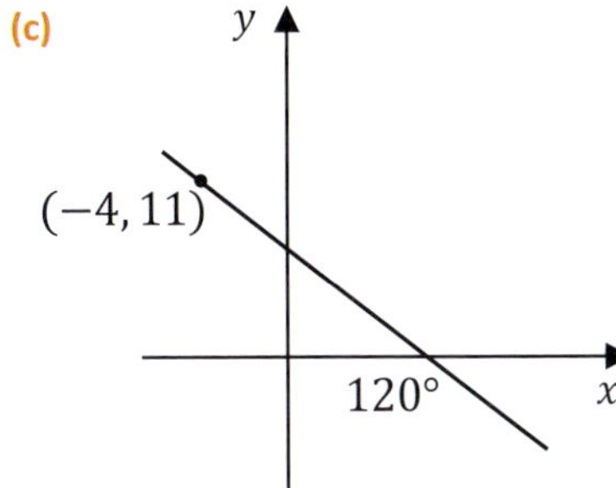

1.7 Finding the Point of Intersection of Lines

National 5 Skills

To find the point of intersection of a pair of lines, we use **simultaneous equations**. For simultaneous equations involving two unknowns, there are two common methods: solving by **substitution** or by **elimination**. Often the easiest method to use is **substitution**, we can do this if one of the equations has an unknown with a coefficient equal to one, or if the unknown is of equal or easily scalable value in both equations.

For example, if you have two lines with equations $2x - y = 7$ and $y = 3x - 11$, the second equation can be substituted straight into the first equation to give $2x - (3x - 11) = 7$. This can then be easily solved.

At Higher level we should be competent using any suitable method to find the point of intersection of any pair of lines.

Worked Examples:

1. Find the point of intersection of the lines $2x - y = 8$ and $3x + y = 17$.

Solution (using substitution):

Rearrange one or both equations:

$$\mathbf{2x - y = 8} \qquad \mathbf{3x + y = 17}$$
$$\mathbf{y = 2x - 8} \qquad \mathbf{y = -3x + 17}$$

Substitute $y = 2x - 8$ into $y = -3x + 17$

$$\mathbf{2x - 8 = -3x + 17}$$
$$5x = 25$$
$$x = 5$$

Substitute $x = 5$ into $y = 2x - 8$

$$y = 10 - 8$$
$$y = 2$$

∴ Point of intersection $(5, 2)$.

2. Find the point of intersection of the lines $2x + 3y = 3$ and $x + 4y = -1$.

Solution (using elimination):

	$2x + 3y = 3$	**(A)**
	$x + 4y = -1$	**(B)**
(A) × 4	$8x + 12y = 12$	**(C)**
(B) × −3	$-3x - 12y = 3$	**(D)**
(C)+(D)	$5x \quad = 15$	
	$x = 3$	

Substitute $x = 3$ into **(A).**

$$2(3) + 3y = 3$$
$$6 + 3y = 3$$
$$3y = -3$$
$$y = -1$$

∴ Point of intersection $(3, -1)$.

Exercise 1.7

Find the point of intersection of each of the following pairs of lines:

1. $x + 2y = 6$, $y = 3x - 4$
2. $y = 3x - 14$, $y = 6 - 2x$
3. $2x + 3y = -3$, $3x - 2y = -11$
4. $3x - 2y - 22 = 0$, $2x + 3y + 20 = 0$
5. $3x - 2y - 13 = 0$, $x - 3y = 2$
6. $3y = 2x - 6$, $5x - 3y = 24$
7. $2x - 5y - 18 = 0$, $x = 2y + 7$
8. $3x + 4y = 27$, $2x + 3y = 19$
9. $y = 10 + 2x$, $y = 5x + 49$
10. $x + 2y = 2$, $3x + 5y - 11 = 0$
11. $3x + 2y - 24 = 0$, $x + y = 11$
12. $3y = 4x + 29$, $6y = 8 - 2x$
13. $6x + 4y - 15 = 0$, $y = 2x + 2$
14. $y = 4x - 15$, $y = 13 - 3x$
15. $4x + 5y = 11$, $x + 3y = 8$
16. $x - 3y - 20 = 0$, $3x + 6y - 15 = 0$
17. $3y = 1 - 5x$, $9x + 6y + 6 = 0$
18. $5x - 4y = 32$, $3x + 2y = 17$
19. $12x + 3y + 21 = 0$, $y = 4x - 9$
20. $x + 3y + 7 = 0$, $3x - 4y = 31$
21. $x + 2y = 4$, $4y = x - 7$
22. $y = 3x + 13$, $y = 8 - 2x$
23. $9x + y = -4$, $3x - 2y = 15$
24. $x + 2y = 0$, $3x + 4y - 2 = 0$

1.8 Perpendicular Bisectors

A **perpendicular bisector** of a line segment is a line that cuts the line segment **in half** (bisects) at **right-angles** (perpendicularly). In the diagram opposite, CD is a perpendicular bisector of AB.

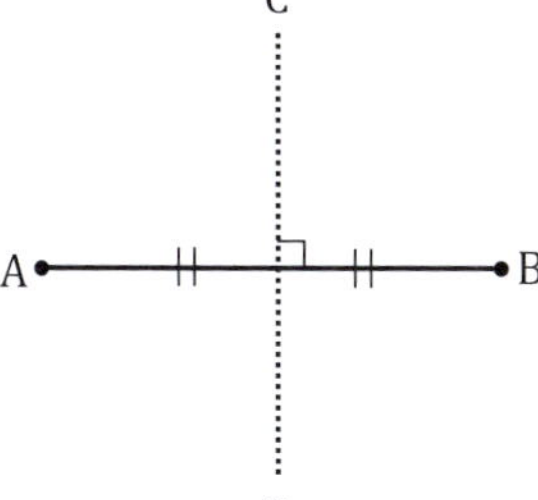

To find the equation of a perpendicular bisector, a **gradient** and a **point** on the line are needed. The **gradient** is normally calculated by finding the gradient of AB and then calculating the perpendicular gradient. The **point** is the midpoint of AB.

NB: it is always good practice to sketch a diagram of the line we need to find.

Worked Examples:

Find the equation of the perpendicular bisector of AB in the diagram.

A(−3, 8)

B(5, 2)

Solution: $A(\underset{x_1}{-3},\underset{y_1}{8}),\ B(\underset{x_2}{5},\underset{y_2}{2})$

Point

$$\text{Midpoint}_{AB} = \left(\frac{x_1+x_2}{2},\frac{y_1+y_2}{2}\right)$$

$$\text{Midpoint}_{AB} = \left(\frac{-3+5}{2},\frac{8+2}{2}\right)$$

$$\text{Midpoint}_{AB} = \left(\frac{2}{2},\frac{10}{2}\right)$$

$$\text{Midpoint}_{AB} = (\underset{a}{1},\underset{b}{5})$$

Gradient

$$m_{AB} = \frac{y_2-y_1}{x_2-x_1}$$

$$m_{AB} = \frac{2-8}{5-(-3)}$$

$$m_{AB} = \frac{-6}{8}$$

$$m_{AB} = -\frac{3}{4}$$

$$\therefore m_{\perp} = \frac{4}{3} \quad \text{as } m_{AB}\times m_{\perp} = -1$$

Equation

$$y - b = m(x - a)$$

$$y - 5 = \frac{4}{3}(x-1)$$

$$3y - 15 = 4x - 4$$

$$4x - 3y + 11 = 0$$

$$\text{or } 3y = 4x + 11$$

Exercise 1.8

1. Find the equation of the perpendicular bisector of the line joining each pair of points. Give your answer in the form $y = mx + c$ or $ay = bx + c$ if the gradient is a fraction:

(a) $A(-3,-2)$ and $B(1,10)$ (b) $C(2,14)$ and $D(-18,4)$ (c) $E(-9,3)$ and $F(1,5)$

(d) $G(-12,1)$ and $H(8,-3)$ (e) $J(-9,2)$ and $K(11,6)$ (f) $L(4,3)$ and $M(-14,-3)$

(g) $N(15,-4)$ and $P(-3,-12)$ (h) $Q(-7,6)$ and $R(11,-10)$ (i) $S(-13,-1)$ and $T(17,5)$

(j) $U(3,-1)$ and $V(9,1)$ (k) $W(4,-5)$ and $X(-8,-2)$ (l) $Y(4,-2)$ and $Z(12,-2)$

2. Find the equation of the perpendicular bisector of the line joining each pair of points. Give your answer in the form $ax + by + c = 0$:

(a) $A(2,6)$ and $B(8,10)$ (b) $C(5,-4)$ and $D(-2,10)$ (c) $E(1,17)$ and $F(-4,-3)$

(d) $G(-7,3)$ and $H(1,-5)$ (e) $J(5,-8)$ and $K(5,4)$ (f) $L(-12,12)$ and $M(-6,8)$

(g) N$(5, 9)$ and P$(1, 3)$ **(h)** Q$(-7, 2)$ and R$(11, -10)$ **(i)** S$(-4, -11)$ and T$(16, 5)$

(j) U$(-1, -1)$ and V$(9, 5)$ **(k)** W$(1, -5)$ and X$(-13, 1)$ **(l)** Y$(7, -18)$ and Z$(1, -10)$

Higher Extension

In any triangle, the perpendicular bisectors of each of the sides are **concurrent**, **i.e.** they all intersect at the same point. The point where three perpendicular bisectors intersect is known as the **circumcentre** of the triangle.

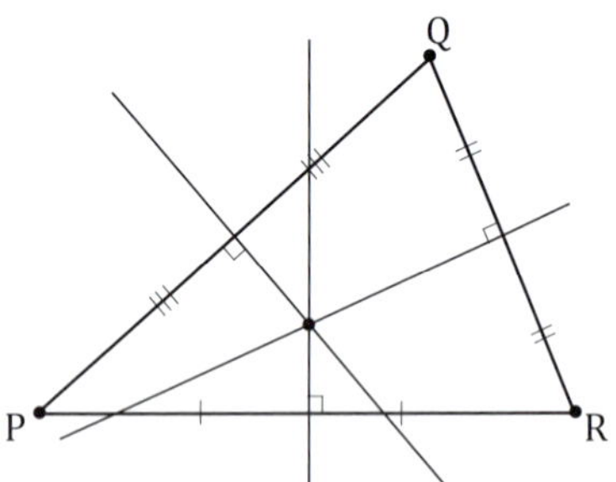

Extra Info

The **circumcentre** of a triangle is the centre of the circle passing through the three vertices of the triangle. This circle is known as the **circumcircle**.

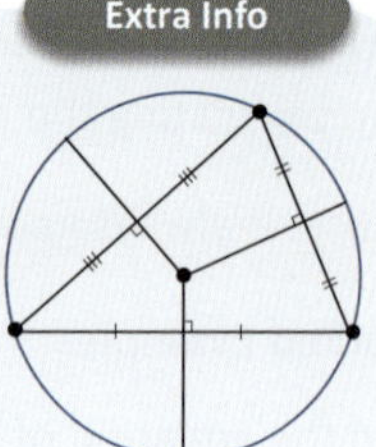

We calculate the circmumcentre by finding the point of intersection of **any two** of the perpendicular bisectors.

3. Calculate the circumcentre of each of the following triangles:

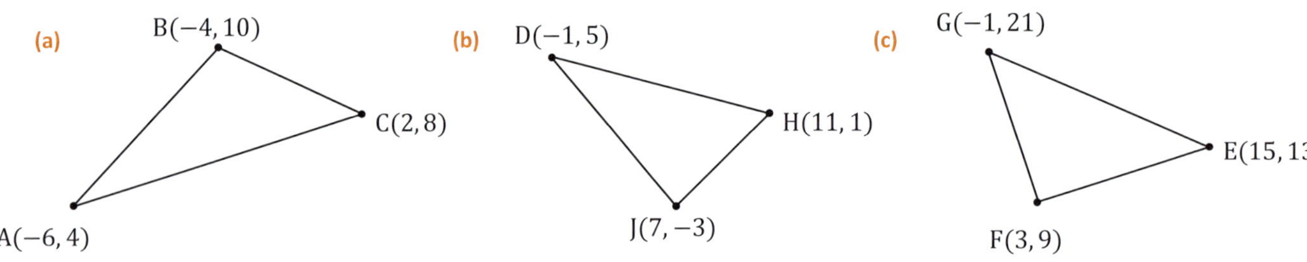

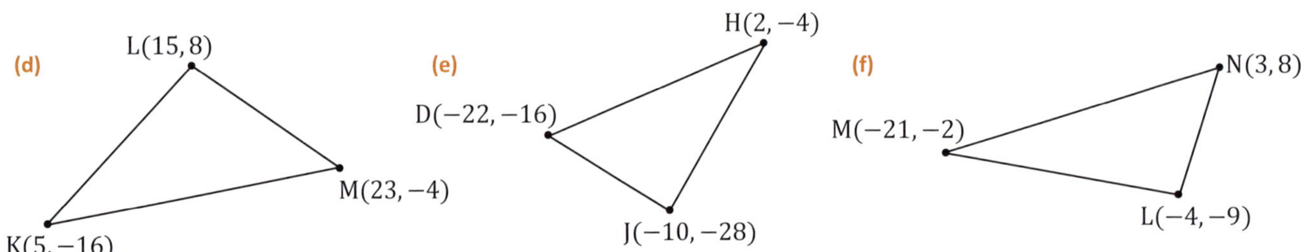

1.9 Medians

A **median** in a triangle is a line segment that connects one vertex to the midpoint of the opposite side.

To find the equation of a median, as always, a **point** and the **gradient** of the line are needed. The **point** can be taken from the given vertex and the **gradient** is calculated by finding the midpoint of the opposite side, then using it with the given vertex to calculate the gradient.

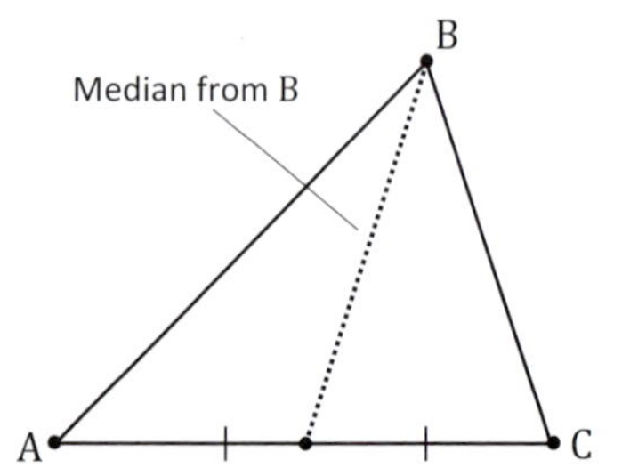

NB: It is always good practice to sketch the triangle and add the line and information.

Worked Example:

Find the equation of the median from B.

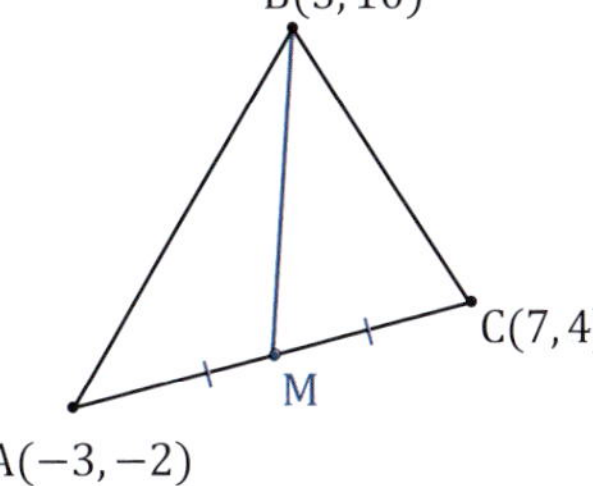

Solution:

Start by drawing the triangle and marking the median and point M in the diagram.

Point	Gradient		Equation
$\overset{x_1\ y_1}{\underset{a\ \ b}{B(3,10)}}$	$M = \left(\frac{x_1 + x_2}{2}, \frac{y_1 + y_2}{2}\right)$	$m_{BM} = \frac{y_2 - y_1}{x_2 - x_1}$	$y - \boldsymbol{b} = m(x - \boldsymbol{a})$
	$M = \left(\frac{-3 + 7}{2}, \frac{-2 + 4}{2}\right)$	$m_{BM} = \frac{1 - 10}{2 - 3}$	$y - 10 = 9(x - 3)$
	$M = \overset{x_2\ y_2}{(2, 1)}$	$m_{BM} = \frac{-9}{-1}$	$y - 10 = 9x - 27$
		$m_{BM} = 9$	$9x - y - 17 = 0$

NB: When sketching a triangle, imagine a coordinate axis and consider the relative positions of each point.

Exercise 1.9

1. Sketch the triangle and find the equation of the median from C in each of the following sets of points. Give your answer in the form $\boldsymbol{y = mx + c}$ or $\boldsymbol{ay = bx + c}$ if the gradient is a fraction:

(a) A(10, 5), B(−8, 3), C(−3, 12)
(b) D(−5, 2), C(3, −10), E(−7, 6)
(c) C(4, 11), F(11, 6), G(−15, −8)
(d) H(−9, 1), C(10, 26), J(23, 15)
(e) K(−19, −3), C(3, 16), L(21, 11)
(f) C(3, 11), M(4, 22), N(26, 8)

2. Sketch the triangle and find the equation of the median from C in each pair of following sets of points. Give your answer in the form $\boldsymbol{ax + by + c = 0}$:

(a) A(−15, −8), C(−10, 23), B(11, −10)
(b) D(−7, 2), C(1, 4), E(3, −4)
(c) F(−11, 1), C(4, 7), G(7, −5)
(d) H(−9, −6), C(−3,7), J(15, 2)
(e) C(−9, 2), K(−1, 9), L(9, 1)
(f) C(−15, 10), M(9, 6), N(1, −2)

Higher Extension

In any triangle, the three medians are **concurrent**, **i.e.** they all intersect at the same point. The point where three medians intersect is known as the **centroid** of the triangle.

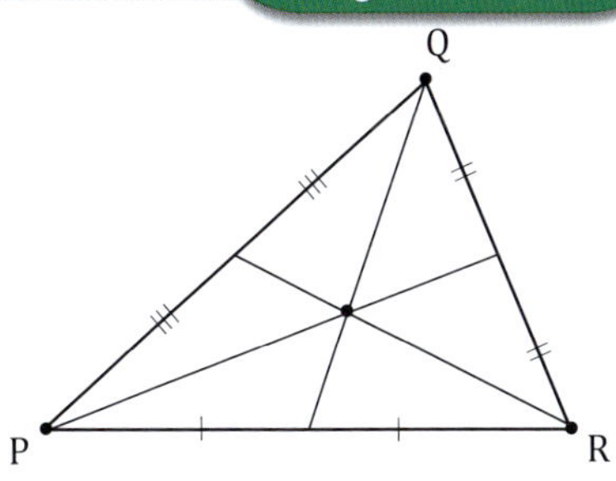

Extra Info

A **median** cuts the area of a triangle in half. The **centroid** of a triangle cuts the medians in the ratio 1:2. The areas of the six small triangles formed by three medians are equal.

We calculate the centroid by finding the point of intersection of **any two** of the medians.

3. Calculate the centroid of each of the following triangles:

(a)

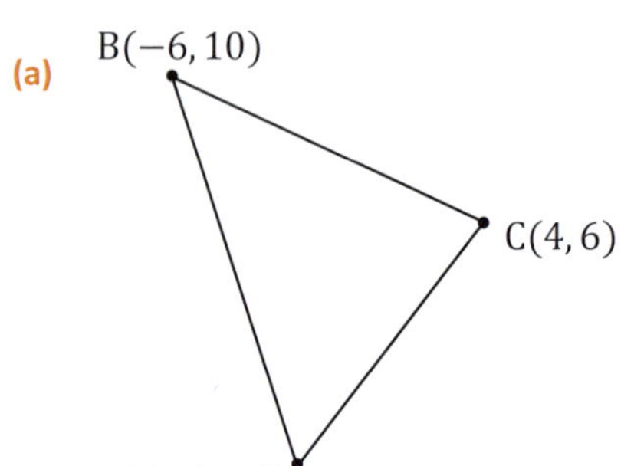

(b)

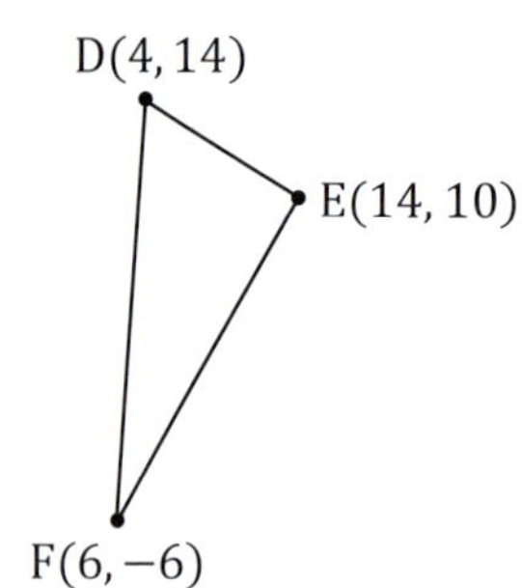

(c)

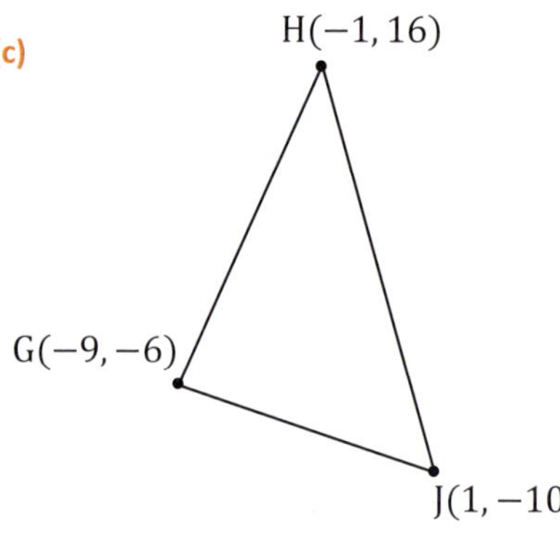

(d)

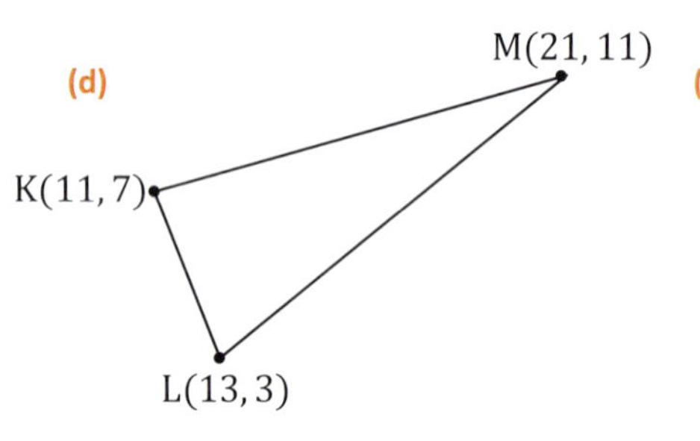

(e)

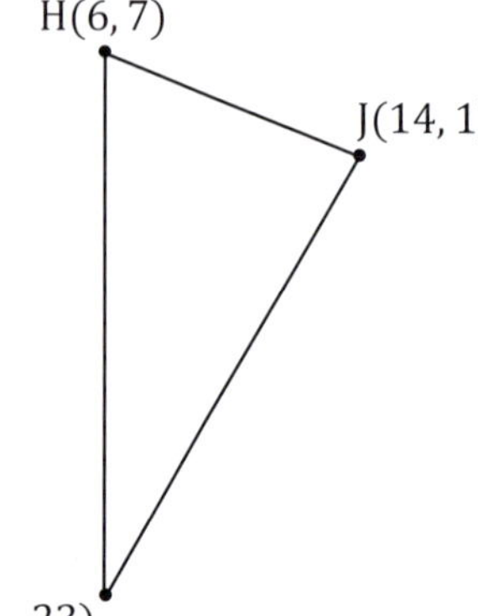

(f)

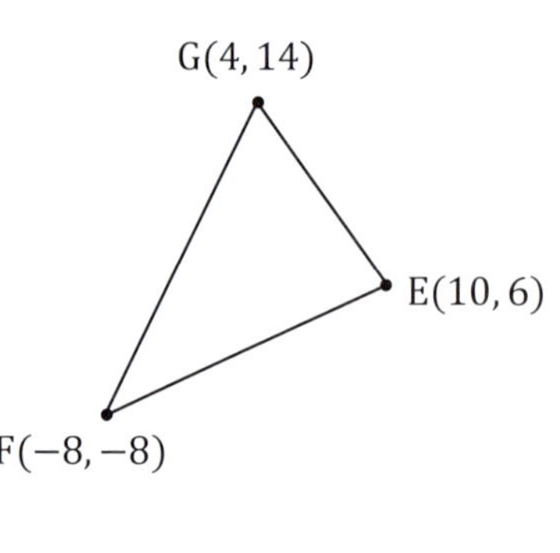

1.10 Altitudes

An **altitude** in a triangle is a line segment from one vertex perpendicular to the opposite side.

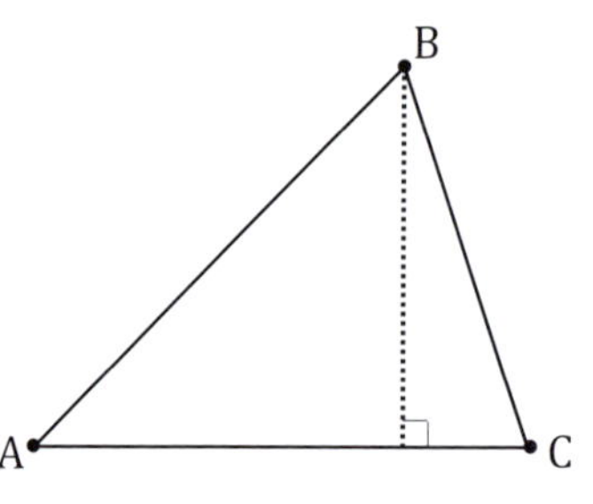

To find the equation of an altitude, as always, a **point** and **gradient** on the line are needed. The **point** can be taken from the given vertex and the **gradient** is calculated by finding the gradient of the opposite side, then using the property of perpendicular gradients.

Worked Example:

Find the equation of the altitude from B.

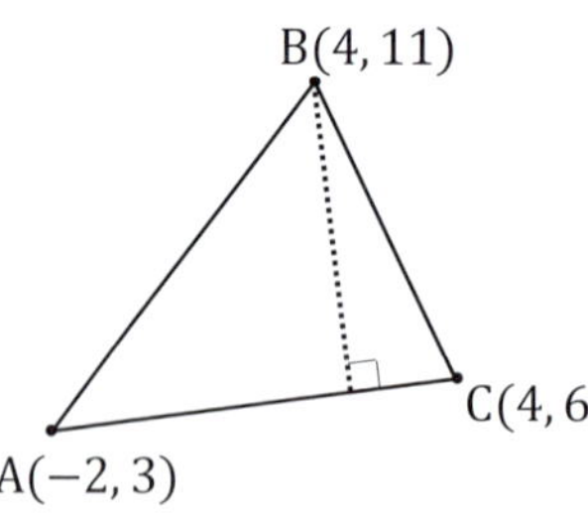

Solution:

Point

B(4, 11)
(a = 4, b = 11)

Gradient

A(−2, 3), C(4, 6)
(x_1, y_1 and x_2, y_2)

$$m_{AC} = \frac{y_2 - y_1}{x_2 - x_1}$$

$$m_{AC} = \frac{6 - 3}{4 - (-2)}$$

$$m_{AC} = \frac{1}{2}$$

$\therefore \boldsymbol{m_\perp} = -2$ as $m_{AC} \times m_\perp = -1$

Equation

$$y - \boldsymbol{b} = \boldsymbol{m}(x - \boldsymbol{a})$$

$$y - 11 = -2(x - 4)$$

$$y - 11 = -2x + 8$$

$$2x + y - 19 = 0$$

Exercise 1.10

1. Sketch the triangle and find the equation of the altitude from A in each of the following sets of points. Give your answer in the form $y = mx + c$ or $ay = bx + c$ if the gradient is a fraction:

(a) $A(-4,-4)$, $B(-6,12)$, $C(4,7)$

(b) $D(-10,-4)$, $E(-5,11)$, $A(1,-1)$

(c) $C(-10,-3)$, $A(-2,13)$, $G(8,3)$

(d) $H(2,-1)$, $A(4,15)$, $J(17,2)$

(e) $A(2,-1)$, $K(2,12)$, $L(20,0)$

(f) $A(-5,5)$, $M(20,65)$, $N(80,-25)$

2. Sketch the triangle and find the equation of the median from A in each pair of the following sets of points. Give your answer in the form $ax + by + c = 0$:

(a) $A(-7,1)$, $C(2,14)$, $B(14,-2)$

(b) $A(-4,-6)$, $D(1,9)$, $E(13,0)$

(c) $F(4,-11)$, $A(8,8)$, $G(19,-5)$

(d) $H(-6,-13)$, $J(0,11)$, $A(13,-5)$

(e) $K(-9,-10)$, $L(-1,2)$, $A(6,-7)$

(f) $A(-16,-13)$, $M(-3,-2)$, $N(3,-17)$

Higher Extension

In any triangle, the three altitudes are **concurrent**, **i.e.** they all intersect at the same point. The point where three altitudes intersect is known as the **orthocentre**.

We calculate the orthocentre by finding the point of intersection of **any two** of the altitudes.

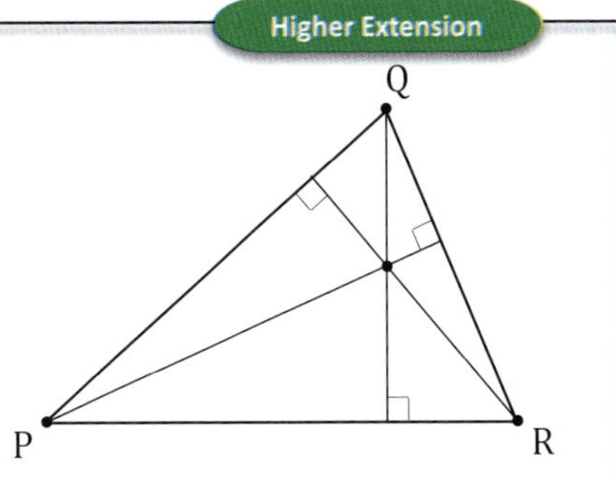

3. Calculate the orthocentre of each of the following triangles:

(a)

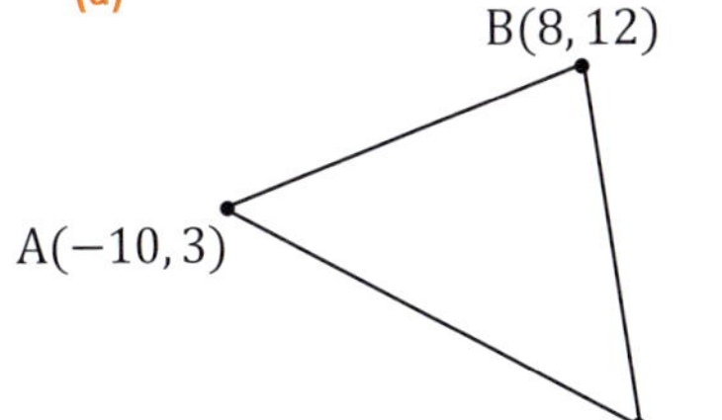

(b)

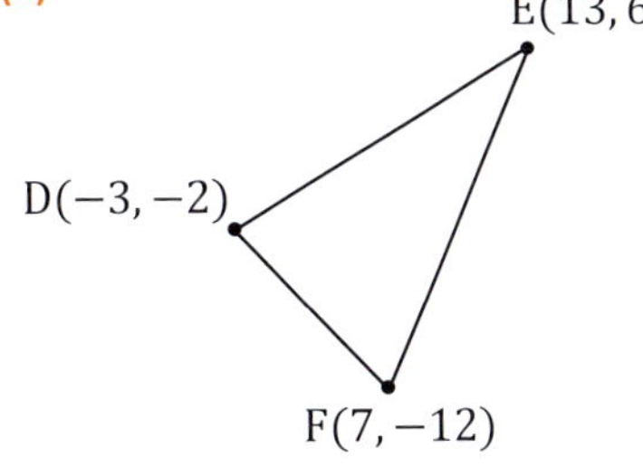

(c)

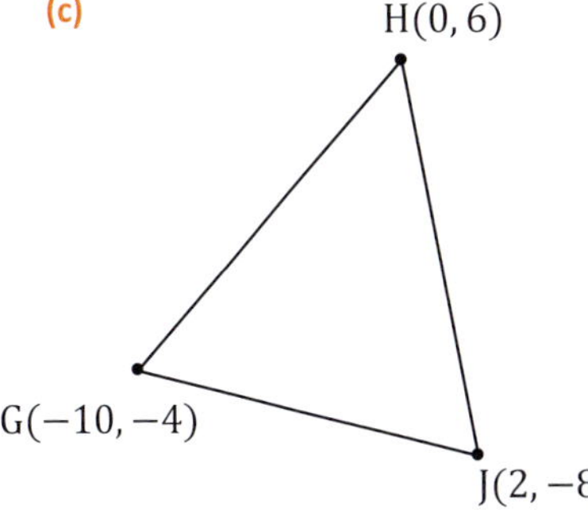

(d)

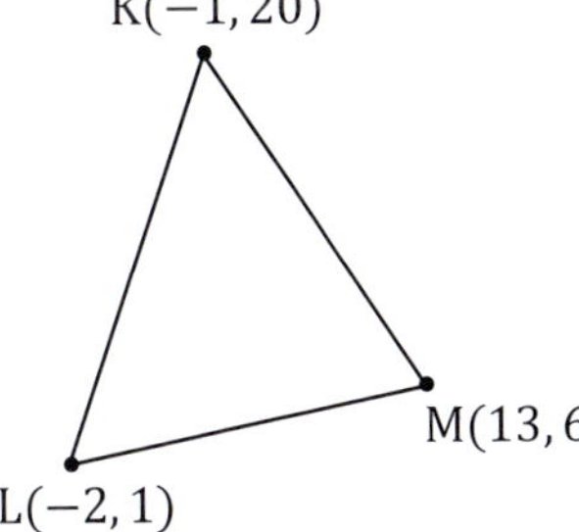

(e)

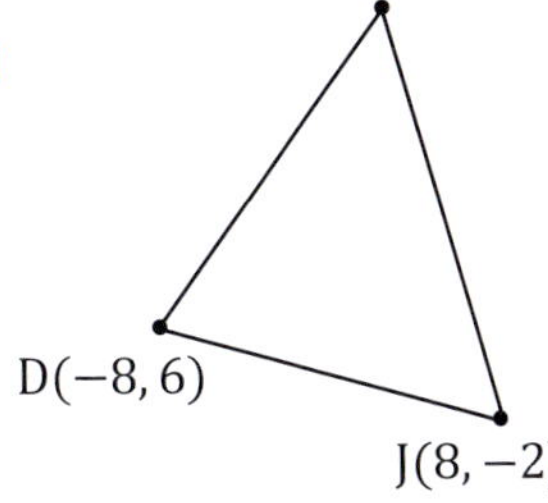

(f)

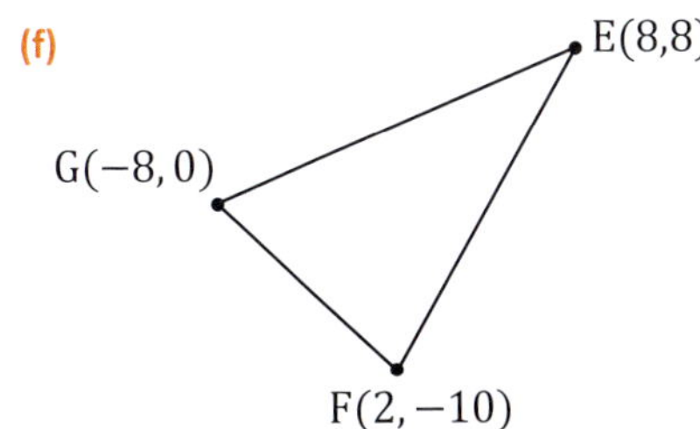

1.11 Review

NB: In the Review exercises, equations that are final answers are given in the form $ax + by + c = 0$; other questions are given in the form $y = mx + c$ or $ay = bx + c$ if the gradient is a fraction.

Exercise 1.11A

1.1 Find the equation of the line joining the following points:

(a) $(1, 1)$ and $(-3, -2)$ (b) $(5, 8)$ and $(3, 12)$ (c) $(7, -2)$ and $(5, 6)$

1.2 Find the midpoint of the line joining the following points:

(a) $A(6, -2)$ and $B(8, 10)$ (b) $C(5, 4)$ and $D(-3, 10)$ (c) $E(1, 17)$ and $F(-1, -3)$

1.3 Find the gradient of a line perpendicular to the line joining each of the following points:

(a) $A(3, -2)$ and $B(5, 4)$ (b) $C(-1, 3)$ and $D(5, 6)$ (c) $E(9, -11)$ and $F(5, 9)$

1.4 (a) A line, l, has the equation $x + y - 4 = 0$. Calculate the angle that the line makes with the positive direction of the x-axis.

(b) Find the equation of the line in the diagram opposite.

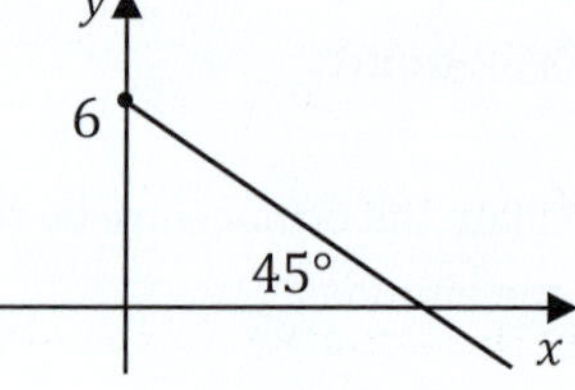

1.5 Determine whether the following sets of points are collinear:

(a) $A(2, 2)$, $B(14, 8)$ and $C(18, 12)$ (b) $D(-8, 6)$, $E(-4, 0)$ and $F(12, -24)$

1.6 (a) Find the equation of the line which intersects the y-axis at $y = -3$ and is perpendicular to the line with equation $3x - 2y - 1 = 0$.

(b) Find the equation of the line which passes through $(9, 1)$ and the midpoint of the line joining points $C(-3, 10)$ and $B(5, 8)$.

1.7 Find the point of intersection of each of the following lines:

(a) $x + 2y = 6$
$y = 3x - 4$

(b) $y = 3x - 14$
$y = 6 - 2x$

(c) $2x + 3y = -3$
$3x - 2y = -11$

1.8 Find the equation of the perpendicular bisector of the line joining each pair of points:

(a) $A(-3, -2)$ and $B(1, 10)$ (b) $C(4, -5)$ and $D(-8, -2)$ (c) $E(-9, 3)$ and $F(1, 5)$

1.9 Sketch the triangle and find the equation of the median from C in each of the following sets of points:

(a) $A(10,5)$, $B(-8,3)$, $C(-3,12)$ (b) $D(-5,2)$, $C(3,-10)$, $E(-7,6)$

1.10 Sketch the triangle and find the equation of the altitude from A in each of the following sets of points:

(a) $A(-4,15)$, $B(-5,4)$, $C(-3,10)$ (b) $A(1,9)$, $D(-4,-8)$, $E(2,4)$

Exercise 1.11B

1. Triangle ABC is shown in the diagram opposite.

   (a) Find the equation of the perpendicular bisector of AC.

   (b) Find the equation of the median from C.

   (c) Find the coordinates of the point of intersection of the perpendicular bisector of AC and the median from C.

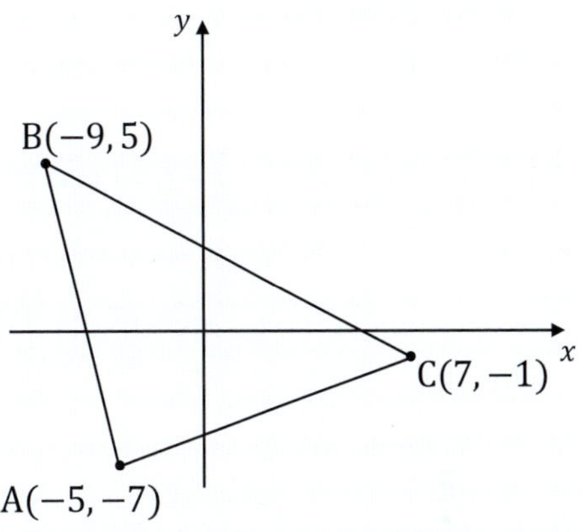

2. Triangle DEF is shown in the diagram opposite.

   (a) Find the equation of the median from E.

   (b) Find the equation of the altitude from D.

   (c) Find the coordinates of the point of intersection of the median from E and the altitude from D.

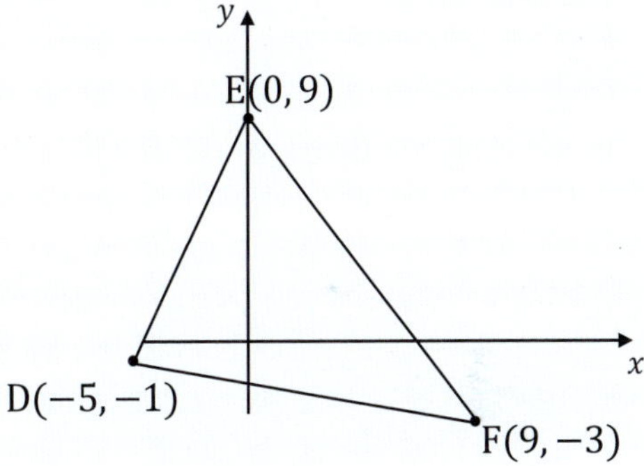

3. Triangle GHJ is shown in the diagram opposite.

   (a) Find the equation of the median from G.

   (b) Find the equation of the perpendicular bisector of GJ.

   (c) Find the coordinates of the point of intersection of the median from G and the perpendicular bisector of GJ.

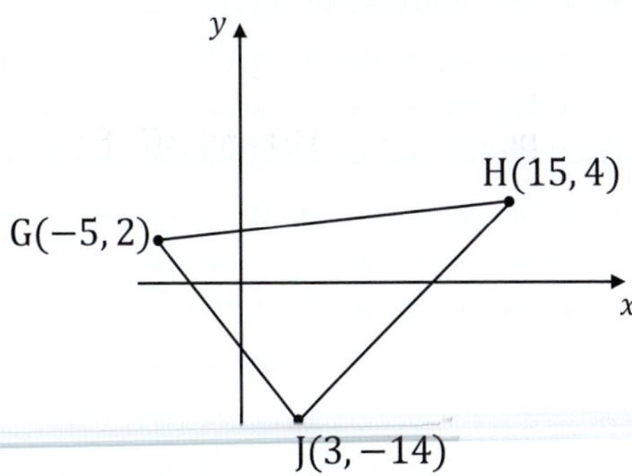

4. Line l_1 is perpendicular to line l_2. Line l_1 has equation $x + 3y = 6$. Lines l_1 and l_2 meet at $x = -9$. Find the equation of l_2

5. The diagram shows rectangle ABCD with $C(6, 13)$ and $D(12, 5)$.

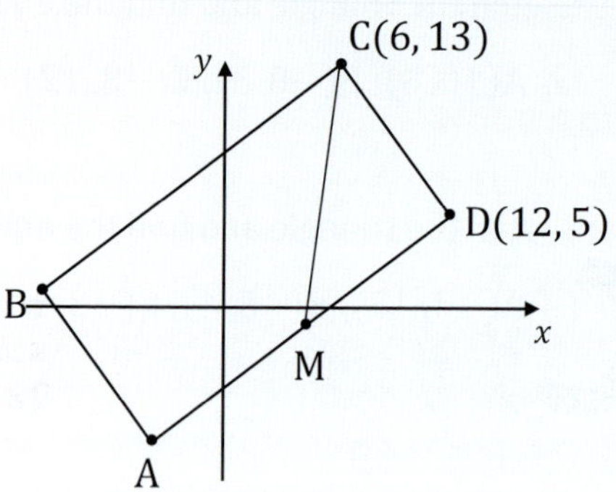

(a) Find the equation of CD.

(b) The line from C to M has the equation $y = 7x - 29$. Find the coordinates of M.

(c) M is the midpoint of AD. Find the coordinates of A and B.

6. The points $K(-8, 3)$, $L(-1, 7)$ and $M(13, y)$ are collinear. Calculate the value of y.

7. The line joining the points $(d, -1)$ and $(4, 15)$ is parallel to the line with gradient, $m = -2$. Find the value of d.

8. The line joining the points $(9, 3)$ and (a^2, a) is perpendicular to the line with gradient, $m = -\frac{1}{2}$. Find the value of a.

9. In the diagram below A and B have coordinates $(-3, 6)$ and $(5, 2)$ respectively.

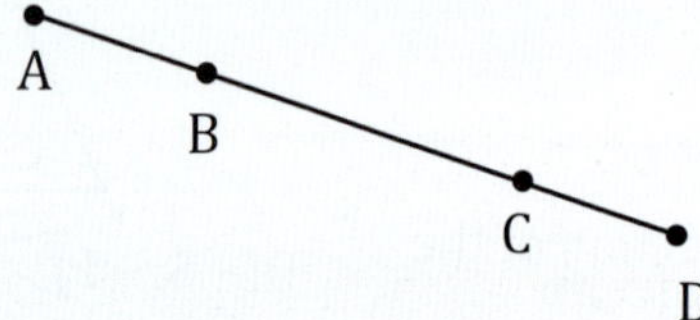

B divides AC in the ratio $1:2$ and C divides AD in the ratio $4:1$.

Find the coordinates of D.

10. Triangle ABC is isosceles, as shown in the diagram.

The gradient of AB is 1.

(a) Find the equation of the perpendicular bisector of AB.

The gradient of AC is $-\frac{1}{3}$.

(b) Find the coordinates of C.

ABCD is a parallelogram.

(c) Find the equation of diagonal AD.

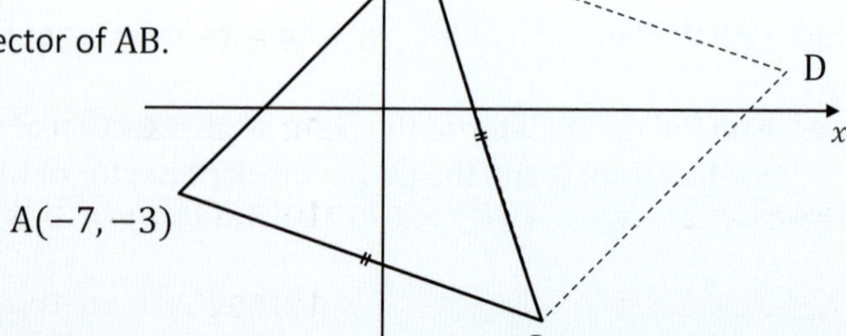

Chapter 2
Quadratic Functions & Graphs

N5 **Exercise 2.1**	Finding the equation of a quadratic function from a turning point
N5 **Exercise 2.2**	Finding the equation of a quadratic graph from the roots
N5 **Exercise 2.3**	Solving quadratics by factorising
Exercise 2.4	Solving quadratics by rearranging
N5 **Exercise 2.5**	Solving quadratics using the quadratic formula
Exercise 2.6	Completing the square
Exercise 2.7	Solving quadratics by completing the square
N5 **Exercise 2.8**	Sketching quadratics from completed square form
N5 **Exercise 2.9**	Sketching quadratics from factorised form
Exercise 2.10	Solving quadratic inequations
N5 **Exercise 2.11**	Determining the nature of roots (the discriminant)
Exercise 2.12	Using the discriminant
Exercise 2.13	Show a line is a tangent to a curve
Exercise 2.14	Nature of the intersection of a line and a curve
Exercise 2.15	Points of intersection of a line and a curve
Exercise 2.16	Points of intersection of two curves
Exercise 2.17	Review

Quadratic Functions

A quadratic is a function or equation in which the highest power of x is 2. For example, $y = x^2$ is a quadratic equation, but $y = x$ is not as the highest power of x is 1. Neither is $y = x^3 - 2x^2$, as the highest power of x is 3.

The diagrams on this page are graphs of quadratic functions. These graphs are commonly called a **parabolas**. Parabolas are either 'n' or 'u' shaped, depending on whether the x^2 term is positive or negative.

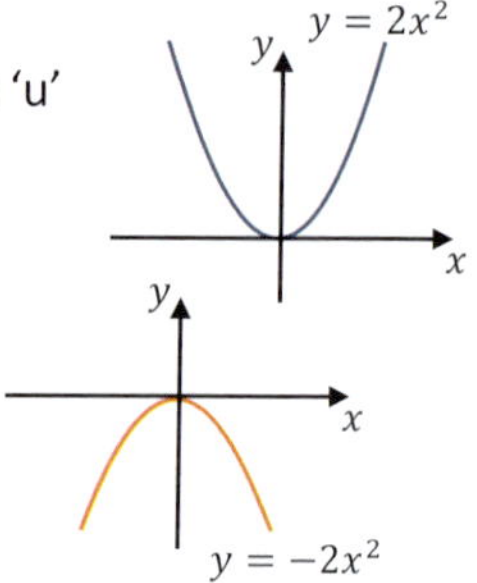

When the coefficient of x^2 is **positive**, the graph has a **minimum turning point**. This produces a 'u' shape (as in the blue graph).

When the coefficient of x^2 is **negative**, the graph has a **maximum turning point**. This produces an 'n' shape (as in the orange graph).

Quadratic Functions are written in three different forms:

Expanded Form — $\boldsymbol{y = ax^2 + bx + c}$. If sketching a graph, or solving the quadratic, this form needs to be put into one or both of the other two forms.

Completed Square Form — $\boldsymbol{y = k(x + p)^2 + q}$. This form is most useful for finding the turning point. In equations of this form, the shape ('u' or 'n') of the graph and nature of the turning point are determined by the value of k. The turning point is $(-p, q)$.

Factorised Form — $\boldsymbol{y = k(x - m)(x - n)}$. This form is used to solve or find the roots of the quadratic (the points where the graph cuts the x-axis). The graph can also be sketched from this form. As above, k gives the shape of the graph and nature of the turning point, m and n allow us to find the roots.

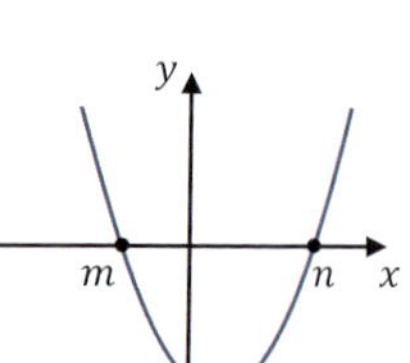

National 5 Skills

2.1 Finding the Equation of a Quadratic Graph from a Turning Point

To find the equation of a quadratic function from its graph, two points are needed (if one of them is the turning point), otherwise three points are needed. When the turning point is given, the **completed square form,** $y = k(x + p)^2 + q$, can be used to determine the equation of the graph.

Step 1: Substitute the turning point. In the completed square form, the turning point of the graph give the values of p and q (notice that the value in the bracket is the negative of the x-coordinate of the turning point).

Step 2: Substitute the other point into the equation to find the value of k.

NB: In an example where the turning point is the origin, p and q are both zero so we are left with $y = kx^2$.

Worked Examples:

Find the equation of the following quadratic functions:

1.

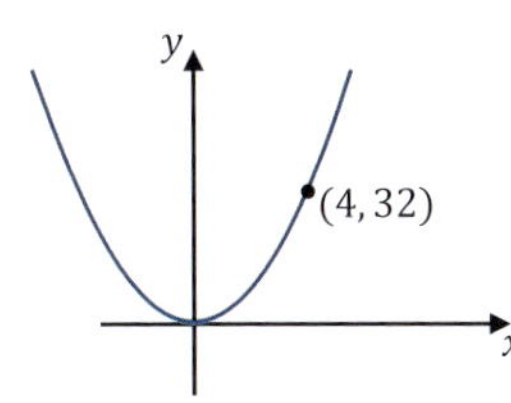

In the graph, the turning point is $(0, 0)$, so $y = k(x + p)^2 + q$ becomes

$y = kx^2$.

Substitute $(4, 32)$

$32 = k(4)^2$

$32 = 16k$

$k = 2$ $\qquad \therefore y = 2x^2$

2.

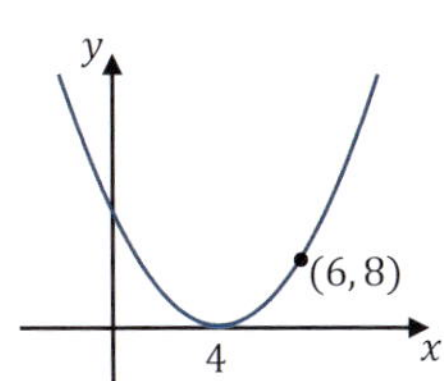

In the graph, the turning point is $(4, 0)$, so $y = k(x + p)^2 + q$ becomes

$y = k(x - 4)^2 + 0$ or just $y = k(x - 4)^2$.

Substitute $(6, 8)$

$8 = k(6 - 4)^2$

$8 = 4k$

$k = 2$ $\qquad \therefore y = 2(x - 4)^2$

3.

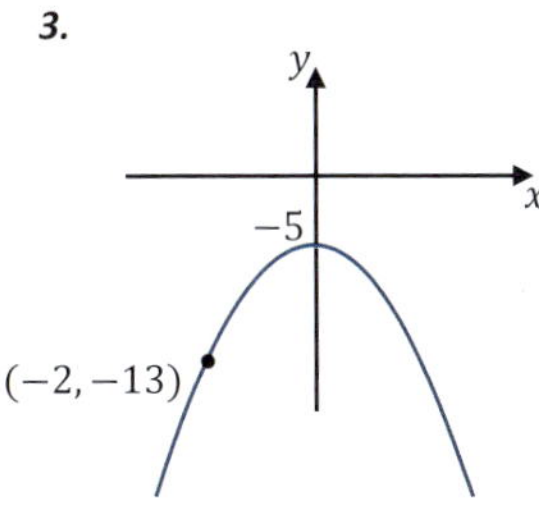

Turning point: $(0, -5)$

$y = k(x - 0)^2 - 5$

$y = kx^2 - 5$.

Substitute $(-2, -13)$

$-13 = k(-2)^2 - 5$

$-13 = 4k - 5$

$k = -2$ $\qquad \therefore y = -2x^2 - 5$

4.

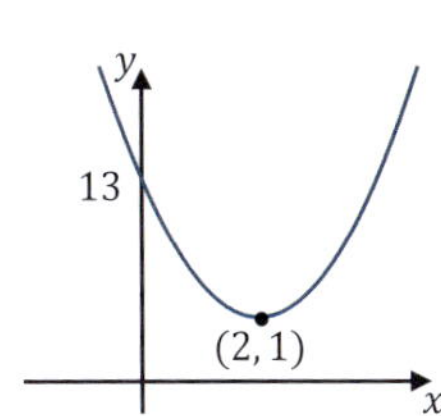

Turning point: $(2, 1)$

$y = k(x - 2)^2 + 1$

Substitute $(0, 13)$

$13 = k(-2)^2 + 1$

$13 = 4k + 1$

$12 = 4k$

$k = 3$ $\qquad \therefore y = 3(x - 2)^2 + 1$

NB: In quadratic graphs, as k becomes a larger positive or negative value, the graph becomes narrower.

Exercise 2.1

Find the equation of each of the following parabolas in the form $y = k(x + p)^2 + q$:

1.

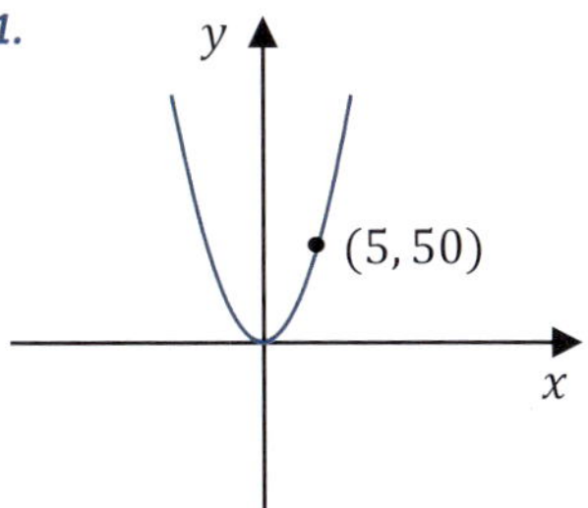

2.

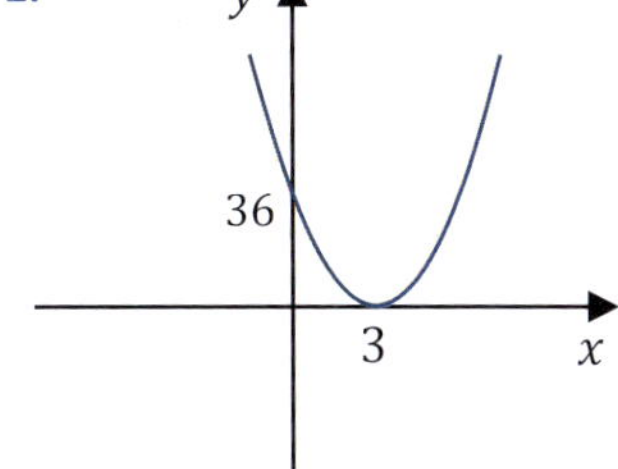

3.

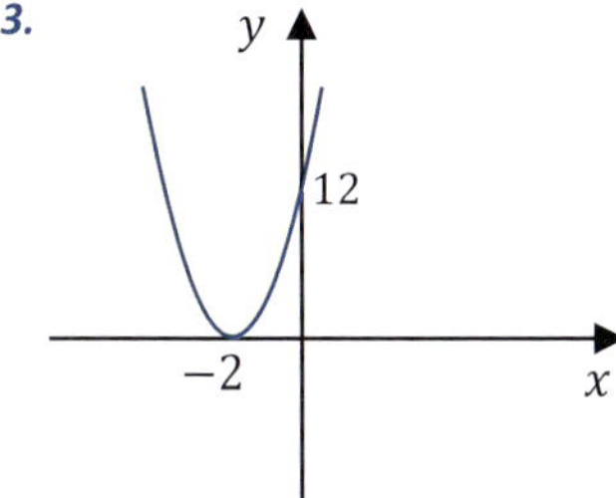

4.

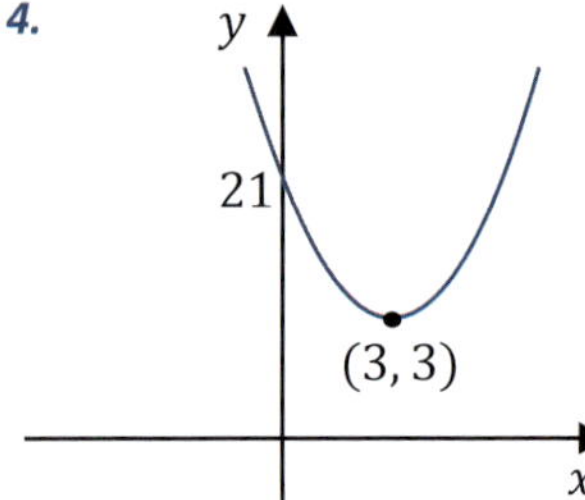

5.

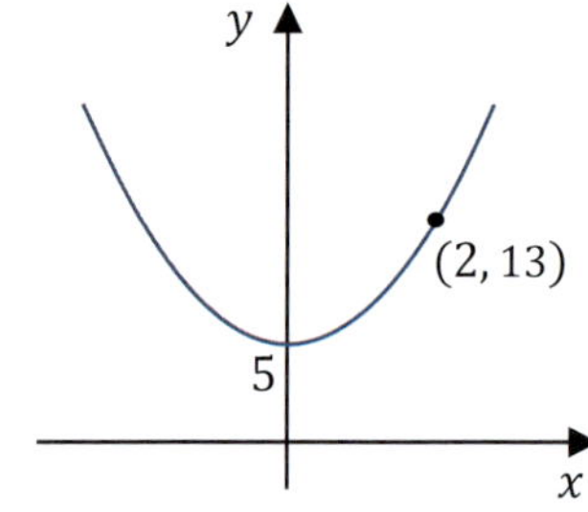

6.

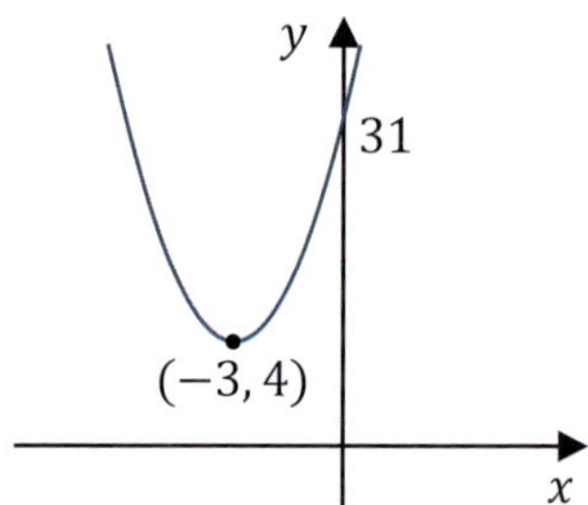

7.

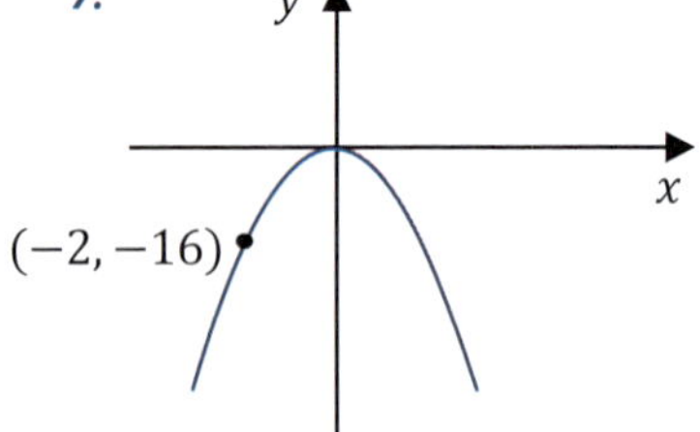

8.

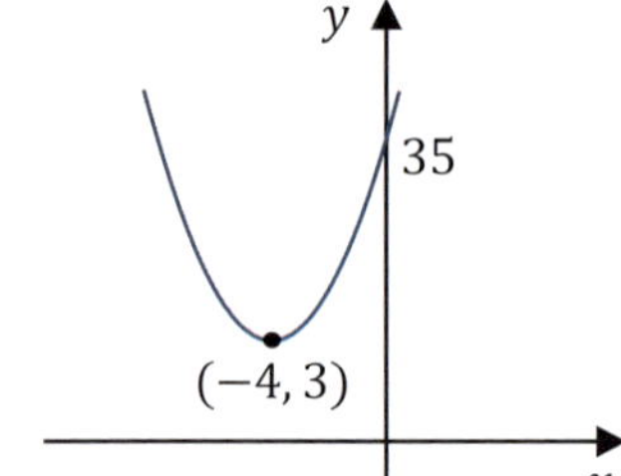

9.

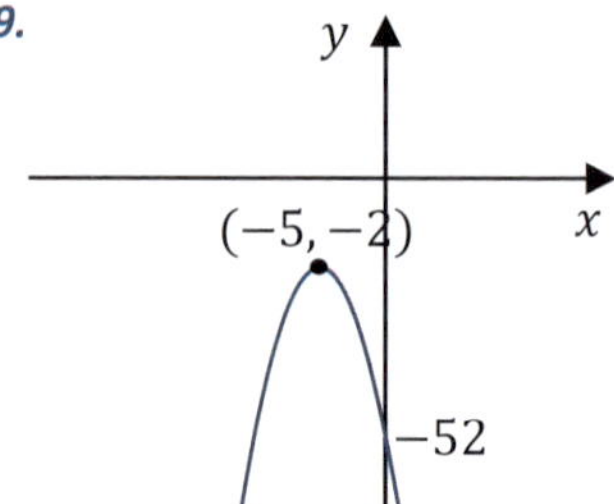

10.

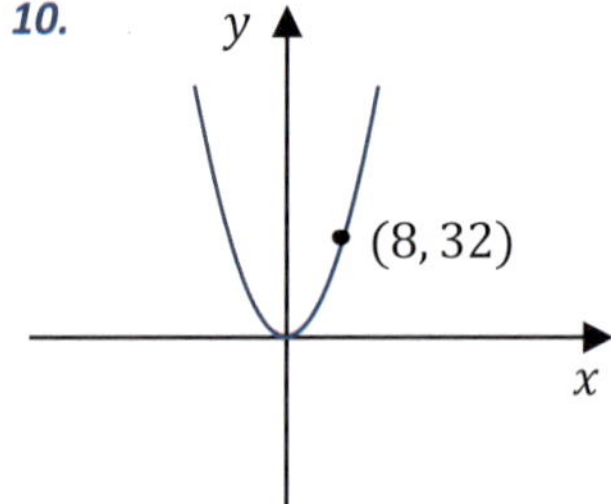

11.

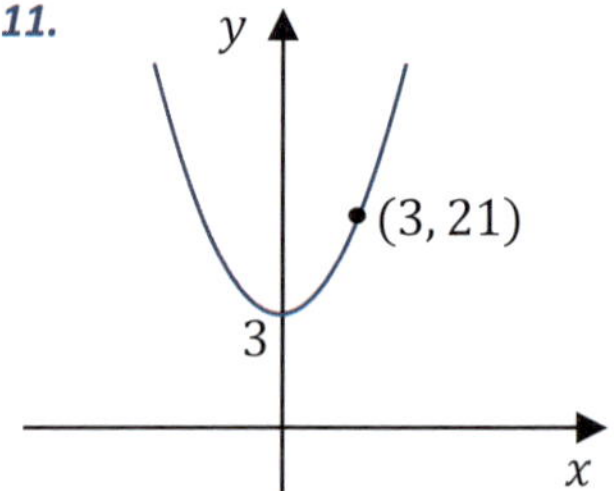

12.

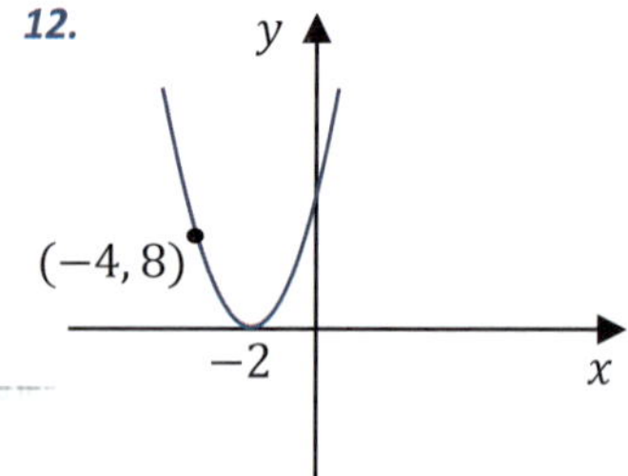

13.

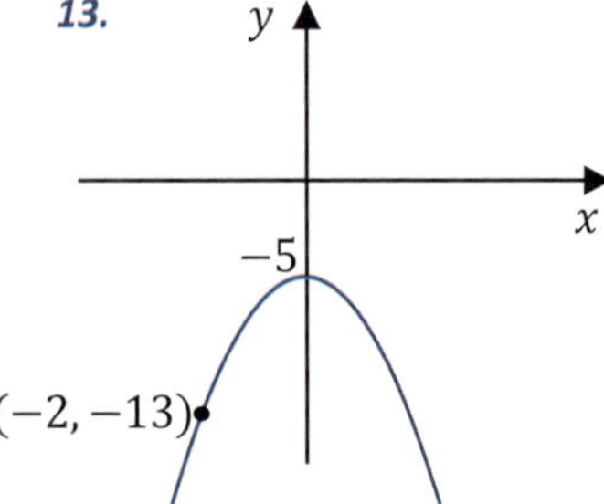

14.

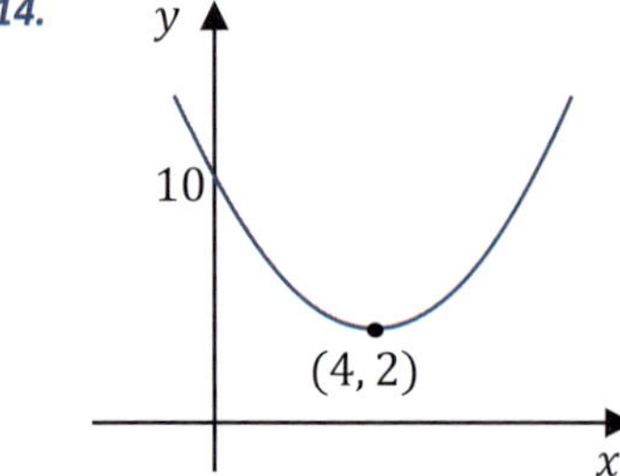

15.

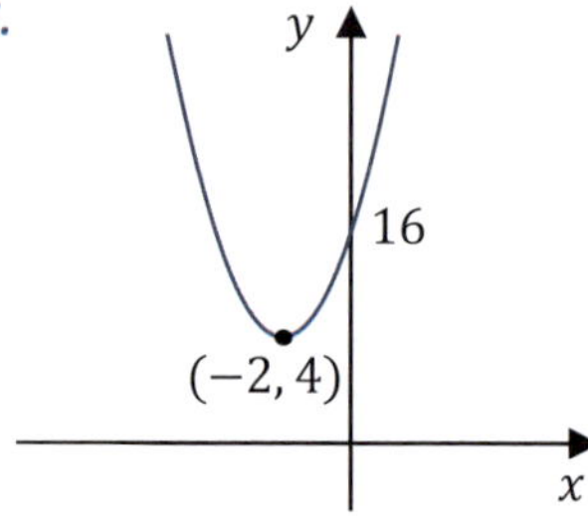

16.

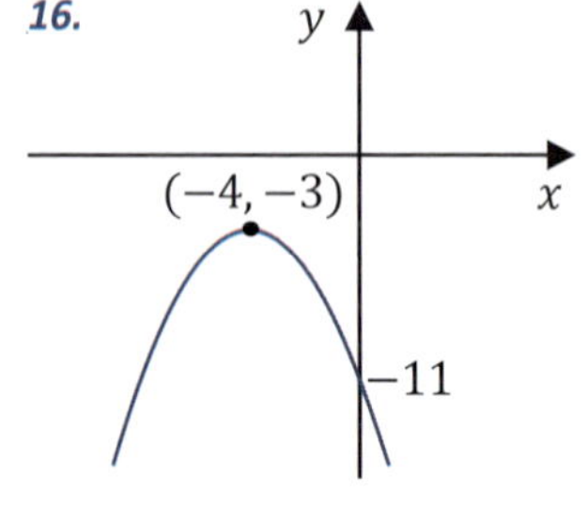

17.

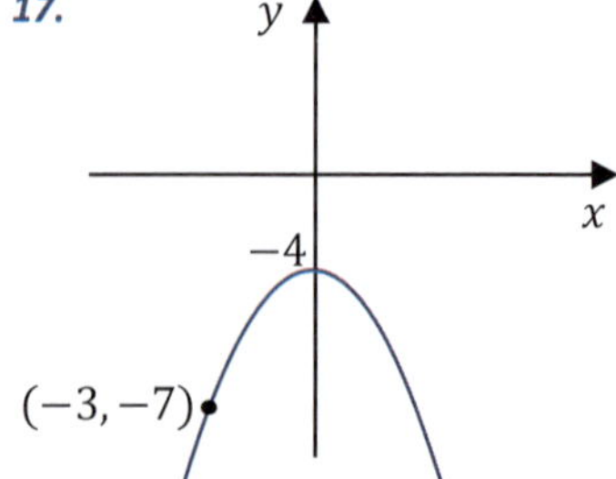

18.

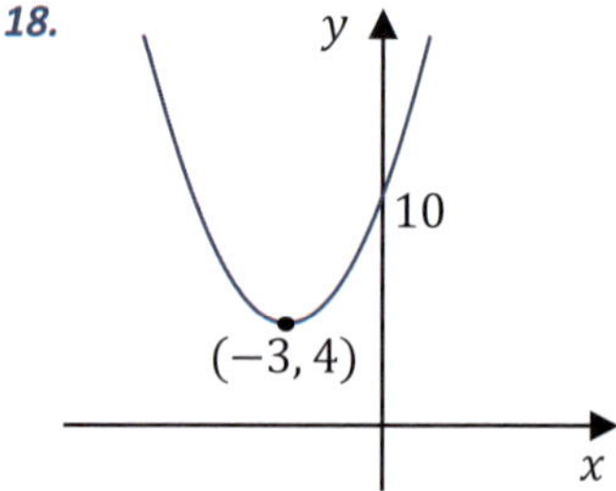

2.2 Finding the Equation of a Quadratic Graph from the Roots

The **roots** of a quadratic function are the x-coordinates at which the graph cuts the x-axis. These values are also known as the **solutions**, the **zeros** or the **x-intercepts** of a quadratic function.

When we have the roots, the equation may be found in the following way:

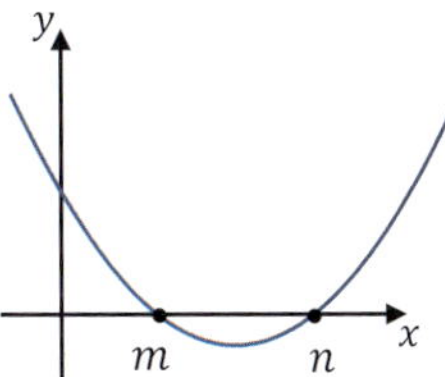

Step 1: Substitute the roots into $\boldsymbol{y = k(x - m)(x - n)}$, (notice that the values in the bracket are the negative of the x-coordinates of the roots).

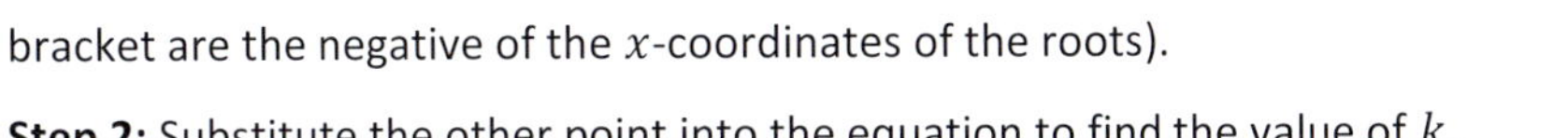

Step 2: Substitute the other point into the equation to find the value of k.

NB: In an example where the roots are at the same place (equal roots), we are left with $y = k(x - m)^2$.

Worked Example:

Find the equation of the following quadratic function in the form $y = k(x - m)(x - n)$.

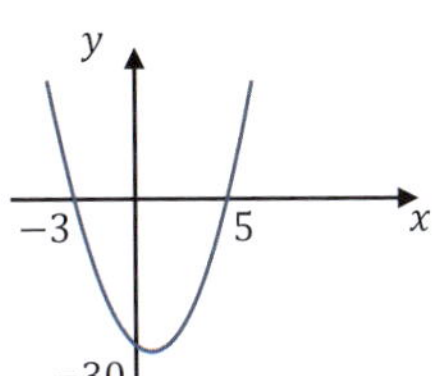

Step 1: Substitute roots

$y = k(x + 3)(x - 5)$

Step 2: Substitute other point $(0, 30)$

$-30 = k(0 + 3)(0 - 5)$

$-30 = -15k$

$k = 2 \qquad \therefore y = 2(x + 3)(x - 5)$

Exercise 2.2

Find the equation of each of the following parabolas in the form $y = k(x - m)(x - n)$:

1. 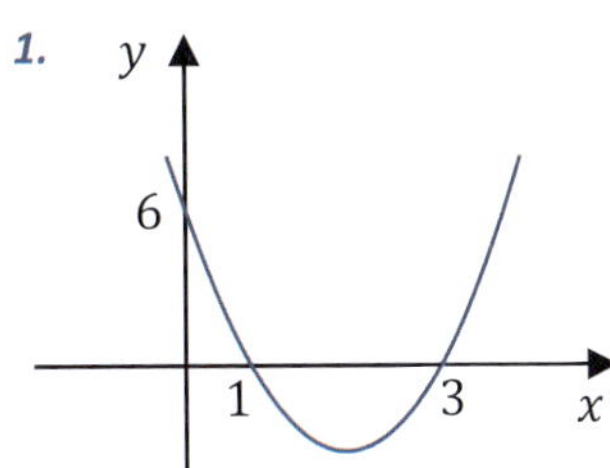

2. 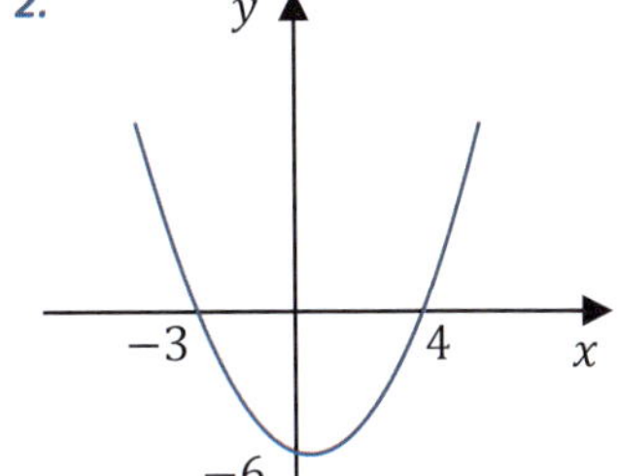

3. 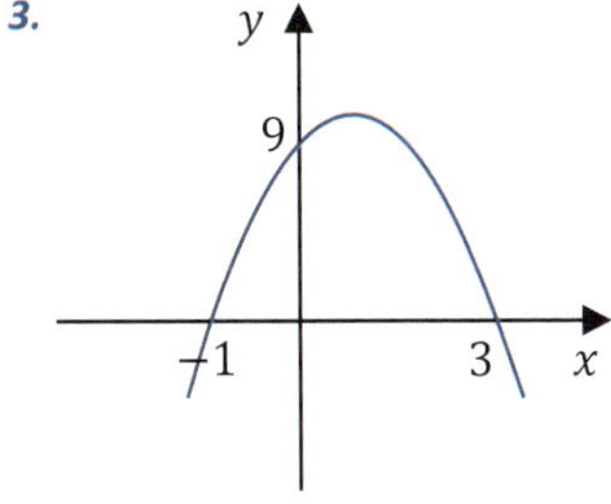

4. 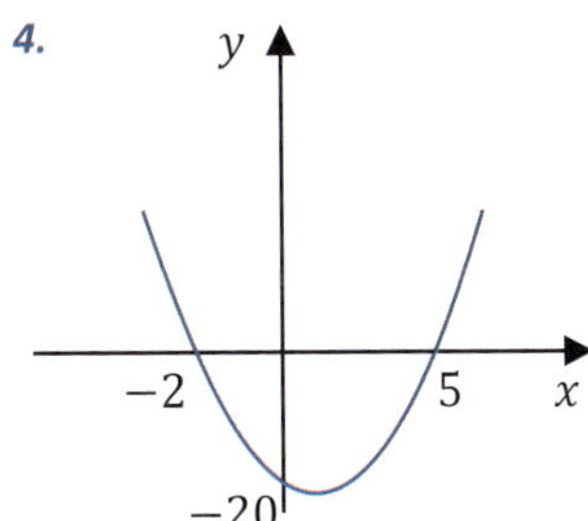

5. 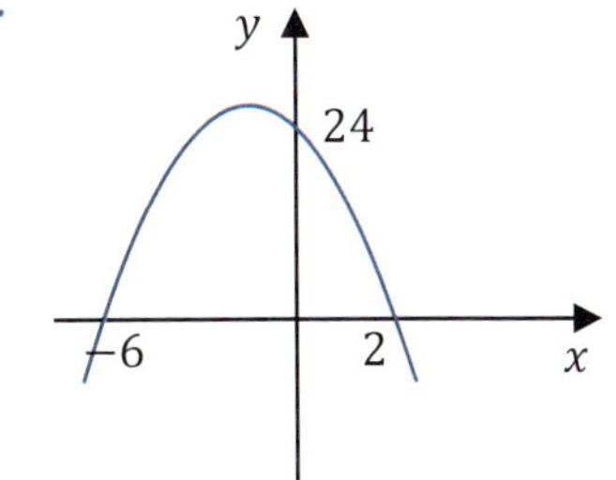

6. 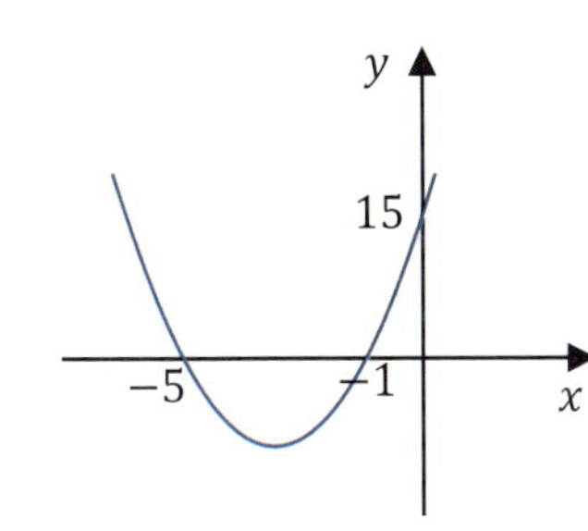

7.

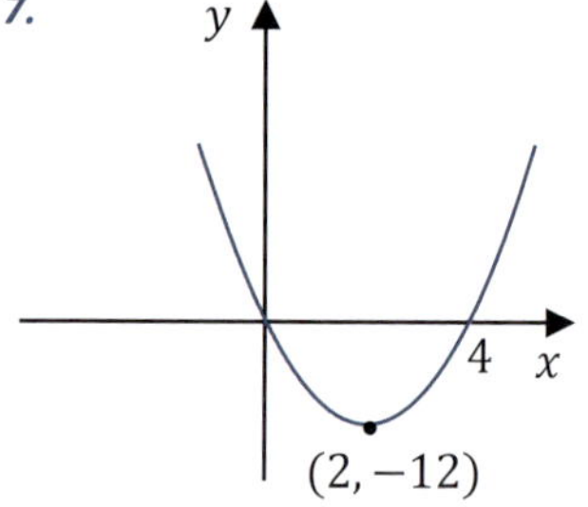

8.

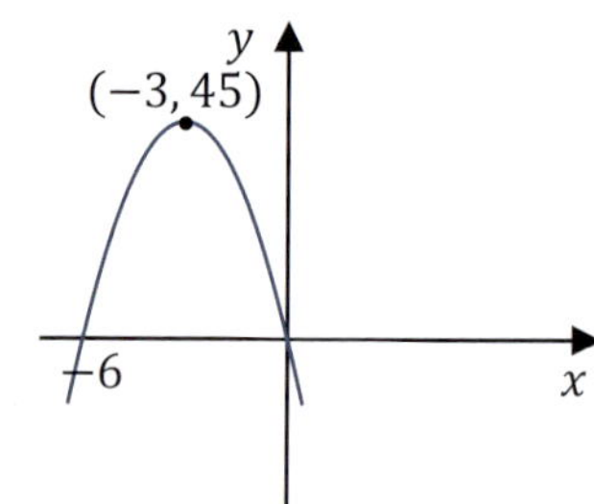

9.

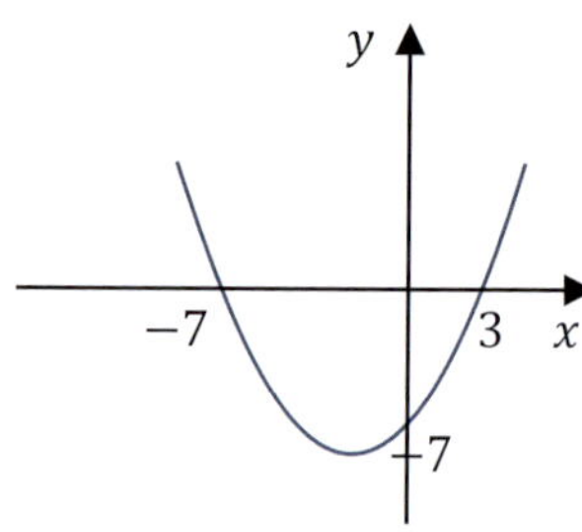

10.

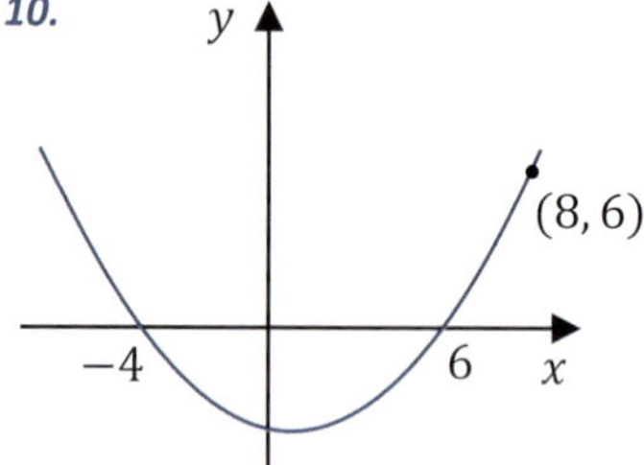

11.

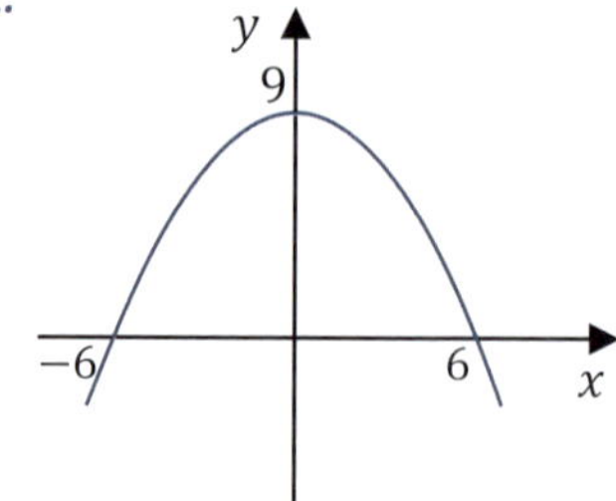

12.

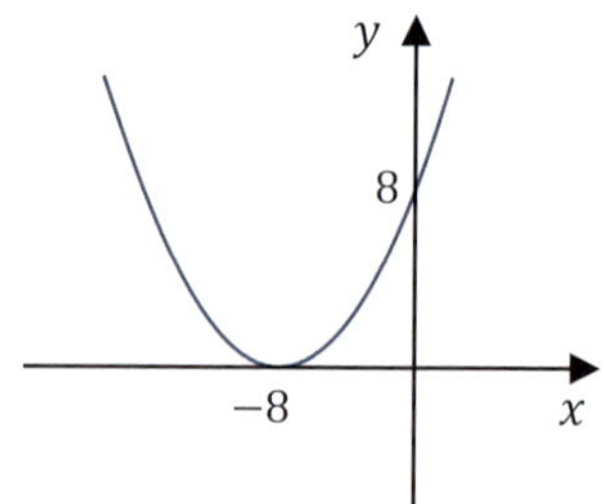

2.3 Solving Quadratics by Factorising

National 5 Skills

Often quadratic equations need to be factorised before they can be solved. Remember to always look for a **common factor** first, then a **difference of two squares** or **trinomial**.

Worked Examples:

Solve the following quadratic equations:

1.
$$x^2 + 4x = 0$$
$$x(x+4) = 0$$
$$x = 0 \quad or \quad x + 4 = 0$$
$$x = 0 \quad or \quad x = -4$$

2.
$$3x^2 - 12 = 0$$
$$3(x^2 - 4) = 0$$
$$3(x+2)(x-2) = 0$$
$$x + 4 = 0 \quad or \quad x - 4 = 0$$
$$x = -4 \quad or \quad x = 4$$

3.
$$2x^2 - x - 6 = 0$$
$$(2x+3)(x-2) = 0$$
$$2x + 3 = 0 \quad or \quad x - 2 = 0$$
$$2x = -3 \quad or \quad x = 2$$
$$x = -\tfrac{3}{2}$$

Exercise 2.3

1. Solve the following quadratic equations by factorising:

(a) $x^2 - 5x = 0$ (b) $x^2 - x = 0$ (c) $x^2 + 9x = 0$

(d) $x^2 - 6x = 0$ (e) $x^2 + 2x = 0$ (f) $3x^2 + 4x = 0$

(g) $4x^2 - 7x = 0$ (h) $5x^2 + 9x = 0$ (i) $6x^2 - 5x = 0$

2. Solve the following quadratic equations by factorising:

(a) $x^2 - 1 = 0$ (b) $x^2 - 25 = 0$ (c) $3x^2 - 27 = 0$

(d) $2x^2 - 50 = 0$ (e) $4x^2 - 100 = 0$ (f) $3x^2 - 12 = 0$

(g) $2x^2 - 8 = 0$ (h) $4x^2 - 1 = 0$ (i) $9x^2 - 1 = 0$

3. Solve the following quadratic equations by factorising:

(a) $x^2 + 5x + 4 = 0$ (b) $x^2 - 7x + 12 = 0$ (c) $x^2 - 5x - 14 = 0$

(d) $x^2 - 10x + 9 = 0$ (e) $x^2 - 2x - 8 = 0$ (f) $x^2 + 6x + 9 = 0$

(g) $2x^2 + x - 3 = 0$ (h) $3x^2 + 10x + 3 = 0$ (i) $5x^2 - 7x - 6 = 0$

4. Solve the following quadratic equations by factorising:

(a) $2x^2 - 3x = 0$ (b) $x^2 - 1 = 0$ (c) $x^2 - 2x - 15 = 0$

(d) $4x^2 - 1 = 0$ (e) $x^2 - 16x = 0$ (f) $x^2 + 4x + 3 = 0$

(g) $2x^2 - 2 = 0$ (h) $9x^2 - 81 = 0$ (i) $6x^2 - 3x = 0$

(j) $x^2 - 5x - 36 = 0$ (k) $5x^2 - 45 = 0$ (l) $x^2 + 11x - 12 = 0$

(m) $2x^2 - 7x + 5 = 0$ (n) $9x^2 - 11x = 0$ (o) $3x^2 + 8x + 4 = 0$

(p) $4x^2 - 16x = 0$ (q) $16x^2 - 1 = 0$ (r) $2x^2 - 1 = 0$

(s) $4x^2 - 5x - 6 = 0$ (t) $8x^2 - 14x - 15 = 0$ (u) $3x^2 - 2x = 0$

2.4 Solving Quadratics by Rearranging

If a quadratic equation is not equal to zero, it needs to be rearranged to be solved.

Worked Examples:

Solve the following quadratic equations:

1. $x^2 = x + 12$

$x^2 - x - 12 = 0$

$(x - 4)(x + 3) = 0$

$x - 4 = 0$ *or* $x + 3 = 0$

$x = 4$ $x = -3$

2. $x^2 + 2x = 6 - 5x - 2x^2$

$3x^2 + 7x - 6 = 0$

$(3x - 2)(x + 3) = 0$

$3x - 2 = 0$ *or* $x + 3 = 0$

$x = \frac{2}{3}$ $x = -3$

3. $\frac{x^2 - 22}{x} = 9$

$x^2 - 22 = 9x$

$x^2 - 9x - 22 = 0$

$(x - 11)(x + 2) = 0$

$x - 11 = 0$ *or* $x + 2 = 0$

$x = 11$ $x = -2$

Exercise 2.4

Solve the following quadratic equations:

1. $3x^2 = 18x$ 2. $4x^2 = 4$ 3. $x^2 = 3x + 4$

4. $x^2 = 2x$ 5. $x^2 - 5x = 6$ 6. $x^2 + 10x - 6 = 3x - 2x^2$

7. $3x^2 + 6x = 8 - 2x^2$

8. $5x^2 - 1 = 2 - 2x - 3x^2$

9. $22x^2 - 5x = 2x - 15x^2$

10. $18 = 2x^2$

11. $8x^2 - 5 = 2x^2 - 13x + 10$

12. $1 - x = 13 - x^2$

13. $\dfrac{x^2 + 3x}{3} + x = -3$

14. $\dfrac{x^2 - 15}{x} = 2$

15. $\dfrac{15 - 13x}{x^2} = 2$

16. $\dfrac{3x^2 + 6x - 4}{(x+2)} - x = 3$

17. $\dfrac{4x^2 - 4x - 14}{(x-1)} = (x+2)$

18. $\dfrac{2x^2 - 23}{(x-3)} = (x+5)$

2.5 Solving Quadratics using the Quadratic Formula

National 5 Skills

When a quadratic function is difficult to factorise (usually because the roots are not whole numbers), the resulting equation can be solved using the **Quadratic Formula**.

The formula is $x = \dfrac{-b \pm \sqrt{b^2 - 4ac}}{2a}$, where $ax^2 + bx + c = 0$

NB: A quadratic function will only have real solutions when $b^2 - 4ac \geq 0$.

Worked Example:

Solve the quadratic equation $4x^2 + 5x - 1 = 0$ correct to one decimal place.

Since $ax^2 + bx + c = 0$, then $a = 4, b = 5, c = -1$

$$x = \frac{-b \pm \sqrt{b^2 - 4ac}}{2a}$$

$$x = \frac{-(5) \pm \sqrt{(5)^2 - 4(4)(-1)}}{2(4)}$$

$x = \dfrac{-(5) - \sqrt{41}}{8}$ $\quad$ $x = \dfrac{-(5) + \sqrt{41}}{8}$

$x = -1.43$ (to 2 d.p.) $\quad$ $x = 0.18$ (to 2 d.p.)

Exercise 2.5

Solve the following quadratic equations correct to two decimal places using the quadratic formula:

1. $x^2 + 4x - 3 = 0$

2. $x^2 - 5x - 7 = 0$

3. $x^2 + 6x - 1 = 0$

4. $x^2 - 2x - 1 = 0$

5. $x^2 - 11x + 6 = 0$

6. $x^2 - 2x - 4 = 0$

7. $3x^2 - 5x - 5 = 0$

8. $2x^2 + 12x + 7 = 0$

9. $3x^2 - 7x - 1 = 0$

10. $4x^2 - 11x - 6 = 0$

11. $1 - 8x^2 - 5x = 0$

12. $10 - 6x - 2x^2 = 0$

13. $5x^2 + 13x + 1 = 0$

14. $x^2 - 9x - 7 = 0$

15. $x^2 - 15 = 0$

16. $8x - 10 = x^2$

17. $9x = 1 - x^2$

18. $5 - 3x^2 = 9x$

19. $7 - 6x^2 = 10x$

20. $x^2 = 15x - 2$

21. $x^2 - 7 = 12x$

2.6 Completing the Square

National 5 Skills

Completing the square is the process of taking a trinomial expression (usually one that does not factorise) and turning it into a perfect square trinomial with something added on or taken away. This form is useful for finding the turning point of a quadratic function (**see 2.1, 2.8**). It can be expressed generally in the following way:

$$ax^2 + bx + c = a\left(x + \frac{b}{2a}\right)^2 + c - \left(\frac{b}{2a}\right)^2$$

This may look quite complicated, but the following illustration may help.

We can find the area of the shape on the left, by considering its component parts, or by considering the shape on the right, less the missing part.

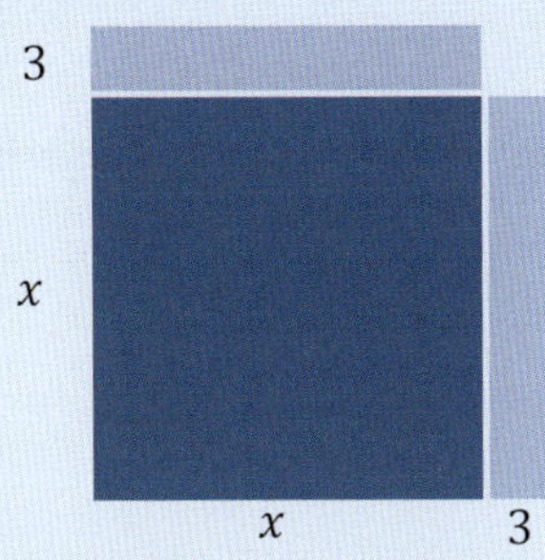

The area of the shape on the left is $x^2 + 3x + 3x = \mathbf{x^2 + 6x}$.

The area of the shape on the right can be written as $(x+3)^2 = \mathbf{x^2 + 6x} + 9$.

To find the area of the shape on the left in terms of the area on the right, it can be written as the whole square, less the missing part,

i.e. $\mathbf{x^2 + 6x} + 9 - 9 = (x+3)^2 - 9$.

This is called completing the square.

Worked Examples:

1. $x^2 + 4x + 5$
$= (x^2 + 4x) + 5$
$= (x + \mathbf{2})^2 + 5 - \mathbf{2}^2$
$= (x + 2)^2 + 5 - 4$
$= (x + 2)^2 + 1$

2. $x^2 - 10x + 32$
$= (x^2 - 10x) + 32$
$= (x - \mathbf{5})^2 + 32 - (\mathbf{-5})^2$
$= (x - 5)^2 + 32 - 25$
$= (x - 5)^2 + 7$

3. $x^2 - 2x + 6$
$= (x^2 - 2x) + 6$
$= (x - \mathbf{1})^2 + 6 - (\mathbf{-1})^2$
$= (x - 1)^2 + 6 - 1$
$= (x - 1)^2 + 5$

NB: In line 3 of each example, the coefficient of the x term is halved inside the bracket. It is then squared and so is always ≥ 0, therefore it is taken away outside the bracket.

Exercise 2.6A

Complete the square of the following:

1. $x^2 + 2x + 3$
2. $x^2 + 8x - 7$
3. $x^2 - 10x + 9$
4. $x^2 + 6x + 4$
5. $x^2 - 4x + 12$
6. $x^2 + 8x - 12$
7. $x^2 - 2x + 7$
8. $x^2 + 20x + 26$
9. $x^2 - 4x + 5$

10. $x^2 + 6x + 15$

11. $x^2 - 14x - 15$

12. $x^2 + 12x - 11$

13. $x^2 - 12x + 9$

14. $x^2 + 18x + 50$

15. $x^2 - 4x - 19$

Worked Examples:

1. $x^2 + 3x + 4$

$= (x^2 + 3x) + 4$

$= \left(x + \frac{3}{2}\right)^2 + 4 - \left(\frac{3}{2}\right)^2$

$= \left(x + \frac{3}{2}\right)^2 + 4 - \frac{9}{4}$

$= \left(x + \frac{3}{2}\right)^2 + \frac{16}{4} - \frac{9}{4}$

$= \left(x + \frac{3}{2}\right)^2 + \frac{7}{4}$

2. $x^2 - 7x + 9$

$= (x^2 - 7x) + 9$

$= \left(x - \frac{7}{2}\right)^2 + 9 - \left(-\frac{7}{2}\right)^2$

$= \left(x - \frac{7}{2}\right)^2 + 9 - \frac{49}{4}$

$= \left(x - \frac{7}{2}\right)^2 + \frac{36}{4} - \frac{49}{4}$

$= \left(x - \frac{7}{2}\right)^2 - \frac{13}{4}$

3. $x^2 - 11x - 1$

$= (x^2 - 11x) - 1$

$= \left(x - \frac{11}{2}\right)^2 - 1 - \left(-\frac{11}{2}\right)^2$

$= \left(x - \frac{11}{2}\right)^2 - 1 - \frac{121}{4}$

$= \left(x - \frac{11}{2}\right)^2 - \frac{4}{4} - \frac{121}{4}$

$= \left(x - \frac{11}{2}\right)^2 - \frac{125}{4}$

Exercise 2.6B

Express the following in the form $(\boldsymbol{x} + \boldsymbol{p})^2 + \boldsymbol{q}$:

1. $x^2 + x + 2$

2. $x^2 + 3x + 3$

3. $x^2 + 5x + 12$

4. $x^2 - 3x + 11$

5. $x^2 - 7x + 22$

6. $x^2 - 11x + 25$

7. $x^2 + 5x + 9$

8. $x^2 + 11x + 18$

9. $x^2 + 13x + 45$

10. $x^2 + x + 11$

11. $x^2 - 9x + 6$

12. $x^2 - 15x + 25$

13. $x^2 + 9x - 15$

14. $x^2 + 13x + 24$

15. $x^2 + 9x - 5$

Worked Examples:

1. $8 - 4x - x^2$

$= -x^2 - 4x + 8$

$= -(x^2 + 4x) + 8$

$= -(x + 2)^2 + 8 - (-1)(2)^2$

$= -(x + 2)^2 + 8 + 4$

$= -(x + 2)^2 + 12$

2. $1 + 3x - x^2$

$= -x^2 + 3x + 1$

$= -(x^2 - 3x) + 1$

$= -\left(x - \frac{3}{2}\right)^2 + 1 - (-1)\left(-\frac{3}{2}\right)^2$

$= -\left(x - \frac{3}{2}\right)^2 + \frac{4}{4} + \frac{3}{4}$

$= -\left(x - \frac{3}{2}\right)^2 + \frac{7}{4}$

Exercise 2.6C

Express the following in the form $\boldsymbol{k}(\boldsymbol{x} + \boldsymbol{p})^2 + \boldsymbol{q}$ where $k \pm 1$:

1. $2 - 2x - x^2$

2. $1 - 4x - x^2$

3. $5 + 8x - x^2$

4. $2 - 3x - x^2$

5. $4 + 5x - x^2$

6. $3 - 7x - x^2$

7. $9 + 5x - x^2$

8. $11 - 5x - x^2$

9. $2 + 6x - x^2$

10. $10 + 10x - x^2$

11. $9 - 13x - x^2$

12. $22 + 11x - x^2$

13. $12 - 5x - x^2$

14. $15 + 24x - x^2$

15. $18 - 15x - x^2$

Higher Skills

Worked Examples: The following examples are Higher level questions.

1. $3x^2 - 12x + 16$

$= (3x^2 - 12x) + 16$

$= 3(x^2 - 4x) + 16$

$= 3(x - 2)^2 + 16 - 3(-2)^2$

$= 3(x - 2)^2 + 16 - 12$

$= 3(x - 2)^2 + 4$

2. $5x^2 - 5x - 5$

$= (5x^2 - 5x) - 5$

$= 5(x^2 - x) - 5$

$= 5\left(x - \frac{1}{2}\right)^2 - 5 - 5\left(-\frac{1}{2}\right)^2$

$= 5\left(x - \frac{1}{2}\right)^2 - 5 - \frac{5}{4}$

$= 5\left(x - \frac{1}{2}\right)^2 - \frac{25}{4}$

3. $10 - 12x - 4x^2$

$= -4x^2 - 12x + 10$

$= -4(x^2 + 3x) + 10$

$= -4\left(x + \frac{3}{2}\right)^2 + 10 - (-4)\left(\frac{3}{2}\right)^2$

$= -4\left(x + \frac{3}{2}\right)^2 + \frac{40}{4} + \frac{36}{4}$

$= -4\left(x + \frac{3}{2}\right)^2 + 19$

Exercise 2.6D

Express the following in the form $\boldsymbol{k(x + p)^2 + q}$:

1. $2x^2 + 4x + 7$

2. $3x^2 - 6x + 9$

3. $5x^2 + 10x + 12$

4. $2x^2 - 8x + 5$

5. $5x^2 + 30x - 5$

6. $4x^2 - 16x - 11$

7. $3x^2 - 9x + 11$

8. $6x^2 + 6x + 5$

9. $7x^2 + 21x - 25$

10. $3 - 6x - 2x^2$

11. $11 + 10x - 2x^2$

12. $4x^2 - 12x + 9$

13. $3x^2 - 3x + 14$

14. $4x^2 - 20x + 13$

15. $10 - 5x - 2x^2$

2.7 Solving Quadratics by Completing the Square

When the roots of a quadratic equation are not rational numbers (**i.e.** they cannot be expressed as an integer or a fraction), the quadratic can be solved by the method of completing the square. This is a non-calculator alternative to the **Quadratic Formula** (see **section 2.5** for more explanation).

Worked Examples:

1.
$$x^2 + 4x - 5 = 0$$
$$(x^2 + 4x) - 5 = 0$$
$$(x + 2)^2 - 5 - 4 = 0$$
$$(x + 2)^2 - 9 = 0$$
$$(x + 2)^2 = 9$$
$$x + 2 = \pm 3$$
$$x = 3 - 2 \quad \text{or} \quad x = -3 - 2$$
$$x = 1 \qquad x = -5$$

2.
$$x^2 - 6x + 7 = 0$$
$$(x^2 - 6x) + 7 = 0$$
$$(x - 3)^2 + 7 - 9 = 0$$
$$(x - 3)^2 - 2 = 0$$
$$(x - 3)^2 = 2$$
$$x - 3 = \pm\sqrt{2}$$
$$x = 3 + \sqrt{2} \quad \text{or} \quad x = 3 - \sqrt{2}$$

NB: Example 1 may be solved by factorising or by completing the square as the solutions are integers.

Exercise 2.7

Solve the following quadratic equations by completing the square:

1. $x^2 - 2x - 8 = 0$
2. $x^2 - 6x + 5 = 0$
3. $x^2 - 10x + 9 = 0$
4. $x^2 + 2x - 24 = 0$
5. $x^2 - 4x - 12 = 0$
6. $x^2 - 8x - 33 = 0$
7. $x^2 - 2x - 12 = 0$
8. $x^2 + 4x - 3 = 0$
9. $x^2 - 6x - 2 = 0$
10. $x^2 - 4x - 7 = 0$
11. $x^2 + 6x - 9 = 0$
12. $x^2 - 8x - 1 = 0$
13. $2x^2 + 8x - 1 = 0$
14. $3x^2 - 12x + 2 = 0$
15. $3x^2 - 8x - 2 = 0$
16. $5x^2 + 20x + 1 = 0$
17. $2x^2 - 12x - 3 = 0$
18. $4x^2 + 12x - 3 = 0$
19. $x^2 + 6x - 11 = 0$
20. $x^2 - 5x + 1 = 0$
21. $x^2 + 7x - 3 = 0$
22. $2x^2 - 6x + 1 = 0$
23. $3x^2 + 9x - 1 = 0$
24. $5x^2 + 15x + 2 = 0$

2.8 Sketching Quadratics from Completed Square Form

National 5 Skills

To sketch a quadratic from completed square form:

Step 1: Identify the turning point and shape of the graph from values of k, p *and* q from the form $\boldsymbol{y = k(x + p)^2 + q}$.

Step 2: Find y-intercept by making $x = 0$.

NB: When $k > 0$ the graph of the function is 'u' shaped.
When $k < 0$ the graph of the function is 'n' shaped.

Step 3: Sketch graph, noting turning point, y-intercept and axis of symmetry. (The axis of symmetry is a vertical line, taken from the x-coordinate of the turning point.)

Worked Example:

Sketch the graph of $y = 2(x - 3)^2 + 4$.

Turning Point: $(3, 4)$

y-intercept (when $x = 0$): $y = 2(0 - 3)^2 + 4$

$y = 22 \quad \therefore (0, 22)$

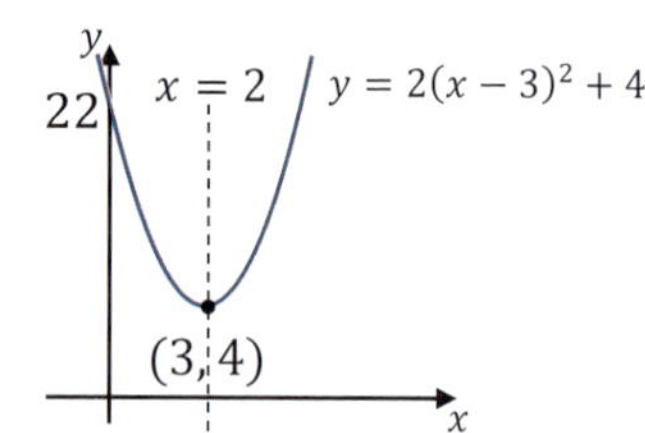

Exercise 2.8

1. Sketch the graph for each of the following quadratic functions:

(a) $y = (x - 2)^2 + 4$
(b) $y = (x + 3)^2 + 5$
(c) $y = (x + 5)^2 + 7$
(d) $y = (x - 3)^2 + 6$
(e) $y = (x - 2)^2 + 8$
(f) $y = (x + 7)^2 + 2$

2. Sketch the graph for each of the following quadratic functions:

(a) $y = -(x - 2)^2 - 6$
(b) $y = -(x - 5)^2 - 8$
(c) $y = -(x + 3)^2 - 7$

(d) $y = -(x-4)^2 - 9$ (e) $y = -(x+5)^2 - 3$ (f) $y = -(x+4)^2 - 11$

3. Sketch the graph for each of the following quadratic functions:

(a) $y = 2(x-3)^2 + 5$ (b) $y = 3(x+3)^2 + 7$ (c) $y = 4(x-2)^2 + 9$

(d) $y = -2(x-5)^2 - 7$ (e) $y = 2(x+1)^2 + 8$ (f) $y = -3(x+1)^2 - 8$

(g) $y = 2(x-2)^2 + 3$ (h) $y = 5(x+2)^2 + 9$ (i) $y = -3(x-3)^2 - 1$

2.9 Sketching Quadratics from Factorised Form

National 5 Skills

To sketch a quadratic from factorised form:

Step 1: Identify the roots and shape from values of k, m and n from the form $\boldsymbol{y = k(x-m)(x-n)}$.

Step 2: Find y-intercept by making $x = 0$.

Step 3: Sketch graph, noting turning point, y-intercept and axis of symmetry.

NB: When $k > 0$ the graph of the function is 'u' shaped.
When $k < 0$ the graph of the function is 'n' shaped.

Worked Example:

Sketch the graph of $y = (x+2)(x-4)$.

Roots: $x = -2, x = 4$

Turning Point: $x = \frac{-2+4}{2} = 1$ (this is the mean of the two roots)

$y = (1+2)(1-4) = (3)(-3) = -9 \therefore (1, -9)$

y-intercept (when $x = 0$): $y = (0+2)(0-4) = -8 \therefore (0, -8)$

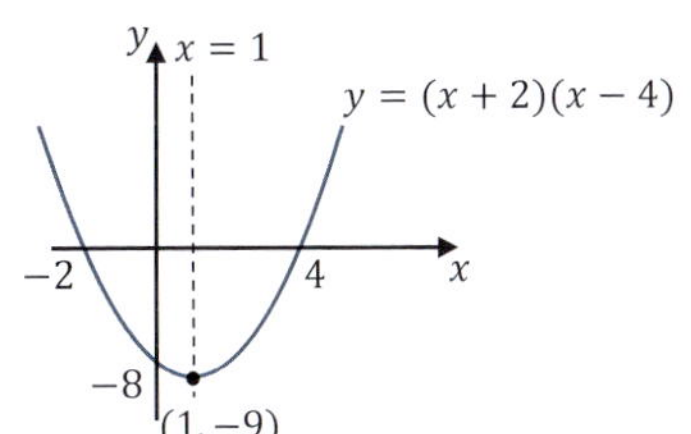

Exercise 2.9

1. Sketch the graph for each of the following quadratic functions:

(a) $y = (x+5)(x-3)$ (b) $y = x(x-6)$ (c) $y = (x+7)(x-3)$

(d) $y = x(x+3)$ (e) $y = (x+1)(x-5)$ (f) $y = (x-2)^2$

(g) $y = (x-5)(x+5)$ (h) $y = (x-4)^2$ (i) $y = (x-3)(x+3)$

2. Sketch the graph for each of the following quadratic functions:

(a) $y = -(x+3)(x-5)$ (b) $y = -x(x+4)$ (c) $y = -x(x-5)$

(d) $y = -(x+2)(x-6)$ (e) $y = -(x+5)^2$ (f) $y = -(x-3)^2$

Worked Example:

Sketch the graph of $y = 2(x-5)(x+3)$.

Roots: $x = 5, x = -3$

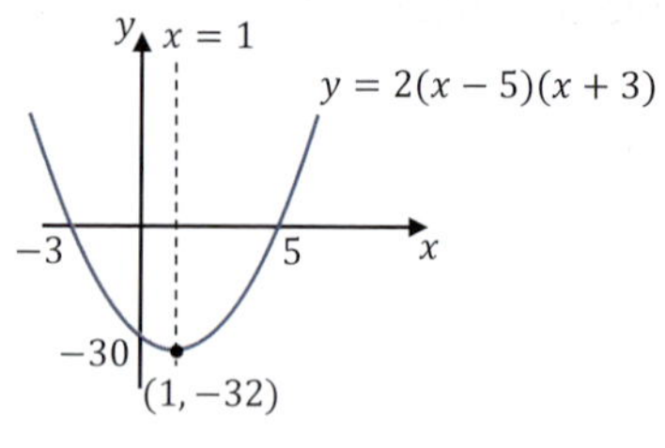

Turning Point: $x = \frac{-3+5}{2} = 1$

$y = 2(1-5)(1+3) = 2(-4)(4) = -32,$

Minimum turning point at $(1, -32)$

y-intercept (when $x = 0$): $y = 2(0-5)(0+3) = -30$

y-intercept at $(0, -30)$

3. Sketch the graph for each of the following quadratic functions:

(a) $y = 2(x+2)(x-6)$ (b) $y = 3(x-3)(x-9)$ (c) $y = 5(x+8)(x-6)$

(d) $y = 2(x-4)(x+2)$ (e) $y = 5x(x-6)$ (f) $y = 2(x+9)^2$

(g) $y = -2x(x-3)$ (h) $y = 3x(x-4)$ (i) $y = -5(x+5)(x-5)$

2.10 Solving Quadratic Inequations

To solve a quadratic inequation: (i) find the roots, (ii) draw a sketch and (iii) answer the question. There are two types of solution to a quadratic inequation, a **bounded solution**, which is enclosed between the two roots of the quadratic (example 1) and an **unbounded solution**, which involves two separate values of x going to $\pm\infty$ (example 2). To find where a quadratic function is **less than zero** is to find where the graph is **below** the x-axis and to find where it is **greater than zero** is to find where the graph is **above** the x-axis.

Worked Examples:

Solve the following quadratic inequations:

1. $x^2 - 6x + 5 < 0$

Roots: $(x-1)(x-5) = 0$

$x - 1 = 0$ *or* $x - 5 = 0$

$x = 1$ $x = 5$

$\therefore x^2 - 6x + 5 < 0$ for $1 < x < 5$

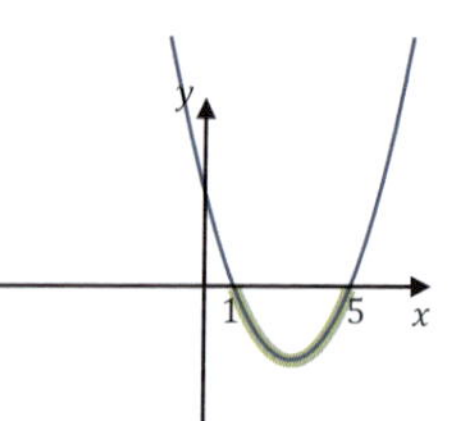

This quadratic is positive as the coefficient of x^2 is greater than zero, therefore the graph has a **minimum turning point**. The roots are $x = 1$ and $x = 5$. To solve the inequation $x^2 - 6x + 5 < 0$ is to find where the graph is below the x-axis.

2. $-x^2 + 3x + 18 \leq 0$

Roots: $(6-x)(x+3) = 0$

$6 - x = 0$ *or* $x + 3 = 0$

$x = 6$ $x = -3$

$\therefore -x^2 + 3x + 18 \leq 0$ for $x \leq -3$ and $x \geq 6$

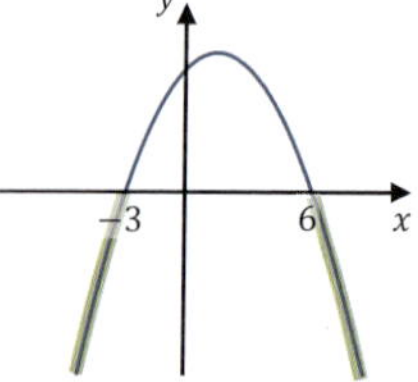

This quadratic is negative as the coefficient of x^2 is less than zero, therefore the graph has a **maximum turning point**. It could also be rearranged to $x^2 - 3x - 18 \geq 0$ and solved to give the correct solution.

Exercise 2.10

Solve the following quadratic inequations:

1. $x^2 - 3x < 0$
2. $4x^2 - 8x < 0$
3. $5x^2 - 125 > 0$
4. $x^2 - 9 \geq 0$
5. $x^2 - 3x + 2 \leq 0$
6. $2x^2 - 2x - 12 > 0$
7. $x^2 + 5x + 6 < 0$
8. $x^2 + 8x + 12 > 0$
9. $x^2 + 2x - 15 \leq 0$
10. $x^2 + 7x - 8 < 0$
11. $x^2 - 9x + 18 \geq 0$
12. $x^2 + 9x + 14 < 0$
13. $8 - 7x - x^2 < 0$
14. $x^2 \leq 5x - 4$
15. $50 - 2x^2 \geq 0$
16. $20 + x - x^2 \leq 0$
17. $x^2 + 5x - 7 < 4x + 5$
18. $x^2 \leq 1$
19. $x^2 + 3x - 54 > 0$
20. $7x^2 + 4x - 2 \geq x^2 + 5x$
21. $x^2 - 5x + 1 \leq 5 + 6x - 2x^2$

2.11 Determining the Nature of Roots (The Discriminant)

National 5 Skills

The formula $b^2 - 4ac$, where $ax^2 + bx + c = 0$ is known as the **discriminant**. The discriminant is used to determine the *nature of the roots*, or the points of intersection between a quadratic curve and the x-axis.

There are three results that matter when calculating the discriminant:

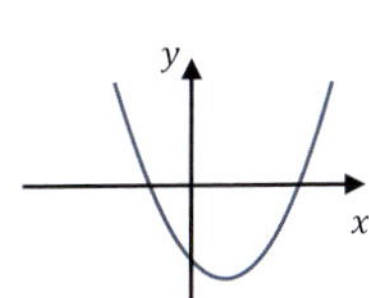

$b^2 - 4ac > 0$
two real and distinct roots
i.e. the curve cuts the x-axis in two different places.

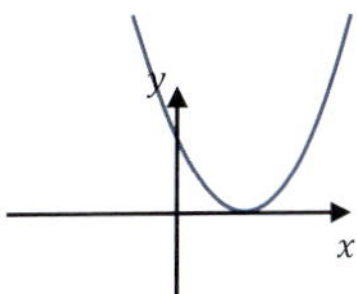

$b^2 - 4ac = 0$
two real and equal roots
i.e. the x-axis is a tangent to the curve.

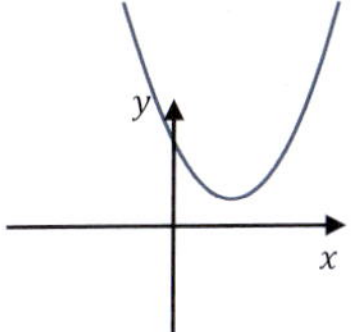

$b^2 - 4ac < 0$
no real roots
i.e. the curve does not cut the x-axis.

Worked Examples:

1. State the nature of the roots of the quadratic equation $x^2 + 3x - 2 = 0$.

   Since $ax^2 + bx + c = 0$, then $a = 1, b = 3, c = -2$

   $b^2 - 4ac = (3)^2 - 4(1)(-2) = 9 + 8 = 17 > 0$

   $b^2 - 4ac > 0$, $\therefore$ there are two real and distinct roots.

2. State the nature of the roots of the quadratic equation $x^2 + 6x + 9 = 0$.

   Since $ax^2 + bx + c = 0$, then $a = 1, b = 6, c = 9$

   $b^2 - 4ac = (6)^2 - 4(1)(9) = 36 - 36 = 0$

   $b^2 - 4ac = 0$, $\therefore$ there are two real and equal roots.

3. State the nature of the roots of the quadratic equation $2x^2 = 4x - 5$.

Since we require $ax^2 + bx + c = 0$, the quadratic needs to be rearranged:

$2x^2 = 4x - 5$

$2x^2 - 4x + 5 = 0$

then $a = 2, b = -4, c = 5$

$b^2 - 4ac = (-4)^2 - 4(2)(5) = 16 - 40 = -24 < 0$

$b^2 - 4ac < 0$, $\therefore$ there are no real roots.

Exercise 2.11

Determine the nature of the roots of the following quadratic equations:

1. $x^2 + 5x + 1 = 0$
2. $2x^2 + x + 5 = 0$
3. $x^2 - 8x + 16 = 0$
4. $2x^2 + 2x - 9 = 0$
5. $x^2 - 2x + 1 = 0$
6. $4x^2 + 5x + 2 = 0$
7. $x^2 + 25 = 10x$
8. $3x^2 - 10x + 9 = 0$
9. $x^2 + 2x - 7 = 0$
10. $2x^2 = 3x$
11. $2x^2 + 3x = x^2 + 8x - 9$
12. $x^2 - 9 = 12x$

2.12 Using the Discriminant

When the roots of a quadratic equation are not known, but the nature of the roots are known, the discriminant can be used to find the value, or range of values, of the unknown coefficients.

Worked Examples:

1. State the values of k for which the equation $2x^2 + kx + 2 = 0$ has equal roots.

Since $ax^2 + bx + c = 0$, then $a = 2, b = k, c = 2$ and the quadratic has equal roots so,

$b^2 - 4ac = 0$

$k^2 - 4(2)(2) = 0$

$k^2 - 16 = 0$

$k^2 = 16$

$k = \pm 4$

2. State the values of k for which the equation $x^2 + (k - 6)x + 1 = 0$ has no real roots.

Since $ax^2 + bx + c = 0$, then $a = 1, b = (k - 6), c = 1$ and the quadratic has no real roots so,

$b^2 - 4ac < 0$

$(k - 6)^2 - 4(1)(1) < 0$

$k^2 - 12k + 36 - 4 < 0$

$k^2 - 12k + 32 < 0$

$(k - 8)(k - 4) = 0$

$k - 8 = 0$ *or* $k - 4 = 0$

$k = 8$ *or* $k = 4$

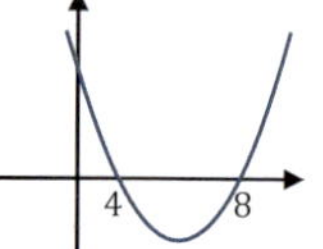

$\therefore k^2 - 12k + 32 < 0$ for $4 < k < 8$

Exercise 2.12

1. Find the value(s) of k for which the following quadratic equations have equal roots:

(a) $kx^2 + 4x + 1 = 0$ (b) $x^2 + kx + 4 = 0$ (c) $x^2 + kx + k = 0$

(d) $x^2 + kx + 1 = 0$ (e) $x^2 + kx + (3 - k) = 0$ (f) $kx^2 - 8x + 1 = 0$

(g) $x^2 + (k + 2)x + 1 = 0$ (h) $x^2 + (k - 1)x + (1 - k) = 0$ (i) $2x^2 - 2kx + 3k = 0$

2. Find the range of values of k for which the following quadratic equations have no real roots:

(a) $x^2 - 4x + k = 0$ (b) $x^2 - kx + 25 = 0$ (c) $2x^2 - kx + 8 = 0$

(d) $x^2 + (3 - k)x + k = 0$ (e) $x^2 + kx + (k + 3) = 0$ (f) $x^2 - kx + (k + 8) = 0$

(g) $x^2 + kx - x - k + 1 = 0$ (h) $x^2 + 2x + kx + 1 = 0$ (i) $2x^2 - 2kx + 3k = 0$

3. Find the range of values of k for which the following quadratic equations have two real roots:

(a) $x^2 + 2x + k = 0$ (b) $x^2 + kx + 25 = 0$ (c) $4x^2 + kx + 4 = 0$

(d) $x^2 + (k - 6)x + 3k - 2 = 0$ (e) $kx^2 + 3kx + (k - 1) = 0$ (f) $kx^2 + (5 + k)x + 9 = 0$

(g) $x^2 + 4x - kx + 7 = k$ (h) $2kx^2 + 2x + kx + 1 = 0$ (i) $x^2 + 3k = 5k - kx$

2.13 Show a Line is a Tangent to a Curve

To show that a line is a tangent to a curve, equate the line and the curve, rearrange so that they equal zero, then either solve and show equal roots, or show that the discriminant equals zero.

Worked Example:

Show that the line with equation $y = 2x + 1$ is a tangent to the curve $y = x^2 + 6x + 5$.

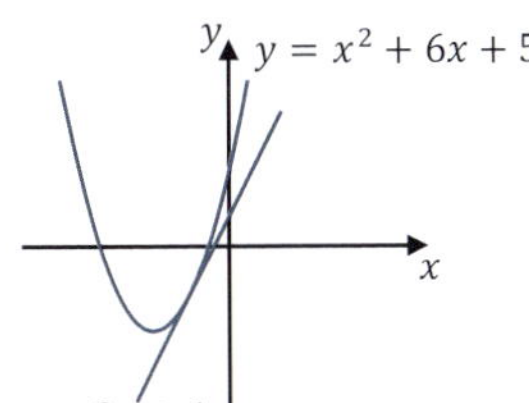

Solution Method 1:

$x^2 + 6x + 5 = 2x + 1$

$x^2 + 4x + 4 = 0$

$(x + 2)(x + 2) = 0$

$x = -2$ twice, $\therefore$ the line is a tangent to the curve.

Solution Method 2:

$x^2 + 6x + 5 = 2x + 1$

$x^2 + 4x + 4 = 0$

then $a = 1, b = 4, c = 4$

$b^2 - 4ac = (4)^2 - 4(1)(4) = 16 - 16 = 0$

$b^2 - 4ac = 0$, $\therefore$ the line is a tangent to the curve.

NB: When we need to find the points of intersection, method 1 is simpler as the x-coordinate has already been calculated.

Exercise 2.13

In each of the following, show that the line is a tangent to the curve:

1. $y = 3x + 2$ and $y = x^2 - x + 6$
2. $y = x + 9$ and $y = x^2 - x + 10$
3. $y = 8x - 16$ and $y = x^2$
4. $y = 7 - 4x$ and $y = x^2 + 2x + 16$
5. $y = x - 9$ and $y = 2x^2 + 9x - 1$
6. $y = x - 19$ and $y = x^2 - 9x + 6$
7. $2x + y - 10 = 0$ and $y = x^2 + 11$
8. $3x - y - 11 = 0$ and $y = 2x^2 - 9x + 7$
9. $7x + y - 5 = 0$ and $y = 2x^2 - 3x + 7$
10. $5x - y - 3 = 0$ and $y = 2x^2 - 11x + 29$
11. $5x - y - 2 = 0$ and $y = x^2 - 7x + 34$
12. $9x + y - 10 = 0$ and $y = 4x^2 - x + 14$

2.14 Nature of the Intersection of a Line and a Curve

To determine the nature of the intersection of a line and a curve: (i) equate the line and the curve, (ii) rearrange so that they equal zero, (iii) calculate the value of the discriminant.

Worked Examples:

1. Determine whether the line with equation $y = x - 2$ and the curve $y = x^2 + 6x + 5$ intersect.

Solution:

$x^2 + 6x + 5 = x - 2$

$x^2 + 5x + 7 = 0$

then $a = 1, b = 5, c = 7$

$b^2 - 4ac = (5)^2 - 4(1)(7) = 25 - 28 = -3$

$b^2 - 4ac < 0$, $\therefore$ the line and curve do not intersect.

2. Determine whether the line with equation $y = 2x - 5$ and the curve $y = x^2 - 4x - 6$ intersect.

Solution:

$x^2 - 4x - 6 = 2x - 5$

$x^2 - 6x - 1 = 0$

then $a = 1, b = 6, c = -1$

$b^2 - 4ac = (6)^2 - 4(1)(-1) = 36 + 4 = 40$

$b^2 - 4ac > 0$, $\therefore$ there are two points of intersection.

Exercise 2.14

In each of the following, determine whether the line and curve intersect and the nature of the intersection (justify your answer):

1. $y = 5x + 1$ and $y = x^2 - 3x + 7$
2. $y = x - 12$ and $y = x^2 - 3x - 4$
3. $y = 4x - 1$ and $y = x^2$
4. $y = 5 - 3x$ and $y = x^2 - 5x + 18$

5. $y = x + 4$ and $y = x^2 + 5x + 8$

6. $y = 6x - 12$ and $y = x^2 - 9x + 6$

7. $2x + y - 9 = 0$ and $y = x^2 + 10$

8. $4x - y + 5 = 0$ and $y = 2x^2 - 7x - 7$

9. $x + y + 8 = 0$ and $y = 2x^2 - 7x + 7$

10. $5x + y - 3 = 0$ and $y = 2x^2 + 8x + 13$

11. $5x - y + 2 = 0$ and $y = 3x^2 - 10x + 11$

12. $6x + y + 10 = 0$ and $y = 4x^2 - 2x + 9$

2.15 Points of Intersection of a Line and a Curve

To find the coordinates of the point(s) of intersection of a line and a curve: (i) equate the line and the curve, (ii) rearrange so that they equal zero, (iii) solve for x, substitute into line to find y.

Worked Example:

Find the coordinates of the points of intersection of the line with equation $y = 4x - 3$ and the curve with equation $y = x^2 + 2x - 11$.

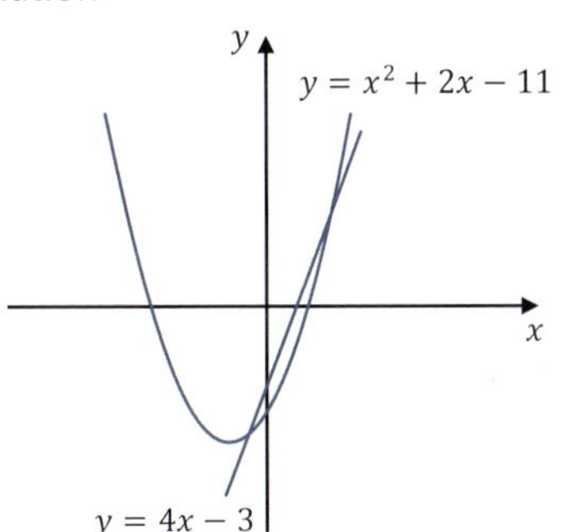

Solution:

Equate: $x^2 + 2x - 11 = 4x - 3$

Solve: $x^2 - 2x - 8 = 0$

$(x + 2)(x - 4) = 0$

$x + 2 = 0$ *or* $x - 4 = 0$

$x = -2$ $\quad$ $x = 4$

Substitute: When $x = -2$, $y = 4(-2) - 3 = -11$

When $x = 4$, $y = 4(4) - 3 = 13$

$\therefore$ Points of intersection are $(-2, -11)$ and $(4, 13)$

Exercise 2.15

1. In each of the following, find the points of intersection between the line and the curve:

(a) $y = 2x + 5$ and $y = x^2 - x - 5$

(b) $y = 4x + 5$ and $y = x^2 - x + 9$

(c) $y = 12 - 2x$ and $y = 5x - x^2$

(d) $y = 5 - 5x$ and $y = x^2 - 9$

(e) $y = 3x + 14$ and $y = x^2 + 3x - 2$

(f) $y = x^2 + 7$ and $y = 19$

(g) $4x - y + 1 = 0$ and $y = 1 - 5x - x^2$

(h) $10x - y + 8 = 0$ and $y = x^2 + 17$

(i) $y = 8x + 1$ and $y = 4x^2 + 1$

(j) $2x - y + 8 = 0$ and $y = 17 + 2x - x^2$

2. In each of the following, show that the line is a tangent to the curve and find the point of contact:

(a) $y = 5x - 1$ and $y = x^2 + 3x$

(b) $y = 5x - 6$ and $y = x^2 - x + 3$

(c) $y = 3x - 4$ and $y = x^2 - x$

(d) $y = 4x - 5$ and $y = x^2 - 1$

(e) $y = 9x + 32$ and $y = 7 - x - x^2$

(f) $y = 8x + 21$ and $y = 5 - x^2$

2.16 Points of Intersection of Two Curves

To find the coordinates of the point(s) of intersection of two curves: (i) equate the two curves, (ii) rearrange so that they equal zero, (iii) solve for x, substitute into one of the curves to find y.

Worked Example:

Two parabolas have equations $y = x^2 - 4x - 21$ and $y = 9 - x^2$. Find the points of intersection of the two parabolas.

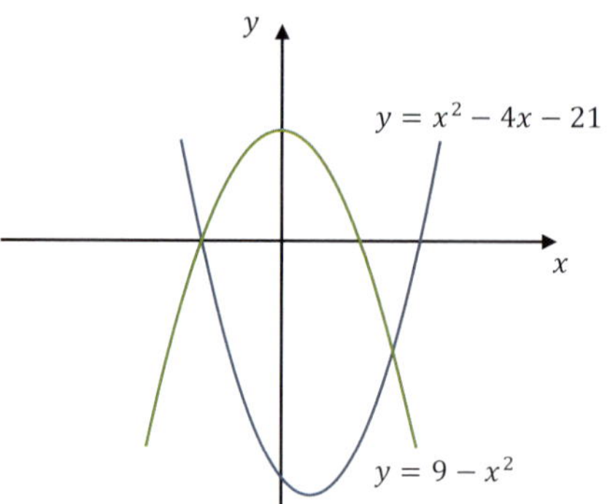

Solution:

Equate: $x^2 - 4x - 21 = 9 - x^2$

Solve: $2x^2 - 4x - 30 = 0$

$2(x + 3)(x - 5) = 0$

$x + 3 = 0$ *or* $x - 5 = 0$

$x = -3$ $\quad$ $x = 5$

Substitute: When $x = -3$, $y = 9 - (-3)^2 = 0$
When $x = 5$, $y = 9 - (5)^2 = -16$

∴ Points of intersection are $(-3, 0)$ and $(5, -16)$

Exercise 2.16

In each of the following, find the points of intersection of the two curves:

1. $y = 9 - 2x^2$ and $y = 2x^2 - 27$
2. $y = x^2 - 15$ and $y = 2x^2 - 5x - 9$
3. $y = 7x - x^2$ and $y = x^2 + x - 8$
4. $y = 5x - x^2$ and $y = x^2 - 5x + 8$
5. $y = 2x^2 + 2x + 12$ and $y = 3x^2 - 5x - 6$
6. $y = x^2 + 2x - 8$ and $y = 2x - x^2$
7. $y = 2x^2 - 2$ and $y = 25 - x^2$
8. $y = x^2 + 2x + 5$ and $y = 2x^2 + 10x + 5$
9. $y = 3x^2 + 15$ and $y = 2x^2 - 7x + 5$
10. $y = x^2 - 7x - 9$ and $y = 15 + x - x^2$

2.17 Review

Exercise 2.17

2.4-5 Solve the following quadratic equations:

(a) $x^2 - 28 = 10x - x^2$ $\quad$ (b) $x^2 - 31 = 5 + 3x - 2x^2$ $\quad$ (c) $x^2 - 16 = 56 - x^2$

(d) $x^2 - 2x = 1 - x^2$ $\quad$ (e) $x^2 + x - 2 = 4x - x^2$ $\quad$ (f) $x^2 + 4x = 3x^2 - 9$

2.6 Express the following in the form $a(x + b)^2 + c$:

(a) $x^2 - 5x + 7$ $\quad$ (b) $5 + 3x - x^2$ $\quad$ (c) $3x^2 - 9x + 20$

2.7 Solve the following quadratic equations:

(a) $x^2 - 4x - 15 = 0$ (b) $x^2 + 8x + 4 = 0$ (c) $2x^2 - 10x + 5 = 0$

2.10 Solve the following quadratic inequations:

(a) $x^2 - 3x - 28 > 0$ (b) $2x^2 + 4x - 6 < 0$ (c) $3x^2 - 14x \geq 5$

2.12 (a) The equation $x^2 + kx + k + 3 = 0$ has two real distinct roots.
Determine the range of values for k.

(b) The equation $x^2 + (k+1)x + 4 = 0$ has equal roots.
Determine the range of values for k.

(c) The equation $3kx^2 + 4kx + (k-1) = 0$ has no real roots.
Determine the range of values for k.

2.13 In each of the following, show the line is a tangent to the curve and find the point of contact:

(a) $y = 4 - 2x$ and $y = x^2 + 4x + 13$ (b) $y = 4x + 3$ and $y = x^2 + 7$

2.14 In each of the following, determine whether the line and the curve intersect (justify your answer):

(a) $y = x - 4$ and $y = x^2 + x + 2$ (b) $y = 3x + 2$ and $y = x^2 + 2x - 9$

2.15 In each of the following, find the points of intersection between the line and the curve:

(a) $y = 5x + 2$ and $y = x^2 - x - 5$ (b) $y = 2x + 5$ and $y = x^2 - 19$

2.16 In each of the following, find the points of intersection between the two curves:

(a) $y = x^2 + 7x + 12$ and $y = 2x^2 + 4x - 16$ (b) $y = x^2 - 13$ and $y = 2x^2 - 5x - 7$

Chapter 3

The Circle

The Circle

Angle Properties

There are four properties to remember from National 5 Mathematics. Firstly, when two radii form a triangle, the triangle is isosceles, **i.e.** two angles and two sides are the same. As in triangle OAB below. The second property is when a diameter forms the longest side of a triangle, whose vertices all lie on the circumference. This triangle is always right angled, as in triangle CDE. Thirdly, when a tangent meets a radius, they always meet at right angles.

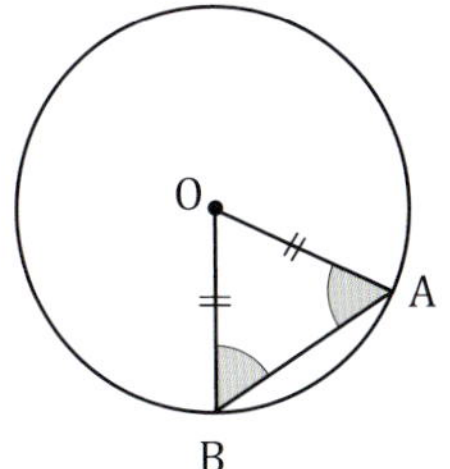

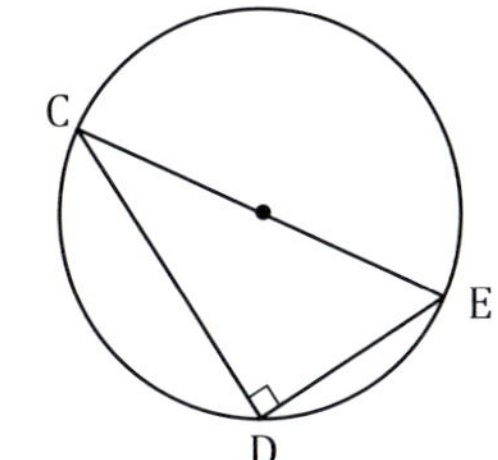

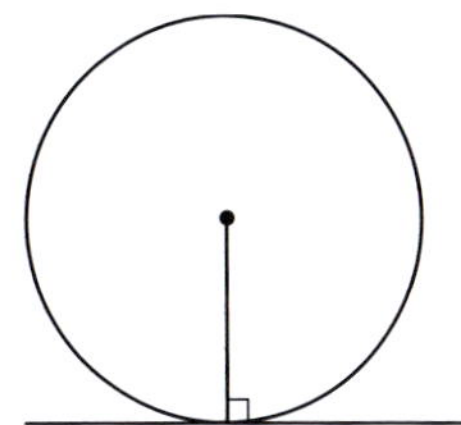

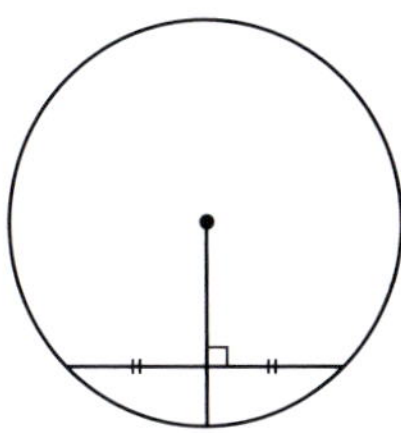

The other relationship to remember is that when a radius intersects a chord at right-angles, the intersecting line is a **perpendicular bisector** (**see 1.8**).

The Equation of a Circle

The equation of a circle is usually written in one of two forms: standard form or general form (see below).

Standard (Centre-Radius) Form: $(x-a)^2+(y-b)^2=r^2$

This is the form used to determine the equation of a circle when a centre (a, b) and a radius r is known. In Higher Mathematics it is adequate to leave the equation in standard form, but the radius must be squared. When the centre of the circle is the origin, the equation then becomes $x^2+y^2=r^2$.

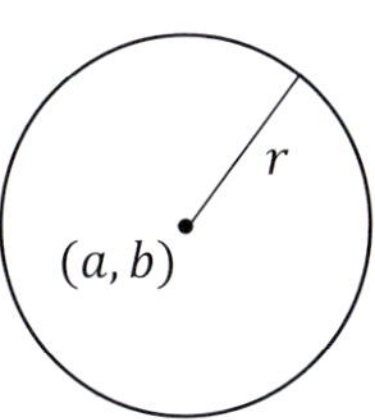

General (Expanded) Form: $x^2+y^2+2gx+2fy+c=0$

This form is the result of expanding the standard form equation and equating to zero. The centre in this form is $(-g,-f)$ and the radius is $r=\sqrt{g^2+f^2-c}$. **NB:** An equation in this form only represents a circle when r or $\sqrt{g^2+f^2-c}>0$.

Common Terms:

Collinear: three or more points on the same line.
Concentric: circles that share the same centre.
Concurrent: three or more lines that intersect at the same point.
Congruent: any two shapes that have all properties identical, **i.e.** same shape and size.

Key Fact

To find the equation of any circle, the most important thing to keep in mind is that two pieces of information are needed: **the centre of the circle** and the **radius** of the circle. This information can be substituted into the Centre-Radius form of the equation:

$$(x-a)^2+(y-b)^2=r^2$$

3.1 The Distance Between Two Points

National 5 Skills

To find the distance between two coordinates, Pythagoras' Theorem is used. This often appears in the form of the **Distance Formula:** $Distance = \sqrt{(x_2 - x_1)^2 + (y_2 - y_1)^2}$, but it may be simpler and often more helpful to sketch a right-angled triangle and work out the vertical and horizontal difference.

Worked Example:

Find the distance between $\mathrm{A}(-1, -2)$ and $\mathrm{B}(5, 6)$.

Method 1: (a) Sketch a triangle.

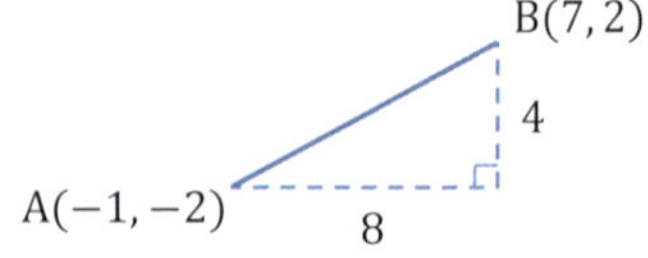

(b) Use Pythagoras' Theorem

$\mathrm{AB}^2 = 8^2 + 4^2$

$\mathrm{AB}^2 = 64 + 16$

$\mathrm{AB} = \sqrt{80}$

$\mathrm{AB} = 4\sqrt{5}\ units$

NB: When the answer is not a whole number, it should be left as a surd in its simplest form.

Method 2: Use the Distance Formula.

$\overset{x_1}{\mathrm{A}(-1}, \overset{y_1}{-2}), \mathrm{B}(\overset{x_2}{7}, \overset{y_2}{2})$

$$\mathrm{AB} = \sqrt{(x_2 - x_1)^2 + (y_2 - y_1)^2}$$
$$\mathrm{AB} = \sqrt{(7 - (-1))^2 + (2 - (-2))^2}$$
$$\mathrm{AB} = \sqrt{8^2 + 4^2}$$
$$\mathrm{AB} = \sqrt{80}$$
$$\mathrm{AB} = 4\sqrt{5}\ units$$

Exercise 3.1

Find the distance between the following pairs of points:

1. $(-1, -1)$ and $(3, 2)$
2. $(2, 3)$ and $(-3, 15)$
3. $(-3, 1)$ and $(12, 9)$
4. $(-19, 1)$ and $(-11, -5)$
5. $(-3, -5)$ and $(12, 15)$
6. $(-7, 3)$ and $(17, 10)$
7. $(-9, 7)$ and $(1, 3)$
8. $(-6, -3)$ and $(4, 5)$
9. $(-10, 3)$ and $(-6, 5)$
10. $(3, 1)$ and $(5, -7)$
11. $(-2, -5)$ and $(13, 1)$
12. $(7, 2)$ and $(5, 9)$
13. $(-1, -3)$ and $(1, 3)$
14. $(-4, 3)$ and $(10, 0)$
15. $(3, -8)$ and $(-8, -3)$

3.2 The Equation of a Circle – Centre, (a, b) and Radius, r

To determine the equation of a circle, it is essential to know two pieces of information: the **centre** of the circle and the **radius** of the circle. Sometimes one or both pieces of information are given, but more often than not, one or both of them needs to be derived. Different skills may be used to find the centre, **e.g.** finding the midpoint, simultaneous equations, the distance between points and simplifying surds.

It is good practice to always identify the centre and radius in any circle question.

Worked Examples:

1. Find the equation of the circle with centre $(5,-3)$ and radius 5. Give your answer in general (expanded) form.

Solution

Centre

$(5,-3)$
$a \quad b$

Radius

$r = 5$

$r^2 = 25$

Equation

$(x-a)^2 + (y-b)^2 = r^2$

$(x-5)^2 + (y-(-3))^2 = 5^2$

$(x-5)^2 + (y+3)^2 = 5^2$

$x^2 - 10x + 25 + y^2 + 6y + 9 = 25$

$x^2 + y^2 - 10x + 6y + 9 = 0$

2. $A(-2,-7)$ and $B(0,3)$ form the diameter of a circle.

Find the equation of the circle.

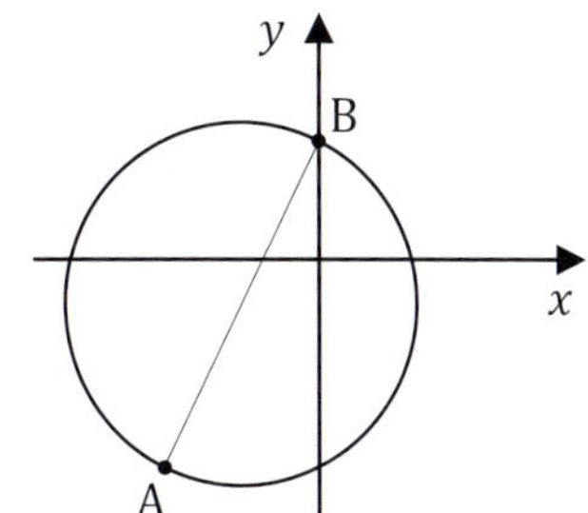

Solution

To find the centre, calculate the midpoint of AB.
To find the radius, find the distance between one of the points and the centre.

Centre (C)

$$\text{Midpoint}_{AB} = \left(\frac{x_1+x_2}{2}, \frac{y_1+y_2}{2}\right)$$

$$\text{Midpoint}_{AB} = \left(\frac{-2+0}{2}, \frac{-7+3}{2}\right)$$

$$\text{Midpoint}_{AB} = \left(\frac{-2}{2}, \frac{-4}{2}\right)$$

$$\text{Midpoint}_{AB} = (-1,-2)$$

$$C = (-1,-2)$$
$a \quad b$

Radius

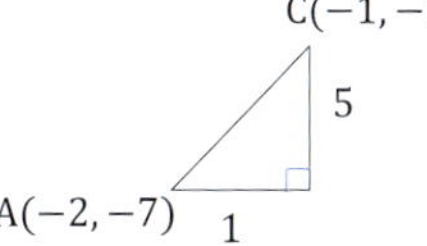

$AC^2 = 1^2 + 5^2$

$AC^2 = 26$

$AC = \sqrt{26}$

$r^2 = 26$

Equation

$(x-a)^2 + (y-b)^2 = r^2$

$(x+1)^2 + (y+2)^2 = 26$

NB: It is easier to calculate the radius than half the diameter when using surds. Standard form does not need to be expanded unless stated.

Exercise 3.2

1. Find the equation of the circles with the following information. Give your answer in general (expanded) form:

(a) centre $(4,1)$, radius 5
(b) centre $(-3,2)$, radius 7
(c) centre $(-6,5)$, radius 4
(d) centre $(9,11)$, radius 8
(e) centre $(5,-9)$, radius 6
(f) centre $(0,0)$, radius 3
(g) centre $(6,2)$, radius $\sqrt{6}$
(h) centre $(-7,3)$, radius $\sqrt{21}$
(i) centre $(0,9)$, radius $4\sqrt{3}$
(j) centre $(3,-8)$, radius $3\sqrt{5}$
(k) centre $(-7,0)$, radius $9\sqrt{6}$
(l) centre $(12,2)$, radius $3\sqrt{11}$

2. The following pairs of points form a diameter of a circle. Find the equation of the circle.

From this point give all your answers in standard (centre-radius) form:

(a) $A(-8,8)$ and $B(0,4)$
(b) $C(2,-17)$ and $D(8,-7)$
(c) $E(-16,4)$ and $F(-2,4)$

(d) $G(9, 12)$ and $H(13, -4)$ (e) $J(16, 12)$ and $K(28, 16)$ (f) $L(-11, 14)$ and $M(1, 12)$

(g) $N(7, -4)$ and $P(11, 18)$ (h) $Q(-9, 15)$ and $R(9, 3)$ (i) $S(-7, 3)$ and $T(17, -3)$

3. In the following circles, AB is either a diameter or radius. Find the equation of the following circles:

(a)

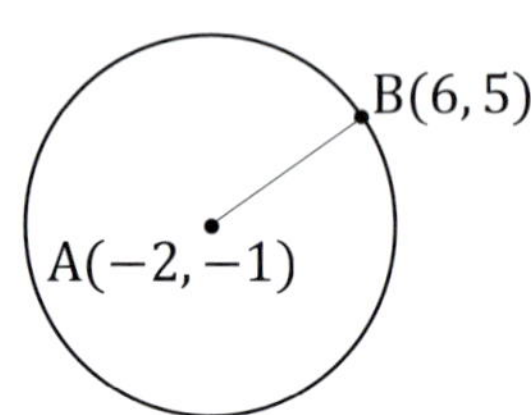

(b)

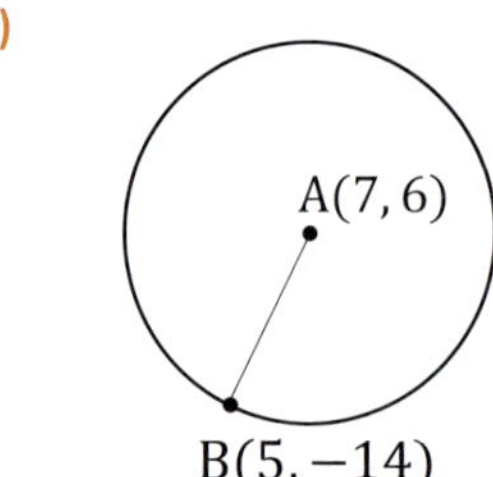

(c)

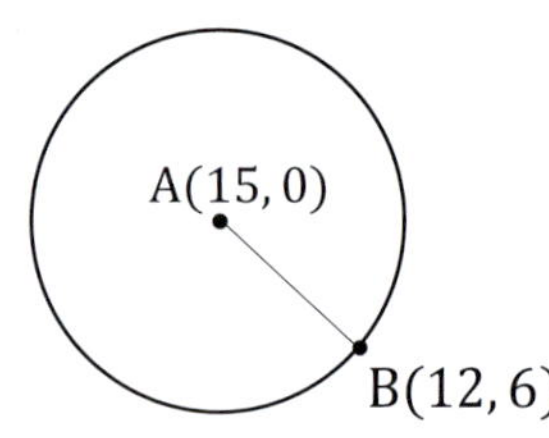

(d)

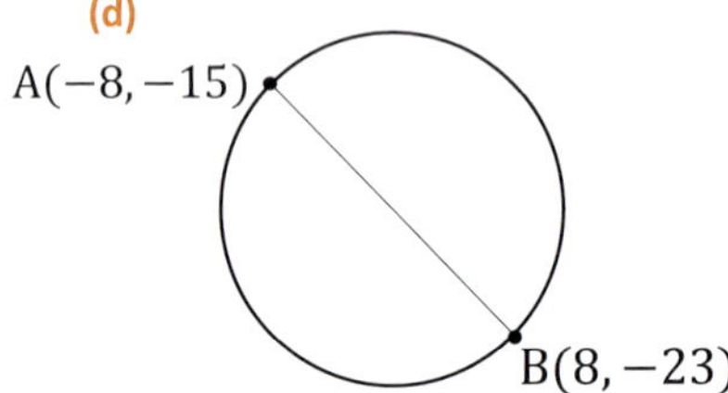

(e)

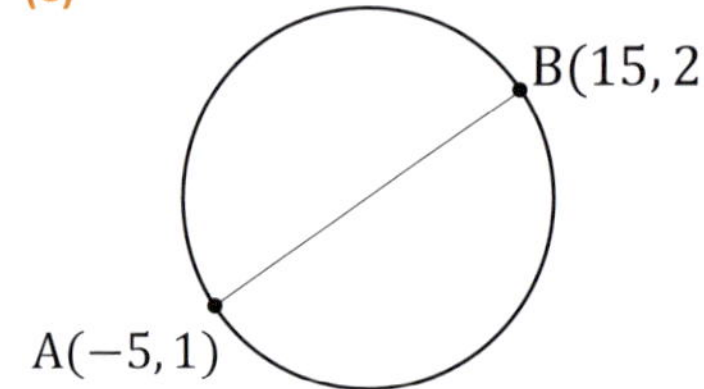

(f)

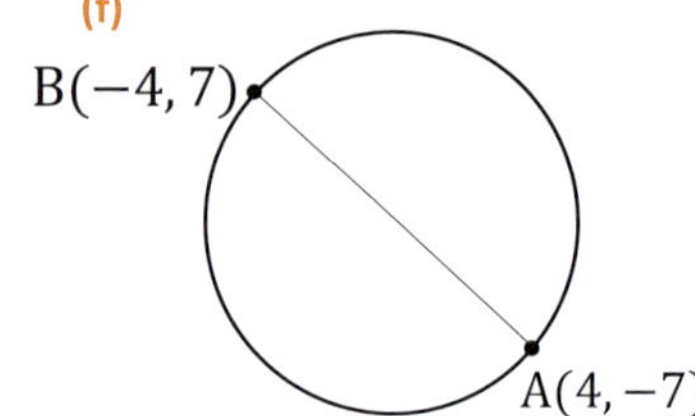

(g)

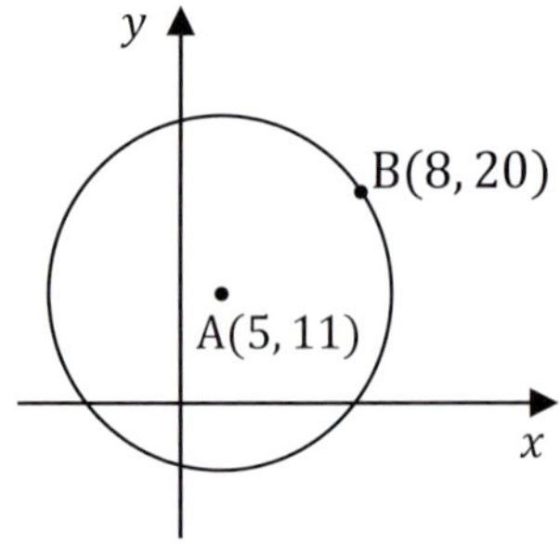

(h)

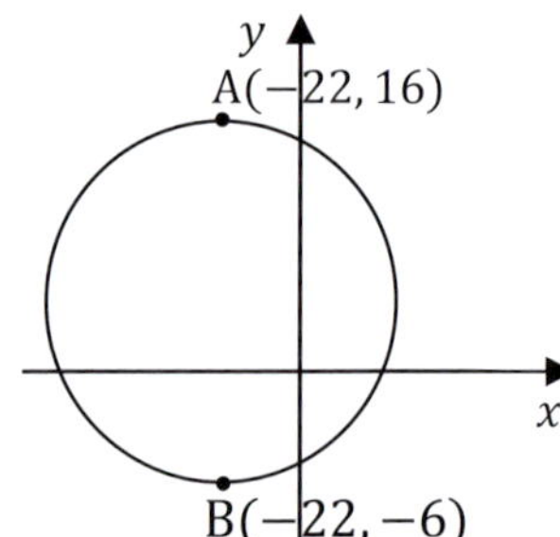

(i)

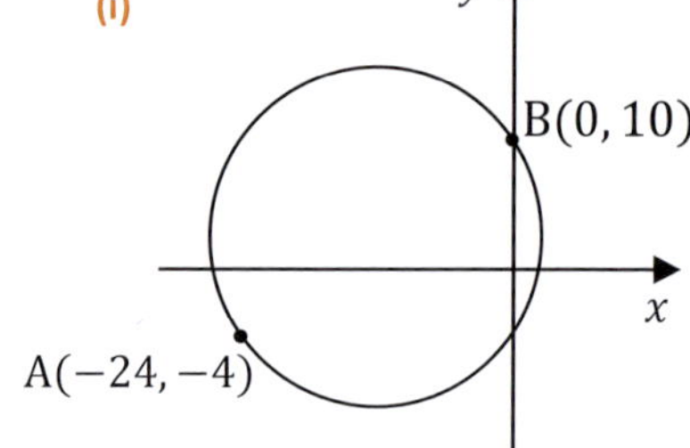

3.3 Finding the Centre and Radius from a Circle Equation

The centre and radius of the equation of a circle can be derived from both forms of the equation.

Standard (Centre-Radius) Form: $(x-a)^2 + (y-b)^2 = r^2$ **Centre:** (a, b) **Radius** $= r$

General (Expanded) Form: $x^2 + y^2 + 2gx + 2fy + c = 0$ **Centre:** $(-g, -f)$ **Radius** $= \sqrt{g^2 + f^2 - c}$

Worked Examples:

NB: the equation only represents a circle when $\sqrt{g^2 + f^2 - c} > 0$.

1. Find the centre and radius of the circle with equation $(x-5)^2 + (y+3)^2 = 50$.

Solution:

Centre: $(5, -3)$ $r = \sqrt{50} = \sqrt{25 \times 2} = 5\sqrt{2}$

2. Find the centre and radius of the circle with equation $x^2 + y^2 - 16x + 6y - 7 = 0$.

Solution: $x^2 + y^2 - 16x + 6y - 7 = 0$

Centre:

$(-g, -f)$

$2g = -16$ $\quad$ $2f = 6$

$g = -8$ $\quad$ $f = 3$

$-g = 8$ $\quad$ $-f = -3$

Circle centre $(8, -3)$

Radius:

$r = \sqrt{g^2 + f^2 - c}$

$r = \sqrt{(-8)^2 + 3^2 - (-7)}$

$r = \sqrt{64 + 9 + 7}$

$r = \sqrt{80}$

$r = 4\sqrt{5}$

Exercise 3.3

1. Find the centre and radius of the circles with the following equations:

(a) $x^2 + y^2 = 25$ $\quad$ (b) $(x - 5)^2 + (y - 3)^2 = 64$ $\quad$ (c) $(x + 12)^2 + (y - 1)^2 = 1$

(d) $x^2 + (y - 32)^2 = 75$ $\quad$ (e) $(x + 9)^2 + (y + 7)^2 = 68$ $\quad$ (f) $(x + 15)^2 + y^2 = 108$

(g) $(x - 21)^2 + (y + 9)^2 = 192$ $\quad$ (h) $x^2 + y^2 = 245$ $\quad$ (i) $(x - 2)^2 + (y - 13)^2 = 252$

(j) $(x + 17)^2 + y^2 = 289$ $\quad$ (k) $(x + 56)^2 + (y + 19)^2 = 243$ $\quad$ (l) $x^2 + (y - 10)^2 = 180$

2. Find the centre and radius of the circles with the following equations:

(a) $x^2 + y^2 - 12x + 6y - 19 = 0$ $\quad$ (b) $x^2 + y^2 - 24x + 10y + 25 = 0$

(c) $x^2 + y^2 + 4x - 14y + 4 = 0$ $\quad$ (d) $x^2 + y^2 - 10x - 8y + 29 = 0$

(e) $x^2 + y^2 - 24x + 6y + 103 = 0$ $\quad$ (f) $x^2 + y^2 - 2x + 14y + 22 = 0$

(g) $x^2 + y^2 + 30x + 4y + 54 = 0$ $\quad$ (h) $x^2 + y^2 + 4x + 24y + 49 = 0$

(i) $x^2 + y^2 - 26y + 106 = 0$ $\quad$ (j) $x^2 + y^2 - 14x + 2y - 275 = 0$

(k) $x^2 + y^2 - 16x + 8y - 176 = 0$ $\quad$ (l) $x^2 + y^2 - 22x - 311 = 0$

Worked Example:

3. Determine whether the equation $x^2 + y^2 - 6x + 10y + 35 = 0$ represents a circle

Solution: Calculate the radius.

$2g = -6$ $\quad$ $2f = 10$

$g = -3$ $\quad$ $f = 5$

$r = \sqrt{g^2 + f^2 - c}$

$r = \sqrt{(-3)^2 + (5)^2 - 35}$

$r = \sqrt{9 + 25 - 35}$

$r = \sqrt{-1}$

$r \notin \mathbb{R}$ $\therefore$ the equation does not represent a circle.

NB: $\notin$ means 'is not an element of'. $\mathbb{R}$ is the set of real numbers (see **chapter 4 – Introduction**).

3. Determine whether each of the following equations represents a circle (justify your answer):

(a) $x^2 + y^2 - 6x + 2y - 18 = 0$ $\quad$ (b) $x^2 + y^2 - 18x + 4y + 85 = 0$

(c) $x^2 + y^2 + 2x - 4y - 5 = 0$ $\quad$ (d) $x^2 + y^2 - 10x - 8y - 11 = 0$

(e) $x^2 + y^2 + 2x + 2y + 10 = 0$

(f) $x^2 + y^2 - 2x + 6y + 40 = 0$

(g) $x^2 + y^2 + 30x + 4y + 54 = 0$

(h) $x^2 + y^2 + 4x + 24y + 49 = 0$

(i) $x^2 + y^2 - 8y + 15 = 0$

(j) $x^2 + y^2 + 2 = 0$

(k) $x^2 + y^2 - 10x + 10y + 50 = 0$

(l) $x^2 + y^2 - 22x + 14y + 200 = 0$

3.4 Coordinates and the Circle 1 – Within, On or Outside a Circle

On a coordinate diagram, any coordinate lies either within, on or outside of any circle. To determine where a coordinate lies, in relation to a circle, substitute the coordinate into the left-hand side of the equation of a circle. If the answer is **less than the right-hand side** of the equation, the coordinate lies **inside** the circle, if it is **equal to the right-hand side**, the point lies **on** the circle, if it is **greater than the right-hand side**, the point lies **outside** the circle.

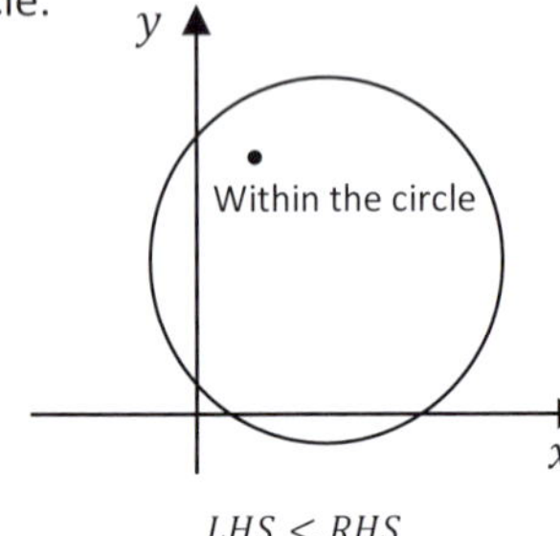

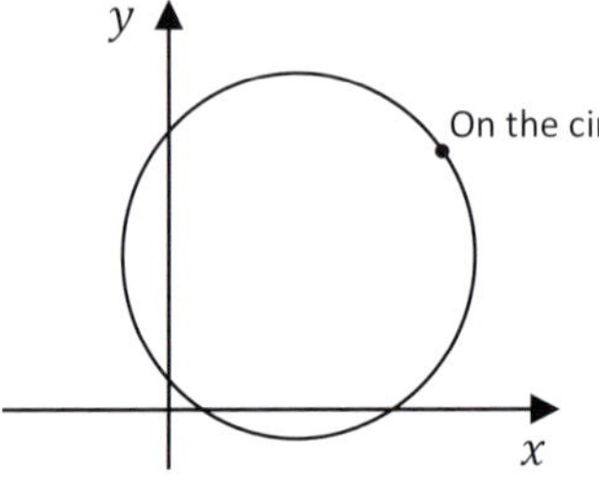

$LHS = RHS$

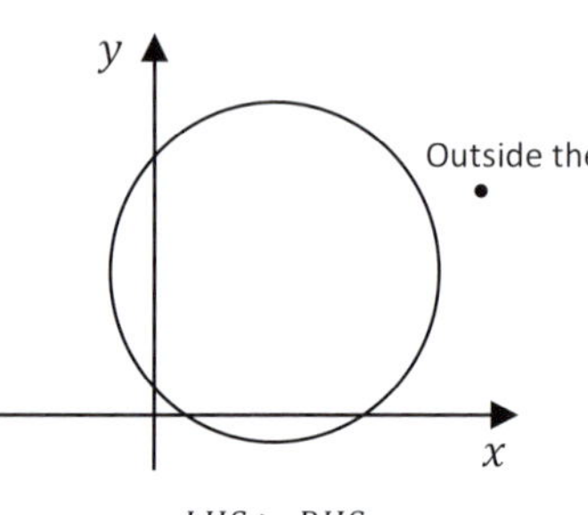

$LHS > RHS$

Worked Examples:

1. Show that the point $(-9, -5)$ lies on the circle $x^2 + y^2 + 24x - 14y + 40 = 0$.

   Solution: Substitute $(-9, -5)$ into left-hand side of equation:

   $LHS = (-9)^2 + (-5)^2 + 24(-9) - 14(-5) + 40 = 81 + 25 - 216 + 70 + 40 = 0 = RHS$

   $\therefore (-9, -5)$ lies on the circle $x^2 + y^2 + 24x - 14y + 40 = 0$.

2. Determine where the point $(5, -2\,)$ lies in relation to the circle $(x - 4)^2 + (y + 9)^2 = 45$.

   Solution: Substitute $(5, -2)$ into left-hand side of equation:

   $(5 - 4)^2 + (-2 + 9)^2 = 1^2 + 7^2 = 50$

   $50 > 45 \;\; \therefore (5, -2)$ lies outside the circle $(x - 4)^2 + (y + 9)^2 = 45$.

3. Determine where the point $(-9, 4)$ lies in relation to the circle $(x + 8)^2 + (y - 6)^2 = 105$.

   Solution: Substitute $(-9, 4)$ into left-hand side of equation:

   $(-9 + 8)^2 + (4 - 6)^2 = (-1)^2 + (-2)^2 = 5$

   $5 < 105 \;\; \therefore (-9, 4)$ lies inside the circle $(x + 8)^2 + (y - 6)^2 = 105$.

Exercise 3.4

1. Determine where the following points lie in relation to the given circles (justify your answer):

(a) $(3, -2)$ and $(x - 4)^2 + (y + 9)^2 = 45$

(b) $(2, -2)$ and $(x + 7)^2 + (y - 3)^2 = 112$

(c) $(-4, -5)$ and $(x + 3)^2 + (y + 2)^2 = 12$

(d) $(10, -7)$ and $(x - 5)^2 + (y + 2)^2 = 50$

(e) $(-11, 5)$ and $(x+7)^2 + (y-6)^2 = 28$

(f) $(0, 3)$ and $x^2 + (y-8)^2 = 17$

(g) $(7, 4)$ and $(x-5)^2 + (y-7)^2 = 72$

(h) $(14, -16)$ and $(x-7)^2 + (y+12)^2 = 65$

(i) $(-2, -9)$ and $(x+6)^2 + (y+5)^2 = 80$

(j) $(-7, 8)$ and $(x+1)^2 + (y+4)^2 = 169$

(k) $(9, 1)$ and $(x-11)^2 + y^2 = 8$

(l) $(-1, 5)$ and $(x-9)^2 + (y-15)^2 = 200$

2. Determine where the following points lie in relation to the given circles (justify your answer):

(a) $(7, 8)$ and $x^2 + y^2 - 12x + 6y - 19 = 0$

(b) $(4, -2)$ and $x^2 + y^2 + 6x - 10y - 70 = 0$

(c) $(-6, -8)$ and $x^2 + y^2 - 4x + 8y - 60 = 0$

(d) $(1, -2)$ and $x^2 + y^2 + 10x - 2y - 19 = 0$

(e) $(0, 9)$ and $x^2 + y^2 - 18x + 4y + 10 = 0$

(f) $(5, -5)$ and $x^2 + y^2 + 6y - 20 = 0$

(g) $(-11, 2)$ and $x^2 + y^2 + 14x + 6y + 6 = 0$

(h) $(-7, 0)$ and $x^2 + y^2 + 16x - 10y + 50 = 0$

(i) $(10, -6)$ and $x^2 + y^2 - 2x + 16y + 5 = 0$

(j) $(12, -6)$ and $x^2 + y^2 - 12x - 36 = 0$

(k) $(4, 7)$ and $x^2 + y^2 - 40x + 2y + 40 = 0$

(l) $(6, 3)$ and $x^2 + y^2 - 6x + 4y - 18 = 0$

3.5 The Nature of the Intersection of a Line and a Circle

Any line and any circle relate to one another in one of three ways. They either have no points of intersection, one point of intersection, or two points of intersection. The best way to determine the nature of the intersection of a line and a circle is to substitute the equation of the line into the equation of the circle, then use the discriminant.

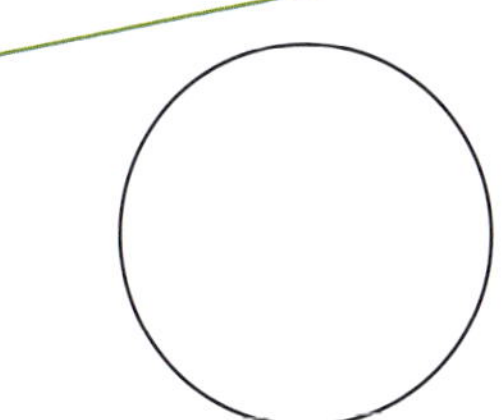

No points of intersection
$b^2 - 4ac < 0$

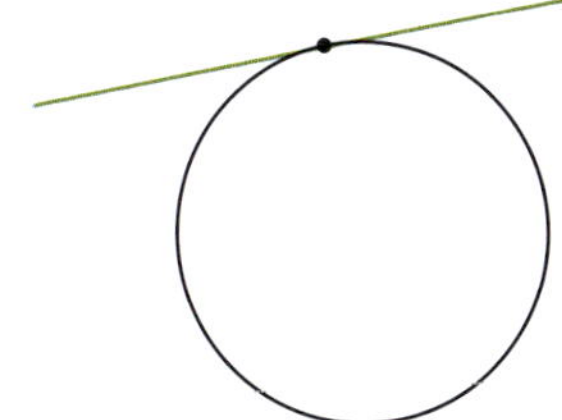

One point of intersection (line is a tangent)
$b^2 - 4ac = 0$

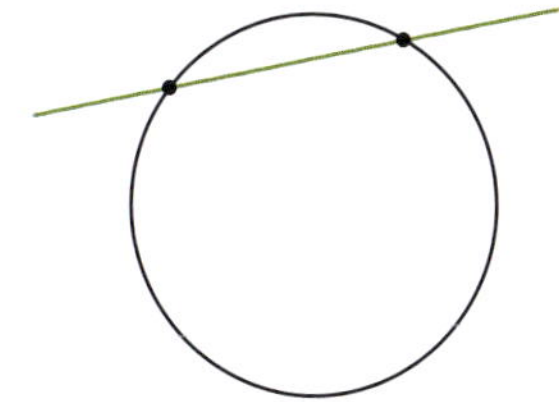

Two points of intersection (line is a chord)
$b^2 - 4ac > 0$

Worked Examples:

1. Determine the nature of intersection of the line $y = 2x - 3$ and the circle $(x-3)^2 + (y+2)^2 = 14$.

Solution: Substitute $y = 2x - 3$ into the circle equation.

$(x-3)^2 + (2x - 3 + 2)^2 = 14$

$(x-3)^2 + (2x-1)^2 = 14$ (expand and equate to zero)

$x^2 - 6x + 9 + 4x^2 - 4x + 1 - 14 = 0$

$5x^2 - 10x - 4 = 0$ (now use the discriminant)

NB: the equation may be substituted into x or y, depending on which is the easier substitution.

$a = 5, b = -10, c = -4$

$b^2 - 4ac = (-10)^2 - 4 \times 5 \times (-4) = 100 - (-80) = 180 > 0$

$b^2 - 4ac > 0$ ∴ there are two points of intersection between the line and the circle.

2. Show that the line $y = x + 9$ is a tangent to the circle $x^2 + y^2 - 10x - 12y + 29 = 0$.

Solution: Substitute $y = x + 9$ into the circle equation

$x^2 + (x + 9)^2 - 10x - 12(x + 9) + 29 = 0$ (expand)

$x^2 + x^2 + 18x + 81 - 10x - 12x - 108 + 29 = 0$

$2x^2 - 4x + 2 = 0$ (now use the discriminant)

$a = 2, b = -4, c = 2$

$b^2 - 4ac = (-4)^2 - 4 \times 2 \times 2 = 16 - 16 = 0$

$b^2 - 4ac = 0$ ∴ the line is a tangent to the circle.

Exercise 3.5

1. Determine whether the line is a tangent to the circle, intersect the circle or neither (justify your answer):

(a) $y = 2x + 2$ and $(x - 5)^2 + (y + 7)^2 = 56$

(b) $y = -x$ and $(x + 1)^2 + (y - 8)^2 = 48$

(c) $2y = x - 6$ and $(x + 9)^2 + y^2 = 26$

(d) $3y = x + 1$ and $(x - 10)^2 + (y + 3)^2 = 40$

(e) $5y = x + 2$ and $x^2 + (y + 9)^2 = 72$

(f) $x + 3y = -7$ and $(x + 7)^2 + (y + 10)^2 = 90$

(g) $y = 3x + 4$ and $(x - 15)^2 + (y - 5)^2 = 17$

(h) $y = \frac{1}{2}x + 3$ and $(x - 4)^2 + (y + 5)^2 = 100$

2. Determine whether the line is a tangent to the circle, intersect the circle or neither (justify your answer):

(a) $y = -x + 8$ and $x^2 + y^2 = 29$

(b) $y = x - 5$ and $x^2 + y^2 - 10x - 8y + 26 = 0$

(c) $y = 3x - 7$ and $x^2 + y^2 - 14x + 4y + 13 = 0$

(d) $y = 8 - x$ and $x^2 + y^2 + 8x - 56 = 0$

(e) $3y + x = -5$ and $x^2 + y^2 - 14x - 12y - 5 = 0$

(f) $x + y = 7$ and $x^2 + y^2 + 6x + 12y - 87 = 0$

(g) $y = x + 12$ and $x^2 + y^2 - 4x + 2y - 6 = 0$

(h) $y = -17$ and $x^2 + y^2 - 6x + 18y + 26 = 0$

3.6 The Points of Intersection of a Line and a Circle

When a line and a circle intersect, we can find the points of intersection by substituting the equation of the line into the equation of the circle and solving to find one of the variables. We find the other variable by substituting the value into the equation of the line.

NB: This method can be used to show the nature of an intersection of a line and a circle, unless they do not intersect. When solving the quadratic equation, two values of x or y show two points of intersection, one repeated value shows that the line is a tangent to the circle.

Worked Examples:

1. The line $y = 2x - 1$ intersects the circle $(x-4)^2 + (y-2)^2 = 10$. Find the coordinates of the points of intersection.

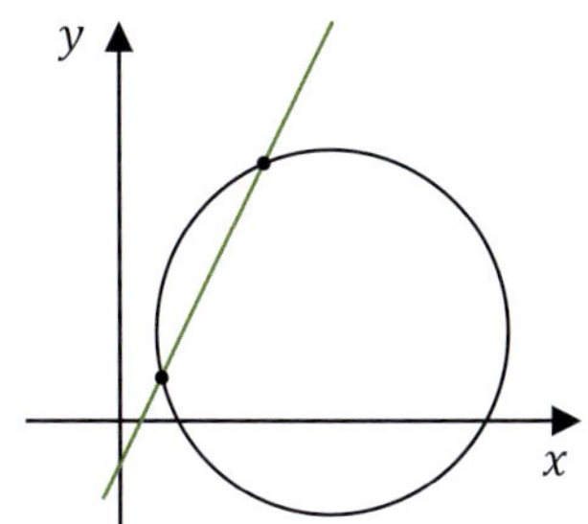

Solution: Substitute $y = 2x - 1$ into the circle equation.

$(x-4)^2 + (2x-1-2)^2 = 10$

$(x-4)^2 + (2x-3)^2 = 10$

$x^2 - 8x + 16 + 4x^2 - 12x + 9 - 10 = 0$

$5x^2 - 20x + 15 = 0$ (now factorise and solve)

$5(x^2 - 4x + 3) = 0$

$5(x-1)(x-3) = 0$

$x - 1 = 0 \quad x - 3 = 0$

$x = 1 \quad x = 3$ (now find y-coordinate)

When $x = 1, y = 2(1) - 1 = 1$. When $x = 3, y = 2(3) - 1 = 5$.

Points of intersection are $(1, 1)$ and $(3, 5)$.

2. Show that the line $x - 3y - 6 = 0$ intersects the circle $x^2 + y^2 + 10x - 6y - 6 = 0$ and find the coordinates of the point(s) of contact.

Solution: Rearrange and substitute $x - 3y - 6 = 0$ into the equation of the circle.

$x - 3y - 6 = 0$

$x = 3y + 6$

$x^2 + y^2 + 10x - 6y - 6 = 0$

$(3y+6)^2 + y^2 + 10(3y+6) - 6y - 6 = 0$

$9y^2 + 36y + 36 + y^2 + 30y + 60 - 6y - 6 = 0$

$10y^2 + 60y + 90 = 0$

$10(y^2 + 6y + 9) = 0$

$10(y+3)(y+3) = 0$

$y + 3 = 0 \quad y + 3 = 0$

$y = -3$ twice $\therefore$ the line is a tangent to the circle.

NB: The repeated root implies one point of contact and therefore tangency.

When $y = -3, x = 3(-3) + 6 = -3$.

Point of contact is $(-3, -3)$.

Exercise 3.6

1. Find the coordinates of the point(s) of intersection of the lines and circles with the following equations:

(a) $y = x - 2$ and $x^2 + y^2 = 100$

(b) $y = 3x - 15$ and $x^2 + y^2 = 45$

(c) $y = 3x + 8$ and $(x+1)^2 + (y-5)^2 = 41$

(d) $x = -6$ and $x^2 + (y-5)^2 = 40$

(e) $y = 2x + 2$ and $(x + 8)^2 + (y - 1)^2 = 45$

(f) $x + y + 1 = 0$ and $(x + 9)^2 + (y - 7)^2 = 13$

(g) $x - 3y + 30 = 0$ and $(x + 9)^2 + (y - 2)^2 = 225$

(h) $2y = x + 5$ and $(x - 12)^2 + (y - 1)^2 = 45$

2. Find the coordinates of the point(s) of intersection of the lines and circles with the following equations:

(a) $y = x + 6$ and $x^2 + y^2 = 68$

(b) $y = 8 - 9x$ and $x^2 + y^2 - 10x - 8y = 0$

(c) $2y = -x - 9$ and $x^2 + y^2 - 14x + 6y - 42 = 0$

(d) $4y + x = -12$ and $x^2 + y^2 - 10x + 8 = 0$

(e) $y = 12 - 2x$ and $x^2 + y^2 + 6x + 4y - 67 = 0$

(f) $y = x + 2$ and $x^2 + y^2 - 24y + 76 = 0$

(g) $3y = x - 5$ and $x^2 + y^2 + 10x - 10y - 75 = 0$

(h) $y = -9$ and $x^2 + y^2 - 16x + 22y + 60 = 0$

3. Show that the line with equation $4y = x + 3$ is a tangent to the circle with equation $x^2 + (y - 5)^2 = 17$ and find the coordinates of the point of contact.

4. Show that the line with equation $3y = x + 7$ is a tangent to the circle with equation $(x - 2)^2 + (y + 7)^2 = 90$ and find the coordinates of the point of contact.

5. Show that the line with equation $2x - y - 1 = 0$ is a tangent to the circle with equation $(x - 1)^2 + (y + 9)^2 = 20$ and find the coordinates of the point of contact.

6. Show that the line with equation $3y = x - 10$ is a tangent to the circle with equation $x^2 + y^2 + 10x - 10y - 40 = 0$ and find the coordinates of the point of contact.

7. Show that the line with equation $x - 4y - 2 = 0$ is a tangent to the circle with equation $x^2 + y^2 - 14x + 6y + 41 = 0$ and find the coordinates of the point of contact.

8. Show that the line with equation $x + 3y - 21 = 0$ is a tangent to the circle with equation $x^2 + y^2 + 22x - 8y + 97 = 0$ and find the coordinates of the point of contact.

3.7 The Equation of a Tangent to a Circle

A tangent to a circle is a line that touches a circle in one place. We already know from National 5 that a tangent to a circle meets the radius of the circle at right-angles. To find the equation of the tangent of a circle, we recall from chapter 1 that two pieces of information are required, a **point** on the line and the **gradient** of the line.

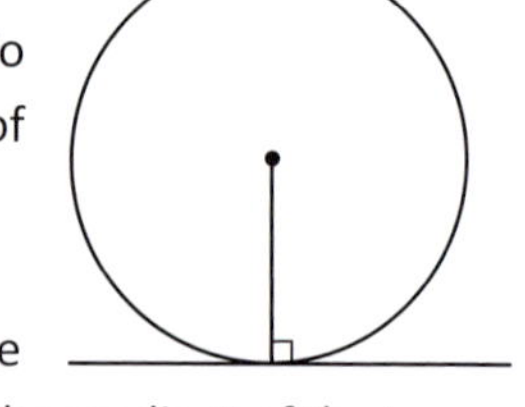

The point on the line will usually be given and the gradient is found by calculating the gradient of the radius, then using the property of perpendicular gradients to calculate the gradient of the tangent.

Worked Example:

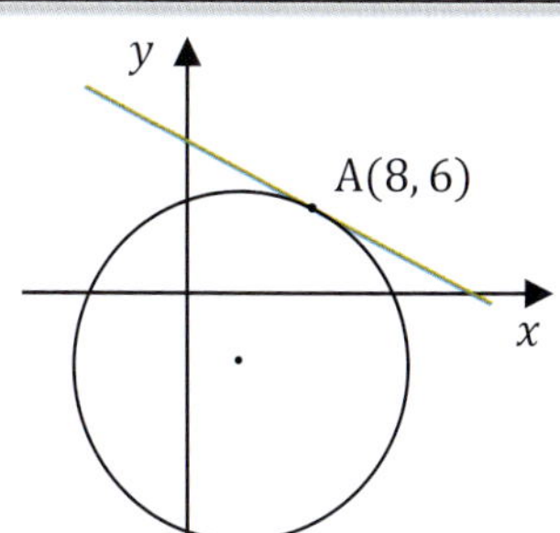

The point $A(8,6)$ lies on the circle $x^2 + y^2 - 4x + 6y - 104 = 0$.
Find the equation of the tangent to the circle at A.

Solution: Find the coordinate of the centre and use for the gradient calculation.

Centre:

$(-g, -f)$

$2g = -4 \qquad 2f = 6$

$g = -2 \qquad f = 3$

$-g = 2 \qquad -f = -3$

Circle centre $(2, -3)$ (x_1 y_1)

Point

$A(8, 6)$ (a b; x_2 y_2)

Gradient

$$m = \frac{y_2 - y_1}{x_2 - x_1}$$

$$m = \frac{6 - (-3)}{8 - 2}$$

$$m = \frac{9}{6} = \frac{3}{2}$$

$$\therefore m_{\perp} = -\frac{2}{3}$$

as $m \times m_{\perp} = -1$

Equation

$$y - b = m(x - a)$$

$$y - 6 = -\frac{2}{3}(x - 8)$$

$$3y - 18 = -2x + 16$$

$$2x + 3y - 34 = 0$$

Exercise 3.7

1. Find the equation of the tangent to the circle with the following equations at the given points:

(a) $(x-4)^2 + (y-9)^2 = 20$ and $(8,7)$

(b) $(x-3)^2 + y^2 = 18$ and $(6,3)$

(c) $(x-3)^2 + (y+1)^2 = 45$ and $(-3,2)$

(d) $(x+5)^2 + (y+2)^2 = 40$ and $(-11,0)$

(e) $(x-9)^2 + (y+1)^2 = 32$ and $(5,-5)$

(f) $(x-10)^2 + (y-8)^2 = 5$ and $(8,9)$

(g) $x^2 + (y-7)^2 = 13$ and $(2,4)$

(h) $(x-5)^2 + (y-6)^2 = 80$ and $(1,14)$

2. Find the equation of the tangent to the circle with the following equations at the given points:

(a) $x^2 + y^2 - 6x + 2y - 10 = 0$ and $(-1,1)$

(b) $x^2 + y^2 + 4x - 6y - 23 = 0$ and $(-2,9)$

(c) $x^2 + y^2 + 10x - 4y - 23 = 0$ and $(1,-2)$

(d) $x^2 + y^2 + 8x + 4y + 3 = 0$ and $(-5,2)$

(e) $x^2 + y^2 - 10y + 15 = 0$ and $(1,2)$

(f) $x^2 + y^2 - 2x - 16y + 39 = 0$ and $(0,3)$

(g) $x^2 + y^2 + 6x + 14y + 45 = 0$ and $(-1,-4)$

(h) $x^2 + y^2 + 8x - 13 = 0$ and $(-2,5)$

3. The point $B(6,7)$ lies on the circle $x^2 + y^2 - 10x - 20y + 115 = 0$
Find the equation of the tangent to the circle at B.

y

B(6, 7)

x

4. The point $C(5,-5)$ lies on the circle $x^2+y^2-6x+16y+60=0$.
Find the equation of the tangent to the circle at C.

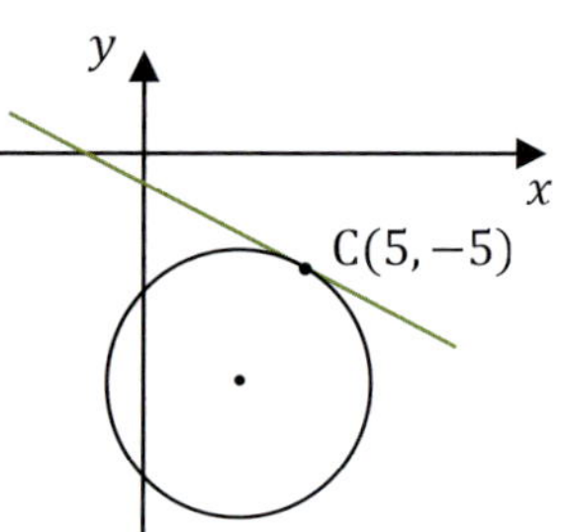

5. The point $D(7,3)$ lies on the circle $x^2+y^2-10x+2y+6=0$.
Find the coordinates of the point where the tangent at D cuts the y-axis.

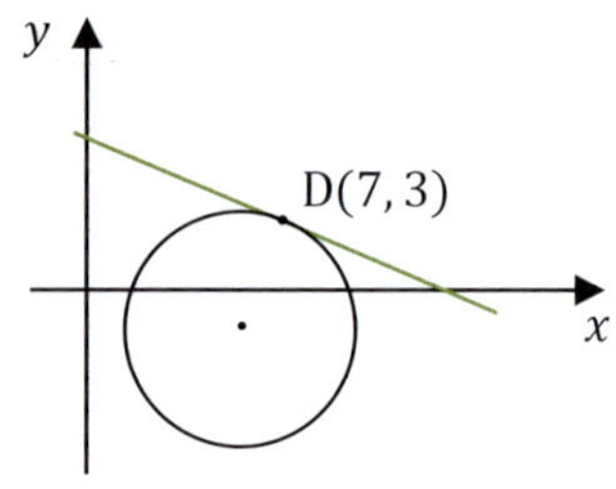

6. Two congruent circles C_1 and C_2 have equations $x^2+y^2-6x+2y-3=0$ and $x^2+y^2-14x-10y+61=0$ respectively. The circles touch externally at the point M. Find the equation of the tangent to the circles at M.

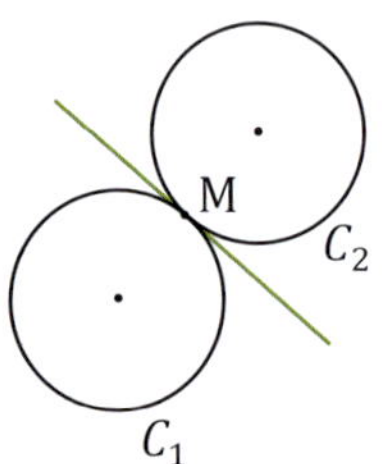

3.8 The Intersection of Two Circles

When two circles intersect, the line passing through the two points of intersection is a **common chord**. When two circles touch externally, the line passing through the point of contact is a **common tangent**.

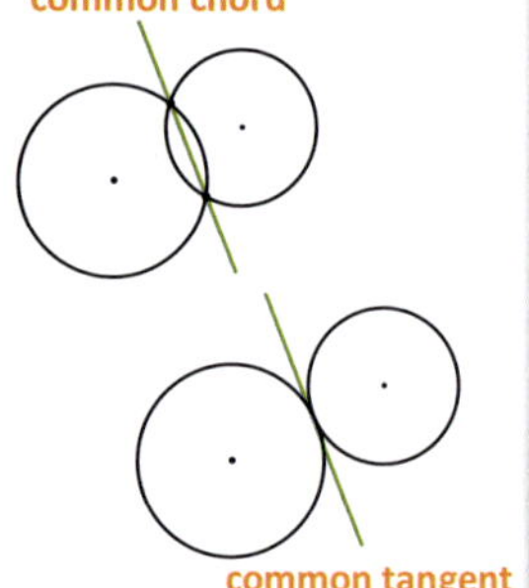

If the sum of the radii is less than the distance between the centres, the circles do not intersect. If the sum of the radii is equal to the distance between the centres, the two circles touch externally. If the sum of the radii of two circles is greater than the distance between the centres, then the two circles intersect. If the difference between the radii is equal to the distance between the centres, the circles touch internally.

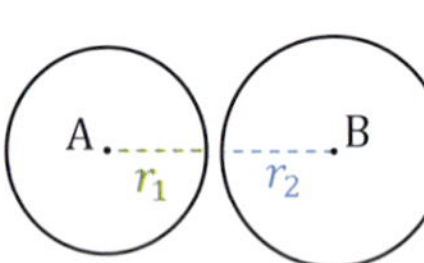

$r_1+r_2<AB$
∴ circles do not intersect

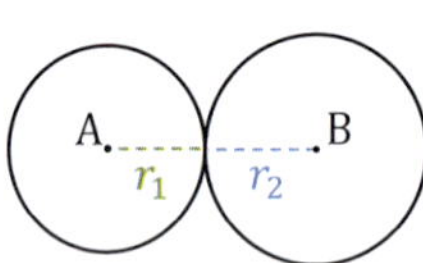

$r_1+r_2=AB$
∴ circles touch externally

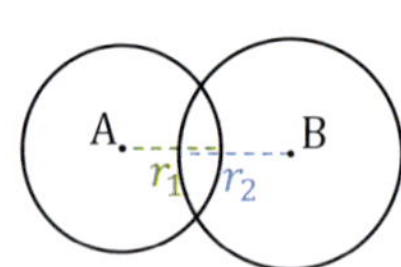

$r_1+r_2>AB$
∴ two points of intersection

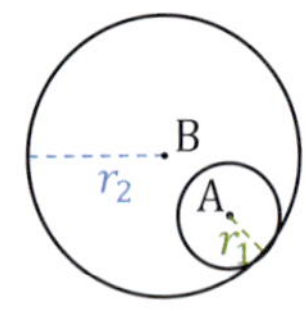

$r_2-r_1=AB$
∴ circles touch internally

Worked Example:
Circles C_1 and C_2 have equations $(x-5)^2+(y+4)^2=25$ and $x^2+y^2-14x-18y+94=0$ respectively. Show that the circles do not intersect.

Solution: Find the sum of the radii and the distance between the centres.

Circle 1

Centre:

$Centre_1=(5,-4)$

Radius:

$r_1=\sqrt{25}=5$

Circle 2

Centre:

$(-g, -f)$

$2g = -14 \qquad 2f = -18$

$g = -7 \qquad f = -9$

$-g = 7 \qquad -f = 9$

$Centre_2 = (7, 9)$

Radius:

$r_2 = \sqrt{g^2 + f^2 - c}$

$r_2 = \sqrt{(-7)^2 + (-9)^2 - 94}$

$r_2 = \sqrt{49 + 81 - 94}$

$r_2 = \sqrt{36}$

$r_2 = 6$

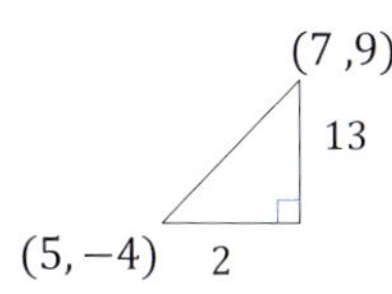

Distance between centres $= \sqrt{2^2 + 13^2}$ $= \sqrt{173}$ $= 13.2$ (1 d.p.)

Sum of radii $= 5 + 6 = 11$

$13.2 > 11$ ∴ the circles do not intersect.

Exercise 3.8

1. In the following pairs of equations, determine whether circles intersect at two points, touch internally/externally, or do not intersect:

(a) $(x + 4)^2 + (y - 9)^2 = 25$ and $x^2 + y^2 - 14x - 18y + 94 = 0$

(b) $(x - 3)^2 + (y + 2)^2 = 5$ and $x^2 + y^2 - 4x - 1 = 0$

(c) $(x + 1)^2 + (y + 3)^2 = 4$ and $x^2 + y^2 - 4x - 2y + 1 = 0$

(d) $(x - 3)^2 + (y + 2)^2 = 4$ and $x^2 + y^2 - 6x - 12y - 55 = 0$

(e) $(x - 7)^2 + (y + 6)^2 = 100$ and $x^2 + y^2 + 4x - 12y + 15 = 0$

(f) $x^2 + (y - 7)^2 = 81$ and $x^2 + y^2 + 10x + 10y + 25 = 0$

(g) $(x + 1)^2 + (y - 3)^2 = 49$ and $x^2 + y^2 + 16x + 4y + 67 = 0$

(h) $(x - 10)^2 + y^2 = 121$ and $x^2 + y^2 + 4x - 10y + 28 = 0$

2. In the following pairs of equations, determine whether circles intersect at two points, touch externally or do not intersect:

(a) $x^2 + (y - 1)^2 = 10$ and $x^2 + y^2 - 8x + 10y + 28 = 0$

(b) $(x - 7)^2 + (y - 12)^2 = 35$ and $x^2 + y^2 - 2x + 8y - 55 = 0$

(c) $(x + 4)^2 + (y + 5)^2 = 1$ and $x^2 + y^2 - 6x + 16y + 19 = 0$

(d) $(x - 7)^2 + (y + 21)^2 = 144$ and $x^2 + y^2 + 2x + 12y + 12 = 0$

3. Circles C_1 and C_2 have equations $(x + 1)^2 + (y + 10)^2 = 153$ and $x^2 + y^2 - 30x - 12y + 76 = 0$ respectively.

(a) Show that the circles intersect.

AB is a common chord with equation $y = 4 - x$.

(b) Find the coordinates of the points A and B.

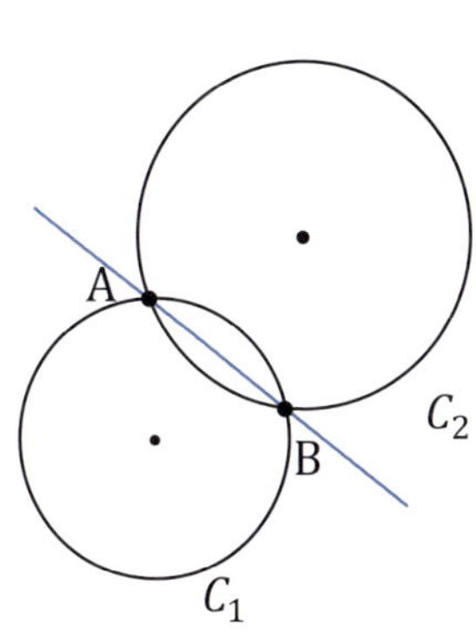

4. Two circles C_1 and C_2 have equations $x^2 + y^2 + 20x + 8y + 80 = 0$ and $x^2 + y^2 - 4x - 2y - 11 = 0$ respectively.
Find the shortest distance between the circles.

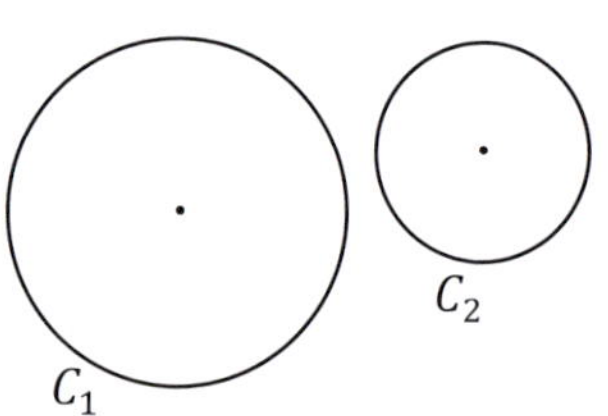

3.9 Coordinates and the Circle 2 – Finding Centres and Radii

Many circle problems involve using the coordinates of the centre and the radius of a circle to work out the equations of other circles.

Worked Examples:

1. Three congruent circles are shown in the diagram. The x-axis is a tangent to each circle. Point $\mathrm{A}(10, 6)$ is the centre of the first circle. Find the equation of the circle with centre C.

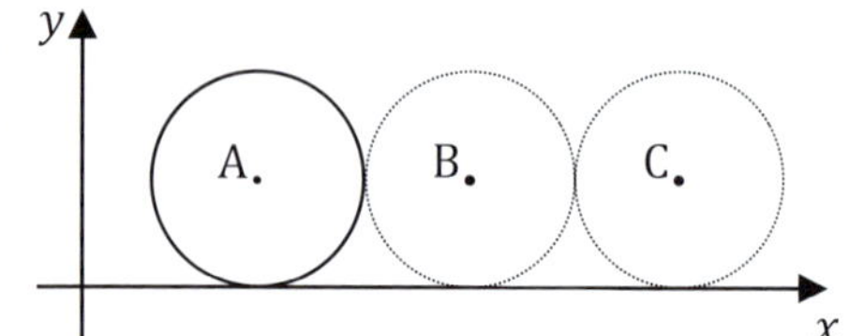

Solution:

Radius

The circles are congruent, so they have the same radius.
The x-axis is a tangent, so the radius of each circle is the same as the y-coordinate of the centre.
$r = 6$.

Centre

The centre is found by counting along four radii from centre A.
$\mathrm{C}(34, 6)$

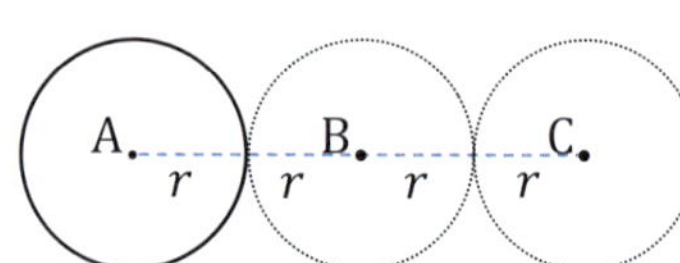

Equation

$(x - 34)^2 + (y - 6)^2 = 36$

2. The circle with centre B has equation $x^2 + y^2 - 12x - 28y + 88 = 0$. It is touched internally by two congruent circles with centres A and C. The centres of the circles lie on a line parallel with the x-axis. Find the equation of the circle with centre C.

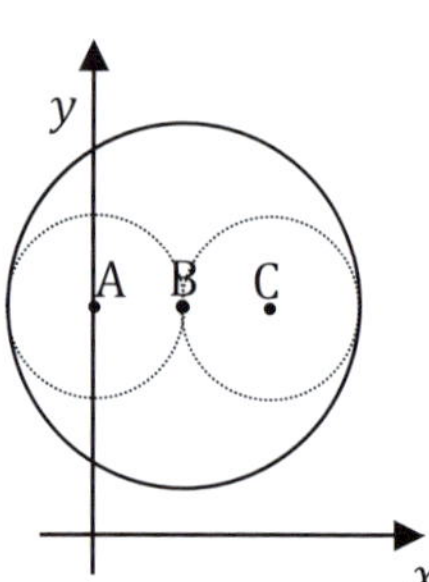

Solution:

Radius

Find the centre and radius of circle with centre B.

$(-g, -f)$ $\qquad r_B = \sqrt{g^2 + f^2 - c}$

$2g = -12 \qquad 2f = -28 \qquad r_B = \sqrt{(-6)^2 + (14)^2 - 88}$

$g = -6 \qquad f = -14 \qquad r_B = \sqrt{36 + 196 - 88}$

$-g = 6 \qquad -f = 14 \qquad r_B = \sqrt{144}$

$Centre_B = (6, 14) \qquad r_B = 12$

The smaller circles are half the radius of the large circle, so the radius of the circle with centre C is 6.

Centre

The centre is found by counting along six from centre B.
$\mathrm{C}(12, 14)$

Equation

$(x - 12)^2 + (y - 14)^2 = 36$

Exercise 3.9A

1. In each of the following questions, the line going through the centres is parallel with the x-axis. Determine the equation of the circle with centre P.

(a) The circle with centre A has equation $x^2 + y^2 - 20x - 12y + 100 = 0$.

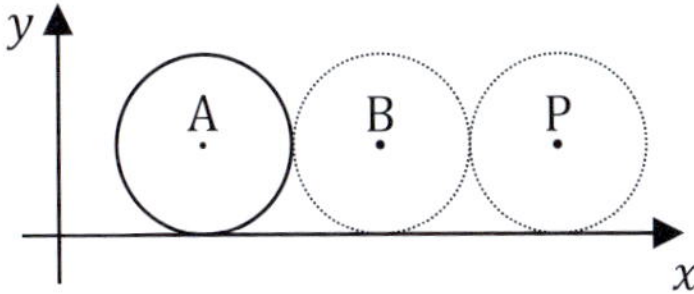

(b) The circle with centre A has equation $x^2 + y^2 - 8x - 22y + 121 = 0$. The circles are congruent.

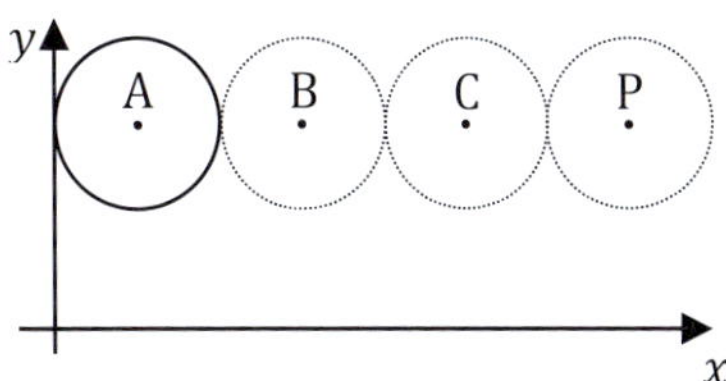

(c) The circle with centre A has equation $x^2 + y^2 - 28x - 30y + 405 = 0$.

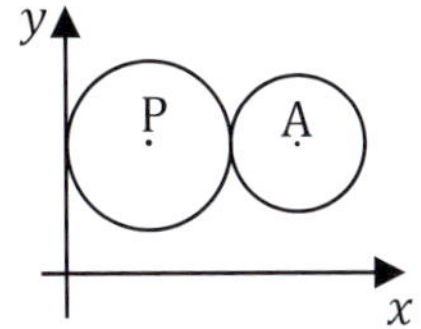

(d) The circle with centre A has equation $x^2 + y^2 - 26x - 24y + 264 = 0$.

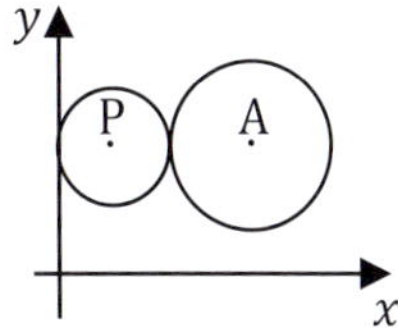

(e) The circle with centre A has equation $x^2 + y^2 - 26x - 10y + 130 = 0$. The smaller circles are congruent.

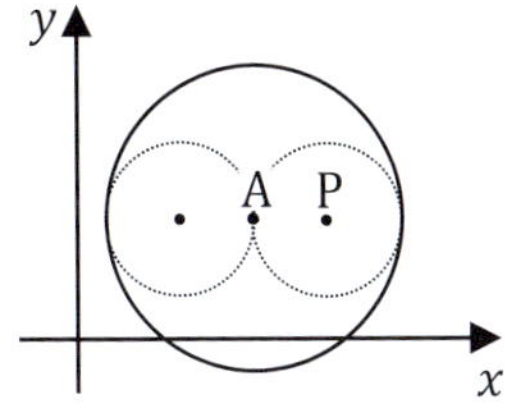

(f) Circle C has equation $x^2 + y^2 - 22x - 22y + 98 = 0$. The smaller circles are congruent.

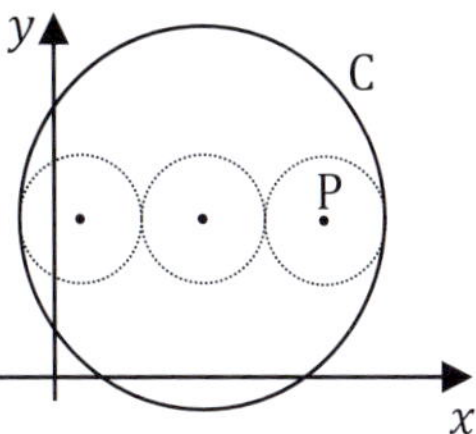

2. In each of the following questions, the line going through the centres is parallel with the y-axis. Determine the equation of the circle with centre P.

(a) The circle with centre A has equation $x^2 + y^2 - 20x - 12y + 100 = 0$.

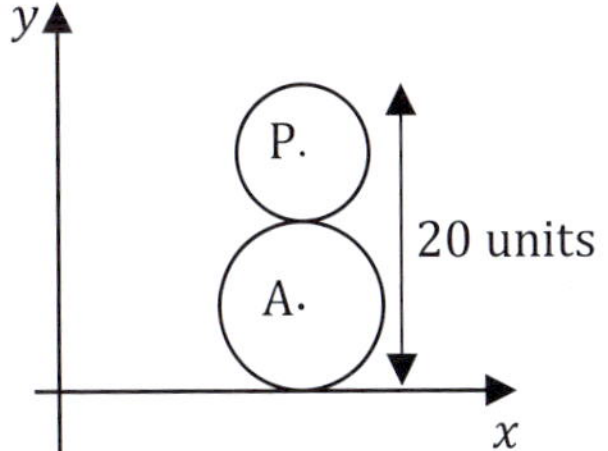

(b) The circle with centre A has equation $x^2 + y^2 - 10x - 28y + 196 = 0$.

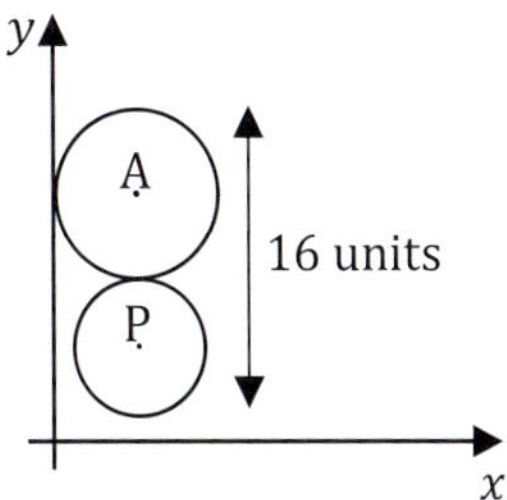

Some circle problems involve circles with different radii and centres that are not parallel to the x or y-axis and require the use of ratios to determine the equation of the unknown circle.

Worked Example:

The equation of the circle with centre A is given $x^2 + y^2 + 10x + 8y + 31 = 0$.
Points A, B and C are collinear. Point B has coordinates $(4, -1)$. The circles have radii r_A, r_B and r_C respectively.

- $r_B = 2r_A$
- $r_C = 3r_A$

Find the equation of the circle with centre C.

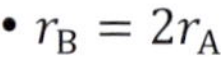

Solution: Find the centre and radius of C.

Radius

$g_A = 5, f_A = 4, c_A = 31$

$r_A = \sqrt{g_A^2 + f_A^2 - c_A} = \sqrt{5^2 + 4^2 - 31} = \sqrt{25 + 16 - 31} = \sqrt{10}$

$\therefore r_C = 3\sqrt{10}$

Centre

$A(-5, -4), B(4, -1)$

AB difference in $x = 4 - (-5) = 9$

AB difference in $y = -1 - (-4) = 3$

$AB : BC = 3 : 5$

BC difference in $x = 9 \div 3 \times 5 = 15$

BC difference in $y = 3 \div 3 \times 5 = 5$

Centre $C = (4 + 15, -1 + 5) = (19, 4)$

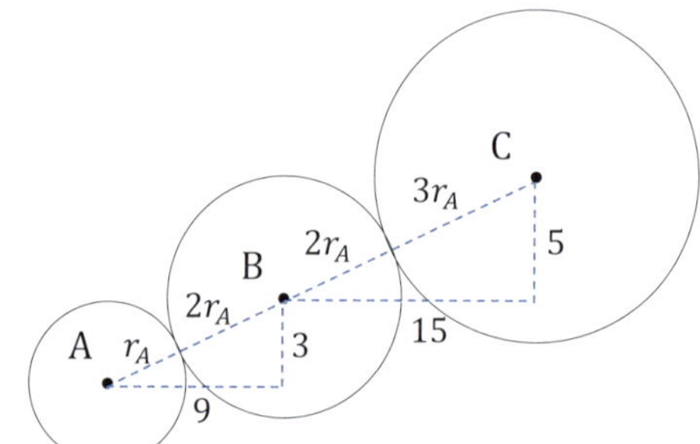

Equation

$(x + 19)^2 + (y - 4)^2 = \left(3\sqrt{10}\right)^2$

$(x + 19)^2 + (y - 4)^2 = 90$

Exercise 3.9B

1. In each of the following questions, determine the equation of the circle with centre P.

(a) The circle with centre A has equation $x^2 + y^2 - 10x + 10y + 9 = 0$.
- B has coordinates $(10, -1)$
- $r_P = 2r_A$

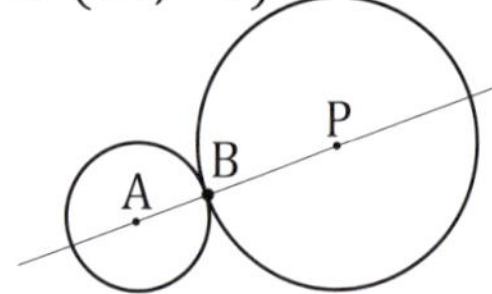

(b) The circle with centre A has equation $x^2 + y^2 - 6x - 4y - 4 = 0$.
- B has coordinates $(-1, 3)$
- $r_P = 3r_A$

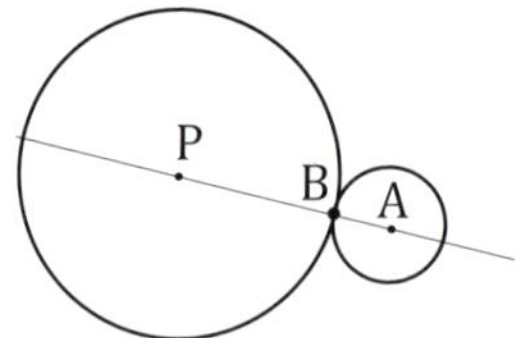

(c) The circle with centre A has equation $x^2 + y^2 - 12x + 6y + 25 = 0$.
- B has coordinates $(-10, 5)$
- $r_P = \frac{3}{2}r_A$

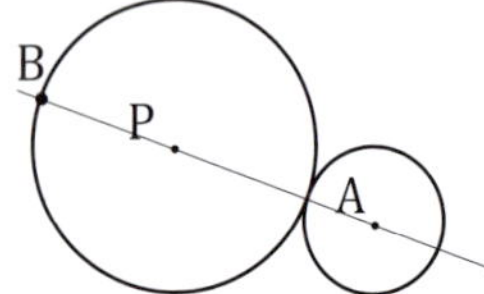

(d) The circle with centre A has equation $x^2 + y^2 - 6x - 8y - 15 = 0$.
- B has coordinates $(9, 2)$
- $r_P = \frac{3}{2}r_A$

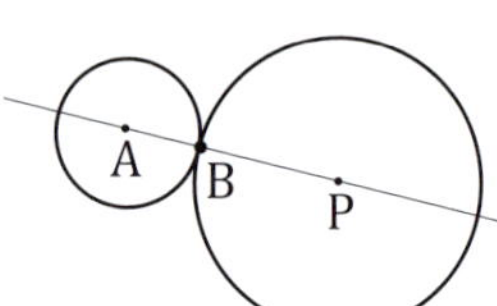

2. Points A,B and C are collinear. The equation of the circle with centre A is given by $x^2 + y^2 + 32x + 2y + 140 = 0$. Point B has coordinates $(-1, 9)$.

The circles have radii r_A, r_B and r_C respectively.

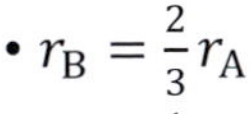

- $r_B = \frac{2}{3} r_A$
- $r_C = \frac{1}{3} r_A$

Find the equation of the circle with centre C.

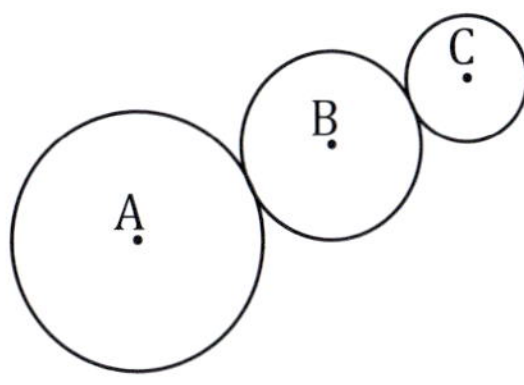

3. The equation of the circle with centre A is given $x^2 + y^2 + 8x - 6y + 12 = 0$.

Point B has coordinates $(8, -5)$. The circles have radii r_A, r_B and r_C respectively.

- $r_B = 3r_A$
- $r_C = 2r_A$

Find the equation of the circle with centre C.

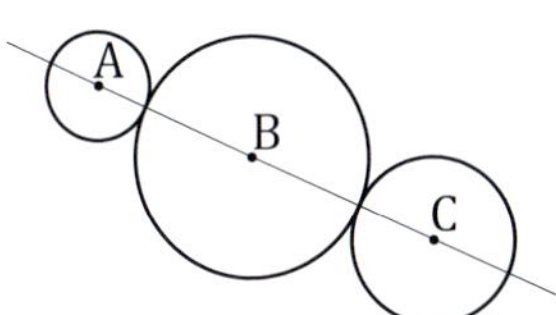

4. The circles with centres A and B are drawn inside the circle with centre C.

The equation of the circle with centre A is given $x^2 + y^2 + 8x + 4y + 4 = 0$.

Point B has coordinates $(8, -2)$. The circles have radii r_A, r_B and r_C.

- $r_B = 2r_A$

Find the equation of the circle with centre C.

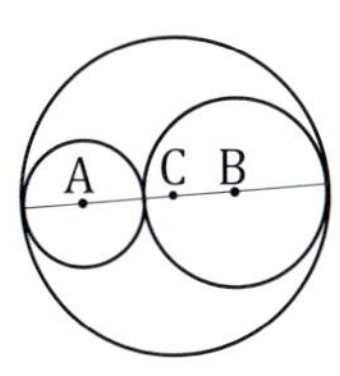

5. The circles with centres A, B and C touch externally. The equation of the circle with centre A is $x^2 + y^2 + 30x + 14y + 264 = 0$. Point C has coordinates $(0, -2)$. The circles have radii r_A, r_B and r_C respectively.

- $r_A = r_B$
- $r_C = 2r_A$

Find the equation of the circle with centre B.

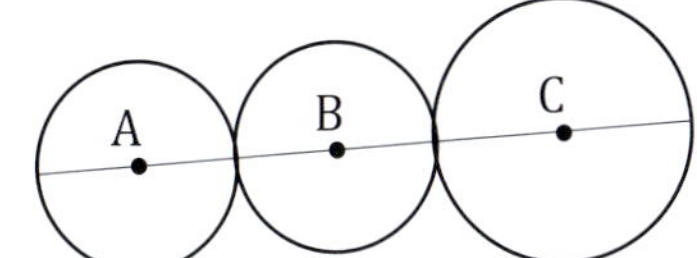

6. The circles with centres A, B and C are drawn inside the circle with centre D.

The equation of the circle with centre A is given $x^2 + y^2 + 16x - 6y - 7 = 0$.

Point B has coordinates $(8, 11)$. The circles have radii r_A, r_B, r_C and r_D.

- $r_A = 2r_C$

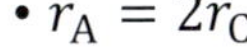

Find the equation of the circle with centre D.

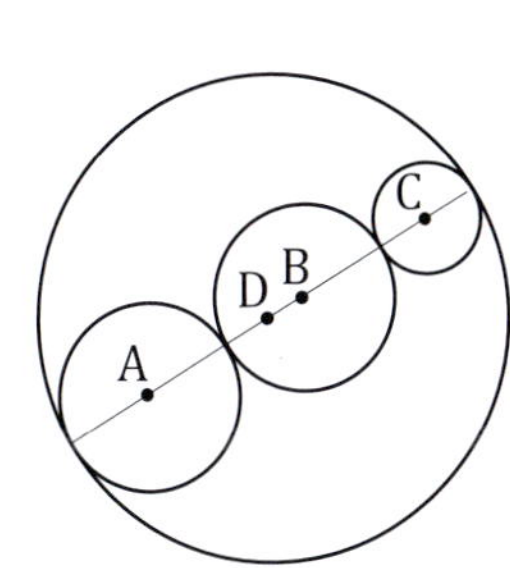

3.10 Review

Exercise 3.10A

2.1 Find the distance between the following points:

(a) $(5,-1)$ and $(8,2)$ (b) $(2,4)$ and $(-3,-8)$ (c) $(-4,1)$ and $(6,-5)$

2.2 Find the equation of the following circles. In each question, AB is a radius or diameter. Give your answer in expanded form:

(a)

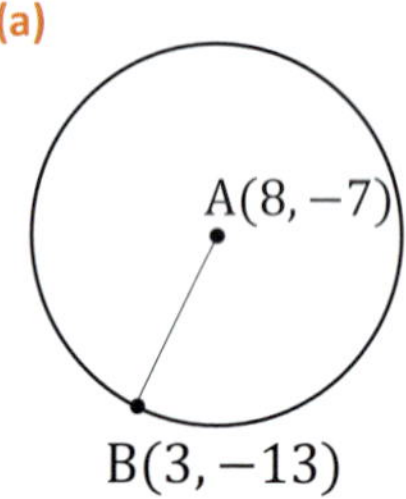

(b)

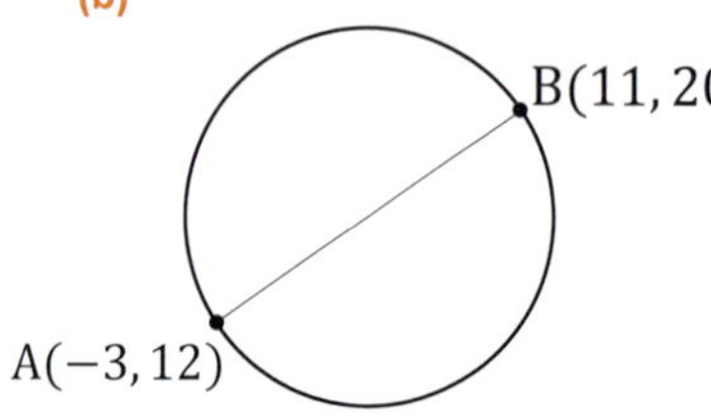

(c)

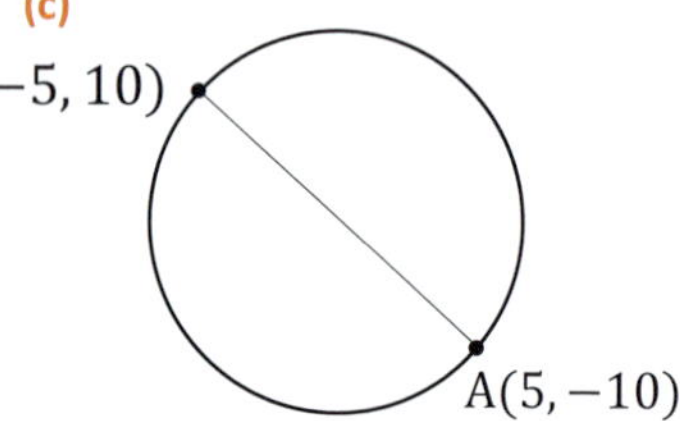

2.3 Find the centre and radius of the circles with the following equations:

(a) $x^2 + y^2 = 144$ (b) $(x+9)^2 + (y-1)^2 = 63$

(c) $x^2 + y^2 + 16x - 8y - 19 = 0$ (d) $x^2 + y^2 - 2x + 6y - 40 = 0$

2.4 Determine where the following points lie in relation to the given circles (justify your answer):

(a) $(11,9)$ and $(x-5)^2 + (y+7)^2 = 50$ (b) $(-1\ -2)$ and $x^2 + y^2 - 10x + 6y - 3 = 0$

2.5 Determine the nature of intersection between the following lines and circles:

(a) $2x + 5y = 10$ and $(x-5)^2 + y^2 = 29$ (b) $y = 3 - x$ and $x^2 + y^2 + 4x + 8y - 12 = 0$

2.6 (a) Find the coordinates of the points of intersection of the following lines and circles:

(i) $x + 3y = 10$ and $(x-6)^2 + (y+2)^2 = 20$ (ii) $y = x + 4$ and $x^2 + y^2 - 8x + 12y - 48 = 0$

(b) Show that the line with equation $x + 3y - 8 = 0$ is a tangent to the circle with equation $x^2 + y^2 - 8x + 4y + 10 = 0$ and find the coordinates of the point of contact.

2.7 Find the equation of the tangent to the circle with the following equations at the given points:

(a) $(x-10)^2 + (y+4)^2 = 8$ and $(12,-2)$ (b) $x^2 + y^2 + 10x - 6y + 29 = 0$ and $(-4,5)$

2.8 In the following pairs of equation, determine whether circles intersect at two points, touch internally/externally or do not intersect:

(a) $(x - 10)^2 + (y + 1)^2 = 80$ and $x^2 + y^2 + 12y + 31 = 0$

(b) $(x - 7)^2 + (y - 12)^2 = 35$ and $x^2 + y^2 - 2x + 8y - 55 = 0$

2.9 In each of the following questions, the line going through the centres is parallel with the x-axis. Determine the equation of the circle with centre P.

(a) The circle with centre A has equation

$x^2 + y^2 - 16x - 10y + 64 = 0$.

(b) The coordinates of point A are $(6, 6)$

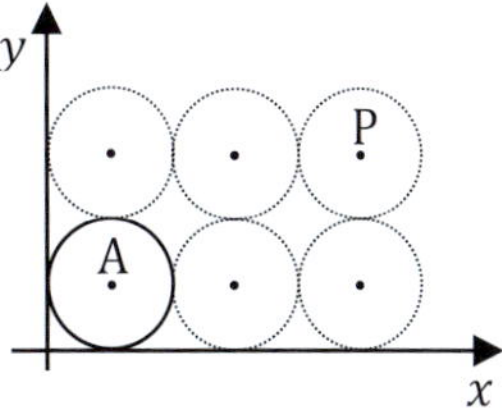

Exercise 3.10B

1. Two circles have equations $x^2 + y^2 + 14x + 2y - 50 = 0$ and $(x - 7)^2 + (y + 8)^2 = 55$. Show that these circles intersect.

2. The equation $x^2 + y^2 + 20x - 4y + 12p - 4 = 0$ represents a circle. Determine the range of values of p.

3. Circle C_1 is represented by the equations $(x - 7)^2 + (y - 2)^2 = 36$. AB is a common chord with equation $y = 3 - x$.

(a) Find the coordinates of the points A and B.

The centre of C_2 has coordinates $(-3, -8)$

(b) Find the equation of circle C_2.

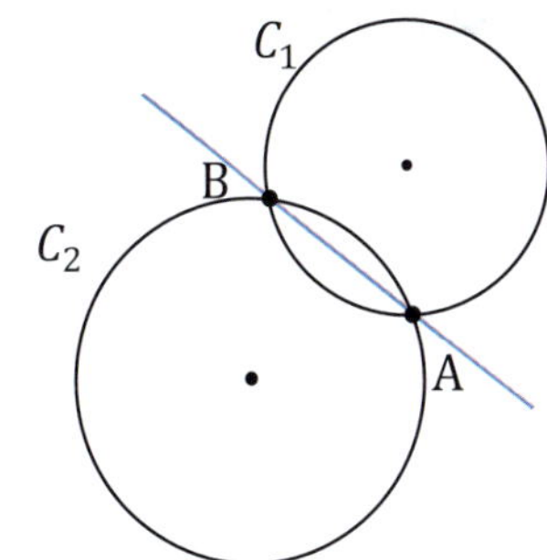

4. Three circles are drawn with centres that are collinear, touching as shown. Circle C_1 has equation $x^2 + y^2 + 10x - 2y - 199 = 0$. The centre of circle C_2 is $(15, 16)$.

(a) Determine the radius of C_2.

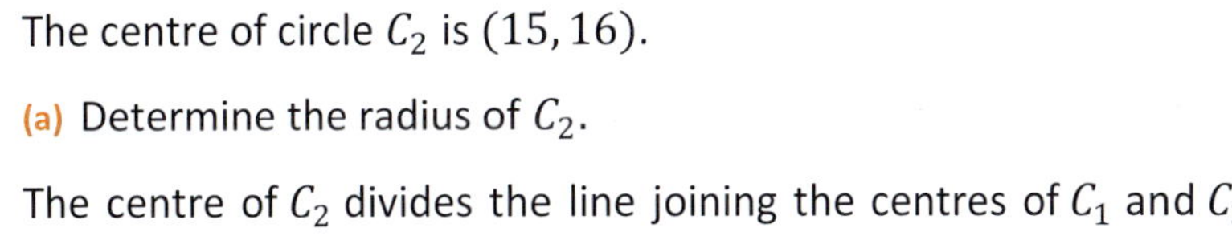

The centre of C_2 divides the line joining the centres of C_1 and C_3 in the ratio 5: 3.

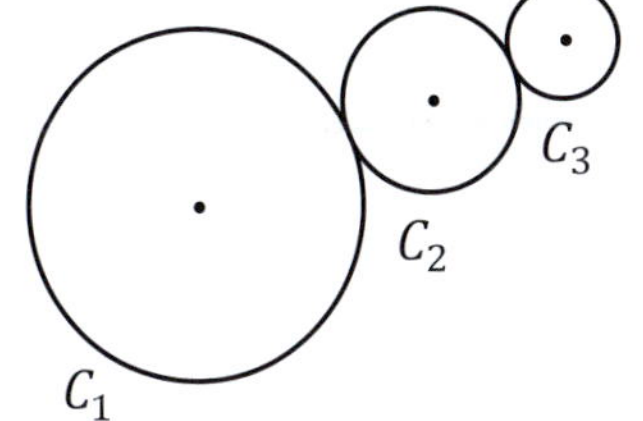

(b) Determine the equation of C_3.

5. The line $x + 2y - 4 = 0$ is a tangent to the circle with centre $(4, -5)$. Find the equation of the circle.

Chapter 4

Functions

Functions

A **function** in mathematics takes an input value, then applies a rule to it and produces an output value or image.

There are many different functions in mathematics: straight lines, quadratic, cubic, trigonometric functions, etc. In fact, any rule that is applied to an input value, that produces **only one** output, may be described as a function. This relationship between the input and output can also be graphed.

Function Notation

A function may be written in one of two ways; either in the form $y = ...$ where y is the output or image and the input would be a value of x, or function notation may be used.

Function notation is usually written in the form $f(x)$ or $g(x)$ meaning a function 'f' or 'g' of x. In such notation, x is the input and $f(x)$ is the output or image. In this notation, $y = f(x)$.

Number Sets

In mathematics, we use numbers all the time and these numbers can be classified or categorised by their type. We categorise many things in life. Just consider a supermarket: there is the fruit and veg section of the supermarket, but within this section there is fruit, and within the fruit, there is the apples section and within the apples section there are green and red apples. Or pupils in a school, they are classified by year-group, house, subjects, level, etc. Numbers are categorised in the same way.

Each number in the set is known as an **element** or **member** of the set. The elements of a set are enclosed in curly brackets or braces **e.g.** $\{1, 2, 3, 4\}$. The **empty set** is a set that contains no elements. It is written as $\{\}$ or $\emptyset$.

We use the following notation.

$\in$ 'is an element of' **e.g.** $3 \in \{0, 1, 2, 3, 4\}$ **i.e.** 3 is an element of the set containing $1, 2, 3$ and 4.

$\notin$ 'is not an element of' **e.g.** $7 \notin \{0, 1, 2, 3, 4\}$ **i.e.** 7 is not an element of the set containing $1, 2, 3$ and 4.

$\subset$ 'is a subset of' **e.g.** $\{1, 2\} \subset \{1, 2, 3, 4\}$ **i.e.** the set containing 1 and 2 is a subset of the set containing $1, 2, 3$ and 4.

Common Number Sets

Sets of numbers are endless, but some sets are well known and commonly used:

Natural numbers: $\mathbb{N} = \{1, 2, 3, 4 ...\}$ These are the numbers we use for counting.

Whole numbers: $\mathbb{W} = \{0, 1, 2, 3, 4 ...\}$ The same as natural numbers, but also including 0.

Integers: $\mathbb{Z} = \{..., -3, -2, 1, 0, 1, 2, 3, ...\}$ The set of positive and negative whole numbers.

Rational numbers: $\mathbb{Q}$ These are all numbers that can be expressed as a division of two integers.

Real numbers: $\mathbb{R}$ These are all the real numbers, including irrational numbers. (**e.g.** $\sqrt{2}, \pi$, etc.)

As can be seen in the diagram below, the smaller sets are subsets of the larger sets. The set of real numbers, $\mathbb{R}$, is as far as we need to go in Higher Mathematics and this is the set that we consider most frequently for Higher Mathematics.

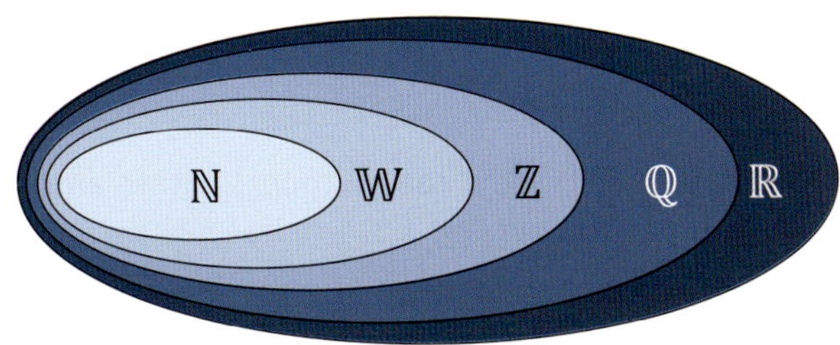

4.1 Domain and Range of Functions

The numbers input into a function, $f(x)$, are known as the **domain** of the function. The numbers output from the function are known as the **range** of the function.

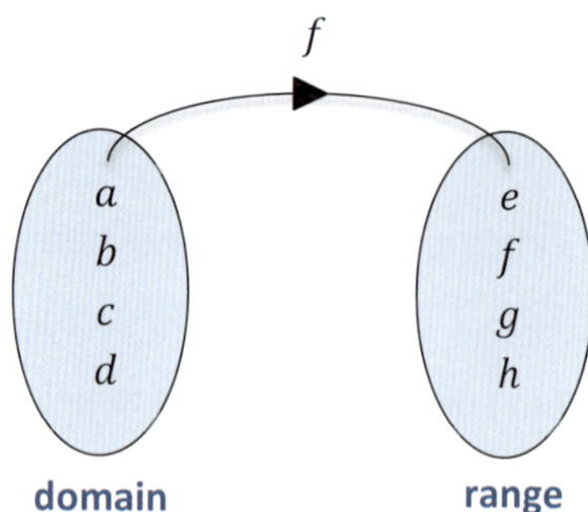

In any function, every value in the domain corresponds to only one value in the range. This means there is only one value of y or $f(x)$ for every value of x (this is why the equation of a circle or an oval is not a function).

Restrictions on the Domain

In some functions there are certain values that cannot be input into the function, these are called **restrictions on the domain** of the function. We have already seen this when studying algebraic fractions in National 5 Mathematics. Typical restrictions on a domain are caused by a dominator of zero (a mathematical impossibility) or a negative square root, which results in an imaginary number which does not lie within the set of real numbers, $\mathbb{R}$.

Worked Examples:

1. Function $f(x)$ is defined on $\mathbb{R}$, the set of real numbers by $f(x) = \dfrac{4}{x + 6x - 16}$. State any restrictions on the domain of $f(x)$.

Solution:

In the function $f(x)$, the denominator $x^2 + 6x - 16 \neq 0$.

$x^2 + 6x - 16 \neq 0$
$(x + 8)(x - 2) \neq 0$
$\therefore x \neq -8, x \neq 2$

2. Function $g(x)$ is defined on $\mathbb{R}$, the set of real numbers by $g(x) = \sqrt{1 - x^2}$. State a suitable domain for $g(x)$.

Solution:

In the function $g(x) = \sqrt{1 - x^2}$, for $g(x) \in \mathbb{R}$ (**i.e.** for values of $g(x)$ to be real numbers), $1 - x^2 \geq 0$.

$1 - x^2 \geq 0$ Now solve the quadratic inequality.
$(1 - x)(1 + x) \geq 0$
Roots: $x = -1, x = 1$

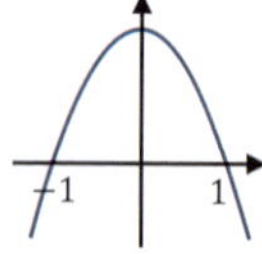

$\therefore -1 \leq x \leq 1$

NB: Before stating any restrictions on a domain, ensure the function is in its simplest form.

Exercise 4.1A

1. The following functions are defined on $\mathbb{R}$, the set of real numbers. State any restrictions on their domains:

(a) $f(x) = \dfrac{3}{x}$ (b) $f(x) = \dfrac{2}{1 - x}$ (c) $f(x) = \dfrac{1}{5x + 2}$

(d) $f(x) = \dfrac{x}{2x-3}$ (e) $f(x) = \dfrac{5x}{1-x^2}$ (f) $f(x) = \dfrac{1}{x^2+2x}$

(g) $f(x) = \dfrac{x+1}{x^2-x-2}$ (h) $f(x) = \dfrac{2}{x^2-9}$ (i) $f(x) = \dfrac{x^2-2x}{x^2+x-6}$

(j) $f(x) = \dfrac{3x-12}{x^2-7x+12}$ (k) $f(x) = \dfrac{x}{1-x^3}$ (l) $f(x) = \dfrac{1}{x^3+8}$

(m) $f(x) = \dfrac{x^2-1}{x^2-x}$ (n) $f(x) = \dfrac{7x}{2x^2+5x-3}$ (o) $f(x) = \dfrac{9-x^2}{x^2+2x-15}$

2. The following functions are defined on $\mathbb{R}$, the set of real numbers. State a suitable domain for each function:

(a) $f(x) = \sqrt{x}$ (b) $f(x) = \sqrt{x-3}$ (c) $f(x) = \sqrt{5-x}$

(d) $f(x) = \sqrt{7+x}$ (e) $f(x) = \sqrt{x-5}$ (f) $f(x) = \sqrt{4-2x}$

(g) $f(x) = \sqrt{x^2-9}$ (h) $f(x) = \sqrt{x^2-4}$ (i) $f(x) = \sqrt{x^2-10}$

(j) $f(x) = \sqrt{16-x^2}$ (k) $f(x) = \sqrt{5x-5x^2}$ (l) $f(x) = \sqrt{x^2-x}$

(m) $f(x) = \dfrac{1}{\sqrt{x^2-4}}$ (n) $f(x) = \dfrac{1}{\sqrt{2x-x^2}}$ (o) $f(x) = \dfrac{1}{\sqrt{x^2-x-2}}$

Range of functions

The range of a function is the range of output values. Some functions range from $-\infty$ to $+\infty$, but others have a limited range.

Worked Examples:

1. Function $f(x)$ is defined on $\mathbb{R}$, the set of real numbers by $f(x) = 3x^2 + 4$, $x \in \mathbb{R}$. State the range of $f(x)$.

   Solution:
   The function $f(x) = 3x^2 + 4$ is quadratic and has a minimum turning point at $(0, 4)$.
   The lowest value of $f(x) = 4$. Therefore, the range of the function is $f(x) \geq 4$.

2. Function $f(x)$ is defined on $\mathbb{R}$, the set of real numbers by $f(x) = x^3 - 5$.
   The domain of f is $0 \leq x \leq 10$, $x \in \mathbb{R}$. State the range of $f(x)$.
   Solution:
   When $x = 0$, $f(0) = -5$, when $x = 10$, $f(10) = 995$.
   The range of $f(x)$ is $-5 \leq f(x) \leq 995$.

Exercise 4.1B

1. The following functions are defined on $\mathbb{R}$, the set of real numbers. State the range of each function:

(a) $f(x) = 6x^2 + 1$ (b) $f(x) = 14 - 2x^2$ (c) $f(x) = x^2 - 9$

(d) $f(x) = (x-3)^2 + 2$ (e) $f(x) = 5 - (x+2)^2$ (f) $f(x) = (x-6)^2 - 12$

(g) $f(x) = x^2 + 4x + 1$ (h) $f(x) = x^2 + 6x + 2$ (i) $f(x) = x^2 + 3x + 9$

(j) $f(x) = 1 - 8x - x^2$ (k) $f(x) = 2 - 5x - x^2$ (l) $f(x) = 2x^2 + 2x + 7$

2. The following functions are defined on $\mathbb{R}$, the set of real numbers. State the range of each function:

(a) $f(x) = x^2 + 1, 0 \leq x \leq 5, x \in \mathbb{R}$ (b) $f(x) = 2x^3 - 1, 0 \leq x \leq 3, x \in \mathbb{R}$

(c) $f(x) = 2 - x^2, 0 < x < 4, x \in \mathbb{R}$ (d) $f(x) = x^3 + 9, -3 \leq x \leq 7, x \in \mathbb{R}$

(e) $f(x) = x^3 + 2, 0 < x \leq 10, x \in \mathbb{R}$ (f) $f(x) = 2x^2 - 4x, 1 \leq x \leq 5, x \in \mathbb{R}$

(g) $f(x) = x^3 + 7, 3 \leq x \leq 10, x \in \mathbb{R}$ (h) $f(x) = 4x - x^2, 2 \leq x < 7, x \in \mathbb{R}$

(i) $f(x) = 3x^3 + 1, -10 \leq x < 0, x \in \mathbb{R}$ (j) $f(x) = 4x^3 - 12, -10 \leq x \leq 1, x \in \mathbb{R}$

(k) $f(x) = \sqrt[3]{x} + 1, -1000 \leq x \leq 64, x \in \mathbb{R}$ (l) $f(x) = \sqrt[3]{x} - 5, -125 \leq x \leq 1000, x \in \mathbb{R}$

4.2 Basic Functions

National 5 Skills

Worked Examples: If $f(x) = 3x + 2$ and $g(x) = x^2 - 2x$

1. Evaluate $f(x)$ when $x = 2$

$f(x) = 3x + 2$
$f(2) = 3(2) + 2$
$f(2) = 6 + 2$
$f(2) = 8$

2. Evaluate $g(x)$ when $x = -3$

$g(x) = x^2 - 2x$
$g(-3) = (-3)^2 - 2(-3)$
$g(-3) = 9 + 6$
$g(-3) = 15$

3. Evaluate $f(-4)$

$f(x) = 3x + 2$
$f(-4) = 3(-4) + 2$
$f(-4) = -12 + 2$
$f(-4) = -10$

4. Evaluate $g\left(\frac{1}{3}\right)$

$g(x) = x^2 - 2x$
$g\left(\frac{1}{3}\right) = \left(\frac{1}{3}\right)^2 - 2\left(\frac{1}{3}\right)$
$g\left(\frac{1}{3}\right) = \frac{1}{9} - \frac{2}{3} = \frac{1}{9} - \frac{6}{9}$
$g\left(\frac{1}{3}\right) = -\frac{5}{9}$

Exercise 4.2

1. For the following functions:

$f(x) = 3x^2 + 1$ $\quad g(x) = 12 - x^3$ $\quad h(x) = 2x^2 + 4x - 5$ $\quad k(x) = \dfrac{x^2 + 6}{x}$

Evaluate:

(a) $f(x)$ when $x = 1$ (b) $h(x)$ when $x = 2$ (c) $k(x)$ when $x = 2$ (d) $f(x)$ when $x = 3$

(e) $g(x)$ when $x = 3$ (f) $k(x)$ when $x = 3$ (g) $h(x)$ when $x = 3$ (h) $g(x)$ when $x = 4$

(i) $f(x)$ when $x = 6$ (j) $h(x)$ when $x = 1$ (k) $g(x)$ when $x = -5$ (l) $k(x)$ when $x = -2$

2. For the following functions:

$f(x) = 4x^3$ $\quad g(x) = 5x - 2x^2$ $\quad h(x) = 6x^3 - 3x^2 + 1$ $\quad k(x) = \dfrac{x^2 + 4x - 1}{x + 2}$

Evaluate:

(a) $f(3)$ (b) $k(1)$ (c) $g(-1)$ (d) $h(2)$

(e) $k(3)$ (f) $g(4)$ (g) $f(-2)$ (h) $k(0)$

(i) $h(-4)$ (j) $f(5)$ (k) $h(5)$ (l) $g(5)$

It is also possible to work backwards using functions to calculate an input, given an output.

Worked Example:

A function is defined as $f(x) = 7x - 5$. If $f(a) = 16$, calculate a.

$$\begin{aligned} 7a - 5 &= 16 \\ 7a &= 21 \\ a &= 3 \end{aligned}$$

3. For each of the following functions, calculate a:

(a) $f(x) = 7x - 5, f(a) = 37$ (b) $f(x) = 3x - 2,\ f(a) = 25$ (c) $f(x) = 57 - 6x, f(a) = 9$

(d) $f(x) = 14 - 2x, f(a) = 36$ (e) $f(x) = 6x + 9,\ f(a) = 27$ (f) $f(x) = 12x - 3, f(a) = 3$

(g) $f(x) = 4x + 5,\ f(a) = -27$ (h) $f(x) = 2x^3 - 3, f(a) = 13$ (i) $f(x) = x^3 - 9, f(a) = 18$

(j) $f(x) = 3x^3 - 8,\ f(a) = -11$ (k) $f(x) = 7 - 2x^3, f(a) = 61$ (l) $f(x) = x^3 - 6, f(a) = 210$

4.3 Composite Functions

Composite Functions consist of more than one function. Substitution is used to determine the resulting composite function when two functions are given. Instead of substituting a value in place of the x term, an entire function is substituted.

Worked Examples: If $f(x) = 5x - 2$ and $g(x) = x^2 + 3x$

1. Find $f(g(x))$

$f(g(x)) = 5(x^2 + 3x) - 2$

$f(g(x)) = 5x^2 + 15x - 2$

2. Find $g(f(x))$

$g(f(x)) = (5x - 2)^2 + 3(5x - 2)$

$g(f(x)) = 25x^2 - 20x + 4 + 15x - 6$

$g(f(x)) = 25x^2 - 5x - 2$

Exercise 4.3A

1. For the following functions:

$f(x) = 2x + 2$ $\quad g(x) = 3x - 1$ $\quad h(x) = 2x - 6$ $\quad k(x) = 10 - 4x$

Find:

(a) $f(g(x))$ (b) $h(g(x))$ (c) $g(k(x))$ (d) $k(g(x))$

(e) $h(k(x))$ (f) $k(h(x))$ (g) $k(f(x))$ (h) $f(k(x))$

(i) $f(f(x))$ (j) $g(g(x))$ (k) $h(h(x))$ (l) $k(k(x))$

2. For the following functions:

$f(x) = 5x - 1$ $\quad g(x) = x^2 + 1$ $\quad h(x) = 2x^2 + 4$ $\quad k(x) = \dfrac{1}{2x + 1}$

Find:

(a) $f(g(x))$ (b) $g(f(x))$ (c) $f(h(x))$ (d) $h(f(x))$

(e) $g(h(x))$ (f) $h(g(x))$ (g) $k(h(x))$ (h) $k(g(x))$

(i) $k(f(x))$ (j) $g(g(x))$ (k) $f(f(x))$ (l) $h(h(x))$

3. For the following functions:

$f(x) = \sin x$ $\quad g(x) = \cos x$ $\quad h(x) = 4x$ $\quad k(x) = x + 3$

Find:

(a) $f(h(x))$ (b) $g(h(x))$ (c) $f(k(x))$ (d) $g(k(x))$

(e) $h(f(x))$ (f) $h(k(x))$ (g) $h(h(x))$ (h) $k(k(x))$

(i) $k(f(x))$ (j) $h(g(x))$ (k) $k(g(x))$ (l) $h(h(h(x)))$

Worked Example: If $f(x) = \frac{1}{x+4}$ and $g(x) = \frac{1}{2-x}$, evaluate $f(g(x))$.

$$f(g(x)) = \frac{1}{\left(\frac{1}{2-x}\right) + 4}$$

$$f(g(x)) = \frac{1}{\left(\frac{1}{2-x}\right) + \frac{4(2-x)}{2-x}}$$

$$f(g(x)) = \frac{1}{\frac{1+8-4x}{2-x}} \left(= \frac{1}{9-4x} \div \frac{1}{2-x} = \frac{1}{9-4x} \times \frac{2-x}{1}\right)$$

$$f(g(x)) = \frac{2-x}{9-4x}$$

NB: From line 3 to 4, the denominator on the denominator multiplies the numerator. This is what happens when dividing fractions.

4. For the following functions:

$f(x) = \frac{1}{x+2}$ $\quad g(x) = \frac{5}{2-x}$ $\quad h(x) = \frac{1}{3x-2}$ $\quad k(x) = \frac{1}{x+4}$

Find:

(a) $k(f(x))$ (b) $g(k(x))$ (c) $h(k(x))$ (d) $k(k(x))$

(e) $f(g(x))$ (f) $h(g(x))$ (g) $k(g(x))$ (h) $g(g(x))$

(i) $g(f(x))$ (j) $h(f(x))$ (k) $f(f(x))$ (l) $f(h(x))$

Worked Examples: If $f(x) = 4x - 2$ and $g(x) = x^2 + 3x$

1. Evaluate $f(g(2))$

$g(2) = (2)^2 + 3(2) = 10$

$f(g(2)) = f(10) = 4(10) - 2$

$f(g(2)) = 38$

2. Evaluate $g(f(-3))$

$f(-3) = 4(-3) - 2 = -14$

$g(f(-3)) = g(-14) = (-14)^2 + 3(-14)$

$g(f(-3)) = 196 - 42$

$g(f(-3)) = 154$

Exercise 4.3B

1. For the following functions:

$f(x) = 2x + 1$ $\quad g(x) = 9 - x$ $\quad h(x) = x^2 - 2x$ $\quad k(x) = \frac{5}{x+3}$

Evaluate:

(a) $f(g(-2))$ (b) $g(f(3))$ (c) $f(h(-4))$ (d) $h(f(3))$

(e) $g(h(-2))$ (f) $h(g(5))$ (g) $h(k(2))$ (h) $k(h(2))$

(i) $k(g(3))$ (j) $g(k(2))$ (k) $k(f(-5))$ (l) $f(k(-4))$

(m) $h(g(-5))$ (n) $k(g(-3))$ (o) $k(h(-2))$ (p) $h(k(-2))$

2. For the following functions:

$f(x) = 3(x+1)$ $g(x) = x - x^2$ $h(x) = (2-x)^2$ $k(x) = \dfrac{1}{5-x}$

Evaluate:

(a) $g(f(1))$ (b) $f(g(2))$ (c) $h(g(2))$ (d) $f(k(2))$

(e) $h(f(3))$ (f) $k(g(-2))$ (g) $h(k(4))$ (h) $g(h(-2))$

(i) $f(f(-2))$ (j) $g(g(-1))$ (k) $k(h(5))$ (l) $h(h(2))$

(m) $f(g(4))$ (n) $g(k(-1))$ (o) $k(h(-2))$ (p) $k(k(7))$

4.4 Inverse Functions

An **Inverse Function** is a function that reverses another function, **i.e.** it returns the values in the range of a function to the values of the domain. The notation used for the inverse function is $f^{-1}(x)$.

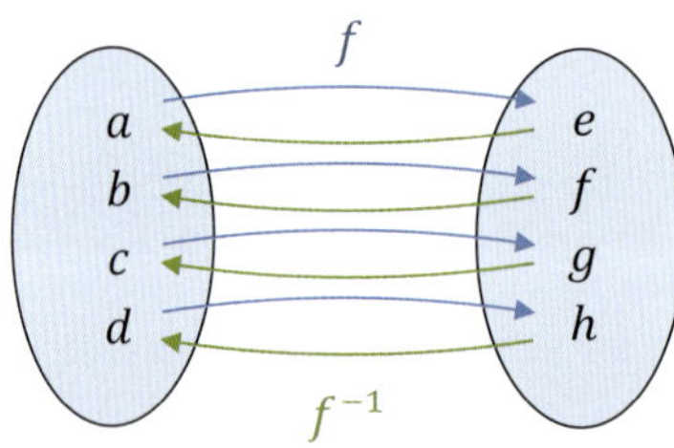

An inverse function only exists when a function has a **one-to-one correspondence**.

Extra Info

One-to-one correspondence

In some functions, each value in the domain corresponds to only one value in the range and vice-versa. This means that there are no values of x that will produce the same value of y.

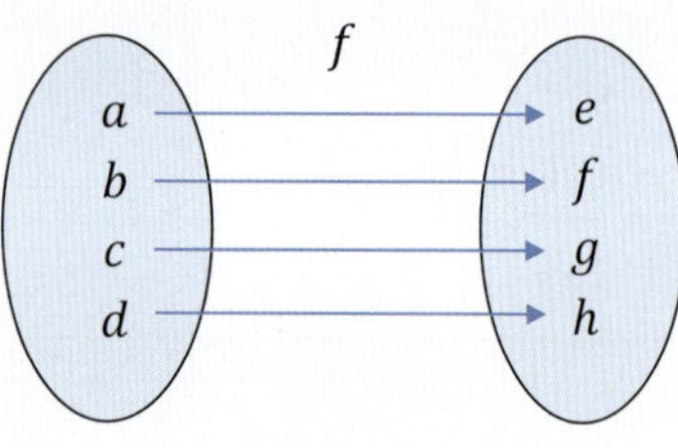

one-to-one

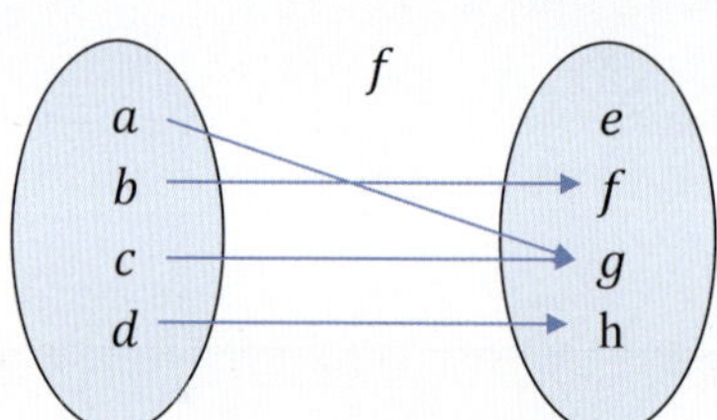

not one-to-one

Straight line functions have inverse functions, as do some cubic functions, but quadratic functions do not have an inverse – as different values in the domain result in the same value in the range.

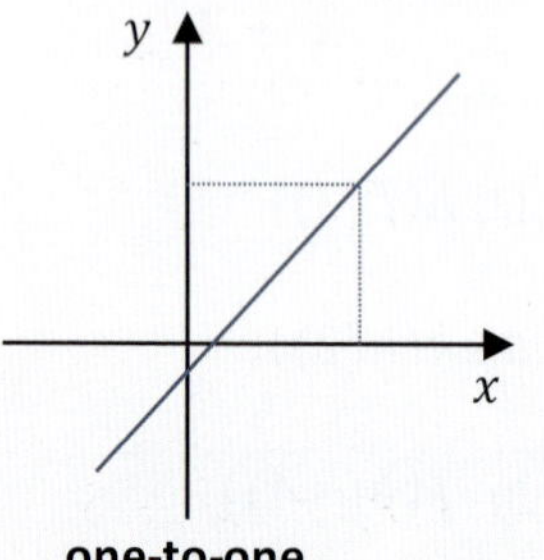

one-to-one

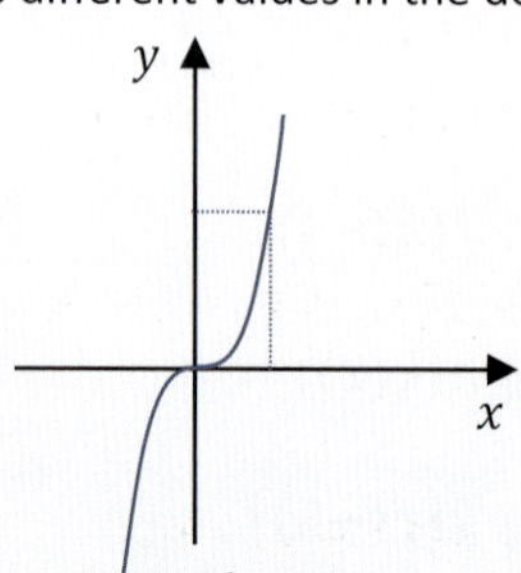

one-to-one

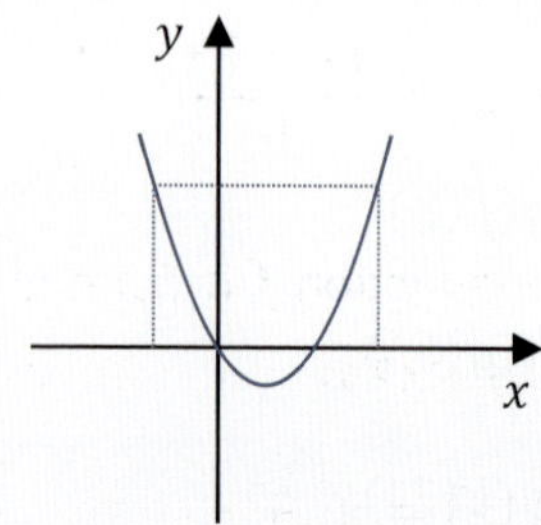

not one-to-one

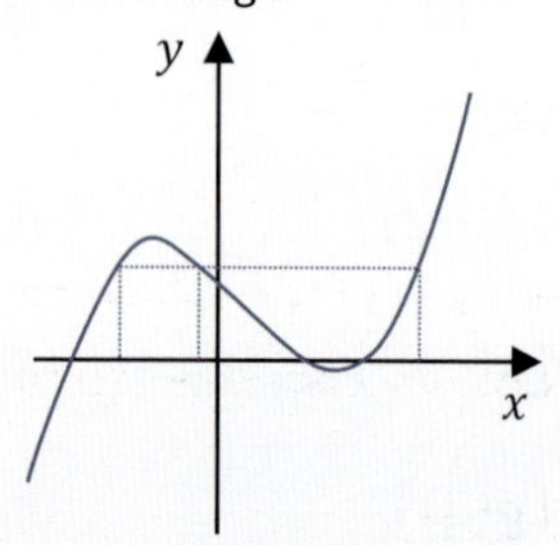

not one-to-one

Extra Info

Trigonometric Functions and Inverses

We are familiar with inverse functions in trigonometry, $y = \sin^{-1} x$, etc. However, these inverse functions are only **partial inverses** within a restricted domain.

Functions and their inverses relate as follows: $f(f^{-1}(x)) = f^{-1}(f(x)) = x$. This means when we graph the inverse of a function, it is symmetrical along the line $y = x$ with the original function (see **section 15.4**).

To find an inverse function:

Step 1: Replace $f(x)$ with y

Step 2: Change the subject to x

Step 3: Replace y with x and x with $f^{-1}(x)$

Worked Example:

A function f is defined by $f(x) = 7x - 3$, where $x \in \mathbb{R}$. Determine an expression for $f^{-1}(x)$.

Solution:

$$y = 7x - 3$$

$$y + 3 = 7x$$

$$\frac{y+3}{7} = x \quad \text{so} \quad x = \frac{y+3}{7}$$

$$f^{-1}(x) = \frac{x+3}{7}$$

Exercise 4.4

1. For each of the following, the function f is defined by $f(x)$, where $x \in \mathbb{R}$. Determine an expression for $f^{-1}(x)$:

(a) $f(x) = 4x + 7$ (b) $f(x) = 5x - 9$ (c) $f(x) = 8 - 2x$ (d) $f(x) = 7x - 20$

(e) $f(x) = \frac{1}{2}x - 2$ (f) $f(x) = \frac{1}{3}x + 9$ (g) $f(x) = \frac{3x-2}{5}$ (h) $f(x) = \frac{3}{4}x + 10$

(i) $f(x) = \frac{5-x}{7}$ (j) $f(x) = \frac{6+5x}{12}$ (k) $f(x) = \frac{3x-5}{9}$ (l) $f(x) = \frac{11x+3}{3}$

(m) $f(x) = \frac{4x-3}{5}$ (n) $f(x) = \frac{12-2x}{5}$ (o) $f(x) = \frac{7x+8}{12}$ (p) $f(x) = \frac{9-2x}{2}$

2. For each of the following, the function f is defined by $f(x)$, where $x \in \mathbb{R}$. Determine an expression for $f^{-1}(x)$:

(a) $f(x) = x^3$ (b) $f(x) = x^3 + 1$ (c) $f(x) = 3 - x^3$ (d) $f(x) = 4x^3 + 5$

(e) $f(x) = 2x^5$ (f) $f(x) = 5x^3 - 7$ (g) $f(x) = 3x^5 + 1$ (h) $f(x) = 4 - 3x^3$

(i) $f(x) = \dfrac{2x^3 - 5}{4}$ (j) $f(x) = \dfrac{6 + x^5}{3}$ (k) $f(x) = \dfrac{3x^3 - 2}{12}$ (l) $f(x) = \dfrac{x^5 - 11}{6}$

3. A function f is defined by $f(x) = 3x^3 + 1$, where $x \in \mathbb{R}$.

   (a) Determine an expression for $f^{-1}(x)$.

   (b) Determine an expression for $f\big(f^{-1}(x)\big)$.

4. A function g is defined by $g(x) = 4x - 7$, where $x \in \mathbb{R}$.

   (a) Determine an expression for $g^{-1}(x)$.

   (b) Determine an expression for $g^{-1}\big(g(x)\big)$.

4.5 Functions Review

Exercise 4.5A

4.1A The following functions are defined on $\mathbb{R}$, the set of real numbers. State any restrictions on their domains:

(a) $f(x) = \dfrac{4}{x - 3}$ (b) $f(x) = \dfrac{5x}{2 - x^2}$ (c) $f(x) = \dfrac{4x - 8}{x^2 - x - 2}$

(d) $f(x) = \sqrt{6 + x}$ (e) $f(x) = \sqrt{x^2 - 4}$ (f) $f(x) = \sqrt{4 - 3x}$

4.1B (a) A function f is defined by $f(x) = x^3 + 2$. The domain of f is $0 \leq x \leq 10, x \in \mathbb{R}$. State the range of the function.

(b) A function g is defined by $g(x) = 2x^3 - 5$. The domain of g is $0 \leq x \leq 5, x \in \mathbb{R}$. State the range of the function.

(c) A function h is defined by $h(x) = 7x^2 + 9$. The domain of f is $0 \leq x \leq 5, x \in \mathbb{R}$. State the range of the function.

4.3A (a) Functions f and g are defined on a suitable domain by $f(x) = x^3 + 2$ and $g(x) = 2x - 1$. Find an expression for $h(x)$ where $h(x) = g\big(f(x)\big)$.

(b) Functions f and g are defined on a suitable domain by $f(x) = 3x^2 - 5$ and $g(x) = 3x + 2$. Find an expression for $h(x)$ where $h(x) = g\big(f(x)\big)$.

(c) Functions f and g are defined on a suitable domain by $f(x) = \dfrac{4}{x - 3}$ and $g(x) = \dfrac{3}{x - 1}$. Find an expression for $h(x)$ where $h(x) = g\big(f(x)\big)$.

4.3B **(a)** Functions f and g are defined on suitable domain by $f(x) = 2x^2 + 2$ and $g(x) = 3x + 4$. Evaluate $g(f(-4))$.

(b) Functions f and g are defined on suitable domain by $f(x) = 3x^3 - 7$ and $g(x) = 2x - 4$. Evaluate $f(g(-2))$.

4.4 For each of the following, the function f is defined by $f(x)$, where $x \in \mathbb{R}$. Determine an expression for $f^{-1}(x)$:

(a) $f(x) = \frac{4}{3}x - 3$ **(b)** $f(x) = \frac{5x - 6}{7}$ **(c)** $f(x) = \frac{2x^3 - 7}{5}$

Exercise 4.5B

1. Functions f and g are defined on suitable domains by $f(x) = \frac{5}{\sqrt{x}}$ and $g(x) = 3 - x$, where $x \in \mathbb{R}$.

   (a) Determine an expression for $f(g(x))$.

   (b) State the range of values for which $f(x)$ is undefined.

2. Functions f and g are defined on suitable domains by $f(x) = \sin 2x$ and $g(x) = 4x$.

   (a) Determine an expression for $g(f(x))$.

   (b) Evaluate $g\left(f\left(\frac{\pi}{6}\right)\right)$.

3. A function, f, is given by $f(x) = \sqrt[3]{x} - 5$. The domain of f is $1 \leq x \leq 125,\ x \in \mathbb{R}$.

   (a) Find $f^{-1}(x)$.

   (b) State the domain of $f^{-1}(x)$.

4. Functions f and g are defined on $\mathbb{R}$ by $f(x) = x^2 + 2x + 5$ and $g(x) = x + 3$.

   (a) Given $h(x) = f(g(x))$, show that $h(x) = x^2 + 8x + 20$.

   (b) Express $h(x)$ in the form $k(x + p)^2 + q$.

5. A function, f, is given by $f(x) = x^2 + 6x$. The domain of f is $-5 \leq x \leq 5,\ x \in \mathbb{R}$.

   (a) Evaluate $f(5)$.

   (b) State the range of $f(x)$.

6. A function, f, is given by $f(x) = x^2 + 6$. The domain of f is $x \geq 0,\ x \in \mathbb{R}$. The function has an inverse.

   (a) Evaluate $f^{-1}(x)$.

   (b) State the domain of $f^{-1}(x)$.

Chapter 5
Graphs of Related Functions

Graphs of Related Functions

In the previous chapter, functions were expressed algebraically, but functions can also be expressed graphically. We are already familiar with the graphs of straight lines and quadratic functions from National 5.

COMMON GRAPHS

Quadratic Functions

These are functions of the form $f(x) = ax^2 \pm ...$ **i.e.** the highest power of x is two. These functions always have one stationary point. This is a point where the function is neither increasing nor decreasing.

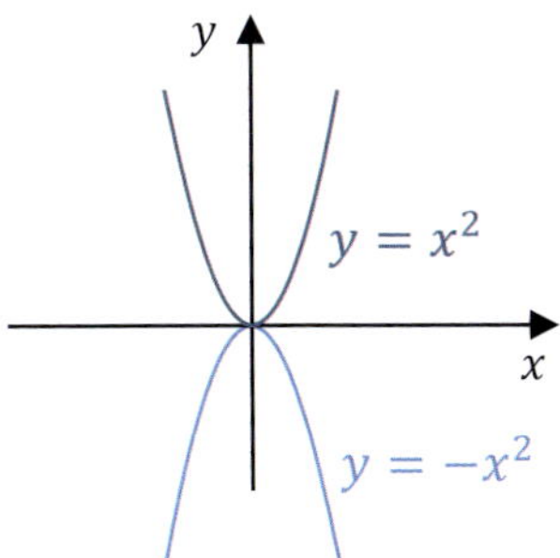

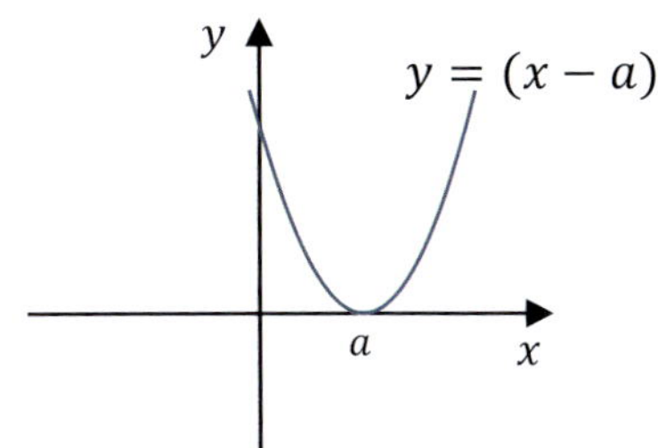

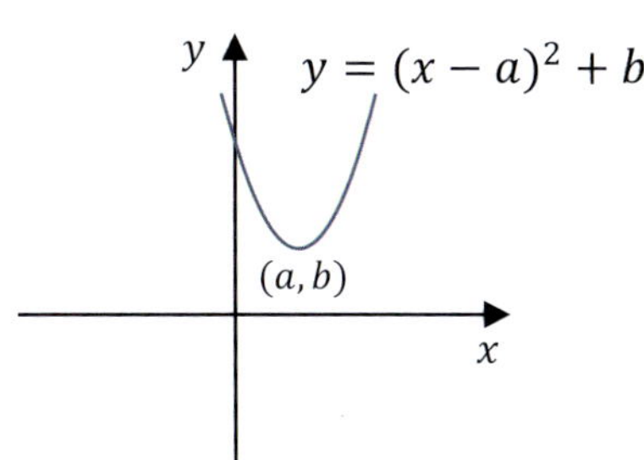

Cubic Functions

These are functions of the form $f(x) = ax^3 \pm ...$ **i.e.** the highest power of x is three. These functions can have zero, one or two stationary points.

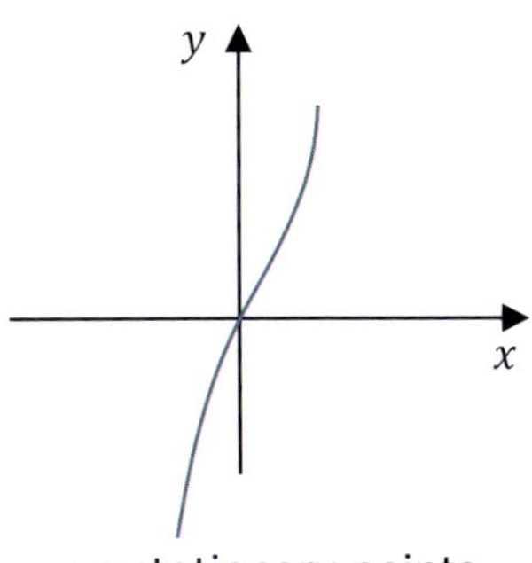

no stationary points

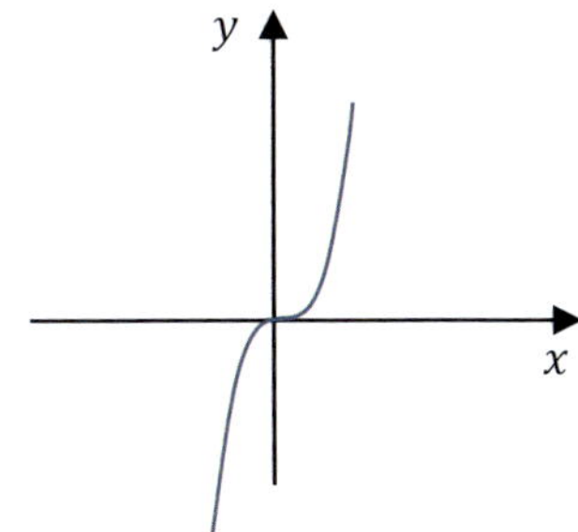

one stationary point

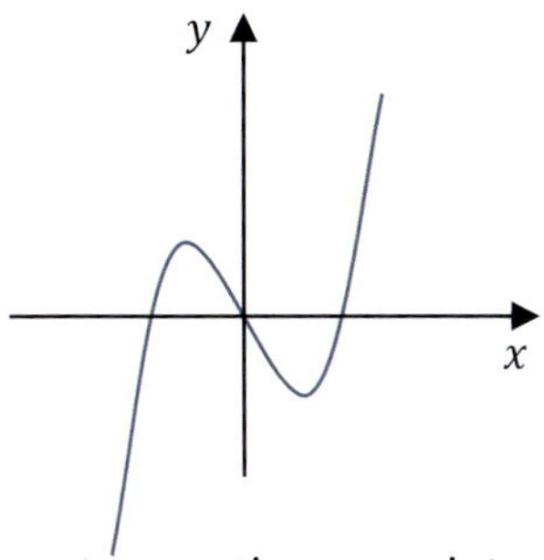

two stationary points

Quartic Functions

These are functions of the form $f(x) = ax^4 \pm ...$ **i.e.** the highest power of x is four. These functions can have one, two or three stationary points.

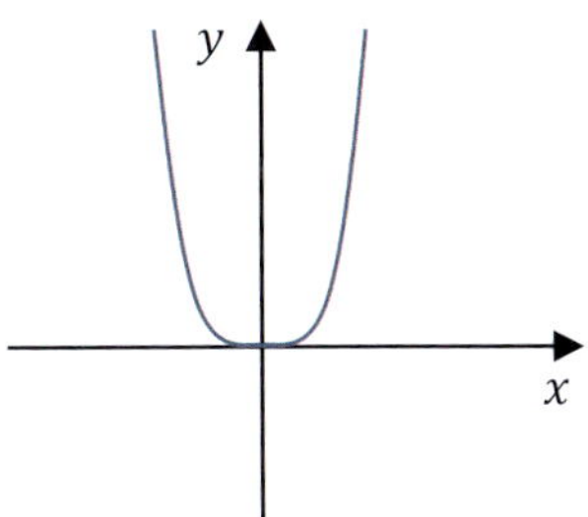

one stationary point

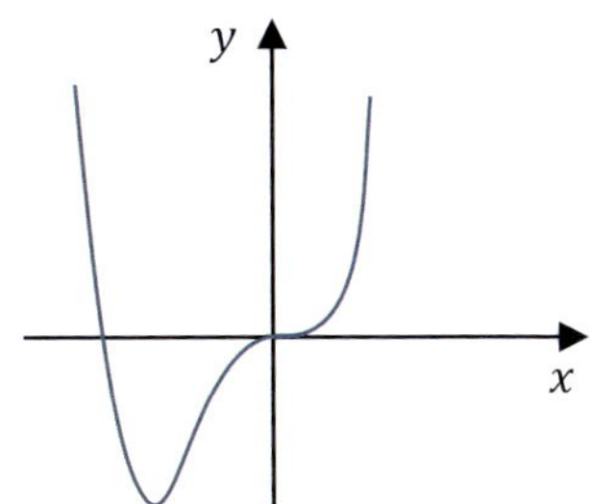

two stationary points

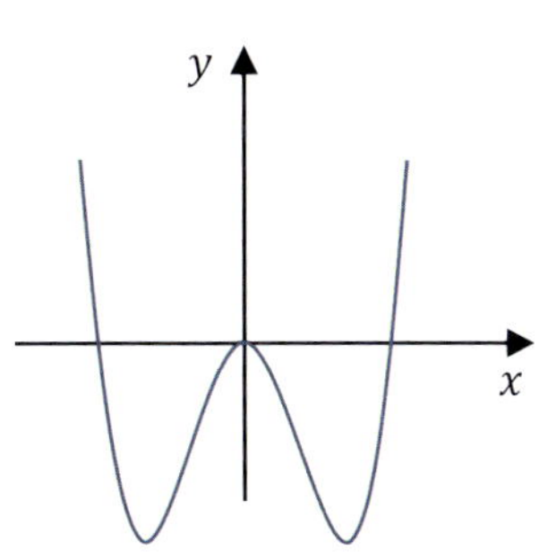

three stationary points

OTHER GRAPHS

The following graphs are less common in Higher Mathematics.

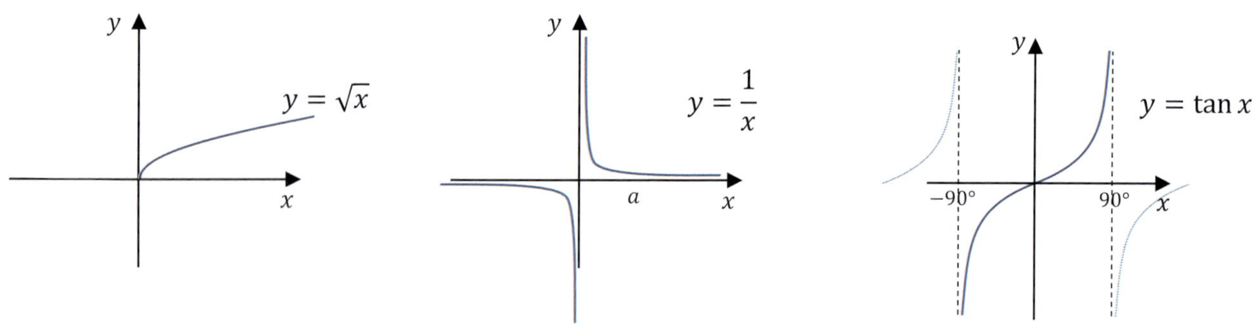

NB: For logarithmic and exponential graphs and their transformations, (see **sections 15.2-5**).

5.1 Graphs of $f(x) \pm k$

In functions of the form $f(x) \pm k$, the graph of the function is moved either up $(+)$ or down $(-)$ by k. We are already familiar with this transformation from National 5 Mathematics with the graphs of quadratic and trigonometric functions.

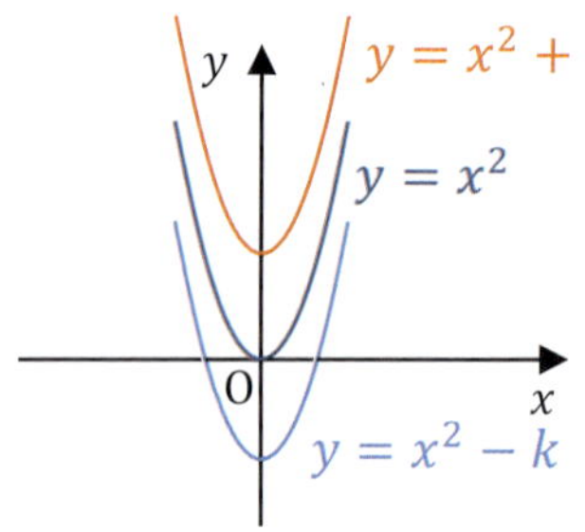

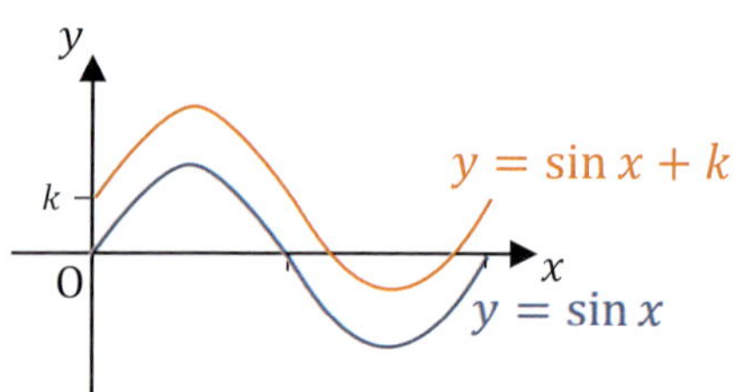

Worked Example:

The diagram shows the graph of $y = f(x)$.

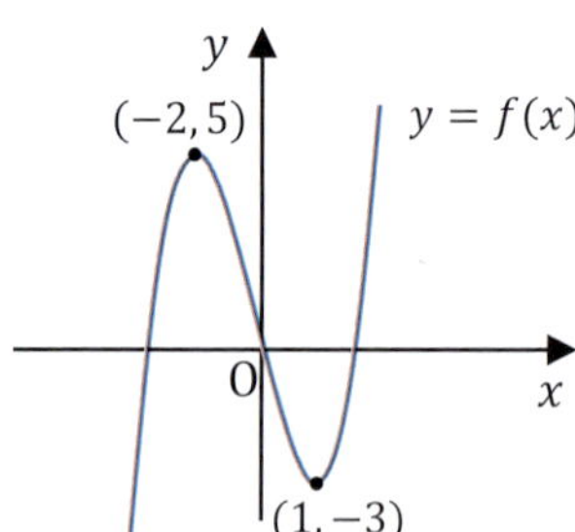

Sketch the graph of $y = f(x) + 3$.

Solution:

- Sketch the graph lightly on the axes.
- Move every known coordinate up by 3.
- Sketch the transformed graph.
- Annotate with the images of given points (including any passing through the origin).

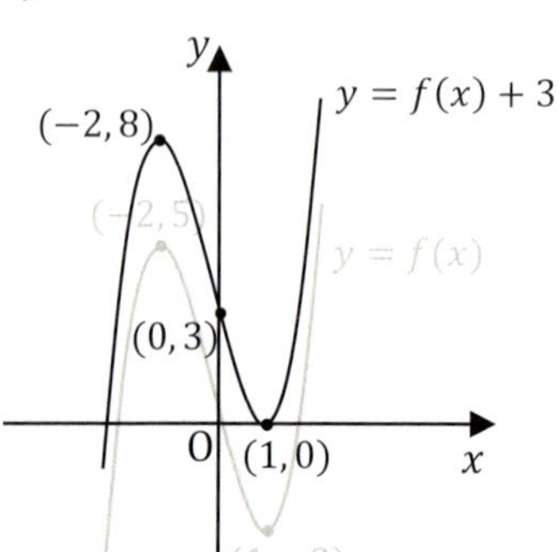

Exercise 5.1

1. In each of the following diagrams the graph of $y = f(x)$ is shown. Sketch the graph with the given transformation:

(a)

$y = f(x)$

$(5, 8)$

Sketch $y = f(x) + 4$

(b)

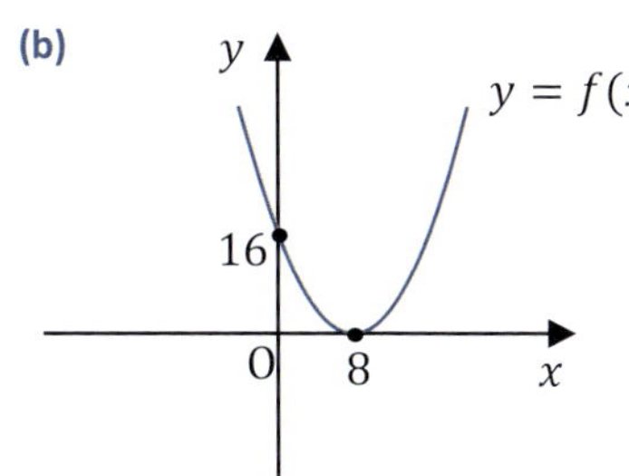

Sketch $y = f(x) + 2$

(c)

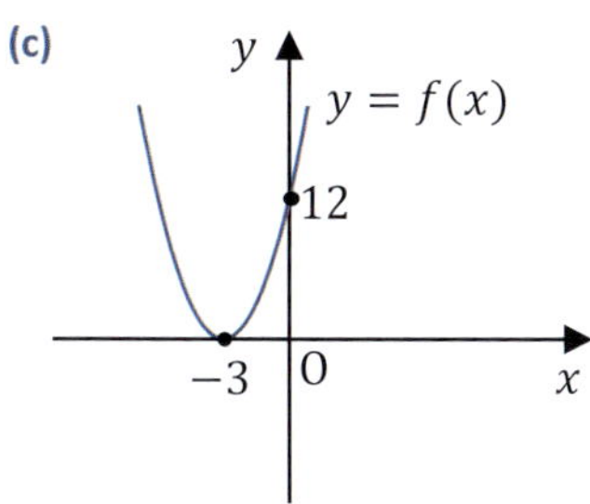

Sketch $y = f(x) - 3$

(d)

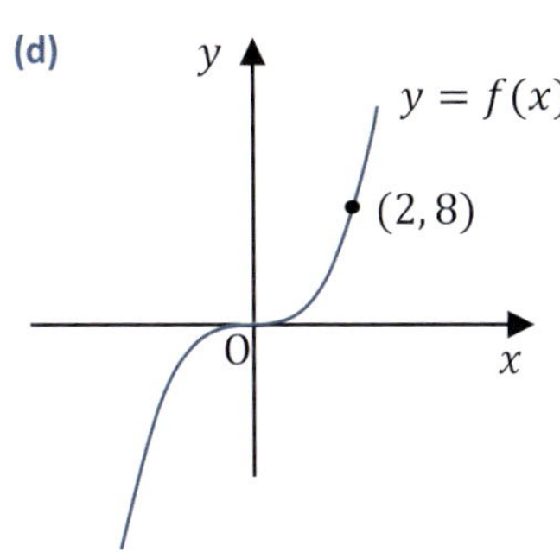

Sketch $y = f(x) - 1$

(e)

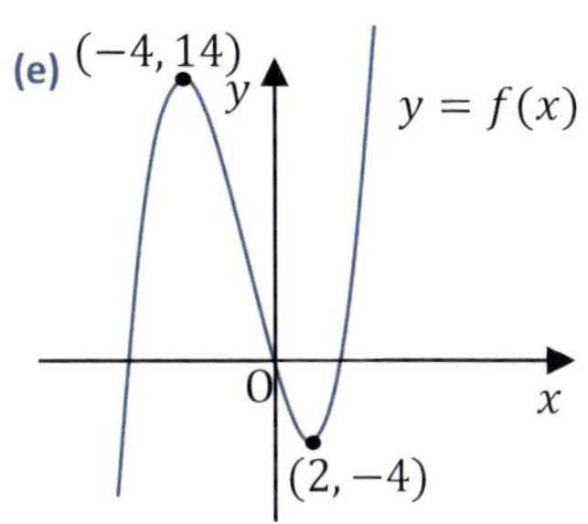

Sketch $y = f(x) - 2$

(f)

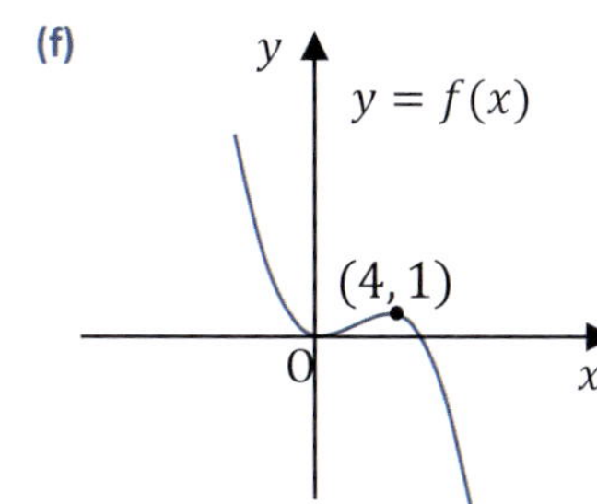

Sketch $y = f(x) - 3$

(g)

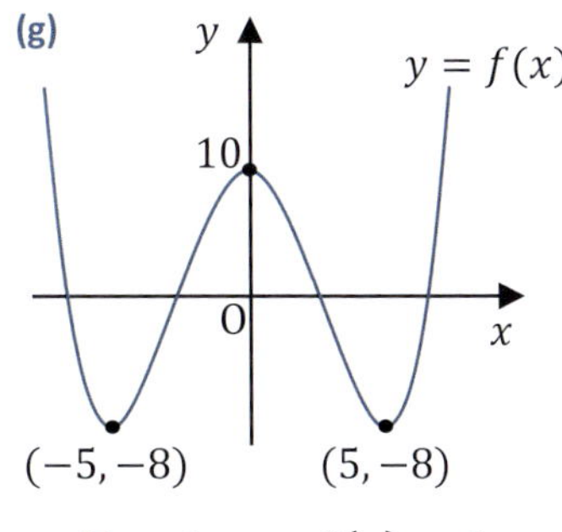

Sketch $y = f(x) - 1$

(h)

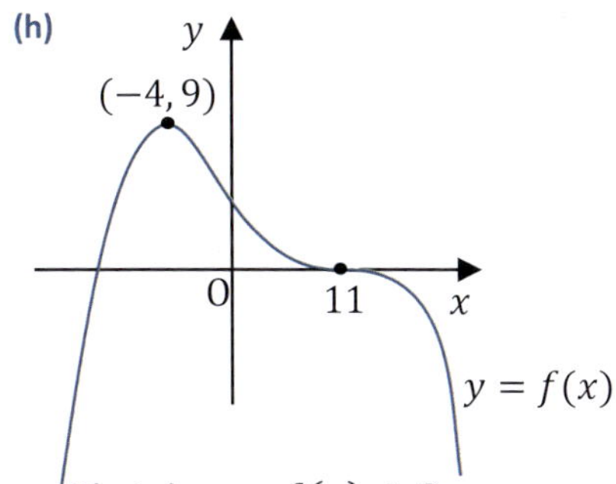

Sketch $y = f(x) + 3$

(i)

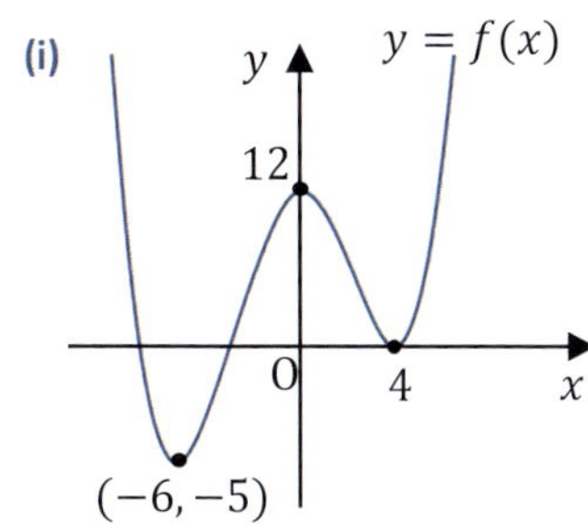

Sketch $y = f(x) + 5$

5.2 Graphs of $f(x \pm k)$

In functions of the form $f(x \pm k)$ where $k > 0$, the graph of the function moves either left $\boldsymbol{f(x+k)}$ or right $\boldsymbol{f(x-k)}$ by k.

Worked Example:

The diagram shows the graph of $y = f(x)$.

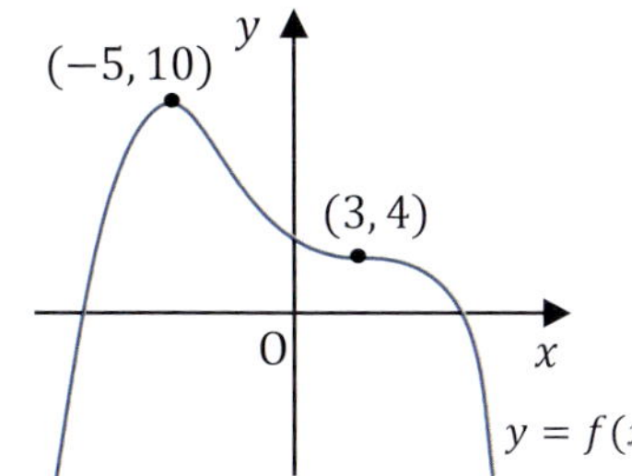

Sketch the graph of $y = f(x - 2)$.

Solution:

- Sketch the graph lightly on the axes.
- Move every known coordinate right by 2.
- Sketch the transformed graph.
- Annotate with the images of given points (including any passing through the origin).

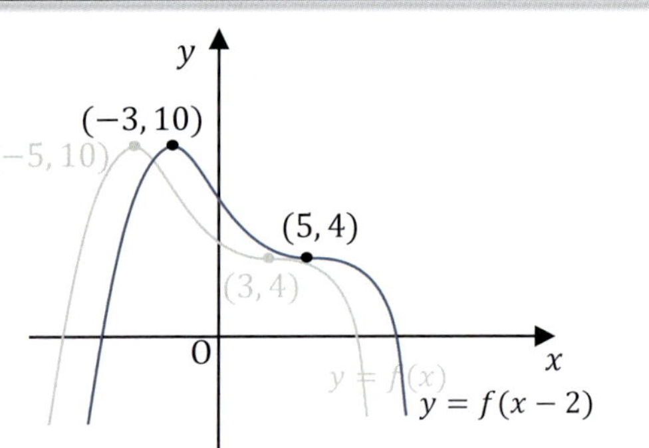

Exercise 5.2

1. In each of the following diagrams the graph of $y = f(x)$ is shown. Sketch the graph with the given transformation:

(a)

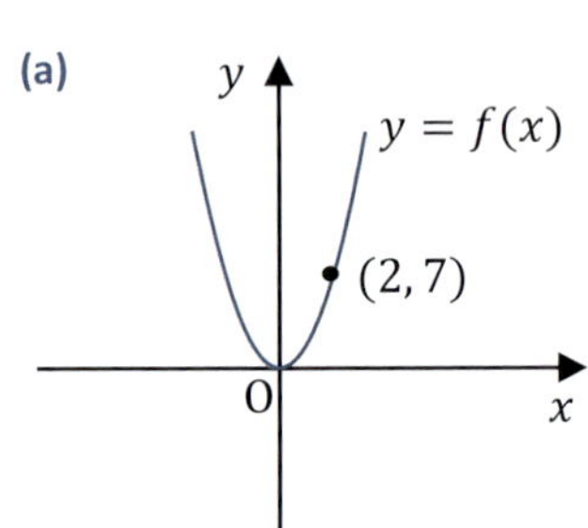

Sketch $y = f(x - 1)$

(b)

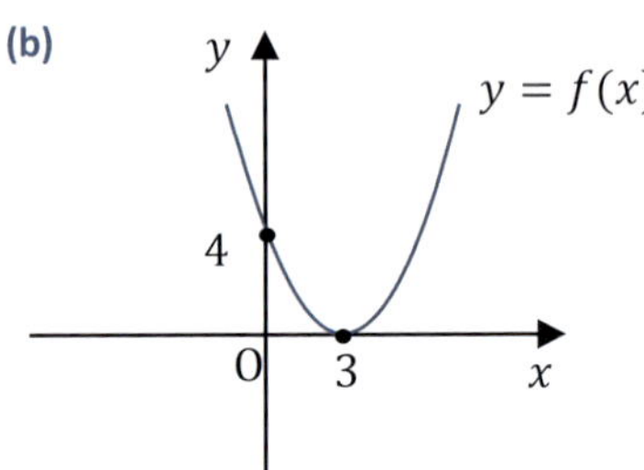

Sketch $y = f(x + 2)$

(c)

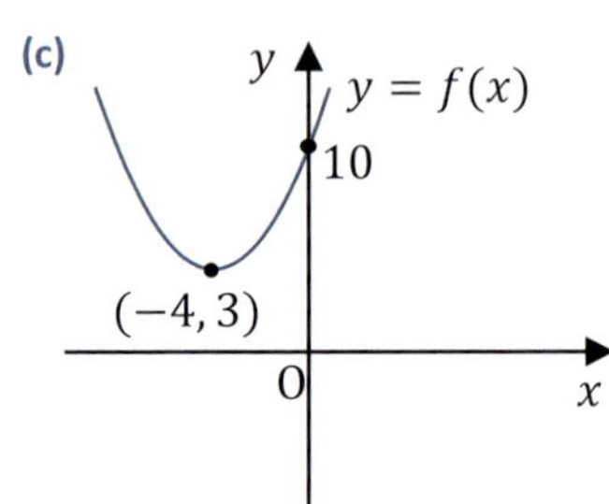

Sketch $y = f(x - 6)$

(d)

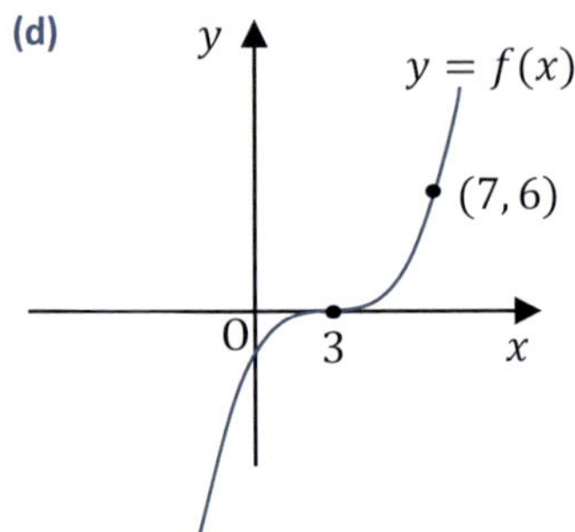

Sketch $y = f(x + 5)$

(e)

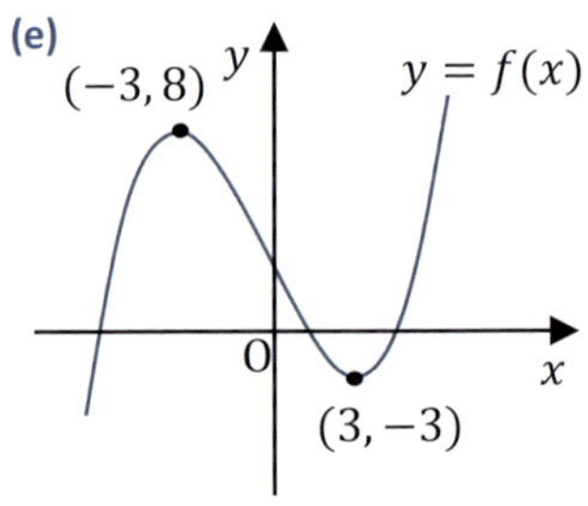

Sketch $y = f(x - 3)$

(f)

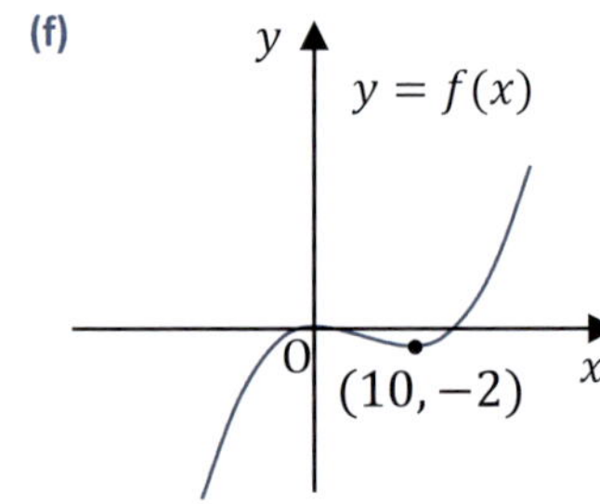

Sketch $y = f(x + 10)$

(g)

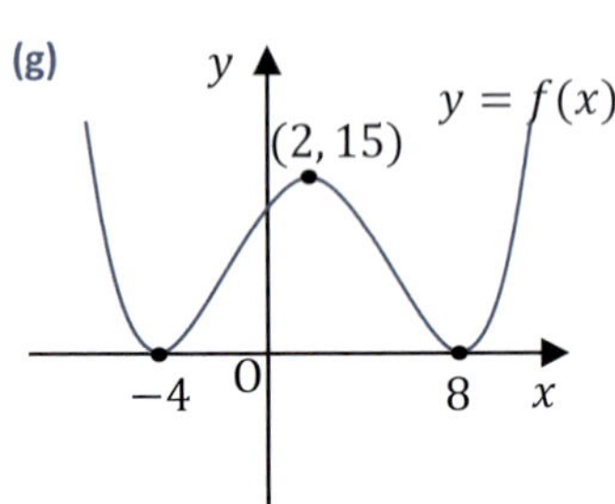

Sketch $y = f(x + 6)$

(h)

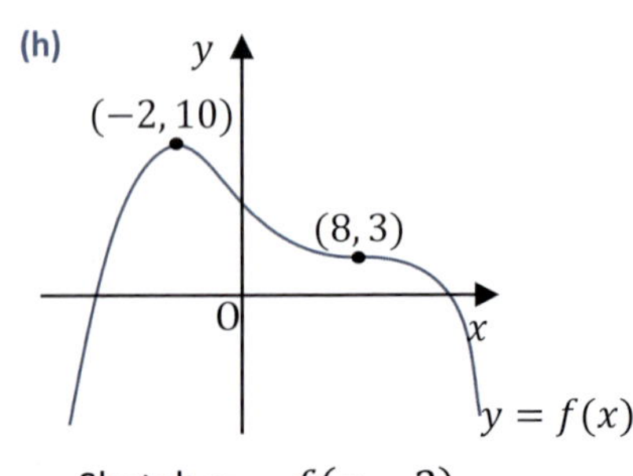

Sketch $y = f(x - 2)$

(i)

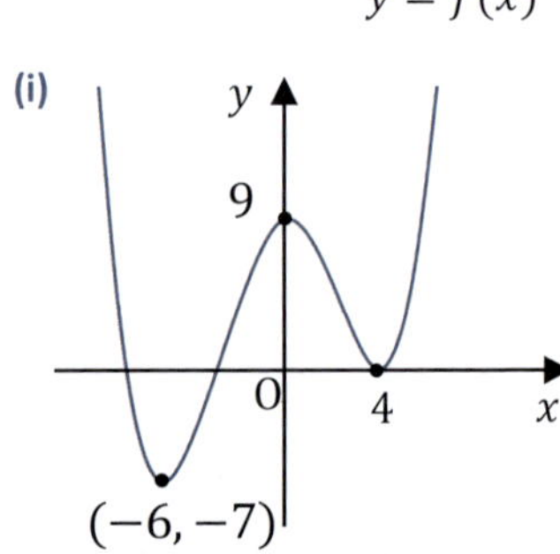

Sketch $y = f(x - 5)$

5.3 Graphs of $kf(x)$

In functions of the form $kf(x)$, the y-coordinate of each point is multiplied by k. When k is a negative number, the graph is reflected in the x-axis (see **example 2**). When $k > 1$ or $k < -1$, the graph is **stretched vertically** from the x-axis. When $-1 < k < 1$, the graph is **squashed vertically** towards the x-axis.

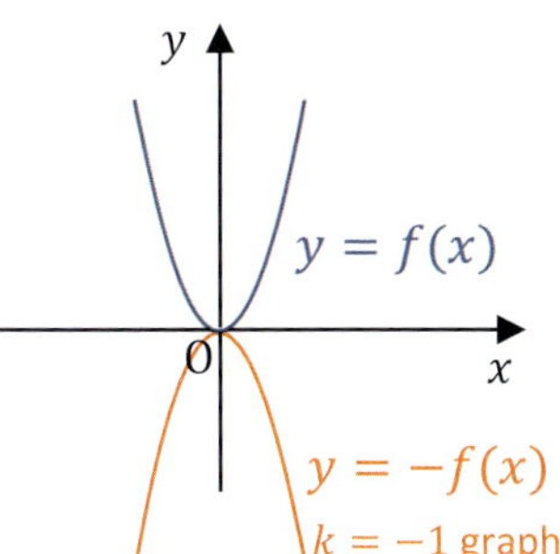

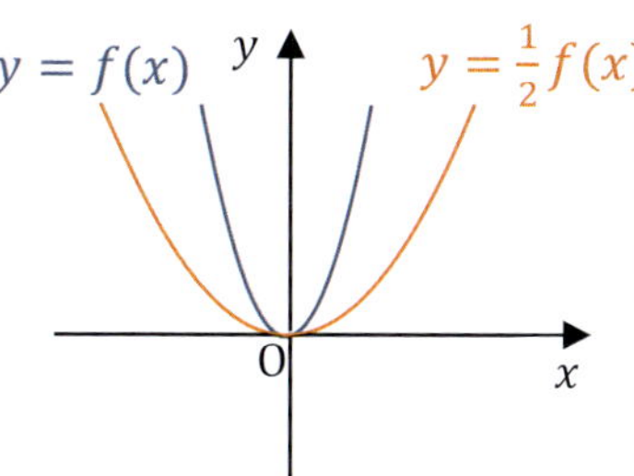

Worked Examples:

1. The diagram shows the graph of $y = f(x)$.

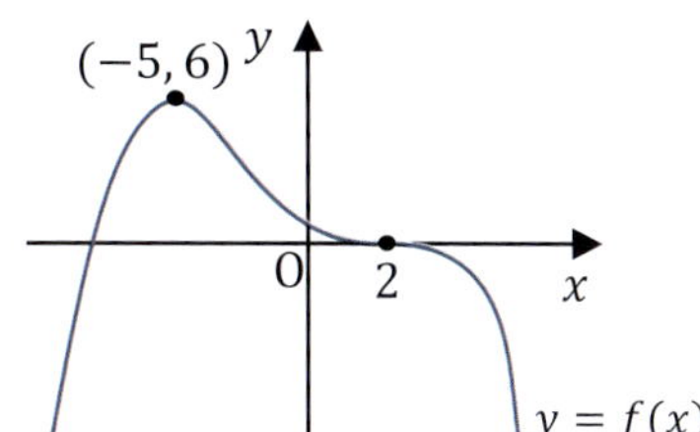

Sketch the graph of $y = 2f(x)$.

Solution:

- Sketch the graph lightly on the axes.
- Multiply every y-coordinate by 2.
- Sketch the transformed graph.

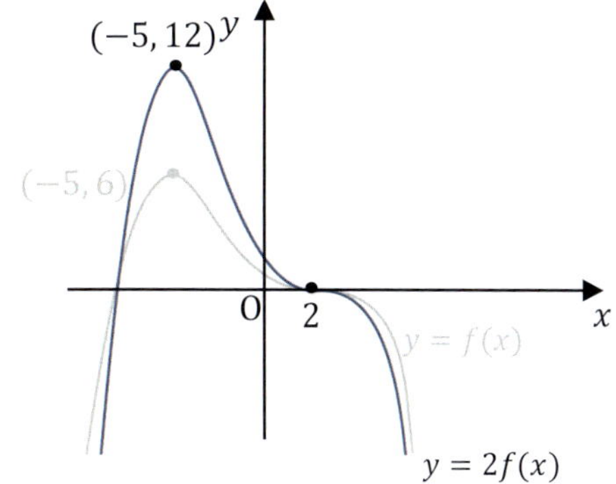

2. The diagram shows the graph of $y = f(x)$.

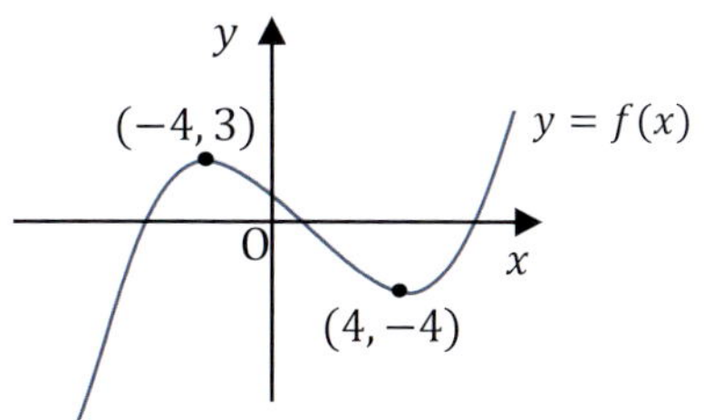

Sketch the graph of $y = -f(x)$.

Solution:

- Sketch the graph lightly on the axes.
- Multiply every y- coordinate by -1.
- Sketch the transformed graph.

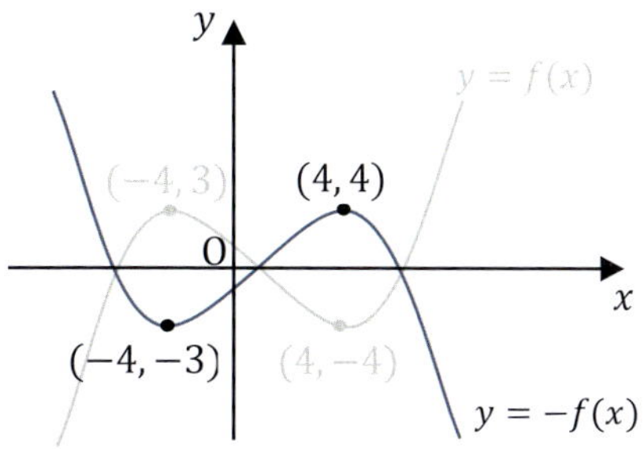

Exercise 5.3

1. In each of the following diagrams the graph of $y = f(x)$ is shown. Sketch the graph with the given transformation:

(a)

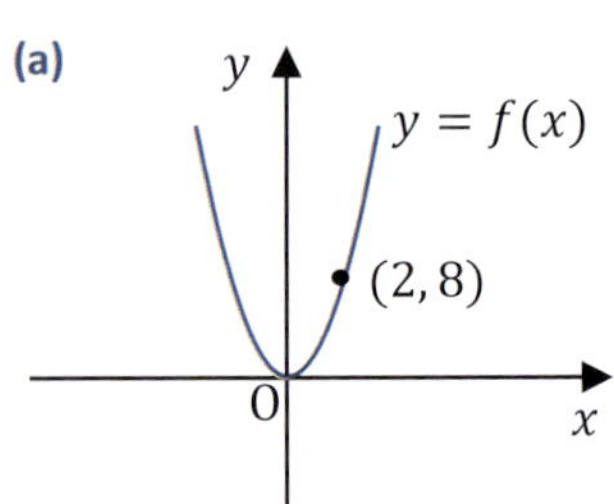

Sketch $y = 2f(x)$

(b)

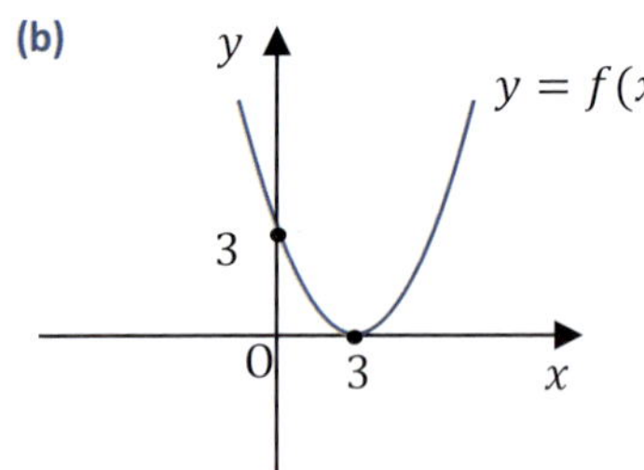

Sketch $y = 3f(x)$

(c)

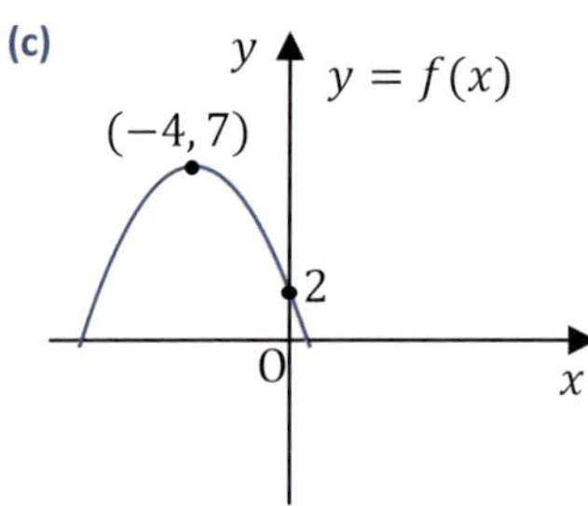

Sketch $y = 2f(x)$

(d)

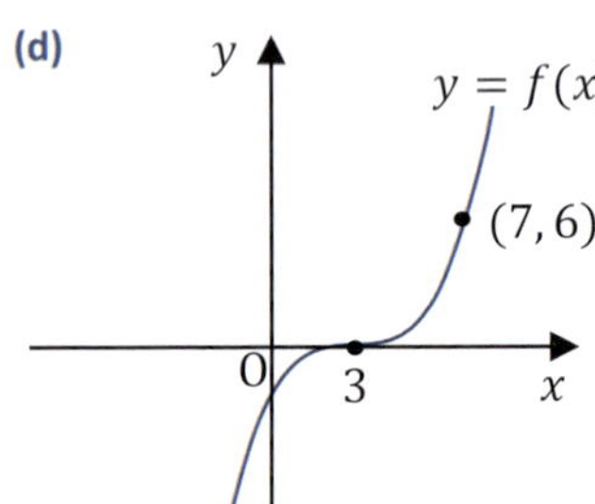

Sketch $y = 4f(x)$

(e)

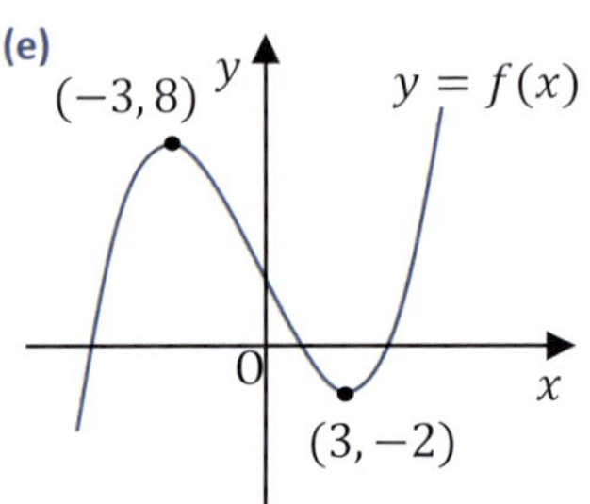

Sketch $y = \frac{1}{2}f(x)$

(f)

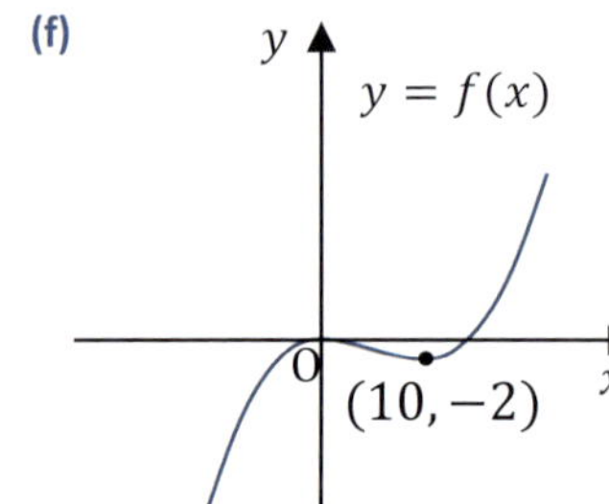

Sketch $y = 3f(x)$

(g)

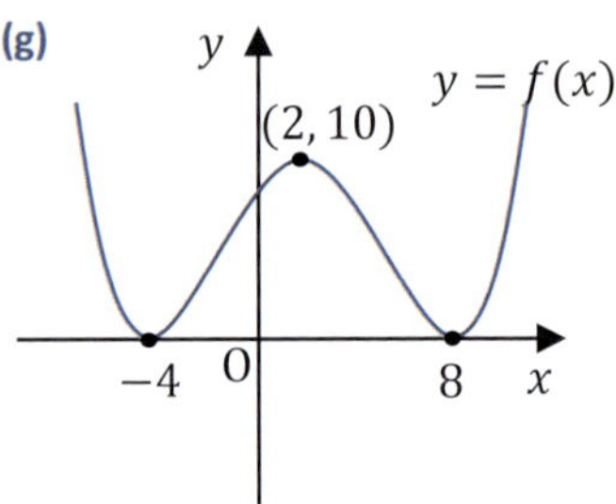

Sketch $y = \frac{1}{2}f(x)$

(h)

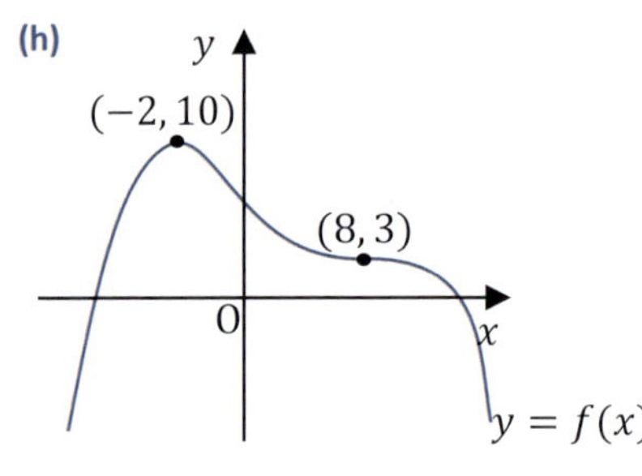

Sketch $y = 3f(x)$

(i)

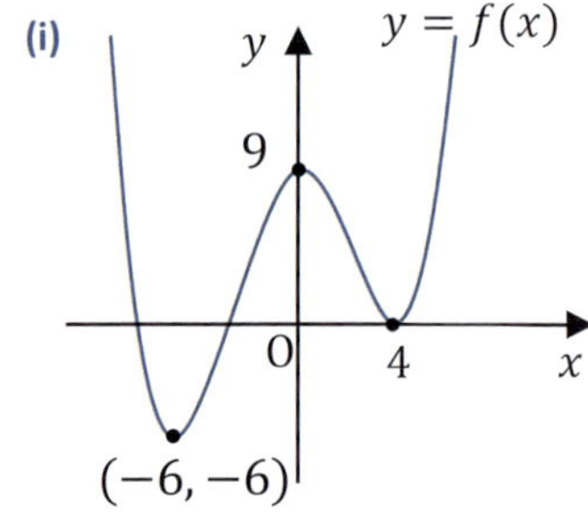

Sketch $y = \frac{1}{3}f(x)$

2. In each of the following diagrams the graph of $y = f(x)$ is shown. Sketch the graph with the given transformation:

(a)

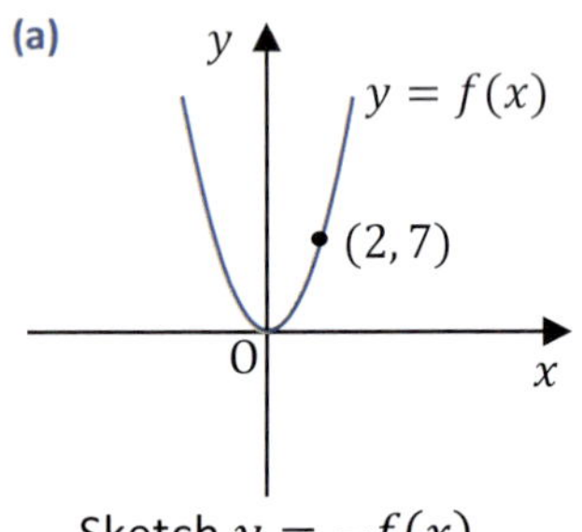

Sketch $y = -f(x)$

(b)

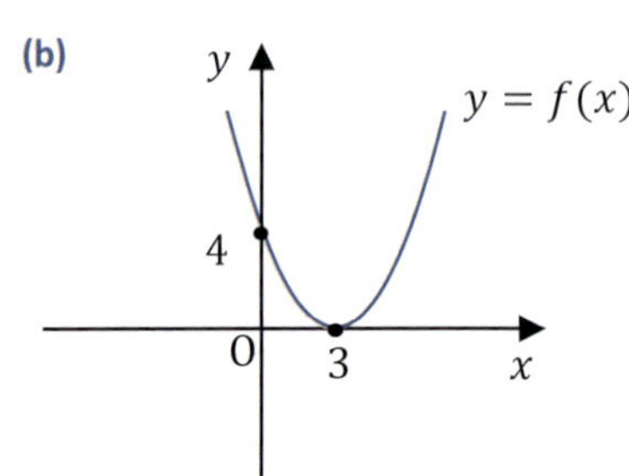

Sketch $y = -f(x)$

(c)

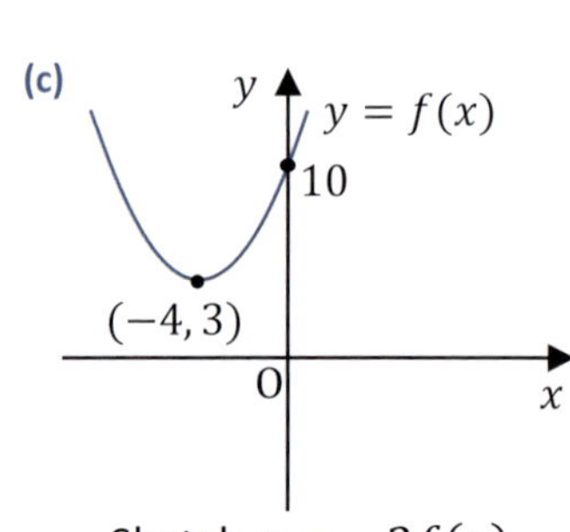

Sketch $y = -2f(x)$

(d)

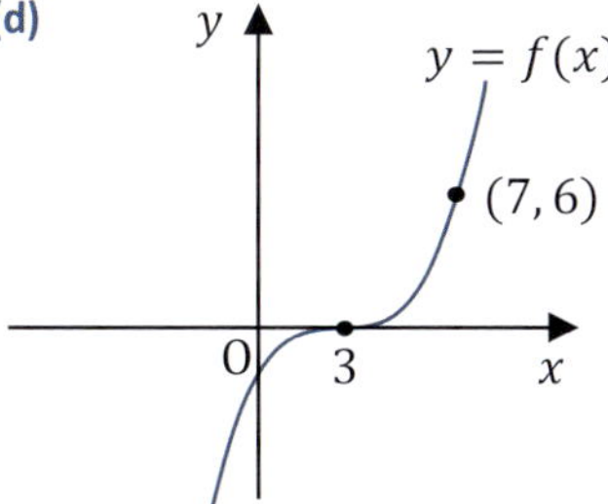

Sketch $y = -f(x)$

(e)

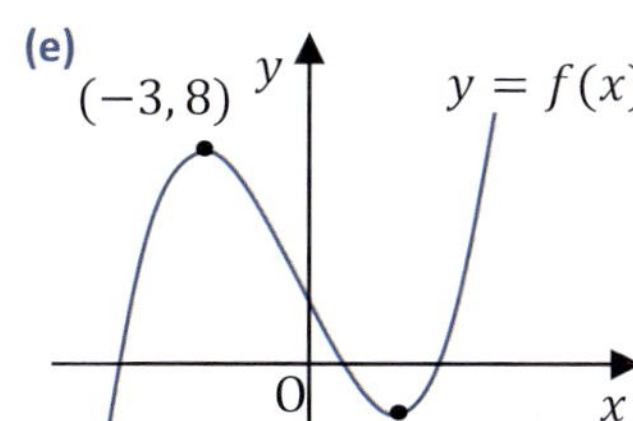

Sketch $y = -2f(x)$

(f)

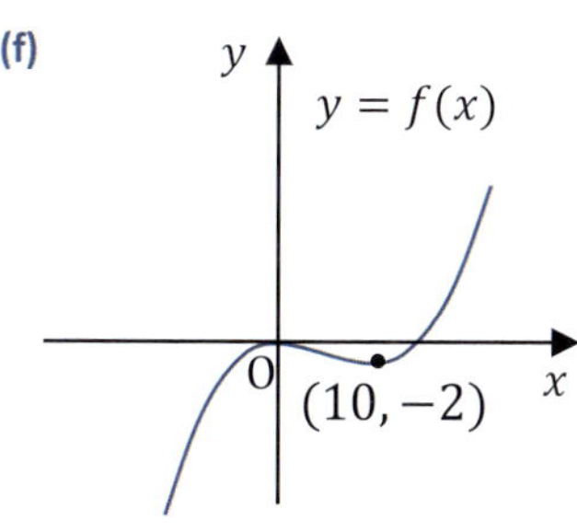

Sketch $y = -3f(x)$

(g)

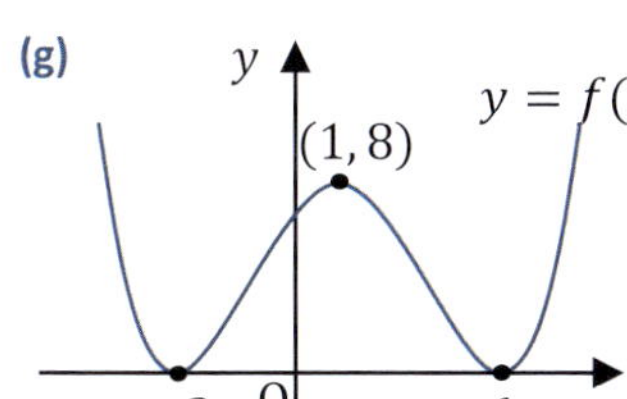

Sketch $y = -f(x)$

(h)

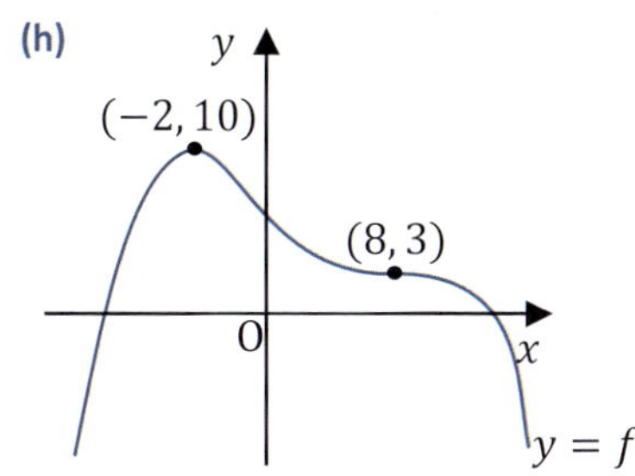

Sketch $y = -2f(x)$

(i)

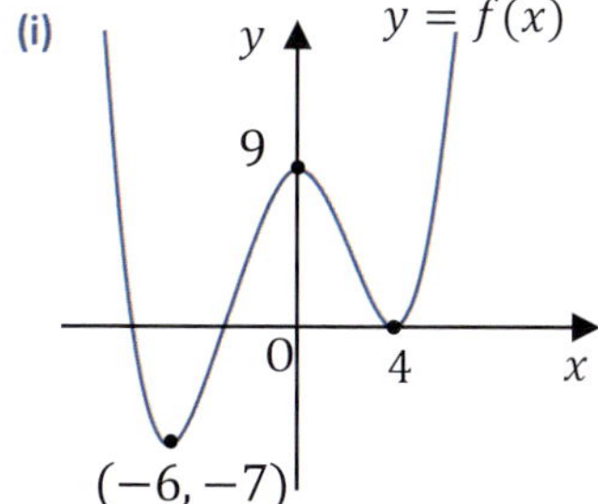

Sketch $y = -4f(x)$

5.4 Graphs of $f(kx)$

In functions of the form $f(x)$, the x-coordinate of each point is divided by k. When k is a negative number, the graph is reflected in the y-axis (see **example 2**). When $k > 1$ or $k < -1$, the graph is **squashed horizontally** towards the y-axis. When $-1 < k < 1$, the graph is **stretched horizontally** away from the y-axis.

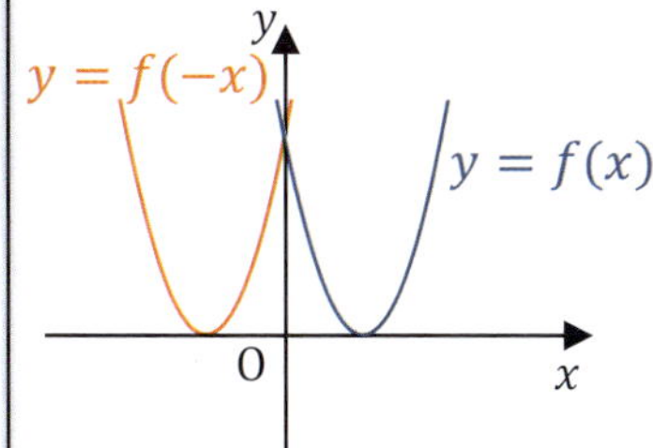

$k = -1$ graph is reflected in y-axis

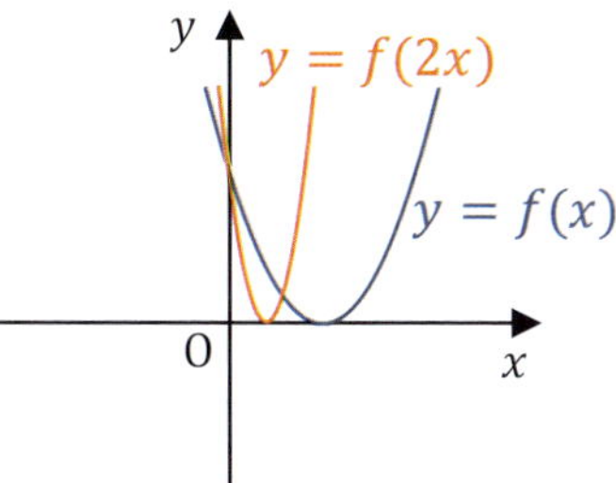

$y = f(x)$ $\quad y = f\left(\frac{1}{2}x\right)$

Worked Examples:

1. The diagram shows the graph of $y = f(x)$.

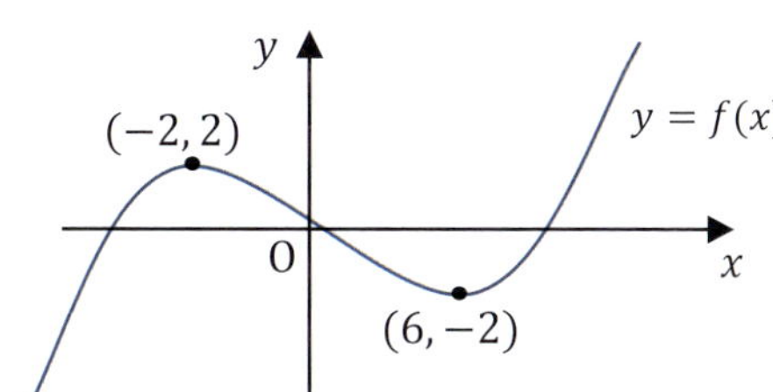

Sketch the graph of $y = f(2x)$.

Solution:

- Sketch the graph lightly on the axes.
- Divide every x-coordinate by 2.
- Sketch the transformed graph.

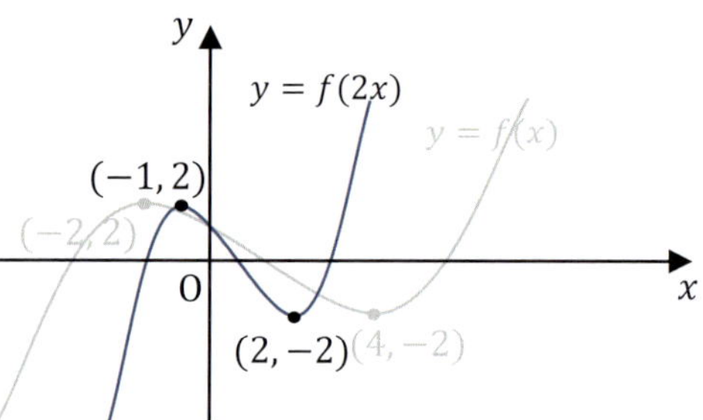

2. The diagram shows the graph of $y = f(x)$.

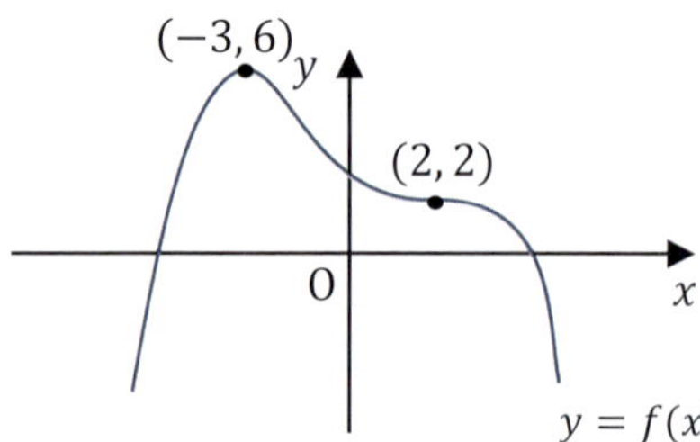

Sketch the graph of $y = f\left(-\frac{1}{2}x\right)$.

Solution:

- Sketch the graph lightly on the axes.
- Divide every x-coordinate by $-\frac{1}{2}$.
- Sketch the transformed graph.

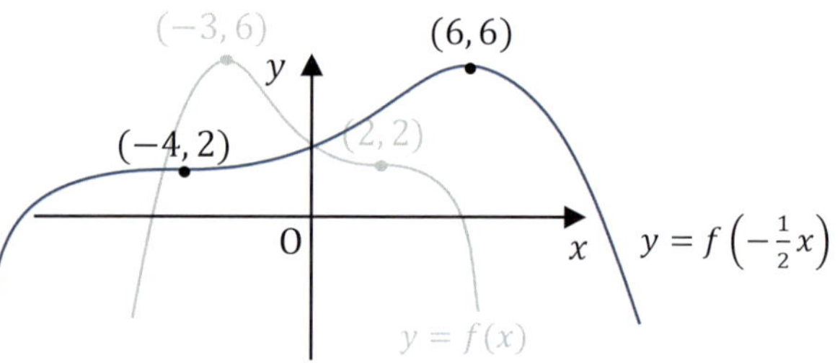

Exercise 5.4

1. In each of the following diagrams the graph of $y = f(x)$ is shown. Sketch the graph with the given transformation:

(a)

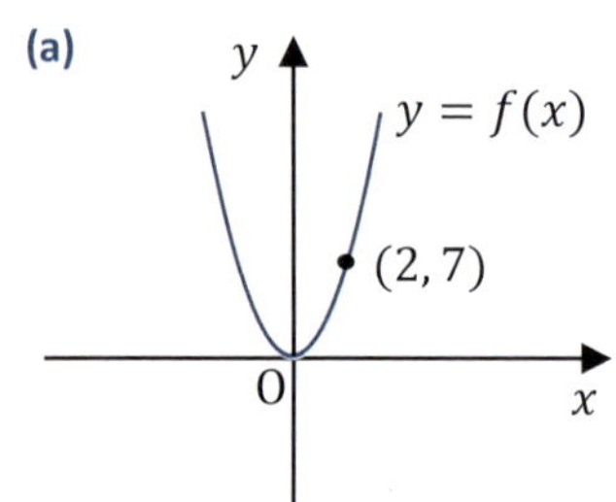

Sketch $y = f(2x)$

(b)

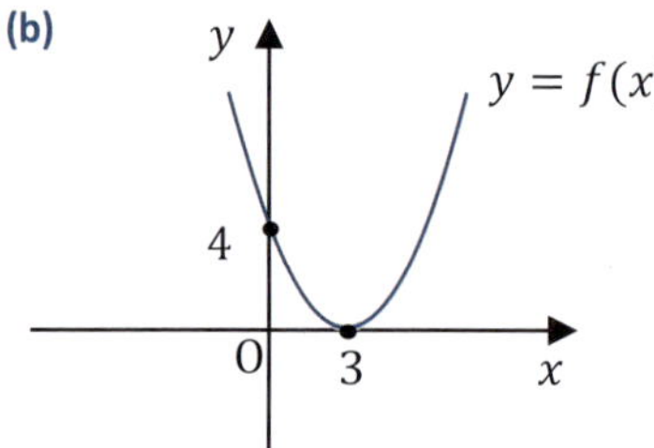

Sketch $y = f(3x)$

(c)

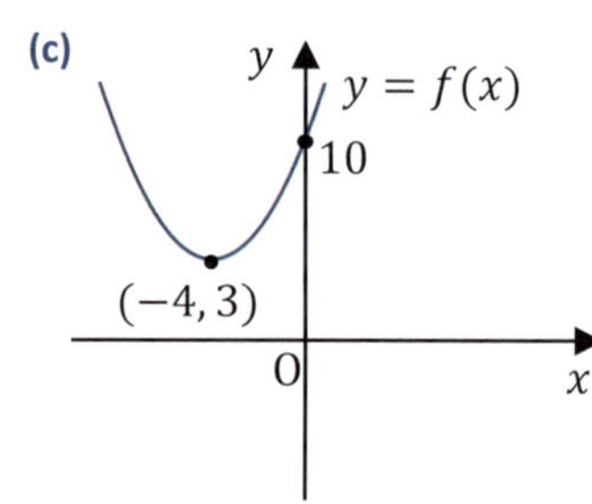

Sketch $y = f\left(\frac{1}{2}x\right)$

(d)

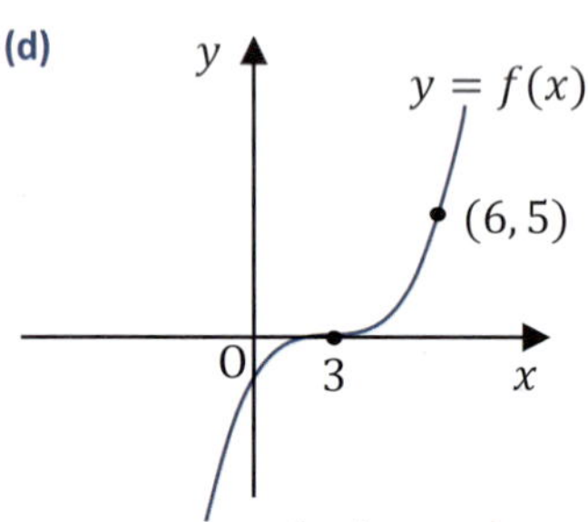

Sketch $y = f(3x)$

(e)

$(-2, 5)$ $y = f(x)$ $(2, -3)$

Sketch $y = f\left(\frac{1}{2}x\right)$

(f)

$(10, 30)$ $(-5, 10)$ $y = f(x)$

Sketch $y = f(5x)$

2. In each of the following diagrams the graph of $y = f(x)$ is shown. Sketch the graph with the given transformation:

(a)

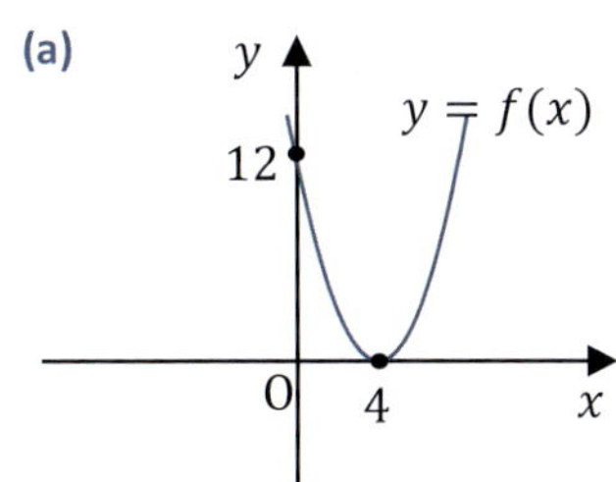

Sketch $y = f(-x)$

(b)

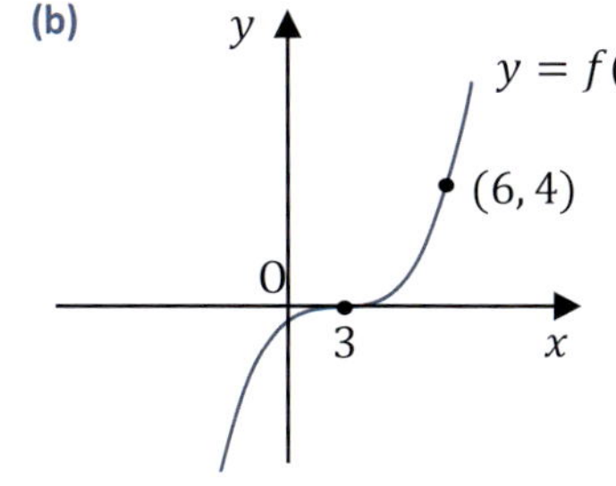

Sketch $y = f(-3x)$

(c)

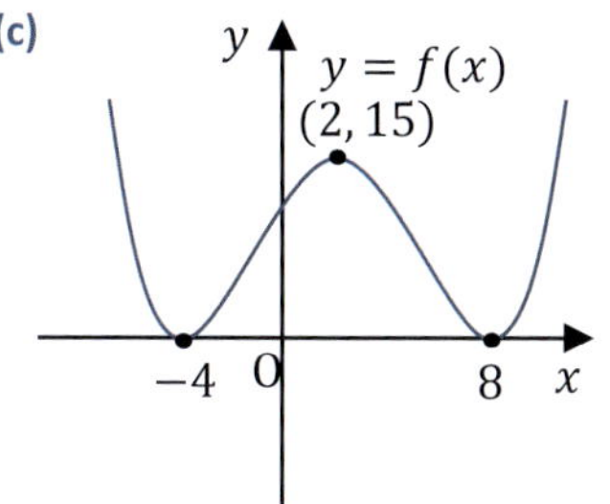

Sketch $y = f(-2x)$

(d)

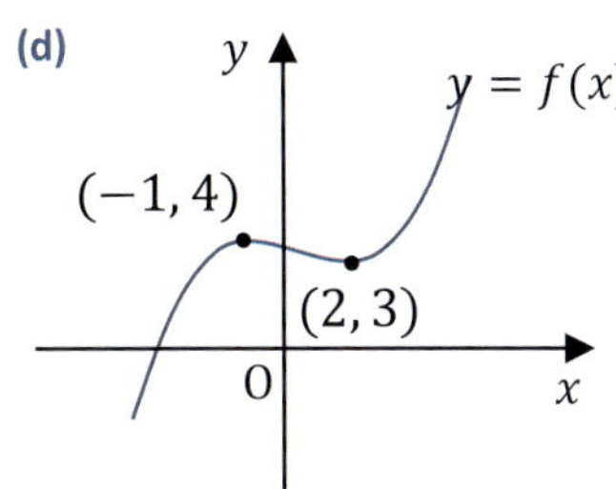

Sketch $y = f\left(-\frac{1}{2}x\right)$

(e)

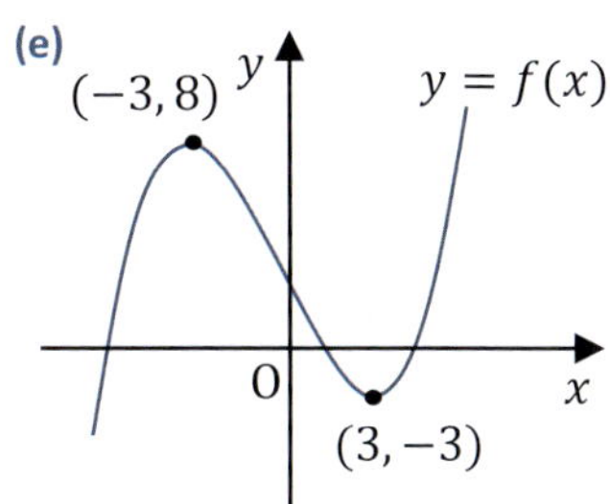

Sketch $y = f(-3x)$

(f)

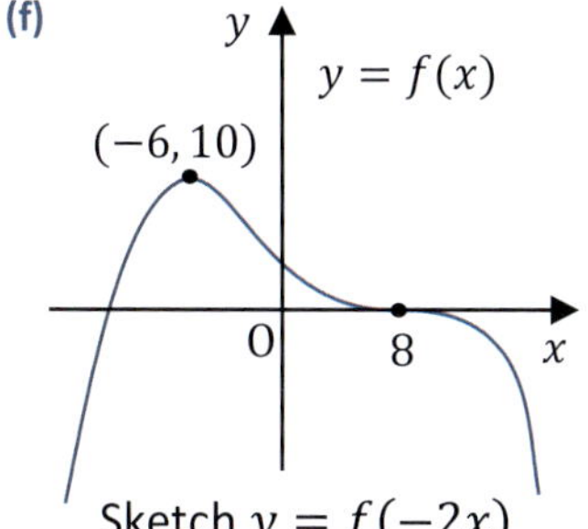

Sketch $y = f(-2x)$

5.5 Review – Combinations of Transformations

In Higher Mathematics we normally need to carry out two or more transformations on a graph of a function.

Worked Examples:

1. The diagram shows the graph of $y = f(x)$.

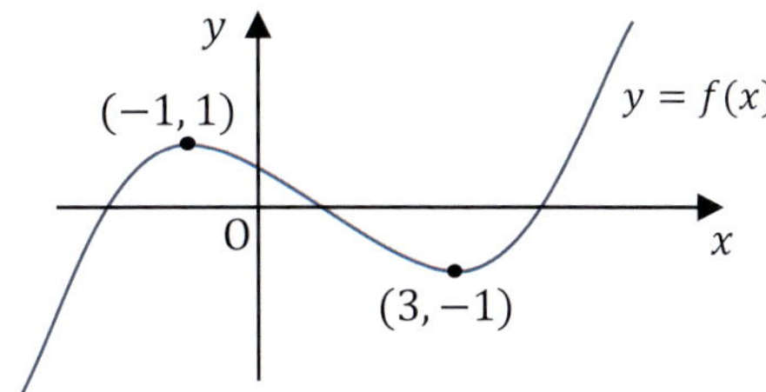

Sketch the graph of $y = f(x - 2) + 1$.

Solution:

- Sketch the original graph lightly on the axes.
- Calculate each new coordinate.

  For each coordinate $(x + 2, y + 1)$

  $(-1, 1) \to (1, 2)$

  $(3, -1) \to (5, 0)$

- Sketch the transformed graph.

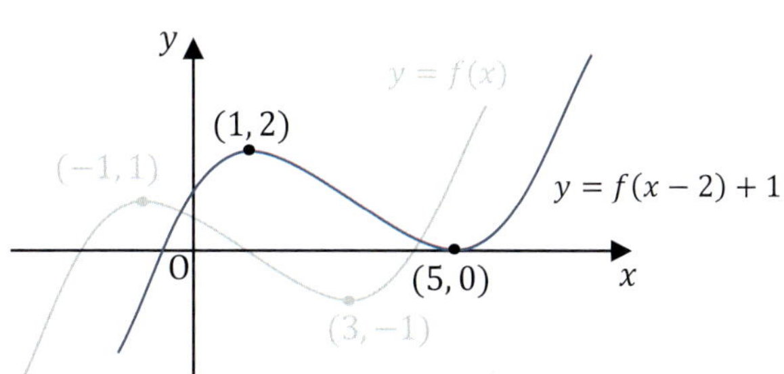

2. The diagram shows the graph of $y = f(x)$.

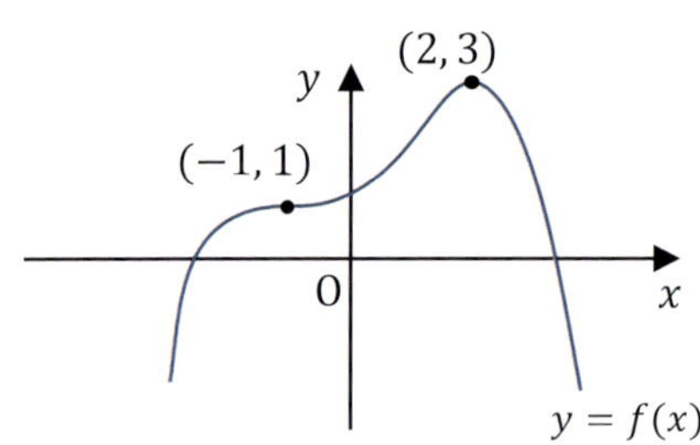

Sketch the graph of $y = 3 - f(x)$.

Solution: $3 - f(x) = -1f(x) + 3$

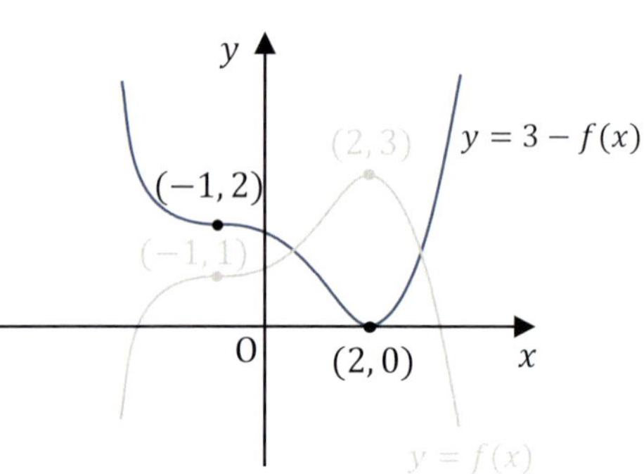

- Sketch the graph lightly on the axes.
- Calculate each new coordinate.

  Use BODMAS so multiply then add, **i.e.** the graph is reflected in x-axis and moved up 3

  For each coordinate $(x, -y + 3)$

  $(-1, 1) \rightarrow (-1, 2)$

  $(2, 3) \rightarrow (2, 0)$
- Sketch the transformed graph.

Exercise 5.5

1. In each of the following diagrams the graph of $y = f(x)$ is shown. Sketch the graph with the given transformation:

(a)

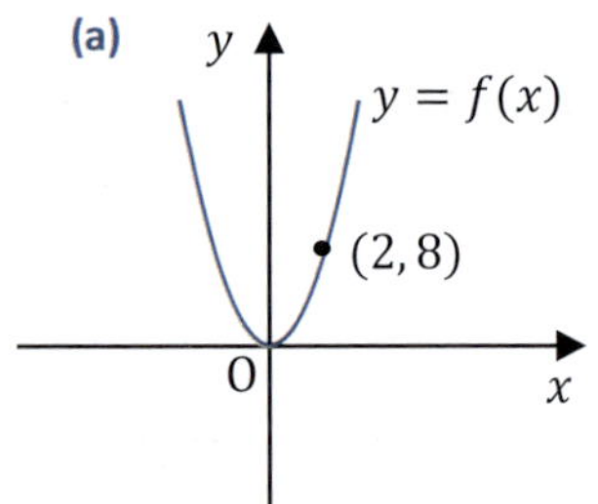

Sketch $y = f(x + 1) + 2$

(b)

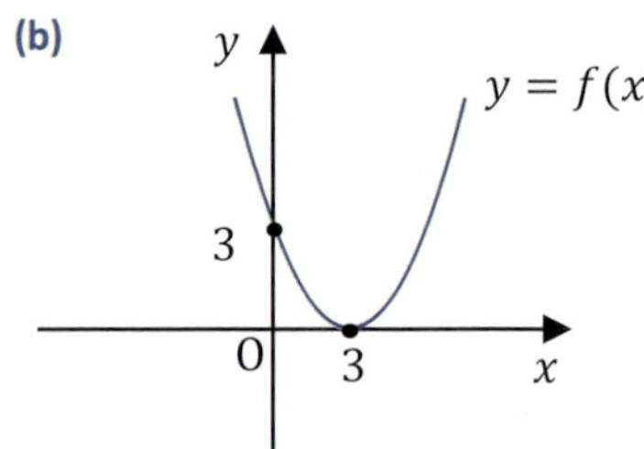

Sketch $y = f(x - 3) + 1$

(c)

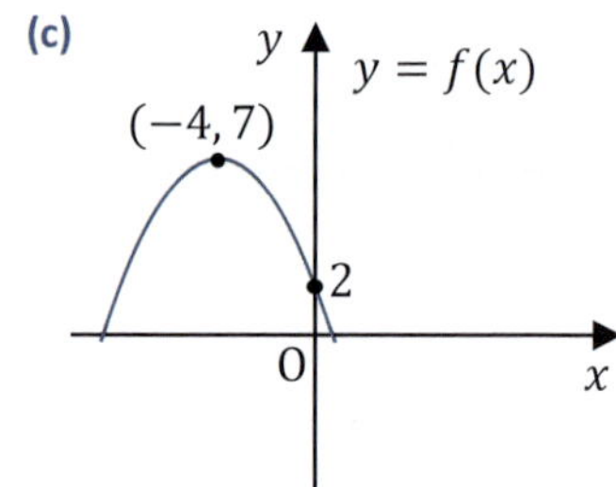

Sketch $y = f(x - 2) - 1$

(d)

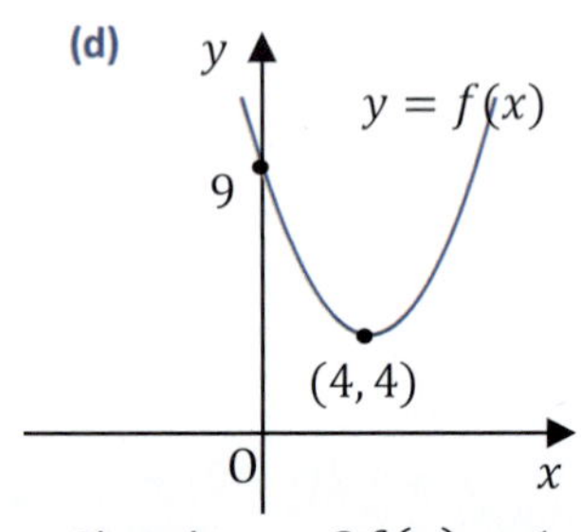

Sketch $y = 2f(x) - 1$

(e)

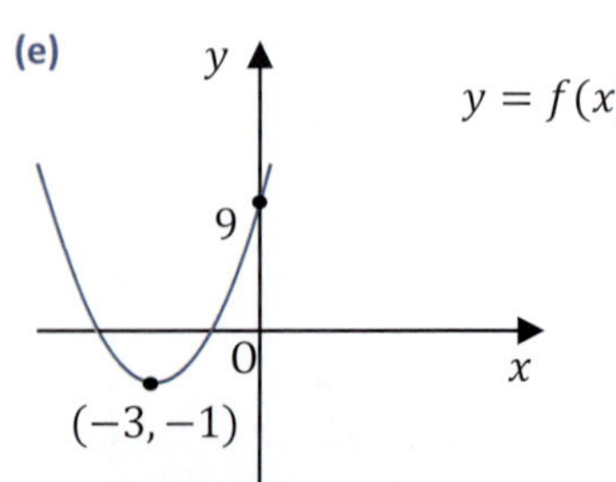

Sketch $y = 2 - f(x)$

(f)

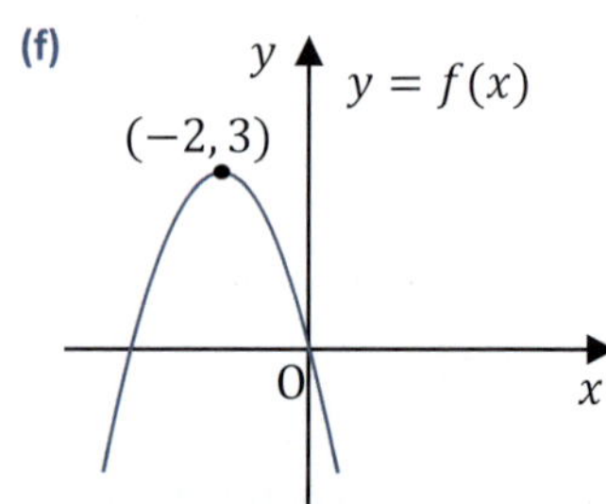

Sketch $y = 1 - f(x)$

(g)

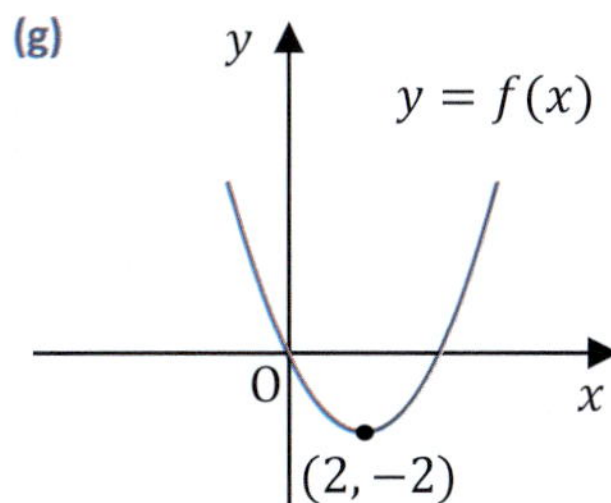

Sketch $y = 2f(x) - 2$

(h)

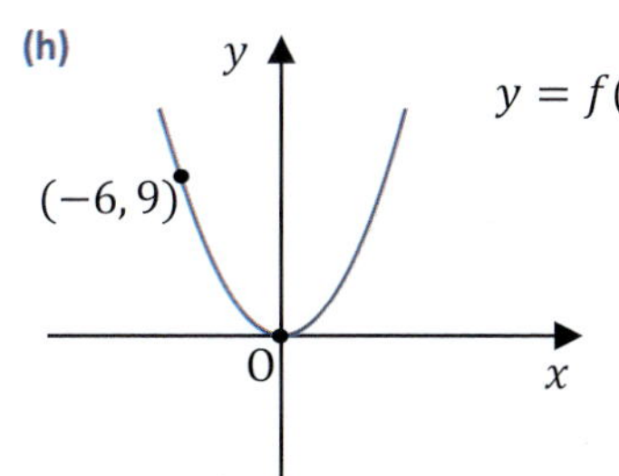

Sketch $y = f(2x) - 1$

(i)

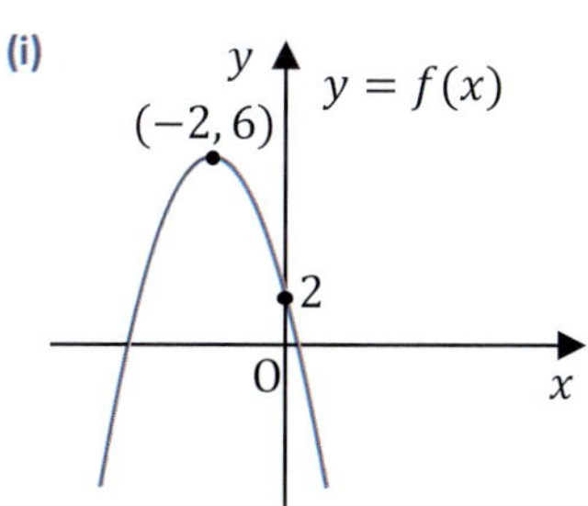

Sketch $y = 3 - f(-2x)$

2. In each of the following diagrams the graph of $y = f(x)$ is shown. Sketch the graph with the given transformation:

(a)

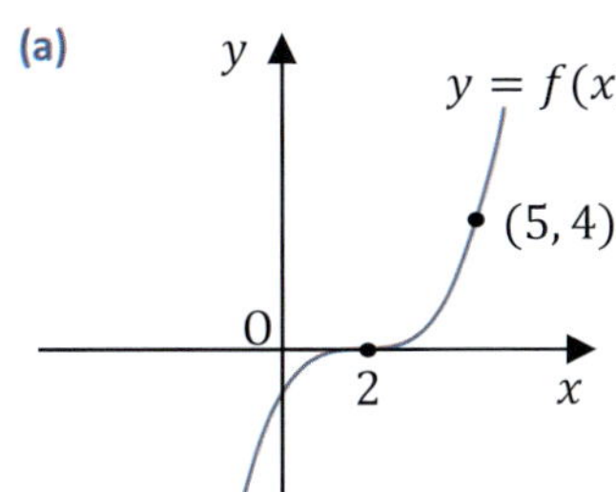

Sketch $y = f(x + 2) - 1$

(b)

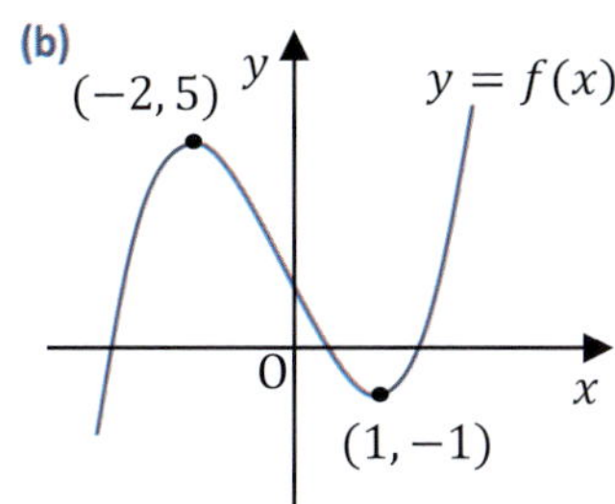

Sketch $y = f(x - 2) - 2$

(c)

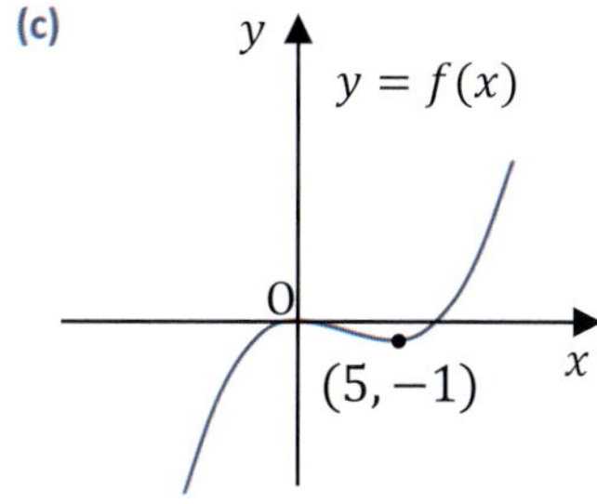

Sketch $y = f(x - 3) + 1$

(d)

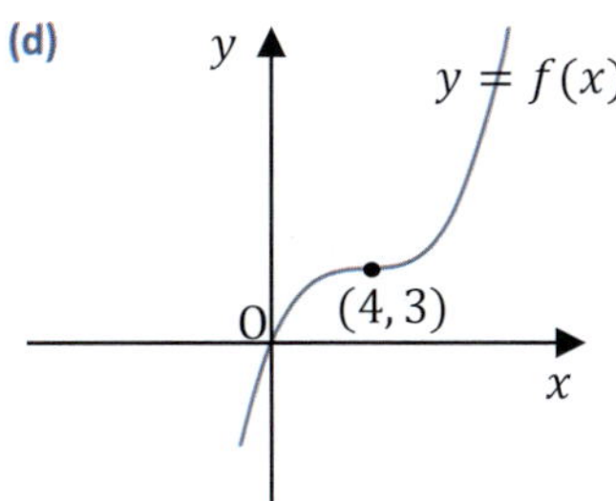

Sketch $y = 2f(x) - 1$

(e)

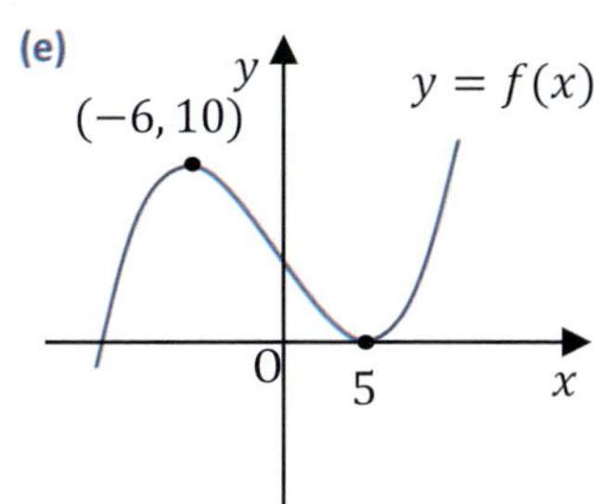

Sketch $y = 10 - f(x)$

(f)

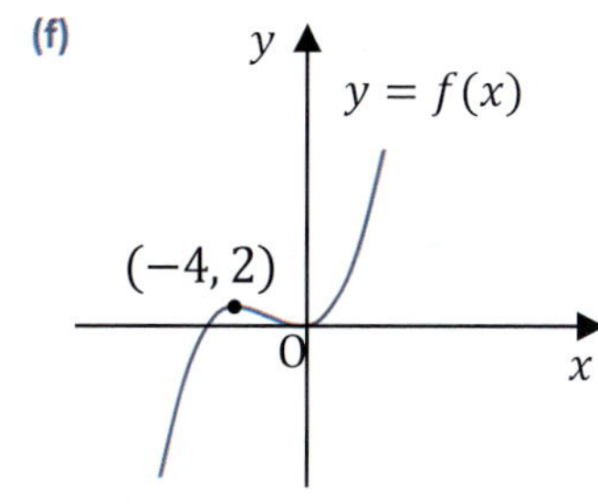

Sketch $y = 6 - 4f(x)$

(g)

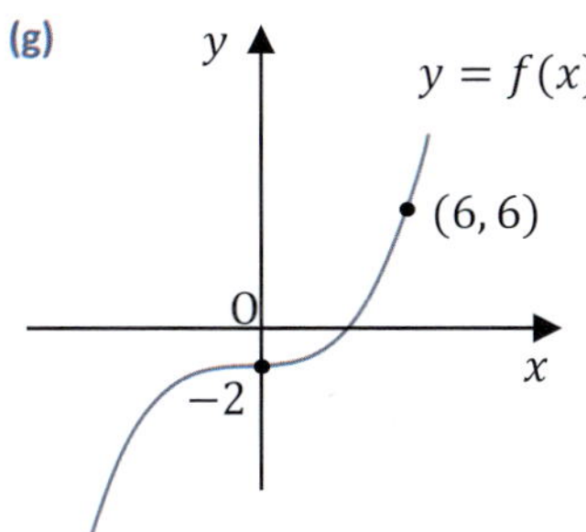

Sketch $y = f(2x) + 2$

(h)

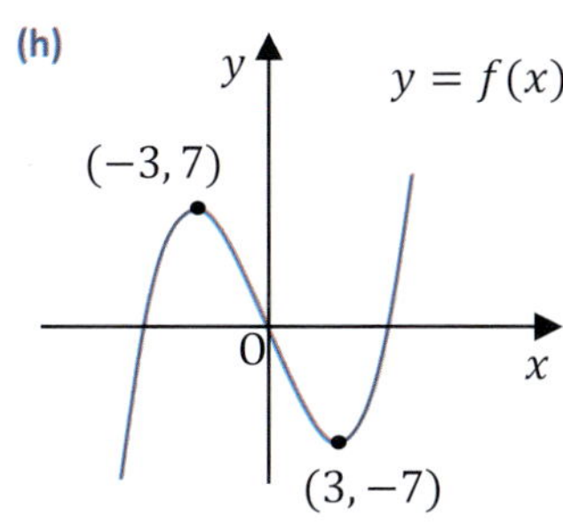

Sketch $y = f(-x) + 3$

(i)

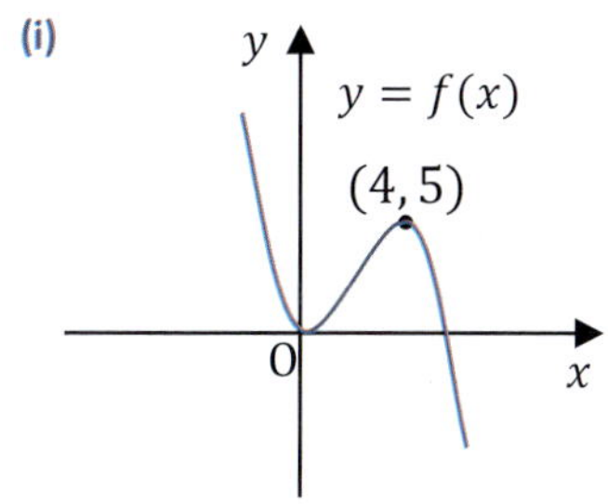

Sketch $y = 1 - f(0.5x)$

3. In each of the following diagrams the graph of $y = f(x)$ is shown. Sketch the graph with the given transformation:

(a)

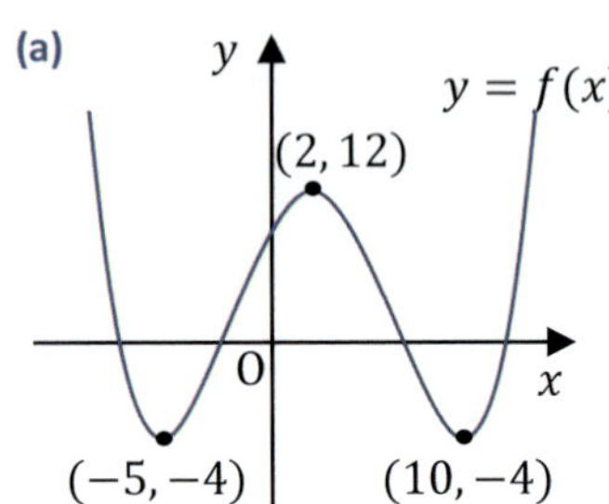

Sketch $y = f(x + 3) + 4$

(b)

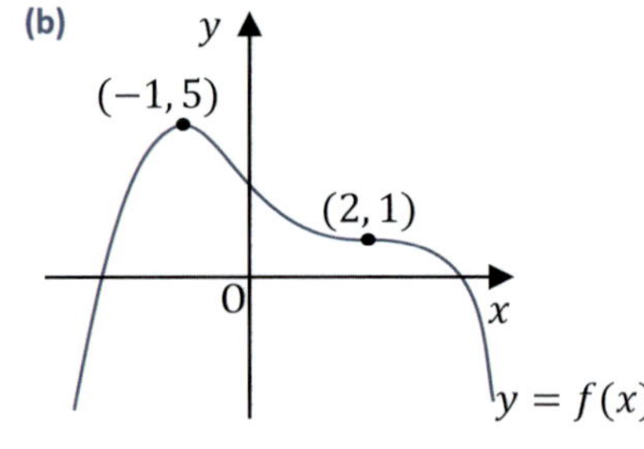

Sketch $y = f(x - 2) - 1$

(c)

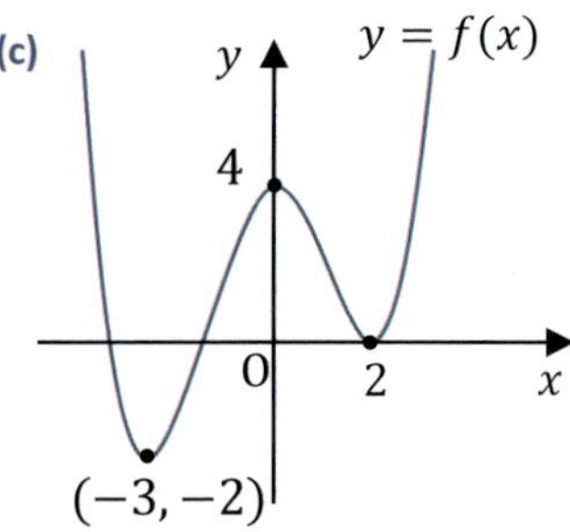

Sketch $y = f(x + 2) + 2$

(d)

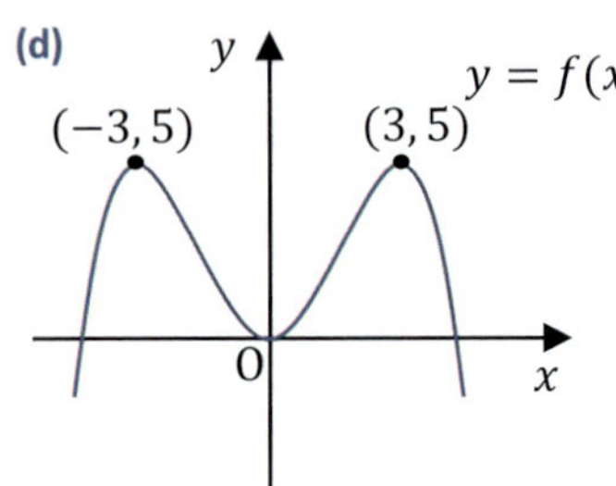

Sketch $y = 2f(x) - 5$

(e)

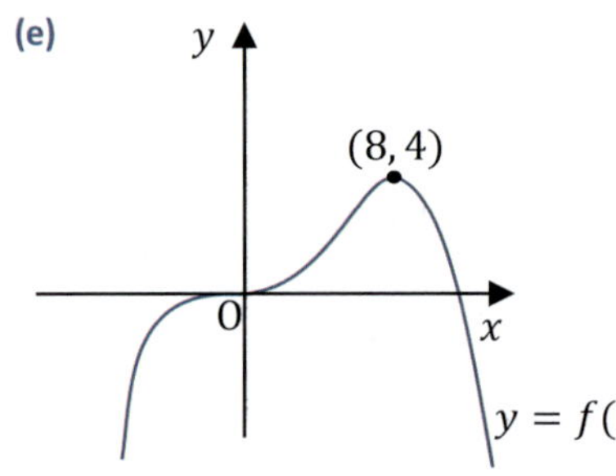

Sketch $y = 2 - \frac{1}{2}f(x)$

(f)

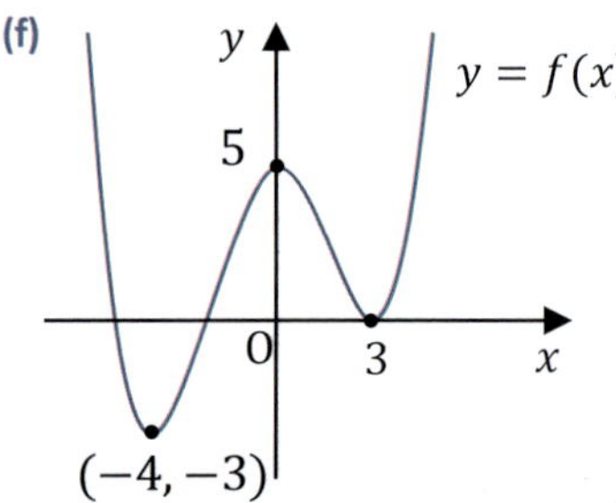

Sketch $y = 3 - 3f(x)$

(g)

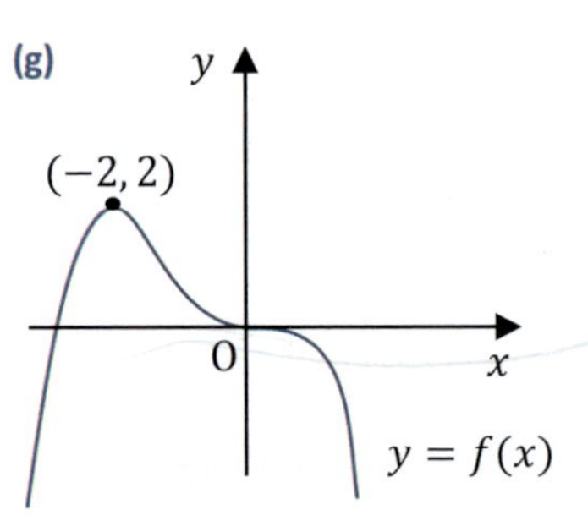

Sketch $y = f(-2x) - 2$

(h)

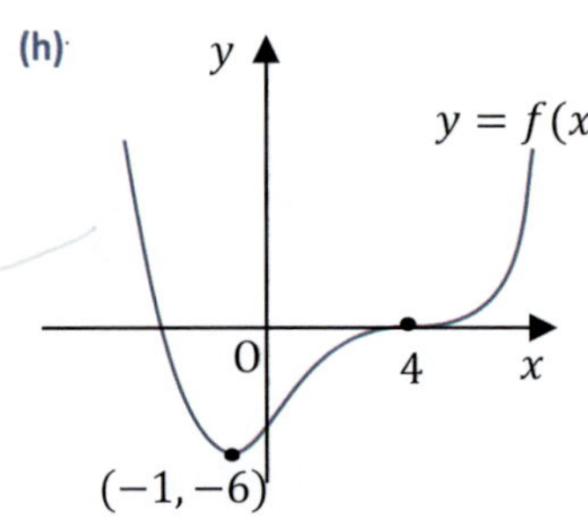

Sketch $y = f(0.5x) + 2$

(i)

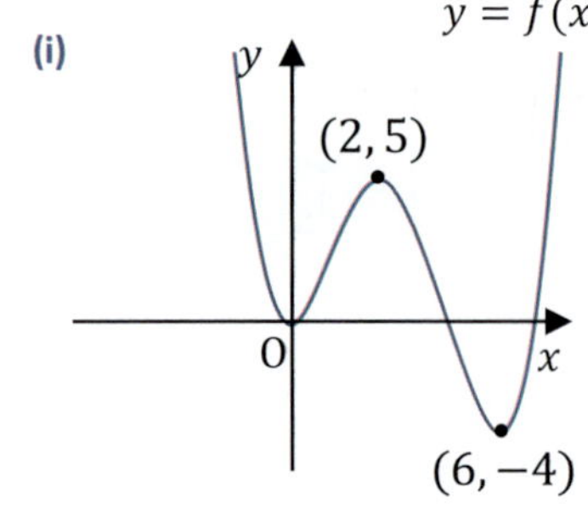

Sketch $y = 4 - f(2x)$

Chapter 6
Recurrence Relations

Recurrence Relations

A **recurrence relation** is a **sequence** in which, once the initial value is determined, each number is a function of the previous number in the sequence. In Higher Mathematics, we are concerned with **linear recurrence relations** of the form $\boldsymbol{u_{n+1} = au_n + b}$, where $\boldsymbol{u_{n+1}}$ is the value being calculated in the sequence, $\boldsymbol{u_n}$ is the **immediately previous** value, and $\boldsymbol{a}$ and $\boldsymbol{b}$ are constants. The initial value of a recurrence relation is usually defined by $\boldsymbol{u_0}$.

Recurrence relations may also appear in the form $\boldsymbol{u_n = au_{n-1} + b}$.

These sequences are used in many applications including science, finance and computing and can be used to model how a sequence of numbers may vary over time.

6.1 Using Recurrence Relations

Worked Examples:

1. A sequence is defined by the recurrence relation $u_{n+1} = 2u_n - 4,\ u_0 = 24$. Find the value of u_4.

Solution:

$u_0 = 24$

$u_1 = 2u_0 - 4 = 2(24) - 4 = 44$

$u_2 = 2u_1 - 4 = 2(44) - 4 = 84$

$u_3 = 2u_2 - 4 = 2(84) - 4 = 164$

$u_4 = 2u_3 - 4 = 2(164) - 4 = 324$

2. A sequence is defined by the recurrence relation $u_{n+1} = 0.6u_n + 52,\ u_0 = 100$. Find the value of u_5.

Solution:

$u_0 = 100$

$u_1 = 0.6u_0 + 52 = 0.6(100) + 52 = 112$

$u_2 = 0.6u_1 + 52 = 0.6(112) + 52 = 119.2$

$u_3 = 0.6u_2 + 52 = 0.6(119.2) + 52 = 123.52$

$u_4 = 0.6u_3 + 52 = 0.6(123.52) + 52 = 126.112$

$u_5 = 0.6u_4 + 52 = 0.6(126.112) + 52 = 127.6672$

NB: We can use our calculator to save writing the substitution for every term. Write down the first two lines of working, then input the u_0 value (100) into your calculator and press '=' then type $0.6(Ans) + 52$ and press '=' for u_1. Continue pressing '=' for the value of u_2, u_3, etc. List all the answers.

Exercise 6.1

1. For each of the following recurrence relations, calculate the value of u_3.

(a) $u_{n+1} = 1.5u_n + 18,\ u_0 = 8$ (b) $u_{n+1} = 0.5u_n - 3,\ u_0 = 6$ (c) $u_{n+1} = 3u_n + 5,\ u_0 = 6$

(d) $u_{n+1} = 2.5u_n - 10,\ u_0 = 12$ (e) $u_{n+1} = 3u_n - 2,\ u_0 = 9$ (f) $u_{n+1} = 2u_n + 18,\ u_0 = 4$

(g) $u_{n+1} = 0.5u_n + 20,\ u_0 = 24$ (h) $u_{n+1} = 2.5u_n + 18,\ u_0 = 16$ (i) $u_{n+1} = 4u_n - 20,\ u_0 = 30$

2. For each of the following recurrence relations, calculate the value of u_5.

(a) $u_{n+1} = 1.5u_n + 18,\ u_0 = 8$ (b) $u_{n+1} = 0.5u_n - 3,\ u_0 = 6$ (c) $u_{n+1} = 3u_n + 5,\ u_0 = 6$

(d) $u_{n+1} = 2.5u_n - 10,\ u_0 = 12$ (e) $u_{n+1} = 3u_n - 2,\ u_0 = 9$ (f) $u_{n+1} = 2u_n + 18,\ u_0 = 4$

(g) $u_{n+1} = 0.5u_n + 20,\ u_0 = 24$ (h) $u_{n+1} = 2.5u_n + 18,\ u_0 = 16$ (i) $u_{n+1} = 4u_n - 20,\ u_0 = 30$

3. For each of the following recurrence relations, calculate the value of u_5.

(a) $u_{n+1} = -2u_n + 20,\ u_0 = 23$ (b) $u_{n+1} = 0.2u_n - 3,\ u_0 = 46$ (c) $u_{n+1} = -1.4u_n + 5,\ u_0 = 18$

(d) $u_{n+1} = 0.4u_n - 5,\ u_0 = 98$ (e) $u_{n+1} = -2.1u_n - 9,\ u_0 = 15$ (f) $u_{n+1} = 3u_n - 50,\ u_0 = 6$

(g) $u_{n+1} = -0.1u_n + 9,\ u_0 = 12$ (h) $u_{n+1} = -1.2u_n + 10,\ u_0 = 16$ (i) $u_{n+1} = 0.3u_n - 9,\ u_0 = 50$

6.2 Finding Constant Values in a Recurrence Relation

If the constant values a and b of a recurrence relation are unknown, they can be calculated – provided we know three consecutive terms of the sequence.

Worked Example:

A sequence is defined by the recurrence relation $u_{n+1} = au_n + b$, where the first three terms of the sequence are 9, 13, 21. Find the values of a and b.

Solution: Substitute values into recurrence relation to form two equations, then solve simultaneously.

$u_0 = 9,\ u_1 = 13,\ u_2 = 21$

$u_1 = au_0 + b \quad \Rightarrow \quad 9a + b = 13$ (A)

$u_2 = au_1 + b \quad \Rightarrow \quad 13a + b = 21$ (B)

(B)−(A) $\quad 4a = 8$

$a = 2$

Substitute $a = 2$ into (A)

$9(2) + b = 13$

$b = -5$

$\therefore u_{n+1} = 2u_n - 5$

Exercise 6.2

1. The first three terms of the recurrence relation defined by $u_{n+1} = au_n + b$ are given in the following questions. Find the values of a and b:

(a) $14, 31, 65$ (b) $10, 29, 86$ (c) $9, 14, 24$

(d) $22, 17, 12$ (e) $-7, -23, -87$ (f) $-3, 24, -30$

(g) $11, 52, 257$ (h) $56, 35, 24.5$ (i) $36, 45, 58.5$

(j) $21, -7.5, 6.75$ (k) $35, 67, 131$ (l) $14, 17, 21.5$

2. The first three terms of the recurrence relation defined by $u_{n+1} = au_n + b$ are given in the following questions. Find the values of a and b:

(a) $15, -3, -13.8$ (b) $11, 13.5, 14.75$ (c) $8, 16.4, 27.32$

(d) $7, 10.7, 18.47$ (e) $22.5, 69, 208.5$ (f) $7, -6.4, 9.68$

(g) $111, 331, 991$

(h) $201, 405, 813$

(i) $6, 1.6, -3.24$

(j) $18.8, 36.4, 71.6$

(k) $98, 129.6, 167.52$

(l) $121, -81.8, 80.44$

6.3 The Limit of a Recurrence Relation

Converging and Diverging Recurrence Relations

The value of $\boldsymbol{a}$ in a relation determines whether the recurrence relation will converge or diverge.

When a recurrence relation continues to increase or decrease in value towards positive or negative infinity, we say this recurrence relation is **diverging**. This happens when $\boldsymbol{a} \leq -1$ or $\boldsymbol{a} \geq 1$.

When a recurrence relation tends towards a particular value, we say the recurrence relation is **converging**. The value that the recurrence relation tends towards is called the **limit**. This happens when $-1 < \boldsymbol{a} < 1$.

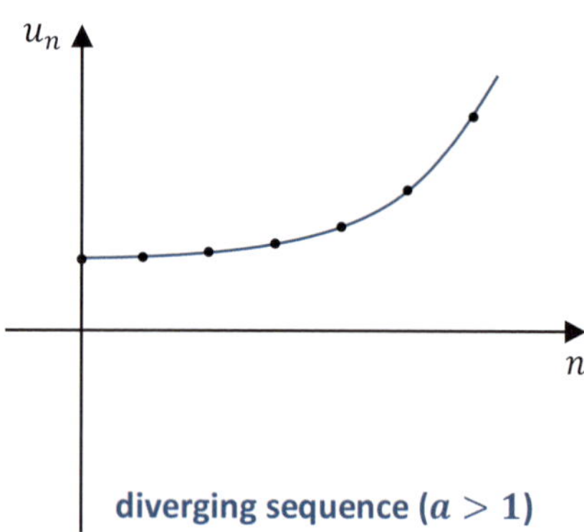

diverging sequence ($a > 1$)

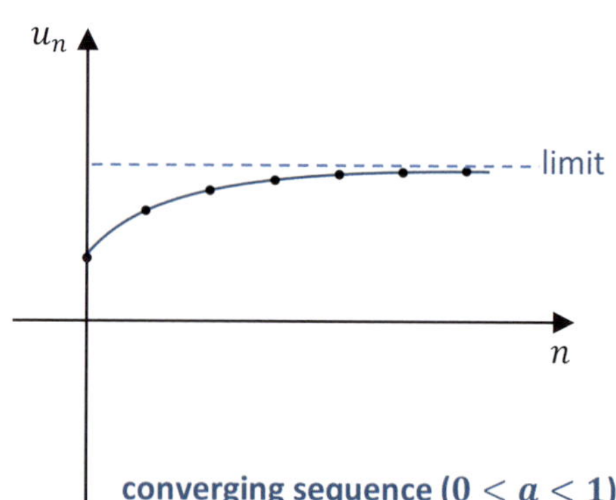

converging sequence ($0 < a < 1$)

Oscillating Sequences

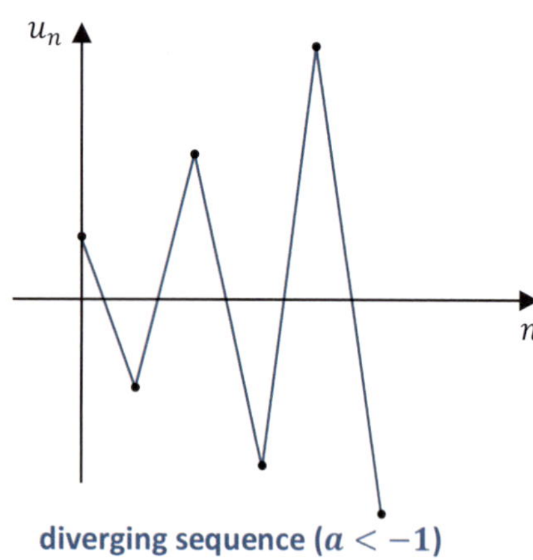

diverging sequence ($a < -1$)

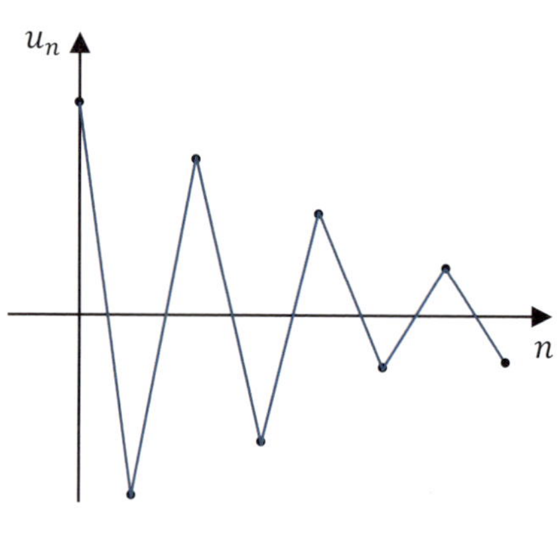

converging sequence ($-1 < a < 0$)

A recurrence relation approaches its limit as $n \to \infty$ (this means as n tends towards infinity, **i.e.** it is very large).

Worked Examples:

1. For each of the following recurrence relations, explain whether the sequence has a limit as $n \to \infty$.

   (a) $u_{n+1} = 0.5u_n + 1$ **Solution:** This sequence has a limit as $-1 < 0.5 < 1$.

   (b) $u_{n+1} = 2u_n - 9$ **Solution:** This sequence does not have a limit as $2 > 1$.

(c) $u_{n+1} = \frac{1}{3}u_n + 15$ **Solution:** This sequence has a limit as $-1 < \frac{1}{3} < 1$.

2. A sequence is defined by the recurrence relation $u_{n+1} = (k+2)u_n + 5$. For what range of values of k does the sequence have a limit?

   Solution: For a limit to exist $-1 < (k+2) < 1$, $\therefore -3 < k < -1$.

Exercise 6.3

1. For each of the following recurrence relations, state whether the sequence has a limit as $n \to \infty$. Give a reason for your answer.

(a) $u_{n+1} = 1.5u_n + 18$ (b) $u_{n+1} = 0.5u_n - 3$ (c) $u_{n+1} = 3u_n + 5$

(d) $u_{n+1} = -\frac{1}{3}u_n - 10$ (e) $u_{n+1} = \frac{1}{4}u_n - 2$ (f) $u_{n+1} = 1.2u_n + 7$

(g) $u_{n+1} = \frac{5}{4}u_n + 20$ (h) $u_{n+1} = -\frac{3}{5}u_n + 6$ (i) $u_{n+1} = \frac{5}{7}u_n - 50$

(j) $u_{n+1} = -\frac{2}{3}u_n + 11$ (k) $u_{n+1} = -\frac{7}{6}u_n - 5$ (l) $u_{n+1} = -4u_n + 1$

2. For each of the following recurrence relations, for what range of values of k does each sequence have a limit?

(a) $u_{n+1} = (k-3)u_n + 3$ (b) $u_{n+1} = (k+9)u_n - 5$ (c) $u_{n+1} = (k-5)u_n + 5$

(d) $u_{n+1} = (4-k)u_n - 23$ (e) $u_{n+1} = \left(k - \frac{1}{2}\right)u_n - 12$ (f) $u_{n+1} = (5-k)u_n + 8$

(g) $u_{n+1} = -(k-1)u_n + 70$ (h) $u_{n+1} = -(2-k)u_n + 91$ (i) $u_{n+1} = -\left(k - \frac{3}{4}\right)u_n - 60$

(j) $u_{n+1} = (2k-3)u_n + 6$ (k) $u_{n+1} = (5k+2)u_n - 17$ (l) $u_{n+1} = (7-4k)u_n + 5$

6.4 Finding The Limit of a Recurrence Relation

The **limit** of a recurrence relation $u_{n+1} = au_n + b$ as $n \to \infty$ can be found using the formula:

$$L = \frac{b}{1-a}$$

Worked Examples:

1. A sequence is defined by the recurrence relation $u_{n+1} = 0.6u_n + 24$. Calculate the limit of this sequence.

Solution: $a = 0.6$, $b = 24$

$$L = \frac{b}{1-a} = \frac{24}{1-0.6} = \frac{24}{0.4} = \frac{24}{4/10} = \frac{240}{4} = 60$$

Extra Info

As a recurrence relation approaches its limit, $u_{n+1} = u_n$. We can calculate the limit by using this fact:

$$L = aL + b$$
$$L - al = b$$
$$L(1-a) = b$$
$$\therefore L = \frac{b}{1-a}$$

2. A sequence is defined by the recurrence relation $u_{n+1} = 0.53u_n - 750$. Calculate the limit of this sequence.

Solution: $a = 0.53, b = -750$

$$L = \frac{b}{1-a} = \frac{-750}{1-0.53} = -1595.74\ (2\ d.p.)$$

Exercise 6.4

1. Calculate the limit of each of the following recurrence relations:

(a) $u_{n+1} = 0.2u_n + 18$ (b) $u_{n+1} = 0.5u_n + 15$ (c) $u_{n+1} = 0.8u_n + 56$

(d) $u_{n+1} = \frac{1}{3}u_n - 60$ (e) $u_{n+1} = \frac{1}{4}u_n - 28$ (f) $u_{n+1} = \frac{3}{4}u_n + 75$

(g) $u_{n+1} = 0.8u_n + 120$ (h) $u_{n+1} = -0.6u_n - 24$ (i) $u_{n+1} = \frac{5}{7}u_n - 50$

(j) $u_{n+1} = \frac{2}{3}u_n + 450$ (k) $u_{n+1} = \frac{5}{6}u_n - 600$ (l) $u_{n+1} = 0.8u_n + 5000$

2. Calculate the limit of each of the following recurrence relations:

(a) $u_{n+1} = 0.8u_n + 210$ (b) $u_{n+1} = 0.65u_n + 80$ (c) $u_{n+1} = 0.4u_n + 140$

(d) $u_{n+1} = \frac{6}{7}u_n - 250$ (e) $u_{n+1} = 0.52u_n - 850$ (f) $u_{n+1} = \frac{2}{9}u_n + 420$

(g) $u_{n+1} = 0.65u_n + 120$ (h) $u_{n+1} = -0.85u_n - 240$ (i) $u_{n+1} = 0.74u_n - 90$

(j) $u_{n+1} = -0.9u_n + 325$ (k) $u_{n+1} = 0.32u_n - 95$ (l) $u_{n+1} = 0.17u_n + 86$

6.5 Using Recurrence Relations in Contexts

When using recurrence relations in context, we use the percentage skills developed in National 5 Mathematics.

Worked Example:

A hospital patient is given a 40mg dose of a drug. Over the course of each hour 20% of the drug passes out of the patient's bloodstream and every hour, on the hour, the nurse administers a further 10mg of the drug.

(a) How many milligrams of the drug are in the patient's bloodstream after 5 hours?

(b) For safety, the amount of drug in the bloodstream should not exceed 55mg after a 10mg re-dose. Is the patient's dosage safe? Give a reason for your answer. (See **Exercise 6.5B**)

Solution: Set up the recurrence relation and use to find (a) u_5 and (b) the limit.

(a) To set up the recurrence relation, determine the percentage value for a

$a = 100\% - 20\% = 80\% = 0.8$

$b = 10$

$u_{n+1} = 0.8u_n + 10$

$u_0 = 40$
$u_1 = 0.8u_0 + 10 = 0.8(40) + 10 = 42$
$u_2 = 43.6$
$u_3 = 44.88$
$u_4 = 45.904$
$u_5 = 46.7232$ ∴ after 5 hours there will be 46.7mg in the patient's bloodstream.

(b) $L = \dfrac{b}{1-a} = \dfrac{10}{1-0.8} = 50$

The drug will not exceed 50mg as this is the limit. 50mg < 55mg ∴ the dosage is safe.

Exercise 6.5A

1. A child's grandmother invests £1200 when their grandchild is born. Each year the investment grows by 3% and the grandmother deposits a further £200. How much will the investment be worth when the child is 18 years old?

2. A person buys a house and takes out an endowment policy to cover their mortgage. They initially invest £25,000. This investment grows by 0.3% each month and they invest a further £600 each month. How much money will the person have saved after 2 years?

3. A sheep farmer owns 2000 sheep. Each year, 13% of the sheep are lost to illness, predators and other factors. The farmer replenishes his stock with a further 300 sheep. How many sheep will the farmer have after 10 years?

4. An island has a population of 8000 people. Each year, 18% of the population move to other places. The local council bring in 250 new residents each year. What will the population of the island be after 10 years?

5. A couple take out a £30,000 bank loan. The monthly interest charged on the loan is 0.8%. After interest is added, the couple make monthly repayments of £800. How much will they owe after two years?

6. A large-scale florist specialises in roses. Their rose bushes are 1.5m high. Each year, during the spring, they prune their rose bushes by 35%. The bushes then grow by 25cm. How tall will the rose bushes be after 3 years?

7. A person invests £500 in an account. The annual interest on the account is 2.5%. Each year the person invests a further £400. How much will the investment be worth after 10 years?

8. A person takes out a mortgage to buy a house. She borrows £200,000 at a monthly interest rate of 0.2%. After the interest is added, she pays back £850 each month. How much will she still have to pay on her mortgage after the first year?

9. A hospital patient receives a 15mg dose of medication. The medication wears off by 15% every hour and the nurse administers a further 2mg booster. How many milligrams of medication will be in the patient's body after 5 hours?

10. A new vaccine is introduced to a population. The vaccine is given in a 10mg dose. Every six months the vaccine loses 45% of its effectiveness and a 3mg booster is given. How much vaccine will a person have in their body after their year 3 booster?

Exercise 6.5B

1. An island has a population of 6500 people. Each year 17% of the population move off the island. The local council bring in 220 new residents each year from other places.

   (a) What will the population of the island be after 4 years?

   In order for there to be a sustainable economy on the island, it is estimated that the population should not fall below 2000.

   (b) Will the island have a sustainable economy in the long term? Give a reason for your answer.

2. A hospital patient undergoes an operation and the anaesthetist administers 15mg of anaesthetic to the patient. Every hour 60% of the anaesthetic wears off and a further 10mg are administered.

   (a) How many milligrams of anaesthetic will be in the patient's body after 6 hours?

   (b) For safety, the anaesthetic must not exceed 17mg. Will the dosage remain safe? Give a reason for you answer.

3. A town has 25,000 inhabitants. Each year 12% of the population move away and a further 500 people move into the town.

   (a) How many inhabitants will the town have after 5 years?

   (b) If the trend continues, how many inhabitants will the town have in the long term?

4. An environmental agency monitors the dissolved oxygen levels in a local loch. During their initial visit, they find the water has 8mg/L of dissolved oxygen, but each month the dissolved oxygen decreases steadily by 7%. To compensate they add additional plant life each month, which increases the dissolved oxygen in the water by 0.3mg/L.

   (a) How much dissolved oxygen will there be in the water after 6 months?

   In order for the water to remain healthy for plant and wildlife, the dissolved oxygen must not fall below 6mg/L.

   (b) In the long term, will the water remain healthy for plants and wildlife? Give a reason for your answer.

5. A new vaccine is introduced to a nation. The vaccine is given in a 6mg dose. Every three months the vaccine reduces by 30% and a 2mg booster is given.

   (a) How much vaccine will a person have in their body after 12 months?

   In order for the vaccine to be effective in the long term, there must be at least 6mg of vaccine in the body.

   (b) Will the vaccine prove effective for the nation? Give a reason for your answer.

6. A gardener uses 6 litres of plant food on the soil of her strawberry plants. Each week 37% of the food is used up or lost to rain, so the gardener adds a further 2 litres of food.

(a) How much food will there be in the soil after 4 weeks?

In order for the plants to continue to bear fruit in the long term, the soil needs to retain 4 litres of the plant food.

(b) Will the plants continue to produce strawberries in the long term? Give a reason for your answer.

7. A person takes out a mortgage of £225,000 to buy a house. After each month, interest at a rate of 0.3% is added to the loan and he then makes a payment of £600.

(a) How much of the mortgage will need to be repaid after 12 months of payments?

(b) Explain why he is not paying enough each month to pay off the mortgage.

8. A local council is monitoring the number of rats in the town centre. One month they record 150 rats. Each month 12% of the rats die or are trapped, but a further 50 are born.

(a) How many rats will there be after 6 months?

The council employ a pest control company to deal with the problem. They promise to reduce the rat population by a further 6% per month.

(b) What will the rat population in the town centre be in the long term? Give a reason for your answer.

9. A charity in the Democratic Republic of Congo is monitoring the number of gorillas in a conservation area. One year they record 105 gorillas. Each year the population grows by 7% but 15 of the gorillas die through old age, illness or poaching.

(a) How many gorillas will remain after 3 years?

(b) At this rate, how many years will it take for there to be less than 20 gorillas in the conservation area?

10. A country has a population of 5.5 million people. The population is decreasing at a rate of 1.1% each year. To compensate, the country allows 50,000 immigrants into the country.

(a) What will the population be after 6 years?

The country wants to increase the population to 7 million people.

(b) How many immigrants should the country allow to enter in order to reach 7 million in the long term? Give a reason for you answer.

6.6 Review

Exercise 6.6A

6.1 For each of the following recurrence relations, calculate the value of u_4.

(a) $u_{n+1} = 2.3u_n + 60,\ u_0 = 91$ (b) $u_{n+1} = 0.5u_n - 120,\ u_0 = 4000$ (c) $u_{n+1} = 6u_n + 41, u_0 = 8$

6.2 The first three terms of the recurrence relation defined by $u_{n+1} = au_n + b$ are given in the following questions. Find the values of a and b:

(a) $26, 80, 242$ (b) $32, 92, 242$ (c) $44, 116, 332$

6.3A In each of the following recurrence relations, state whether the sequence has a limit as $n \to \infty$. Give a reason for your answer.

(a) $u_{n+1} = 7u_n + 18$ (b) $u_{n+1} = 0.1u_n - 3$ (c) $u_{n+1} = -0.9u_n + 5$

6.3B In each of the following recurrence relations, for what range of values of k does each sequence have a limit?

(a) $u_{n+1} = (k-3)u_n + 3$ (b) $u_{n+1} = (5-k)u_n - 5$ (c) $u_{n+1} = (3k-5)u_n + 1$

6.4 Calculate the limit of each of the following recurrence relations:

(a) $u_{n+1} = 0.6u_n + 100$ (b) $u_{n+1} = 0.8u_n + 200$ (c) $u_{n+1} = \frac{5}{7}u_n + 80$

6.5A A person takes out a £25,000 loan for a car with an interest rate of 6.3% per annum. Each year he pays back £5400. How much does he owe after four years of payments?

6.5B A forester sprays 500 litres of insecticide on an area of freshly planted trees. Each week 23% of the insecticide is lost to rain and evaporation, so the forester sprays a further 45 litres of insecticide.

(a) How much insecticide will there be after 7 weeks?

In order for the trees to survive in the long term, they need to retain 200 litres of the insecticide.

(b) Will the trees survive? Give a reason for your answer.

Exercise 6.6B

1. A conservation group record the number of tigers in a province in South East Asia. One year they record 280 tigers, the next year, 240 tigers and the following year, 208 tigers. This population of tigers can be modelled using the recurrence relation $u_{n+1} = au_n + b$ where n is the number of years recorded.

   (a) Use the information above to find the values of a and b.

   (b) How many tigers will survive in this province in the long term?

2. A sequence is defined by the recurrence relation $u_{n+1} = 0.4u_n + 140$.

   (a) Find the value of u_3

   (b) Explain why this sequence approaches a limit as $n \to \infty$.

   (c) Calculate the limit of the sequence.

3. A sequence takes the form $u_{n+1} = au_n + 12$. Find the value of a which produces a limit of 4.

4. A sequence takes the form $u_{n+1} = au_n + 56$. Find the value of a which produces a limit of 36.

5. A sequence takes the form $u_{n+1} = 0.85u_n + b$. Find the value of b which produces a limit of 142.

6. A sequence is defined by the recurrence relation $u_{n+1} = au_n + b$. The first three terms of the sequence are 15, 36 and 78.

   (a) Find the values of a and b.

   (b) Calculate the fourth term in the sequence.

7. A sequence is defined by the recurrence relation $u_{n+1} = au_n + b$. The first three terms of the sequence are 20, 54 and 105.

   (a) Find the values of a and b.

   (b) Calculate the fourth term in the sequence.

   (c) Why does this sequence not have a limit?

8. A sequence is defined by the recurrence relation $u_{n+1} = au_n + b$. The first three terms of the sequence are 150, 140 and 132.

   (a) Find the values of a and b.

   (b) Calculate the fourth term in the sequence.

   (c) Why does this sequence approach a limit as $n \to \infty$?

9. A sequence is defined by the recurrence relation $u_{n+1} = ku_n - 16$, with $u_0 = 4$.

   (a) Show that $u_2 = 4k^2 - 16k - 16$.

   (b) For what range of values is $u_2 > u_0$.

10. A sequence is defined by the recurrence relation $u_{n+1} = ku_n - 12$, with $u_0 = 6$.

    (a) Show that $u_2 = 6k^2 - 12k - 12$.

    (b) For what range of values is $u_2 < u_0$.

11. A sequence is defined by the recurrence relation $u_{n+1} = ku_n - 15$, with $u_0 = 5$.

    (a) Show that $u_2 = 5k^2 - 15k - 15$.

    (b) For what range of values is $u_2 > u_0$.

12. A florist specialises in roses. The bushes grow by 25cm each year. In order to maintain healthy roses, he aims to prune them by a certain percentage. This can be modelled using the recurrence relation $u_{n+1} = mu_n + 25$. If he wants the roses to reach 1.7m tall in the long term, what should the value of m be?

13. A sheep farmer owns 3000 sheep. Each year, 17% of the sheep are lost to illness, predators and other factors. The farmer replenishes his stock with a further 250 sheep each year.

    (a) How many sheep will the farmer have after 8 years?

    The farmer wants to maintain 3000 sheep each year in the long term.

    (b) How many sheep should the farmer add each year to retain a stock of 3000? Give a reason for your answer.

14. A person takes out a mortgage of £162,000 to buy a house. After the first month, interest at a rate of 0.5% is added to the loan and he then makes a payment of £550.

    (a) How much of the mortgage will need to be repaid after 4 months?

    (b) Explain why he is not paying enough each month to pay off the mortgage.

Chapter 7
Polynomials

Polynomials

A polynomial is a name that derives from the Greek word *polus* meaning many and the Latin word *nomen* meaning name. It is an expression with multiple terms of **decreasing positive whole number** powers of x. In Higher Mathematics, these are usually considered to be expressions with a power higher than 2, such as $x^3 - 7x + 6$.

7.1 Factorising Polynomials

Polynomials can be factorized using **synthetic division** or **algebraic long division**.

Worked Examples:

1. Factorise $x^3 + 2x^2 - 5x - 6$.

Method 1: Synthetic Division

Step 1: Set up synthetic division using coefficients from the polynomial in decreasing powers of x. For the example, $x^3 + 2x^2 - 5x - 6$, the coefficients are 1, 2, -5 and -6. If there is no term the coefficient is 0.

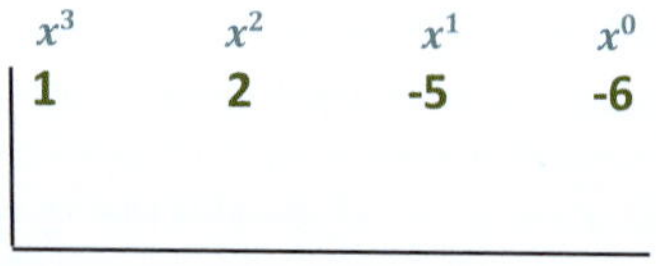

	x^3	x^2	x^1	x^0
	1	2	-5	-6

Step 2: The value outside of the division is derived from factors of the last term (in the example above, factors of -6).

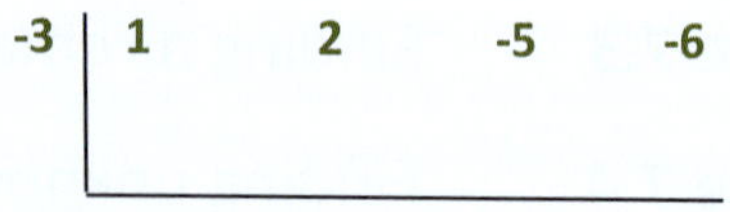

-3	1	2	-5	-6

Step 3: Add each number vertically, then multiply by the value outside of the division. The last number that you have is the remainder. If the remainder of the division is 0 then the value outside the division is a root and from the root the factor may be derived, **e.g.** if -3 is a root, $(x + 3)$ is a factor.

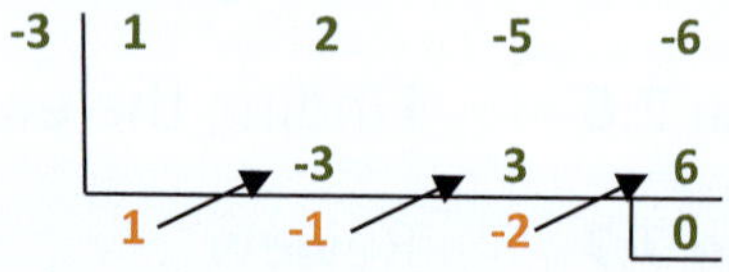

-3	1	2	-5	-6
		-3	3	6
	1	-1	-2	0

$\therefore\ x^3 + 2x^2 - 5x - 6$
$= (x + 3)(x^2 - x - 2)$
$= (x + 3)(x - 2)(x + 1)$

NB: The remaining values under the line are the coefficients of the quotient.

Step 4: If the quotient is not a quadratic, repeat the process with the quotient until it can be factorised normally.

Method 2: Algebraic Long Division

Step 1: Set up division with the factor as the divisor.

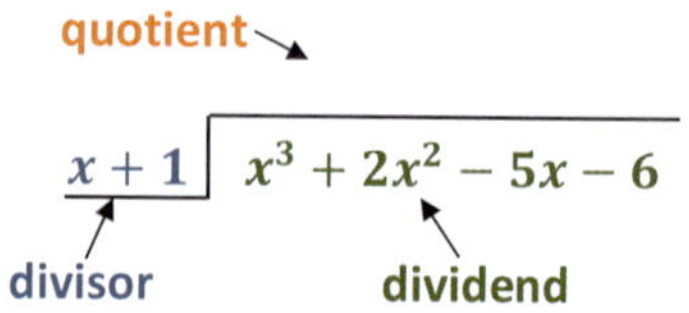

$$x + 1 \,\overline{)\, x^3 + 2x^2 - 5x - 6}$$

quotient (above the line); divisor ($x + 1$); dividend ($x^3 + 2x^2 - 5x - 6$)

Step 2: Multiply the **divisor** by a term that will make the leading term equal to the highest power of the polynomial and write it underneath the **dividend**. Write the term in the **quotient**. In the example, $x^2 \times (x + 1) = x^3 + x^2$.

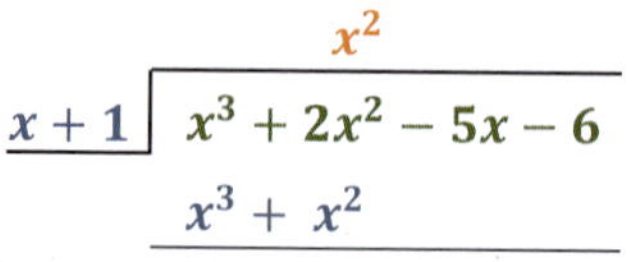

$$\begin{array}{r} x^2 \\ x + 1 \,\overline{)\, x^3 + 2x^2 - 5x - 6} \\ x^3 + x^2 \qquad\qquad \\ \hline \end{array}$$

Step 3: Take away the multiplied factor from the dividend and write the answer below the line. Then bring down the next term from the dividend.

Step 3: Repeat the process until the division is complete. The term at the end of the calculation is the remainder.

NB: If the remainder is 0, then the divisor is a factor of the dividend.

$$\begin{array}{r|l} & x^2 + x + 6 \\ \hline x+1 & x^3 + 2x^2 - 5x - 6 \\ & x^3 + x^2 \\ \hline & \quad x^2 - 5x \\ & \quad x^2 + x \\ \hline & \quad -6x - 6 \\ & \quad 6x + 6 \\ \hline & \qquad 0 \text{ (remainder)} \end{array}$$

2. (a) Show that $(x-1)$ is a factor of $x^3 + 4x^2 + x - 6$.

(b) Fully factorise $x^3 + 4x^2 + x - 6$.

Solution:

(a) If $(x-1)$ is a factor, then $x = 1$ is a root. If we are not being asked to factorise, we can substitute the value $x = 1$ into the polynomial and if the answer is 0, then $x = 1$ is a root and $(x-1)$ is a factor.

e.g. $(1)^3 + 4(1)^2 + (1) - 6 = 6 - 6 = 0$, $\therefore (x-1)$ is a factor of $x^3 + 4x^2 + x - 6$.

However, this does not leave a quotient to further factorise, so synthetic division or algebraic long division is necessary when being asked to fully factorise.

e.g.

$$\begin{array}{r|rrrr} 1 & 1 & 4 & 1 & -6 \\ & & 1 & 5 & 6 \\ \hline & 1 & 5 & 6 & \boxed{0} \end{array}$$

$\therefore (x-1)$ is a factor of $x^3 + 4x^2 + x - 6$.

(b) The quotient coefficients can now be used to complete the factorisation.

$x^3 + 4x^2 + x - 6 = (x+1)(x^2 + 5x + 6) = (x+1)(x+2)(x+3)$

Exercise 7.1A

1. Show that the following are factors of each of the given polynomials:

(a) $(x+1)$ is a factor of $x^3 + 6x^2 + 11x + 6$.

(b) $(x-2)$ is a factor of $x^3 + 2x^2 - 5x - 6$.

(c) $(x-4)$ is a factor of $x^3 - 6x^2 - 7x + 60$.

(d) $(x+3)$ is a factor of $x^3 + 9x^2 + 11x - 21$.

(e) $(x+5)$ is a factor of $x^3 + 8x^2 + 5x - 50$.

(f) $(x-3)$ is a factor of $x^3 + x^2 - 24x + 36$.

(g) $(x+1)$ is a factor of $x^4 - 5x^2 + 4$.

(h) $(x-4)$ is a factor of $x^3 - 21x + 20$.

2. (i) Show that the following are factors of each of the given polynomials and (ii) fully factorise:

(a) $(x-1)$ is a factor of $x^3 - 2x^2 - 11x + 12$.

(b) $(x-3)$ is a factor of $x^3 - 4x^2 - 17x + 60$.

(c) $(x+2)$ is a factor of $x^3 + 6x^2 - 13x - 42$.

(d) $(x-4)$ is a factor of $x^3 - 5x^2 - 2x + 24$.

(e) $(x-6)$ is a factor of $x^3 - 7x^2 + 36$.

(f) $(x+9)$ is a factor of $x^3 - 63x + 162$.

(g) $(x-7)$ is a factor of $x^3 - 13x^2 + 51x - 63$.

(h) $(x-8)$ is a factor of $x^3 - 4x - 8x^2 + 32$.

Exercise 7.1B

1. Fully factorise:

(a) $x^3 - 2x^2 - x + 2$ (b) $x^3 - 5x^2 - 2x + 24$ (c) $x^3 - 2x^2 - 5x + 6$

(d) $x^3 - 2x^2 - 4x + 8$ (e) $x^3 - x - 3x^2 + 3$ (f) $x^3 - 9x^2 + 23x - 15$

2. Fully factorise:

(a) $x^3 + x^2 - 9x - 9$ (b) $x^3 - 3x - 2$ (c) $x^4 - 6x^2 - 27$

(d) $x^3 - 12x - 16$ (e) $x^3 + 3x^2 - 4$ (f) $x^3 + 7x^2 - 36$

3. Fully factorise:

(a) $x^4 + x^3 - 7x^2 - x + 6$ (b) $x^4 - 5x^2 + 4$ (c) $x^4 - 9x^2 + 4x + 12$

(d) $x^4 - 17x^2 + 16$ (e) $x^4 - x^3 - 3x^2 + 5x - 2$ (f) $x^4 - 18x^2 + 81$

4. Fully factorise:

(a) $2x^3 - 3x^2 - 8x - 3$ (b) $2x^3 - 5x^2 - 6x + 9$ (c) $3x^3 - 10x^2 + 9x - 2$

(d) $3x^3 - 4x^2 - x + 2$ (e) $3x^3 - 5x^2 - 6x + 8$ (f) $5x^3 - 9x^2 - 17x - 3$

5. Fully factorise:

(a) $x^3 + x^2 - 3x - 3$ (b) $x^4 - 4x^3 - 2x + 8$ (c) $x^4 + x^3 + 2x - 4$

7.2 Solving Polynomial Equations

Polynomials include quadratic functions but are not limited to them. To solve polynomials, they need to be factorised using **synthetic division** or **algebraic long division** and then solved in the same way as quadratic functions.

Worked Example:

Solve the equation $x^3 - 3x + 2 = 0$.

Solution:

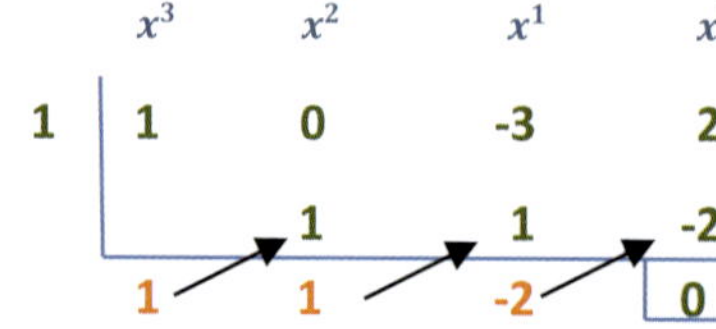

$$x^3 - 3x + 2 = 0$$

$$(x-1)(x^2 + x - 2) = 0$$

$$(x-1)(x-1)(x+2) = 0$$

$(x+2) = 0$ or $(x-1) = 0$ twice

$x = -2$ or $x = 1$ twice

Exercise 7.2

Solve each of the following polynomial equations:

1.

(a) $x^3 - 4x^2 + x + 6 = 0$ (b) $x^3 + 3x^2 - x - 3 = 0$ (c) $x^3 + 3x^2 - 6x - 8 = 0$

(d) $x^3 - x^2 - 8x + 12 = 0$ (e) $x^3 + 5x^2 + 2x - 8 = 0$ (f) $x^3 - 5x^2 + 8x - 4 = 0$

2.

(a) $x^3 - 3x - 2 = 0$ (b) $x^3 + 7x^2 - 36 = 0$ (c) $x^3 - 7x - 6 = 0$

(d) $x^3 - 12x - 16 = 0$ (e) $x^3 - 13x - 12 = 0$ (f) $x^3 - 3x^2 + 4 = 0$

3.

(a) $x^4 - 9x^2 + 4x + 12 = 0$ (b) $x^4 - x^3 - 11x^2 + 9x + 18 = 0$ (c) $x^4 - 2x^3 - 4x^2 + 2x + 3 = 0$

(d) $x^4 - 5x^2 + 4 = 0$ (e) $x^4 + 2x^3 - 7x^2 - 8x + 12 = 0$ (f) $x^4 - 23x^2 + 18x + 40 = 0$

4.

(a) $3x^3 - 10x^2 + 9x - 2 = 0$ (b) $2x^3 + 7x^2 + 2x - 3 = 0$ (c) $2x^3 - 3x^2 - 9x + 10 = 0$

(d) $3x^3 - 17x^2 + 28x - 12 = 0$ (e) $2x^3 - 3x^2 - 5x + 6 = 0$ (f) $5x^3 + 4x^2 - 61x + 12 = 0$

5.

(a) $x^3 - 2x^2 + 4x - 8 = 0$ (b) $x^3 + 3x^2 + 5x + 15 = 0$ (c) $x^3 + 3x^2 - 20 = 0$

7.3 Finding a Remainder when Dividing a Polynomial

To find a remainder when dividing a polynomial, use **substitution**, **synthetic division** or **algebraic long division**.

Worked Example:

Find the remainder when $x^3 - 7x^2 - 4x + 26$ is divided by $(x + 2)$.

Solution:

Method 1: $(-2)^3 - 7(-2)^2 - 4(-2) + 26 = -8 - 28 + 8 + 26 = -2$

$\therefore$ the remainder when $x^3 - 7x^2 - 4x + 26$ is divided by $(x + 2)$ is -2

Method 2:

-2	1	-7	-4	26
		-2	18	-28
	1	-9	14	-2

$\therefore$ the remainder when $x^3 - 7x^2 - 4x + 26$ is divided by $(x + 2)$ is -2

Exercise 7.3

1. Find the remainder in each of the following:

(a) $x^3 + 6x^2 + 11x + 9$ is divided by $(x - 2)$ (b) $x^3 - 12x^2 + 15$ is divided by $(x + 2)$

(c) $x^4 - 3x^2 - 2x + 4$ is divided by $(x + 3)$

(d) $x^3 - 15x + 11$ is divided by $(x + 5)$

(e) $x^3 - 6x^2 + 21x - 3$ is divided by $(x - 4)$

(f) $x^4 + 5x^3 + 2x^2 - 7$ is divided by $(x - 2)$

(g) $x^3 - 3x^2 + 16$ is divided by $(x + 5)$

(h) $x^3 + 5x^2 - 12x + 6$ is divided by $(x + 3)$

(i) $x^3 - 23$ is divided by $(x + 7)$

(j) $x^4 + 6x^2 - 5$ is divided by $(x + 4)$

7.4 Finding the Unknown Coefficients of a Polynomial

If there are unknown coefficients in a polynomial, these can be determined, provided we know other information about the polynomial.

Worked Examples:

1. For the polynomial, $x^3 + 3x^2 + ax - 8$, $(x - 2)$ is a factor. Determine the value of a.

Solution: Use synthetic division, then solve the equation.

$x^3 + 3x^2 + ax - 8$

2	1	3	a	-8
		2	10	$20 + 2a$
	1	5	$10 + a$	$\mathbf{12 + 2a} = 0$

NB: The question states that $(x - 2)$ is a factor, so using $x = 2$, we know that the remainder of the division will be zero. This means we can equate our expression for the remainder to zero. If a different remainder is given, then we use that (**see example 2**).

$\mathbf{12 + 2a = 0}$

$\therefore a = -6$

2. For the polynomial, $x^3 + 3x^2 + ax + b$, $(x + 2)$ is a factor and the remainder when the polynomial is divided by $(x + 1)$ is 4. Determine the value of a and b.

Solution: Use synthetic division twice to form two equations then solve them simultaneously.

Dividing by $(x + 2)$.

-2	1	3	a	b
		-2	-2	$-2a + 4$
	1	1	$a - 2$	$\mathbf{b - 2a + 4} = 0$

Dividing by $(x + 1)$.

-1	1	3	a	b
		-1	-2	$-a + 2$
	1	2	$a - 2$	$\mathbf{b - a + 2} = 4$

$b - 2a + 4 = 0$ (A)

$b - a + 2 = 4$ (B)

(A) - (B) $-a + 2 = -4$

$a = 6$ substitute $a = 6$ into (B) $b - 6 + 2 = 4$, $b = 8$

Exercise 7.4

1. In each of the following, find the unknown coefficient, given:

(a) $(x - 1)$ is a factor of $x^3 + ax^2 - 4$.

(b) $(x - 1)$ is a factor of $x^3 - 2x^2 + ax + 6$.

(c) $(x - 3)$ is a factor of $x^3 - 4x^2 + ax + 18$.

(d) $(x + 4)$ is a factor of $x^3 + 2x^2 + ax - 12$.

(e) $(x + 5)$ is a factor of $x^3 + ax^2 - 7x - 10$.

(f) $(x - 6)$ is a factor of $x^3 + ax^2 - 12x + 36$.

2. In each of the following, find the unknown coefficient, given:

(a) When $x^3 + 3x^2 + ax - 4$ is divided by $(x - 2)$, the remainder is 2.

(b) When $x^3 - 5x^2 + ax - 11$ is divided by $(x + 3)$, the remainder is -95.

(c) When $x^3 + ax^2 - 3x + 8$ is divided by $(x - 2)$, the remainder is 34.

(d) When $x^3 + ax^2 - 3x - 1$ is divided by $(x + 1)$, the remainder is -6.

(e) When $x^3 + 3x^2 + ax + 5$ is divided by $(x - 4)$, the remainder is 81.

(f) When $x^3 - 9x^2 + ax - 7$ is divided by $(x - 2)$, the remainder is -29.

3. In each of the following, find the unknown coefficients:

(a) For the polynomial $x^3 + 4x^2 + ax + b$, $(x + 1)$ is a factor and the remainder is 12 when the polynomial is divided by $(x - 1)$.

(b) For the polynomial $x^3 + 4x^2 + ax + b$, $(x + 2)$ is a factor and the remainder is 20 when the polynomial is divided by $(x - 2)$.

(c) For the polynomial $x^3 - 2x^2 + ax + b$, $(x - 1)$ is a factor and the remainder is -12 when the polynomial is divided by $(x - 3)$.

(d) For the polynomial $x^3 - 2x^2 + ax + b$, $(x + 1)$ is a factor and the remainder is -16 when the polynomial is divided by $(x + 3)$.

(e) For the polynomial $2x^3 + x^2 + ax + b$, $(x - 2)$ is a factor and the remainder is -4 when the polynomial is divided by $(x - 1)$.

(f) For the polynomial $x^3 + 7x^2 + ax + b$, $(x + 3)$ is a factor and the remainder is 35 when the polynomial is divided by $(x - 2)$.

(g) For the polynomial $x^3 + ax^2 - x + b$, $(x + 1)$ is a factor and the remainder is -15 when the polynomial is divided by $(x - 2)$.

(h) For the polynomial $2x^3 - 9x^2 + ax + b$, $(x - 2)$ is a factor and the remainder is -30 when the polynomial is divided by $(x + 1)$.

(i) For the polynomial $6x^3 - 31x^2 + ax + b$, the remainder is -75 when the polynomial is divided by $(x + 1)$ and -3 when the polynomial is divided by $(x - 1)$.

(j) For the polynomial $10x^3 - 27x^2 + ax + b$, the remainder is -45 when the polynomial is divided by $(x - 2)$ and -24 when the polynomial is divided by $(x + 1)$.

7.5 Finding the Points of Intersection of Curves

To find the points of intersection of two curves: equate the curves, rearrange to equal zero, solve to find x-coordinates (using synthetic division if necessary) and substitute values into the curve to find the y-coordinates.

Worked Example:

1. Find the coordinates of the points of intersection of the graphs with equations $y = f(x)$ and $y = g(x)$, where $f(x) = x^3 - x^2 - 3x + 3$ and $g(x) = x^2 + 2x - 3$.

Solution:

$x^3 - x^2 - 3x + 3 = x^2 + 2x - 3$

$x^3 - 2x^2 - 5x + 6 = 0$

1	1	-2	-5	6
		1	-1	-6
	1	-1	-6	0

$(x-1)(x^2-x-6)=0$ When $x=1, g(1)=(1)^2+2(1)-3=0$

$(x-1)(x-3)(x+2)=0$ When $x=3, g(3)=(3)^2+2(3)-3=12$

$x=1, x=3, x=-2$ When $x=-2, g(-2)=(-2)^2+2(-2)-3=-3$

Points of intersection are $(1,0)$, $(3,12)$ and $(-2,-3)$.

Exercise 7.5

1. Find the coordinates of the points of intersection of the graphs with equations $y=f(x)$ and $y=g(x)$, for each of the following:

(a) $f(x)=x^2+x+3$
$g(x)=2x+9$

(b) $f(x)=x^2-3x+1$
$g(x)=2x+7$

(c) $f(x)=8x-7$
$g(x)=x^2+x+5$

(d) $f(x)=3x^2+7x-8$
$g(x)=2x^2+9x$

(e) $f(x)=7x^2+3x-15$
$g(x)=6x^2+3x+1$

(f) $f(x)=x^2+5x+3$
$g(x)=x^2-x$

2. Find the coordinates of the points of intersection of the graphs with equations $y=f(x)$ and $y=g(x)$, for each of the following:

(a) $f(x)=x^3+x^2+4x-1$
$g(x)=4x^2+5x-4$

(b) $f(x)=x^3+3x^2+3x+2$
$g(x)=2x^2+7x+6$

(c) $f(x)=x^3+4x+7$
$g(x)=x^2+9x+10$

(d) $f(x)=x^3+4x^2-8$
$g(x)=2x^2+19x+12$

(e) $f(x)=x^3+13x^2+40$
$g(x)=3x^2-33x+4$

(f) $f(x)=x^3-x^2-8x+13$
$g(x)=7x^2+3x-5$

3. Find the coordinates of the points of intersection of the graphs with equations $y=f(x)$ and $y=g(x)$, for each of the following:

(a) $f(x)=2x^3+x^2-5x+1$
$g(x)=x^3+3x^2+6x-11$

(b) $f(x)=3x^3-2x^2-12x+9$
$g(x)=2x^3-x^2+2x-15$

(c) $f(x)=3x^3+5x^2-8x-2$
$g(x)=x^3+2x^2-5$

7.6 Finding the Equation of a Polynomial From a Graph

The **roots** of a polynomial are the x-coordinates at which the graph of the function cuts the x-axis. At the roots, the equation of the function $f(x)=0$. We can use the roots and the y-intercept of the function to determine the equation.

Step 1: Turn the roots into factors of the polynomial, $\boldsymbol{y=k(x-a)(x-b)(x-c)}$

Step 2: Substitute the y-intercept or other coordinate into the equation to find the value of k.

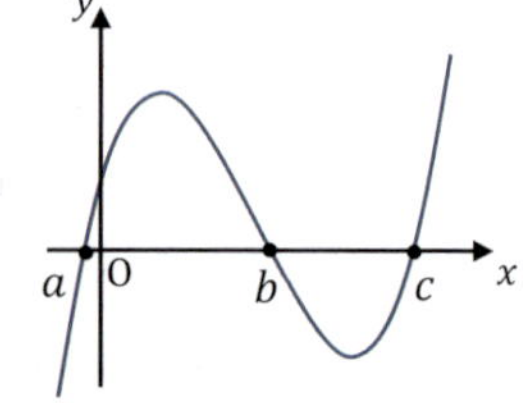

NB: In an example where the roots are at the same place (equal roots), use the factor twice in the equation.

Worked Example:

The graph of $y = f(x)$ is shown. Determine the equation of the function $f(x)$.

Step 1: $f(x) = 0$ where $x = -2, 1, 3$

$\therefore f(x) = k(x+2)(x-1)(x-3)$

Step 2: Substitute other point (in this case the y-intercept)

$3 = k(0+2)(0-1)(0-3)$

$3 = 6k$

$k = \frac{1}{2} \qquad \therefore y = \frac{1}{2}(x+2)(x-1)(x-3)$

Exercise 7.6

1. In each of the diagrams the graph of $y = f(x)$ is shown. Determine the equation of the function $f(x)$:

(a)

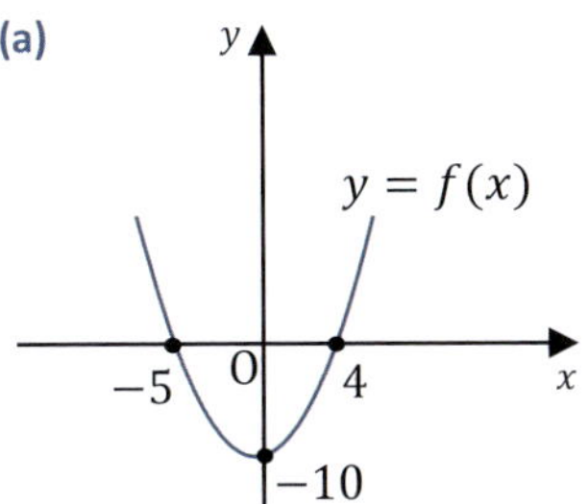

(b)

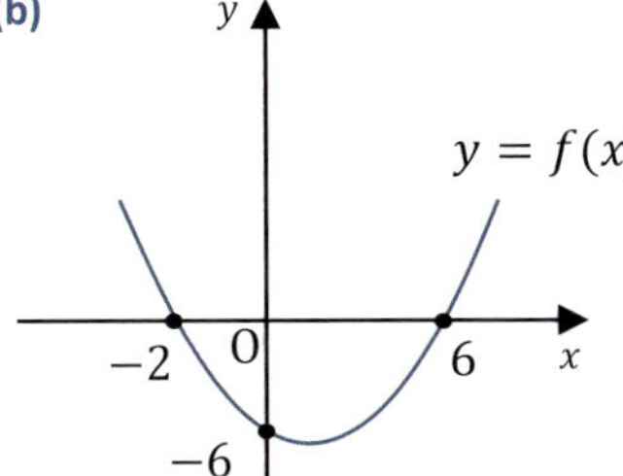

(c)

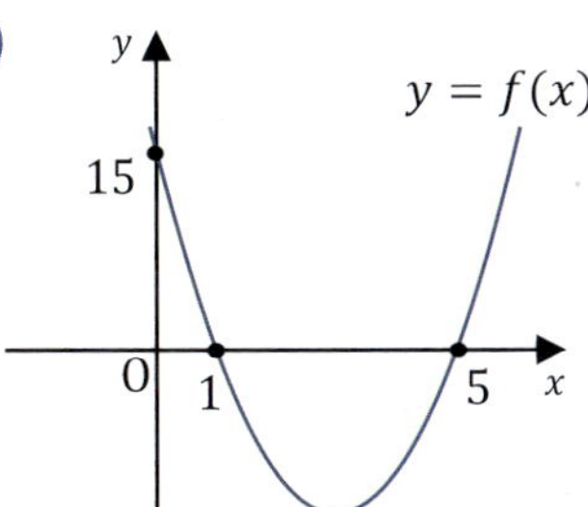

(d)

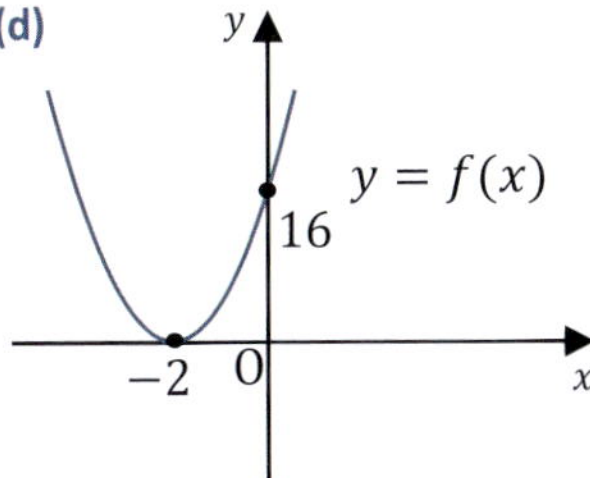

(e)

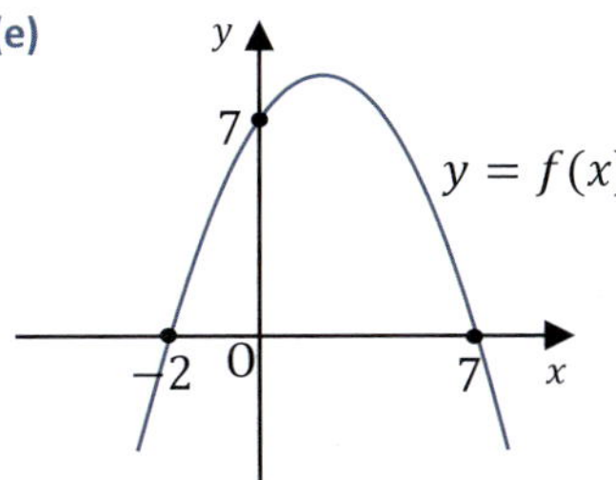

(f)

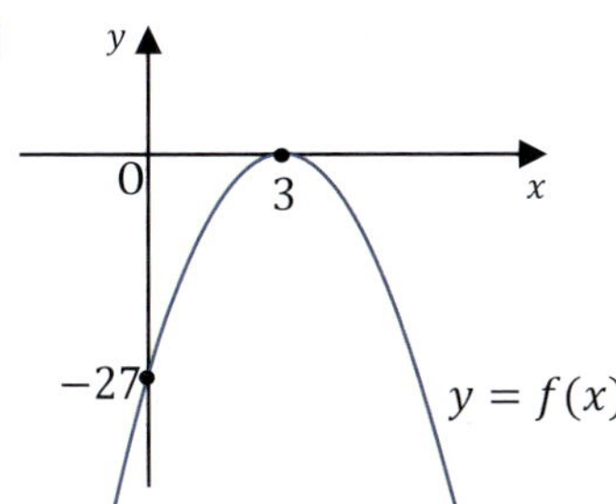

2. In each of the diagrams the graph of $y = f(x)$ is shown. Determine the equation of the function $f(x)$:

(a)

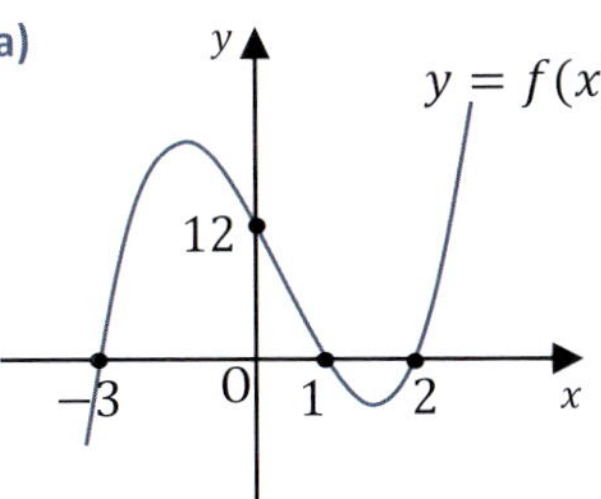

(b)

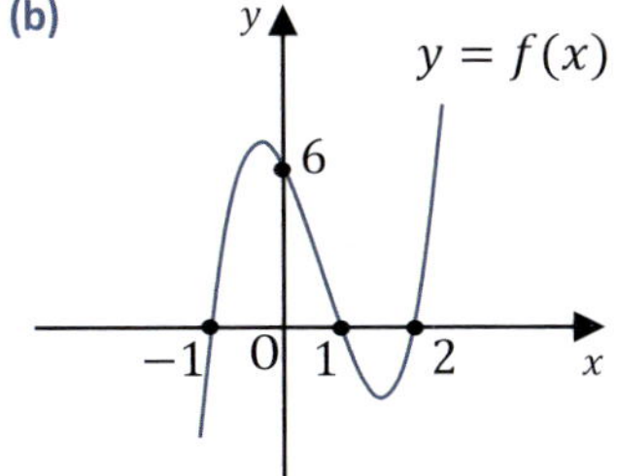

(c)

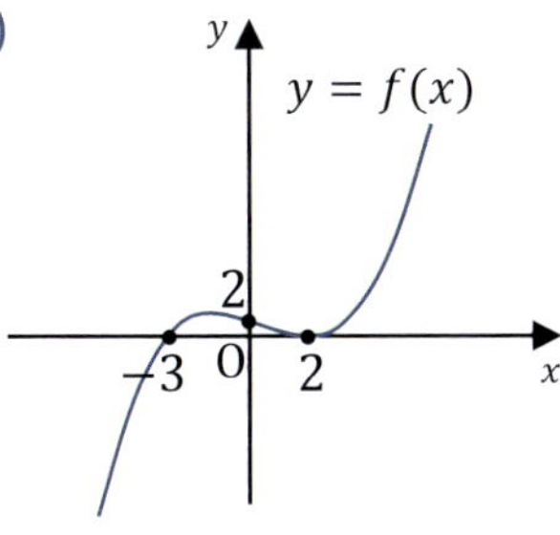

(d)

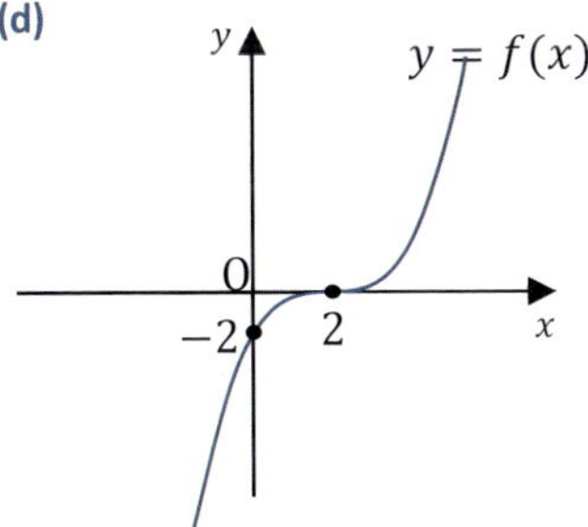

(e)

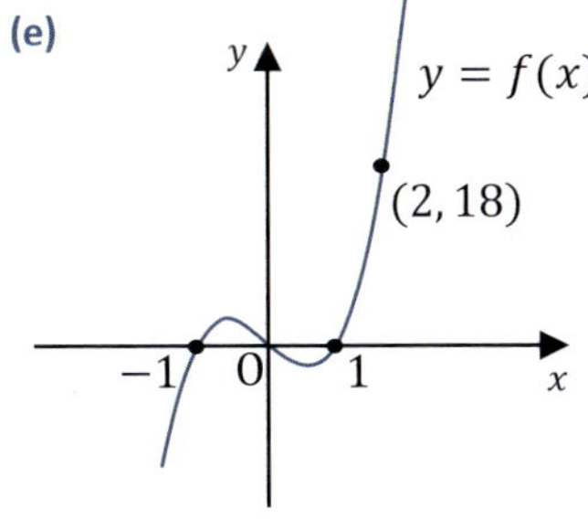

(f)

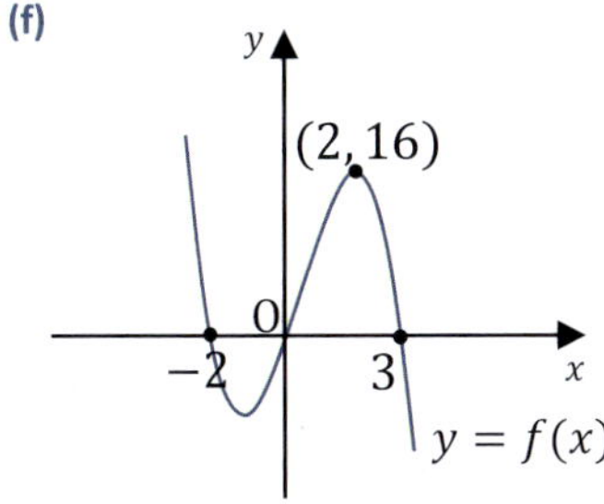

3. In each of the diagrams the graph of $y = f(x)$ is shown. Determine the equation of the function $f(x)$:

(a)

(b) 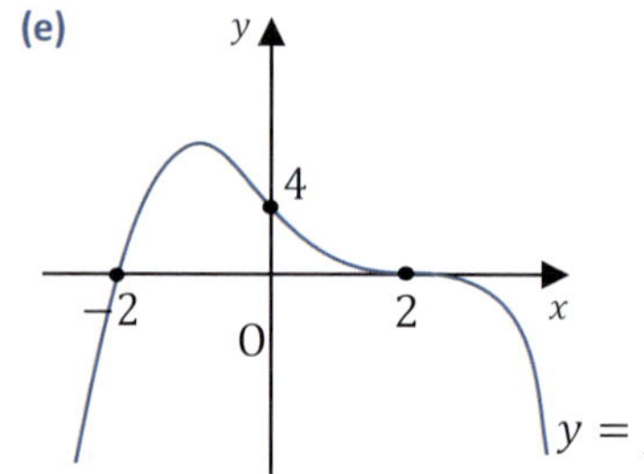

(c) 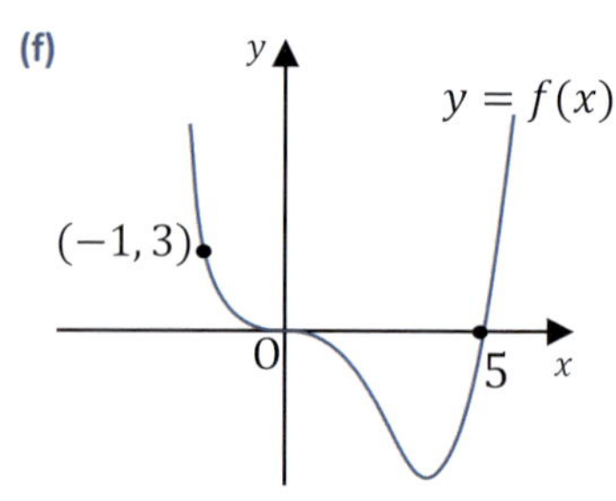

(d)

(e)

(f)

7.7 Polynomials Review

Exercise 7.7

7.1 (a) Show that $(x - 2)$ is a factor of $x^3 + 7x^2 + 2x - 40$.

(b) Show that $(x - 3)$ is a factor of $x^3 - 4x^2 - 27x + 90$.

(c) Fully factorise: (i) $x^3 - 5x^2 - 4x + 20$ (ii) $x^3 + 3x^2 - 13x - 15$

7.2 Solve:

(a) $x^3 - 6x^2 + 5x + 12 = 0$ (b) $x^3 - 12x - 16 = 0$ (c) $x^3 - 5x^2 - 8x + 12 = 0$

7.3 Find the remainder when:

(a) $x^3 - 13x^2 + 2$ is divided by $(x - 2)$. (b) $x^3 - 7x^2 + x - 3$ is divided by $(x - 3)$.

7.4. In each of the following, determine the values of a and b:

(a) For the polynomial $x^3 + x^2 + ax + b$, $(x - 1)$ is a factor and the remainder is 24 when the polynomial is divided by $(x + 2)$.

(b) For the polynomial $x^3 - 4x^2 + ax + b$, $(x + 2)$ is a factor and the remainder is -20 when the polynomial is divided by $(x - 3)$.

7.5 Find the coordinates of the points of intersection of the graphs with equations $y = f(x)$ and $y = g(x)$:

(a) $f(x) = x^3 + 5x^2 + 5x - 13$
$g(x) = 3x - 5$

(b) $f(x) = x^3 + x^2 + 8x - 1$
$g(x) = x^2 + 11x + 1$

(c) $f(x) = 2x^3 + x$
$g(x) = x^3 + 4x^2 - 6$

7.6 In each of the diagrams the graph of $y = f(x)$ is shown. Determine the equation of the function $f(x)$:

(a)

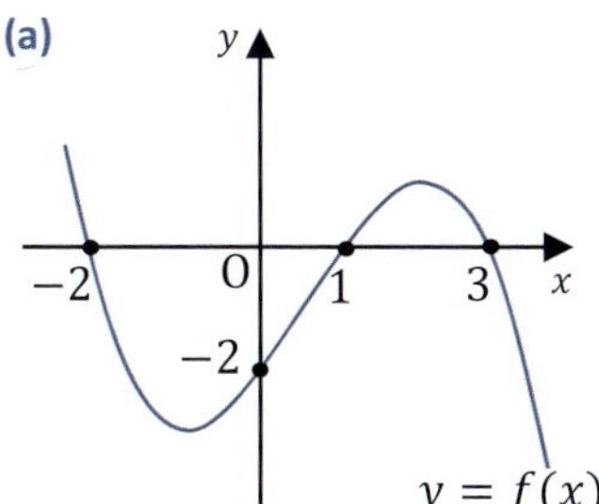

(b)

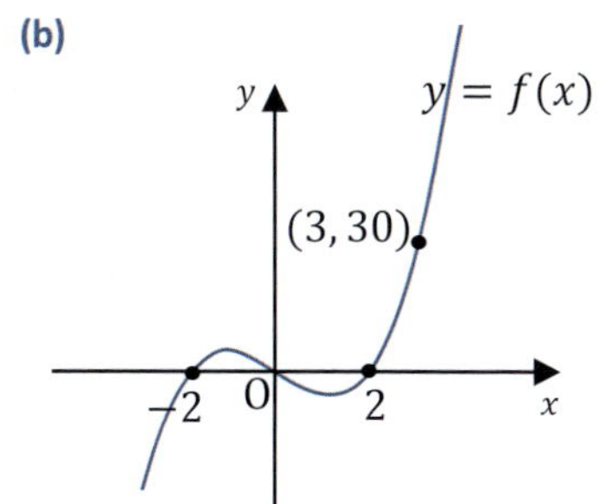

(c)

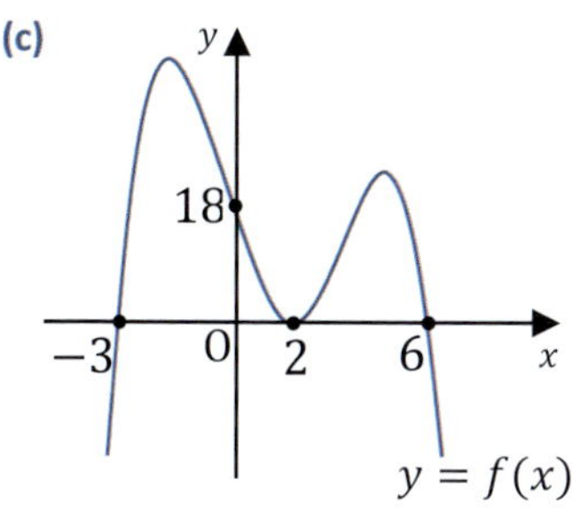

Chapter 8

Trigonometric Functions

Trigonometric Functions

Trigonometric Functions are functions that relate the angles of a right-angled triangle to the ratio of two of its sides. In National 5 and Higher Mathematics three trigonometric functions are of interest: **Sine** (**sin**), **Cosine** (**cos**) and **Tangent** (**tan**).

For any right-angled triangle:

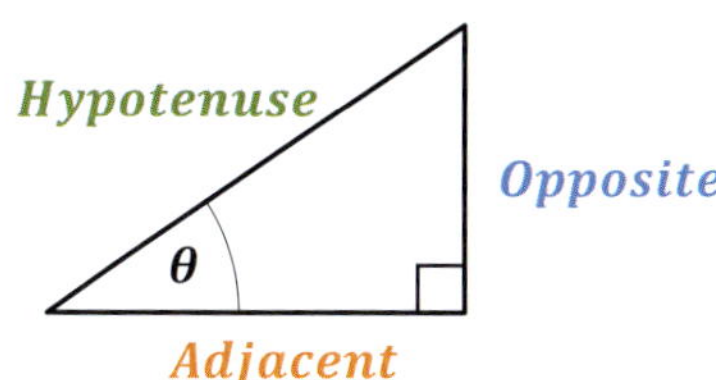

$$\sin\theta = \frac{Opposite}{Hypotenuse} \qquad \cos\theta = \frac{Adjacent}{Hypotenuse} \qquad \tan\theta = \frac{Opposite}{Adjacent}$$

These relationships may be remembered using the acronym **SOH CAH TOA**.

Trigonometric Graphs

The Sine Graph

The graph of $y = \sin x°$ has an **amplitude** of 1 and a **period** of $360°$. This amplitude means that each graph reaches a maximum value of 1 and a minimum value of -1 and it has a range of 2. The period means that the graph repeats itself every $360°$.

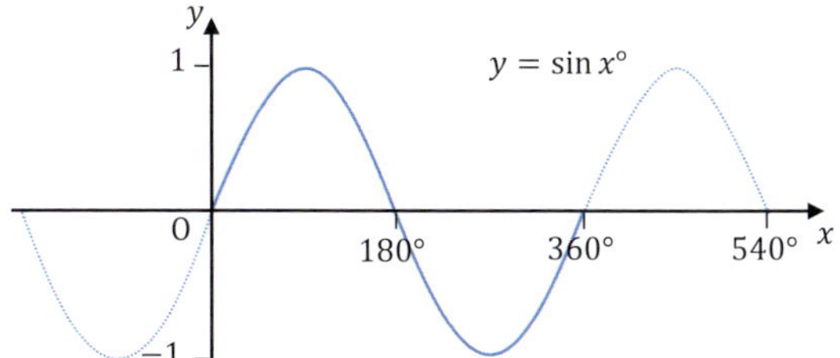

The Cosine Graph

The graph of $y = \cos x°$ also has an **amplitude** of 1 and a **period** of $360°$. The difference between $y = \sin x°$ and $y = \cos x°$ can be seen in the diagrams opposite. The graph of $y = \sin x°$ starts at $(0, 0)$ and the graph of $y = \cos x°$ starts at $(0, 1)$.

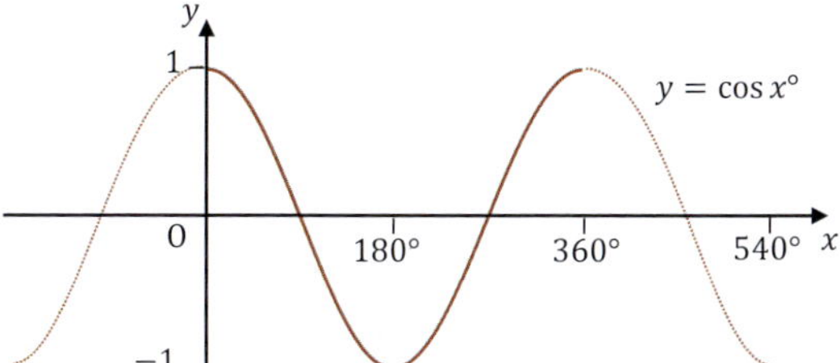

The Tangent Graph

The graph of the tangent function is different, it has no amplitude as the graph tends towards positive and negative infinity as the graph nears $90°$ and $-90°$. The dotted lines in the graphs are **vertical asymptotes** and correspond with the values for which the function is undefined. The period of $y = \tan x°$ is $180°$.

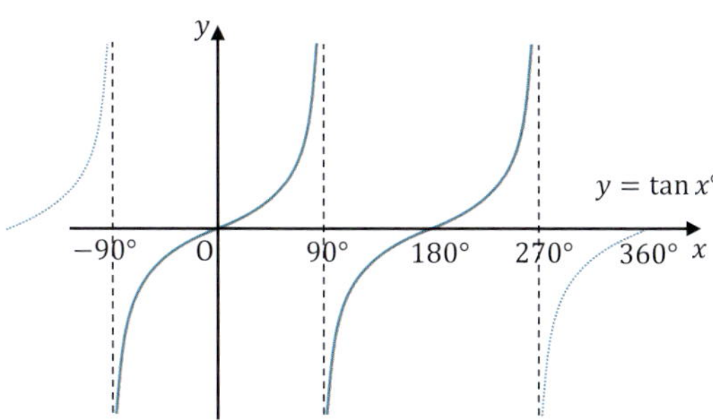

Trigonometric Identities

Trigonometric identities are facts that are true for any value of the given variable. In National 5 we learned two trigonometric identities:

$$\tan x = \frac{\sin x}{\cos x} \quad \text{and} \quad \sin^2 x + \cos^2 x = 1$$

$$\sin^2 x = 1 - \cos^2 x$$

$$\cos^2 x = 1 - \sin^2 x$$

The above identities should be memorised for Higher Mathematics.

National 5 Skills

8.1 Finding the Equation of a Trigonometric Function from a Graph

In trigonometric functions of the form $y = a \sin bx$ and $y = a \cos bx$, the **amplitude** of the graph is the positive value of a. This is half of the range, **i.e.** half the distance from the maximum to the minimum value. The amplitude of $y = \sin x$ and $y = \cos x$ is 1, the amplitude of $y = 3\cos x$ is 3, etc. The graph of $y = \tan x$ does not have an amplitude as it has no maximum or minimum value.

The **period** of the graph is the length of one full wave. For cosine and sine graphs, the period can be derived by dividing $360°$ by b. Alternatively, to find the value of b, divide $360°$ by the period of one wave.

Worked Examples:

Find the equation of each of the following trigonometric functions:

1. $y = a \sin bx°$

$a = 4$
$b = 1$
$y = 4 \sin x°$

2.

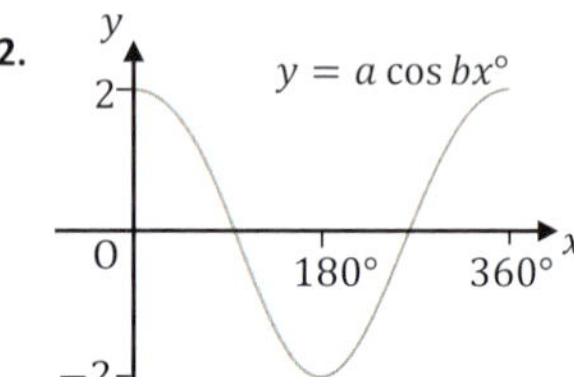

$a = 2$
$b = 1$
$y = 2 \cos x°$

3. $y = a \sin bx°$

$a = 1$
$b = \frac{360}{180} = 2$
$y = \sin 2x°$

4.

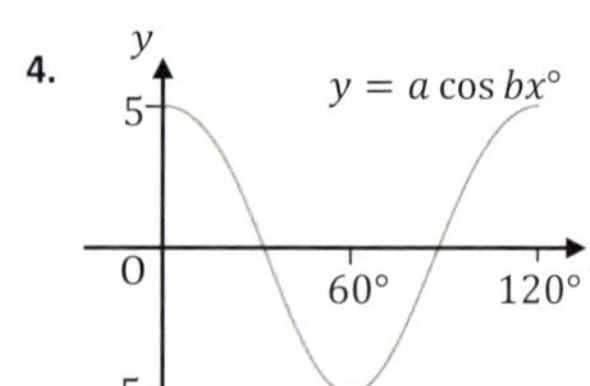

$a = 5$
$b = \frac{360}{120} = 3$
$y = 5 \cos 3x°$

Exercise 8.1A

State the equation of each of the following trigonometric functions:

1.

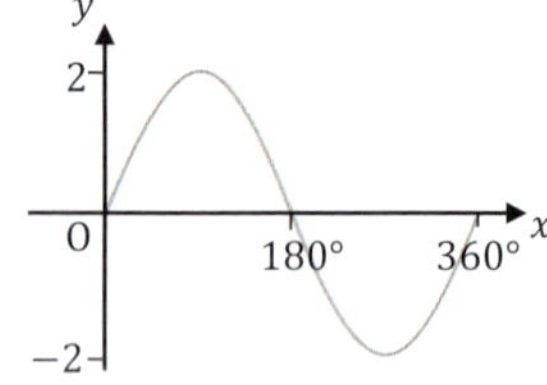

2.

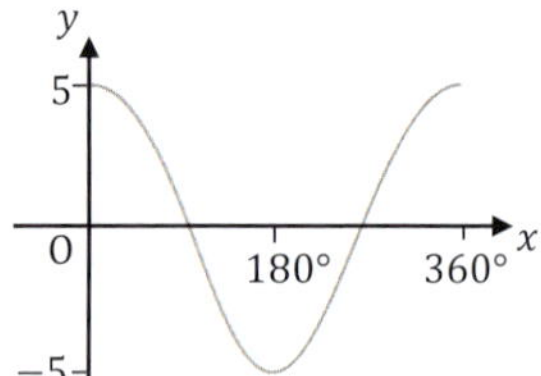

3.

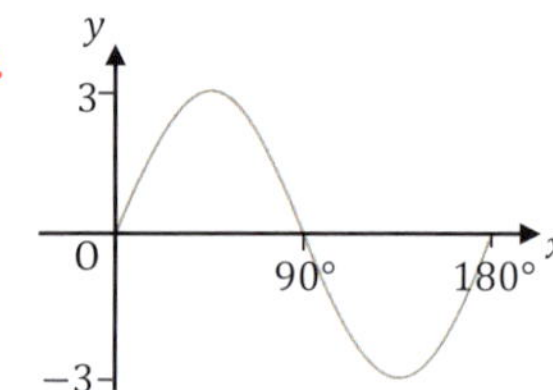

4.

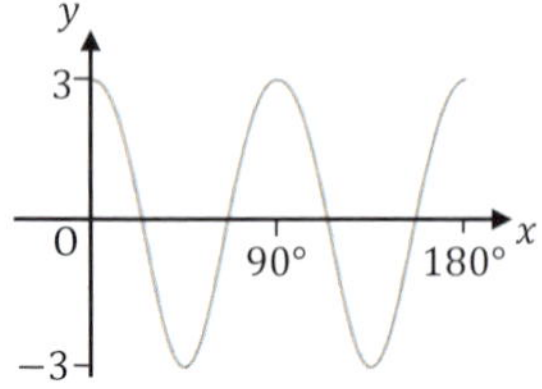

5.

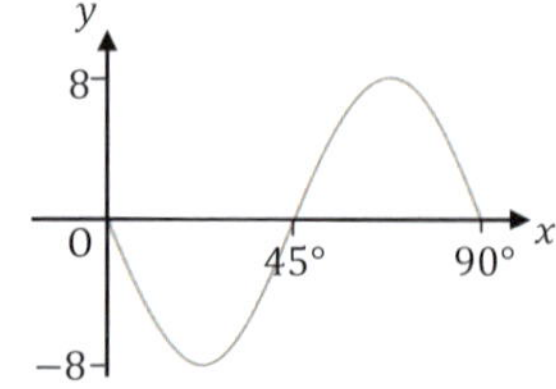

6.

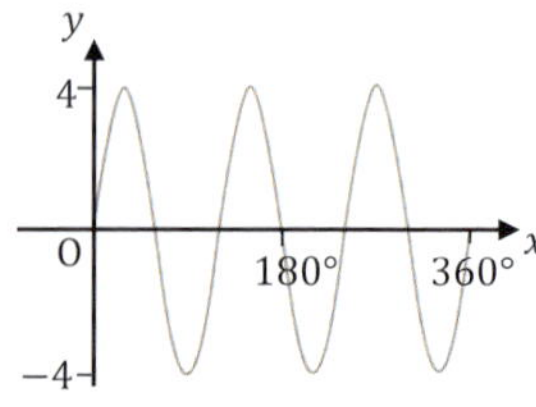

7.

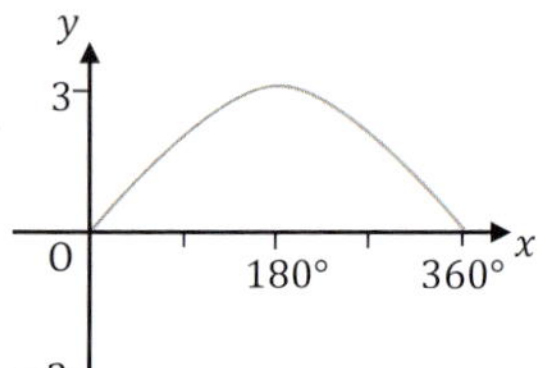

8.

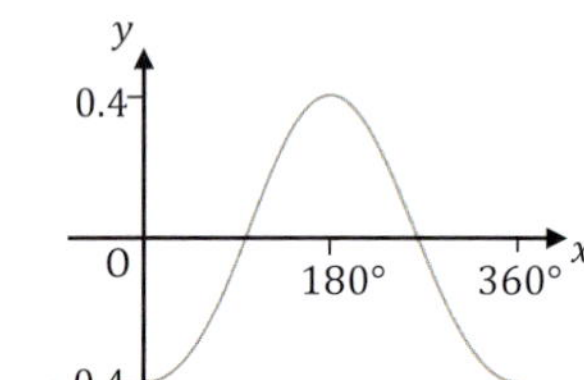

9.

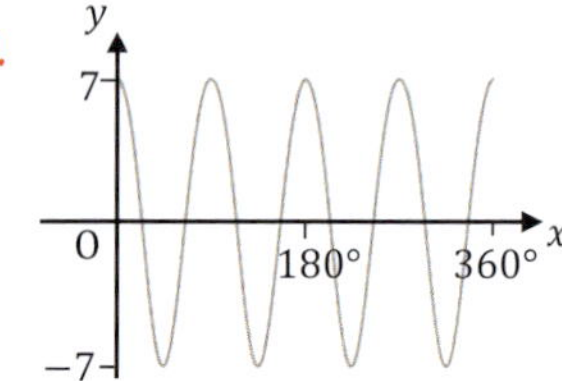

In trigonometric functions of the form $y = a \sin bx + c$ and $y = a \cos bx + c$, a and b are derived as above, and the value of c translates the graph **vertically**.

Worked Examples:

Find the equation of each of the following trigonometric functions:

1.

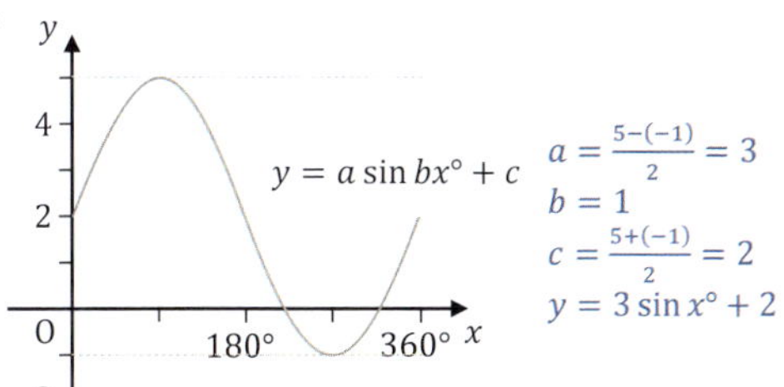

$a = \frac{5-(-1)}{2} = 3$
$b = 1$
$c = \frac{5+(-1)}{2} = 2$
$y = 3 \sin x° + 2$

2.

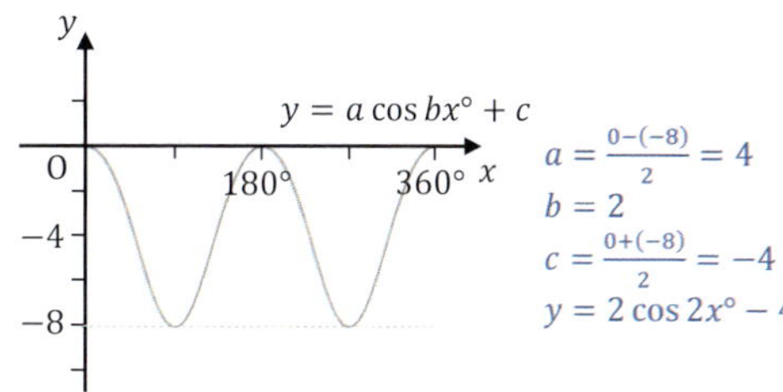

$a = \frac{0-(-8)}{2} = 4$
$b = 2$
$c = \frac{0+(-8)}{2} = -4$
$y = 2 \cos 2x° - 4$

NB: The value of a is half of the range, **i.e.** half of the *difference* between the maximum and the minimum value. The value of c is half of the *sum* of the maximum and the minimum value.

Exercise 8.1B

Find the equation of each of the following trigonometric functions in the form given:

1.

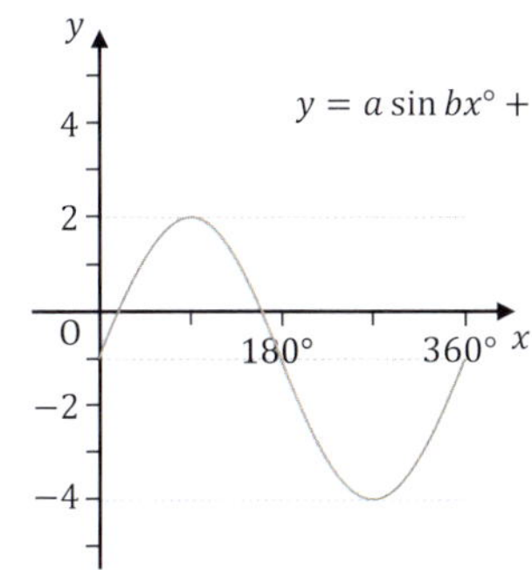

2.

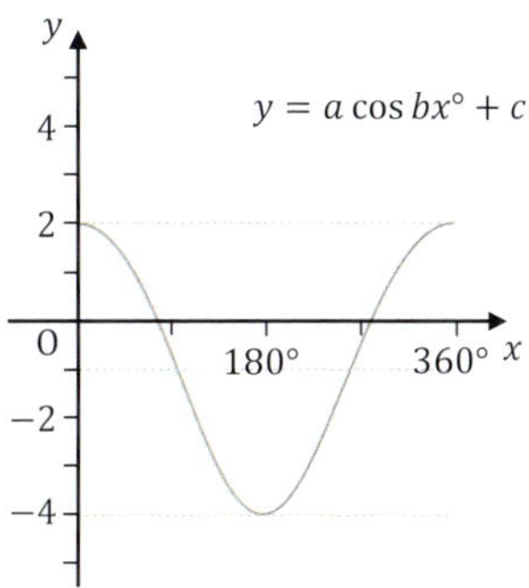

3.

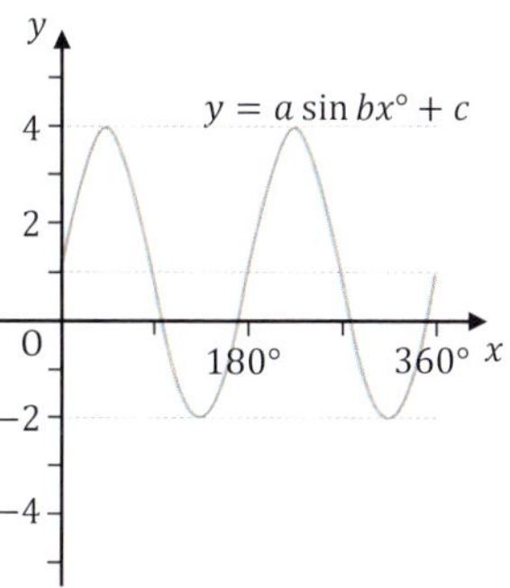

4.

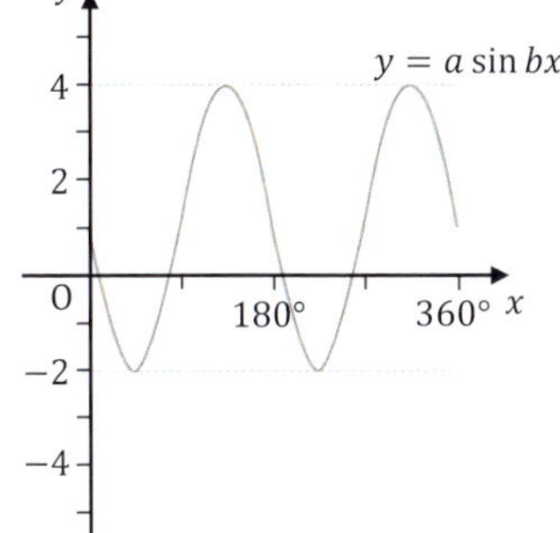

5.

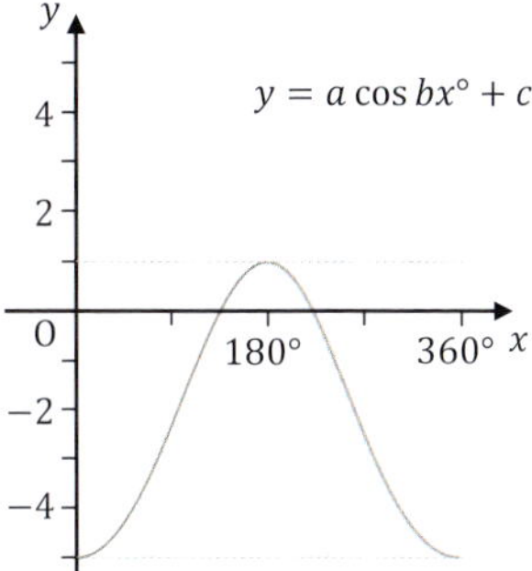

6.

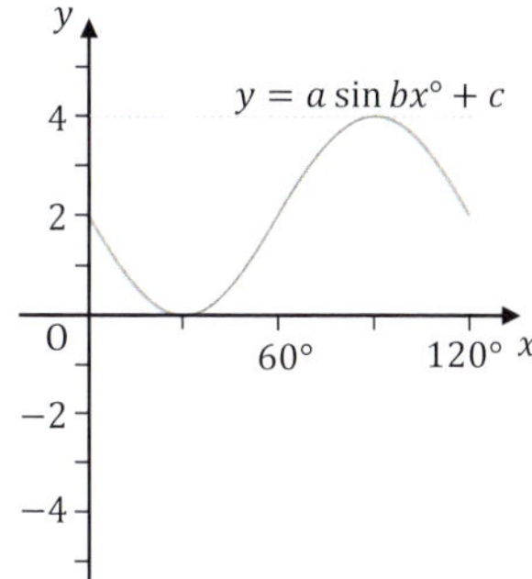

7.

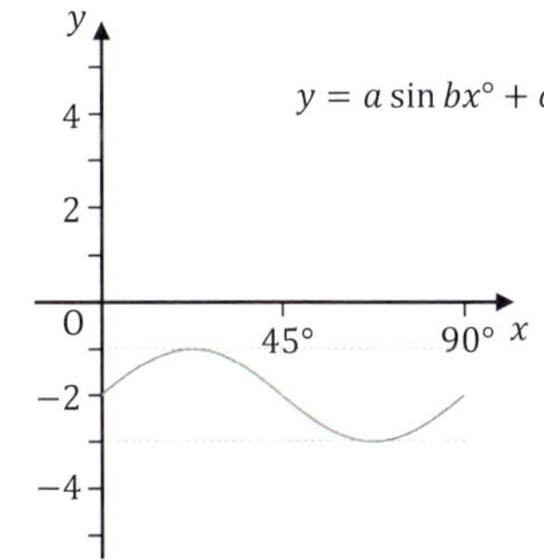

8.

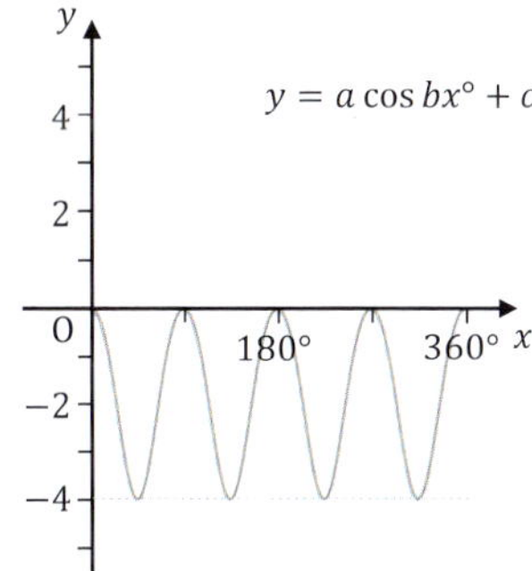

9.

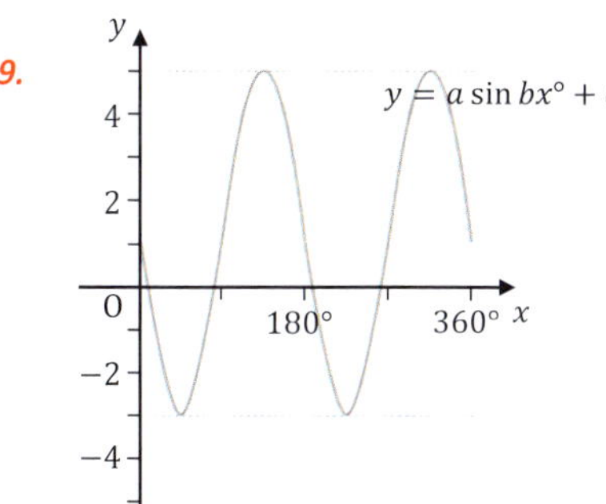

In trigonometric functions of the form $y = a\sin(x + b)$ and $y = a\cos(x + b)$, a is the amplitude and the value of b translates the graph **horizontally**. As with quadratic functions, the value in the bracket is the negative of the direction that the graph shifts.

Worked Examples:

Find the equation of each of the following trigonometric functions:

1.

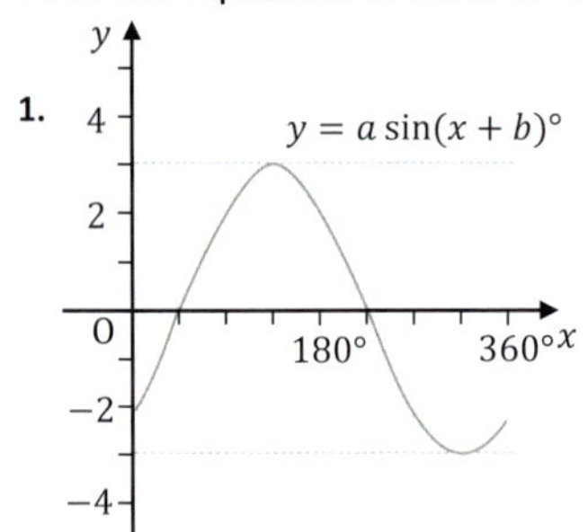

$a = 3$
$b = -45°$
$y = 3\sin(x - 45)°$

2.

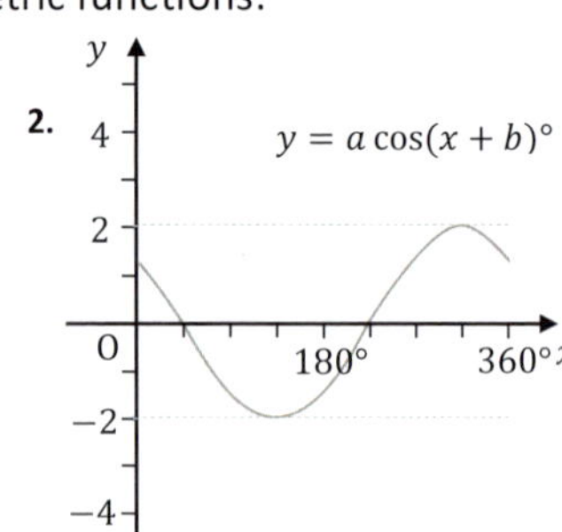

$a = 2$
$b = 45°$
$y = 2\cos(x + 45)°$

Exercise 8.1C

Find the equation of each of the following trigonometric functions in the form given:

1.

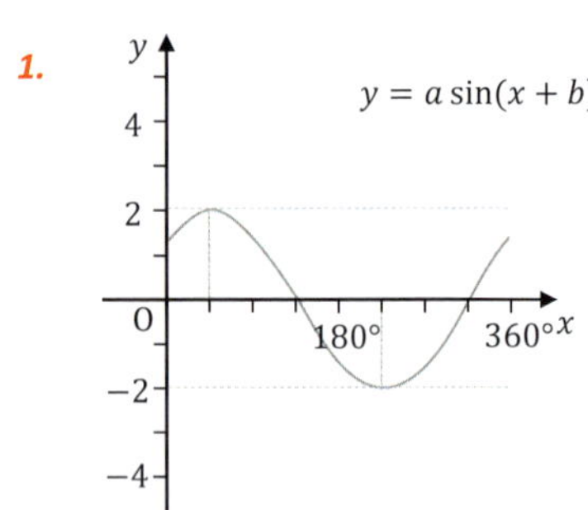

2.

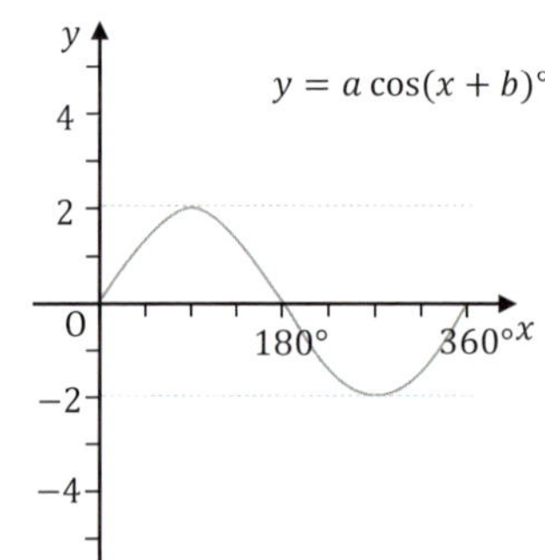

3.

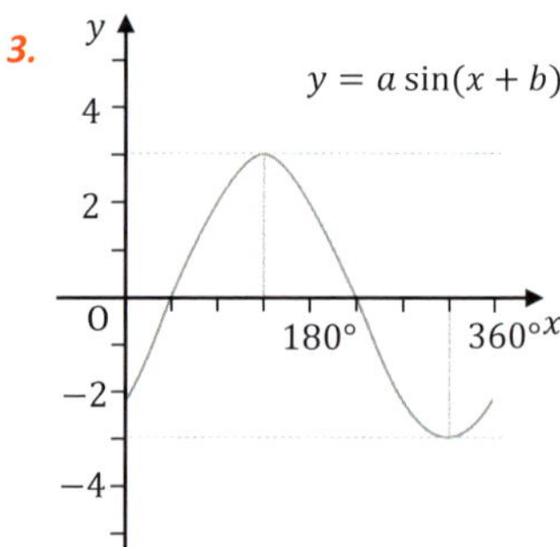

4.

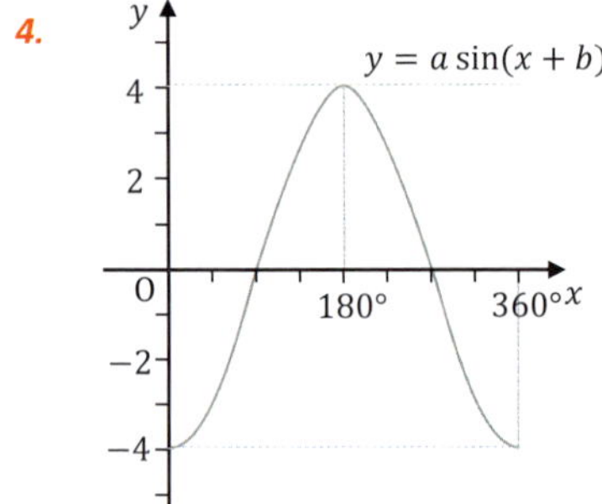

5.

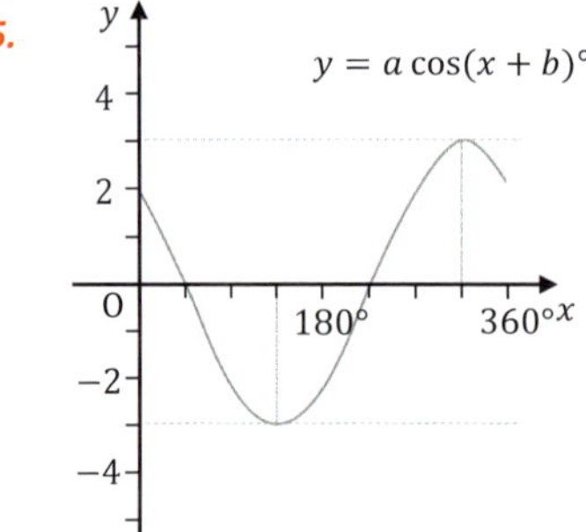

6.

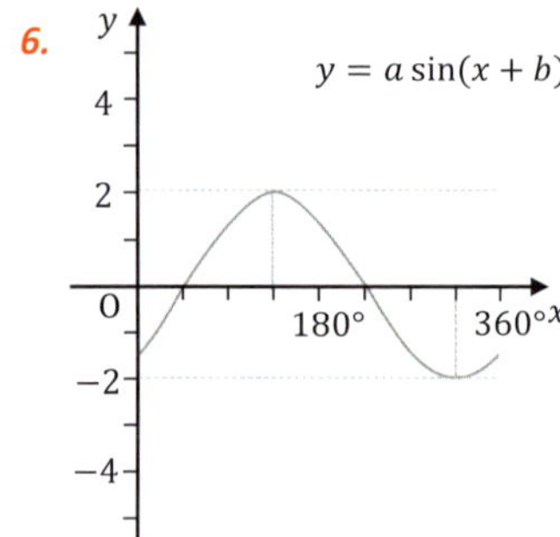

7.

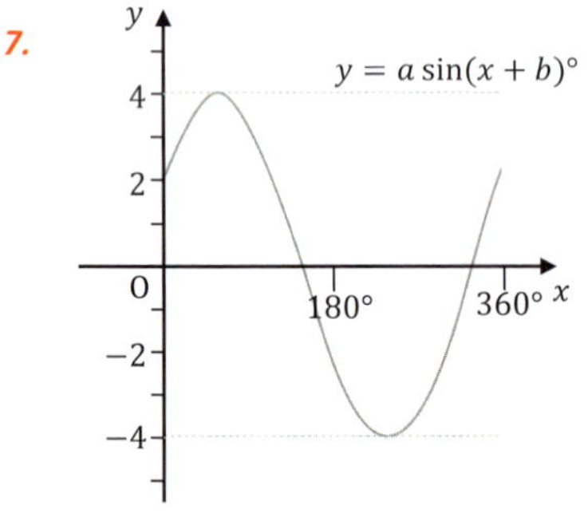

8.

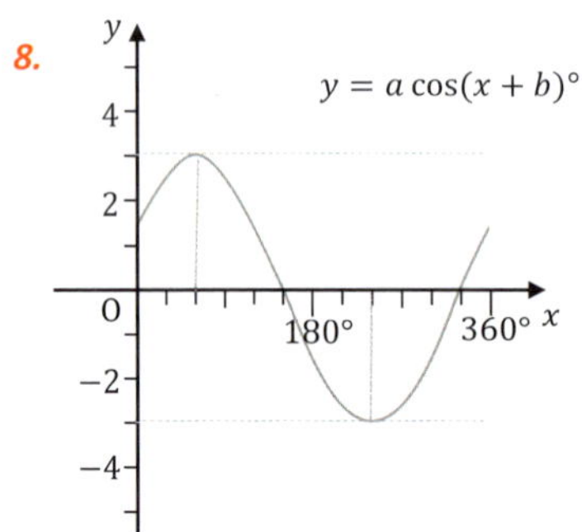

9.

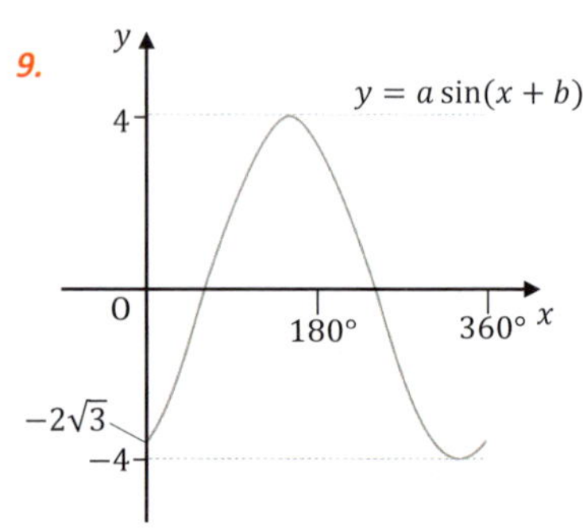

8.2 Solving Trigonometric Equations

National 5 Skills

As the graphs of trigonometric functions repeat indefinitely, trigonometric equations have either an infinite number of solutions, or none. In order to solve them, it is helpful to have a knowledge of the graphs. The diagram on the right shows the graphs of $y = \frac{1}{2}$ and $y = \sin x$, we can see that $\sin x = \frac{1}{2}$ in two places. If these graphs were to continue another $360°$ in either direction, there would be another two solutions.

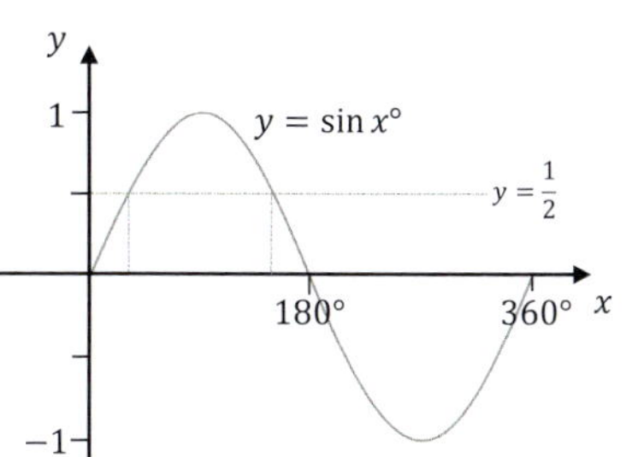

A helpful memory aid for finding the solutions of trigonometric equations is the **CAST** diagram. The diagram shows where each of the functions are **positive**. In the first quadrant (**A** from CAST), **all** of the functions are positive as all of the graphs are above the x-axis between $0°$ and $90°$. In the second quadrant (**S**), only the sine graph (**sin**) is positive (above the x-axis) and both cosine and tangent are negative (below the x-axis). In the third quadrant (**T**), only the tangent graph (**tan**) is positive and in the fourth quadrant (**C**), only the cosine graph (**cos**) is positive.

Sin $+ve$ $180 - x$	**All** $+ve$ x
Tan $+ve$ $180 + x$	**Cos** $+ve$ $360 - x$

To determine where the graphs are **negative**, we simply take the two quadrants where the graph is **not** positive, **e.g.** if sine is positive in the first two quadrants it is negative in the third and fourth.

NB: The name CAST diagram does not help us remember the order of the quadrants as it starts in quadrant four. The order we should remember should be **ASTC** a helpful memory aid (**A**ll **S**tudents **T**ake **C**are).

Worked Examples:

1. Solve the equations $\sin x° = \frac{1}{2}$, for $0 \leq x \leq 360$.

$\sin x° = \frac{1}{2}$

$x° = \sin^{-1}\left(\frac{1}{2}\right)$

$x° = 30°, 180° - 30°$

$x° = 30°, 150°$

The first part of the equation is solved as normal. Because $\frac{1}{2}$ is a positive value, the two solutions are taken from the 'all' and 'sin' quadrants. The blue text in the cast diagram explains how to calculate the solution.

2. Solve the equations $3\cos x° - 1 = 0$, for $0 \leq x \leq 360$.

$3\cos x° - 1 = 0$

$3\cos x° = 1$

$\cos x° = \frac{1}{3}$

$x° = \cos^{-1}\left(\frac{1}{3}\right)$

$x° = 70.5°, 360° - 70.5°$

$x° = 70.5°, 289.5°$ (to 1 d.p.)

In the question, rearrange to $\cos x° = \frac{1}{3}$. Because $\frac{1}{3}$ is a positive value, this time the two solutions are taken from the 'all' and 'cos' quadrants. Again, the blue text in the cast diagram explains how to calculate the solution.

3. Solve the equations $5\tan x° + 2 = 0$, for $0 \le x \le 360$.

$5\tan x° + 2 = 0$

$5\tan x° = -2$

$\tan x° = -\frac{2}{5}$

$x_A = \tan^{-1}\left(\frac{2}{5}\right) = 21.8°$

$x° = 180° - 21.8°, 360° - 21.8°$

$x° = 158.2°,\ 338.2°$ (to 1 d.p.)

Rearranging we get $\tan x° = -\frac{2}{5}$. This time $-\frac{2}{5}$ is a negative value, so the two solutions are taken from where tan is negative, **i.e.** the sin and cos quadrants.

NB: Do not put the negative in the calculator as in line 4. Notice the answer from the calculator is not a solution, rather the *acute* angle is used to calculate the solutions. This angle can be called x_A.

Exercise 8.2A

1. Solve the following equations for $0 \le x \le 360$. Give your answer correct to 1 decimal place:

(a) $\cos x° = \frac{1}{3}$ (b) $\sin x° = \frac{1}{2}$ (c) $\tan x° = \frac{1}{2}$

(d) $\cos x° = \frac{1}{2}$ (e) $\cos x° = \frac{1}{\sqrt{2}}$ (f) $\tan x° = 1$

(g) $4\sin x° = 1$ (h) $3\cos x° = 2$ (i) $5\sin x° = 3$

2. Solve the following equations for $0 \le x \le 360$. Give your answer correct to 1 decimal place:

(a) $\sin x° = -\frac{1}{\sqrt{2}}$ (b) $\cos x° = -\frac{\sqrt{3}}{2}$ (c) $\tan x° = -1$

(d) $\sin x° = -\frac{1}{2}$ (e) $\cos x° = -\frac{2}{3}$ (f) $\tan x° + 4 = 0$

(g) $\tan x° + 3 = 0$ (h) $2\cos x° + 1 = 0$ (i) $3\sin x° + 2 = 0$

3. Solve the following equations for $0 \le x \le 360$. Give your answer correct to 1 decimal place:

(a) $5\cos x° - 1 = 1$ (b) $2\cos x° + 3 = 2$ (c) $2\tan x° - 1 = 3$

(d) $6\sin x° - 3 = 2$ (e) $5\sin x° + 1 = 0$ (f) $\sqrt{3}\tan x° + 1 = 0$

(g) $4\tan x° + 3 = 2$ (h) $5\cos x° - 3 = 2$ (i) $2\sin x° + 3 = 4$

Worked Example:

Solve the following equations for $0 \le x \le 360$.

$\sin 2x° = \frac{\sqrt{3}}{2}$

$2x° = 60°, 120°, 60° + 360°, 120° + 360°$

$2x° = 60°, 120°, 420°, 480°$

$x° = 30°, 60°, 210°, 240°$

$\sin 2x$ has four solutions for $0 \le x \le 360$. To find the third and fourth solution, add one period of the graph, **i.e.** 360° to each of the first two solutions in line 2. If there are further solutions, add 360° to each of the previous two solutions.

NB: Generally, perform any of the angle calculations as a last step. As above, divide each solution by two.

Exercise 8.2B

1. Solve the following equations for $0 \leq x \leq 360$:

(a) $\sin 2x^\circ = \frac{1}{2}$ (b) $\cos 2x^\circ = \frac{1}{3}$ (c) $\tan 3x^\circ = 1$

(d) $\cos 2x^\circ = -\frac{1}{4}$ (e) $\sin 3x^\circ = -\frac{2}{3}$ (f) $\tan 2x^\circ = 5$

2. Solve the following equations for $0 \leq x \leq 360$:

(a) $2\cos 2x^\circ + 2 = 1$ (b) $2\sin 3x^\circ - 2 = 0$ (c) $3\cos 3x^\circ - 1 = 0$

(d) $3\cos 4x^\circ + 2 = 1$ (e) $4\sin 3x^\circ - 2 = -4$ (f) $2\tan 3x^\circ - 1 = 0$

Worked Example:

Solve the following equations for $0 \leq x \leq 360$.

$\cos(x - 30)^\circ = \frac{1}{5}$

$(x - 30)^\circ = 78.5^\circ, 360^\circ - 78.5^\circ$

$(x - 30)^\circ = 78.5^\circ, 281.5^\circ$

$x^\circ = 78.5^\circ + 30^\circ, 281.5^\circ + 30^\circ$

$x^\circ = 108.5^\circ, 311.5^\circ$

As already stated, perform any of the angle calculations as a last step. In this example, add 30° to each solution.

Exercise 8.2C

1. Solve the following equations for $0 \leq x \leq 360$:

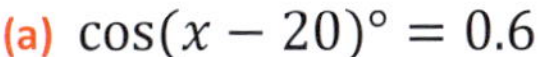

(a) $\cos(x - 20)^\circ = 0.6$ (b) $\sin(x - 30)^\circ = \frac{1}{3}$ (c) $\tan(x - 15)^\circ = 3$

(d) $\tan(x + 20)^\circ = -2$ (e) $\cos(x + 25)^\circ = 0.4$ (f) $\sin(x - 35)^\circ = -0.7$

2. Solve the following equations for $0 \leq x \leq 360$:

(a) $5\cos(x + 30)^\circ = 1$ (b) $4\sin(x - 20)^\circ + 1 = 0$ (c) $4\tan(x - 15)^\circ - 3 = 0$

(d) $4\tan(x + 20)^\circ + 3 = 2$ (e) $6\cos(x + 35)^\circ + 5 = 4$ (f) $5\sin(x - 35)^\circ - \sqrt{3} = 0$

8.3 Exact Values

There are certain angles in trigonometry that produce exact values. Some of these we already know from National 5 from the graphs of $y = \sin x$ and $y = \cos x$.

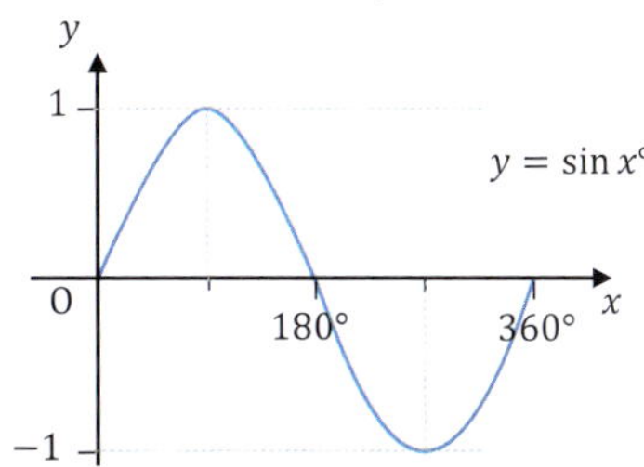

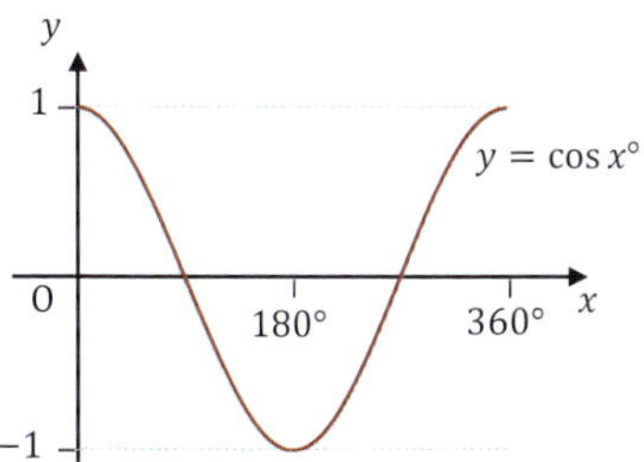

$x°$	$\sin x°$	$\cos x°$
0	0	1
90	1	0
180	0	-1
270	-1	0
360	0	1

There are other exact values that can be seen in the exact values triangles below:

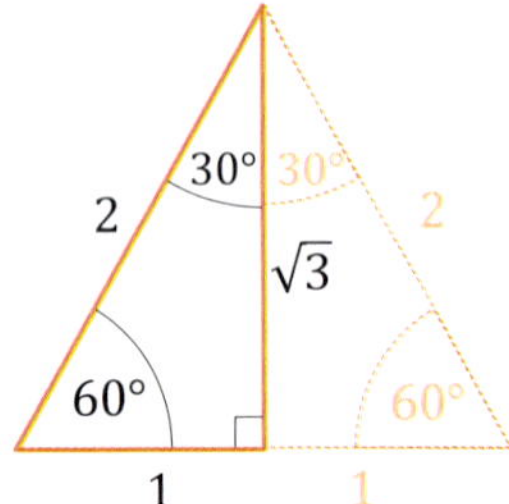

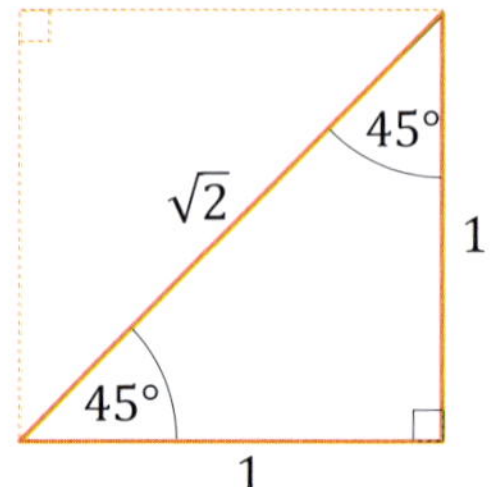

From these triangles we can determine the exact value of sin, cos or tan of 30°, 45° and 60°.

$x°$	$\sin x°$	$\cos x°$	$\tan x°$
30	$\frac{1}{2}$	$\frac{\sqrt{3}}{2}$	$\frac{1}{\sqrt{3}}$
45	$\frac{1}{\sqrt{2}}$	$\frac{1}{\sqrt{2}}$	1
60	$\frac{\sqrt{3}}{2}$	$\frac{1}{2}$	$\sqrt{3}$

Exercise 8.3

1. Find the exact value of:

(a) $\sin 45°$ (b) $\cos 60°$ (c) $\tan 45°$ (d) $\sin 60°$

(e) $\sin 180°$ (f) $\cos 360°$ (g) $\tan 60°$ (h) $\sin 90°$

(i) $\cos 270°$ (j) $\cos 180°$ (k) $\tan 30°$ (l) $\sin 0°$

(m) $\cos 90°$ (n) $\cos 0°$ (o) $\tan 0°$ (p) $\sin 270°$

2. Find the exact value of:

(a) $\cos 150°$ (b) $\sin 150°$ (c) $\cos 405°$ (d) $\sin 240°$

(e) $\cos 120°$ (f) $\tan 225°$ (g) $\sin 330°$ (h) $\sin 420°$

(i) $\sin 225°$ (j) $\cos 210°$ (k) $\tan 315°$ (l) $\tan 135°$

(m) $\tan 480°$ (n) $\sin 300°$ (o) $\cos 300°$ (p) $\sin 315°$

8.4 Solving Trigonometric Equations with Exact Values

Exact values can be used to solve trigonometric equations without a calculator.

Worked Examples:

Solve the following equations for $0 \leq x \leq 360$.

1. $2\cos x° - \sqrt{3} = 0$

$$2\cos x° = \sqrt{3}$$
$$\cos x° = \frac{\sqrt{3}}{2}$$
$$x° = 30°, 330°$$

2. $\sin 2x° = \frac{\sqrt{3}}{2}$

$$2x° = 60°, 120°, 420°, 480°$$
$$x° = 30°, 60°, 210°, 240°$$

3. $\cos(x - 30)° = \frac{1}{\sqrt{2}}$

$$(x - 30)° = 45°, 315°$$
$$x° = 75°, 345°$$

Exercise 8.4

1. Solve the following equations for $0 \leq x \leq 360$:

(a) $\sin x° = \frac{1}{2}$
(b) $\cos x° = \frac{\sqrt{3}}{2}$
(c) $\tan x° = \frac{1}{\sqrt{3}}$
(d) $\tan x° = \sqrt{3}$
(e) $\cos x° = \frac{1}{\sqrt{2}}$
(f) $\tan x° = 1$
(g) $\tan x° = -1$
(h) $2\sin x° = -\sqrt{3}$
(i) $\sqrt{2}\cos x° = -1$

2. Solve the following equations for $0 \leq x \leq 360$:

(a) $\sqrt{2}\sin 2x° - 1 = 0$
(b) $\sqrt{2}\cos 2x° + 1 = 0$
(c) $\tan 2x° - \sqrt{3} = 0$
(d) $2\sin 2x° + 1 = 0$
(e) $2\cos 2x° - 1 = 0$
(f) $\tan 3x° + \sqrt{3} = 0$
(g) $\sqrt{2}\sin 3x° + 2 = 1$
(h) $\sqrt{2}\cos 3x° - 5 = -4$
(i) $\sqrt{3}\tan 2x° + 1 = 0$

3. Solve the following equations for $0 \leq x \leq 360$:

(a) $\sqrt{2}\sin(x - 25)° = 1$
(b) $\sqrt{2}\cos(x + 10)° + 1 = 0$
(c) $3\tan(x - 20)° - 3 = 0$
(d) $\sqrt{3}\tan(x - 15)° + 3 = 2$
(e) $\sqrt{2}\sin(x + 20)° + 4 = 3$
(f) $2\cos(x - 15)° - \sqrt{3} = 0$
(g) $2\sin(x - 30)° - \sqrt{3} = 0$
(h) $2\cos(x + 10)° + \sqrt{3} = 0$
(i) $\tan(x - 45)° - \sqrt{3} = 0$

8.5 Solving Trigonometric Equations with Radians

So far, we have always used degrees to measure angles, but in trigonometry it is more common to use **radians**. Instead of using degrees, radians are measured as the distance around a circle of radius 1. Consider the circle with centre the origin and radius 1. The circumference of this circle is 2π, this means that 2π in radians is equivalent to $360°$. Half of the circumference would be π, so this is equivalent to $180°$, etc.

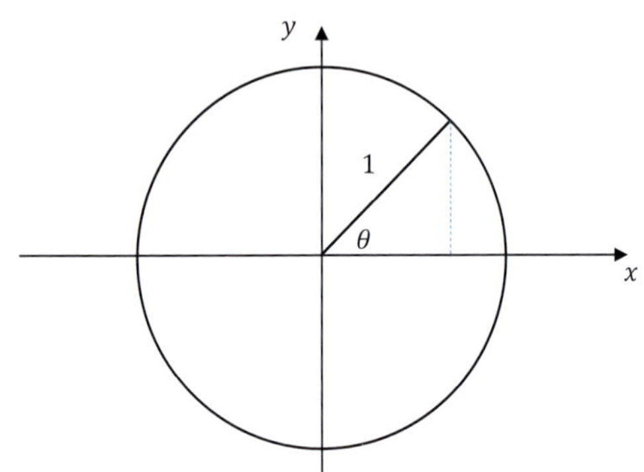

Degrees	Radians
360°	2π
180°	π
90°	$\frac{\pi}{2}$
60°	$\frac{\pi}{3}$
45°	$\frac{\pi}{4}$
30°	$\frac{\pi}{6}$
270°	$\frac{3\pi}{2}$

Trigonometric equations are often solved using **radians**. If no unit for angles is specified (**i.e.** no degrees symbol) or no degrees mentioned in the question, then radians should be used. Most radians questions will make some mention of π.

Worked Examples:

Solve the following equations for $0 \leq x \leq 2\pi$.

1. $2\cos x - \sqrt{3} = 0$

$$2\cos x = \sqrt{3}$$

$$\cos x = \frac{\sqrt{3}}{2}$$

$$x = \frac{\pi}{6}, 2\pi - \frac{\pi}{6}$$

$$x = \frac{\pi}{6}, \frac{12\pi}{6} - \frac{\pi}{6}$$

$$x = \frac{\pi}{6}, \frac{11\pi}{6}$$

2. $\text{Sin } 2x = \frac{\sqrt{3}}{2}$

$$2x = \frac{\pi}{3}, \pi - \frac{\pi}{3}, 2\pi + \frac{\pi}{3}, 3\pi - \frac{\pi}{3}$$

$$2x = \frac{\pi}{3}, \frac{3\pi}{3} - \frac{\pi}{3}, \frac{6\pi}{3} + \frac{\pi}{3}, \frac{9\pi}{3} - \frac{\pi}{3}$$

$$2x = \frac{\pi}{3}, \frac{2\pi}{3}, \frac{7\pi}{3}, \frac{8\pi}{3}$$

$$x = \frac{\pi}{6}, \frac{2\pi}{6}, \frac{7\pi}{6}, \frac{8\pi}{6}$$

$$x = \frac{\pi}{6}, \frac{\pi}{3}, \frac{7\pi}{6}, \frac{4\pi}{3}$$

Exercise 8.5A

1. Solve the following equations for $0 \leq x \leq 2\pi$:

(a) $\sin x = \frac{1}{2}$ **(b)** $\cos x = \frac{\sqrt{3}}{2}$ **(c)** $\tan x = \sqrt{3}$

(d) $\tan x = \frac{1}{\sqrt{3}}$ **(e)** $\cos x = \frac{1}{\sqrt{2}}$ **(f)** $\tan x = 1$

(g) $\tan x = -1$ **(h)** $2\sin x = -\sqrt{3}$ **(i)** $\sqrt{2}\cos x = -1$

2. Solve the following equations for $0 \leq x \leq 2\pi$:

(a) $\sqrt{2}\sin 2x - 1 = 0$ **(b)** $\sqrt{2}\cos 2x + 1 = 0$ **(c)** $\tan 2x - \sqrt{3} = 0$

(d) $2\sin 2x + 1 = 0$ **(e)** $2\cos 2x - 1 = 0$ **(f)** $\tan 3x + \sqrt{3} = 0$

(g) $\sqrt{2}\sin 3x + 2 = 1$ **(h)** $\sqrt{2}\cos 3x - 5 = -4$ **(i)** $\sqrt{3}\tan 2x - 1 = 0$

3. Solve the following equations for $0 \leq x \leq 2\pi$:

(a) $\sqrt{2}\sin\left(x - \frac{\pi}{6}\right) = 1$
(b) $\sqrt{2}\cos\left(x - \frac{\pi}{6}\right) + 1 = 0$
(c) $2\cos\left(x - \frac{\pi}{4}\right) - 1 = 0$
(d) $2\sin\left(x + \frac{\pi}{6}\right) + 2 = 1$
(e) $\sqrt{2}\sin\left(x + \frac{\pi}{4}\right) + 5 = 4$
(f) $2\cos\left(x - \frac{\pi}{4}\right) - \sqrt{3} = 0$
(g) $2\sin\left(x + \frac{\pi}{3}\right) + 1 = 0$
(h) $\sqrt{2}\cos\left(x - \frac{\pi}{3}\right) + 2 = 1$
(i) $2\cos\left(x + \frac{\pi}{3}\right) - \sqrt{3} = 0$

When using radians that are not exact values, we need to change our calculator to radians mode. Equations are then solved in the usual way. However, when finding additional solutions, it is important to remember to add multiples of 2π and not $360°$.

Exercise 8.5B

1. Solve the following equations for $0 \leq x \leq 2\pi$. Give your answer correct to 2 decimal places:

(a) $\sin x = \frac{1}{6}$
(b) $\cos x = \frac{2}{3}$
(c) $\tan x = 4$
(d) $\tan x = 5$
(e) $\cos x = 0.7$
(f) $\tan x = \frac{1}{2}$
(g) $\sin x = -0.6$
(h) $3\sin x = -2$
(i) $4\cos x = -1$

2. Solve the following equations for $0 \leq x \leq 2\pi$. Give your answer correct to 2 decimal places:

(a) $5\cos x - 1 = 1$
(b) $3\sin x + 3 = 2$
(c) $5\tan x - 3 = 3$
(d) $6\sin 2x - 3 = 2$
(e) $3\cos x + 2 = 0$
(f) $\sqrt{2}\tan 2x + 1 = 0$
(g) $3\tan 2x + 4 = 2$
(h) $3\sin 3x + 5 = 3$
(i) $5\cos 2x + 3 = 5$

3. Solve the following equations for $0 \leq x \leq 2\pi$. Give your answer correct to 2 decimal places:

(a) $\sqrt{3}\sin(x - 0.2) = 1$
(b) $\sqrt{2}\cos(x - 0.3) + 1 = 0$
(c) $4\tan(x - 1.2) - 3 = 0$
(d) $\sqrt{3}\tan(x + 1.1) + 4 = 2$
(e) $\sqrt{5}\sin(x + 0.4) + 5 = 4$
(f) $3\cos(x - 0.1) - \sqrt{3} = 0$
(g) $\sqrt{5}\cos(x + 0.3) + 2 = 1$
(h) $3\sin(x - 0.3) + 2 = 3$
(i) $4\cos(x + 0.3) - 3 = 0$

8.6 Points of Intersection between a Trigonometric Graph and a Line

Worked Example:

Find the coordinates of the points of intersection between the line and the trigonometric graph in the range $0 \leq x \leq 360$. Give your answer correct to 1 decimal place.

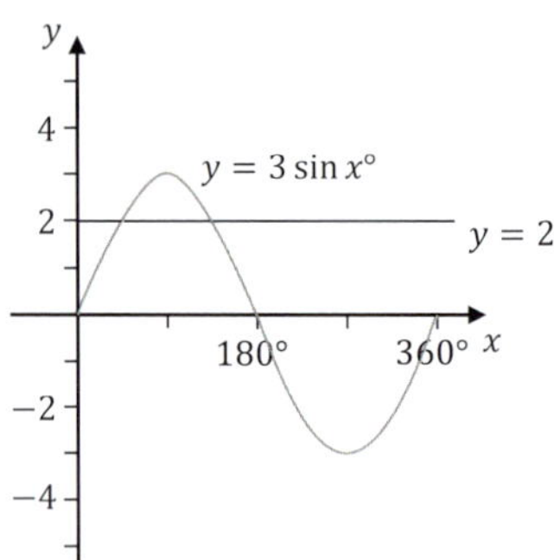

$3 \sin x° = 2$

$\sin x° = \frac{2}{3}$

$x° = 41.8°, 180° - 41.8°$

$x° = 41.8°, 138.2°$

Points of intersection $(41.8°, 2)$ and $(138.2°, 2)$

Exercise 8.6

1. Find the coordinates of the points of intersection between the line and the trigonometric graph in the range $0 \leq x \leq 360$. Give your answer correct to 1 decimal place:

(a)

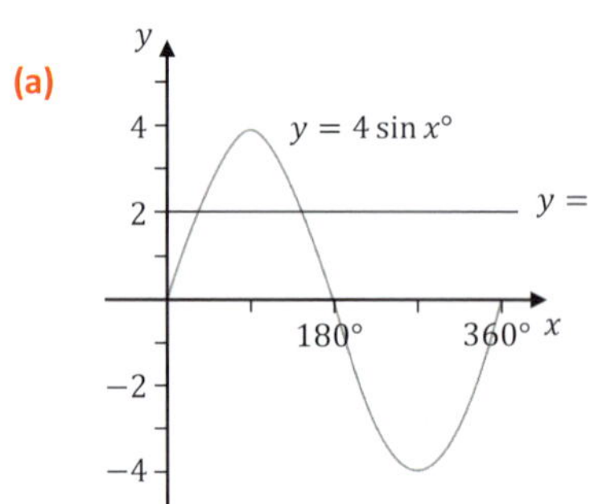

(b)

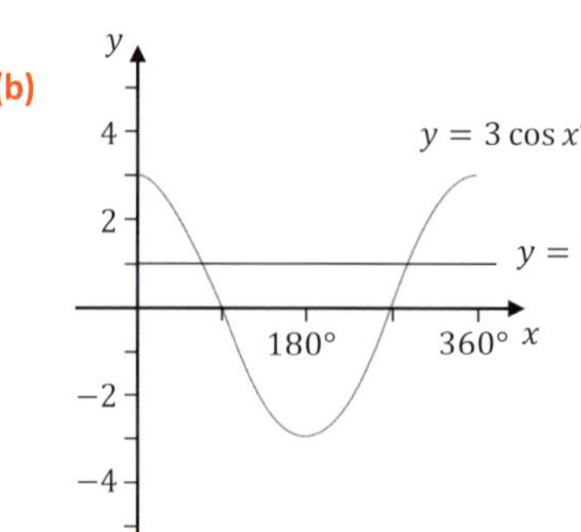

(c)

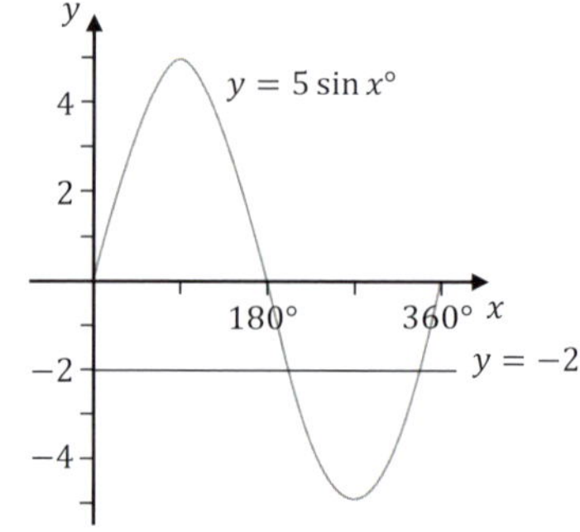

(d)

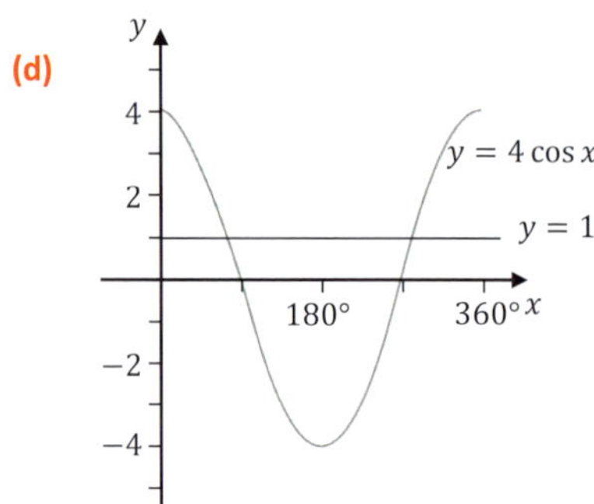

(e)

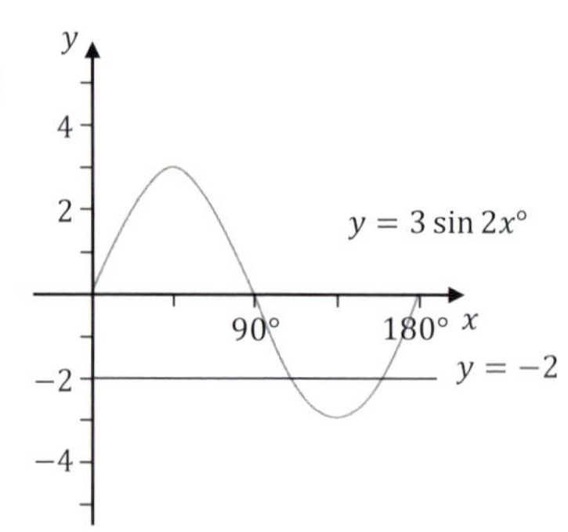

(f)

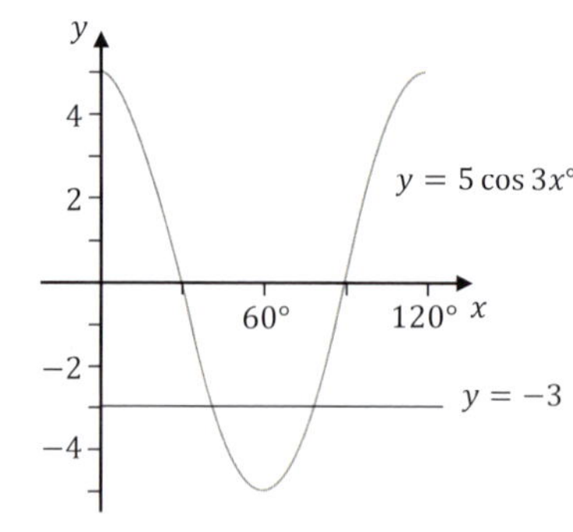

(g)

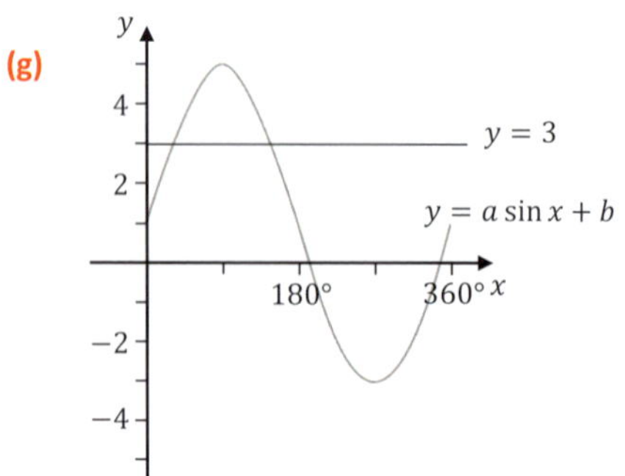

(h)

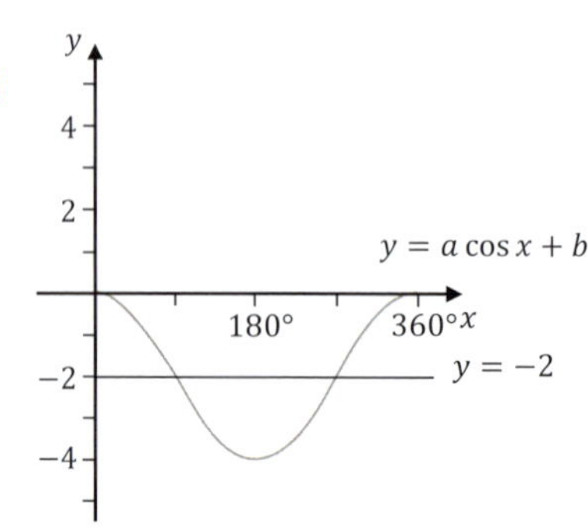

(i)

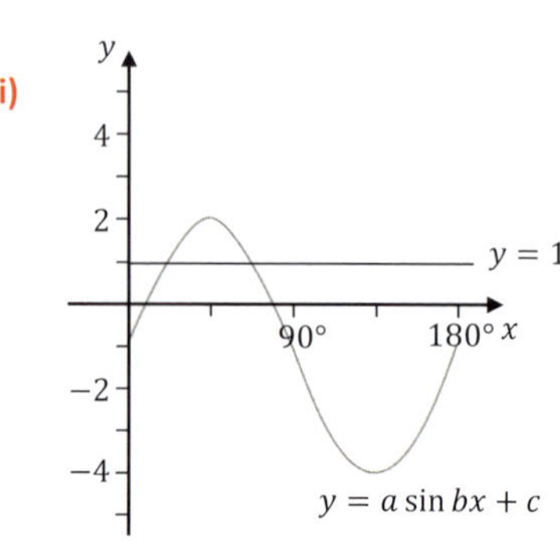

2. Find the points of intersection between the line and the trigonometric graph in the range $0 \leq x \leq 2\pi$. Give your answer correct to 2 decimal places:

(a)

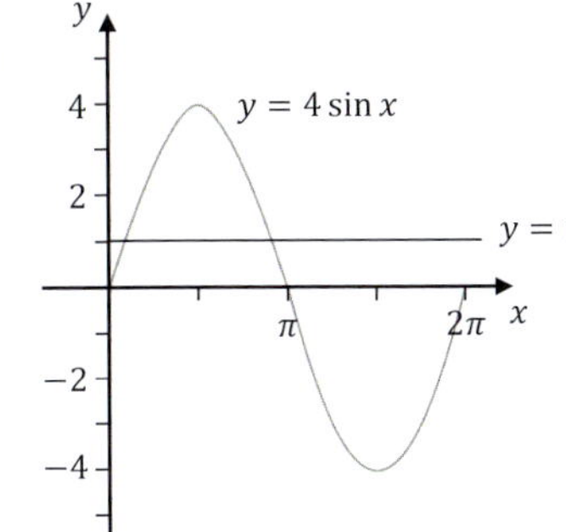

(b)

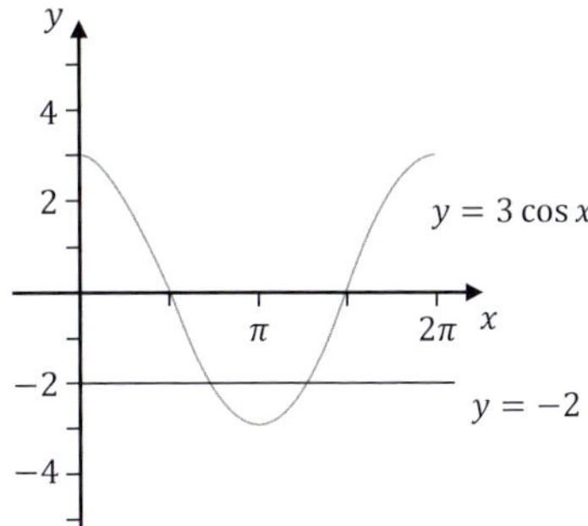

(c)

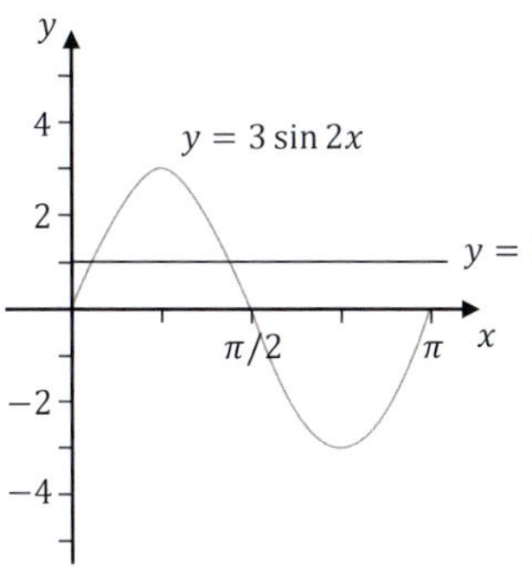

(d)

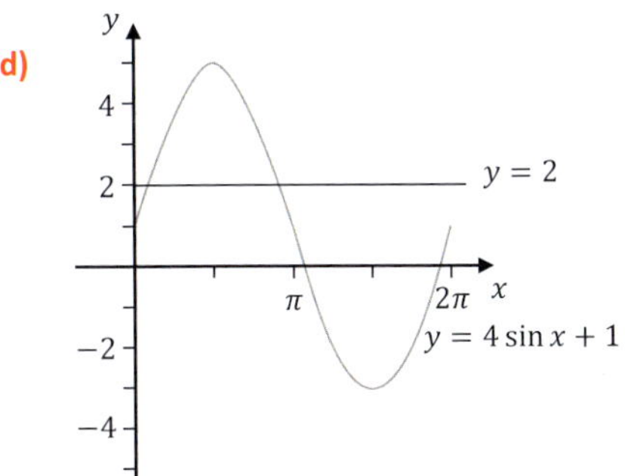

(e)

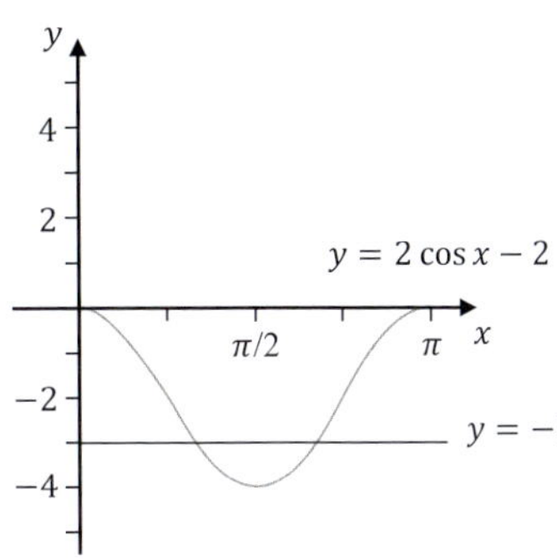

(f)

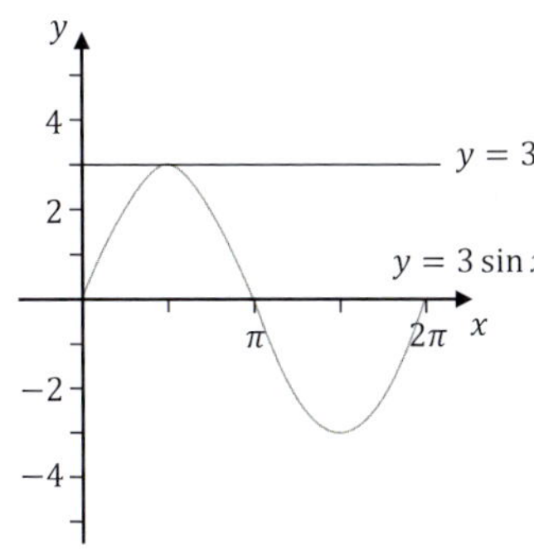

(g)

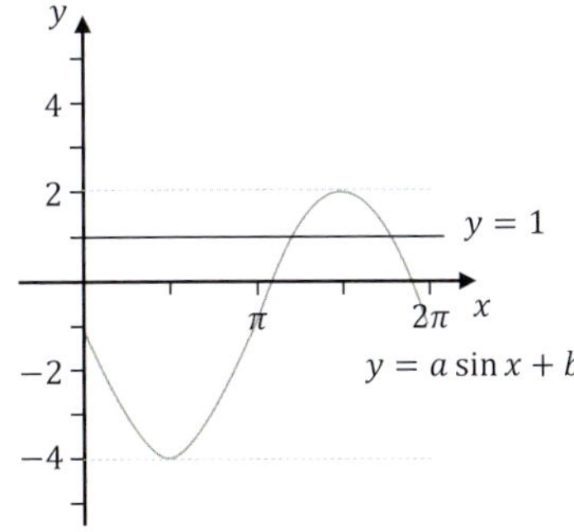

(h)

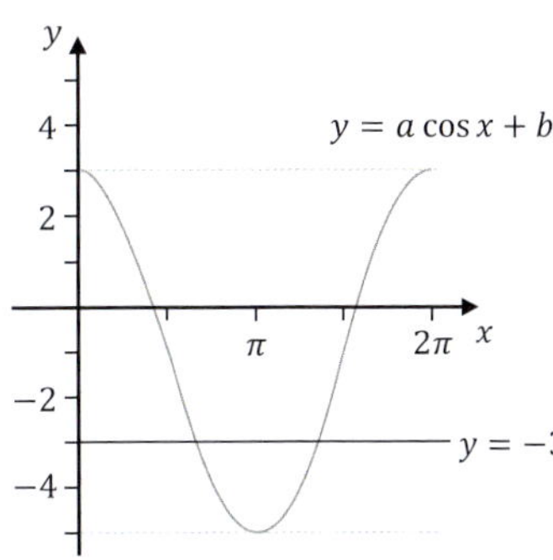

(i)

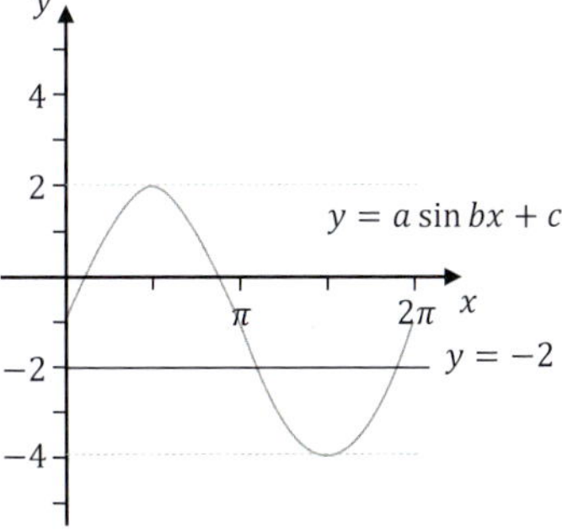

8.7 Review

Exercise 8.7

8.1 State the equation of each of the following trigonometric functions:

(a)

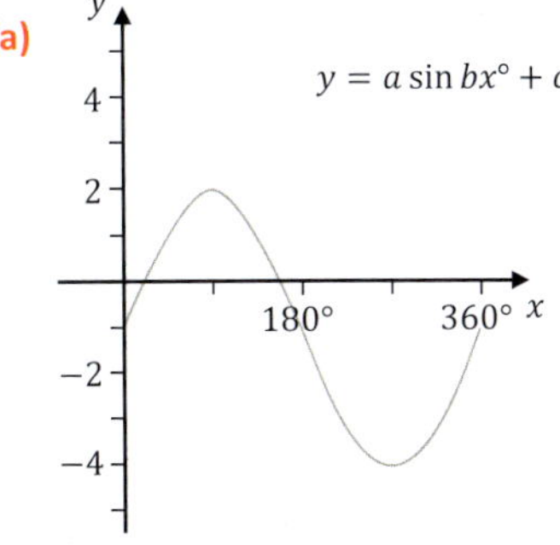

(b)

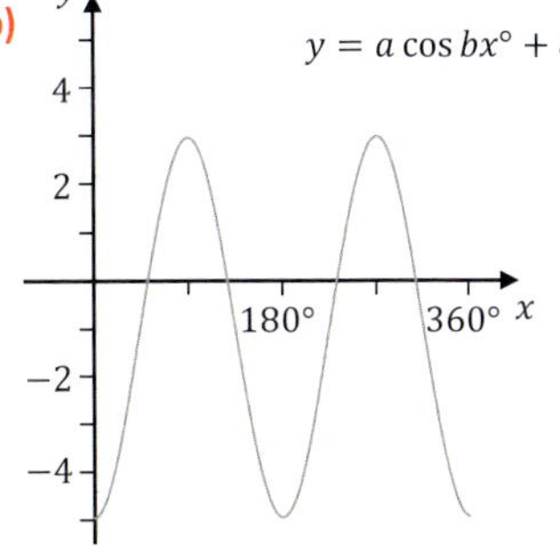

(c)

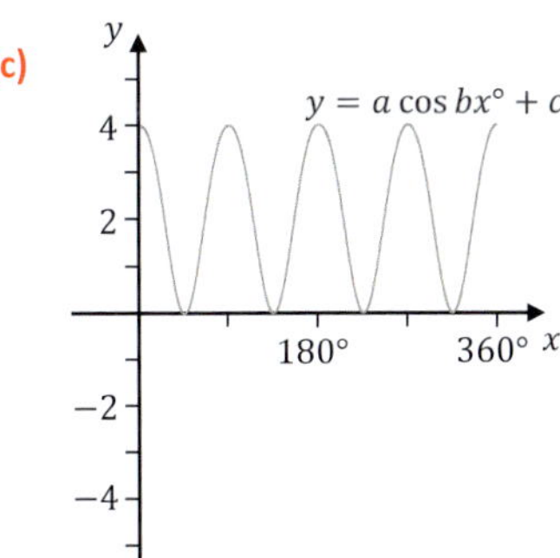

(d)

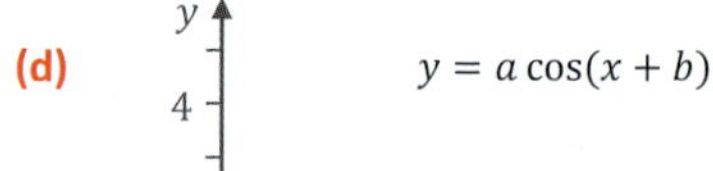

(e)

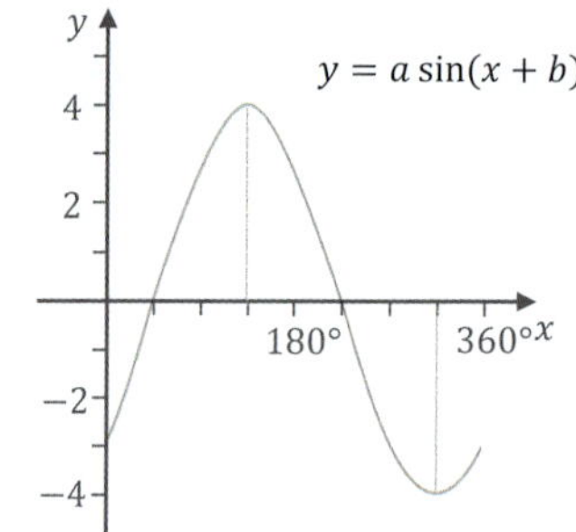

(f)

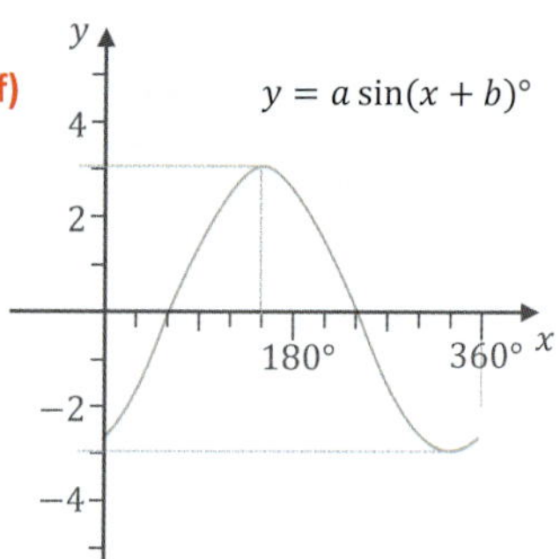

8.2 Solve the following equations for $0 \le x \le 360$. Give your answer correct to 1 decimal place:

(a) $3\tan x^\circ + 2 = 4$ **(b)** $4\sin x^\circ + 5 = 3$ **(c)** $2\cos 2x^\circ + 3 = 2$

(d) $2\sin 2x^\circ + 2 = 1$ **(e)** $4\cos(x - 10)^\circ + 5 = 3$ **(f)** $3\sin(x + 20)^\circ + 3 = 2$

8.3 Without using a calculator, find the exact value of:

(a) $\sin 45^\circ$ **(b)** $\cos 60^\circ$ **(c)** $\tan 135^\circ$ **(d)** $\sin 240^\circ$

(e) $\cos 270^\circ$ **(f)** $\cos 225^\circ$ **(g)** $\tan 315^\circ$ **(h)** $\sin 270^\circ$

(i) $\cos\frac{\pi}{3}$ **(j)** $\cos\frac{5\pi}{4}$ **(k)** $\tan\frac{2\pi}{3}$ **(l)** $\sin\frac{7\pi}{6}$

8.4 Without using a calculator, solve the following equations for $0 \le x \le 360$:

(a) $\tan x^\circ + 3 = 4$ **(b)** $4\sin x^\circ + 3 = 1$ **(c)** $2\cos 2x^\circ - \sqrt{3} = 0$

(d) $2\sin 2x^\circ - 1 = 0$ **(e)** $4\cos(x - 10)^\circ + 5 = 3$ **(f)** $2\sin(x + 25)^\circ + \sqrt{3} = 0$

8.5A Without using a calculator, solve the following equations for $0 \le x \le 2\pi$.

(a) $\sqrt{2}\sin x - 3 = 4$ **(b)** $6\tan x - 5 = 1$ **(c)** $2\cos 3x + 2 = 3$

8.5B Solve the following equations for $0 \le x \le 2\pi$. Give your answer correct to 2 decimal places:

(a) $3\tan x - 2 = 4$ **(b)** $4\sin x + 2 = 1$ **(c)** $2\cos 2x + 3 = 2$

(d) $3\sin 2x - 2 = 0$ **(e)** $4\cos(x - 0.2) + 3 = 1$ **(f)** $4\sin(x + 0.4) + 5 = 2$

8.6 Find the points of intersection between the line and the trigonometric graph in the range $0 \le x \le 2\pi$. Give your answer correct to 1 decimal place:

(a)

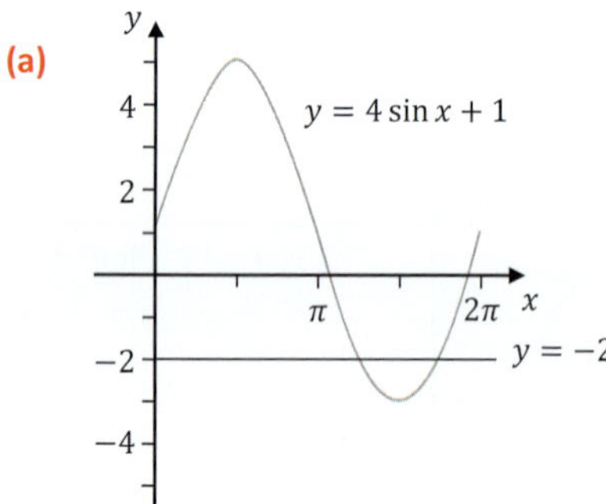

(b)

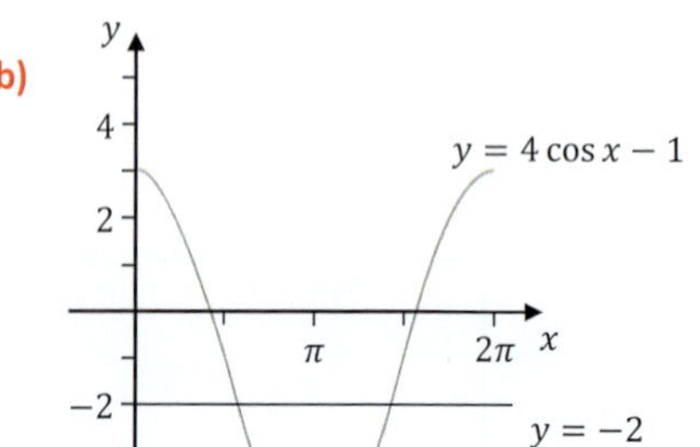

y = −2

(c)

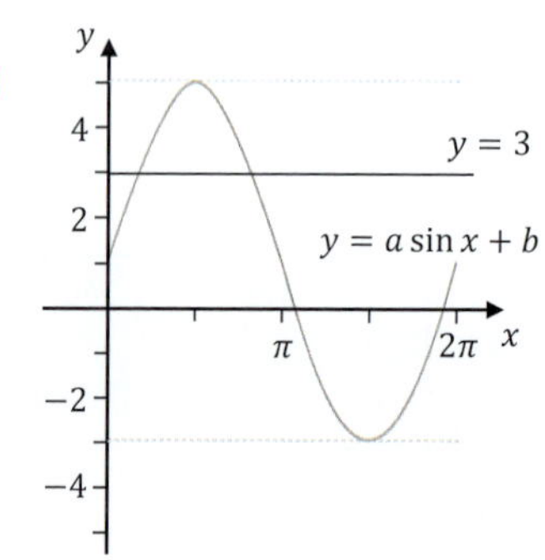

Chapter 9
Addition Formulae

Addition Formulae

The **Addition Formulae** are used as a way of expressing trigonometric functions of the sum or difference of two angles as functions of the two angles. There are four formulae to be familiar with and use for Higher Mathematics:

$$\cos(\alpha+\beta)=\cos\alpha\cos\beta-\sin\alpha\sin\beta$$
$$\cos(\alpha-\beta)=\cos\alpha\cos\beta+\sin\alpha\sin\beta$$
$$sin(\alpha+\beta)=\sin\alpha\cos\beta+\cos\alpha\sin\beta$$
$$sin(\alpha-\beta)=\sin\alpha\cos\beta-\cos\alpha\sin\beta$$

These formulae are given on a formulae sheet in Higher Mathematics.

Trigonometric Identities

Trigonometric identities are facts that are true for any value of the given variable. In National 5 we learned two trigonometric identities:

$$\tan x=\frac{\sin x}{\cos x} \quad \text{and} \quad \sin^2 x+\cos^2 x=1$$
$$\sin^2 x=1-\cos^2 x$$
$$\cos^2 x=1-\sin^2 x$$

The above identities should be memorised for Higher Mathematics.

9.1 Expanding the Addition Formulae

When expanding the addition formulae, pay careful attention to the signs in the bracket. In Higher Mathematics the formulae appear in the formula sheet, but there is value in learning and becoming familiar with them.

It is useful to come up with a memory aid to help remember these formulae. One may be that the **sine** expansions have the **same** sign as the sign in the bracket. The **cosine** expansions have a **contrasting** sign.

Exercise 9.1A

1. Expand each of the following using the addition formulae above:

(a) $\cos(\alpha+\beta)$ (b) $\cos(\alpha-\beta)$ (c) $\cos(a+b)$ (d) $\cos(a-b)$

(e) $\cos(\theta-q)$ (f) $\cos(2b+c)$ (g) $\cos(4b-2c)$ (h) $\cos(a+a)$

2. Using the trigonometric identities from National 5 (above), write your answer to **1(h)** in two other ways.

3. Expand each of the following using the addition formulae above:

(a) $\sin(\alpha+\beta)$ (b) $\sin(\alpha-\beta)$ (c) $\sin(a+b)$ (d) $\sin(a-b)$

(e) $\sin(\theta-\phi)$ (f) $\sin(3b+c)$ (g) $\sin(2b-3c)$ (h) $\sin(a+a)$

Worked Example:

Use the addition formulae to expand and simplify $\sin(x+30)°$.

Solution:

$$\sin(x+30)°=\sin x°\cos 30°+\cos x°\sin 30°=\sin x°\times\frac{\sqrt{3}}{2}+\cos x°\times\frac{1}{2}=\frac{\sqrt{3}}{2}\sin x°+\frac{1}{2}\cos x°$$

Exercise 9.1B

1. Use the addition formulae to expand and simplify each of the following:

(a) $\cos(x + 45)°$ (b) $\sin(x - 60)°$ (c) $\cos(x - 30)°$ (d) $\sin(x + 45)°$

(e) $\sin(x - 90)°$ (f) $\cos(x + 90)°$ (g) $\sin(x - 30)°$ (h) $\cos(x - 45)°$

(i) $\cos(x - 60)°$ (j) $\sin(x + 60)°$ (k) $\cos(x - 90)°$ (l) $\sin(x + 90)°$

2. Using the trigonometric identities from National 5 to expand and simplify:

(a) $\tan(x + 90)°$ (b) $\tan(x - 90)°$

3. Use the addition formulae to expand and simplify each of the following:

(a) $\cos\left(x + \frac{\pi}{3}\right)$ (b) $\sin\left(x - \frac{\pi}{6}\right)$ (c) $\cos\left(x - \frac{\pi}{2}\right)$ (d) $\sin\left(x + \frac{\pi}{3}\right)$

(e) $\sin\left(x - \frac{\pi}{4}\right)$ (f) $\cos\left(x + \frac{\pi}{6}\right)$ (g) $\sin\left(x - \frac{\pi}{2}\right)$ (h) $\cos\left(x - \frac{\pi}{4}\right)$

9.2 Using the Addition Formulae

The addition formulae can be used to evaluate expressions or find exact values for functions of the form $\cos(a \pm b)$ and $\sin(a \pm b)$.

Worked Example:

Given $0 \leq a \leq 90$ and $0 \leq b \leq 90$, find the exact value of $\cos(a + b)$, if $\sin a = \frac{2}{\sqrt{9}}$ and $\cos b = \frac{3}{5}$.

Solution:

Step 1: Sketch a triangle for each angle given and use right-angled trigonometry and Pythagoras' Theorem to find values for $\cos a$ and $\sin b$.

$\sin a = \frac{2}{3} = \frac{opp}{hyp}$

$\sqrt{(3)^2 - 2^2} = \sqrt{5}$

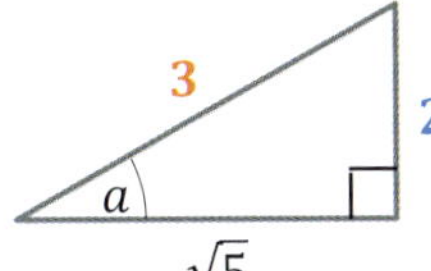

$\cos b = \frac{3}{5} = \frac{adj}{hyp}$

Pythagorean triple

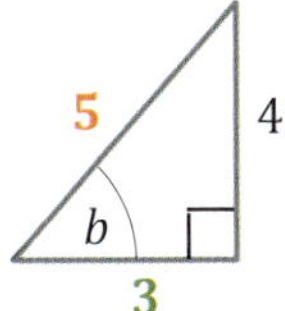

Step 2: List all the values:

$\sin a = \frac{2}{3}$, $\cos a = \frac{\sqrt{5}}{3}$, $\sin b = \frac{4}{5}$, $\cos b = \frac{3}{5}$

Step 3: Expand the trigonometric function and substitute values.

$\cos(a + b) = \cos a \cos b - \sin a \sin b = \frac{\sqrt{5}}{3} \times \frac{3}{5} - \frac{2}{3} \times \frac{4}{5} = \frac{3\sqrt{5} - 8}{15}$

Exercise 9.2

1. Given $0 \leq a \leq 90$, use the information to write an expression for each of the following:

(a) $\cos(x + a)$, if $\sin a = \frac{3}{5}$ (b) $\sin(x + a)$, if $\cos a = \frac{3}{\sqrt{10}}$ (c) $\cos(x - a)$, if $\sin a = \frac{4}{5}$

(d) $\cos(x - a)$, if $\cos a = \frac{5}{13}$ (e) $\sin(x - a)$, if $\sin a = \frac{2}{3}$ (f) $\cos(x + a)$, if $\cos a = \frac{12}{13}$

(g) $\cos(x+a)$, if $\sin a = \frac{2}{\sqrt{11}}$ **(h)** $\sin(x+a)$, if $\cos a = \frac{2}{\sqrt{10}}$ **(i)** $\cos(x-a)$, if $\sin a = \frac{15}{17}$

2. Given $0 \le a \le 90$ and $0 \le b \le 90$, use the information to find an exact value for each of the following:

(a) $\cos(a+b)$, if $\sin a = \frac{3}{5}$ and $\cos b = \frac{5}{13}$ **(b)** $\sin(a+b)$, if $\sin a = \frac{4}{5}$ and $\cos b = \frac{12}{13}$

(c) $\sin(a-b)$, if $\sin a = \frac{3}{\sqrt{10}}$ and $\cos b = \frac{1}{\sqrt{5}}$ **(d)** $\cos(a-b)$, if $\sin a = \frac{8}{17}$ and $\cos b = \frac{3}{5}$

(e) $\cos(a+b)$, if $\sin a = \frac{12}{13}$ and $\cos b = \frac{2}{3}$ **(f)** $\sin(a+b)$, if $\sin a = \frac{5}{6}$ and $\cos b = \frac{15}{17}$

(g) $\sin(a-b)$, if $\sin a = \frac{1}{\sqrt{5}}$ and $\cos b = \frac{1}{3}$ **(h)** $\cos(a-b)$, if $\sin a = \frac{2}{\sqrt{13}}$ and $\cos b = \frac{4}{5}$

3. Use the information given in the diagrams below to find the exact of: **(a)** $\cos(a+b)$, **(b)** $\sin(a+b)$.

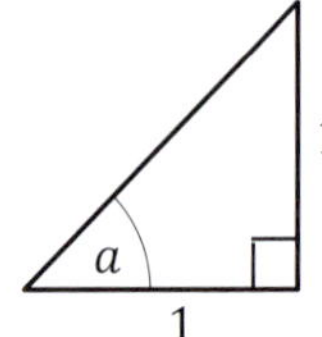

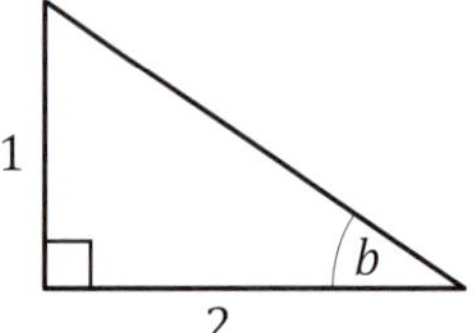

4. Use the information given in the diagrams below to find the exact of: **(a)** $\cos(a+b)$, **(b)** $\sin(a+b)$.

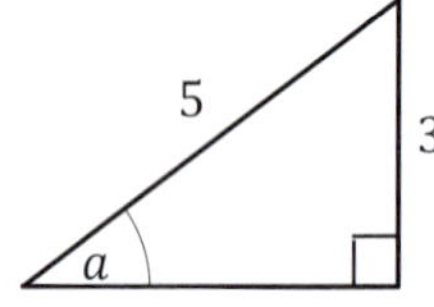

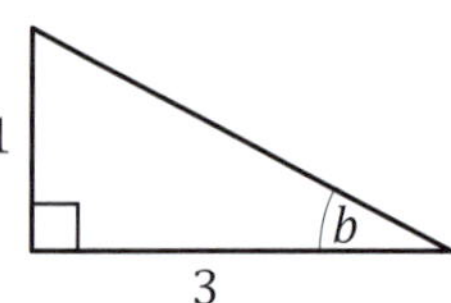

5. Use the information given in the diagrams below to find the exact of: **(a)** $\cos(b-a)$, **(b)** $\sin(b-a)$.

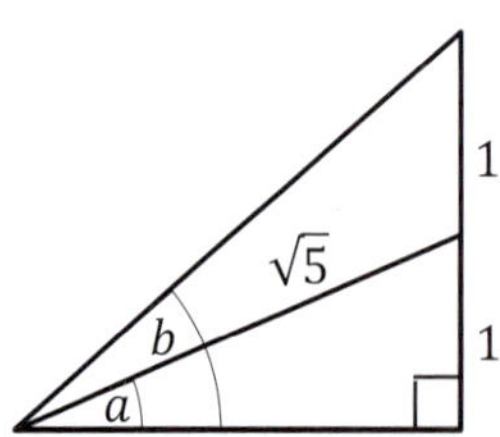

6. By expressing each of the following as the sum or difference of two angles, find the exact value of:

(a) $\cos 105°$ **(b)** $\sin 15°$ **(c)** $\cos 15°$ **(d)** $\sin 75°$

(e) $\cos 120°$ **(f)** $\sin 105°$ **(g)** $\cos 75°$ **(h)** $\sin \frac{\pi}{12}$

(i) $\cos \frac{7\pi}{12}$ **(j)** $\sin \frac{5\pi}{12}$ **(k)** $\cos \frac{\pi}{12}$ **(l)** $\sin \frac{7\pi}{12}$

7. By expressing each of the following as the sum or difference of two angles, find the exact value of:

(a) $\sin 165°$ **(b)** $\sin 255°$ **(c)** $\cos 345°$ **(d)** $\cos 195°$

(e) $\sin 345°$ **(f)** $\cos 165°$ **(g)** $\sin 195°$ **(h)** $\cos 255°$

9.3 Using the Double Angle Formulae

The **double angle formulae** are the result of using the addition formulae on a trigonometric function with a repeated angle, **i.e.** $\sin(a + a) = \sin 2a$ and $\cos(a + a) = \cos 2a$.

$$\sin 2a = 2 \sin a \cos a$$

$$\cos 2a = \cos^2 a - \sin^2 a$$

$$= 2\cos^2 a - 1$$

$$= 1 - 2\sin^2 a$$

$\sin 2a$

Expanding the sine function gives just one formula:

$\sin 2a = \sin(a + a) = \sin a \cos a + \cos a \sin a = 2 \sin a \cos a$

$\cos 2a$

The cosine function gives three possibilities. These are derived from rearranging $\sin^2 x + \cos^2 x = 1$ into the form $\sin^2 x = 1 - \cos^2 x$ or $\cos^2 x = 1 - \sin^2 x$, then substituting:

$\cos 2a = \cos(a + a) = \cos a \cos a - \sin a \sin a = \cos^2 a - \sin^2 a$

$\cos^2 a - \sin^2 a = \cos^2 a - (1 - \cos^2 a) = 2\cos^2 a - 1$

$\cos^2 a - \sin^2 a = (1 - \sin^2 a) - \sin^2 a = 1 - 2\sin^2 a$

Worked Example:

Given $\sin x = \frac{3}{4}$, find the exact value of **(a)** $\sin 2x$ and **(b)** $\cos 2x$.

Solution:

$\sin x = \frac{3}{4}$

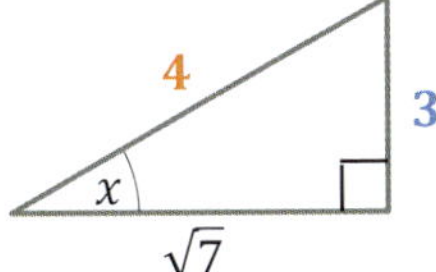

$\sqrt{(4)^2 - 3^2} = \sqrt{7}$

$\sin x = \frac{3}{4}, \cos x = \frac{\sqrt{7}}{4}$

(a) $\sin 2x = 2 \sin x \cos x = 2 \times \frac{3}{4} \times \frac{\sqrt{7}}{4} = \frac{6\sqrt{7}}{16} = \frac{3\sqrt{7}}{8}$ **(b)** $\cos 2x = 2\cos^2 x - 1 = 2 \times \frac{7}{16} - \frac{16}{16} = \frac{-2}{16} = -\frac{1}{8}$

NB: When using $\cos 2x$, any of the alternatives may be substituted, but $\cos^2 x - \sin^2 x$ is rarely used.

Exercise 9.3

1. Given $0 \leq x \leq 90$, use the information to find the exact value of:

(a) $\cos 2x$, if $\sin x = \frac{3}{5}$

(b) $\sin 2x$, if $\cos x = \frac{5}{13}$

(c) $\cos 2x$, if $\tan x = \frac{5}{\sqrt{11}}$

(d) $\sin 2x$, if $\cos x = \frac{15}{17}$

(e) $\cos 2x$, if $\sin x = \frac{4}{7}$

(f) $\sin 2x$, if $\cos x = \frac{9}{10}$

(g) $\cos 2x$, if $\tan x = \frac{2}{3}$

(h) $\sin 2x$, if $\cos x = \frac{1}{4}$

(i) $\cos 2x$, if $\tan x = \frac{8}{15}$

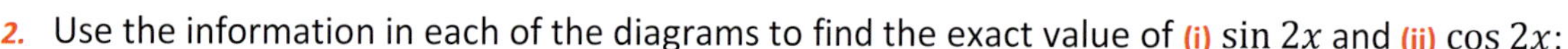

2. Use the information in each of the diagrams to find the exact value of (i) $\sin 2x$ and (ii) $\cos 2x$:

(a)

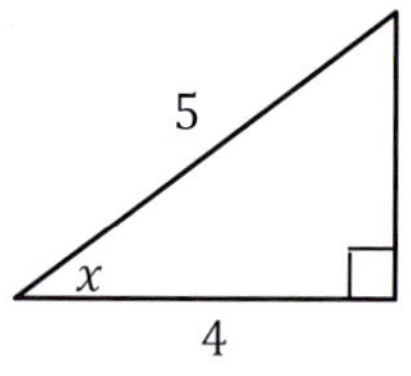

(b)

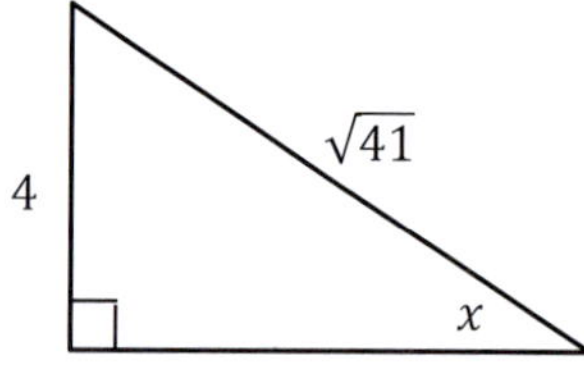

(c)

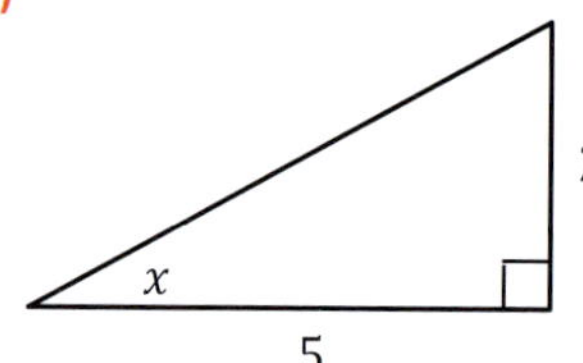

(d)

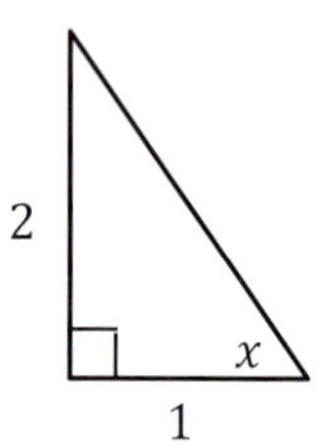

(e)

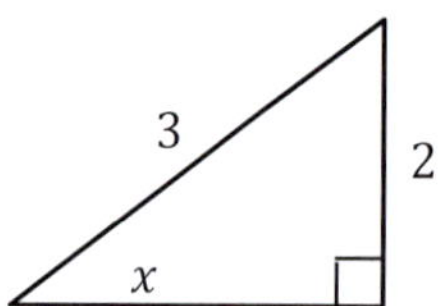

(f)

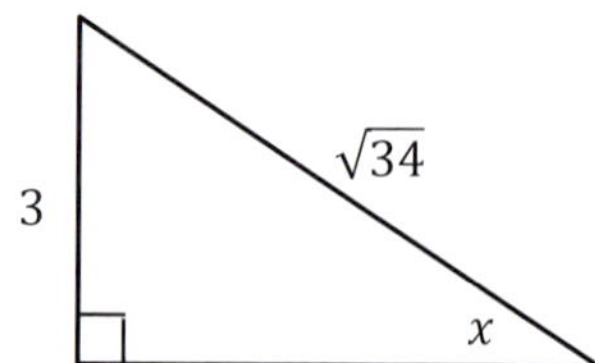

(g)

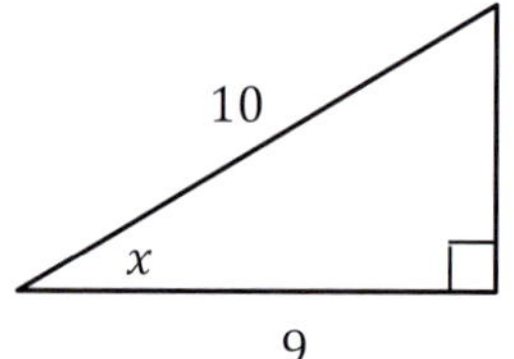

(h)

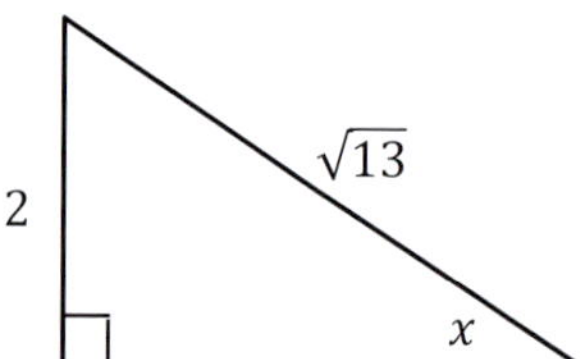

(i)

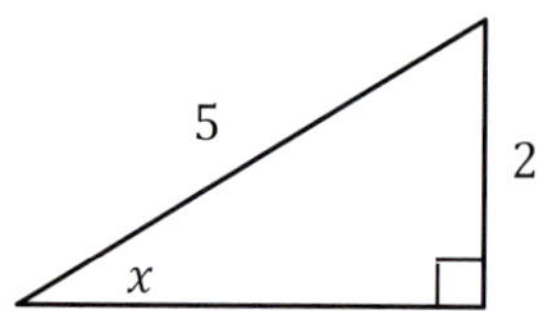

3. Use the information in each of the diagrams to find the exact value of (i) $\sin 2\theta$ and (ii) $\cos 2\theta$:

(a)

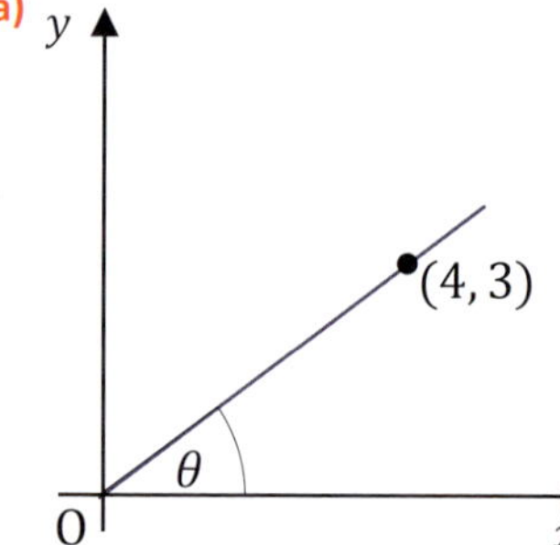

(b)

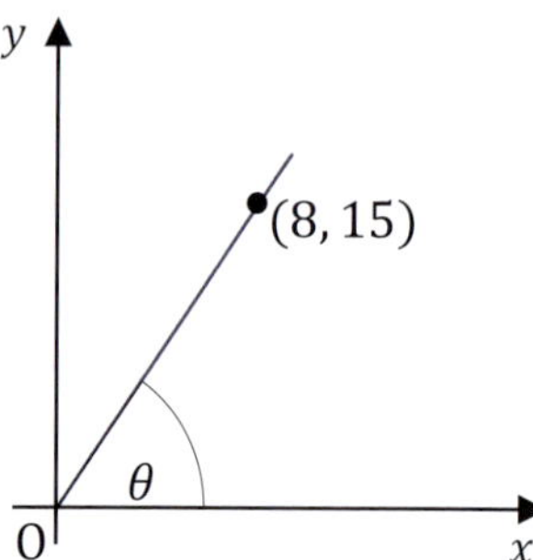

(c)

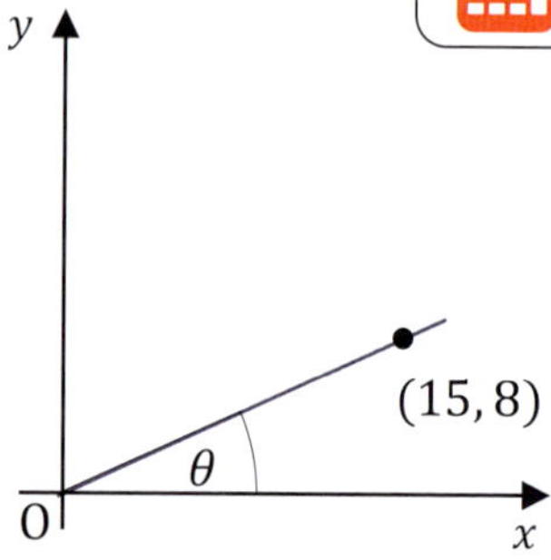

(d)

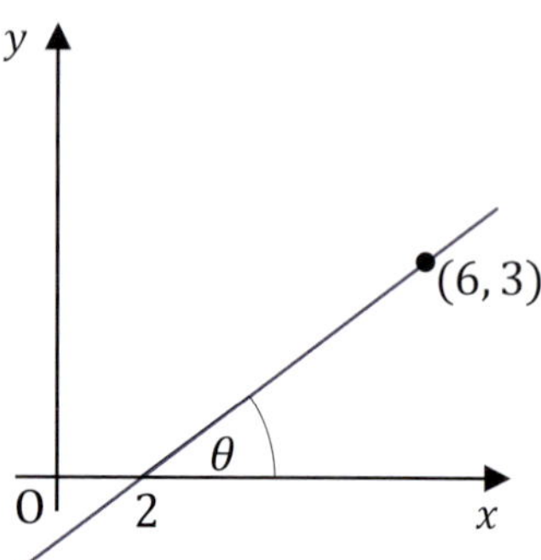

(e)

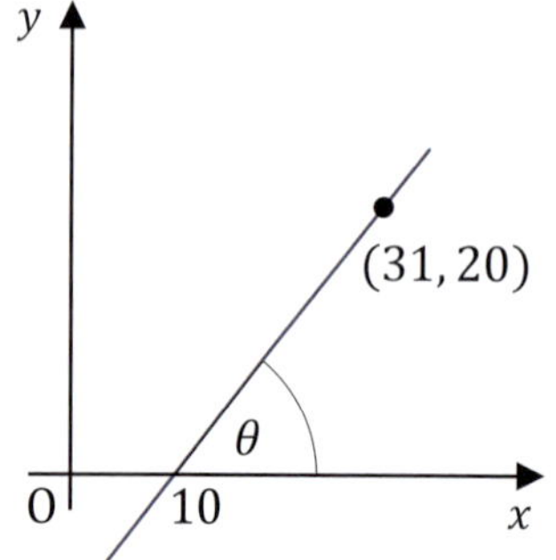

(f)

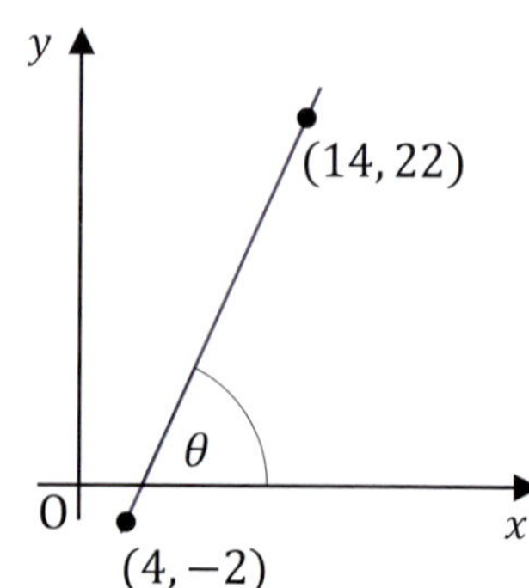

4. Given that $\sin\theta = \frac{3}{4}$, find the exact value of (a) $\sin 2\theta$, (b) $\cos 2\theta$ and (c) $\tan 2\theta$.

5. Given that $\cos\theta = \frac{1}{\sqrt{5}}$, find the exact value of (a) $\sin 2\theta$, (b) $\cos 2\theta$ and (c) $\tan 2\theta$.

6. Given that $\tan\theta = \frac{2}{3}$, find the exact value of (a) $\sin 2\theta$, (b) $\cos 2\theta$ and (c) $\tan 2\theta$.

7. (a) Given that $\tan\theta = \frac{1}{2}$, find the exact value of $\sin 2\theta$.

   (b) By expressing $\sin 4\theta$ as $\sin(2\theta + 2\theta)$, find the exact value of $\sin 4\theta$.

8. (a) Given that $\tan\theta = \frac{1}{3}$, find the exact value of $\cos 2\theta$.

   (b) By expressing $\cos 3\theta$ as $\cos(2\theta + \theta)$, find the exact value of $\cos 3\theta$.

9.4 Using Trigonometric Identities

We are familiar with trigonometric identities from National 5 Mathematics. These are facts or equalities that are true for every value of the trigonometric function. In National 5, we learned two identities, which we have already used in this chapter:

$$\tan x = \frac{\sin x}{\cos x} \text{ and } \sin^2 x + \cos^2 x = 1$$

In Higher Mathematics, we now also need to use the double angle formulae to prove identities.

$$\sin 2a = 2\sin a\cos a$$

$$\begin{aligned}\cos 2a &= \cos^2 a - \sin^2 a\\ &= 2\cos^2 a - 1\\ &= 1 - 2\sin^2 a\end{aligned}$$

Worked Example:

Show that $3\cos^2 x - \sin^2 x - 1 = 2\cos 2x$.

Solution: Start with the left-hand-side and work towards the right.

$LHS = 3\cos^2 x - \sin^2 x - 1$

$= 3\cos^2 x - (1 - \cos^2 x) - 1$

$= 4\cos^2 x - 2$

$= 2(2\cos^2 x - 1)$

$= 2\cos 2x$

$= RHS.$

Trigonometric identities at Higher level are more difficult as there is often more than one substitution that can be carried. Attention needs to be paid to what the right-hand-side of the equation needs to look like.

Exercise 9.4

1. Show that:

(a) $\cos 2x - 1 = -2\sin^2 x$

(b) $\cos 2x + 1 = 2\cos^2 x$

(c) $\sin 2x\tan x = 2\sin^2 x$

(d) $\dfrac{\cos 2x + 1}{2} = \cos^2 x$

(e) $\dfrac{\sin 2x}{\tan x} = 2\cos^2 x$

(f) $\dfrac{\cos 2x\tan 2x}{\cos x} = 2\sin x$

(g) $\dfrac{\sin 2x}{2\sin x} - \cos^3 x = \cos x\sin^2 x$

(h) $\dfrac{\cos 2x}{\cos x + \sin x} = \cos x - \sin x$

(i) $\dfrac{2\sin x\cos x}{2\cos^2 x - 1} = \tan 2x$

(j) $\dfrac{\sin 4x}{2\cos 2x} = 2\sin x\cos x$

(k) $\dfrac{\cos 2x + 1}{\cos x} = 2\cos x$

(l) $\dfrac{2 - 2\cos 2x}{\sin x\cos x} = 4\tan x$

2. By using the addition formulae, show that:

(a) $\cos 3x = 4\cos^3 x - 3\cos x$

(b) $\sin 3x = 3\sin x - 4\sin^3 x$

3. Show that:

(a) $\tan(a+b) = \dfrac{\tan a + \tan b}{1 - \tan a \tan b}$

(b) $\tan 2x = \dfrac{2\tan x}{1 - \tan^2 x}$

9.5 Solving Trigonometric Equations using the Double Angle Formulae

We have already solved equations of the form $\cos(x \pm a) = b$ and $\sin ax = b$. If there is a combination of trigonometric functions, **e.g.** $\sin 2x + \sin x = b$ or $\cos 2x + \cos x = b$, we can use the double angle formulae to solve these equations. To do so, we substitute the double angle function and then factorise the equation.

Worked Examples:

1. Solve the equation $\sin 2x° - \cos x° = 0$ for $0 \le x \le 360$.

Solution:

$\sin 2x° - \cos x° = 0$

$2\sin x° \cos x° - \cos x° = 0$

$\cos x°(2\sin x° - 1) = 0$

$\cos x° = 0$ or $2\sin x° - 1 = 0$

$x° = 90°, 270°$ or $\sin x° = \frac{1}{2}$

$x° = 30°, 150°$

$x° = 30°, 90°, 150°, 270°$

In this example, the only option is to replace $\sin 2x$ with $2\sin x\cos x$. Then factorise the expression. There are now two equations to solve, the blue and the green, in the same way as solving a quadratic equation.

2. Solve the equation $\cos 2x - \cos x = 0$ for $0 \le x \le 2\pi$.

Solution:

$\cos 2x - \cos x = 0$

$(2\cos^2 x - 1) - \cos x = 0$

$2\cos^2 x - \cos x - 1 = 0$

$(2\cos x + 1)(\cos x - 1) = 0$

$2\cos x + 1 = 0$ or $\cos x - 1 = 0$

$\cos x = -\frac{1}{2}$ or $\cos x = 1$

$x_A = \frac{\pi}{3}$ $\quad x = 0, 2\pi$

$x = \frac{2\pi}{3}, \frac{4\pi}{3}$

$x = 0, \frac{2\pi}{3}, \frac{4\pi}{3}, 2\pi$

In this example, there are three possibilities for $\cos 2x$ but as the other term is $-\cos x$, we should use the identity that only contains $\cos x$. This gives a trinomial expression to factorise (line 3).

NB: It may be easier to let $\cos x = c$ and factorise the expression $2c^2 - c - 1$. As before, there are now two equations to solve: the blue and the green.

NB: If the solutions of one of the equations do not exist, simply score that equation out.

Exercise 9.5A

1. Solve the following equations for $0 \le x \le 360$:

(a) $2\sin^2 x° - \sin x° - 1 = 0$

(b) $2\cos^2 x° + \cos x° - 1 = 0$

(c) $2\sin^2 x° - 3\sin x° + 1 = 0$

2. Solve the following equations for $0 \leq x \leq 2\pi$:

(a) $2\sin^2 x + 3\sin x + 1 = 0$ (b) $2\cos^2 x + 3\cos x + 1 = 0$ (c) $4\sin^2 x - 1 = 0$

3. Solve the following equations for $0 \leq x \leq 360$:

(a) $\sin 2x° - \sin x° = 0$ (b) $\sin 2x° + \cos x° = 0$ (c) $2\cos x° - 2\sin 2x° = 0$

4. Solve the following equations for $0 \leq x \leq 2\pi$:

(a) $\sin 2x = \sqrt{3}\sin x$ (b) $\sin 2x - \sqrt{2}\cos x = 0$ (c) $\sin 2x = \sqrt{3}\cos x$

5. Solve the following equations for $0 \leq x \leq 360$:

(a) $\cos 2x° + \cos x° = 0$ (b) $\cos 2x° + 3\cos x° + 2 = 0$ (c) $\sin x° - \cos 2x° = 0$

6. Solve the following equations for $0 \leq x \leq 2\pi$:

(a) $\cos 2x = 5\sin x + 3$ (b) $\cos 2x - 2\cos x - 3 = 0$ (c) $\cos 2x = \cos x$

7. Solve the following equations for $0 \leq x \leq 360$:

(a) $2\sin 2x° = \tan x°$ (b) $\sin 2x° = 2\sin^2 x°$ (c) $\sin 2x° = 2\cos^2 x°$

Exercise 9.5B

1. Solve the following equations for $0 \leq x \leq 360$. Give your answers correct to 1 decimal place:

(a) $\cos 2x° - 2 = \cos x°$ (b) $\cos 2x° + 18\sin x° + 17 = 0$ (c) $\cos 2x° + 7\cos x° + 6 = 0$

2. Solve the following equations for $0 \leq x \leq 2\pi$. Give your answers correct to 2 decimal places:

(a) $3\cos 2x - 7\cos x = 0$ (b) $\sin x - 1 = 2\cos 2x$ (c) $2\cos 2x - 5\cos x + 3 = 0$

9.6 Review

Exercise 9.6A

9.1 Use the addition formulae to expand and evaluate each of the following:

(a) $\sin(x + 45)°$ (b) $\cos\left(x + \frac{\pi}{6}\right)$ (c) $\sin\left(x + \frac{\pi}{3}\right)$

9.2 Given $0 \leq a \leq \frac{\pi}{2}$ and $0 \leq b \leq \frac{\pi}{2}$, find an exact value for each of the following:

(a) $\cos(a + b)$, if $\sin a = \frac{4}{5}$ and $\cos b = \frac{2}{3}$ (b) $\sin(a + b)$, if $\sin a = \frac{3}{\sqrt{10}}$ and $\cos b = \frac{5}{13}$

9.3 Given $0 \leq x \leq 90$, find the exact value of:

(a) $\cos 2x°$, if $\sin x° = \frac{2}{\sqrt{5}}$ (b) $\sin 2x°$, if $\cos x° = \frac{5}{\sqrt{34}}$ (c) $\cos 2x°$, if $\tan x° = \frac{2}{3}$

9.4 Show:

(a) $\dfrac{\sin 2x}{2\sin x} - \cos x \sin^2 x = \cos^3 x$ (b) $\dfrac{\cos 2x}{\cos x + \sin x} = \cos x - \sin x$ (c) $\cos 2x - \cos^2 x = -\sin^2 x$

9.5 Solve the following equations for $0 \leq x \leq 2\pi$:

(a) $\sin 2x = \sqrt{3}\cos x$ (b) $3\cos 2x - 11\cos x + 7 = 0$

Exercise 9.6B

1. A right-angled triangle has sides and angles as shown in the diagram.

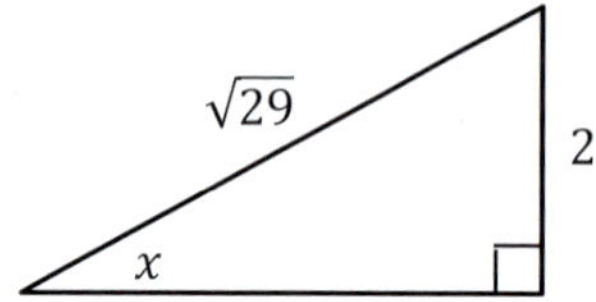

Find exact values of:

(a) $\sin 2x$,

(b) $\cos 2x$.

2. Given $\tan 2x = \frac{5}{12}$, find the exact values of:

(a) $\sin 2x$,

(b) $\sin x$.

3. Line OA is inclined at an angle of θ radians to the x-axis. A is point $(5, 12)$. Find the exact values of:

(a) $\sin 2\theta$,

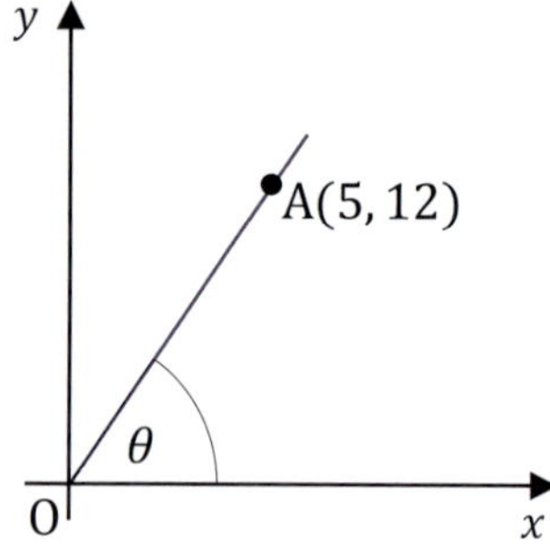

(b) $\cos 2\theta$,

(c) $\tan 2\theta$.

4. Functions $f(x) = \cos x$ and $g(x) = \left(x - \frac{\pi}{4}\right)$, $h(x) = 2x$.

(a) Find an expression for $f\big(g(x)\big)$.

(b) Find an expression for $f\big(h(x)\big)$.

(c) Given $\tan x = \frac{1}{2}$, find an exact value for $f\big(h(x)\big)$.

5. A line is given by the equation $2y - x + 4 = 0$. The angle the line makes with the positive direction of the x-axis is θ radians. Find the exact values of:

(a) $\sin 2\theta$,

(b) $\cos 2\theta$.

6. Using the information given in the diagram opposite, find an exact value for:

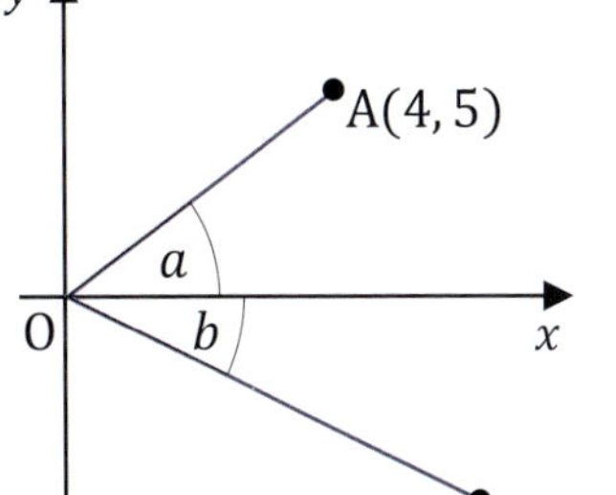

(a) $\sin(a + b)$,

(b) $\cos(a + b)$.

7. Functions $f(x) = \sin x$ and $g(x) = \left(x + \frac{\pi}{6}\right)$.

(a) Find an expression for $f\big(g(x)\big)$.

(b) Expand and evaluate $f\big(g(x)\big)$.

8. A right-angled triangle has sides and angles as shown in the diagram.

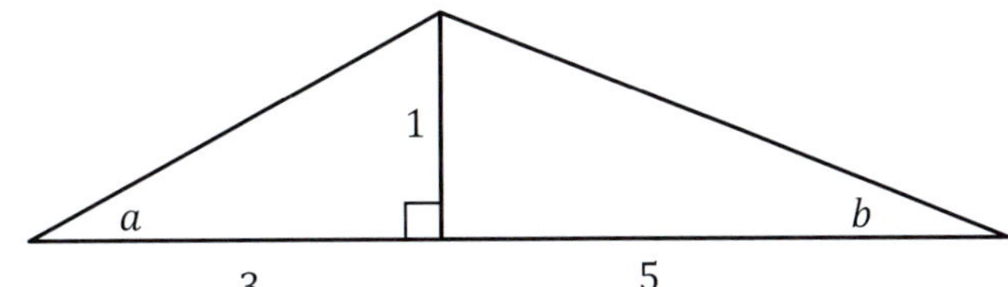

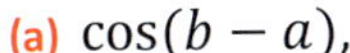

Find the exact values of:

(a) $\cos(a + b)$,

(b) $\sin(a + b)$,

(c) $\sin 2a$.

9. A right-angled triangle has sides and angles as shown in the diagram. Find the exact values of:

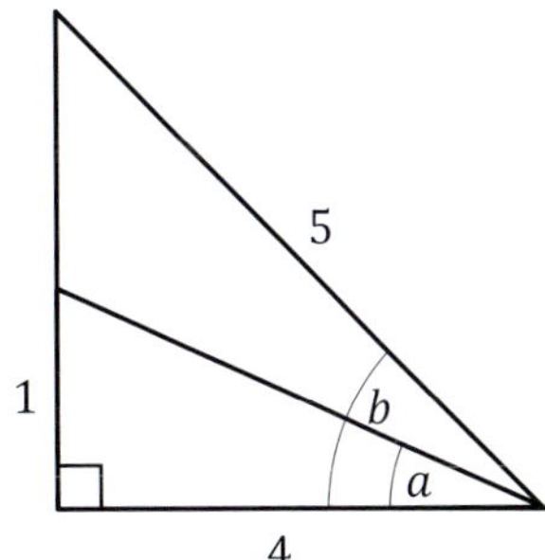

(a) $\cos(b - a)$,

(b) $\sin(b - a)$,

(c) $\cos 2a$.

10. A line is given by the equation $4y - 3x + 4 = 0$. The angle the line makes with the positive direction of the x-axis is 2θ radians. Find the exact values of:

(a) $\sin 2\theta$,

(b) $\cos 2\theta$,

(c) $\cos \theta$.

11. Functions $f(x) = \cos x$ and $g(x) = \left(x + \frac{\pi}{4}\right)$, $h(x) = 2x$.

(a) Find an expression for $f\big(g(x)\big)$.

(b) Find an expression for $h\big(g(x)\big)$.

(c) Given $\tan x = \frac{1}{3}$, find an exact value for $f\big(h(g(x))\big)$.

Chapter 10
The Wave Function

The Wave Function

The **Wave Function** is a trigonometric function that can express the sum or difference of two trigonometric functions. When using the addition formulae, we expanded a trigonometric function of the sum or difference of angles. With the wave function we do the opposite.

10.1 Using the Wave Function

When an expression is made up of two different trigonometric functions in the form $\mathbf{a}\cos x \pm \mathbf{b}\sin x$, we can express this function as one trigonometric function of the form $k\sin(x \pm \alpha)$ or $k\cos(x \pm \alpha)$, where $k > 0$. We need to identify the values of k and α: in order to do this, we need to use the addition formulae to expand the wave function, then equate the coefficients a and b with their respective trigonometric functions.

Step 1: Expand using the addition formula, for example:

$$k\cos(x - \alpha) = k(\cos x \cos \alpha + \sin x \sin \alpha)$$

$$= k\cos x \cos\alpha + k\sin x \sin\alpha = k\cos\alpha \cos x + k\sin\alpha \sin x$$

Step 2: Equate the coefficients of $\mathbf{a}\cos x + \mathbf{b}\sin x$ with the correct trigonometric function, being careful to ensure the correct coefficient.

e.g. $k\cos\alpha = \mathbf{a}$ and $k\sin\alpha = \mathbf{b}$

NB: In step 1 the $\cos\alpha$ and $\sin\alpha$ were moved to the front to make equating the coefficients easier.

Step 3: To calculate k, square and sum the coefficients, then square root the answer. This will eliminate $\sin\alpha$ and $\cos\alpha$.
(**Proof:** $k^2\sin^2\alpha + k^2\cos^2\alpha = k^2(\sin^2\alpha + \cos^2\alpha) = k^2\,(1) = k^2$)

Step 4: To calculate α, use $\sin\alpha$ and $\cos\alpha$ to find $\tan\alpha$.

$$\tan\alpha = \frac{k\sin\alpha}{k\cos\alpha} = \frac{\sin\alpha}{\cos\alpha}$$

Now use trigonometry to determine the quadrant. A good idea is to draw a CAST diagram and tick which quadrants are positive or negative (see worked examples).

Step 5: Write answer in desired form.

Worked Examples:

1. Express $2\cos x° + 3\sin x°$ in the form $k\cos(x - \alpha)°$, where $k > 0$ and $0 < \alpha < 360$.

Solution:

Step 1: $k\cos(x - \alpha)° = k(\cos x° \cos\alpha° + \sin x° \sin\alpha°)$
$= k\cos x° \cos\alpha° + k\sin x° \sin\alpha° = k\cos\alpha° \cos x° + k\sin\alpha° \sin x°$

Step 2: $2\cos x° + 3\sin x°$
$\therefore k\cos\alpha° = 2$ and $k\sin\alpha° = 3$

Step 3: $k = \sqrt{2^2 + 3^2} = \sqrt{13}$

Step 4: $\tan \alpha^\circ = \dfrac{\sin \alpha^\circ}{\cos \alpha^\circ} = \dfrac{3}{2}$

$\alpha^\circ = \tan^{-1}\dfrac{3}{2} = 56.3^\circ$ (1 d.p.)

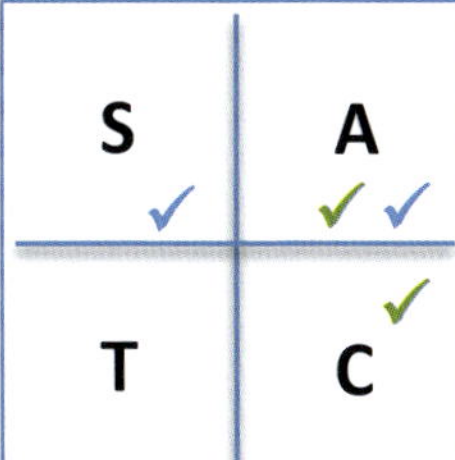

NB: In step 4 the signs for each function tell us the quadrant of α. Tick the quadrants where each is positive (in this question both $k\cos\alpha$ and $k\sin\alpha$ are positive). The quadrant with two ticks is the quadrant we use.

Step 5: $2\cos x^\circ + 3\sin x^\circ = \sqrt{13}\cos(x - 56.3)^\circ$

Exercise 10.1A

1. Express the following expressions in the required form:

(a) $\cos x^\circ + \sqrt{3}\sin x^\circ$ in the form $k\cos(x - \alpha)^\circ$ where $k > 0$ and $0 < x < 360$.

(b) $2\cos x^\circ - \sqrt{3}\sin x^\circ$ in the form $k\cos(x + \alpha)^\circ$ where $k > 0$ and $0 < x < 360$.

(c) $2\sin x^\circ + 5\cos x^\circ$ in the form $k\sin(x + \alpha)^\circ$ where $k > 0$ and $0 < x < 360$.

(d) $\cos x - 2\sin x$ in the form $k\cos(x + \alpha)^\circ$ where $k > 0$ and $0 < x < 360$.

(e) $\sin x - 2\cos x$ in the form $k\sin(x - \alpha)^\circ$ where $k > 0$ and $0 < x < 360$.

(f) $5\cos x^\circ - 2\sin x^\circ$ in the form $k\cos(x + \alpha)^\circ$ where $k > 0$ and $0 < x < 360$.

(g) $3\sin x^\circ + 2\cos x^\circ$ in the form $k\sin(x + \alpha)^\circ$ where $k > 0$ and $0 < x < 360$.

(h) $\sin x^\circ - 4\cos x^\circ$ in the form $k\sin(x - \alpha)^\circ$ where $k > 0$ and $0 < x < 360$.

2. Express the following expressions in the required form:

(a) $\cos x + \sqrt{3}\sin x$ in the form $k\cos(x - \alpha)$ where $k > 0$ and $0 < x < 2\pi$.

(b) $2\sin x + \cos x$ in the form $k\sin(x + \alpha)$ where $k > 0$ and $0 < x < 2\pi$.

(c) $4\cos x - \sin x$ in the form $k\cos(x + \alpha)$ where $k > 0$ and $0 < x < 2\pi$.

(d) $3\sin x - 5\cos x$ in the form $k\sin(x - \alpha)$ where $k > 0$ and $0 < x < 2\pi$.

(e) $2\sin x - 3\cos x$ in the form $k\sin(x - \alpha)$ where $k > 0$ and $0 < x < 2\pi$.

(f) $2\cos x + \sqrt{2}\sin x$ in the form $k\cos(x - \alpha)$ where $k > 0$ and $0 < x < 2\pi$.

(g) $3\sin x + 4\cos x$ in the form $k\sin(x + \alpha)$ where $k > 0$ and $0 < x < 2\pi$.

(h) $4\cos x + 3\sin x$ in the form $k\cos(x - \alpha)$ where $k > 0$ and $0 < x < 2\pi$.

2. Express $3\cos x + 4\sin x$ in the form $k\sin(x - \alpha)$, where $k > 0$ and $0 < \alpha < 2\pi$.

Solution:

Step 1: $k\sin(x - \alpha) = k(\sin x\cos\alpha - \cos x\sin\alpha)$

$= k\sin x\cos\alpha - k\cos x\sin\alpha = k\cos\alpha\sin x - k\sin\alpha\cos x$

Step 2: $3\cos x + 4\sin x$

NB: The coefficients are in a different order to the expansion.

$\therefore$ $k\cos\alpha° = 4$ and $-k\sin\alpha° = 3$ so $k\sin\alpha° = -3$

Step 3: $k = \sqrt{4^2 + (-3)^2} = 5$

Step 4: $\tan\alpha = \dfrac{\sin\alpha}{\cos\alpha} = \dfrac{-3}{4}$

$\alpha_A = \tan^{-1}\dfrac{3}{4} = 0.64$ (2 d.p.)

$\alpha = 2\pi - 0.64 = 5.64$

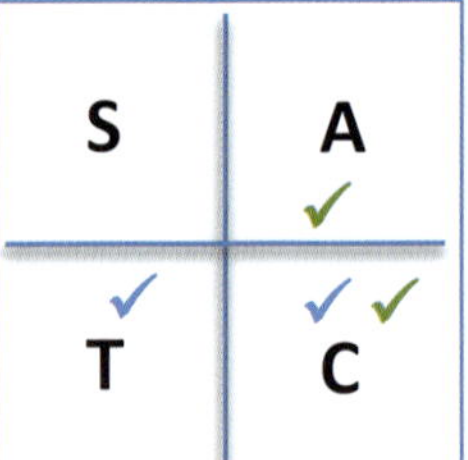

This time $\sin\alpha$ is negative and $\cos\alpha$ is positive. Tick the corresponding quadrants and again, the quadrant with two ticks is the quadrant we use.

Step 5: $3\cos x + 4\sin x = 5\sin(x - 5.64)$

Exercise 10.1B

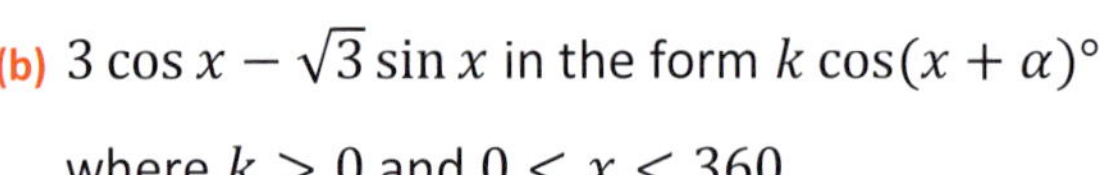

1. Express the following expressions in the required form:

(a) $\cos x° - \sqrt{2}\sin x°$ in the form $k\cos(x-\alpha)°$ where $k > 0$ and $0 < x < 360$.

(b) $3\cos x - \sqrt{3}\sin x$ in the form $k\cos(x+\alpha)°$ where $k > 0$ and $0 < x < 360$.

(c) $2\sin x° - 5\cos x°$ in the form $k\sin(x+\alpha)°$ where $k > 0$ and $0 < x < 360$.

(d) $2\sin x° - \cos x°$ in the form $k\sin(x+\alpha)°$ where $k > 0$ and $0 < x < 360$.

(e) $\sin x + 2\cos x$ in the form $k\sin(x-\alpha)°$ where $k > 0$ and $0 < x < 360$.

(f) $5\cos x° - 2\sin x°$ in the form $k\cos(x+\alpha)°$ where $k > 0$ and $0 < x < 360$.

(g) $3\sin x° + 2\cos x°$ in the form $k\sin(x+\alpha)°$ where $k > 0$ and $0 < x < 360$.

(h) $\sin x - 4\cos x$ in the form $k\sin(x-\alpha)°$ where $k > 0$ and $0 < x < 360$.

2. Express the following expressions in the required form:

(a) $3\sin x° - \sqrt{2}\cos x°$ in the form $k\cos(x-\alpha)$ where $k > 0$ and $0 < x < 2\pi$.

(b) $2\sin x + \cos x$ in the form $k\cos(x+\alpha)$ where $k > 0$ and $0 < x < 2\pi$.

(c) $3\cos x° - 2\sin x°$ in the form $k\sin(x+\alpha)$ where $k > 0$ and $0 < x < 2\pi$.

(d) $\cos x° - 4\sin x°$ in the form $k\sin(x+\alpha)$ where $k > 0$ and $0 < x < 2\pi$.

(e) $4\cos x - 2\sin x$ in the form $k\sin(x+\alpha)$ where $k > 0$ and $0 < x < 2\pi$.

(f) $3\sin x° - \cos x°$ in the form $k\cos(x+\alpha)$ where $k > 0$ and $0 < x < 2\pi$.

(g) $5\cos x° + 2\sin x°$ in the form $k\sin(x+\alpha)$ where $k > 0$ and $0 < x < 2\pi$.

(h) $2\cos x - 3\sin x$ in the form $k\sin(x-\alpha)$ where $k > 0$ and $0 < x < 2\pi$.

10.2 Solving Trigonometric Equations with the Wave Function

Worked Examples:

Solve the following equations:

1. $\sqrt{5}\cos(x-30)^\circ = 2$ for $0 \le x \le 360$

2. $\sqrt{3}\sin(x+0.43) = 1$ for $0 \le x \le 2\pi$

Solutions:

$$\begin{aligned} \sqrt{5}\cos(x-30)^\circ &= 2 \\ \cos(x-30)^\circ &= \tfrac{2}{\sqrt{5}} \\ (x-30)^\circ &= 45^\circ, 360^\circ - 45^\circ \\ (x-30)^\circ &= 45^\circ, 315^\circ \\ x^\circ &= 45^\circ + 30^\circ, 315^\circ + 30^\circ \\ x^\circ &= 75^\circ, 345^\circ \end{aligned}$$

$$\begin{aligned} \sqrt{3}\sin(x+0.43) &= 1 \\ \sin(x+0.43) &= \tfrac{1}{\sqrt{3}} \\ (x+0.43) &= 0.62, \pi - 0.62 \\ (x+0.43) &= 0.62, 2.52 \\ x &= 0.62 - 0.43, 2.52 - 0.43 \\ x &= 0.19, 2.52 + 2.03 \end{aligned}$$

Exercise 10.2

1. Solve the following equations for $0 \le x \le 360$:

(a) $3\sin(x-25)^\circ = 1$
(b) $\sqrt{3}\cos(x+10)^\circ = 1$
(c) $3\sin(x-20)^\circ = 3$
(d) $3\cos(x-15)^\circ = 2$
(e) $5\sin(x+20)^\circ = 3$
(f) $5\cos(x-15)^\circ = \sqrt{3}$

2. Solve each of the following by first expressing them in the form $k\sin(x \pm \alpha)^\circ$ or $k\cos(x \pm \alpha)^\circ$, where $k > 0$ and $0 \le x \le 360$:

(a) $3\cos x^\circ - \sqrt{2}\sin x^\circ = 1$
(b) $2\cos x^\circ + \sin x^\circ = 1$
(c) $3\cos x^\circ + 5\sin x^\circ = 2$
(d) $\sin x^\circ - 4\cos x^\circ = -1$
(e) $2\sin 2x^\circ + 3\cos 2x^\circ = 2$
(f) $5\sin 3x^\circ - 3\cos 3x^\circ = 1$

3. Solve the following equations for $0 \le x \le 2\pi$:

(a) $\sqrt{2}\cos\left(x - \frac{\pi}{6}\right) = 1$
(b) $\sqrt{2}\sin\left(x - \frac{\pi}{6}\right) + 1 = 0$
(c) $2\sin(x-0.76) = 1$
(d) $2\cos(x+0.34) = 1$
(e) $3\cos\left(x + \frac{\pi}{4}\right) = \sqrt{2}$
(f) $2\sin(x-0.56) = \sqrt{3}$

4. Solve each of the following by first expressing them in the form $k\sin(x \pm \alpha)$ or $k\cos(x \pm \alpha)$, where $k > 0$ and $0 \le x \le 2\pi$:

(a) $2\cos x - \sqrt{2}\sin x = 1$
(b) $2\cos x - 4\sin x = \sqrt{2}$
(c) $\sqrt{3}\cos x + 5\sin x = 1$
(d) $3\sin x - \cos x = 2$
(e) $\sqrt{5}\sin 2x + 3\cos 2x = 1$
(f) $5\sin 4x - \sqrt{2}\cos 4x = 2$

10.3 Sketching the Graph of $y = k\sin(x \pm \alpha)$ and $y = k\cos(x \pm \alpha)$

In trigonometric functions of the form $y = k\sin(x \pm \alpha)$ and $y = k\cos(x \pm \alpha)$, k is the **amplitude**, and α translates the graph **horizontally**.

NB: When the value of α is **positive**, the graph moves **left**; when α is negative, the graph moves right.

In the sketch of the graph mark where the **roots** and **turning points** are, and **calculate the y-intercept** by making $x = 0$ in the equation.

Sketching trigonometric graphs of the form $y = k\sin(x \pm \alpha)$ and $y = k\cos(x \pm \alpha)$ can be difficult. One method to make this easier is to start with an x-axis only and draw the $\sin x$ or $\cos x$ wave. Then draw a y-axis in an appropriate place, then complete and remove the parts of the graph needed for the given range.

Worked Example:

Sketch and annotate the graph of $y = 3\sin(x - 45)°$ in the interval $0 \leq x \leq 360$.

Solution:

Step 1: Draw the wave on an x-axis and mark the roots.

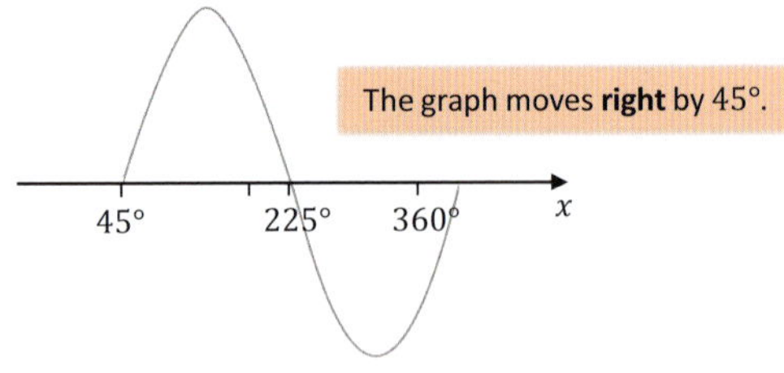

The graph moves **right** by 45°.

Step 2: Draw a y-axis.

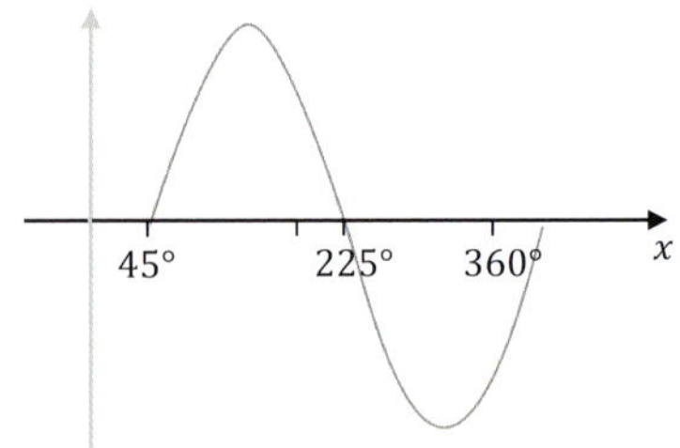

Step 3: Fill in the rest of the information and add and remove the sections of the wave to fit the required range.

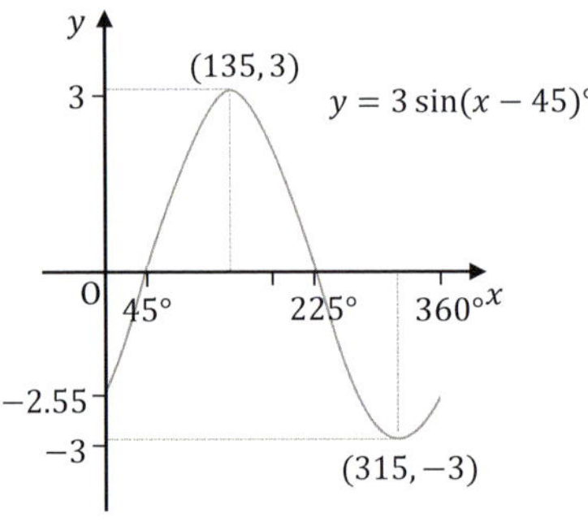

Exercise 10.3

1. Sketch and annotate the graph of each of the following functions in the given range:

(a) $y = \cos(x + 45)°\ (0 \leq x \leq 360)$

(b) $y = \sin\left(x - \frac{\pi}{4}\right)\ (0 \leq x \leq 2\pi)$

(c) $y = 2\sin(x - 45)°\ (0 \leq x \leq 360)$

(d) $y = 3\cos\left(x + \frac{\pi}{6}\right)\ (0 \leq x \leq 2\pi)$

(e) $y = 3\cos(x - 30)°\ (0 \leq x \leq 360)$

(f) $y = 2\sin\left(x + \frac{\pi}{3}\right)\ (0 \leq x \leq 2\pi)$

(g) $y = 2\sin(x + 30)^\circ \ (0 \leq x \leq 360)$

(h) $y = 3\cos\left(x - \frac{\pi}{4}\right) \ (0 \leq x \leq 2\pi)$

(i) $y = 2\cos(x + 60)^\circ \ (0 \leq x \leq 360)$

(j) $y = -\sin\left(x - \frac{\pi}{6}\right) \ (0 \leq x \leq 2\pi)$

(k) $y = 4\sin(x - 60)^\circ \ (0 \leq x \leq 360)$

(l) $y = 4\cos\left(x - \frac{\pi}{3}\right) \ (0 \leq x \leq 2\pi)$

2. Sketch and annotate the graph of each the following functions in the given range:

(a) $y = \sqrt{3}\cos(x + 20)^\circ \ (0 \leq x \leq 360)$

(b) $y = \sqrt{5}\cos(x + 120)^\circ \ (0 \leq x \leq 360)$

(c) $y = -4\sin(x - 15)^\circ \ (0 \leq x \leq 360)$

(d) $y = 2\cos(x - 200)^\circ \ (0 \leq x \leq 360)$

(e) $y = \sqrt{5}\cos(x - 340)^\circ \ (0 \leq x \leq 360)$

(f) $y = 5\cos(x + 320)^\circ \ (0 \leq x \leq 360)$

3. Answer each of the following:

(a) (i) Express $2\cos x^\circ - \sqrt{2}\sin x^\circ$ in the form $k\cos(x + \alpha)^\circ$, $k > 0$ and $0 \leq x \leq 360$.

(ii) Hence sketch $y = 2\cos x^\circ - \sqrt{2}\sin x^\circ$, where $0 \leq x \leq 360$.

(b) (i) Express $5\sin x^\circ - \sqrt{2}\cos x^\circ$ in the form $k\sin(x + \alpha)^\circ$, $k > 0$ and $0 \leq x \leq 360$.

(ii) Hence sketch $y = 5\sin x^\circ - \sqrt{2}\cos x^\circ$, where $0 \leq x \leq 360$.

(c) (i) Express $3\sin x^\circ - 2\cos x^\circ$ in the form $k\cos(x + \alpha)^\circ$, $k > 0$ and $0 \leq x \leq 360$.

(ii) Hence sketch $y = 3\sin x^\circ - 2\cos x^\circ + 2$, where $0 \leq x \leq 360$.

(d) (i) Express $2\sin x^\circ + \sqrt{2}\cos x^\circ$ in the form $k\sin(x + \alpha)^\circ$, $k > 0$ and $0 \leq x \leq 360$.

(ii) Hence sketch $y = 3 - 2\sin x^\circ - \sqrt{2}\cos x^\circ$, where $0 \leq x \leq 360$.

10.4 Maximum and Minimum Values

The maximum or minimum value of a trigonometric function of the form $y = k\sin(x \pm \alpha)$ or $y = k\cos(x \pm \alpha)$ within a given range can simply be found by determining the value of k. To find the x-coordinate where this value occurs, equate the function to the maximum or minimum value, then solve.

Worked Examples:

1. (a) State the maximum value of the function $y = 3\sin(x - 45)^\circ$.

(b) The x-coordinate for which it occurs, where $0 \leq x \leq 360$.

Solution:

(a) Maximum value is 3.

(b) $3\sin(x - 30)^\circ = 3$

$\sin(x - 30)^\circ = 1$

$(x - 30)^\circ = 90^\circ$

$x^\circ = 120^\circ$

Maximum occurs where $x^\circ = 120^\circ$.

2. (a) State the minimum value of the function $y = 2\cos(x + 0.4)$.

(b) The x-coordinate for which it occurs, where $0 \leq x \leq 2\pi$.

Solution:

(a) Maximum value is 2.

(b) $2\cos(x + 0.4) = 2$

$\cos(x + 0.4) = 1$

$(x + 0.4) = \pi$

$x = \pi + 0.4 = 3.54$ (2 d.p)

Maximum occurs where $x = 3.54$

Exercise 10.4

1. Answer each of the following:

(a) (i) State the maximum value of the function $y = 3\sin(x - 45)°$.
(ii) The x-coordinate for which it occurs, where $0 \le x \le 360$.

(b) (i) State the maximum value of the function $y = 7\sin\left(x - \frac{\pi}{3}\right)$.
(ii) The x-coordinate for which it occurs, where $0 \le x \le 2\pi$.

(c) (i) State the maximum value of the function $y = 5\sin(x + 20)°$.
(ii) The x-coordinate for which it occurs, where $0 \le x \le 360$.

(d) (i) State the maximum value of the function $y = -4\sin\left(x + \frac{\pi}{4}\right)$.
(ii) The x-coordinate for which it occurs, where $0 \le x \le 2\pi$.

(e) (i) State the maximum value of the function $y = 5\cos(x + 45)°$.
(ii) The x-coordinate for which it occurs, where $0 \le x \le 360$.

(f) (i) State the maximum value of the function $y = 2\cos(x + 15)°$.
(ii) The x-coordinate for which it occurs, where $0 \le x \le 360$.

(g) (i) State the maximum value of the function $y = -2\cos(x - 0.3)$.
(ii) The x-coordinate for which it occurs, where $0 \le x \le 2\pi$.

(h) (i) State the maximum value of the function $y = 6\cos(x + 0.5)$.
(ii) The x-coordinate for which it occurs, where $0 \le x \le 2\pi$.

2. Answer each of the following:

(a) (i) Express $2\cos x° - \sqrt{2}\sin x°$ in the form $k\cos(x + \alpha)°$, $k > 0$ and $0 \le x \le 360$.
(ii) Hence, state the maximum value of the function $y = 2\cos x° - \sqrt{2}\sin x°$.
(iii) The x-coordinate for which it occurs, where $0 \le x \le 360$.

(b) (i) Express $3\sin x - 5\cos x$ in the form $k\sin(x - \alpha)$, $k > 0$ and $0 \le x \le 2\pi$.
(ii) Hence, state the minimum value of the function $y = 3\sin x - 5\cos x$.
(iii) The x-coordinate for which it occurs, where $0 \le x \le 2\pi$.

(c) (i) Express $3\cos x - 5\sin x$ in the form $k\cos(x - \alpha)$, $k > 0$ and $0 \le x \le 2\pi$.
(ii) Hence, state the minimum value of the function $y = 9\cos x - 15\sin x$.
(iii) The x-coordinate for which it occurs, where $0 \le x \le 2\pi$.

(d) (i) Express $5\sin x° - 2\cos x°$ in the form $k\sin(x + \alpha)°$, $k > 0$ and $0 \le x \le 360$.
(ii) Hence, state the maximum value of the function $y = 10\sin x° - 4\cos x°$.
(iii) The x-coordinate for which it occurs, where $0 \le x \le 360$.

(e) (i) Express $3\sin x° - 2\cos x°$ in the form $k\cos(x + \alpha)°$, $k > 0$ and $0 \le x \le 360$.
(ii) Hence, state the minimum value of the function $y = 3\sin x° - 2\cos x° + 3$.
(iii) The x-coordinate for which it occurs, where $0 \le x \le 360$.

(f) (i) Express $\cos x - \sqrt{2}\sin x$ in the form $k\sin(x - \alpha)$, $k > 0$ and $0 \le x \le 2\pi$.
(ii) Hence, state the maximum value of the function $y = \cos x - \sqrt{2}\sin x - 4$.
(iii) The x-coordinate for which it occurs, where $0 \le x \le 2\pi$.

(g) (i) Express $5 \sin x° - 3 \cos x°$ in the form $k \sin(x + \alpha)°$, $k > 0$ and $0 \leq x \leq 360$.

(ii) Hence, state the maximum value of the function $y = 10 \sin x° - 6 \cos x° + 1$.

(iii) The x-coordinate for which it occurs, where $0 \leq x \leq 360$.

(h) (i) Express $\cos x - 3 \sin x$ in the form $k \sin(x - \alpha)$, $k > 0$ and $0 \leq x \leq 2\pi$.

(ii) Hence, state the maximum value of the function $y = 3 \cos x - 9 \sin x - 4$.

(iii) The x-coordinate for which it occurs, where $0 \leq x \leq 2\pi$.

10.5 Review

Exercise 10.5

10.1 Write the following expressions in the required form:

(a) $2 \cos x° + \sin x°$ in the form $k \cos(x - \alpha)°$ where $k > 0$ and $0 < x < 360$.

(b) $2 \sin x + \sqrt{3} \cos x$ in the form $k \sin(x + \alpha)$ where $k > 0$ and $0 < x < 2\pi$.

(c) $4 \cos x + 2 \sin x$ in the form $k \cos(x + \alpha)$ where $k > 0$ and $0 < x < 2\pi$.

(d) $3 \cos x° - 5 \sin x°$ in the form $k \sin(x - \alpha)°$ where $k > 0$ and $0 < x < 360$.

10.2 Solve each of the following by first expressing them in the form $k \sin(x \pm \alpha)$ or $k \cos(x \pm \alpha)$, where $k > 0$ and $0 \leq x \leq 2\pi$:

(a) $2 \cos x - \sqrt{2} \sin x = 1$

(b) $2 \cos x - 4 \sin x = \sqrt{2}$

(c) $\sqrt{3} \cos x + 5 \sin x = 1$

(d) (i) Express $3 \cos x° + \sin x°$ in the form $k \cos(x - \alpha)°$, $k > 0$ and $0 < x < 360$.

(ii) Hence solve $3 \cos x° + \sin x° = 2$.

(e) (i) Express $2 \sin x° + \cos x°$ in the form $k \sin(x + \alpha)°$, $k > 0$ and $0 < x < 360$.

(ii) Hence solve $2 \sin x° + \cos x° = 1$.

(f) (i) Express $2 \cos x + 2 \sin x$ in the form $k \cos(x + \alpha)$, $k > 0$ and $0 < x < 2\pi$.

(ii) Hence solve $2 \cos 2x + 2 \sin 2x = 1$.

(g) (i) Express $\sqrt{5} \cos x + 2 \sin x$ in the form $k \sin(x - \alpha)$, $k > 0$ and $0 < x < 2\pi$.

(ii) Hence solve $\sqrt{5} \cos 3x° + 2 \sin 3x° = 3$.

10.3 Answer each of the following:

(a) (i) Express $\sqrt{3} \cos x° + \sin x°$ in the form $k \cos(x - \alpha)°$, $k > 0$ and $0 < x < 360$.

(ii) Hence sketch $y = \sqrt{3} \cos x° + \sin x°$.

(b) (i) Express $\sqrt{2} \sin x° + \sqrt{2} \cos x°$ in the form $k \sin(x + \alpha)°$, $k > 0$ and $0 < x < 360$.

(ii) Hence sketch $y = \sqrt{2} \sin x° + \sqrt{2} \cos x°$.

(c) (i) Express $\sqrt{3}\sin x° + \cos x°$ in the form $k\sin(x-\alpha)°$, $k > 0$ and $0 < x < 360$.

(ii) Hence sketch $y = \sqrt{3}\sin x° + \cos x° - 1$.

(d) (i) Express $\sqrt{3}\sin x° + \cos x°$ in the form $k\cos(x+\alpha)°$, $k > 0$ and $0 < x < 360$.

(ii) Hence sketch $y = 1 - \sqrt{3}\sin x° - \cos x°$.

10.4 Answer each of the following:

(a) (i) Express $5\cos x° - 3\sin x°$ in the form $k\cos(x+\alpha)°$, $k > 0$ and $0 \leq x \leq 360$.

(ii) Hence, state the maximum value of the function $y = 5\cos x° - 3\sin x° - 2$.

(iii) The x-coordinate for which it occurs, where $0 \leq x \leq 360$.

(b) (i) Express $3\cos x - 2\sin x$ in the form $k\sin(x+\alpha)$, $k > 0$ and $0 \leq x \leq 2\pi$.

(ii) Hence, state the minimum value of the function $y = 6\cos x - 4\sin x + 3$.

(iii) The x-coordinate for which it occurs, where $0 \leq x \leq 2\pi$.

Chapter 11

Calculus 1 - Differentiation

Differentiation

Differentiation or **differential calculus** is a branch of mathematics that calculates the rate of change of one variable with respect to another. For example, the rate at which the position of an object changes with respect to time, **i.e.**, the velocity of the object; or the rate of change of the velocity of an object with respect to time, **i.e.**, the acceleration of the object. The rate of change of a function is known as the derivative of the function.

We **differentiate** a function to find the **derivative** or the **rate of change** of the function. This is also the **gradient of the tangent** to the function at any given point.

The theory of differential calculus was developed in the 17th century independently by two mathematicians, Isaac Newton and Gottfried Leibniz. These mathematicians both developed their own notation for differentiation. Both forms of the notation are still used for differentiation.

Leibniz' Notation	**Newton's (Function) Notation**
$y = ax^n$	$f(x) = ax^n$
$\frac{dy}{dx} = nax^{n-1}$	$f'(x) = nax^{n-1}$

Using Leibniz' notation, the derivate is called $\frac{dy}{dx}$ where dy represents a small change in y, and dx represents a small change in x. In function notation the derivate is called $f'(x)$.

Extra Info

The rate at which a straight-line function changes is constant, hence the straight line – the rate at which one variable changes with respect to the other is simply the gradient. But the rate of change of a function that is a curve is always changing – this is more difficult to determine.

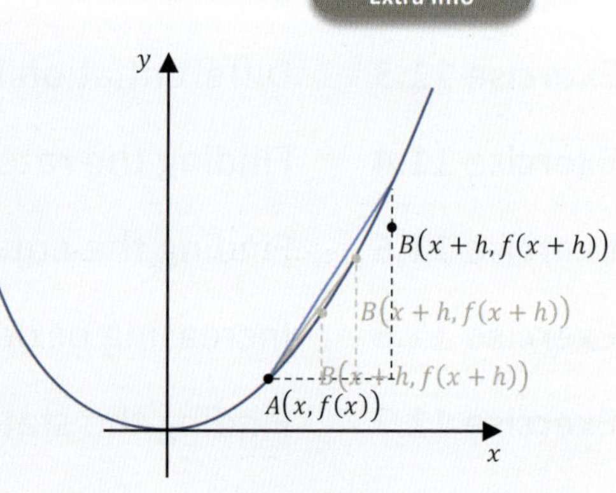

We may find an approximate of the rate of change, or the gradient of the tangent at point A by selecting another coordinate on the line, B, then calculating the gradient between these two points.

The closer point B is to point A, the more accurate the estimation of the gradient of the tangent at A will be. As $h \to 0$, (h tends towards zero), the difference between the gradient of AB and the gradient of the tangent at A will be the same.

$$f'(x) = m_{AB} = \lim_{h\to 0}\frac{f(x+h)-f(x)}{(x+h)-x} = \lim_{h\to 0}\frac{f(x+h)-f(x)}{h}$$

Example: Differentiate the curve $y = f(x)$, where $f(x) = 3x^2$

$$f'(x) = \lim_{h\to 0}\frac{f(x+h)-f(x)}{(x+h)-x} = \lim_{h\to 0}\frac{(3x+h)^2-3x^2}{h}$$

$$= \lim_{h\to 0}\frac{3(x+h)^2-3x^2}{h}$$

$$= \lim_{h\to 0}\frac{3(x^2+2xh+h^2)-3x^2}{h}$$

$$= \lim_{h\to 0}\frac{3x^2+6xh+3h^2-3x^2}{h} = \lim_{h\to 0}\frac{6xh+3h^2}{h} = \lim_{h\to 0}\frac{h(6x+3h)}{h} = \lim_{h\to 0} 6x+3h$$

As $h \to 0$, $f'(x) = 6x$

11.1 Using Indices

One of the most important mathematical skills in both differential and integral calculus is using indices. When differentiating a function, it is often necessary to prepare the function – this is called expressing the function in **differentiable form**. To do this, each term must be in index form, expressed on the numerator of any fraction.

Worked Examples:

1. Express each of the following in differentiable form:

(a) $\frac{1}{x} = x^{-1}$ (b) $\frac{1}{3x^2} = \frac{1}{3}x^{-2}$ (c) $\frac{3}{x^4} = 3x^{-4}$ (d) $\frac{5}{2x^3} = \frac{5}{2}x^{-3}$

Exercise 11.1

1. Express each of the following in negative index form:

(a) $\frac{2}{x}$ (b) $\frac{1}{2x}$ (c) $\frac{2}{x^2}$ (d) $\frac{4}{x^3}$ (e) $\frac{1}{4x^5}$ (f) $\frac{6}{x^2}$

(g) $\frac{1}{3x^6}$ (h) $\frac{2}{3x}$ (i) $\frac{3}{5x^4}$ (j) $\frac{5}{x^2}$ (k) $\frac{1}{12x^3}$ (l) $\frac{7}{3x^4}$

Worked Examples:

2. Express each of the following in index form with x in the numerator:

(a) $\sqrt{x} = x^{\frac{1}{2}}$ (b) $\sqrt[3]{x^2} = x^{\frac{2}{3}}$ (c) $\frac{3}{\sqrt{x}} = \frac{3}{x^{\frac{1}{2}}} = 3x^{-\frac{1}{2}}$ (d) $\frac{5}{2\sqrt[3]{x^2}} = \frac{5}{2x^{\frac{2}{3}}} = \frac{5}{2}x^{-\frac{2}{3}}$

2. Express each of the following in index form with x in the numerator:

(a) $\sqrt[3]{x}$ (b) $\sqrt[4]{x^3}$ (c) $\sqrt{x^3}$ (d) $\sqrt[3]{x^4}$ (e) $3\sqrt{x^5}$ (f) $4\sqrt[3]{x^2}$

(g) $\frac{2}{\sqrt{x^3}}$ (h) $\frac{1}{\sqrt[3]{x^5}}$ (i) $\frac{5}{\sqrt[4]{x^3}}$ (j) $\frac{1}{4\sqrt[3]{x^2}}$ (k) $\frac{3}{4\sqrt{x^5}}$ (l) $\frac{11}{5\sqrt[4]{x^3}}$

It is good practice to express answers in both positive index and root form. This makes evaluating any rates of change at a given point much simpler without a calculator (**section 11.4**).

Worked Examples:

3. Express each of the following in positive index and root form:

(a) $4x^{-2} = \frac{4}{x^2}$ (b) $\frac{x^{-3}}{3} = \frac{1}{3x^3}$ (c) $x^{\frac{2}{5}} = \sqrt[5]{x^2}$ (d) $2x^{-\frac{3}{4}} = \frac{2}{\sqrt[4]{x^3}}$

3. Express each of the following in positive index and root form:

(a) x^{-3} (b) x^{-4} (c) $2x^{-3}$ (d) $\frac{x^{-5}}{2}$ (e) $\frac{2}{3}x^{-3}$ (f) $\frac{3}{4}x^{-5}$

(g) $x^{\frac{3}{5}}$ (h) $x^{\frac{3}{2}}$ (i) $x^{\frac{3}{4}}$ (j) $x^{\frac{4}{3}}$ (k) $3x^{\frac{1}{2}}$ (l) $2x^{\frac{2}{3}}$

(m) $3x^{-\frac{1}{4}}$ (n) $2x^{-\frac{3}{5}}$ (o) $\frac{1}{2}x^{-\frac{2}{3}}$ (p) $\frac{x^{-\frac{1}{3}}}{2}$ (q) $\frac{3x^{-\frac{2}{3}}}{2}$ (r) $\frac{2}{3}x^{-\frac{4}{3}}$

11.2 Differentiating Functions

When differentiating a function, we multiply each term of the function by its power, then we take away 1 from the power:

Worked Examples:

1. Differentiate each of the following:

(a) $y = x^4$

$\frac{dy}{dx} = 4x^3$

(b) $y = 2x^3$

$\frac{dy}{dx} = 6x^2$

(c) $y = 3x^{-2}$

$\frac{dy}{dx} = -6x^{-3}$

$\frac{dy}{dx} = -\frac{6}{x^3}$

(d) $y = 4x^{\frac{1}{2}}$

$\frac{dy}{dx} = 2x^{-\frac{1}{2}}$

$\frac{dy}{dx} = \frac{2}{\sqrt{x}}$

NB: $y = x = x^1$

$\frac{dy}{dx} = x^0 = 1$

Exercise 11.2A

1. Differentiate each of the following:

(a) $y = x^2$ (b) $y = x^3$ (c) $y = x$ (d) $y = x^4$

(e) $y = x^7$ (f) $y = x^5$ (g) $y = x^6$ (h) $y = x^9$

(i) $y = x^{-2}$ (j) $y = x^{-4}$ (k) $y = x^{-6}$ (l) $y = x^{-3}$

(m) $y = 2x^2$ (n) $y = 3x^2$ (o) $y = 2x^3$ (p) $y = 3x^4$

(q) $y = 4x^3$ (r) $y = 5x$ (s) $y = 3x^{-1}$ (t) $y = 2x^{-2}$

Using function notation, we write:

$$\boldsymbol{f(x) = ax^n}$$

$$\boldsymbol{f'(x) = nax^{n-1}}$$

Worked Examples:

2. Differentiate each of the following:

(a) $f(x) = 5x^2$

$f'(x) = 10x$

(b) $f(x) = 4x$

$f'(x) = 4$

(c) $f(x) = \frac{2}{3}x^{-2}$

$f'(x) = -\frac{4}{3}x^{-3}$

$f'(x) = -\frac{4}{3x^3}$

(d) $f(x) = \frac{3}{2}x^{\frac{1}{3}}$

$f'(x) = \frac{3}{6}x^{-\frac{2}{3}}$

$f'(x) = \frac{1}{2\sqrt[3]{x^2}}$

2. Differentiate each of the following functions:

(a) $f(x) = 3x^3$ (b) $f(x) = 4x^7$ (c) $f(x) = 2x$ (d) $f(x) = 3x^{-2}$

(e) $f(x) = 4x^{-3}$ (f) $f(x) = 7x^5$ (g) $f(x) = 5x^{-1}$ (h) $f(x) = 4x^6$

3. Find the derivative of each of the following functions, using the correct notation. Give your answers in both positive index **and** root form:

(a) $f(x) = x^{\frac{1}{2}}$ (b) $y = x^{\frac{1}{3}}$ (c) $f(x) = x^{\frac{2}{3}}$ (d) $y = x^{-\frac{2}{3}}$

(e) $y = 2x^{\frac{1}{2}}$ (f) $f(x) = 4x^{\frac{3}{4}}$ (g) $y = 6x^{-\frac{1}{3}}$ (h) $f(x) = 12x^{\frac{5}{6}}$

(i) $f(x) = \frac{1}{2}x^{\frac{1}{2}}$ (j) $y = \frac{3}{4}x^{\frac{1}{3}}$ (k) $f(x) = \frac{3}{2}x^{\frac{2}{3}}$ (l) $y = \frac{1}{8}x^{-\frac{2}{3}}$

When differentiating functions that consist of more than one term, differentiate each term individually.

Worked Examples:

3. Find the derivative of each of the following:

(a) $f(x) = 3x^3 - 4x$

$f'(x) = 9x^2 - 4$

(b) $y = 4x^2 - 2x + 1$

$\frac{dy}{dx} = 8x - 2$

(c) $f(x) = x^5 - 4x^{-2} + 3x$

$f'(x) = 5x^4 + 8x^{-3} + 3$

$f'(x) = 5x^4 + \frac{8}{x^3} + 3$

Exercise 11.2B

1. Differentiate each of the following:

(a) $f(x) = x^2 + x$ (b) $y = 2x^2 - 4x$ (c) $f(x) = x^2 - 9x + 1$

(d) $y = x^3 - 2x^2$ (e) $f(x) = x^3 - 6x + 1$ (f) $y = 4x^2 - 18x + 2$

(g) $f(x) = x^2 - x + 1$ (h) $y = x^3 - x^2 + 6x + 2$ (i) $f(x) = x^3 + x^2 + 3x + 9$

(j) $y = 7 - 6x^2 - x^3$ (k) $f(x) = x^4 + 3x^3 - 2x$ (l) $y = 3x^4 - 23x + 12$

2. Find the derivative of each of the following:

(a) $f(x) = x^4 + x^{-1}$ (b) $y = x^3 - 3x^{-1}$ (c) $f(x) = x^5 - 2x^{-3}$

(d) $y = x^7 - 5x^{-2}$ (e) $f(x) = x^{-3} - 6x^{-1}$ (f) $y = x^{\frac{2}{3}} - x^{-2}$

(g) $f(x) = 3x^{-\frac{1}{3}} - \frac{2}{3}x^{\frac{1}{2}}$ (h) $y = 4x^{-\frac{2}{3}} - \frac{1}{2}x^{\frac{1}{2}}$ (i) $f(x) = 4x^{\frac{3}{4}} + \frac{3}{4}x^{-\frac{1}{4}}$

11.3 Differentiation Involving Preparation of the Function

When differentiating a function, it is often necessary to prepare the function so that it is in a differentiable form. This involves breaking the function down into individual terms and expressing each term on the numerator of any fraction and in index form (**section 11.1**).

Worked Examples:

1. Differentiate each of the following:

(a) $y = \sqrt[3]{x^2}$

$y = x^{\frac{2}{3}}$

$\frac{dy}{dx} = \frac{2}{3}x^{-\frac{1}{3}}$

$\frac{dy}{dx} = \frac{2}{3\sqrt[3]{x}}$

(b) $f(x) = \frac{4}{x^2}$

$f(x) = 4x^{-2}$

$f'(x) = -8x^{-3}$

$f'(x) = -\frac{8}{x^3}$

(c) $y = \frac{3}{\sqrt{x}}$

$y = 3x^{-\frac{1}{2}}$

$\frac{dy}{dx} = -\frac{3}{2}x^{-\frac{3}{2}}$

$\frac{dy}{dx} = -\frac{3}{2\sqrt{x^3}}$

Exercise 11.3A

1. Differentiate each of the following:

(a) $f(x) = \sqrt[3]{x}$ (b) $y = \sqrt{x^3}$ (c) $f(x) = \sqrt[4]{x^5}$ (d) $y = 10\sqrt[5]{x^3}$

(e) $y = \frac{2}{x}$ (f) $f(x) = \frac{1}{x^2}$ (g) $y = \frac{1}{2x^2}$ (h) $f(x) = \frac{4}{x^3}$

(i) $f(x) = \frac{4}{3x}$ (j) $y = \frac{3}{x^4}$ (k) $f(x) = \frac{1}{\sqrt{x}}$ (l) $y = \frac{2}{\sqrt[3]{x^2}}$

Worked Examples:

2. Differentiate each of the following:

(a) $y = x^2(x - 2)$

$y = x^3 - 2x^2$

$\frac{dy}{dx} = 3x^2 - 4x$

(b) $f(x) = \sqrt{x}(x - 2x^2)$

$f(x) = x^{\frac{1}{2}}(x - 2x^2)$

$f(x) = x^{\frac{3}{2}} - 2x^{\frac{5}{2}}$

$f'(x) = \frac{3}{2}x^{\frac{1}{2}} - 5x^{\frac{3}{2}}$

(c) $f(x) = \frac{4x^2 - 5x}{\sqrt{x}}$

$f(x) = x^{-\frac{1}{2}}(4x^2 - 5x^1)$

$f(x) = 4x^{\frac{3}{2}} - 5x^{\frac{1}{2}}$

$f'(x) = \frac{12}{2}x^{\frac{1}{2}} - \frac{5}{2}x^{-\frac{1}{2}}$

$f'(x) = 6\sqrt{x} - \frac{5}{2\sqrt{x}}$

Exercise 11.3B

1. Differentiate each of the following functions:

(a) $f(x) = x(x + 1)$ (b) $f(x) = 4x(x - 2)$ (c) $f(x) = 3x(x^2 - 1)$

(d) $f(x) = (x - 3)^2$ (e) $f(x) = x^2\left(2x + \frac{1}{x}\right)$ (f) $f(x) = \left(x + \frac{1}{x}\right)\left(3x + \frac{1}{x}\right)$

(g) $f(x) = x^2(\sqrt{x} - 2)$ (h) $f(x) = x^3(\sqrt{x} - x)$ (i) $f(x) = \sqrt[3]{x^2}(\sqrt{x} - 2)$

(j) $f(x) = x^{-1}(\sqrt{x} - \sqrt[3]{x})$ (k) $f(x) = x^{-2}\left(\sqrt{x} - 3x^{-\frac{1}{2}}\right)$ (l) $f(x) = \sqrt[4]{x^3}(\sqrt{x} - 3x)$

(m) $f(x) = x\left(x^2 + \frac{1}{\sqrt{x}}\right)$ (n) $f(x) = x\left(\sqrt{x} - \frac{3}{\sqrt{x}}\right)$ (o) $f(x) = \sqrt{x}\left(\sqrt{x^3} + \frac{4}{\sqrt{x}}\right)$

2. Differentiate each of the following:

(a) $y = \dfrac{x^2 + 2x}{x}$ (b) $y = \dfrac{x^3 - 3x^2}{x^2}$ (c) $y = \dfrac{4x^2 - x^3}{x}$ (d) $y = \dfrac{5x^3 + 6x^2}{x}$

(e) $y = \dfrac{2x^2 + 2x}{x^3}$ (f) $y = \dfrac{2x^2 - x}{x^4}$ (g) $y = \dfrac{x + 3x^3}{x^2}$ (h) $y = \dfrac{5x^5 + 3x}{x^3}$

(i) $y = \dfrac{x^2 + 2x}{3x^2}$ (j) $y = \dfrac{4x^2 - 5x}{2x^4}$ (k) $y = \dfrac{3x^3 - x^2 - 3}{2x^4}$ (l) $y = \dfrac{x^3 - 5x^2 + x}{3x^4}$

(m) $y = \dfrac{x^2 - 3x}{\sqrt{x}}$ (n) $y = \dfrac{3x^2 + 5x}{2\sqrt{x}}$ (o) $y = \dfrac{2x^2 + 3}{5\sqrt[3]{x}}$ (p) $y = \dfrac{x^2 + 2x - 1}{4\sqrt{x}}$

11.4 Finding the Rate of Change of a Function

When differentiating functions, the derivative of the function is the **rate of change** of the function, this rate of change is the **gradient of the tangent** to the curve of the function at any given point.

Worked Examples:

1. Given the function $f(x) = 4x^3$, evaluate $f'(-2)$.

$f(x) = 4x^3$

$f'(x) = 12x^2$

$f'(-2) = 12(-2)^2 = 12(4) = 48$

2. Given $y = 4\sqrt{x}$, find the gradient of the tangent to the function when $x = 9$.

$y = 4\sqrt{x}$

$y = 4x^{\frac{1}{2}}$

$\dfrac{dy}{dx} = 2x^{-\frac{1}{2}} = \dfrac{2}{\sqrt{x}}$

When $x = 9$,

$\dfrac{dy}{dx} = \dfrac{2}{\sqrt{9}} = \dfrac{2}{3}$

NB: It is always good practice to return the answer to positive index and root form as it makes evaluating the derivative with given values much more straightforward.

3. Given the function $f(x) = 3x^3 + 3x^2 - 2x$, determine the rate of change of the function when $x = 3$.

$f(x) = x^3 + 3x^2 - 2x$

$f'(x) = 9x^2 + 6x - 2$

$f'(3) = 9(3)^2 + 6(3) - 2 = 81 + 18 - 2 = 97$

Exercise 11.4A

1. Evaluate each of the following:

(a) $f'(2)$, when $f(x) = x^2 - 2x$ (b) $g'(-1)$, when $g(x) = 2x^3 - 10x$

(c) $h'(3)$, when $h(x) = x^3 - \dfrac{1}{x}$ (d) $f'(-4)$, when $f(x) = 4x^3 - 2x^2 - 3x$

(e) $g'(4)$, when $g(x) = \sqrt{x} - \frac{2}{x}$

(f) $h'(4)$, when $h(x) = x^3 - \sqrt{x}$

(g) $f'(1)$, when $f(x) = 3x^3 - \frac{1}{\sqrt{x}}$

(h) $g'(-8)$, when $g(x) = x^2 - \sqrt[3]{x}$

(i) $h'(4)$, when $h(x) = \frac{4x^2 - 5x}{\sqrt{x}}$

(j) $f'(1)$, when $f(x) = \frac{\sqrt{x} - 3x}{x^2}$

(k) $g'(-2)$, when $g(x) = \frac{x^2 + 5x - 1}{x^3}$

(l) $h'(9)$, when $h(x) = \frac{x^2 + 5x - 1}{\sqrt{x}}$

2. Find the gradient of the tangent to each of the following curves at the given point:

(a) $y = 2x^2$, when $x = -1$.

(b) $y = x^2(x - 3)$, when $x = 2$.

(c) $y = 5x^3 - 2x^2 + x$, when $x = 3$.

(d) $y = 1 - x^3$, when $x = 4$.

(e) $y = \sqrt{x}(1 - 2\sqrt{x})$, when $x = 4$.

(f) $y = \sqrt{x}(5\sqrt{x} - 1)$, when $x = 1$.

(g) $y = \frac{x^3 - 2x}{x^2}$, when $x = -3$.

(h) $y = \frac{x^3 - 2x^2 - 1}{x}$, when $x = 3$.

(i) $y = \frac{4x^3 + 6x - 1}{2x}$, when $x = 2$.

(j) $y = \frac{\sqrt{x} - 2x}{x^2}$, when $x = 4$.

(k) $y = \frac{x^2 + 2}{\sqrt{x}}$, when $x = 1$.

(l) $y = \frac{\sqrt{x} - 4}{x^2}$, when $x = 4$.

3. Find the rate of change of each of the following functions at the given value:

(a) $f(x) = x^2 - x$, when $x = 2$.

(b) $f(x) = x(x + 4)$, when $x = -3$.

(c) $f(x) = 2(2 - x^2)$, when $x = -1$.

(d) $f(x) = x^3 + 4x - 2$, when $x = 5$.

(e) $f(x) = 4x - \sqrt{x^3}$, when $x = 4$.

(f) $f(x) = \sqrt{x}(1 - 12\sqrt{x})$, when $x = 25$.

(g) $f(x) = \frac{5x^2 + 11x}{x^3}$, when $x = -2$.

(h) $f(x) = \frac{9x - 2x^2}{3x^3}$, when $x = -3$.

(i) $f(x) = \frac{x^2 + 2x - 1}{x}$, when $x = 4$.

(j) $f(x) = \frac{x^3 - \sqrt{x}}{x}$, when $x = 9$.

(k) $f(x) = \frac{x^3 + 3}{\sqrt{x}}$, when $x = 4$.

(l) $f(x) = \frac{\sqrt{x} + 2}{x}$, when $x = 1$.

NB: The rate of change of distance with respect to time is the **velocity** and the rate of change of velocity with respect to time is the **acceleration**.

Worked Example:

The distance, d metres, of a projectile being fired from its starting point is given by $d(t) = 10t - t^2, 0 \leq t \leq 5$, where t is the time in seconds after firing. Calculate the speed of the object after 3 seconds.

Solution:

$d'(t) = 10 - 2t$

$d'(3) = 10 - 2(3) = 4$

After 3 seconds, the object will be travelling at 4 metres per second.

Exercise 11.4B

1. The distance, d metres, an object has travelled with respect to time is given by $d(t) = 8t - t^2$, $0 \leq t \leq 9$, where t is the time in seconds after the object begins its journey. Calculate the speed of the object after 3 seconds.

2. The volume, V litres, of liquid in a container is given by $V(x) = 7 - 0.25x^2, -\sqrt{28} \leq x \leq \sqrt{28}$, where x is the time in seconds after the container begins to drain. Calculate the rate of change of the volume after 8 seconds.

3. The velocity, v, of a projectile is given by the function $v(t) = 12t - 3t^2, 0 \leq t \leq 4$, where t is the time in seconds after the object begins its journey. Calculate the acceleration of the projectile after 1 second.

4. If $v(t) = 5t^2 - 4t + 7$, what is the rate of change of v with respect to t when $t = 4$?

5. Calculate the rate of change of $d(t) = \frac{1}{4t}, t \neq 0$, when $t = 6$.

6. The depth, D centimetres, of water in a new reservoir is given by the function $D(t) = \sqrt{4x}, x \geq 0$, where x is the time in hours after beginning to fill the reservoir. Calculate the rate of change of the depth after 40 hours.

7. The velocity, v, of an object is given by the function $v(t) = 4\sqrt{t}, t \geq 0$, where t is the time in seconds after the object begins its journey. Calculate the acceleration of the object after 25 seconds.

8. Calculate the rate of change of $V(x) = \frac{1}{x^2}, x \neq 0$, when $x = 7$.

9. The volume, V litres, of gas in a balloon being inflated is represented by the formula $V(t) = t^3 - \frac{4}{t^2}$, $t \geq \sqrt[5]{4}$, t seconds after the beginning of the inflation. Calculate the rate of change of the volume after 7 seconds.

10. If $r(s) = 4s^3 - 2s^2 + 3s$, what is the rate of change of r with respect to s when $s = 7$?

11.5 Finding the Equation of a Tangent

We have already determined how to find the equation of the tangent to a circle (**section 3.7**); the method for finding the equation of the tangent to a curve is the same. A tangent is straight line and so we need the two pieces of information – the **gradient** of the tangent and **a point** on the line.

Worked Example:

Find the equation of the tangent to the curve $y = x^2 - 7x + 10$ at the point where $x = 4$.

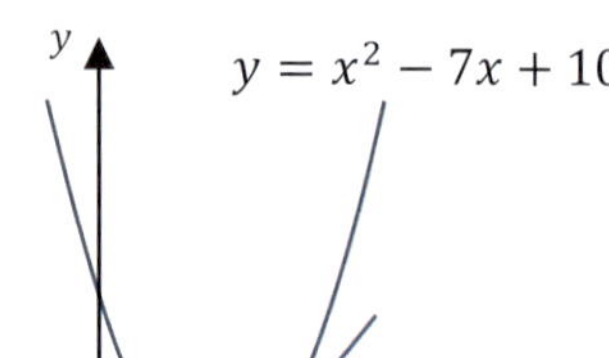

Solution:

Point

When $x = 4$

$y = (4)^2 - 7(4) + 10$

$y = -2$

$(4, -2)$
$a \quad b$

Gradient

$y = x^2 - 7x + 10$

$\frac{dy}{dx} = 2x - 7$

When $x = 4$

$\frac{dy}{dx} = m = 2(4) - 7 = 1$

Equation

$y - b = m(x - a)$

$y + 2 = (x - 4)$

$y = x - 6$

Exercise 11.5

1. In each of the following, find the equation of the tangent at the given point:

(a) $f(x) = x^2 - 5x$, when $x = 4$

(b) $f(x) = x^2 - 5x$, when $x = -1$

(c) $f(x) = x^2 - x - 6$, when $x = 2$

(d) $f(x) = 3x^2 + 2$, when $x = 1$

(e) $f(x) = 16 - x^2$, when $x = 3$

(f) $f(x) = x^2 - 5x + 6$, when $x = 7$

2. In each of the following, find the equation of the tangent at the given point:

(a) $f(x) = x^3 - 3x + 1$, when $x = 2$

(b) $f(x) = x^3 + x^2 + x - 2$, when $x = 1$

(c) $f(x) = x^3 + x^2 - 2$, when $x = -2$

(d) $f(x) = x^3 - 3x^2 + 4$, when $x = 0$

(e) $f(x) = x^3 - 2x^2 + 3x - 5$, when $x = 2$

(f) $f(x) = x(x - 2)(x + 4)$, when $x = 0$

(g) $f(x) = x^3 - 2x^2 - 5$, when $y = -5$

(h) $f(x) = (x + 1)(x - 3)(x + 6)$, when $x = -5$

3. In each of the following, find the equation of the tangent at the given point:

(a) $f(x) = \frac{6}{x}$, when $x = -3$.

(b) $f(x) = x - \frac{8}{x}$, when $x = 2$.

(c) $f(x) = \sqrt{x}$, when $y = 3$.

(d) $f(x) = 4x - \frac{4}{x}$, when $x = 4$.

(e) $f(x) = 6\sqrt{x} - 2x$, when $x = 4$.

(f) $f(x) = \sqrt{x} - \frac{18}{x}$, when $x = 9$.

11.6 Increasing and Decreasing Functions

A function is said to be **strictly increasing** at a given point or within a given range, when the graph of the function is moving **up** along the positive direction of the x-axis. The gradient of the tangent to the function at that point, or within the range, is **positive**, **i.e.** $\boldsymbol{f'(x) > 0}$.

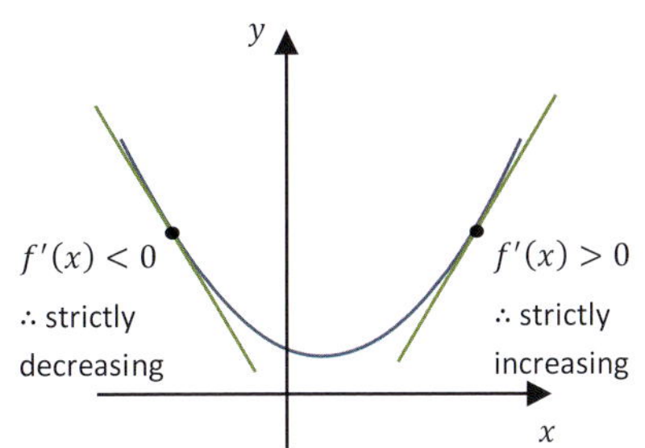

In like manner, a function is said to be **strictly decreasing** at a given point or within a given range, when the graph of the function is moving **down** along the positive direction of the x-axis. The gradient of the tangent to the function at that point, or within the range, is **negative**, **i.e.** $\boldsymbol{f'(x) < 0}$.

NB: When the graph is neither increasing nor decreasing, the gradient of the tangent to the function is zero. In this case, $f'(x) = 0$ (**section 11.7**).

Worked Examples:

1. Show that the function $f(x) = x^3 - 4x^2 + 3$ is strictly increasing at the point where $x = 3$.

Solution:

$f(x) = x^3 - 4x^2 + 3$
$f'(x) = 3x^2 - 8x$
When $x = 3$
$f'(3) = 3(3)^2 - 8(3) = 81 - 24 = 57$
$57 > 0 \therefore f(x)$ is strictly increasing when $x = 3$.

2. Determine the range of values for which $f(x) = x^3 + 6x^2 - 2$ is strictly decreasing.

Solution:

$f(x) = x^3 + 6x^2 - 2$
$f'(x) = 3x^2 + 12x$
For $f(x)$ decreasing, $f'(x) < 0$
$3x^2 + 12x < 0$
$3x(x + 4) = 0$
$x = 0$ or $x = -4$
$\therefore f(x)$ is strictly decreasing when for $-4 < x < 0$.

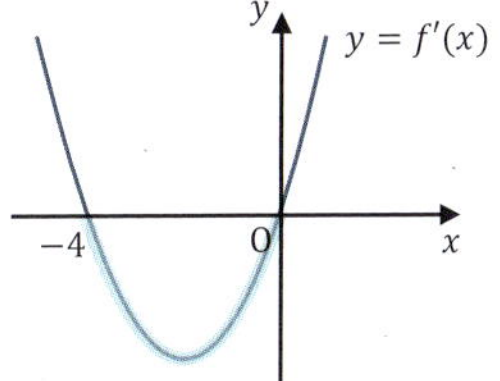

Sketch a graph to solve the quadratic inequation (see **section 2.9**).

3.
(a) Given that $f(x) = x^3 + 3x^2 + 5x + 2$, find $f'(x)$.
(b) Explain why the curve with equation $y = f(x)$ is strictly increasing for all values of x.

Solution:

(a) $f(x) = x^3 + 3x^2 + 5x + 2$
$f'(x) = 3x^2 + 6x + 5$

(b) $f'(x) = 3x^2 + 6x + 5$
$f'(x) = 3(x^2 + 2x) + 5$
$f'(x) = 3(x + 1)^2 + 5 - 3$
$f'(x) = 3(x + 1)^2 + 2$
$(x + 1)^2 \geq 0 \;\forall x$
$\therefore f'(x) > 0$
$\Rightarrow f(x)$ is always strictly increasing.

NB: $\forall x$ means 'for all values of x'.

Exercise 11.6

1. Show that the following functions are strictly increasing at the given point:

(a) $f(x) = x^2 - 2x + 1$, when $x = 4$.

(b) $f(x) = 3x - x^2$, when $x = -1$.

(c) $f(x) = x^2 - x - 2$, when $x = 6$.

(d) $f(x) = 3x^2 + 5$, when $x = 1$.

(e) $f(x) = x^3 + 4x^2 + 3$, when $x = -3$.

(f) $f(x) = x^3 - 5x^2 - 2x + 1$, when $x = 5$.

(g) $f(x) = 4\sqrt{x}$, when $x = 2$.

(h) $f(x) = \sqrt{x} - \frac{1}{x}$, when $x = 4$.

(i) $f(x) = 2x - \frac{5}{x}$, when $x = 4$.

(j) $f(x) = 2x^2 - \frac{2}{3x}$, when $x = 5$.

2. Show that the following functions are strictly decreasing at the given point:

(a) $f(x) = x^2 - 3x + 1$, when $x = -2$.

(b) $f(x) = 5x - 2x^2$, when $x = 3$.

(c) $f(x) = 3x^2 - 4x + 3$, when $x = -1$.

(d) $f(x) = 2x^3 - 2x + 3$, when $x = 1$.

(e) $f(x) = 4x^2 - 5x^3$, when $x = 2$.

(f) $f(x) = x^3 + 5x^2 - 2$, when $x = -1$.

(g) $f(x) = \frac{1}{\sqrt{x}}$, when $x = 4$.

(h) $f(x) = 2x + \frac{5}{\sqrt{x}}$, when $x = 1$.

(i) $f(x) = 3x + \frac{7}{x}$, when $x = -1$.

(j) $f(x) = \frac{1}{x} + x^2$, when $x = -2$.

3. Determine the range of values where the following are strictly increasing:

(a) $f(x) = x^2 + 2x$

(b) $f(x) = x^2 - 4x + 1$

(c) $f(x) = 9 + 2x - x^2$

(d) $f(x) = x^3 - 3x + 8$

(e) $f(x) = 12 + 3x^2 - x^3$

(f) $f(x) = 3x^3 - 9x^2 + 8$

(g) $f(x) = x^3 - 3x^2 - 45x + 4$

(h) $f(x) = x^3 + 3x^2 + 3x + 2$

(i) $f(x) = x^3 - 3x^2 - 9x + 9$

(j) $f(x) = x^3 - 6x^2 - 63x + 9$

(k) $f(x) = 1 - x^2 - \frac{1}{3}x^3$

(l) $f(x) = x^3 + 6x^2 + 8$

4. Determine the range of values where the following are strictly decreasing:

(a) $f(x) = x^2 - 6x$

(b) $f(x) = x^2 - 4x + 1$

(c) $f(x) = 16 - x^2$

(d) $f(x) = x^3 - 6x^2$

(e) $f(x) = 10 + 6x^2 - x^3$

(f) $f(x) = x^3 + 9x^2 + 15x$

(g) $f(x) = 2x^3 - 6x^2 - 90x - 2$

(h) $f(x) = x^3 - 6x^2 - 15x + 19$

(i) $f(x) = 72x - 3x^2 - x^3$

(j) $f(x) = x^3 - 3x + 9$

(k) $f(x) = 6 - 6x^2 - 2x^3$

(l) $f(x) = \frac{1}{3}x^3 - x^2 - 3$

5. Explain why each of the curves with equation $y = f(x)$ are strictly increasing for all values of x:

(a) $f(x) = x^3 - 6x^2 + 15x + 2$

(b) $f(x) = \frac{1}{3}x^3 + 2x^2 + 6x - 3$

(c) $f(x) = x^3 - 3x^2 + 5x - 1$

(d) $f(x) = \frac{1}{3}x^3 + x^2 + 5x + 7$ (e) $f(x) = x^3 + 12x^2 + 50x - 12$ (f) $f(x) = x^3 + 4x^2 + 7x + 9$

6. Explain why each of the curves with equation $y = f(x)$ are strictly decreasing for all values of x:

(a) $f(x) = 4 - 13x - 6x^2 - x^3$ (b) $f(x) = 9 - 5x - 2x^2 - \frac{1}{3}x^3$ (c) $f(x) = 1 - 4x + 3x^2 - x^3$

(d) $f(x) = 7 - 35x + 9x^2 - x^3$ (e) $f(x) = 11 - 2x - x^3$ (f) $f(x) = 14 - 5x - 2x^3$

11.7 Finding the Stationary Points and their Nature

In this section we will consider what happens when a curve is neither increasing nor decreasing – when this happens the curve is stationary. To find the **stationary points** of a curve, we need to find where the gradient of the tangent to the curve is equal to zero, **i.e.** where $\boldsymbol{f'(x) = 0}$.

The graph of a function is stationary in one of four ways; this is the **nature** of the stationary point.

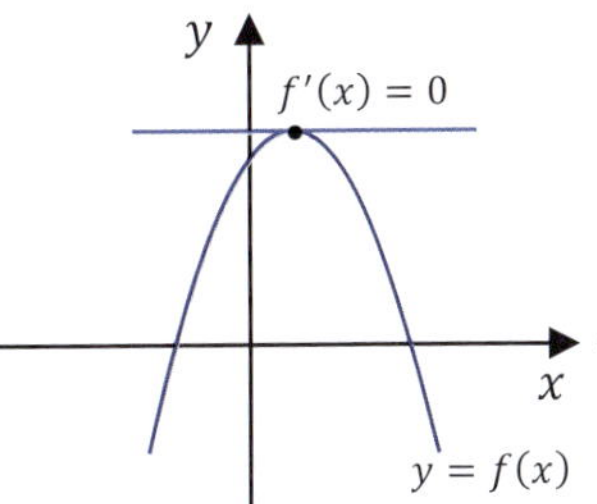

maximum turning point

y
y = f(x)
x
f′(x) = 0

minimum turning point

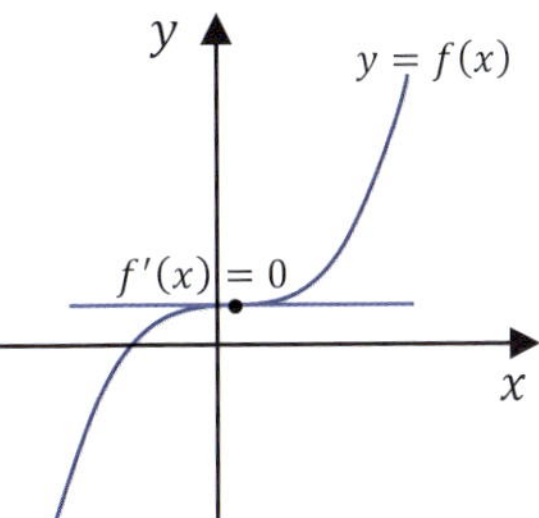

rising point of inflection

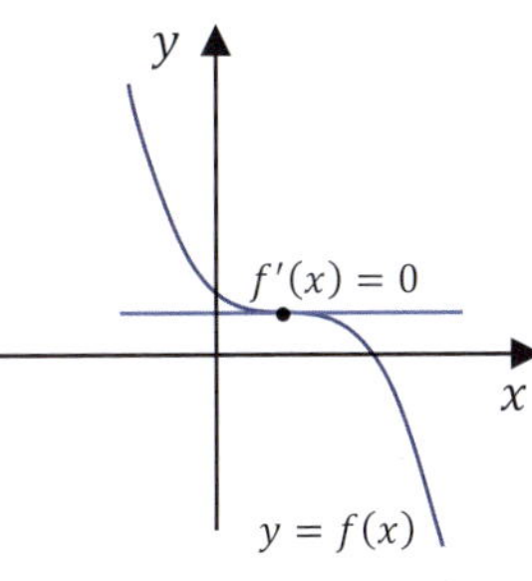

falling point of inflection

To find the coordinates of the stationary points of a curve:

i. differentiate the function
ii. equate to zero
iii. solve to find x-coordinate
iv. substitute into original curve to y-coordinate
v. draw a nature table to determine their nature
vi. answer the question

Nature table:

x	SP^-	SP	SP^+
$\frac{dy}{dx}$	$-$	0	$+$
Slope	\	—	/

Worked Examples:

1. Find the coordinates of the stationary points of the graph with equation $y = x^3 + 3x^2 - 24x + 5$ and determine their nature.

Solution:

i. $y = x^3 + 3x^2 - 24x + 5$

$\frac{dy}{dx} = 3x^2 + 6x - 24$

ii. Stationary points occur when $\frac{dy}{dx} = 0$.

$3x^2 + 6x - 24 = 0$

iii. $3(x^2 + 2x - 8) = 0$

$3(x + 4)(x - 2) = 0$

$x = -4$ or $x = 2$

iv. when $x = -4$, $y = (-4)^3 + 3(-4)^2 - 24(-4) + 5$

$y = -64 + 48 + 96 + 5 = 85$

when $x = 2$, $y = (2)^3 + 3(2)^2 - 24(2) + 5$

$y = 8 + 12 - 48 + 5 = -23$

v.

x	-4^-	-4	-4^+
$\frac{dy}{dx}$	+	0	−
Slope	/	—	\

x	2^-	2	2^+
$\frac{dy}{dx}$	−	0	+
Slope	\	—	/

vi. Maximum turning point at $(-4, 85)$ and minimum turning point at $(2, -23)$.

For the table on the left, select a value less than -4, for example -5 and evaluate $\frac{dy}{dx}$. A simple way to do this is to substitute -5 into the factorised form and check the signs, **e.g.** $3(-5+4)(-5-2) = 3(-1)(-7)$, which is positive. Do the same for a value greater than -4, but notice that this must be less than 2. Repeat the process for the other table.

2. Find the coordinates of the stationary points of the graph with equation $y = x^3 - 9x^2 + 27x - 25$ and determine their nature.

Solution:

i. $y = x^3 - 9x^2 + 27x - 22$

$\frac{dy}{dx} = 3x^2 - 18x + 27$

ii. Stationary points occur when $\frac{dy}{dx} = 0$.

$3x^2 - 18x + 27 = 0$

iii. $3(x^2 - 6x + 9) = 0$

$3(x-3)(x-3) = 0$

$x = 3 \; twice$

iv. when $x = 3$, $y = (3)^3 - 9(3)^2 + 27(3) - 22$

$y = 27 - 81 + 81 - 22 = 5$

v.

x	3^-	3	3^+
$\frac{dy}{dx}$	+	0	+
Slope	/	—	/

vi. Rising point of inflection at $(3, 5)$.

Exercise 11.7

1. Find the stationary points of the curves with the following equations and determine their nature:

(a) $f(x) = x^2 + 2x$
(b) $f(x) = x^2 - 4x + 1$
(c) $y = 11 + 6x - x^2$
(d) $f(x) = x^3 - 3x^2 + 3x - 2$
(e) $y = 15 - 12x + 6x^2 - x^3$
(f) $f(x) = x^3 + x^2$
(g) $y = x^3 - 3x^2 - 45x + 4$
(h) $f(x) = 1 - 3x^2 - \frac{1}{3}x^3$
(i) $f(x) = x^3 + x^2 + 3x + 9$
(j) $f(x) = x^3 - 6x^2 - 63x + 9$
(k) $f(x) = 1 - x^2 - \frac{1}{3}x^3$
(l) $y = 18 - 16x + 4x^2 - \frac{1}{3}x^3$

2. Find the stationary points of the curves with the following equations and determine their nature:

(a) $f(x) = 3x^4 + 8x^3 + 6$
(b) $f(x) = x^3(x+4)$
(c) $y = \frac{1}{4}x^4 - \frac{1}{2}x^2$
(d) $f(x) = 9 + 2x^2 - x^4$
(e) $y = x^2(8 - x^2)$
(f) $f(x) = x^4 - 4x^3 - 6$

3. Find the stationary points of the curves with the following equations and determine their nature:

(a) $f(x) = x + \frac{4}{x}$
(b) $f(x) = 16x + \frac{1}{x}$
(c) $y = 2x + \frac{32}{x}$

11.8 Sketching the Graph of a Function

To sketch the graph of a polynomial function, we need to determine four things: the **roots**, the **y-intercept**, the **stationary points** and their nature, and what the curve does when x is a **large positive** and **negative** value.

Worked Example:

Sketch the graph of $y = f(x)$ where $f(x) = x^3 + 6x^2 - 32$.

Solution:

Roots:

$x^3 + 6x^2 - 32 = 0$
$(x+4)(x^2 + 2x - 8) = 0$
$(x+4)(x+4)(x-2) = 0$
$x = -4$ twice or $x = 2$

-4	1	6	0	-32
		-4	-8	32
	1	2	-8	0

$\therefore (x+4)$ is a factor.

y-intercept (when $x = 0$):

$(0)^3 + 6(0)^2 - 32 = -32$

Stationary Points:

$f(x) = x^3 + 6x^2 - 32$
$f'(x) = 3x^2 + 12x$
Stationary points occur when $f'(x) = 0$.
$3x^2 + 12x = 0$
$3x(x+4) = 0$
$x = 0$ or $x = -4$

x	-4^-	-4	-4^+
$f'(x)$	$+$	0	$-$
Slope	/	—	\

x	0^-	0	0^+
$f'(x)$	$-$	0	$+$
Slope	\	—	/

when $x = -4$

$y = (-4)^3 + 6(-4)^2 - 32 = -64 + 96 - 32 = 0$

when $x = 0$

$y = (0)^3 + 6(0)^2 - 32 = -32$

Maximum turning point at $(-4, 0)$ and minimum turning point at $(0, -32)$.

Large positive and negative x:

$f(x) = x^3 + 6x^2 - 32$

As $x \to \infty, f(x) \to \infty$

As $x \to -\infty, f(x) \to -\infty$

At this stage consider what is happening as $x \to \pm\infty$ (tends towards positive and negative infinity). In this case, as x becomes larger, $f(x)$ becomes larger and as x becomes larger negative, $f(x)$ becomes larger negative.

Sketch:

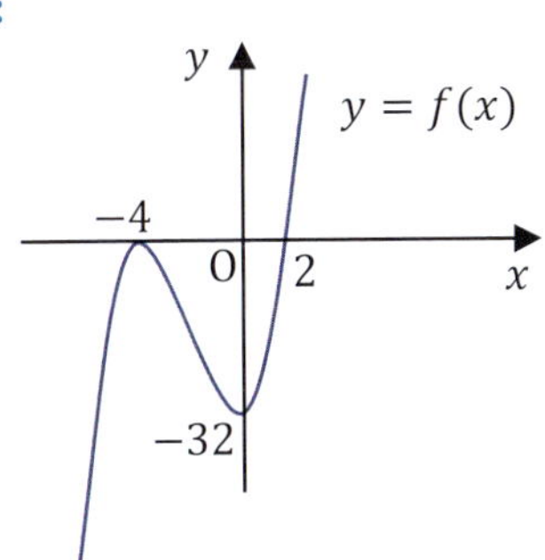

NB: When sketching the curve, ensure the roots, y-intercept and turning points are all clearly labelled.

Exercise 11.8

1. Sketch the graph of $y = f(x)$ when:

(a) $f(x) = x^2 + 4x$ (b) $f(x) = x^2 - 2x - 15$ (c) $y = 16 - 6x - x^2$

(d) $f(x) = x^3 + 3x^2$ (e) $y = 6x^2 - x^3$ (f) $f(x) = x(x+3)^2$

2. Sketch the graph of $y = f(x)$ when:

(a) $f(x) = \frac{1}{3}x^3 - 9x - 18$ (b) $f(x) = x^3 - 8$ (c) $y = (x-3)(x-6)^2$

(d) $f(x) = 2x^3 - 12x^2 + 64$ (e) $y = x^4 - 4x^3 + 4x^2$ (f) $f(x) = x^4 + 4x^3 + 27$

11.9 Optimisation

Optimisation is the process of finding an **optimal solution** to a given problem. To find an optimal solution, we find the stationary points of the given function.

Worked Examples:

1. The area of a rectangle is given by the $A(x) = 3x^2 - 2x^3$, $x > 0$. Find the value of x which maximises the area and calculate the maximum area of the rectangle.

Solution:

Stationary Points:

$A(x) = 3x^2 - 2x^3$

$A'(x) = 6x - 6x^2$

Stationary points occur when $A'(x) = 0$.

$6x - 6x^2 = 0$

$6x(1-x) = 0$

~~$x = 0$~~ or $x = 1$

x	1^-	1	1^+
$A'(x)$	$+$	0	$-$
Slope	/	—	\

when $x = 1$

$A(1) = 3(1)^2 - 2(1)^3 = 1$ $\therefore$ maximum area is 1 unit^2 when $x = 1$.

NB: The solution $x = 0$ is disregarded as it is not valid. The rectangle could not have an area of 0 units^2.

2. The surface area of a box is given by $A(x) = 2x^2 + \dfrac{256}{x}$, $x > 0$. Find the value of x which maximises the surface area and calculate the maximum surface area of the box.

Solution:

Stationary Points:

$A(x) = 2x^2 + \dfrac{256}{x} = 2x^2 + 256x^{-1}$

$A'(x) = 4x - 256x^{-2}$

Stationary points occur when $A'(x) = 0$.

$4x - 256x^{-2} = 0$

$4x = \dfrac{256}{x^2}$

$4x^3 = 256$

$x^3 = 64$

x	4^-	4	4^+
$A'(x)$	$+$	0	$-$
Slope	/	—	\

$x = 4$ $A(4) = 2(4)^2 + \dfrac{256}{4} = 32 + 64 = 96$ $\therefore$ maximum surface area is 96 units^2 when $x = 4$.

Exercise 11.9A

1. In each of the following questions, the area of a shape is given by function. Calculate the value of x, where $x > 0$, which maximises the area and calculate the maximum area.

(a) $A(x) = 12x^2 - 2x^3$
(b) $A(x) = 24x^2 - 4x^3$
(c) $A(x) = 48x^2 - x^3$
(d) $A(x) = 1500 + 36x^2 - 4x^3$
(e) $A(x) = 8x^3 - x^4$
(f) $A(x) = 15 + 8x^3 - 2x^4$

2. In each of the following questions, the surface area of a shape is given by function. Calculate the value of x, where $x > 0$, which minimises the surface area and calculate the minimum area.

(a) $A(x) = 2x + \dfrac{18}{x}$
(b) $A(x) = 5x + \dfrac{45}{x}$
(c) $A(x) = 7x + \dfrac{112}{x}$
(d) $A(x) = 8x + \dfrac{392}{x}$
(e) $A(x) = 11x + \dfrac{891}{x}$
(f) $A(x) = 15x + \dfrac{240}{x}$

3. In each of the following questions, the surface area of a shape is given by function. Calculate the value of x which minimises the surface area and calculate the minimum surface area.

(a) $A(x) = 2x^2 + \dfrac{32}{x}$
(b) $A(x) = 3x^2 + \dfrac{162}{x}$
(c) $A(x) = x^2 + \dfrac{432}{x}$
(d) $A(x) = 2x^2 + \dfrac{1372}{x}$
(e) $A(x) = 3x^2 + \dfrac{7986}{x}$
(f) $A(x) = 4x^2 + \dfrac{8000}{x}$

In many cases, optimisation questions involve proving a formula from the given information. This typically involves using common formulae to express one of the variables in terms of the other, and then substituting the replaced variable.

Worked Example:

The roof of a new bungalow is in the shape of a triangular prism. The volume of the roof space is 32 cubic metres. The roof must be covered in roofing felt before tiling, including both ends.

The cross-section of the roof is a right-angled, isosceles triangle of sides x and the length of the prism is l.

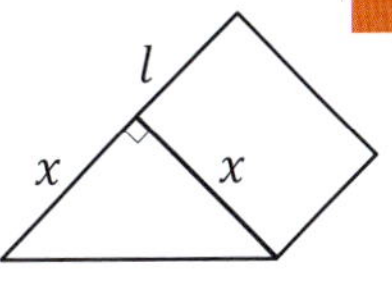

(a) Show that the surface area of the roof $A\ m^2$ requiring felt, is given by $A(x) = x^2 + \dfrac{128}{x}$

(b) Find the value of x which minimises the surface area.

Solution: Find an expression for the volume and surface area, and substitute to prove the formula.

(a) **Volume of the prism:**

$$V = \frac{1}{2}lbh$$

$$32 = \frac{1}{2} \times x^2 \times l$$

$$l = \frac{64}{x^2}$$

Surface area of the prism:

$$A(x) = 2\left(\frac{1}{2}x^2\right) + 2(lx)$$

$$A(x) = x^2 + 2lx = x^2 + 2x\left(\frac{64}{x^2}\right)$$

$$A(x) = x^2 + \frac{128x}{x^2} = x^2 + \frac{128}{x}$$

(b) $A(x) = x^2 + \frac{128}{x} = x^2 + 128x^{-1}$

$A'(x) = 2x - 128x^{-2} = 2x - \frac{128}{x^2}$

Stationary points occur when $A'(x) = 0$.

$2x - \frac{128}{x^2} = 0$

$2x = \frac{128}{x^2}$

$2x^3 = 128$

$x^3 = 64$

x	4^-	4	4^+
$A'(x)$	$-$	0	$+$
Slope	╲	—	╱

$x = 4$ $\qquad A(4) = (4)^2 + \frac{128}{4} = 16 + 32 = 48$ $\therefore$ maximum surface area is $96\ m^2$ when $x = 4$.

NB: Since the answer to part (a) is usually given, it is often possible to answer part (b) without doing part (a).

Exercise 11.9B

1. A tank is in the shape of a triangular prism. The volume of the tank is 62.5 litres.

   The cross-section of the tank is a right-angled, isosceles triangle of sides x and the length of the prism is l.

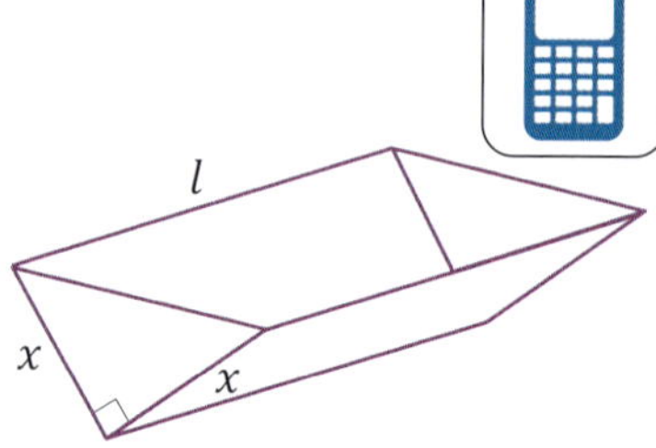

(a) Show that the internal surface area of the tank, $A\ cm^2$, is given by $A(x) = x^2 + \frac{250{,}000}{x}$.

(b) Find the value of x which minimises the surface area.

2. An allotment is fenced into six different plots – each plot is l metres by b metres as shown in the diagram.

   The total length of fencing required for all the allotment is 270 metres.

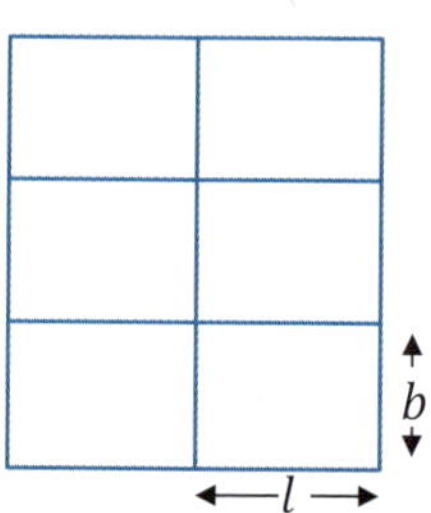

(a) Show that the total area of the allotments, $A\ m^2$, is given by $A(l) = 180l - \frac{16}{3}l^2$.

(b) Find the value of l which maximises the area.

3. A half-cylinder has a volume of 12 cubic centimetres. The radius of the half-cylinder is r centimetres and the height h centimetres. The curved surface and the semi-circular ends of the half-cylinder are painted.

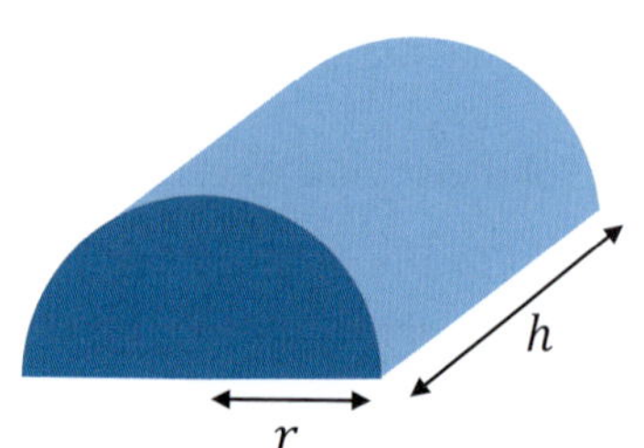

(a) Show that the surface area of the half-cylinder to be painted, $A\ cm^2$, is given by the formula:

$A = \pi r^2 + \frac{24}{r}$.

(b) Determine the value of r which minimises the surface area.

4. A rectangle must be cut out of a right-angled, isosceles triangle. The length of the equal sides of the triangle are 8 centimetres.

(a) Show that the area of the rectangle, $A\ cm^2$, is given by $A(x) = 8\sqrt{2}x - 2x^2$.

(b) Determine the value of x which maximises the area and calculate the maximum area.

5. A rectangle is placed between two parabolas with equations $y = 16 - 4x^2$ and $y = \frac{5}{8}(16 - 4x^2)$. The lower two vertices of the rectangle touch the upper parabola and the sides of the rectangle are parallel to the x and y-axes. The length of the rectangle is x units.

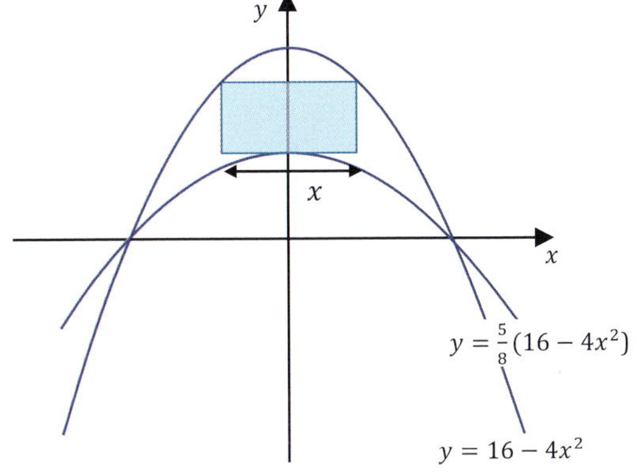

(a) Show that the total area of the rectangle, $A\ units^2$, is given by $A(x) = 6x - x^3$.

(b) Determine the value of x which maximises the area and calculate the minimum area.

6. A scoop on a small construction loader is in the shape of a triangular prism. The volume of the scoop is 171.5 litres.

The cross-section of the scoop is a right-angled, isosceles triangle of sides x and the length of the prism is l.

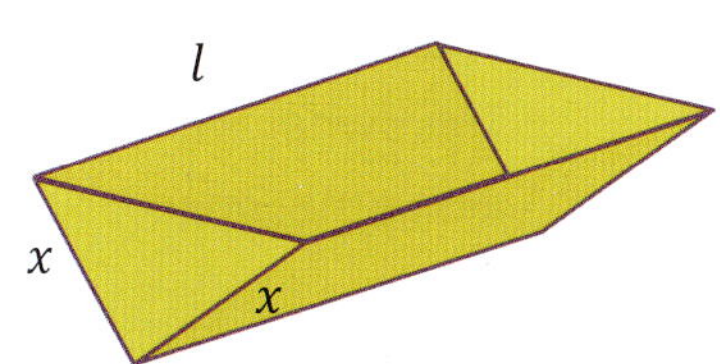

(a) Show that the internal surface area of the tank, $A\ cm^2$, is given by $A(x) = x^2 + \dfrac{686{,}000}{x}$.

(b) Find the value of x which minimises the surface area.

7. An industrial estate is fenced into eight identical plots – each plot is fenced around its perimeter, l metres by b metres, as shown in the diagram.

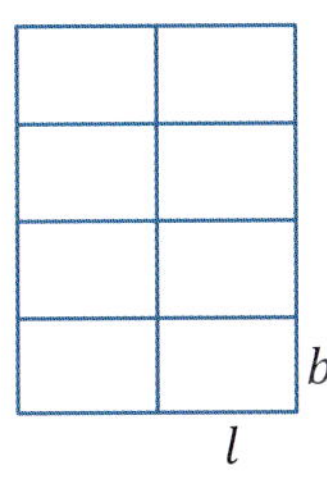

The length of fencing required for the estate is 8 kilometres.

(a) Show that the total area of the industrial estate, $A\ m^2$, is given by $A(b) = 6400b - \dfrac{48}{5}b^2$.

(b) Find the value of b which maximises the area.

8. A cylinder has a volume of 1357 cubic centimetres. The radius of the cylinder is r centimetres and the height h centimetres.

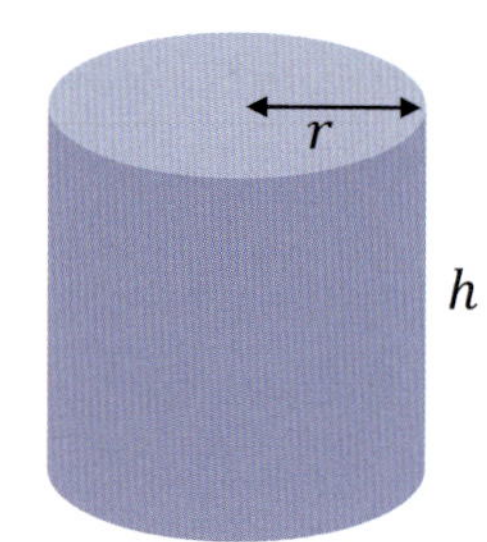

(a) Show that the surface area of the cylinder, $A\ cm^2$, is given by

$A = 2\pi r^2 + \dfrac{2714}{r}$.

(b) Determine the value of r which minimises the surface area.

9. An open top, square based box has a volume of 256 cubic centimetres. The inside of the box is lined with paper. Its base has dimensions x centimetres and height h centimetres.

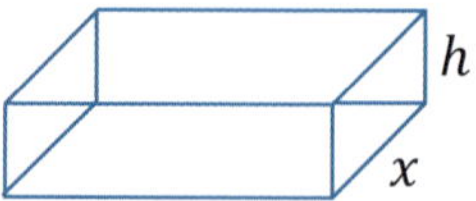

(a) Show that the area, $A\ cm^2$, of paper required to line the box is given by

$A(x) = x^2 + \dfrac{1024}{x}$.

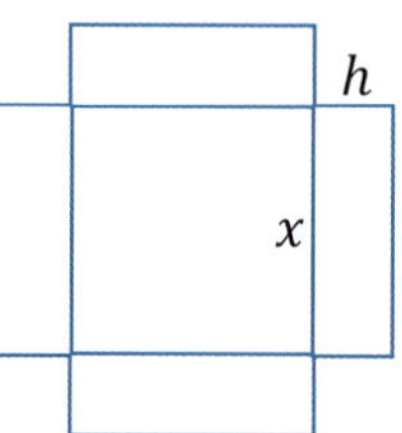

(b) Determine the value of x which minimises the area and calculate the minimum area of cardboard required.

10. A garden is in the shape of a right-angled, isosceles triangle. The length of the equal sides of the triangle are 12 metres. The owner wants to cultivate a rectangular lawn in the garden along the longest side.

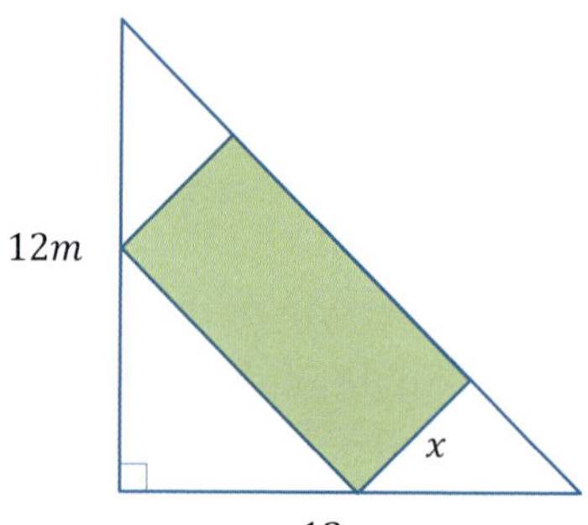

(a) Show that the total area of the lawn, $A\ m^2$, is given by
$A(x) = 12\sqrt{2}x - 2x^2$.

(b) Determine the value of x which maximises the area and calculate the maximum area.

11. A rectangle is placed between two parabolas with equations $y = 36 - 4x^2$ and $y = \frac{1}{3}(36 - 4x^2)$. The upper two vertices of the rectangle touch the upper parabola and the sides of the rectangle are parallel to the x and y-axes. The length of the rectangle is x units.

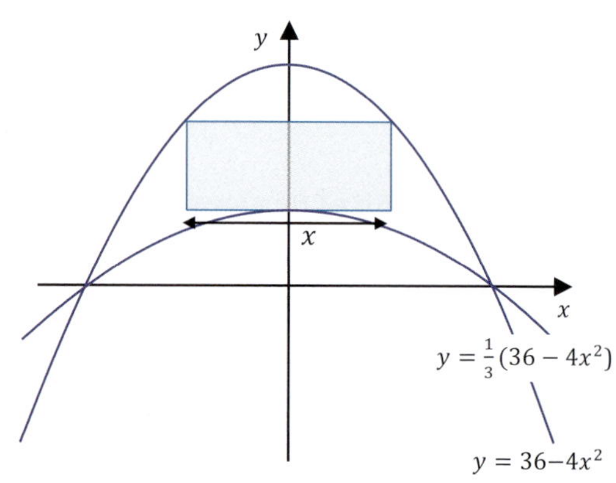

(a) Show that the total area of the rectangle, $A\ units^2$, is given by
$A(x) = 24x - x^3$.

(b) Determine the value of x which maximises the area and calculate the maximum area.

11.10 Closed Intervals

A closed interval is a defined interval on the domain (the x-values) of the function. When determining the maximum and minimum values of a function within a closed interval, we need to know two pieces of information: the value of the function at the stationary points and the value of the function at the extents of the interval.

Worked Example:

The function $f(x) = x^3 - 6x^2 + 5$ is defined on the domain $-1 \leq x \leq 2$. Determine the maximum and minimum values of the function.

Solution:

Stationary Points:

$f(x) = x^3 - 6x^2 + 5$

$f'(x) = 3x^2 - 12x$

Stationary points occur when $f'(x) = 0$.

$3x^2 - 12x = 0$

$3x(x - 4) = 0$

$x = 0$ or $x = 4$

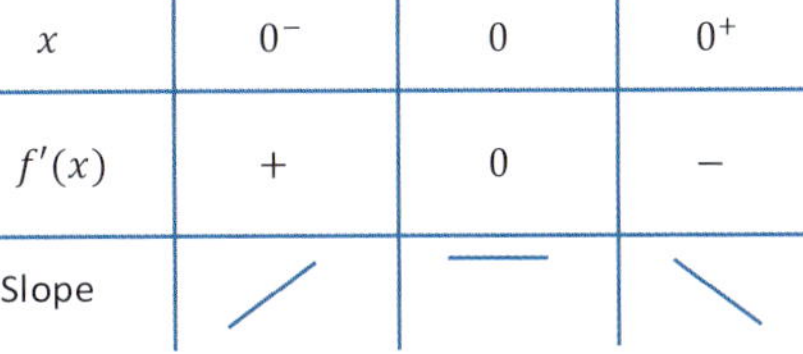

x	0^-	0	0^+
$f'(x)$	$+$	0	$-$
Slope	/	—	\

when $x = 0$

$f(0) = (0)^3 - 6(0)^2 + 5 = 5$ $\quad\therefore$ maximum turning point at $(0, 5)$.

Extents of domain:

when $x = -1$

$f(0) = (-1)^3 - 6(-1)^2 + 5 = -2$

when $x = 2$

$f(2) = (2)^3 - 6(2)^2 + 5 = -11$

$\therefore$ maximum value is 5 when $x = 0$ and minimum value is -11 when $x = 2$.

Exercise 11.10

1. For each of the following functions defined on the given domain, determine the maximum and minimum values of f:

(a) $f(x) = x^2 - 6x,\ 1 \leq x \leq 4$

(b) $f(x) = x^2 - 2x - 8,\ 0 \leq x \leq 3$

(c) $f(x) = 5 - 4x - x^2, -4 \leq x \leq 2$

(d) $f(x) = (3 + x)(7 - x), -4 \leq x \leq 4$

2. For each of the following functions defined on the given domain, determine the maximum and minimum values of f:

(a) $f(x) = x^3 - x^2 + 9,\ 0 \leq x \leq 3$

(b) $f(x) = x^3 - 9x^2 + 15x - 2,\ 0 \leq x \leq 3$

(c) $f(x) = 2x^3 - 24x - 2, -2 \leq x \leq 5$

(d) $f(x) = 7 - 24x^2 - 4x^3, -5 \leq x \leq 0$

(e) $f(x) = x^4 - 8x^2 + 2, -1 \leq x \leq 3$

(f) $f(x) = x^4 - 4x^3 + 2, -1 \leq x \leq 4$

(g) $f(x) = x^4 - 8x^3 + 10x^2 - 3, 0 \leq x \leq 7$

(h) $f(x) = 4 - 6x^3 + x^4, 0 \leq x \leq 5$

11.11 Sketching the Derived Function

To sketch the graph of the derivative of a function, **i.e.** the derived function, we use what we already know. The derivative is the rate of change of the function or, more helpfully, the gradient of the tangent of the curve. As we know from a nature table, when the derivative of a function is **positive**, the slope of the curve is **increasing**, when the derivative is **negative**, the slope is **decreasing** and when the derivative is **zero**, the curve is **stationary**.

Keep these facts in mind when sketching the derived function.

Worked Example:

The diagram shows the graph of $y = f(x)$ with stationary points at (a, b) and $(4, 0)$.
Sketch the graph of $y = f'(x)$.

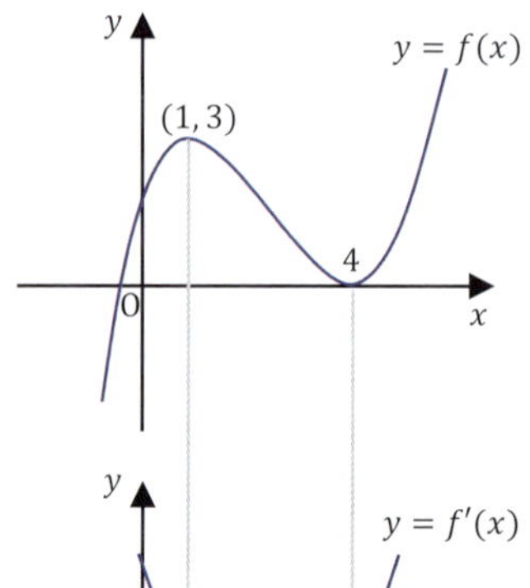

NB: When sketching the derived function, the graph of $f'(x)$ is always of a power 1 degree less than $f(x)$. A quartic will result in a cubic, a cubic will result in a quadratic and a quadratic will result in a straight line.

Solution:

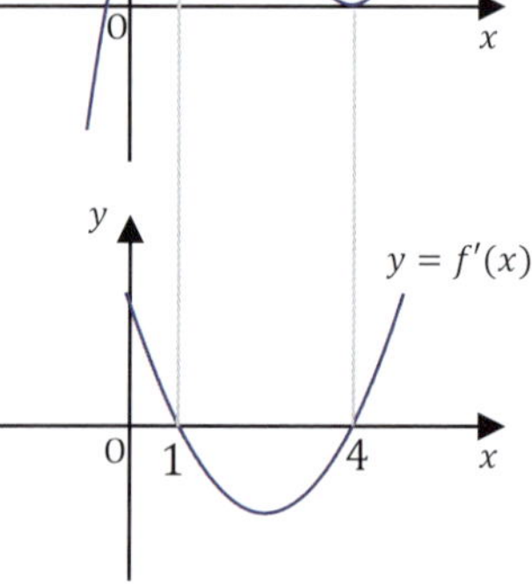

Step 1: Identify the stationary points. Draw a set of axes directly below the graph and then draw a dotted line from the stationary points of $f(x)$ to the x-axis below.

Step 2: Consider the graph of the derived function as a graph of the gradient of the function. Where $f(x)$ is increasing, $x < 1$ and $x > 4$, the graph of $f'(x)$ is positive, **i.e.** above the x-axis. Where $f(x)$ is decreasing, $1 < x < 4$, the graph of $f'(x)$ is negative, **i.e.** below the x-axis.

Exercise 11.11

1. In each of the following diagrams the graph of $y = f(x)$ is shown. Sketch the graph of $f'(x)$:

(a)

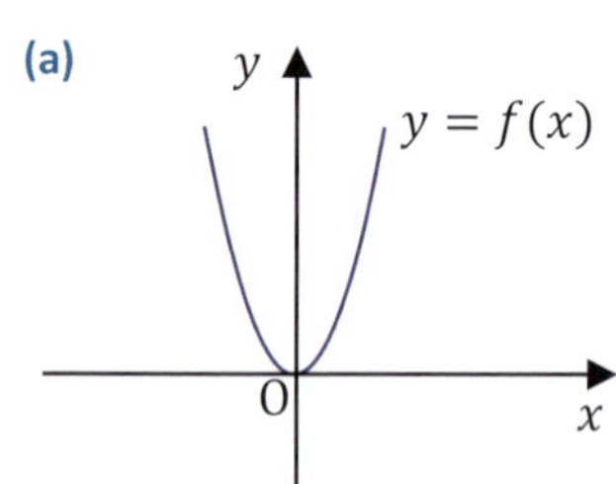

(b)

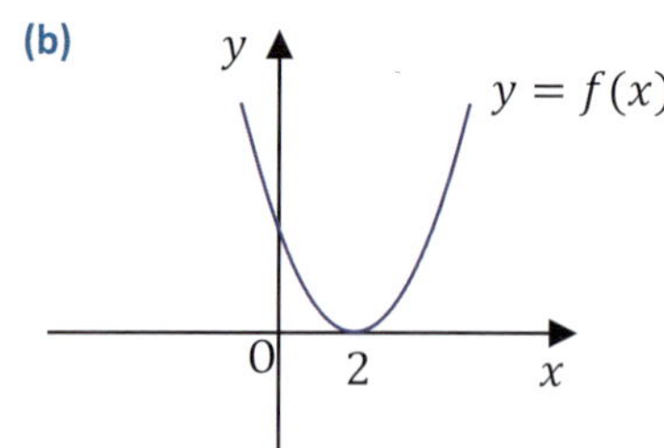

(c)

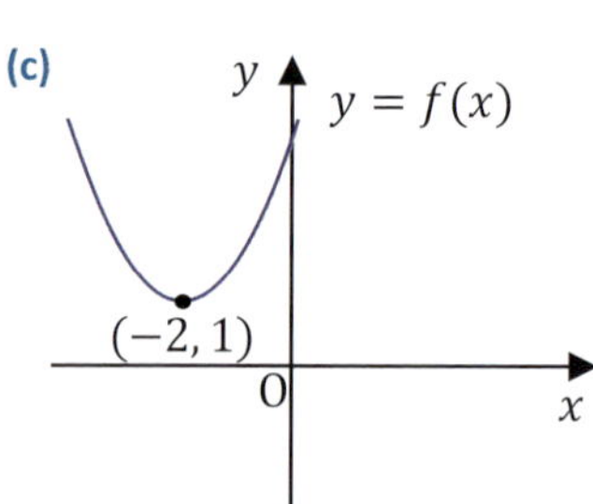

(d)

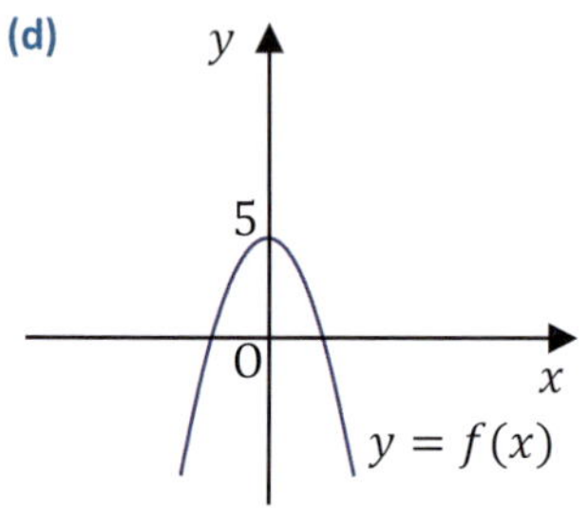

(e)

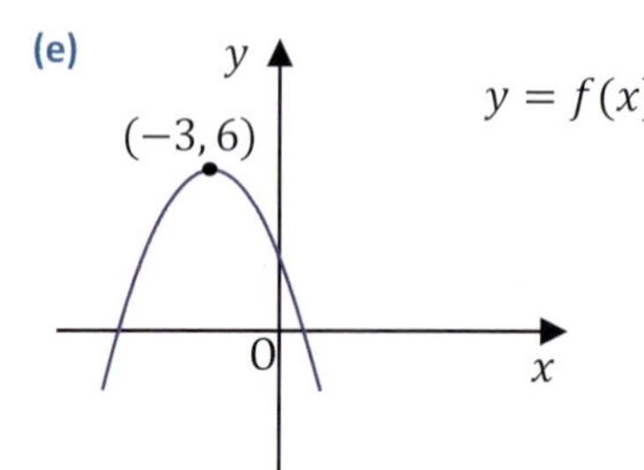

(f)

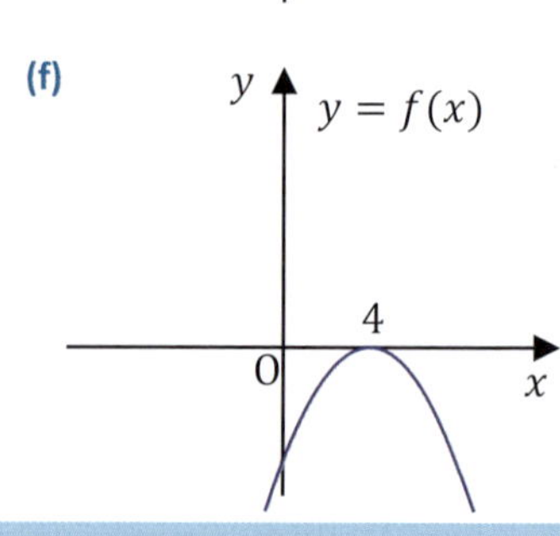

2. In each of the following diagrams the graph of $y = f(x)$ is shown. The stationary points are marked on each diagram. Sketch the graph of $f'(x)$:

(a)

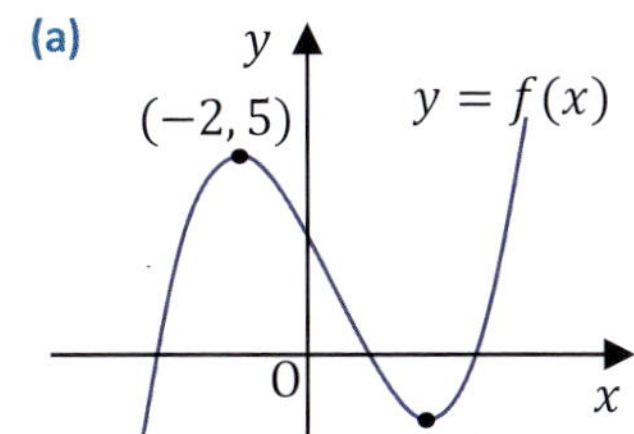

(b)

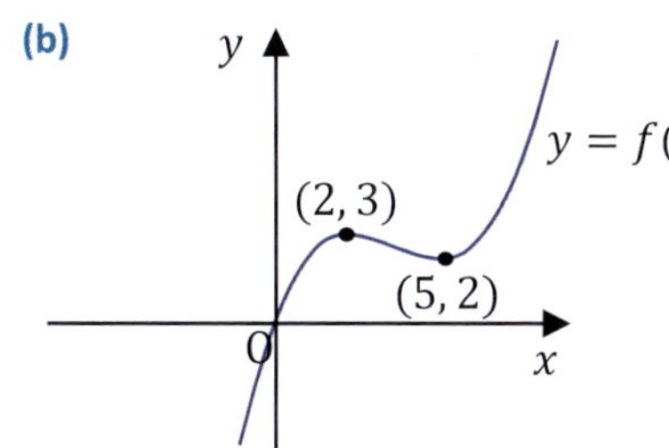

(c)

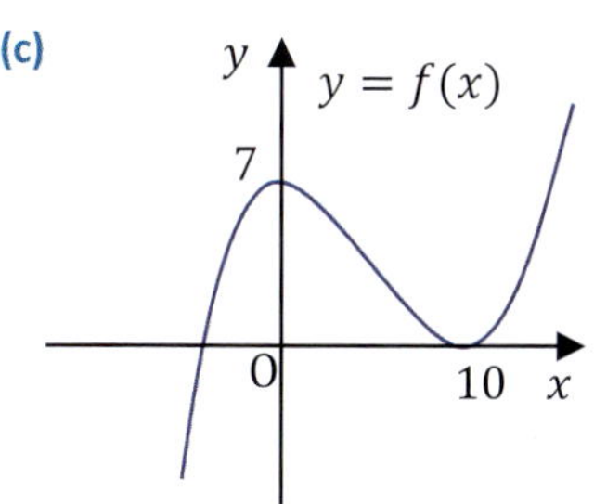

(d)

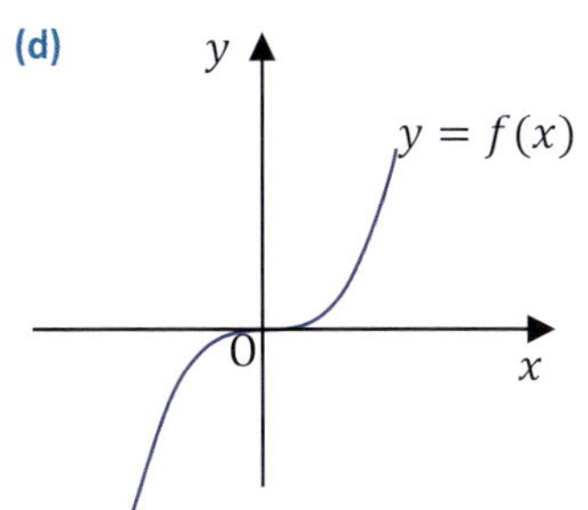

(e)

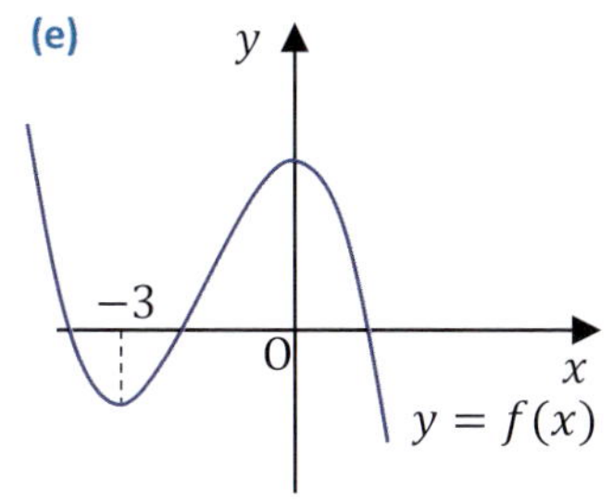

(f)

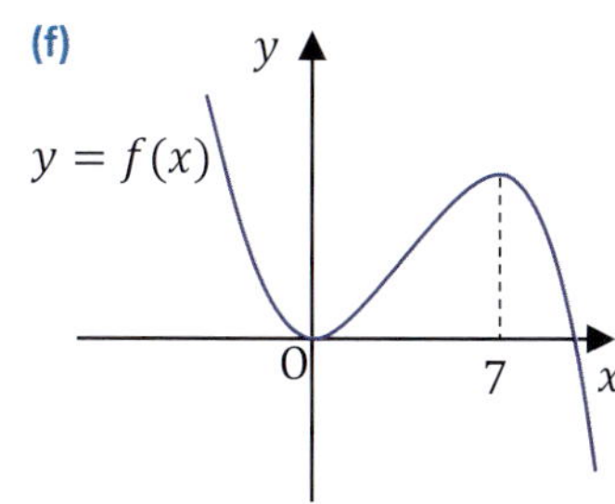

(g)

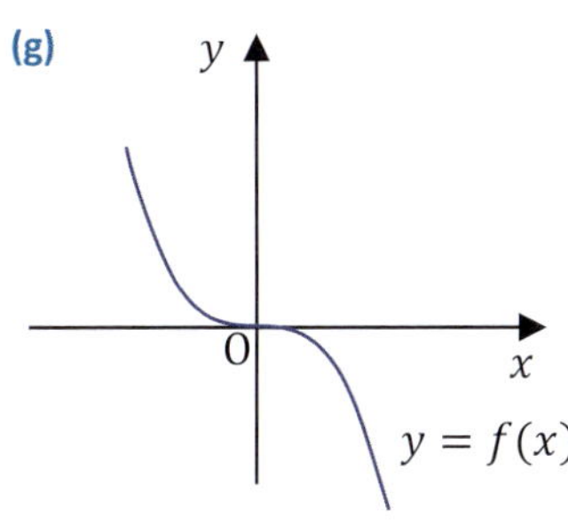

(h)

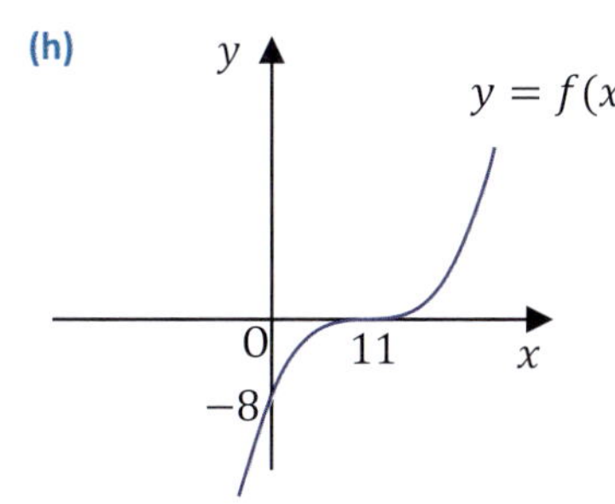

(i)

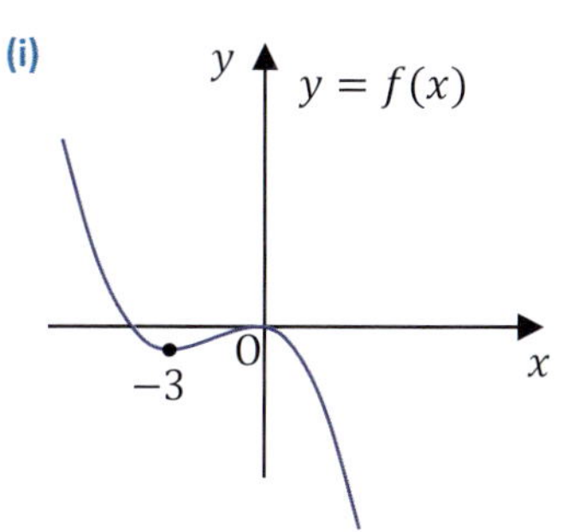

3. In each of the following diagrams the graph of $y = f(x)$ is shown. The stationary points are marked on each diagram. Sketch the graph of $f'(x)$:

(a)

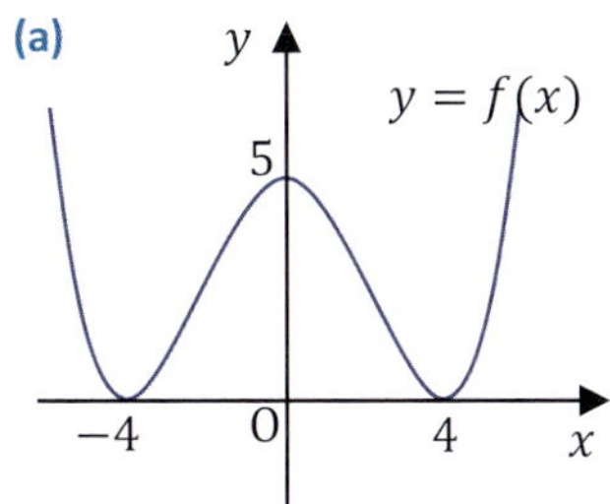

(b)

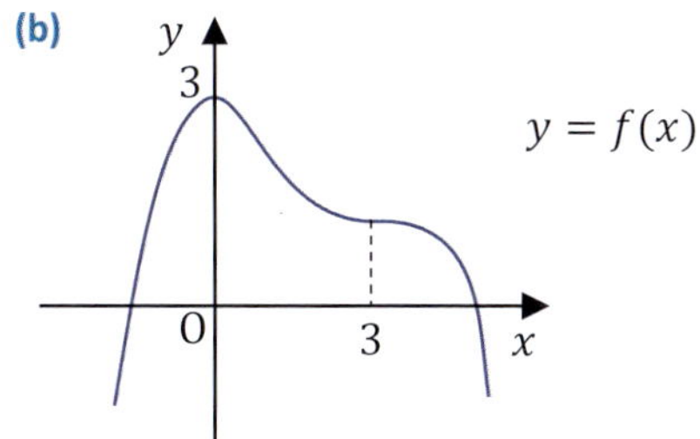

(c)

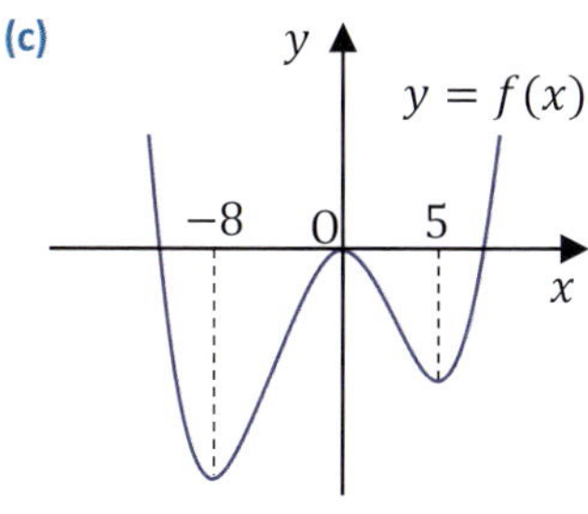

(d)

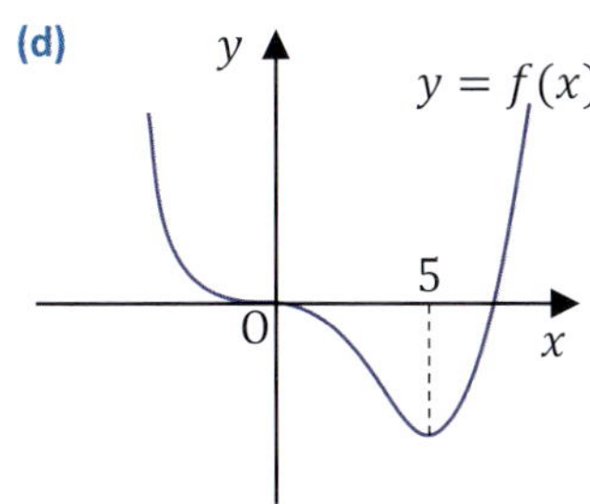

(e)

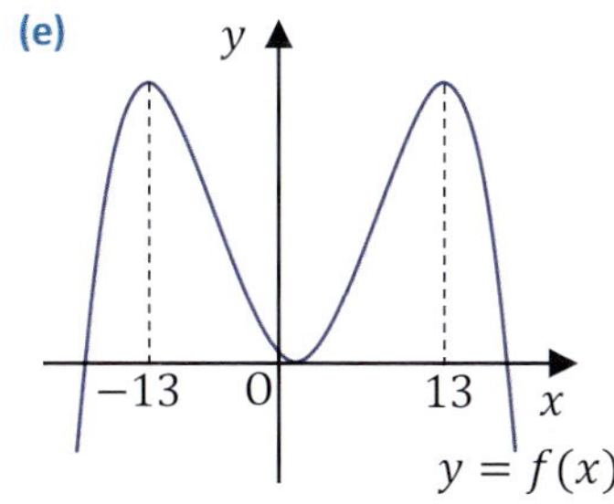

(f)

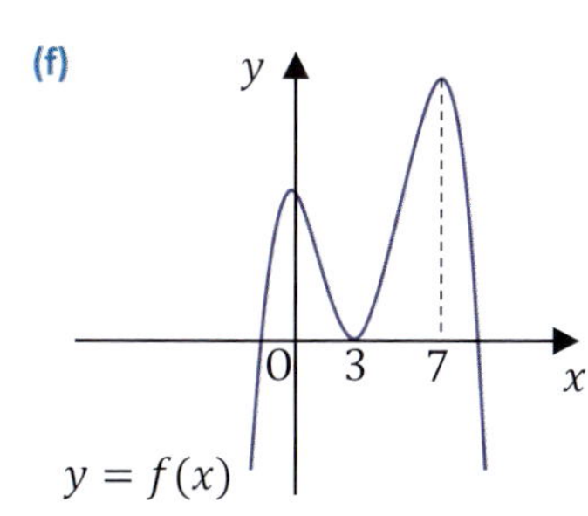

(g)

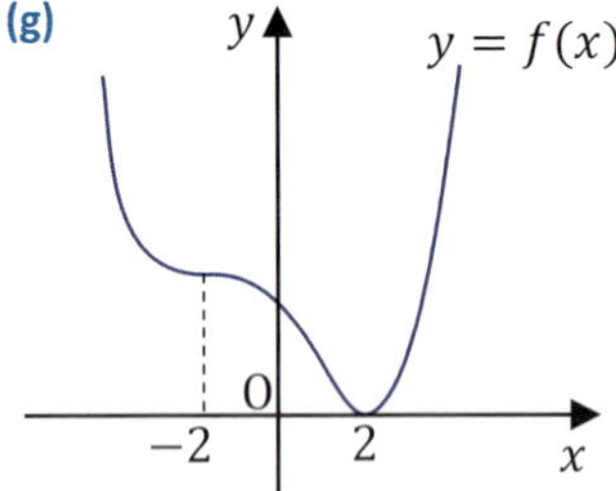

(h)

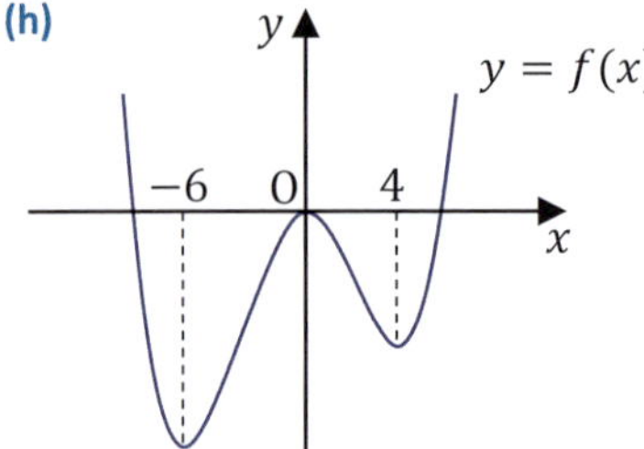

(i)

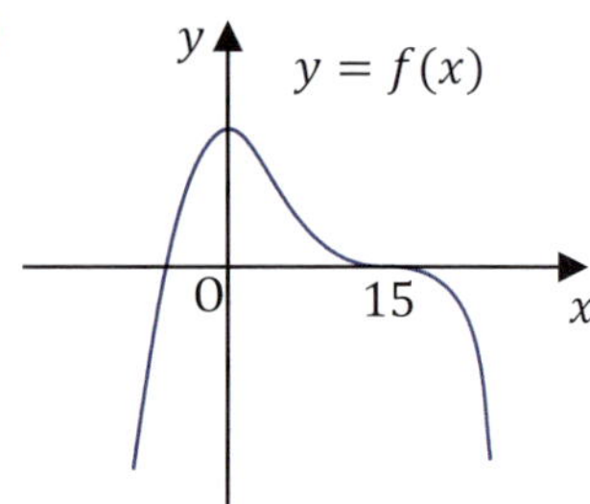

11.12 Review

Exercise 11.12

11.2 Differentiate each of the following functions:

(a) $f(x) = 10x^{\frac{3}{5}}$ (b) $y = 4x^2 - 18x + 2$ (c) $f(x) = \dfrac{3}{\sqrt{x}}$

11.3 Differentiate each of the following functions:

(a) $f(x) = x^2(\sqrt{x} - x)$ (b) $y = \dfrac{5x^3 - x^2 - 4}{2x^4}$ (c) $y = \dfrac{x^2 + 2x - 1}{4\sqrt{x}}$

11.4 (a) Given that $f(x) = 4\sqrt{x^3} - 2x^2$, find $f'(9)$.

(b) Find the gradient of the tangent to the curve $y = x^3 - 3x^2 + x$ when $x = 3$.

(c) A function f is defined on a suitable domain by $f(x) = \dfrac{x^2 + 3}{\sqrt{x}}$. Calculate the rate of change of f when $x = 4$.

11.5 Find the equation of the tangent to the curve $y = x^3 + 2x^2 - 3x + 2$ at the point where $x = -2$.

11.6 (a) A function f is defined on a suitable domain by $f(x) = 5x + \dfrac{3}{x}$. Show that the function is strictly increasing at the point where $x = -1$.

(b) A function f is defined on a suitable domain by $f(x) = 12 + 3x^2 - x^3$. Determine the range of values of x for which f is strictly increasing.

(c) A function f is defined on a suitable domain by $f(x) = 6 - 6x^2 - 2x^3$. Determine the range of values of x for which f is strictly decreasing.

(d) Given that $f(x) = x^3 - 6x^2 + 19x$. Explain why the curve $y = f(x)$ is increasing for all values of x.

11.7 Find the stationary points on the curve with equation $y = x^3 - 6x^2 + 18$ and determine their nature.

11.8 Sketch the graph of the curve with equation $y = \frac{1}{2}x^3 - 8x$.

11.9 A half-cylinder feeding trough has a volume of 80 litres. The radius of the half-cylinder is r centimetres and the length l centimetres.

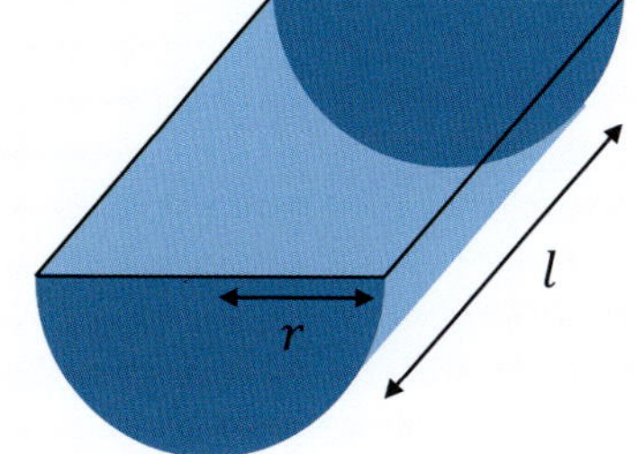

(a) Show that the internal surface area of the feeding trough, $A\ cm^2$, is given by:

$$A = \pi r^2 + \frac{160}{r}.$$

(b) Determine the value of r which minimises the surface area.

11.10 A function f is defined on the domain $1 \le x \le 7$ by $f(x) = \frac{1}{2}x^3 - 4x^2 + 2$.
Determine the maximum and minimum values of f.

11.11 The diagram shows the graph of $y = f(x)$, with stationary points at $(-5, 8)$ and $(5, 0)$.

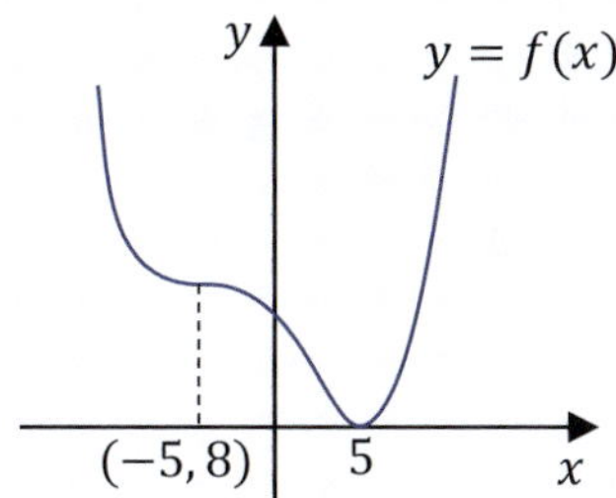

Sketch the graph of $y = f'(x)$.

Chapter 12

Calculus 2 - Integration

Integration

Integration or **integral calculus** is the reverse process of differentiation. If we have a differentiated function, $f(x)$, we can integrate that function to arrive at the antiderivative of the function, $F(x)$. Integration is used to solve mathematical and physics problems relating to area, volume, length of curves, etc.

The notation for integration is: $\int ax^n \, dx$. The integral symbol $\int$ is a long 's', which was used in older English writing as a lower case 's'. In integral calculus it means 'the sum of', much like the Greek letter sigma in other mathematical operations. The dx means 'a small change in x', or to be more accurate, an infinitesimally small change in x. When we integrate, we sum together all the infinitesimally small parts of x.

When we integrate, we add one to the power of x and divide by the new power:

$$\int x^n \, dx = \frac{x^{n+1}}{n+1}$$

What we do next depends on whether we have an **indefinite** or **definite integral**.

Indefinite Integrals

When we integrate indefinite integrals, we add one to the power of x and divide by the new power:

$$\int f(x) \, dx = F(x) + C$$

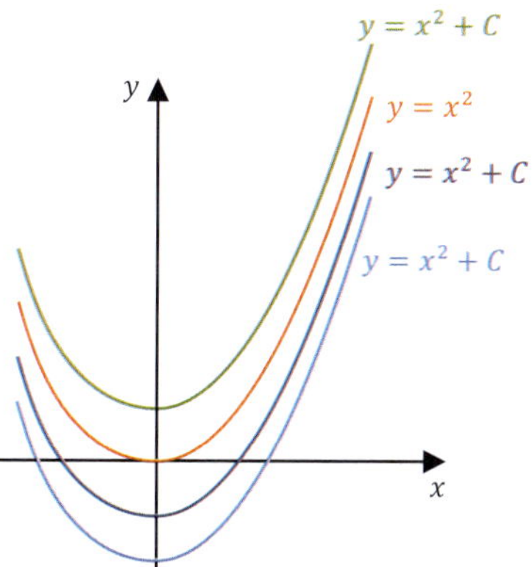

We also add on the value C. This is known as the constant of integration. This is because the antiderivative of any function has an unlimited number of possible solutions. If we differentiate x^2 we have $2x$, but if we differentiate $x^2 + 4$, we also have $2x$. If we differentiate $x^2 + C$, where C is any value, we end up with $2x$. Therefore, when we find the antiderivative of $2x$, or any function, we find the set of all antiderivatives of that function.

Definite Integrals

Definite integrals differ from indefinite both in what they do and how they appear. A definite integral is used to find the area between the graph and the x-axis, or between two curves, bounded by two limits:

$$\int_a^b f(x) \, dx = F(b) - F(a)$$

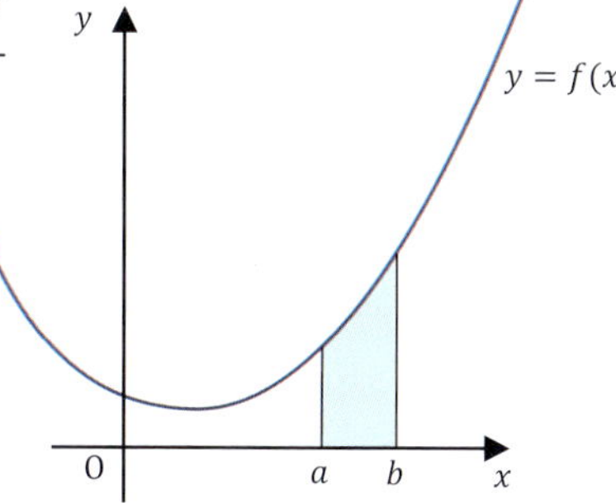

12.1 Basic Integration

When we integrate, we add one to the power and divide by the new power:

$$\int x^n \, dx = \frac{x^{n+1}}{n+1} + C$$

When the integral is indefinite, **i.e.** it has no limits, we also add on the value C. This is known as the constant of integration.

Worked Examples:

1. Integrate each of the following:

(a) $\int x^2 \, dx$

$= \frac{x^{2+1}}{2+1} + C$

$= \frac{x^3}{3} + C$

(b) $\int 6 \, dx$

$= \int 6x^0 \, dx$

$= \frac{6x^{0+1}}{0+1} + C$

$= 6x + C$

(c) $\int 2x^{-3} \, dx$

$= \frac{2x^{-3+1}}{-3+1} + C$

$= \frac{2x^{-2}}{-2} + C$

$= -\frac{1}{x^2} + C$

(d) $\int x^{\frac{2}{3}} \, dx$

$= \frac{x^{\frac{2}{3}+1}}{\frac{2}{3}+1} + C$

$= \frac{x^{\frac{5}{3}}}{\frac{5}{3}} + C$

$= \frac{3x^{\frac{5}{3}}}{5} + C$

Exercise 12.1A

1. Integrate each of the following:

(a) $\int x \, dx$ (b) $\int 2x \, dx$ (c) $\int 5 \, dx$ (d) $\int 8 \, dx$

(e) $\int x^2 \, dx$ (f) $\int x^3 \, dx$ (g) $\int x^6 \, dx$ (h) $\int x^4 \, dx$

(i) $\int 3x^{-2} \, dx$ (j) $\int 4x^{-3} \, dx$ (k) $\int 10x^{-2} \, dx$ (l) $\int 3x^{-5} \, dx$

(m) $\int 4x^2 \, dx$ (n) $\int 5x^{-5} \, dx$ (o) $\int 3x^7 \, dx$ (p) $\int 6x^{-9} \, dx$

2. Integrate each of the following:

(a) $\int x^{\frac{1}{2}} \, dx$ (b) $\int 2x^{\frac{1}{2}} \, dx$ (c) $\int 5x^{\frac{1}{3}} \, dx$ (d) $\int 8x^{\frac{1}{4}} \, dx$

(e) $\int x^{-\frac{1}{3}} \, dx$ (f) $\int 4x^{-\frac{1}{2}} \, dx$ (g) $\int 2x^{\frac{2}{3}} \, dx$ (h) $\int 6x^{\frac{3}{4}} \, dx$

(i) $\int 3x^{\frac{2}{3}} \, dx$ (j) $\int 4x^{-\frac{3}{2}} \, dx$ (k) $\int \frac{3}{4}x^{\frac{3}{4}} \, dx$ (l) $\int 8x^{-\frac{1}{4}} \, dx$

(m) $\int \frac{1}{4}x^{-\frac{2}{3}} \, dx$ (n) $\int 5x^{-\frac{1}{6}} \, dx$ (o) $\int \frac{2}{5}x^{-\frac{2}{3}} \, dx$ (p) $\int \frac{1}{3}x^{-\frac{1}{4}} \, dx$

When integrating functions that consist of more than one term, integrate each term individually.

Worked Examples:

2. Find the derivative of each of the following:

(a) $\int (x^3 + 2x^2)\, dx$

$= \frac{x^4}{4} + \frac{2x^3}{3} + C$

(b) $\int (4x^2 - 2x + 1)\, dx$

$= \frac{4x^3}{3} - \frac{2x^2}{2} + x + C$

$= \frac{4x^3}{3} - x^2 + x + C$

(c) $\int (5 - x^{-2} + 3x^{-3})\, dx$

$= 5x - \frac{x^{-1}}{-1} + \frac{3x^{-2}}{-2} + C$

$= 5x + \frac{1}{x} - \frac{3}{2x^2} + C$

Exercise 12.1B

1. Integrate each of the following:

(a) $\int (x^2 + 2)\, dx$ (b) $\int (x^3 + x)\, dx$ (c) $\int (2x^2 + 3x)\, dx$

(d) $\int (4x^2 + 2x - 1)\, dx$ (e) $\int (5x^2 - x + 3)\, dx$ (f) $\int (x^2 - 7x - 4)\, dx$

(g) $\int (8 - 3x + x^2)\, dx$ (h) $\int (x^3 + x^2 - 6)\, dx$ (i) $\int (2x^3 + 6x^2 - 4x)\, dx$

(j) $\int (x^4 + 2x^3)\, dx$ (k) $\int (1 + x + x^4)\, dx$ (l) $\int (2x^3 - 5x + 1)\, dx$

2. Integrate each of the following:

(a) $\int (x^{-2} + 5)\, dx$ (b) $\int (x^{-4} + 3x)\, dx$ (c) $\int (5x^3 - x)\, dx$

(d) $\int \left(4x^{\frac{1}{2}} + x^{-3}\right) dx$ (e) $\int \left(x^2 - x^{\frac{1}{2}} + 7\right) dx$ (f) $\int \left(x^{-\frac{1}{2}} - \frac{1}{4}x + 1\right) dx$

(g) $\int \left(8x^{-\frac{1}{3}} + 4x^2\right) dx$ (h) $\int \left(x^3 + \frac{x^2}{2} - 6\right) dx$ (i) $\int (2x^3 - 5x^2 + 3)\, dx$

(j) $\int \left(\frac{1}{3}x - 2x^{-2} + 5\right) dx$ (k) $\int \left(\frac{x^{-3}}{2} + x^{-\frac{1}{4}}\right) dx$ (l) $\int \left(2x^{\frac{3}{2}} - \frac{5x}{2} + x^{-\frac{3}{4}}\right) dx$

12.2 Integration Involving Preparation of the Function

When integrating a function, it is often necessary to prepare the function so that it is in an integrable form. This involves breaking the function down into individual terms, and expressing each term on the numerator of any fraction and in index form (**section 11.1**).

Worked Examples:

1. Integrate each of the following:

(a) $\int \sqrt{x^3}\, dx$

$= \int x^{\frac{3}{2}}\, dx = \cdots$

(b) $\int \frac{5}{x^3} dx$

$= \int 5x^{-3}\, dx = \cdots$

(c) $\int \frac{2}{\sqrt{x}} dx$

$= \int 2x^{-\frac{1}{2}}\, dx = \cdots$

$$= \frac{x^{\frac{5}{2}}}{\frac{5}{2}} + C \qquad = \frac{5x^{-2}}{-2} + C \qquad = \frac{2x^{\frac{1}{2}}}{\frac{1}{2}} + C$$

$$= \frac{2\sqrt{x^5}}{5} + C \qquad = -\frac{5}{2x^2} + C \qquad = 4\sqrt{x} + C$$

Exercise 12.2A

1. Integrate each of the following. Give your answer in positive index, root form:

(a) $\int \frac{1}{x^2}\,dx$ (b) $\int \frac{2}{x^2}\,dx$ (c) $\int \frac{1}{x^3}\,dx$ (d) $\int \frac{1}{x^4}\,dx$

(e) $\int \frac{4}{x^3}\,dx$ (f) $\int \frac{1}{2x^3}\,dx$ (g) $\int \frac{3}{5x^4}\,dx$ (h) $\int \frac{6}{7x^5}\,dx$

(i) $\int \sqrt[3]{x}\,dx$ (j) $\int \sqrt{x}\,dx$ (k) $\int \sqrt{x^3}\,dx$ (l) $\int \sqrt[3]{x^2}\,dx$

(m) $\int \frac{2}{\sqrt[3]{x}}\,dx$ (n) $\int \frac{5}{\sqrt{x^3}}\,dx$ (o) $\int \frac{3}{2\sqrt{x^5}}\,dx$ (p) $\int \frac{2}{3\sqrt[5]{x^3}}\,dx$

Worked Examples:

2. Integrate each of the following:

(a) $\int x^2(x+1)\,dx$

$= \int x^3 + x^2\,dx$

$= \frac{x^4}{4} + \frac{x^3}{3} + C$

(b) $\int \sqrt{x}(x+3x^2)\,dx$

$= \int x^{\frac{3}{2}} + 3x^{\frac{5}{2}}\,dx$

$= \frac{x^{\frac{5}{2}}}{\frac{5}{2}} + \frac{3x^{\frac{7}{2}}}{\frac{7}{2}} + C$

$= \frac{2\sqrt{x^5}}{5} + \frac{6\sqrt{x^7}}{7} + C$

(c) $\int \frac{2x^2-5x}{\sqrt{x}}\,dx$

$= \int 2x^{\frac{3}{2}} - 5x^{\frac{1}{2}}\,dx$

$= \frac{2x^{\frac{5}{2}}}{\frac{5}{2}} + \frac{5x^{\frac{3}{2}}}{\frac{3}{2}} + C$

$= \frac{4\sqrt{x^5}}{5} + \frac{10\sqrt{x^3}}{3} + C$

Exercise 12.2B

1. Integrate each of the following:

(a) $\int x(x+2)\,dx$ (b) $\int x(x^2+2x)\,dx$ (c) $\int 2x(x^3+1)\,dx$

(d) $\int (x+1)(x+2)\,dx$ (e) $\int (x+3)^2\,dx$ (f) $\int (x-4)(x^2+1)\,dx$

(g) $\int x^2(\sqrt{x}-2)\,dx$ (h) $\int \left(x+\frac{1}{x}\right)\left(3x+\frac{1}{x}\right)dx$ (i) $\int x^3(\sqrt{x}-x)\,dx$

(j) $\int x\left(x^2+\frac{1}{\sqrt{x}}\right)dx$ (k) $\int \left(x+\sqrt{x}\right)^2 dx$ (l) $\int x\left(\sqrt{x}-\frac{3}{\sqrt{x}}\right)dx$

(m) $\int \sqrt{x}\left(\sqrt{x^3}+\frac{4}{\sqrt{x}}\right)dx$ (n) $\int \left(\sqrt{x}+\frac{1}{x}\right)^2 dx$ (o) $\int \sqrt[3]{x}(\sqrt{x}-3x)\,dx$

2. Integrate each of the following functions:

(a) $\int \frac{x^2 + 2x}{x} dx$ (b) $\int \frac{x^3 - 3x^2}{x^2} dx$ (c) $\int \frac{4x^2 - x^3}{x} dx$

(d) $\int \frac{2x^2 + 2x}{x^4} dx$ (e) $\int \frac{4x^2 - 6x}{x^4} dx$ (f) $\int \frac{5x^5 + 3x}{x^3} dx$

(g) $\int \frac{3x^3 - x^2 - 3}{2x^5} dx$ (h) $\int \frac{5x^2 + x + 1}{3x^4} dx$ (i) $\int \frac{x^2 - 3x}{\sqrt{x}} dx$

(j) $\int \frac{x^2 + 5}{\sqrt{x}} dx$ (k) $\int \frac{3x^2 + 5x}{2\sqrt{x}} dx$ (l) $\int \frac{x^2 + 2x - 1}{4\sqrt{x}} dx$

12.3 Definite Integrals

Definite integrals are integrals that involve limits. The limits are placed at the top and bottom of the integral sign. The upper limit b is the higher of the two numbers. Once we have integrated the expression, the limits are then substituted, and the lower limit taken away from the upper. Let $F(x)$ be the indefinite integral of $f(x)$, then:

$$\int_a^b f(x)\,dx$$

$$= (F(b) + C) - (F(a) + C)$$

$$= F(b) - F(a)$$

NB: For definite integrals, the constant of integration is not required, as it is effectively cancelled out during the substitution.

Worked Examples:

1. Evaluate $\int_{-1}^{2} x^2\,dx$

$$= \left[\frac{x^3}{3}\right]_{-1}^{2}$$

$$= \left(\frac{(2)^3}{3}\right) - \left(\frac{(-1)^3}{3}\right)$$

$$= \left(\frac{8}{3}\right) - \left(\frac{-1}{3}\right)$$

$$= \frac{9}{3} = 3$$

2. Evaluate $\int_{-2}^{3} (x^2 + x + 1)\,dx$

$$= \left[\frac{x^3}{3} + \frac{x^2}{2} + x\right]_{-2}^{3}$$

$$= \left(\frac{(3)^3}{3} + \frac{(3)^2}{2} + 3\right) - \left(\frac{(-2)^3}{3} + \frac{(-2)^2}{2} - 2\right)$$

$$= \left(\frac{27}{3} + \frac{9}{2} + 3\right) - \left(\frac{-8}{3} + \frac{4}{2} - 2\right)$$

$$= \frac{115}{6}$$

Exercise 12.3A

1. integrate each of the following:

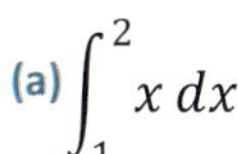

(a) $\int_1^2 x\,dx$ (b) $\int_2^5 x^2\,dx$ (c) $\int_{-4}^3 2\,dx$ (d) $\int_1^2 5x^2\,dx$

(e) $\int_{-2}^0 3x^3\,dx$ (f) $\int_1^3 4x^2\,dx$ (g) $\int_{-3}^2 2x^3\,dx$ (h) $\int_2^7 4\,dx$

(i) $\int_{1}^{2} x^{-2}\,dx$ (j) $\int_{0}^{5} \sqrt{x}\,dx$ (k) $\int_{2}^{4} \frac{4}{x^2}\,dx$ (l) $\int_{1}^{125} \sqrt[3]{x}\,dx$

(m) $\int_{81}^{256} \frac{2}{\sqrt[4]{x}}\,dx$ (n) $\int_{5}^{9} \frac{5}{3x^2}\,dx$ (o) $\int_{49}^{144} \frac{3}{\sqrt{x}}\,dx$ (p) $\int_{-8}^{343} \frac{6}{\sqrt[3]{x}}\,dx$

2. Evaluate each of the following:

(a) $\int_{0}^{2} (x^2 - 2x)\,dx$ (b) $\int_{-1}^{2} (2x + 3)\,dx$ (c) $\int_{-1}^{6} (x^2 + x + 3)\,dx$

(d) $\int_{-2}^{0} (x^3 - 5x + 2)\,dx$ (e) $\int_{-3}^{3} (x^3 + 5x + 4)\,dx$ (f) $\int_{1}^{3} (x^2 - 4x - 2)\,dx$

3. Evaluate each of the following:

(a) $\int_{1}^{6} x(x + 4)\,dx$ (b) $\int_{-3}^{10} (x - 2)(x + 3)\,dx$ (c) $\int_{-2}^{4} (x^2 + 5)^2\,dx$

(d) $\int_{1}^{4} x^2(\sqrt{x} - 3)\,dx$ (e) $\int_{1}^{4} \left(x + \frac{2}{x}\right)^2 dx$ (f) $\int_{1}^{3} x^3(\sqrt{x} - x)\,dx$

4. Evaluate each of the following:

(a) $\int_{-3}^{2} \frac{x^2 - x}{x}\,dx$ (b) $\int_{6}^{5} \frac{x^2 + 2x}{x^4}\,dx$ (c) $\int_{1}^{4} \frac{x^2 - 3x}{\sqrt{x}}\,dx$

(d) $\int_{1}^{3} \frac{x^2 + 3x + 1}{x^4}\,dx$ (e) $\int_{1}^{4} \frac{4 + 5\sqrt{x}}{x^2}\,dx$ (f) $\int_{4}^{9} \frac{5\sqrt{x} - 2}{3x^2}\,dx$

Exercise 12.3B

1. Find the value of a in each of the following questions:

(a) $\int_{2}^{a} x\,dx = 6$ (b) $\int_{1}^{a} x^2\,dx = 114$ (c) $\int_{a}^{3} 4\,dx = 36$ (d) $\int_{-4}^{a} 3x^2\,dx = 72$

(e) $\int_{-2}^{a} x^3\,dx = 60$ (f) $\int_{-6}^{a} 5x^2\,dx = 405$ (g) $\int_{a}^{2} 7x\,dx = -112$ (h) $\int_{a}^{3} 4x^2\,dx = 72$

2. Find the value(s) of a in each of the following questions:

(a) $\int_{0}^{a} (x + 6)\,dx = 80$ (b) $\int_{a}^{2} (3x - 2)\,dx = -30$ (c) $\int_{a}^{6} (2x + 3)\,dx = 56$

(d) $\int_{-3}^{a} (4x - 7)\,dx = -24$ (e) $\int_{-1}^{a} (10x - 8)\,dx = 35$ (f) $\int_{1}^{a} (6x - 2)\,dx = 132$

3. Find the value of a in each of the following questions:

(a) $\int_{a}^{4} 3\sqrt{x}\,dx = 14$ (b) $\int_{1}^{a} \frac{1}{\sqrt{x}}\,dx = 4$ (c) $\int_{4}^{a} \frac{2}{\sqrt{x}}\,dx = 12$

12.4 Area Under Curves

Definite integrals are used to calculate the area under a curve, or the area between curves. As with the previous exercise, the area under a curve may be expressed as the definite integral:

$$\int_a^b f(x)\,dx = F(b) - F(a)$$

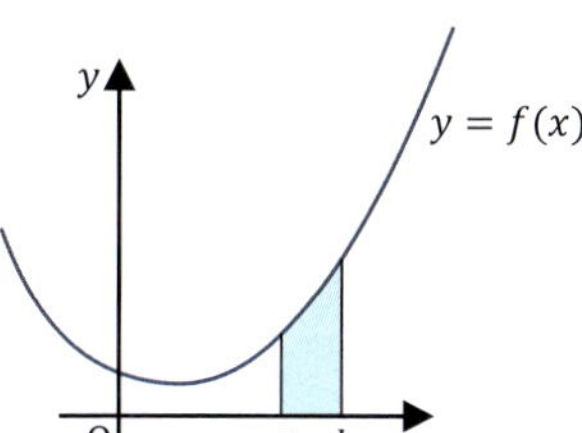

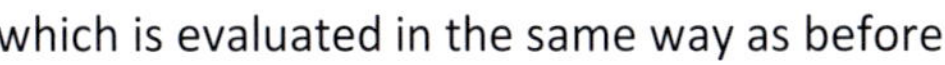
which is evaluated in the same way as before.

Worked Example:

The diagram shows the curve with equation $y = x^2 - 2x + 2$.
Calculate the shaded area.

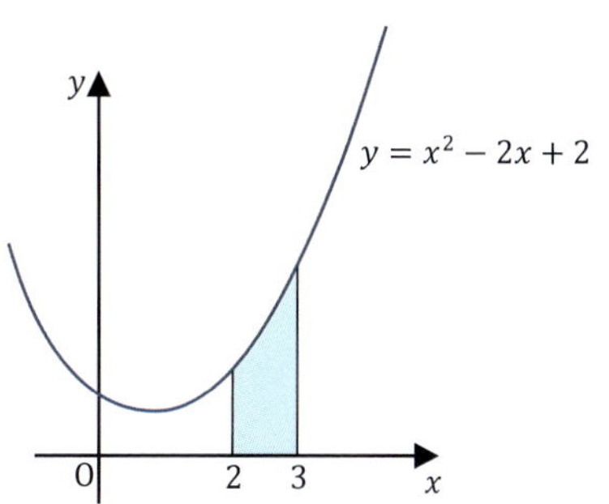

Solution:

$$\int_2^3 (x^2 - 2x + 2)\,dx$$

$$= \left[\frac{x^3}{3} - \frac{2x^2}{2} + 2x\right]_2^3$$

$$= \left(\frac{(3)^3}{3} - \frac{2(3)^2}{2} + 2(3)\right) - \left(\frac{(2)^3}{3} - \frac{2(2)^2}{2} + 2(2)\right)$$

$$= \frac{10}{3} \text{ units}^2$$

Exercise 12.4A

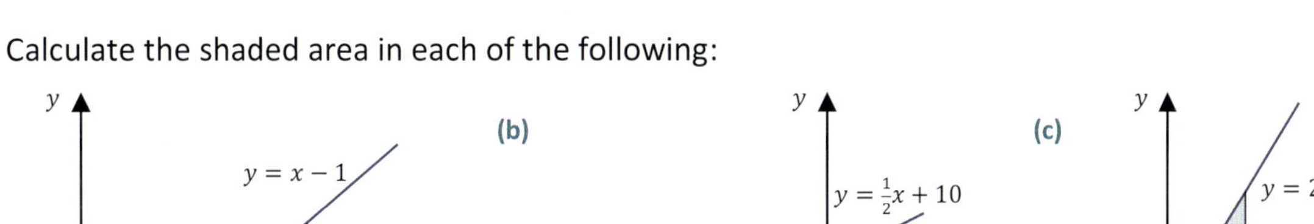

1. Calculate the shaded area in each of the following:

(a)

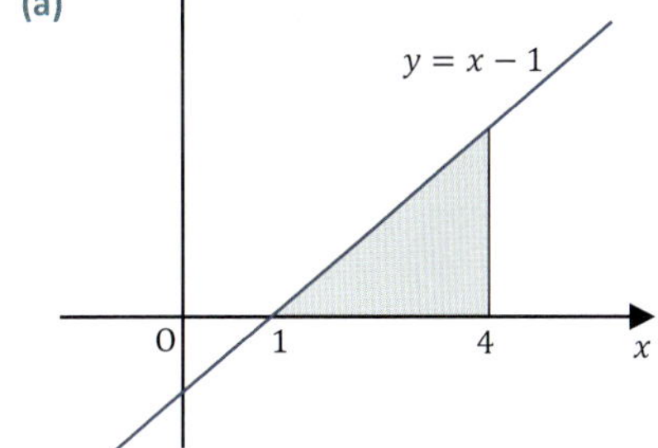

(b)

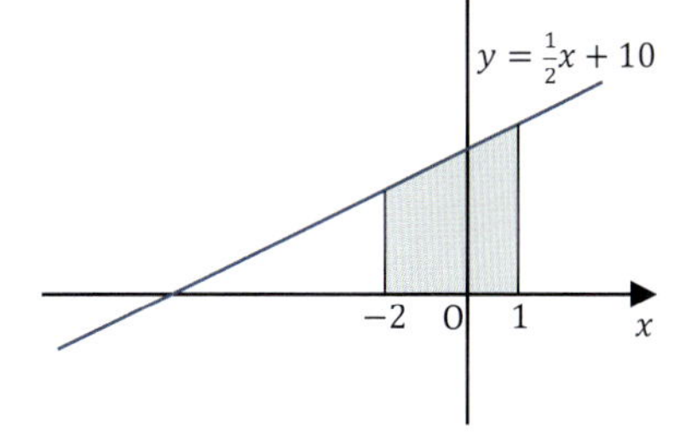

(c)

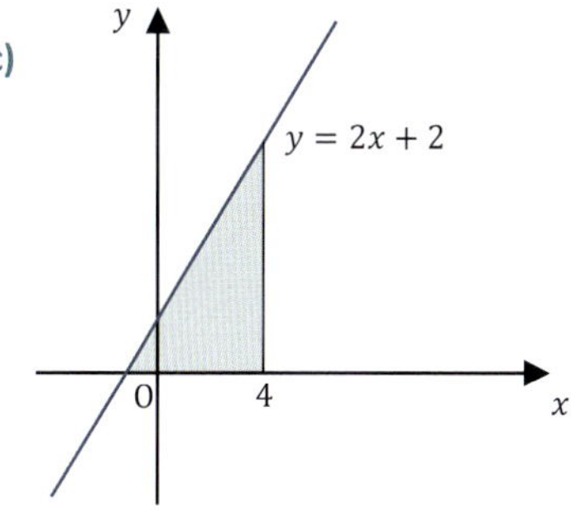

(d)

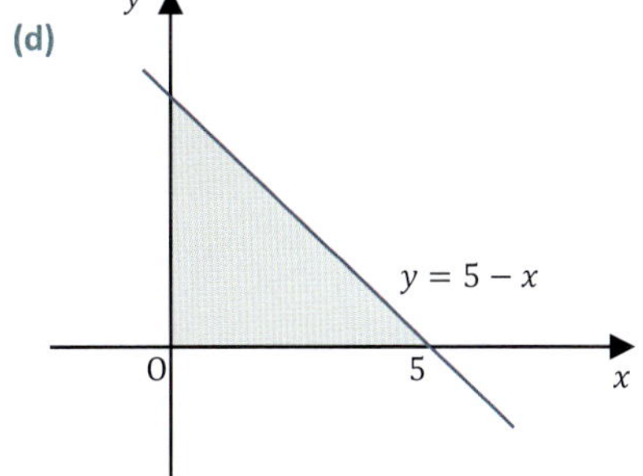

(e)

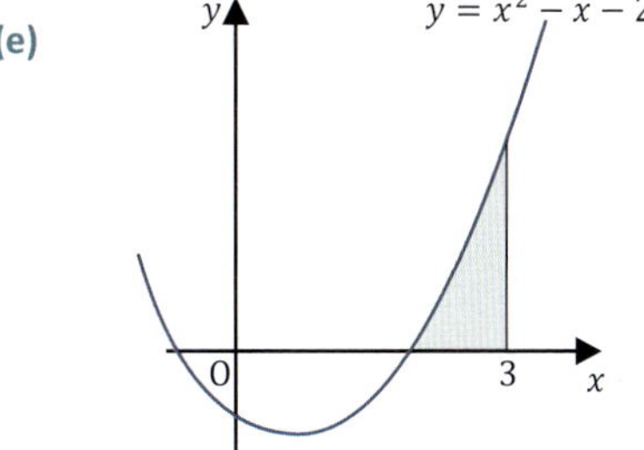

(f)

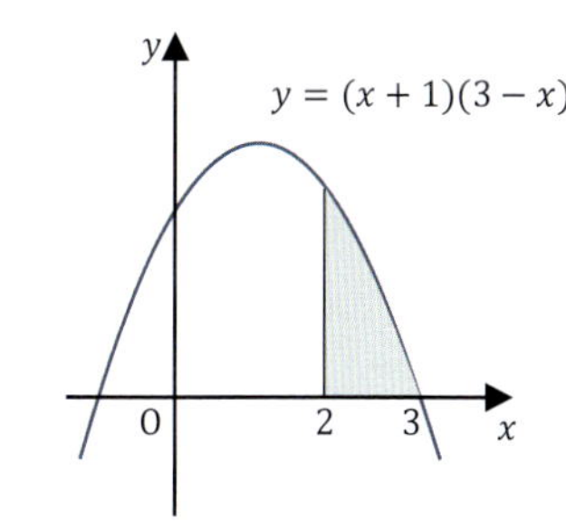

When the area to be calculated is below the x-axis, the answer to the integration will be negative.

Worked Example:

The diagram shows the curve with equation $y = x^2 - 2x - 3$.
Calculate the shaded area.

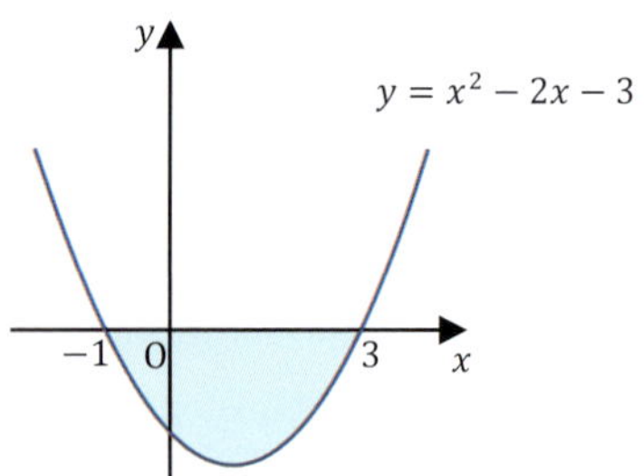

Solution:

$$\int_{-1}^{3} (x^2 - 2x - 3)\, dx$$

$$= \left[\frac{x^3}{3} - \frac{2x^2}{2} - 3x\right]_{-1}^{3}$$

$$= \left(\frac{(3)^3}{3} - \frac{2(3)^2}{2} - 3(3)\right) - \left(\frac{(-1)^3}{3} - \frac{2(-1)^2}{2} - 2(-1)\right)$$

$$= -\frac{29}{3}$$

$\therefore$ shaded area is $\frac{29}{3}$ units².

NB: When we are calculating a shaded area and the result is negative, we must conclude that the area is a positive value and thus answer the question on a separate line without the negative. We cannot write $-\frac{29}{3} = \frac{29}{3}$ units².

Exercise 12.4B

1. Calculate the shaded area in each of the following:

(a)

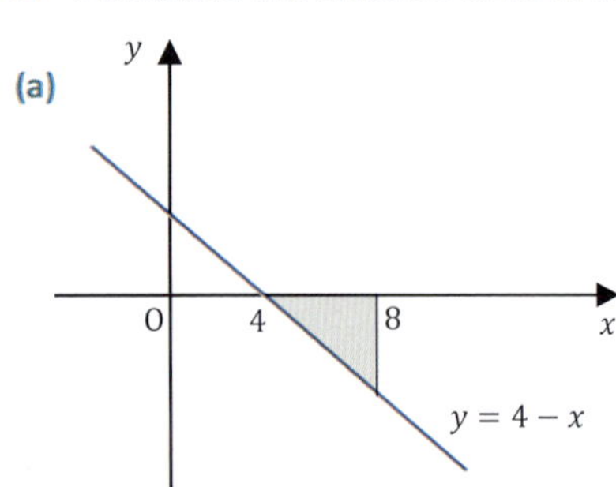

(b)

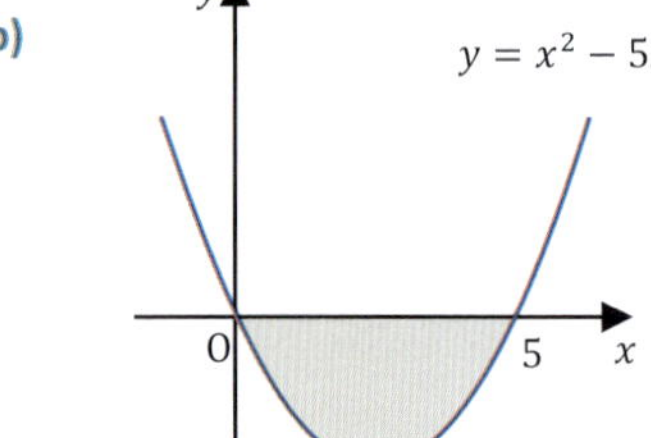

(c)

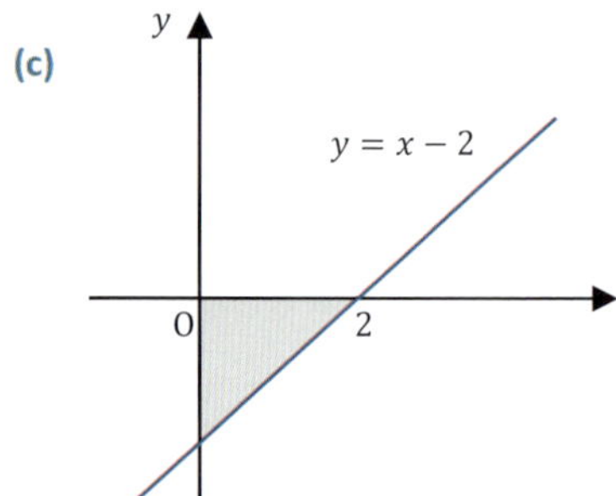

(d)

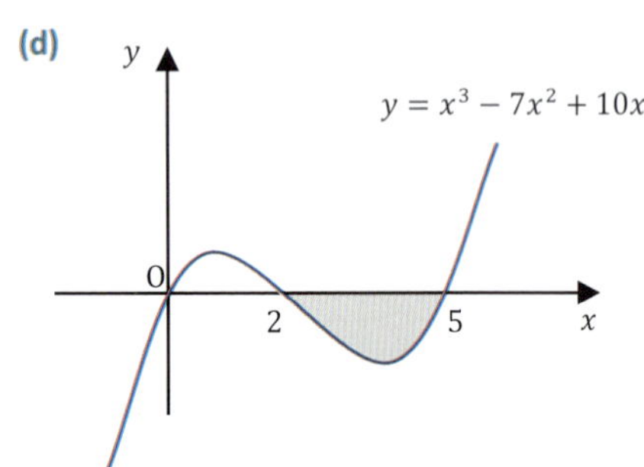

(e)

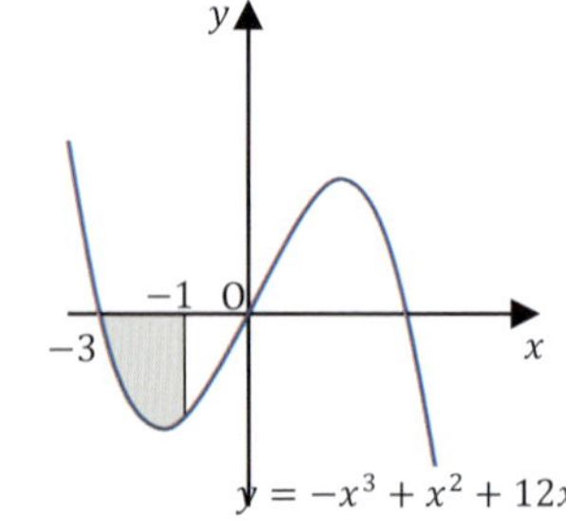

(f)

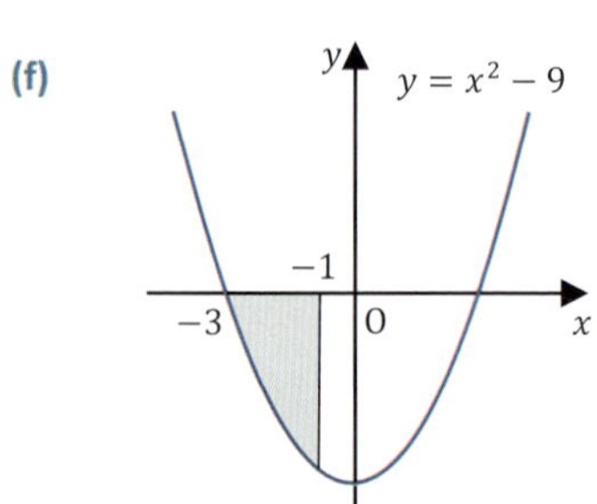

Sometimes the area to be calculated is both above and below the x-axis. In this case, the area above and below must be calculated separately and then the positive values should be added together. It may be necessary to first find the roots of the function, **i.e.** the cross-over points of the curve for the limits of the integration.

Worked Example:

The diagram shows the curve with equation $y = x^2 - 6x - 7$. Calculate the shaded area.

Solution:

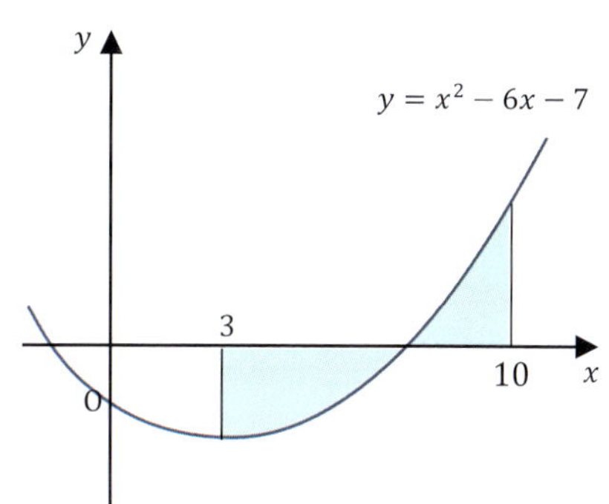

Find the missing limit by calculating the root:

$x^2 - 6x - 7 = 0$

$(x - 7)(x + 1) = 0$

$x = 7$ or ~~$x = -1$~~

Below the x-axis:

$$\int_3^7 (x^2 - 6x - 7)\,dx$$

$$= \left[\frac{x^3}{3} - \frac{6x^2}{2} - 7x\right]_3^7$$

$$= \left(\frac{(7)^3}{3} - \frac{6(7)^2}{2} - 7(7)\right) - \left(\frac{(3)^3}{3} - \frac{6(3)^2}{2} - 7(3)\right)$$

$$= -\frac{128}{3}$$

NB: In questions that involve the use of a calculator, type line three into the calculator including all the brackets.

Above the x-axis:

$$\int_7^{10} (x^2 - 6x - 7)\,dx$$

$$= \left[\frac{x^3}{3} - \frac{6x^2}{2} - 7x\right]_7^{10}$$

$$= \left(\frac{(10)^3}{3} - \frac{6(10)^2}{2} - 7(10)\right) - \left(\frac{(7)^3}{3} - \frac{6(7)^2}{2} - 7(7)\right)$$

$$= 45$$

Total Area $= 45 + \dfrac{128}{3} = \dfrac{263}{3}$ units^2

Exercise 12.4C

1. Calculate the shaded area in each of the following:

(a)

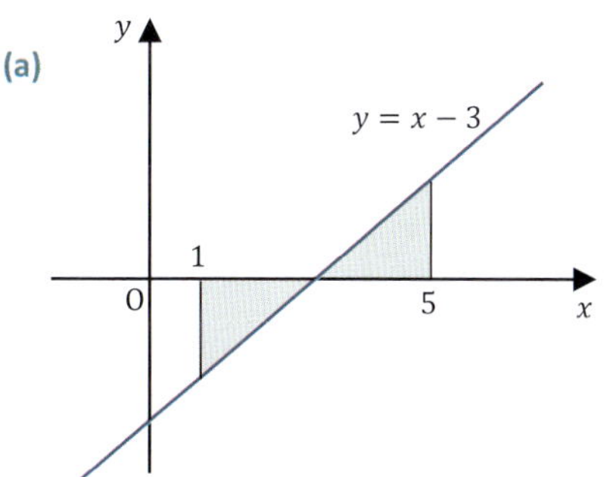

(b)

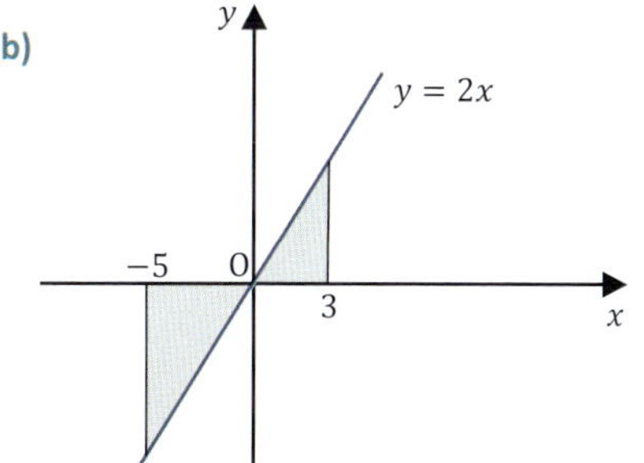

(c)

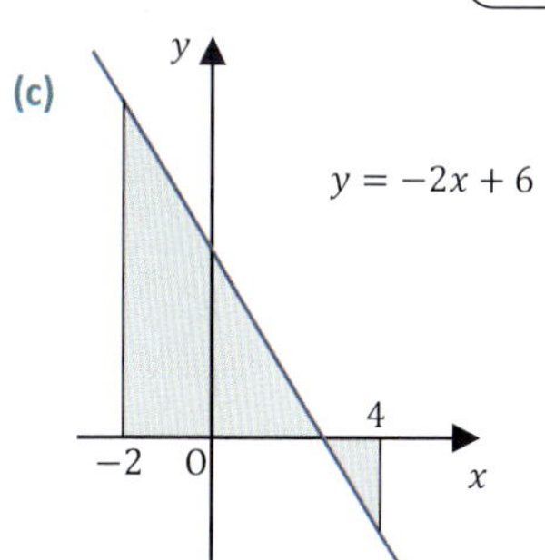

(d)

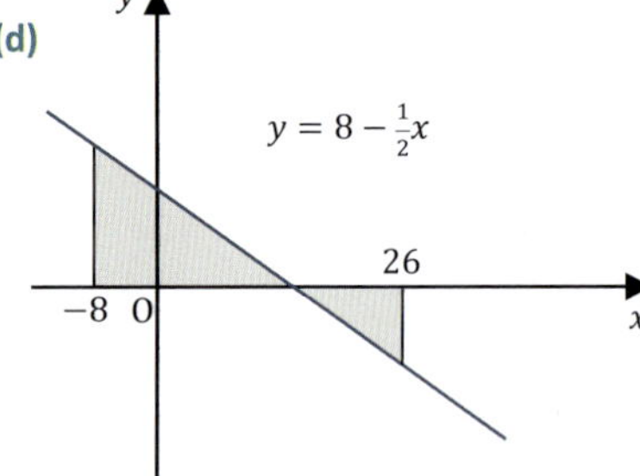

(e)

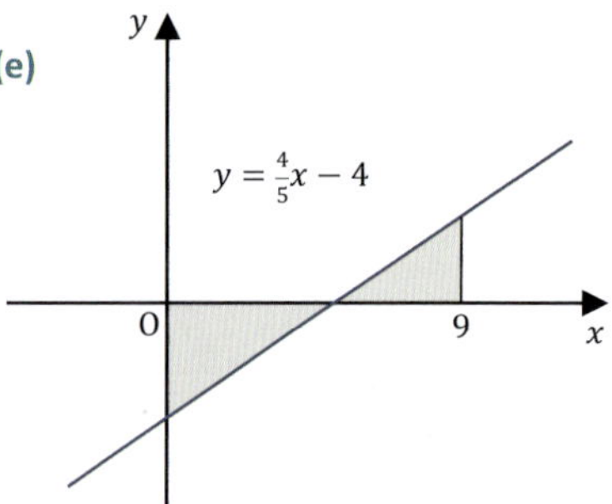

(f)

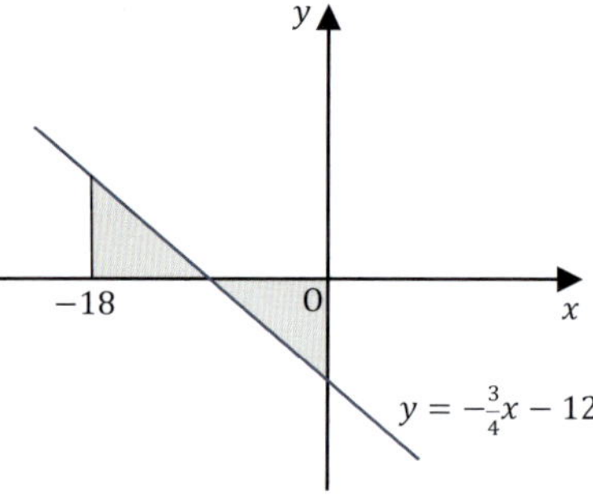

2. Calculate the shaded area in each of the following:

(a)

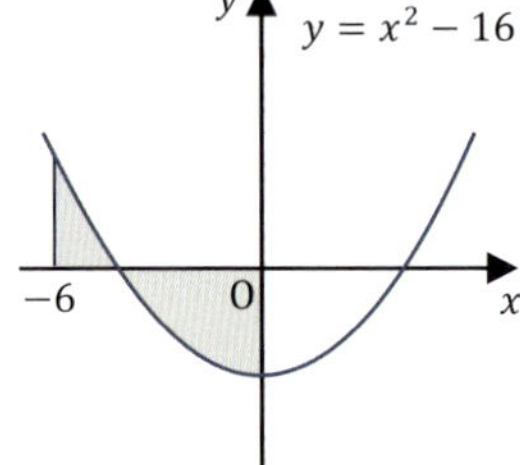

(b)

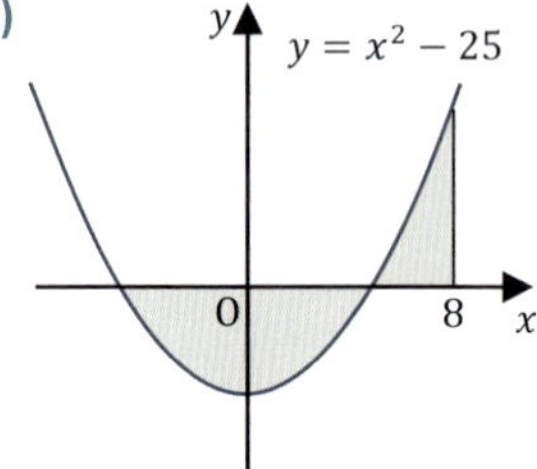

(c)

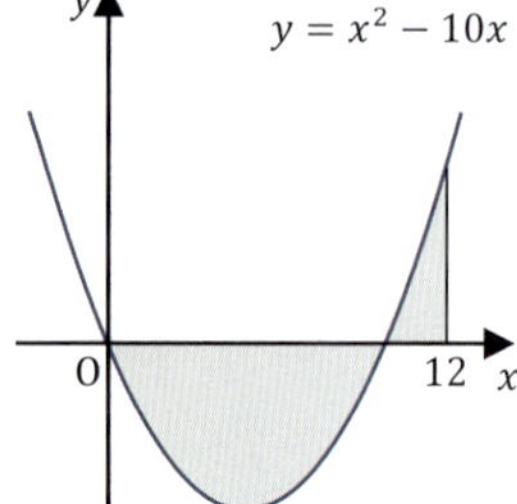

(d)

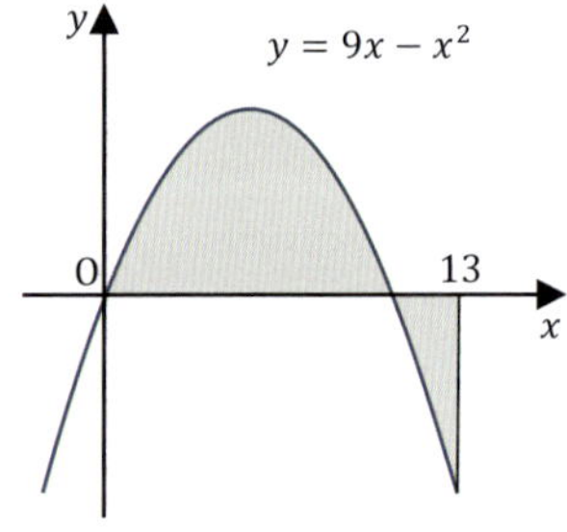

(e)

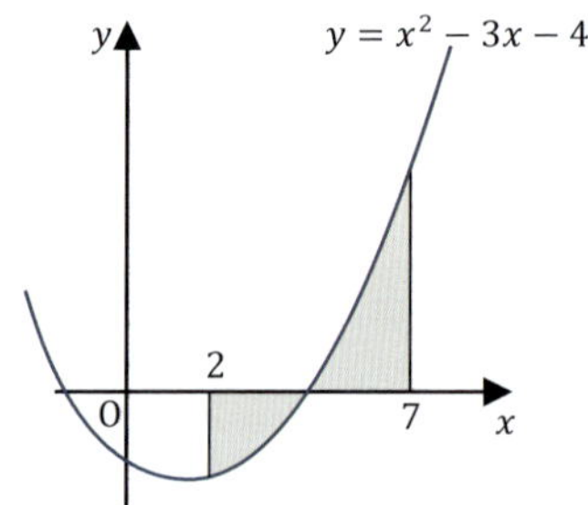

(f)

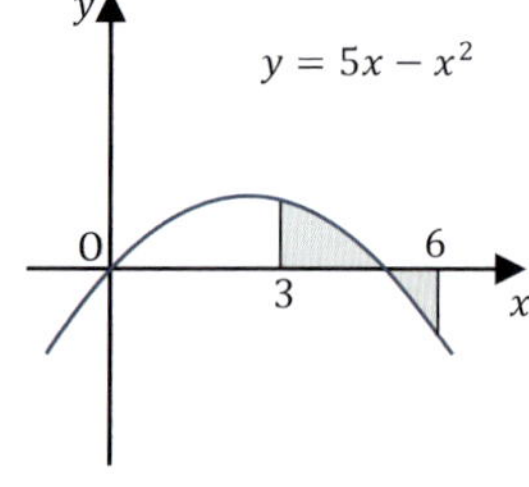

3. Calculate the shaded area in each of the following:

(a)

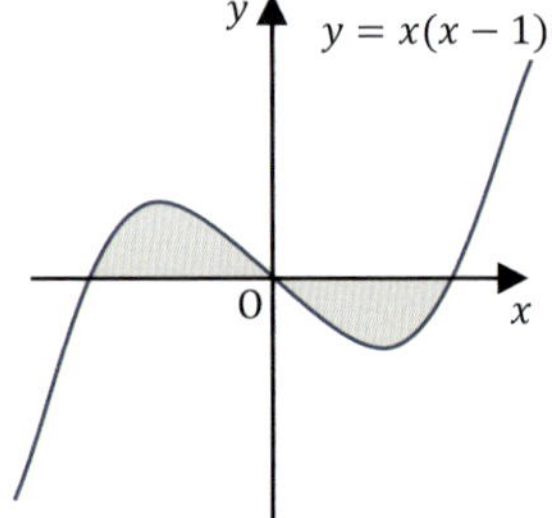

(b)

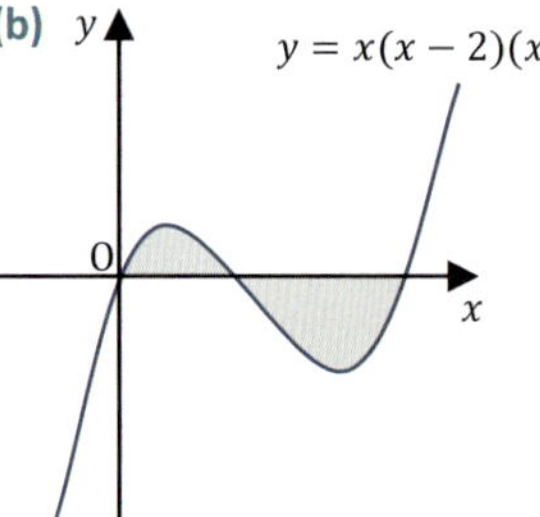

(c)

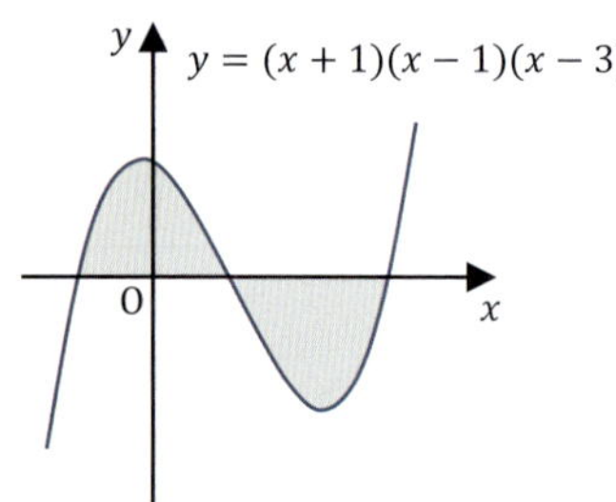

(d)

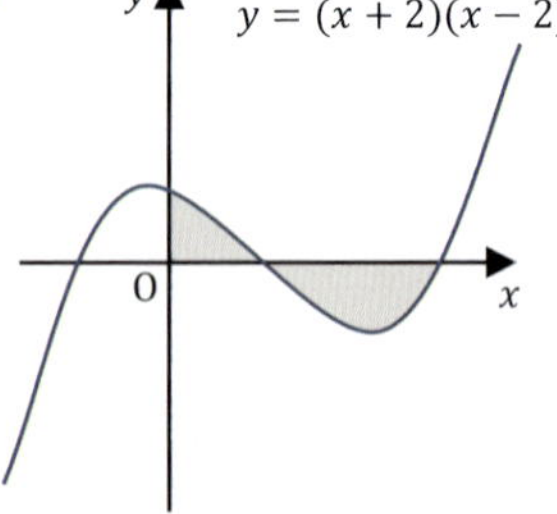

(e)

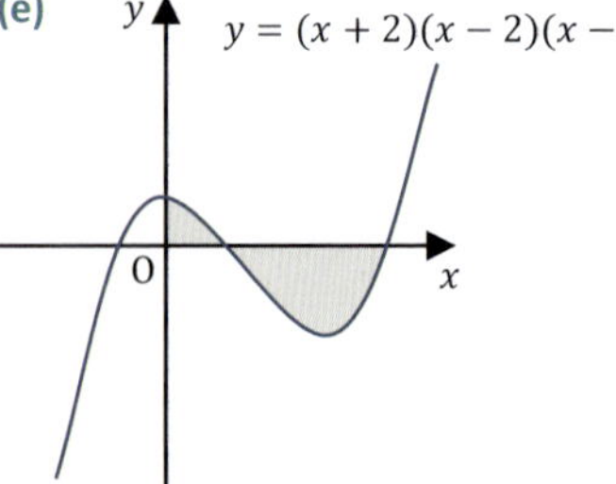

(f)

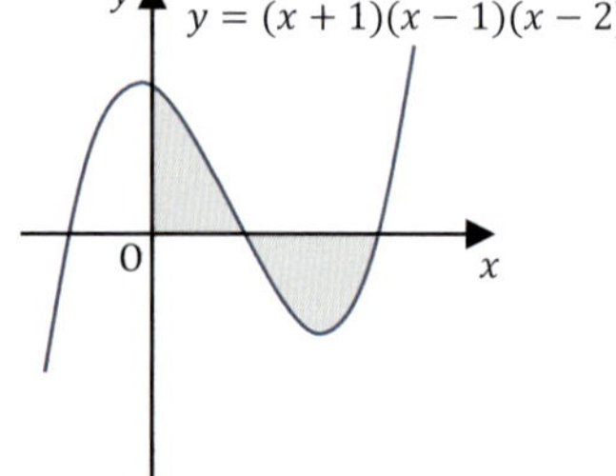

12.5 Area Between Two Curves

We already know how to find the area under a curve, so we can use that skill to calculate the area between two curves, or between a curve and a straight line. If we calculate the area under both curves, or the curve and the straight line, then we can take the smaller of the two areas away from the larger to calculate the area between the curves. This is illustrated in the diagrams below:

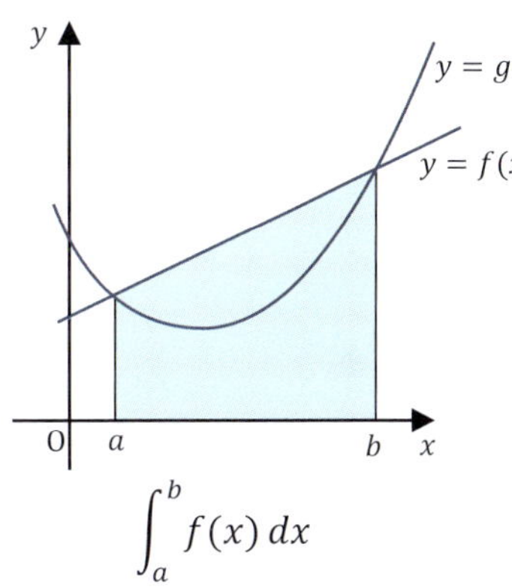

$\int_a^b f(x)\,dx$

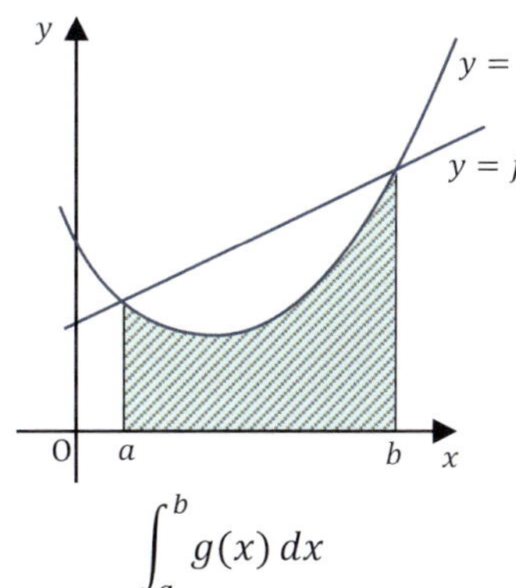

$\int_a^b g(x)\,dx$

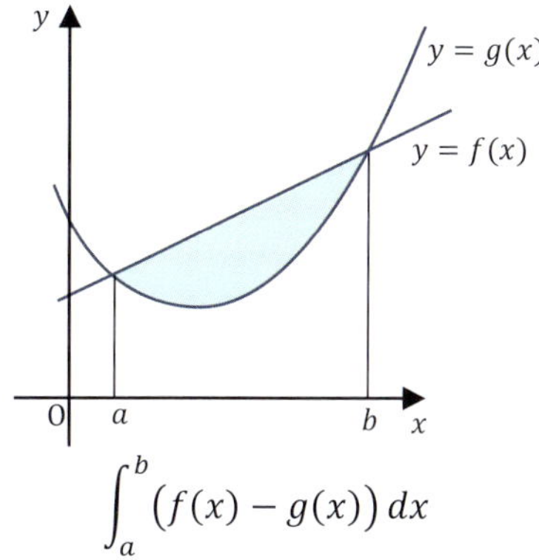

$\int_a^b \big(f(x) - g(x)\big)\,dx$

As a principle, **between the points of intersection**, the lower curve is taken away from the upper curve. This is typically described as: **upper curve minus lower curve**.

As before, it is often necessary to calculate the points of intersection first, to find the limits of the integration.

Worked Example:

The diagram shows the curve with equation $y = x^2 - 4x + 7$ and the straight line with equation $y = x + 3$. Calculate the shaded area.

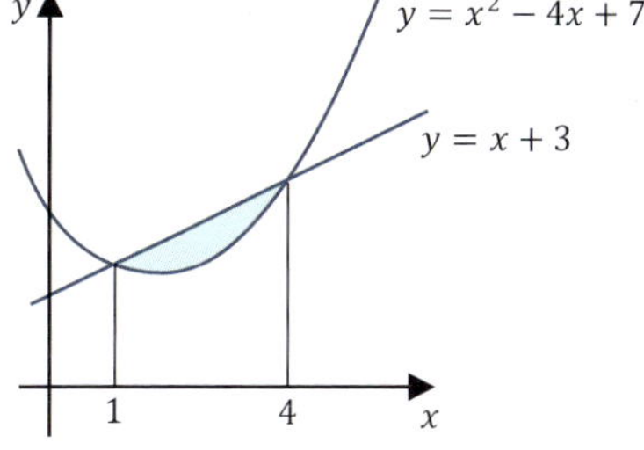

Solution: Between the two limits the straight line is above the curve.

$$\int_1^4 upper - lower\,dx$$

$$= \int_1^4 \big((x+3) - (x^2 - 4x + 7)\big)\,dx$$

$$= \int_1^4 (-x^2 + 5x - 4)\,dx$$

$$= \left[-\frac{x^3}{3} + \frac{5x^2}{2} - 4x\right]_1^4$$

$$= \left(-\frac{(4)^3}{3} + \frac{5(4)^2}{2} - 4(4)\right) - \left(-\frac{(1)^3}{3} + \frac{5(1)^2}{2} - 4(1)\right)$$

$$= \frac{9}{2}\ \text{units}^2$$

NB: It does not matter if the area between the curves is above or below the x-axis, provided the lower curve is taken away from the upper curve. If the answer to the question turns out to be negative, we have either taken the upper curve away from the lower, or not considered any cross-over points of the curves.

Exercise 12.5A

1. Calculate the shaded area in each of the following:

(a)

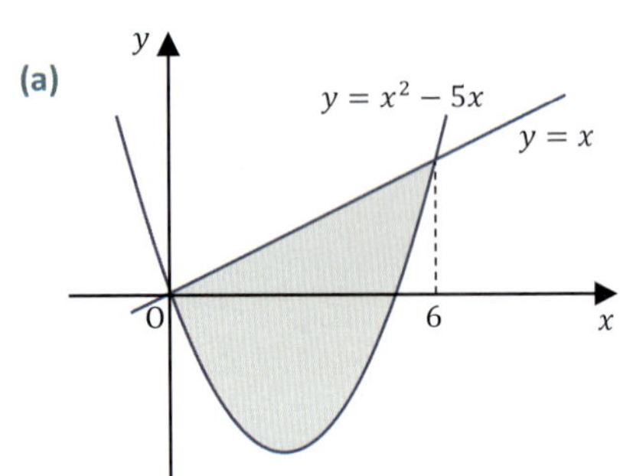

(b)

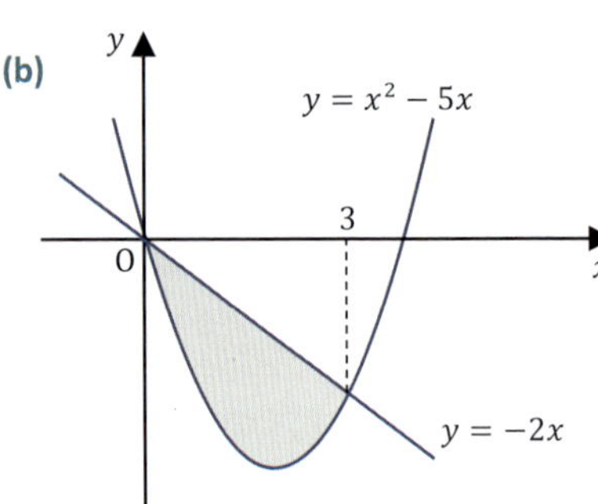

(c)

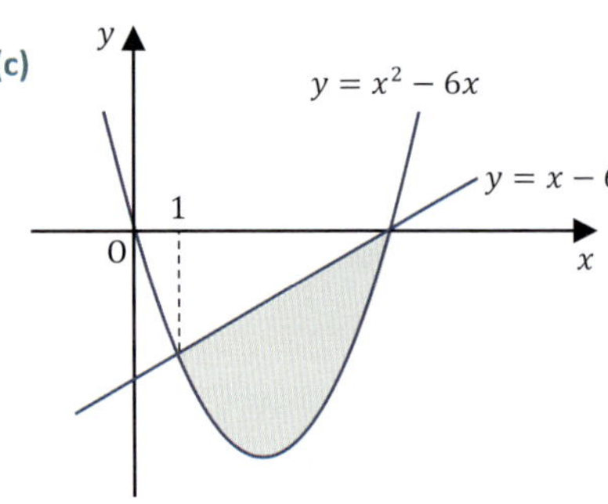

(d)

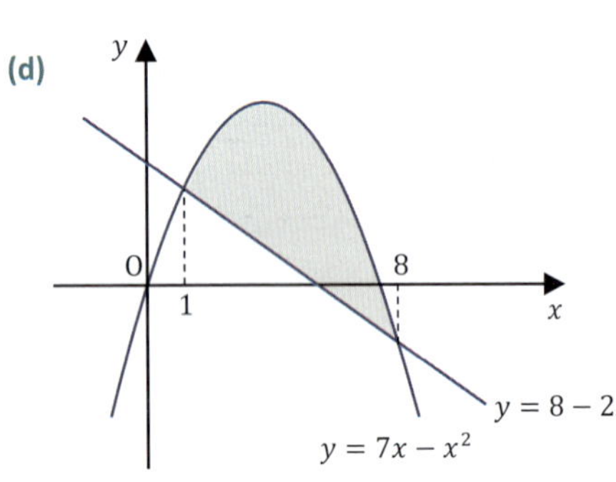

(e)

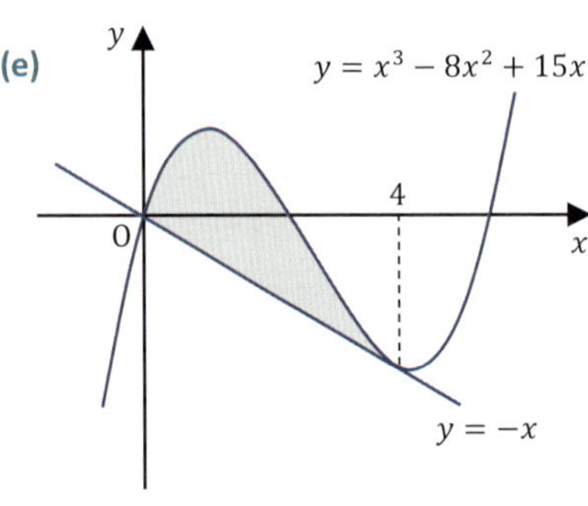

(f)

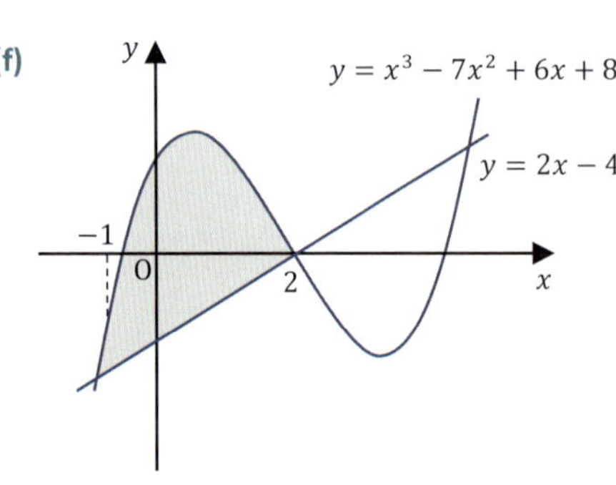

(g)

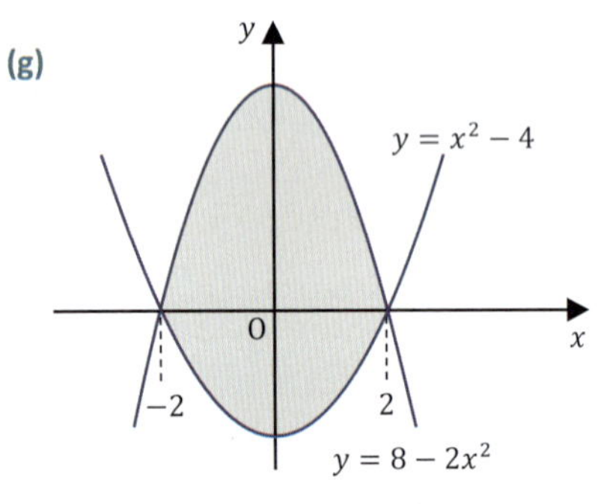

(h)

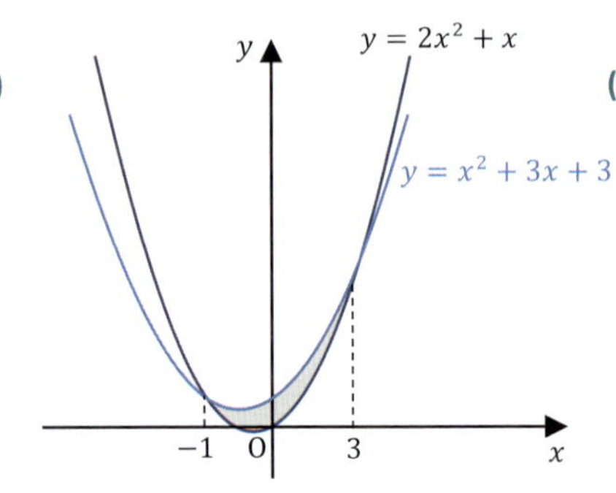

(i)

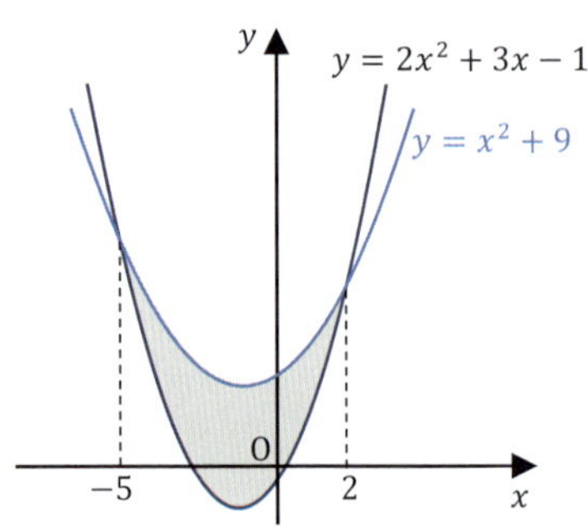

Worked Example:

The diagram shows the curves with equation $y = 2x^2 - 2x + 3$ and $y = x^2 + 11$.
Calculate the shaded area.

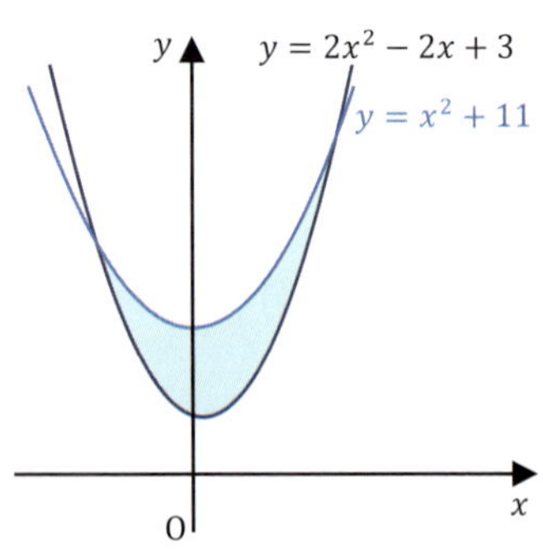

Solution: Equate and solve to find the limits, then integrate.

$2x^2 - 2x + 3 = x^2 + 11$
$x^2 - 2x - 8 = 0$
$(x - 4)(x + 2) = 0$
$x = 4$ or $x = -2$

$$\int_{-2}^{4} upper - lower\, dx$$

$$= \int_{-2}^{4} \left((x^2 + 11) - (2x^2 - 2x + 3)\right) dx$$

$$= \int_{-2}^{4} (-x^2 + 2x + 8)\, dx$$

$$= \left[-\frac{x^3}{3} + \frac{2x^2}{2} + 8x\right]_{-2}^{4}$$

$$= \left(-\frac{(4)^3}{3} + \frac{2(4)^2}{2} + 8(4)\right) - \left(-\frac{(-2)^3}{3} + \frac{2(-2)^2}{2} + 8(-2)\right)$$

$= 36$ units^2

Exercise 12.5B

1. Calculate the shaded area in each of the following:

(a)

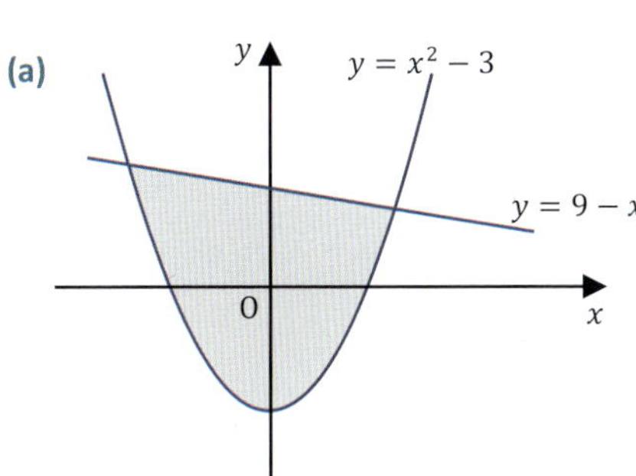

(b)

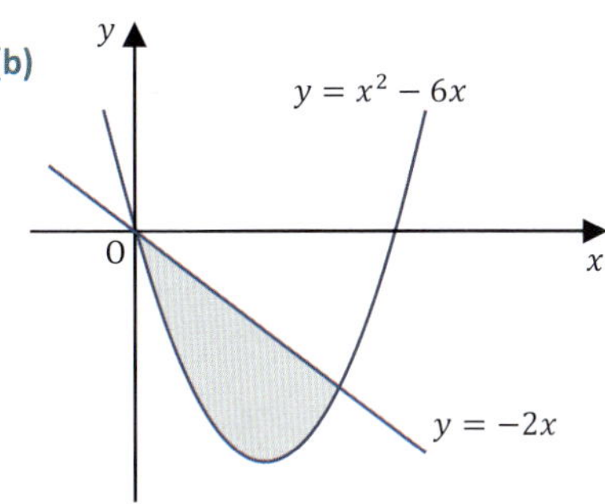

(c)

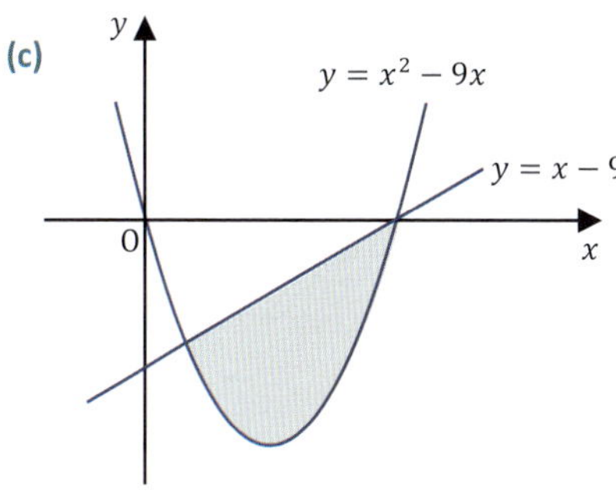

(d)

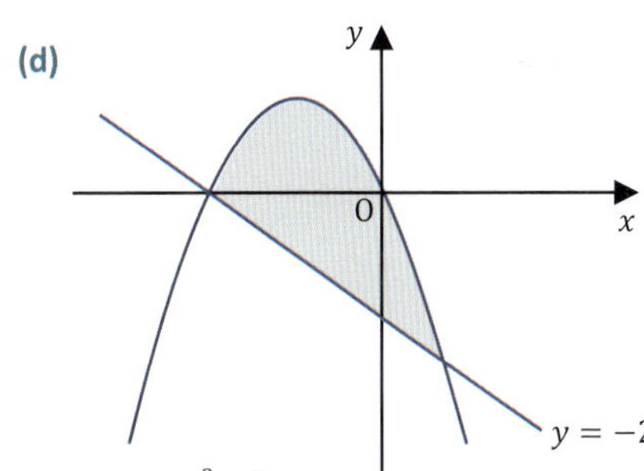

(e)

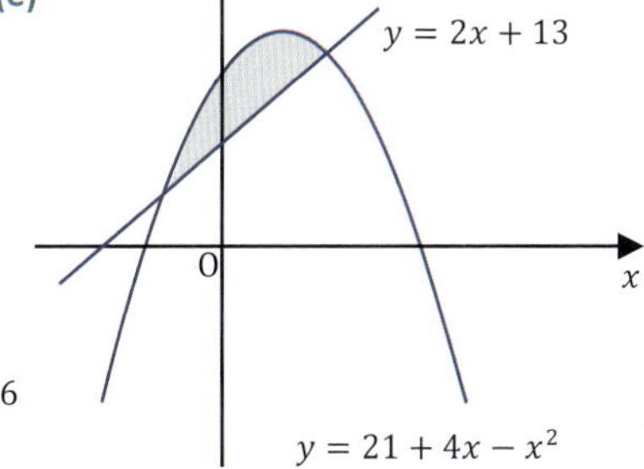

(f)

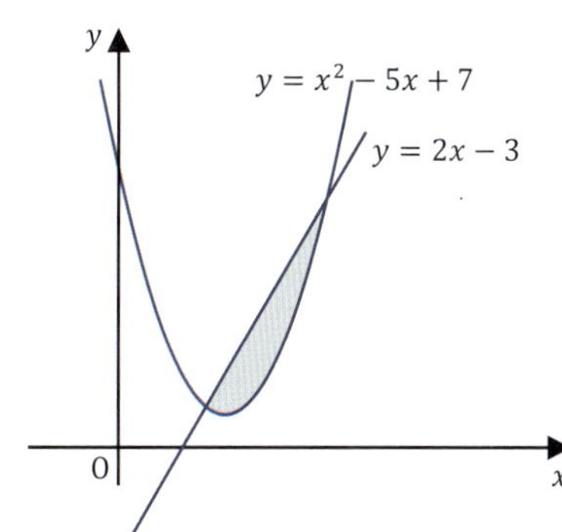

2. Calculate the shaded area in each of the following:

(a)

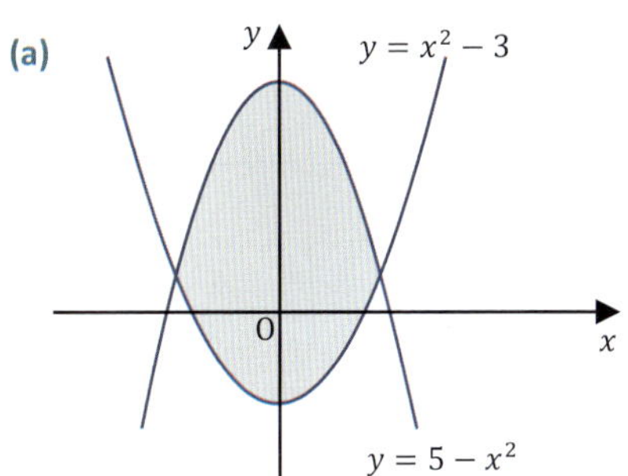

(b)

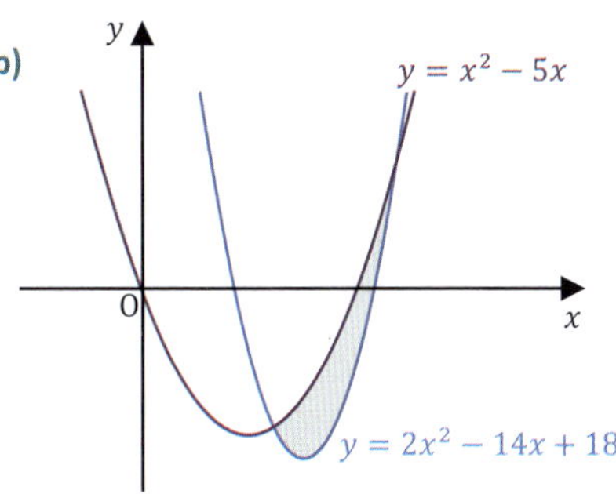

(c)

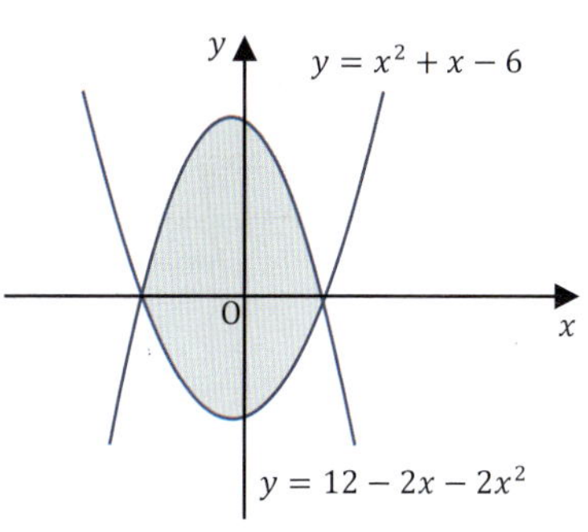

(d)

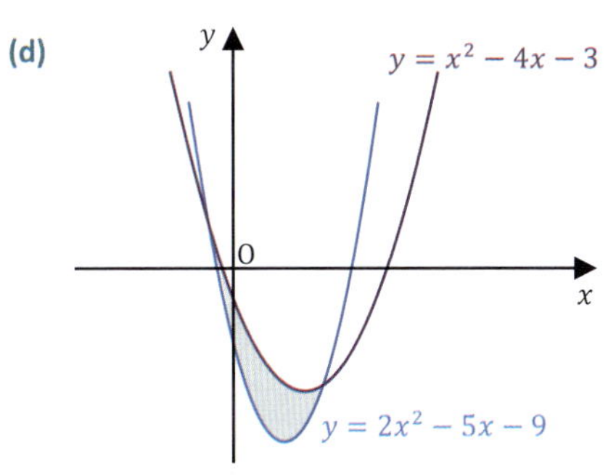

(e)

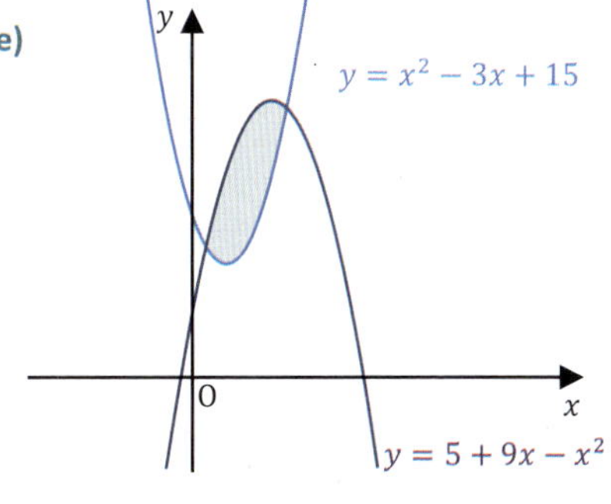

(f)

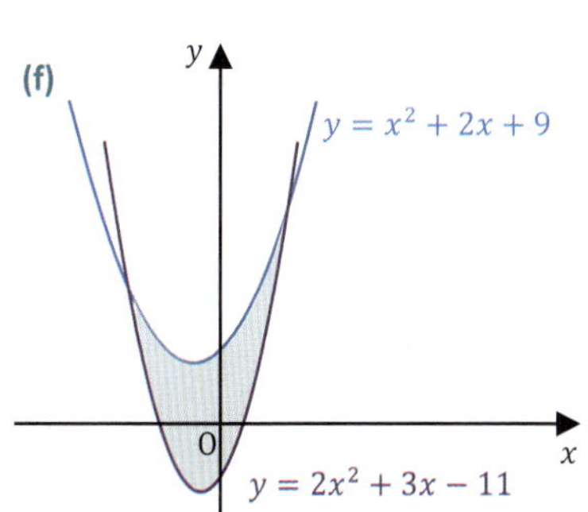

In the following exercise, synthetic or polynomial long division will be required to determine the limits for the integration (**section 7.1-2**). In questions where there are two areas, each area needs to be worked out individually and then added together.

Exercise 12.5C

1. Calculate the shaded area in each of the following:

(a)

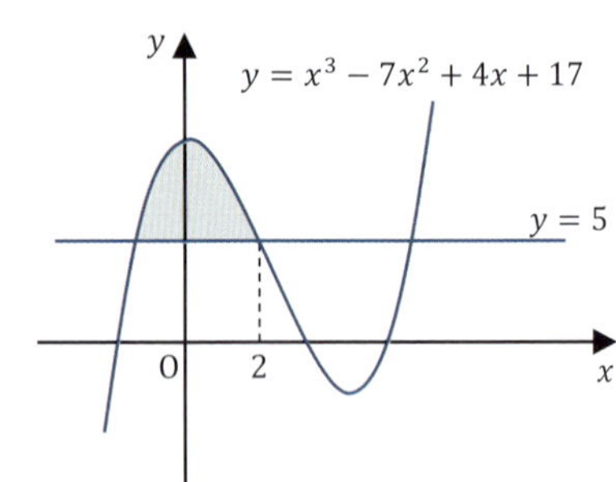

(b)

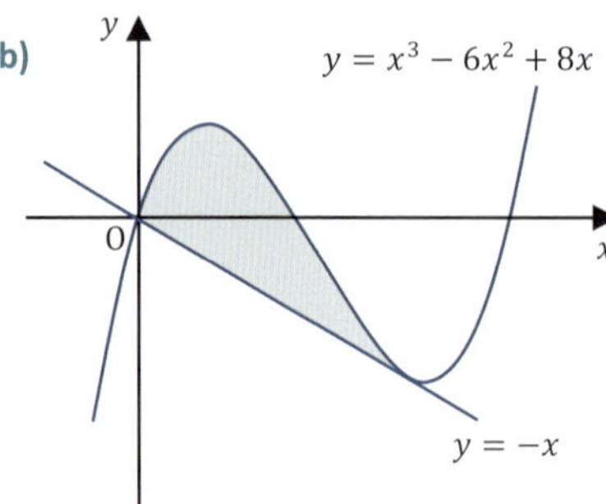

(c)

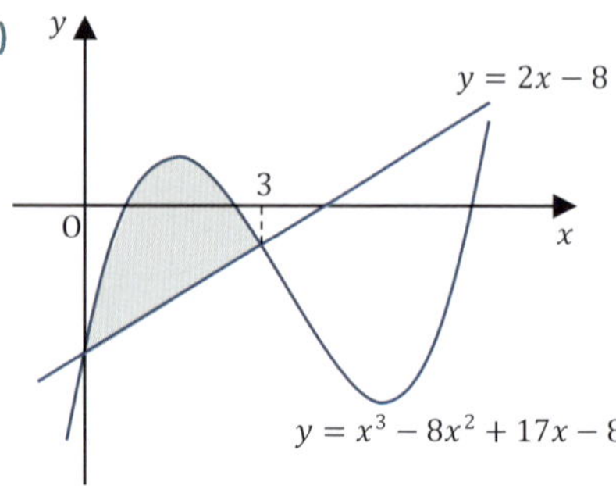

(d)

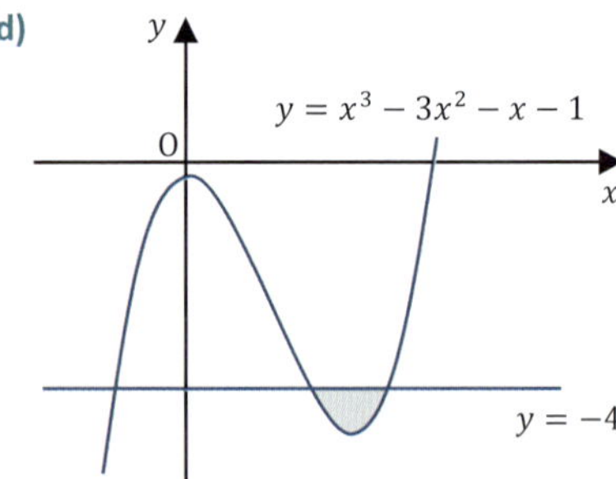

(e)

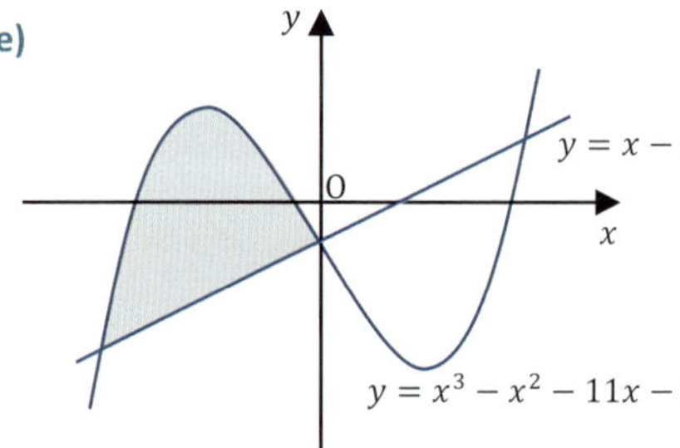

(f)

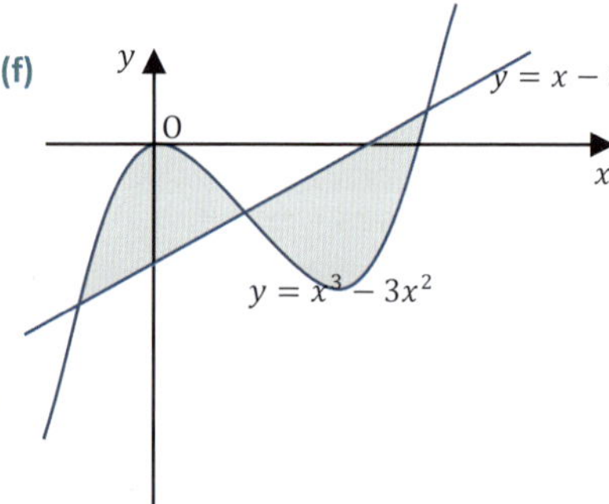

2. Calculate the shaded area in each of the following:

(a)

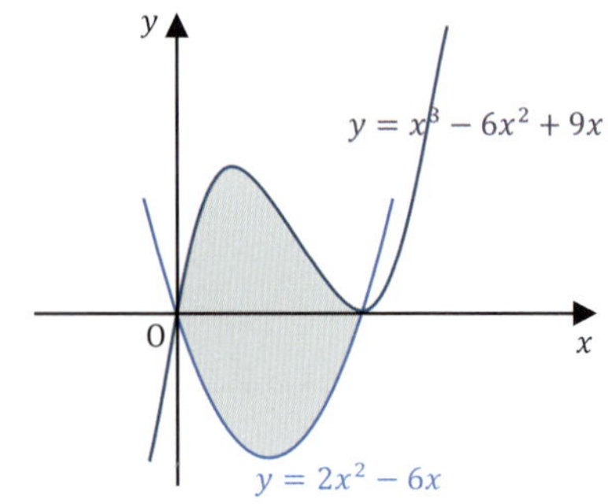

(b)

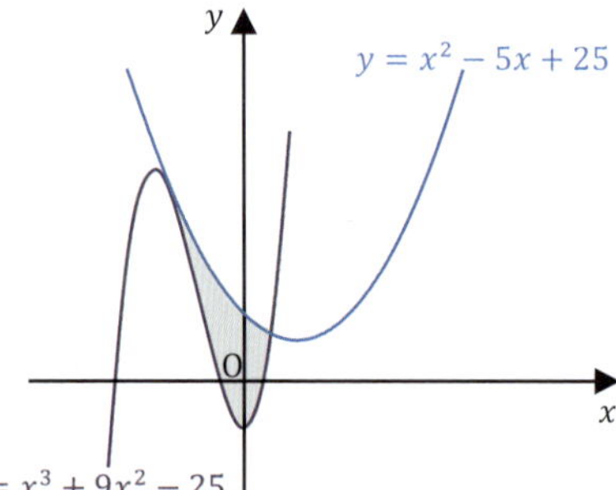

(c)

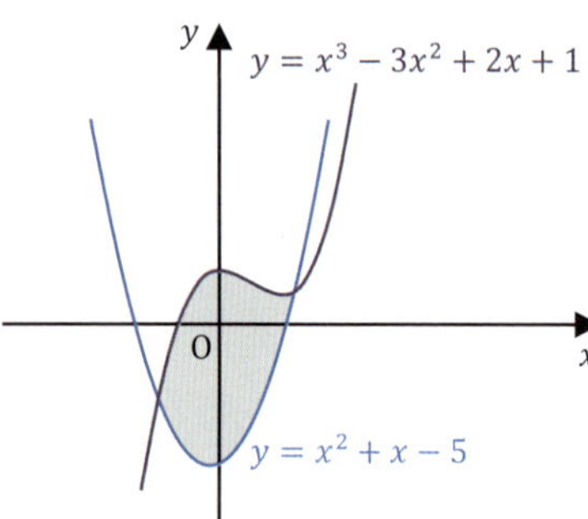

(d)

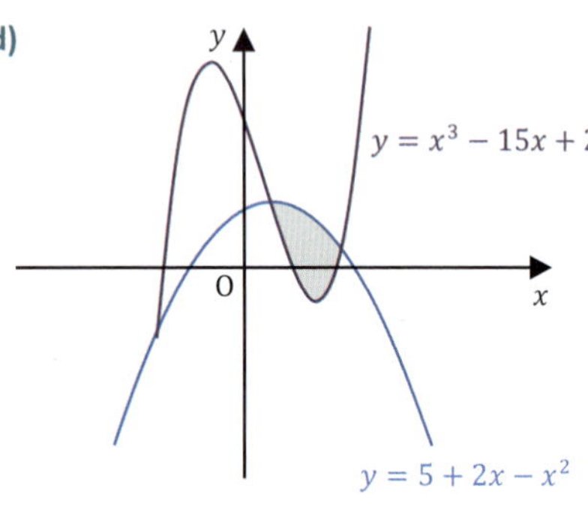

(e)

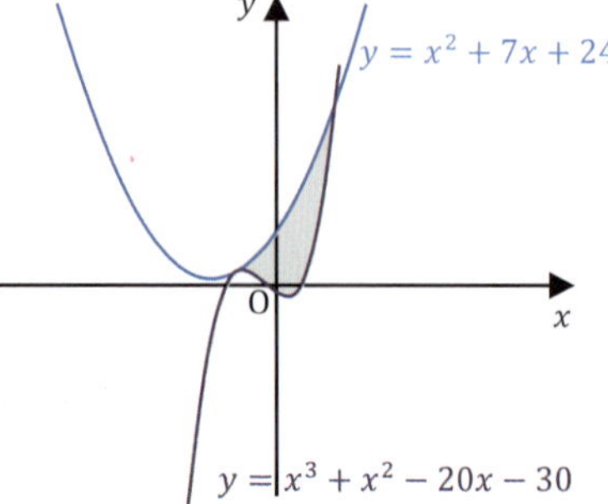

(f)

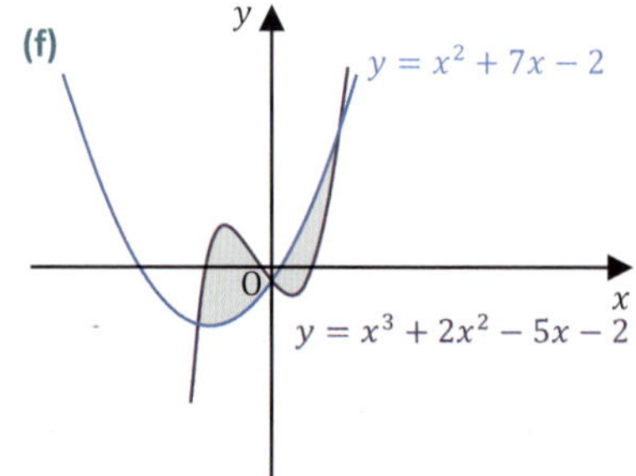

12.6 Differential Equations

If we are given an equation for a rate of change, **i.e.** an equation representing a function that has already been differentiated, we saw at the beginning of this chapter that such an equation can represent an infinite number of possible functions. Therefore, the constant of integration is required. However, if we are given further information relating to the original function, such as a point on the curve or some initial conditions in the question context, we can determine the original equation.

Worked Examples:

1. A curve is such that $\frac{dy}{dx} = 3x^2 - 6x$. The curve passes through the point $(2, -16)$. Express y in terms of x.

   Solution:

   Step 1: Integrate $\frac{dy}{dx}$.

   $$y = \int (3x^2 - 6x)\ dx$$

   $$y = x^3 - 3x^2 + C$$

   Step 2: Substitute the coordinate $(2, -16)$ into integrated form.

   $$-16 = 2^3 - 3(2)^2 + C$$

   $$C = -16 - 8 + 12 = -12$$

   $$\therefore y = x^3 - 3x^2 - 12$$

2. For a function f, defined on a suitable domain, it is known that $f'(x) = 4x + \frac{1}{\sqrt{x}}$ and $f(4) = 29$. Express $f(x)$ in terms of x.

   Solution:

   Step 1: Integrate $f'(x)$.

   $$f(x) = \int \left(4x + \frac{1}{\sqrt{x}}\right)\ dx$$

   $$f(x) = \int \left(4x + x^{-\frac{1}{2}}\right)\ dx$$

   $$f(x) = 2x^2 + 2x^{\frac{1}{2}} + C$$

   Step 2: Substitute the coordinate $(4, 29)$ into integrated form.

   $$f(x) = 2x^2 + 2\sqrt{x} + C$$

   $$29 = 2(4)^2 + 2\sqrt{4} + C$$

   $$C = 29 - 32 - 4 = -7$$

   $$\therefore y = 2x^2 + 2\sqrt{x} - 7$$

Exercise 12.6

1. Use the following information to express y in terms of x:

(a) A curve is such that $\frac{dy}{dx} = 4x - 2$.
The curve passes through the point $(1, 8)$.

(b) A curve is such that $\frac{dy}{dx} = 9 - 6x$.
The curve passes through the point $(2, 15)$.

(c) A curve is such that $\frac{dy}{dx} = 3x^2 + 6x$.
The curve passes through the point $(1, 10)$.

(d) A curve is such that $\frac{dy}{dx} = x^2 + 2x$.
The curve passes through the point $(3, 30)$.

(e) A curve is such that $\frac{dy}{dx} = 6x^2 + 12x + 2$.
The curve passes through the point $(-2, 14)$.

(f) A curve is such that $\frac{dy}{dx} = 1 - 4x^3$.
The curve passes through the point $(3, 81)$.

(g) A curve is such that $\frac{dy}{dx} = 3x^2 + 2x - 5$.
The curve passes through the point $(-4, -15)$.

(h) A curve is such that $\frac{dy}{dx} = 9x^2 + 8x - 4$.
The curve passes through the point $(-2, 28)$.

2. For each of the following functions f, defined on suitable domains, use the information to express $f(x)$ in terms of x:

(a) $f'(x) = 3x + 5$ and $f(4) = 20$.

(b) $f'(x) = 9 - 2x$ and $f(-1) = 7$.

(c) $f'(x) = 3x^2 - 5$ and $f(2) = 18$.

(d) $f'(x) = 6x^2 - x$ and $f(-1) = 8$.

(e) $f'(x) = x^2 + 9$ and $f(3) = 15$.

(f) $f'(x) = \sqrt{x} - 2$ and $f(9) = 25$.

(g) $f'(x) = \frac{2x^2 + 5x}{x}$ and $f(4) = 6$.

(h) $f'(x) = \sqrt{x}\left(\sqrt{x} - 3\right)$ and $f(4) = 20$.

(i) $f'(x) = \frac{6x + 8}{\sqrt{x}}$ and $f(4) = 20$.

(j) $f'(x) = \frac{9x - 6}{\sqrt{x}}$ and $f(16) = 45$.

3. The gradient of the tangent to a curve is given by $\frac{dy}{dx} = 8x - \frac{4}{x^2}$. The curve passes through the point $(2, 8)$. Find the equation of the curve.

4. The velocity of an object is given by $\frac{dS}{dt} = 16t - 3t^2$, where S is the distance in metres from a given point, t seconds after its journey began. After 3 seconds the object is 49 metres from the point. How far away is it after 9 seconds?

5. The rate of change of the volume, V litres of an object with respect to time, t hours, is given by $\frac{dV}{dt} = 6t^2 - 12t$. The volume of the object after 5 hours is 320 litres. Calculate the volume of the object after 9 hours.

6. The gradient of the tangent to a curve is given by $\frac{dy}{dx} = 6x - \frac{10}{x^2}$. The curve passes through the point $(-2, 9)$. Find the equation of the curve.

7. The acceleration of an object is given by $\frac{dv}{dt} = 4t + 9$, where v is the velocity in metres per second, t seconds after the journey began. After 3 seconds, the velocity is 18 ms^{-1}. Find the velocity of the object after 10 seconds.

12.7 Review

Exercise 12.7

12.1 Find:

(a) $\int 3x^2\,dx$ (b) $\int (x^2 - x + 3)\,dx$ (c) $\int 9x^{\frac{1}{2}}\,dx$

12.2 Find:

(a) $\int \frac{2}{\sqrt{x}}\,dx$ (b) $\int \left(x + \frac{2}{x}\right)^2 dx$ (c) $\int 2x\left(\sqrt{x} - \frac{1}{\sqrt{x}}\right) dx$

12.3

(a) Evaluate:

(i) $\int_{-1}^{4} \frac{4}{x^3}\,dx$ (ii) $\int_{-1}^{3} (x^3 + 2x + 3)\,dx$ (iii) $\int_{1}^{4} \frac{x^2 - 3x}{\sqrt{x}}\,dx$

(b) Find the value of a in each of the following questions:

(i) $\int_{a}^{4} (3x - 4)\,dx = -70$ (ii) $\int_{a}^{2} 6x^2\,dx = 144$ (iii) $\int_{4}^{a} \frac{5}{\sqrt{x}}\,dx = 30$

12.4 Calculate the shaded area:

(a)

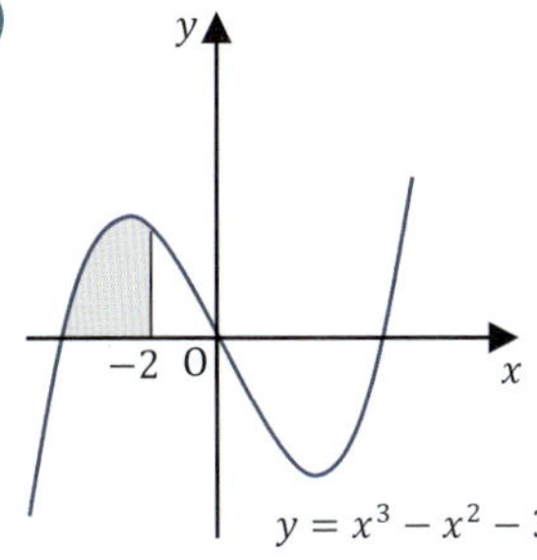

(b)

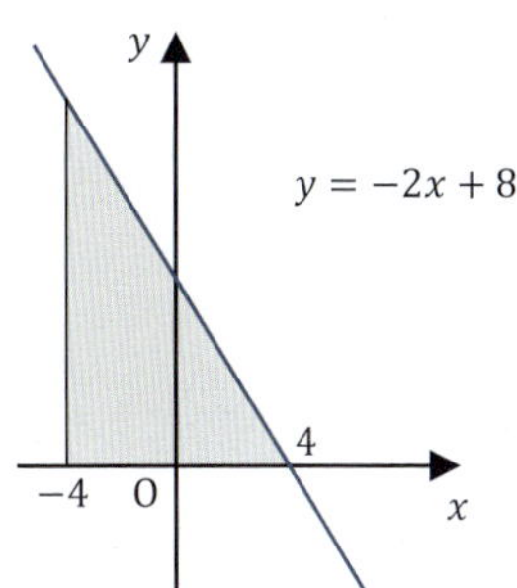

(c)

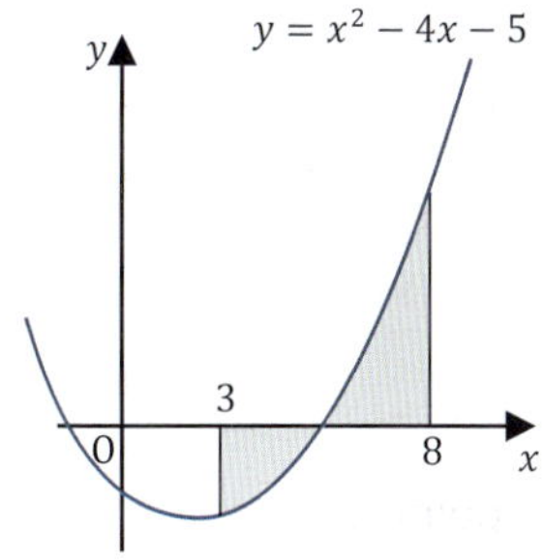

12.5 Calculate the shaded area:

(a)

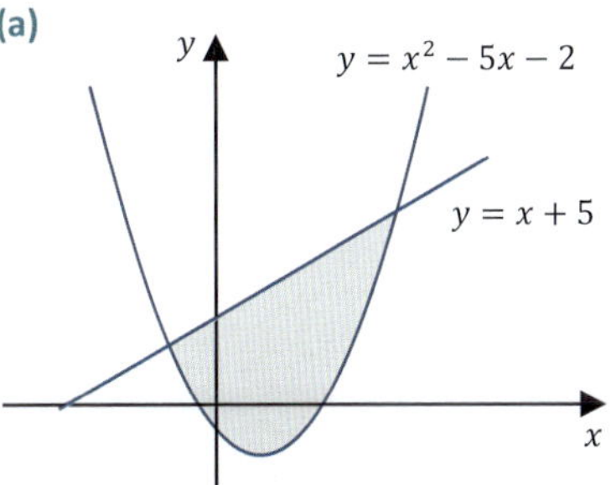

(b)

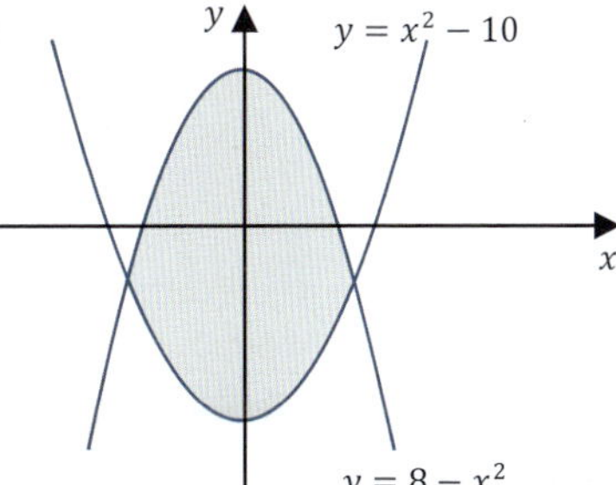

(c)

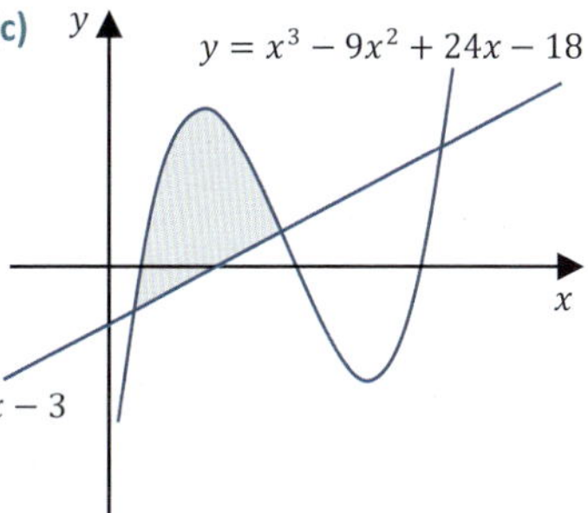

12.6 The rate of change of the volume, V litres of an object with respect to time, t hours, is given by $\frac{dV}{dt} = 9\sqrt{t} + 4t$. The volume of the object after 4 hours is 130 litres. Calculate the volume of the object after 8 hours.

Chapter 13

Calculus 3 – Further Calculus

Further Calculus

We have already covered the two main parts of calculus: differential and integral calculus. This chapter takes us further in our study of both topics. In this chapter we will differentiate and integrate **composite** and **trigonometric** functions.

13.1 Differentiating Composite Functions – The Chain Rule

When we differentiate **composite functions** (**see chapter 4**), we can use the **Chain Rule**. With this rule, we differentiate the **outer** function and multiply by the derivative of the **inner** function:

$$f(x) = (ax+b)^n$$

$$f'(x) = n(ax+b)^{n-1} \times a$$

When identifying the **outer** and **inner** function, consider where the brackets would be that surround the inner function.

Worked Examples:

The following functions are given on suitable domains. Find the derivative, giving your answers in positive index and root form:

(a) $f(x) = (4x+3)^3$ (b) $f(x) = 2(x^2+3x)^4$ (c) $f(x) = 2(x^2-5)^{\frac{1}{2}}$

Solutions:

Step 1: Identify the inner and outer function

Step 2: Cover up the inner function and differentiate the outer function,

i.e. $f(x) = (\quad)^n \Rightarrow f'(x) = n(\quad)^{n-1}$

Step 3: Multiply by the derivative of the inner function and simplify.

(a) $f(x) = (4x+3)^3$

$f'(x) = 3(4x+3)^2 \times 4$

$f'(x) = 12(4x+3)^2$

(b) $f(x) = 2(x^2+3x)^4$

$f'(x) = 8(x^2+3x)^3 \times (2x+3)$

$f'(x) = 8(x^2+3x)^3(2x+3)$

(c) $f(x) = 2(x^2-5)^{\frac{1}{2}}$

$f'(x) = 1(x^2-5)^{-\frac{1}{2}} \times 2x$

$f'(x) = \dfrac{2x}{\sqrt{x^2-5}}$

Exercise 13.1A

1. Differentiate each of the following:

(a) $f(x) = (2x-1)^3$ (b) $y = (3x+2)^7$ (c) $f(x) = (6x+5)^3$

(d) $y = (9x-2)^5$ (e) $f(x) = 3(4x+5)^5$ (f) $y = 2(6x-11)^4$

(g) $y = 6(2x+3)^3$ (h) $f(x) = 5(6x-1)^5$ (i) $f(x) = 6(3x+11)^{10}$

2. Differentiate each of the following:

(a) $y = (x^2+1)^3$ (b) $f(x) = (2x^3+5)^4$ (c) $f(x) = (3x^2-10)^7$

(d) $f(x) = (4x^3+1)^4$ (e) $g(x) = 2(x^4+5)^6$ (f) $y = 5(2x^2-7)^7$

(g) $f(x) = 9(3x^5+5)^3$ (h) $y = 4(3x^6-2)^5$ (i) $h(x) = 6(2x^9+15)^{10}$

3. Differentiate each of the following:

(a) $f(x) = (x^2 + x)^3$ (b) $y = (x^3 - x)^3$ (c) $f(x) = 2(x^2 - 4x)^5$

(d) $y = 3(x^3 + x)^6$ (e) $g(x) = 5(2x - x^2)^3$ (f) $y = 4(5x^2 - x^3)^7$

(g) $h(x) = 2(x^4 - 2x^2)^5$ (h) $y = (2x^3 - x^4)^3$ (i) $k(x) = 2(3x^4 + 2x)^9$

4. The following functions are given on suitable domains. Find the derivative, giving your answers in positive index and root form:

(a) $f(x) = (x^2 + 2)^{-2}$ (b) $f(x) = (x^3 - 2)^{-3}$ (c) $g(x) = 2(x^2 + 4)^{-3}$

(d) $f(x) = 2(x^3 + 1)^{-4}$ (e) $y = 5(2x - 3)^{-4}$ (f) $f(x) = 4(6 - x^3)^{-7}$

(g) $h(x) = 3(x^2 - 2x)^{-4}$ (h) $f(x) = 2(x^3 - 3x)^{-3}$ (i) $g(x) = 3(5x + x^2)^{-2}$

5. The following functions are given on suitable domains. Find the derivative, giving your answers in positive index and root form:

(a) $f(x) = (4x + 2)^{\frac{1}{2}}$ (b) $g(x) = (2x - 2)^{\frac{1}{2}}$ (c) $f(x) = (x^2 + 4)^{\frac{3}{2}}$

(d) $f(x) = (2x^2 + 1)^{-\frac{1}{2}}$ (e) $y = (2x - 3)^{-\frac{3}{2}}$ (f) $h(x) = 4(x^2 + 2)^{\frac{2}{3}}$

(g) $f(x) = 3(x^2 + x)^{-\frac{2}{3}}$ (h) $f(x) = 4(2x^2 - x)^{-\frac{1}{2}}$ (i) $g(x) = 2(4x^3 + x)^{-\frac{2}{3}}$

Worked Examples:

Differentiate each of the following:

(a) $f(x) = \dfrac{3}{(2x + 5)^2}$ (b) $g(x) = \dfrac{7}{(x - x^2)^3}$ (c) $f(x) = \dfrac{6}{\sqrt{3x^2 - 2}}$

Solutions:

(a) $f(x) = \dfrac{3}{(2x + 5)^2}$

$f(x) = 3(2x + 5)^{-2}$

$f'(x) = -6(2x + 5)^{-3} \times 2$

$f'(x) = \dfrac{-12}{(2x + 5)^3}$

$f'(x) = -\dfrac{12}{(2x + 5)^3}$

(b) $g(x) = \dfrac{7}{(x - x^2)^3}$

$g(x) = 7(x - x^2)^{-3}$

$g'(x) = -21(x - x^2)^{-4} \times (1 - 2x)$

$g(x) = \dfrac{-21(1 - 2x)}{(x - x^2)^4}$

$g(x) = -\dfrac{21(1 - 2x)}{(x - x^2)^4}$

(c) $f(x) = \dfrac{6}{(3x^2 - 2)^{\frac{1}{2}}}$

$f'(x) = 6(3x^2 - 2)^{-\frac{1}{2}}$

$f'(x) = -3(3x^2 - 2)^{-\frac{3}{2}} \times 6x$

$f(x) = \dfrac{-18x}{\sqrt{(3x^2 - 2)^3}}$

$f(x) = -\dfrac{18x}{\sqrt{(3x^2 - 2)^3}}$

Exercise 13.1B

1. Find the derivative of each of the following. Give your answers in positive index and root form:

(a) $f(x) = \dfrac{4}{(3x + 2)^2}$ (b) $f(x) = \dfrac{4}{(5x + 2)^3}$ (c) $f(x) = \dfrac{9}{(4 - 2x)^5}$

(d) $g(x) = \dfrac{3}{(x^2 + 2x)^2}$ (e) $f(x) = \dfrac{5}{(2x^3 + x)^3}$ (f) $h(x) = \dfrac{7}{(5x - x^2)^3}$

(g) $f(x) = \dfrac{4}{(4x+3)^{\frac{1}{2}}}$ (h) $k(x) = \dfrac{4}{(5x-2)^{\frac{2}{3}}}$ (i) $f(x) = \dfrac{2}{(4x-x^2)^{\frac{3}{2}}}$

2. Find the derivative of each of the following. Give your answers in positive index and root form:

(a) $f(x) = \dfrac{4}{\sqrt{x+2}}$ (b) $f(x) = \dfrac{3}{\sqrt{4x+2}}$ (c) $g(x) = \dfrac{5}{\sqrt{7-3x}}$

(d) $f(x) = \dfrac{1}{\sqrt{x^2+2}}$ (e) $h(x) = \dfrac{5}{\sqrt{x^2+x}}$ (f) $f(x) = \dfrac{2}{\sqrt{2x^2+x}}$

(g) $k(x) = \dfrac{3}{\sqrt{(x^2+2)^3}}$ (h) $g(x) = \dfrac{7}{\sqrt[3]{x^3-5x}}$ (i) $f(x) = \dfrac{3}{\sqrt{(x^2+2x)^3}}$

Exercise 13.1C

1. Evaluate each of the following:

(a) $f'(2)$, when $f(x) = (x^2+4)^3$ (b) $g'(-1)$, when $g(x) = (4x-2)^4$

(c) $h'(1)$, when $h(x) = (7x-6)^3$ (d) $f'(-2)$, when $f(x) = (2x^2-3)^4$

(e) $g'(-2)$, when $g(x) = (3x-6)^4$ (f) $h'(3)$, when $h(x) = (5x^2-3)^3$

2. The following functions are given on suitable domains – evaluate:

(a) $f'(-1)$, when $f(x) = (6x+4)^{-3}$ (b) $g'(1)$, when $g(x) = (2x+1)^{-5}$

(c) $h'(3)$, when $h(x) = (2x^2-3)^{-3}$ (d) $f'(-2)$, when $f(x) = (x^2-5)^{-4}$

(e) $g'(2)$, when $g(x) = (x^3-4)^{-\frac{1}{2}}$ (f) $h'(4)$, when $h(x) = (x^2-9)^{\frac{1}{2}}$

3. Evaluate each of the following:

(a) $f'(2)$, when $f(x) = \dfrac{1}{(3x+2)^2}$ (b) $g'(1)$, when $g(x) = \dfrac{1}{\sqrt{6x-2}}$

(c) $h'(2)$, when $h(x) = \dfrac{1}{(x^2-5)^3}$ (d) $f'(-1)$, when $f(x) = \dfrac{2}{(x^3+2)^4}$

(e) $g'(-3)$, when $g(x) = \dfrac{6}{\sqrt{x^2-5}}$ (f) $h'(2)$, when $h(x) = \dfrac{6}{\sqrt[3]{2x-1}}$

4. In each of the following, calculate the rate of change at the given point:

(a) $f(x) = (x^2-1)^3$ when $x = 2$ (b) $f(x) = (3x^2-1)^3$ when $x = -1$

(c) $f(x) = (x^2-1)^{-2}$ when $x = 3$ (d) $f(x) = (x^3-1)^4$ when $x = 1$

(e) $f(x) = \dfrac{1}{(3x-2)^2}$ when $x = -2$ (f) $f(x) = \dfrac{1}{\sqrt{2x-3}}$ when $x = 4$

5. In each of the following, calculate the gradient of the tangent to the curve at the given point:

(a) $f(x) = (x^2 + 5)^3$ when $x = 2$

(b) $f(x) = (2x^2 + 3)^3$ when $x = -2$

(c) $f(x) = (3x^2 + 2)^{-2}$ when $x = -2$

(d) $f(x) = (2x^2 - x)^3$ when $x = 1$

(e) $f(x) = \dfrac{1}{(5x + 3)^2}$ when $x = 3$

(f) $f(x) = \dfrac{1}{\sqrt{x^2 + 1}}$ when $x = -3$

13.2 Differentiating Trigonometric Functions

The derivative of a trigonometric function can be most easily seen in the graph of the derived function of each function.

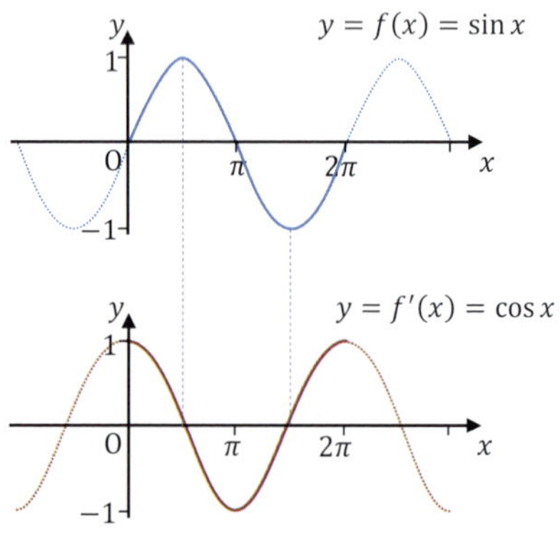

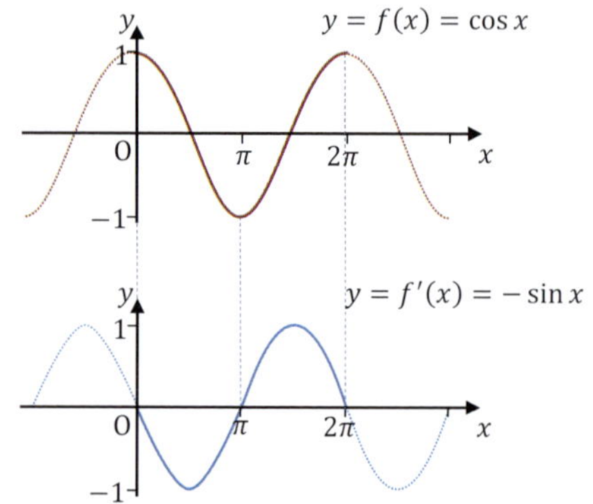

When we differentiate **trigonometric functions**, we use the following:

$$\frac{d}{dx}\sin x = \cos x \qquad \frac{d}{dx}\cos x = -\sin x$$

These derivatives are given in the formula sheet for Higher Mathematics.

It should be noted that these values are only true when using radians. For this reason, in calculus, when differentiating or integrating trigonometric functions, always use radians (see **extra info**).

Extra Info

Radians are essential in calculus because the **angle in radians equates to the linear distance**. This is not the case when we use degrees. We can see this in the unit circle. The radius of the unit circle is 1 unit. In this circle, the length of the arc of the circle is always the radian measure of the angle.

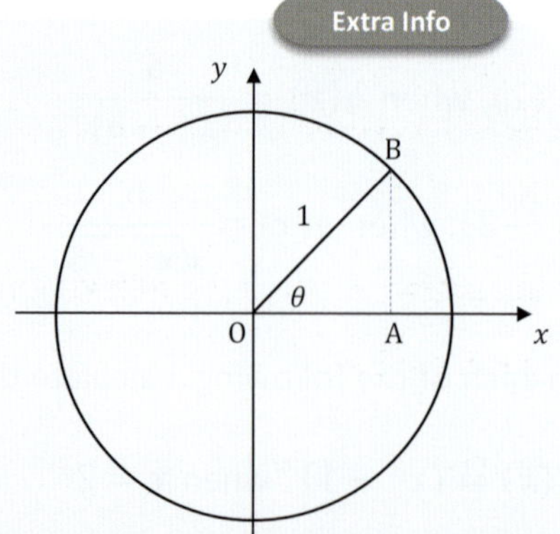

$$\textit{length of arc} = \frac{\theta}{2\pi} \times \pi D = \frac{\theta}{2\pi} \times 2\pi = \theta$$

Therefore, we can say that: $\mathrm{OA} = \cos\theta$, $\mathrm{AB} = \sin\theta$ and $\mathrm{OB} = \tan\theta$.

When using radians, on a trigonometric graph, one unit in the x-direction is the same as one unit in the y-direction. Again, this is not the case when using degrees.

Worked Examples:

Differentiate each of the following:

(a) $f(x) = 2\sin x$

$f'(x) = 2\cos x$

(b) $f(x) = 5\cos x$

$f'(x) = -5\sin x$

(c) $f(x) = 7\sin x - 3\cos x$

$f'(x) = 7\cos x + 3\sin x$

Exercise 13.2A

1. Differentiate each of the following:

(a) $f(x) = 4\sin x$ (b) $y = 2\cos x$ (c) $f(x) = 6\sin x$

(d) $y = 10\cos x$ (e) $f(x) = 7\cos x$ (f) $y = 8\sin x$

2. Differentiate each of the following:

(a) $y = \cos x + \sin x$ (b) $f(x) = \cos x - \sin x$ (c) $y = 3\cos x + 2\sin x$

(d) $y = \sin x + 4\cos x$ (e) $f(x) = 2\sin x - 4\cos x$ (f) $f(x) = 9\cos x - 2\sin x$

When differentiating and integrating trigonometric functions, we most frequently have composite functions. We differentiate these using **the chain rule**. It is important to identify the **inner** and **outer** function, which is not as obvious as algebraic questions. It is important to recognise where the brackets would be, **e.g.**

$$\frac{d}{dx}\sin ax = \frac{d}{dx}\sin(ax) = \cos(ax) \times a \qquad \frac{d}{dx}\cos ax = \frac{d}{dx}\cos(ax) = -\sin(ax) \times a$$

Worked Examples:

Differentiate each of the following:

(a) $f(x) = \sin 2x$ (b) $f(x) = 2\cos 3x$ (c) $f(x) = 3\sin(5x - 2)$

Solutions:

(a) $f(x) = \sin(2x)$

$f'(x) = \cos(2x) \times 2$

$f'(x) = 2\cos(2x)$

(b) $f(x) = 2\cos(3x)$

$f'(x) = -2\sin(3x) \times 3$

$f'(x) = -6\sin(3x)$

(c) $f(x) = 3\sin(5x - 2)$

$f'(x) = 3\cos(5x - 2) \times 5$

$f'(x) = 15\cos(5x - 2)$

Exercise 13.2B

1. Differentiate each of the following:

(a) $f(x) = \sin 3x$ (b) $y = \cos 2x$ (c) $f(x) = \sin 5x$

(d) $y = \cos 4x$ (e) $f(x) = 2\cos 3x$ (f) $y = 2\sin 4x$

2. Differentiate each of the following:

(a) $y = 3\cos 5x$ (b) $f(x) = -2\cos 2x$ (c) $f(x) = -2\sin 2x$

(d) $y = 3\cos 5x + \sin 2x$ (e) $f(x) = 2\sin 4x - 3\cos 2x$ (f) $f(x) = \cos x - 3\sin 5x$

(g) $y = 6\sin 2x + \cos 3x$

(h) $f(x) = \cos 3x - 5\cos 2x$

(i) $f(x) = \cos x - 3\sin 2x$

3. Differentiate each of the following:

(a) $y = \cos(2x - 3)$

(b) $f(x) = \sin(4x + 2)$

(c) $f(x) = \cos(5x + 1)$

(d) $y = \sin\left(x + \frac{\pi}{3}\right)$

(e) $f(x) = \cos\left(3x - \frac{\pi}{3}\right)$

(f) $f(x) = \sin\left(2x + \frac{3\pi}{2}\right)$

(g) $y = \sin(x^2 + 1)$

(h) $f(x) = \cos(2x^2 - 2)$

(i) $f(x) = -\cos(3x^2 - 2)$

When dealing with $\sin^n x$, $\cos^n x$, or any other power of the trigonometric functions, these functions may be written as $(\sin x)^n$. It is important to identify the **Inner** and **outer** function, which can be more challenging with these functions as there are no obvious brackets, **e.g.**

$$\sin^n x = (\sin x)^n = (\sin x)^n$$

Worked Examples:

Differentiate each of the following:

(a) $f(x) = \sin^2 x$

(b) $f(x) = \cos^3 x$

(c) $f(x) = 3\sin^4 x$

Solutions:

(a) $f(x) = (\sin x)^2$

$f'(x) = 2(\sin x)^1 \times \cos x$

$f'(x) = 2\sin x \cos x$

(b) $f(x) = (\cos x)^3$

$f'(x) = 3(\cos x)^2 \times -\sin x$

$f'(x) = -3\cos^2 x \sin x$

(c) $f(x) = 3(\sin x)^4$

$f'(x) = 12(\sin x)^3 \times \cos x$

$f'(x) = 12\sin^3 x \cos x$

Exercise 13.2C

1. Differentiate each of the following:

(a) $f(x) = \sin^3 x$

(b) $y = \cos^2 x$

(c) $f(x) = \sin^5 x$

(d) $y = \cos^7 x$

(e) $f(x) = \cos^4 x$

(f) $y = \sin^6 x$

2. Differentiate each of the following:

(a) $f(x) = 5\sin^2 x$

(b) $y = 6\cos^3 x$

(c) $f(x) = 11\sin^4 x$

(d) $y = 3\cos^4 x$

(e) $f(x) = 8\sin^2 x$

(f) $y = 6\sin^4 x$

3. Differentiate each of the following:

(a) $f(x) = \sin^2 x - \cos^2 x$

(b) $y = \cos^2 x - 2\sin 2x$

(c) $f(x) = \cos^3 x + \sin^3 x$

(d) $y = 4\sin 3x - \cos^2 x$

(e) $f(x) = 5\sin^3 x - \cos^2 x$

(f) $y = 7\cos 3x + \sin^5 x$

Exercise 13.2D

1. Evaluate:

(a) $f'\left(\frac{\pi}{6}\right)$, when $f(x) = \cos 2x$.

(b) $f'\left(\frac{\pi}{3}\right)$, when $f(x) = \sin 3x$.

(c) $f'\left(\frac{\pi}{4}\right)$, when $f(x) = 2\sin 4x$.

(d) $f'\left(\frac{\pi}{4}\right)$, when $f(x) = 3\cos 2x$.

(e) $f'\left(\frac{3\pi}{4}\right)$, when $f(x) = \cos^2 x$.

(f) $f'\left(\frac{\pi}{6}\right)$, when $f(x) = \sin^2 x$.

(g) $f'\left(\frac{\pi}{3}\right)$, when $f(x) = 3\sin\left(2x - \frac{\pi}{3}\right)$.

(h) $f'\left(\frac{5\pi}{6}\right)$, when $f(x) = 5\cos^3 x$.

2. In each of the following, calculate the rate of change at the given point:

(a) $f(x) = \sin 2x$ when $x = \frac{\pi}{6}$.

(b) $f(x) = 4\cos 3x$ when $x = \frac{\pi}{3}$.

(c) $f(x) = 3\cos 5x$ when $x = \frac{\pi}{3}$.

(d) $f(x) = 2\sin\left(2x - \frac{\pi}{6}\right)$ when $x = \frac{5\pi}{6}$.

(e) $f(x) = \cos^2 x$ when $x = \frac{\pi}{4}$.

(f) $f(x) = \sin^2 x$ when $x = \frac{2\pi}{3}$.

(g) $f(x) = 2\cos^3 x$ when $x = \frac{\pi}{6}$.

(h) $f(x) = 3\sin^3 x$ when $x = \frac{5\pi}{6}$.

13.3 Integrating Composite Functions

When we integrate **composite functions** (**see chapter 4**), provided the inner function is linear (this will always be the case in Higher Mathematics), we can use the reverse process to the chain rule. To do this, we **integrate** the outer function and divide by the **derivative** of the inner function:

$$\int (ax+b)^n \, dx$$

$$= \frac{(ax+b)^{n+1}}{(n+1)\times a} + C$$

Consider integration as the reverse of differentiation. When a composite function has been differentiated, the function has been multiplied by the derivative of the inner function. Therefore, the reverse of this is not to multiply by the integral of the inner function, but to divide by the derivative.

Worked Examples:

Find:

(a) $\int (2x+1)^3 \, dx$

(b) $\int 3(3x-2)^{-2} \, dx$

(c) $\int 2(5x+2)^{-\frac{1}{2}} \, dx$

Step 1: Identify the inner and outer function

Step 2: Cover up the inner function and integrate the outer function,

i.e. $\int (\quad)^n \, dx = \frac{(\quad)^{n+1}}{n+1} \dots$

Step 3: Divide by the derivative of the inner function.

Step 4: Add constant of integration and simplify.

Solutions:

(a) $\int (2x+1)^3 \, dx$

(b) $\int 3(3x-2)^{-2} \, dx$

(c) $\int 2(5x+2)^{-\frac{1}{2}} \, dx$

$$= \frac{(2x+1)^4}{4 \times 2} + C \qquad = \frac{3(3x-2)^{-1}}{-1 \times 3} + C \qquad = \frac{2(5x+2)^{\frac{1}{2}}}{{}^1/_2 \times 5} + C$$

$$= \frac{(2x+1)^4}{8} + C \qquad = -\frac{1}{(3x-2)} + C \qquad = \frac{4\sqrt{x^2+5}}{5} + C$$

NB: The inner (blue) function in each of these questions is a linear function.

Exercise 13.3A

1. Find:

(a) $\int (x+2)^2\,dx$ (b) $\int (4x+3)^2\,dx$ (c) $\int (5x-2)^3\,dx$

(d) $\int 5(5x+1)^4\,dx$ (e) $\int 2(3x-3)^3\,dx$ (f) $\int 3(7x+1)^6\,dx$

(g) $\int 2(3-x)^5\,dx$ (h) $\int 2(1-3x)^7\,dx$ (i) $\int 8(5-x)^4\,dx$

(j) $\int \frac{1}{2}(2x+4)^2\,dx$ (k) $\int \frac{1}{4}(3x-2)^3\,dx$ (l) $\int \frac{1}{2}(5-4x)^3\,dx$

(m) $\int \frac{1}{3}(4x+7)^5\,dx$ (n) $\int 3(5x-3)^3\,dx$ (o) $\int 2(7x+1)^5\,dx$

(p) $\int \frac{2}{3}(3-x)^5\,dx$ (q) $\int \frac{3}{4}(4-5x)^2\,dx$ (r) $\int \frac{4}{5}(1-5x)^2\,dx$

2. The following are given on suitable domains – find:

(a) $\int (2x+4)^{-3}\,dx$ (b) $\int (2x-4)^{-2}\,dx$ (c) $\int 2(1-4x)^{-3}\,dx$

(d) $\int 5(3x+5)^{-4}\,dx$ (e) $\int 2(7x-2)^{-3}\,dx$ (f) $\int 4(3x-2)^{-5}\,dx$

(g) $\int \frac{1}{2}(5x-3)^{-2}\,dx$ (h) $\int \frac{1}{2}(3x-2)^{-5}\,dx$ (i) $\int \frac{2}{3}(4x-1)^{-7}\,dx$

3. The following are given on suitable domains – find:

(a) $\int (4x-3)^{\frac{1}{2}}\,dx$ (b) $\int (2x+2)^{\frac{1}{3}}\,dx$ (c) $\int 4(3x+5)^{-\frac{1}{2}}\,dx$

(d) $\int 6(3x-1)^{-\frac{1}{3}}\,dx$ (e) $\int 5(5x-4)^{\frac{2}{3}}\,dx$ (f) $\int 7(4x+1)^{-\frac{1}{3}}\,dx$

(g) $\int \frac{2}{3}(4+2x)^{-\frac{2}{3}}\,dx$ (h) $\int \frac{3}{4}(3x+2)^{-\frac{3}{4}}\,dx$ (i) $\int \frac{1}{2}(5x+1)^{-\frac{1}{5}}\,dx$

Worked Examples:

Find:

(a) $\int \frac{2}{(3x-2)^2}\,dx$ (b) $\int \frac{4}{(2x-3)^3}\,dx$ (c) $\int \frac{4}{\sqrt{3x+1}}\,dx$

Method:

Step 1: Identify the inner and outer function

Step 2: Cover up the inner function and integrate the outer function,

i.e. $\int (\quad)^n \, dx = \frac{(\quad)^{n+1}}{n+1} \ldots$

Step 3: Divide by the derivative of the inner function.

Step 4: Add constant of integration and simplify.

(a) $\int 2(3x-2)^{-2} \, dx$

$= \frac{2(3x-2)^{-1}}{-1 \times 3} + C$

$= -\frac{2}{3(3x-2)} + C$

(b) $\int 4(2x-3)^{-3} \, dx$

$= \frac{4(2x-3)^{-2}}{-2 \times 2} + C$

$= -\frac{1}{(2x-3)^2} + C$

(c) $\int 4(3x+1)^{-\frac{1}{2}} \, dx$

$= \frac{4(3x+1)^{\frac{1}{2}}}{{}^1\!/_2 \times 3} + C$

$= \frac{8\sqrt{3x+1}}{3} + C$

Exercise 13.3B

1. The following are given on suitable domains – find:

(a) $\int \frac{2}{(2x+1)^2} \, dx$

(b) $\int \frac{5}{(5x-2)^4} \, dx$

(c) $\int \frac{4}{(2x-1)^3} \, dx$

(d) $\int \frac{3}{(3x+2)^2} \, dx$

(e) $\int \frac{1}{(x-2)^5} \, dx$

(f) $\int \frac{8}{(9-2x)^3} \, dx$

(g) $\int \frac{3}{(2x+4)^{\frac{1}{2}}} \, dx$

(h) $\int \frac{3}{(1-x)^{\frac{1}{3}}} \, dx$

(i) $\int \frac{6}{(4x+7)^{\frac{2}{3}}} \, dx$

2. The following are given on suitable domains – find:

(a) $\int \frac{1}{\sqrt{x+2}} \, dx$

(b) $\int \frac{2}{\sqrt{3x+2}} \, dx$

(c) $\int \frac{4}{\sqrt{3x-2}} \, dx$

(d) $\int \frac{2}{\sqrt{4x+5}} \, dx$

(e) $\int \frac{6}{\sqrt[3]{5-2x}} \, dx$

(f) $\int \frac{1}{\sqrt{6-5x}} \, dx$

(g) $\int \frac{9}{\sqrt{(7x+2)^3}} \, dx$

(h) $\int \frac{2}{\sqrt[3]{(6-4x)^2}} \, dx$

(i) $\int \frac{3}{\sqrt{(5x+9)^3}} \, dx$

Exercise 13.3C

1. Evaluate:

(a) $\int_{-1}^{2} (4x+2)^2 \, dx$

(b) $\int_{-1}^{2} (3x-4)^3 \, dx$

(c) $\int_{-1}^{1} (6x-2)^4 \, dx$

(d) $\int_{-2}^{1} (2x-5)^3 \, dx$

(e) $\int_{0}^{1} (3x+1)^4 \, dx$

(f) $\int_{1}^{1.1} (5-3x)^3 \, dx$

2. The following are given on suitable domains – evaluate:

(a) $\int_{-3}^{1} (2x-3)^{-2}\,dx$ (b) $\int_{1}^{3} (5x-2)^{-2}\,dx$ (c) $\int_{-1}^{1} (3x-4)^{-3}\,dx$

(d) $\int_{-1}^{0} (4-3x)^{-3}\,dx$ (e) $\int_{-1}^{1} (2-x)^{-4}\,dx$ (f) $\int_{-2}^{0} (6x-1)^{-3}\,dx$

3. The following are given on suitable domains – evaluate:

(a) $\int_{-2}^{-1} \frac{1}{(2x-2)^2}\,dx$ (b) $\int_{1}^{3} \frac{2}{(2x+4)^3}\,dx$ (c) $\int_{-1}^{1} \frac{1}{(4-x)^2}\,dx$

(d) $\int_{2}^{7} \frac{1}{\sqrt{x+2}}\,dx$ (e) $\int_{-2}^{1} \frac{2}{\sqrt{x+3}}\,dx$ (f) $\int_{3}^{6} \frac{1}{\sqrt{x-2}}\,dx$

(g) $\int_{4}^{10} \frac{1}{\sqrt{2x-4}}\,dx$ (h) $\int_{1}^{14} \frac{4}{\sqrt[3]{2x-1}}\,dx$ (i) $\int_{-12}^{2} \frac{3}{\sqrt[3]{2x-3}}\,dx$

13.4 Integrating Trigonometric Functions

We have already differentiated trigonometric functions. When we integrate, we do the reverse process. It is helpful to become familiar with the derivatives and integrals of the sine and cosine functions. The diagram on the right may be a helpful memory aid.

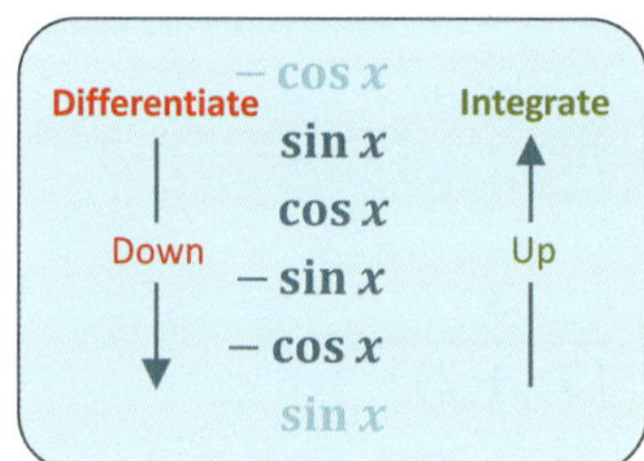

When we integrate **trigonometric functions**, we have the following:

$$\int \cos ax\,dx = \frac{\sin ax}{a} + C \qquad \int \sin ax\,dx = -\frac{\cos ax}{a} + C$$

Worked Examples:

Find:

(a) $\int \sin 2x\,dx$ (b) $\int 2\cos 3x\,dx$ (c) $\int 4\sin(2x-1)\,dx$

Method:

Step 1: Identify the inner and outer function and bracket the inner function.

Step 2: Cover up the inner function and integrate the outer function.

Step 3: Divide by the derivative of the inner function.

Step 4: Add constant of integration and simplify.

(a) $\int \sin(2x)\,dx$

$= \frac{-\cos(2x)}{2} + C$

(b) $\int 2\cos(3x)\,dx$

$= \frac{2\sin(3x)}{3} + C$

(c) $\int 4\sin(2x-1)\,dx$

$= \frac{-4\cos(2x-1)}{2} + C$

$= -2\cos(2x-1) + C$

Exercise 13.4A

1. Find:

(a) $\int \sin 3x\,dx$ (b) $\int \cos 2x\,dx$ (c) $\int \sin 5x\,dx$

(d) $\int \cos 7x\,dx$ (e) $\int \cos\left(\frac{x}{3}\right)dx$ (f) $\int \sin\left(\frac{1}{2}x\right)dx$

2. Find:

(a) $\int 3\cos 2x\,dx$ (b) $\int 4\sin 3x\,dx$ (c) $\int 2\sin 2x\,dx$

(d) $\int 4\cos 2x\,dx$ (e) $\int 5\sin 6x\,dx$ (f) $\int 3\cos 5x\,dx$

3. Find:

(a) $\int \cos(2x-2)\,dx$ (b) $\int \sin(3x-2)\,dx$ (c) $\int \sin(4x+1)\,dx$

(d) $\int \cos\left(3x-\frac{\pi}{3}\right)dx$ (e) $\int \sin(2x-1)\,dx$ (f) $\int \cos\left(2x+\frac{\pi}{6}\right)dx$

4. Find:

(a) $\int 3\cos(2x-2)\,dx$ (b) $\int 2\sin(2x+1)\,dx$ (c) $\int \frac{1}{3}\sin(3x+1)\,dx$

(d) $\int \frac{1}{2}\cos\left(3x-\frac{\pi}{3}\right)dx$ (e) $\int 2\sin(2x-1)\,dx$ (f) $\int \frac{4}{5}\cos\left(2x-\frac{\pi}{3}\right)dx$

It is not possible to integrate $\sin^2 x$ or $\cos^2 x$ using the reverse chain rule method – as the integrated form is not the same as the antiderivative, **i.e.** if we were to differentiate the integral of $\sin^2 x$, we would not end up with $\sin^2 x$. Instead, we must use double angle formulae and integrate these.

Worked Example:

Find $\int \sin^2 x\,dx$.

Solution:

$$\cos 2x = 1 - 2\sin^2 x$$
$$2\sin^2 x = 1 - \cos 2x$$
$$\sin^2 x = \frac{1}{2} - \frac{\cos 2x}{2}$$

$$\int \sin^2 x\,dx = \int \left(\frac{1}{2} - \frac{\cos 2x}{2}\right)dx$$
$$= \frac{1}{2}x - \frac{\sin 2x}{2\times 2} + C$$
$$= \frac{1}{2}x - \frac{\sin 2x}{4} + C$$

Exercise 13.4B

1. Find, by substitution of the double angle formulae:

(a) $\int \cos^2 x\,dx$ (b) $\int 2\sin^2 x\,dx$ (c) $\int 3\sin^2 x\,dx$

(d) $\int (\cos^2 x + \sin^2 x)\,dx$ (e) $\int 2\sin x\cos x\,dx$ (f) $\int 4\cos 2x\sin 2x\,dx$

Definite integrals are evaluated in the same way as before.

Worked Examples:

1. Evaluate $\int_0^{\pi/3} \sin 2x \, dx$

2. Evaluate $\int_0^{\pi/2} \cos(3x-1) \, dx$

Solution:

1. $\int_0^{\pi/3} \sin(2x) \, dx$

$= \left[\frac{-\cos(2x)}{2}\right]_0^{\pi/3}$

$= \left(\frac{-\cos\left(2 \times \frac{\pi}{3}\right)}{2}\right) - \left(\frac{-\cos(2 \times 0)}{2}\right)$

$= \left(\frac{1}{4}\right) - \left(-\frac{1}{2}\right)$

$= \frac{3}{4}$

2. $\int_0^{\pi/2} \cos(3x-1) \, dx$

$= \left[\frac{\sin(3x-1)}{3}\right]_0^{\pi/2}$

$= \left(\frac{\sin\left(3 \times \frac{\pi}{2} - 1\right)}{3}\right) - \left(\frac{\sin(2 \times 0 - 1)}{3}\right)$

$= (-0.180 \ldots) - (-280 \ldots)$

$= 0.100$ (3 s.f.)

NB: When evaluating trigonometric definite integrals, it is important to always calculate the subtractions. In algebraic integration, when substituting zero, the result is zero. This is not always the case with trigonometry (see lines 3 and 4 in the examples).

Exercise 13.4C

1. Evaluate (answer (a) to (d) without using a calculator):

(a) $\int_0^{\pi/3} \sin x \, dx$ (b) $\int_0^{\pi/6} \cos x \, dx$ (c) $\int_0^{\pi/4} \sin 2x \, dx$ (d) $\int_0^{\pi/4} \cos 2x \, dx$

(e) $\int_0^{1} 2 \sin 3x \, dx$ (f) $\int_0^{0.3} 3 \cos 4x \, dx$ (g) $\int_0^{0.6} 4 \sin 5x \, dx$ (h) $\int_{-\pi/6}^{0.3} 2 \cos 3x \, dx$

2. Evaluate:

(a) $\int_{-1}^{0} \sin(x+1) \, dx$ (b) $\int_0^{\pi/6} \cos(x-1) \, dx$ (c) $\int_{0.3}^{\pi/3} \sin\left(2x - \frac{\pi}{6}\right) dx$

(d) $\int_0^{\pi/8} 7 \cos\left(2x + \frac{\pi}{4}\right) dx$ (e) $\int_{\pi/8}^{1} 3 \sin\left(2x + \frac{\pi}{8}\right) dx$ (f) $\int_0^{0.5} 3 \cos\left(3x - \frac{\pi}{10}\right) dx$

13.5 Review

Exercise 13.5A

13.1A Find the derivative:

(a) $f(x) = (2x-3)^3$ (b) $y = (x^2+9)^5$ (c) $f(x) = (6x+5)^{-3}$

(d) $f(x) = 2(x^3 - x)^3$ **(e)** $y = (2x^3 + x)^{-\frac{1}{2}}$ **(f)** $f(x) = \frac{1}{2}(2x^3 + 4x)^4$

13.1B Differentiate:

(a) $f(x) = \dfrac{3}{(7x+3)^3}$ **(b)** $f(x) = \dfrac{1}{(5x-2)^{\frac{1}{3}}}$ **(c)** $f(x) = \dfrac{5}{\sqrt[3]{(x-x^2)}}$

13.1C Evaluate:

(a) $f'(3)$, when $f(x) = (x^2 + 2)^3$.

(b) $g'(-2)$, when $g(x) = (5x + 4)^{-2}$.

(c) $g'(-1)$, when $g(x) = \dfrac{6}{(2x+4)^3}$.

(d) $h'(2)$, when $h(x) = \dfrac{5}{\sqrt{4x^3 - 9}}$.

(e) Calculate the rate of change of $f(x) = (x^2 + 2x)^3$ when $x = -1$.

(f) Calculate the gradient of the tangent to the curve $y = \sqrt{x^3 + 2}$ when $x = 2$.

13.2B Differentiate:

(a) $y = 3\cos 5x$ **(b)** $f(x) = -2\sin 2x - 3\cos 2x$ **(c)** $f(x) = 4 - 2\sin 2x$

(d) $y = \sin(x^2 + 1)$ **(e)** $f(x) = \cos(2x^2 - 2)$ **(f)** $f(x) = -\cos(3x^2 - 2)$

13.2C Differentiate:

(a) $f(x) = 4\sin^2 x$ **(b)** $y = 3\cos^4 x$ **(c)** $f(x) = \cos^3 x + \sin^3 x$

13.2D Evaluate:

(a) $f'(2)$, when $f(x) = 4\cos 5x$.

(b) $f'\left(\frac{\pi}{6}\right)$, when $f(x) = 3\sin^2 x$.

(c) $f'\left(\frac{\pi}{3}\right)$, when $f(x) = 2\sin\left(2x - \frac{\pi}{6}\right)$.

(d) $f'\left(\frac{\pi}{4}\right)$, when $2\sin(3x + 1)$.

13.3A Find:

(a) $\int (2x-3)^3\,dx$ **(b)** $\int 4(5x+2)^{\frac{1}{2}}\,dx$ **(c)** $\int 4(7-3x)^4\,dx$

(d) $\int 6(5x-3)^{-2}\,dx$ **(e)** $\int 5(4x+1)^{-\frac{1}{2}}\,dx$ **(f)** $\int 4(5-4x)^{-\frac{2}{3}}\,dx$

13.3B Find:

(a) $\int \dfrac{2}{(6x+2)^3}\,dx$ **(b)** $\int \dfrac{2}{\sqrt[3]{(3x-2)}}\,dx$ **(c)** $\int \dfrac{3}{\sqrt{(5x-1)^3}}\,dx$

13.3C Evaluate:

(a) $\int_0^1 (3x+2)^2\,dx$ (b) $\int_{-1}^1 (5-2x)^2\,dx$ (c) $\int_3^5 \frac{1}{(4x-2)^2}\,dx$

(d) $\int_{-2}^0 \frac{1}{(2x-2)^2}\,dx$ (e) $\int_1^3 \frac{2}{(3x+4)^3}\,dx$ (f) $\int_0^1 \frac{1}{\sqrt{4-3x}}\,dx$

13.4A Find:

(a) $\int \sin 3x\,dx$ (b) $\int 2\cos 5x\,dx$ (c) $\int (1-3\sin 2x)\,dx$

(d) $\int \cos\left(3x-\frac{\pi}{3}\right)dx$ (e) $\int 4\sin\left(2x-\frac{\pi}{2}\right)dx$ (f) $\int (1+\sin(5x-1.2))\,dx$

13.4B Use the double angle formulae to find:

(a) $\int \sin^2 x\,dx$ (b) $\int (1-\sin^2 x)\,dx$ (c) $\int \sin x\cos x\,dx$

13.4C Evaluate:

(a) $\int_{-1}^0 \sin 2x\,dx$ (b) $\int_0^{\pi/3} 2\cos(2x-1)\,dx$ (c) $\int_{0.2}^{3\pi/8} \frac{1}{2}\sin\left(3x-\frac{\pi}{8}\right)dx$

Exercise 13.5B

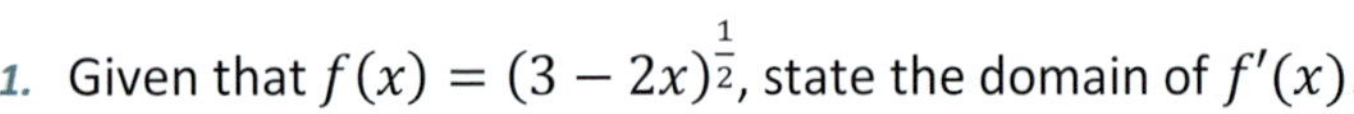

1. Given that $f(x) = (3-2x)^{\frac{1}{2}}$, state the domain of $f'(x)$.

2. Given $f(x) = \sin 2x - 2\cos 3x$, find the exact value of $f'\left(\frac{\pi}{6}\right)$.

3. (a) Express the function $f(x) = 2\sin x - 3\cos x$ in the form $f(x) = k\sin(x-a)$. Give k and a to 1 decimal place.

   (b) Hence find the value of b, where $1 \le b \le 3$ for which $\int_1^b (2\sin x - 3\cos x)\,dx = 2.4$.

4. The rate of change of a function is given by $\frac{dy}{dx} = 5\sin 2x$. The curve passes through the point $\left(\frac{\pi}{6}, 0\right)$. Express y in terms of x.

5. Calculate the rate of change of $f(x) = \sin^2 x - 4x$, when $x = 1.2$.

6. Given that $\int_{\pi/8}^{a} 3\cos\left(2x-\frac{\pi}{4}\right)dx = \frac{3}{2}, 0 \le a \le 2$, calculate the value of a.

7. The graphs of $y = f(x)$ and $y = g(x)$ are shown.

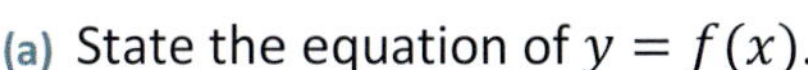

(a) State the equation of $y = f(x)$.

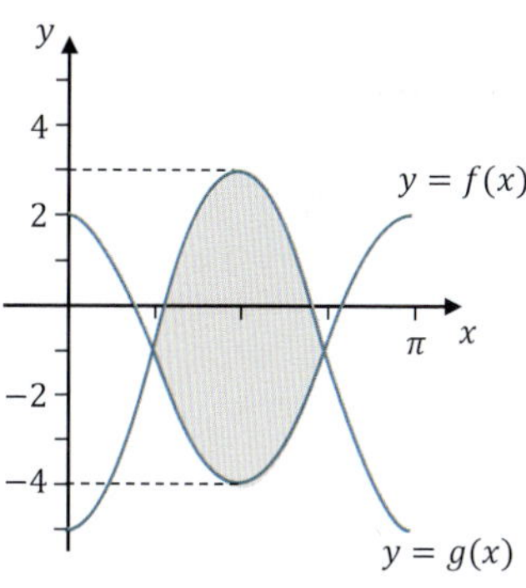

(b) State the equation of $y = g(x)$.

(c) Find the coordinates of the points of intersection of the two graphs.

(d) Calculate the shaded area.

8. Given that $f(x) = (5 - x^2)^{-\frac{1}{2}}$, state the domain of $f'(x)$.

9. Given $f(x) = 3\cos 2x + 2\sin 3x$, find the exact value of $f'\left(\frac{\pi}{3}\right)$.

10. The rate of change of a function is given by $f(x) = 3\cos\left(2x - \frac{\pi}{6}\right)$. The curve passes through the point $\left(\frac{\pi}{4}, 0\right)$. Express y in terms of x.

11. Calculate the rate of change of $f(x) = 3\cos 2x + x^2$, when $x = 0.4$.

12. Given that $\int_{5\pi/18}^{a} 2\sin\left(3x - \frac{5\pi}{6}\right) dx = \frac{2}{3}, 0 \leq a \leq 2$, calculate the value of a.

13. The graphs of $y = f(x)$ and $y = g(x)$ are shown.

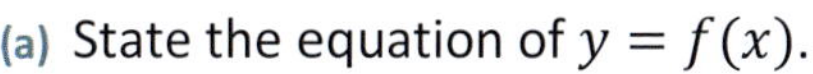

(a) State the equation of $y = f(x)$.

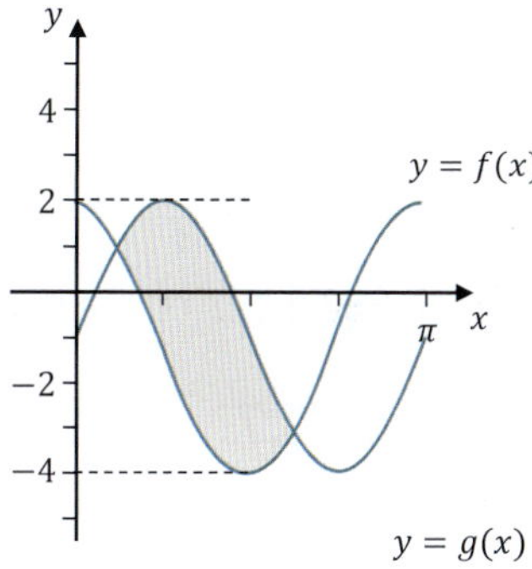

(b) State the equation of $y = g(x)$.

(c) Find the coordinates of the points of intersection of the two graphs.

(d) Calculate the shaded area.

Chapter 14

Vectors

N5 **Exercise 14.1**	Adding and subtracting vectors in component form
N5 **Exercise 14.2**	Using position vectors
N5 **Exercise 14.3**	Magnitude of vectors
Exercise 14.4	Finding unit vectors
Exercise 14.5	Working with unit vectors
Exercise 14.6	Collinearity
Exercise 14.7	Determining the coordinates of a division point on a line
Exercise 14.8	Determining the ratio of division of a line segment
Exercise 14.9	The scalar product
Exercise 14.10	Finding the angle between two vectors
Exercise 14.11	Properties of the scalar product
Exercise 14.12	Vector pathways
Exercise 14.13	Review

VECTORS

A vector is a quantity that has both a **magnitude** and a **direction**. Vectors can be expressed as line segments with an arrow to indicate direction. These can be named in one of two ways, either using a lower-case bold letter, such as $\mathbf{u}$, or by the letters at the end of each line segment, such as $\overrightarrow{AB}$, as in the example below.

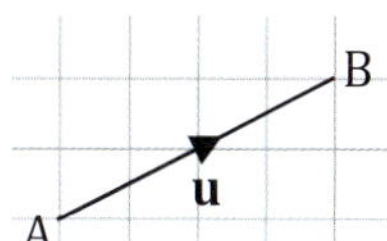

NB: When writing vectors using the lower-case form, vectors should be underlined, i.e. vector $\mathbf{u}$ would be written as $\underline{u}$.

In vector notation the direction of the arrow is important and shows the direction that the vector is travelling, **e.g.** $\overrightarrow{AB}$ is the vector from point A to point B. So it is also the case that $\overrightarrow{AB} = \overleftarrow{BA} \neq \overrightarrow{BA} = \overleftarrow{AB}$ and if $\overrightarrow{AB} = \mathbf{u}$ then $\overleftarrow{AB} = -\mathbf{u}$.

The vector can be expressed either as a line segment or in component form. Component form gives the vector's direction in two or three dimensions. **Three-dimensional coordinates** allow us to reference points in three-dimensional space. In two dimensions we refer to (x, y), but in three dimensions we use (x, y, z). Vectors are written in component form by finding their difference in the x, y and z directions.

In component form, **vector components** are written as $\mathbf{u} = \begin{pmatrix} x \\ y \\ z \end{pmatrix}$, where x, y and z are the difference in each direction. These components should be distinguished from coordinates, which represent the points at the end of the line segment of the vector and are written horizontally $A(p, q, r)$.

14.1 Adding and Subtracting Vectors in Component Form

National 5 Skills

To add or subtract vector components, add or subtract the x-components of each vector and do the same to the y-components. If components are multiplied by a scalar, multiply each of the components by the scalar value outside the bracket.

Worked Examples:

Given that $\mathbf{a} = \begin{pmatrix} 2 \\ 3 \end{pmatrix}$, $\mathbf{b} = \begin{pmatrix} 4 \\ -5 \end{pmatrix}$ and $\mathbf{c} = \begin{pmatrix} -2 \\ 8 \end{pmatrix}$, calculate the resultant vector for each of the following:

(a) $\mathbf{a} + \mathbf{b}$

$= \begin{pmatrix} 2 \\ 3 \end{pmatrix} + \begin{pmatrix} 4 \\ -5 \end{pmatrix}$

$= \begin{pmatrix} 6 \\ -2 \end{pmatrix}$

(b) $\mathbf{b} - \mathbf{c}$

$= \begin{pmatrix} 4 \\ -5 \end{pmatrix} - \begin{pmatrix} -2 \\ 8 \end{pmatrix}$

$= \begin{pmatrix} 6 \\ -13 \end{pmatrix}$

(c) $2\mathbf{a} - 3\mathbf{b}$

$= 2\begin{pmatrix} 2 \\ 3 \end{pmatrix} - 3\begin{pmatrix} 4 \\ -5 \end{pmatrix}$

$= \begin{pmatrix} 4 \\ 6 \end{pmatrix} - \begin{pmatrix} 12 \\ -15 \end{pmatrix} = \begin{pmatrix} -8 \\ 21 \end{pmatrix}$

Exercise 14.1A

$\mathbf{a} = \begin{pmatrix} 1 \\ 2 \end{pmatrix}$ $\mathbf{b} = \begin{pmatrix} 6 \\ 4 \end{pmatrix}$ $\mathbf{c} = \begin{pmatrix} -3 \\ 3 \end{pmatrix}$ $\mathbf{d} = \begin{pmatrix} -1 \\ -8 \end{pmatrix}$ $\mathbf{e} = \begin{pmatrix} -4 \\ 0 \end{pmatrix}$

Using the vectors above, find the resultant vector of each of the following. Express your answer in component form:

1. $\mathbf{a} + \mathbf{b}$
2. $\mathbf{b} + \mathbf{c}$
3. $\mathbf{c} - \mathbf{a}$
4. $\mathbf{d} - \mathbf{e}$
5. $2\mathbf{b} + \mathbf{a}$
6. $3\mathbf{c} - 2\mathbf{a}$
7. $4\mathbf{c} + 2\mathbf{e}$
8. $3\mathbf{c} - 2\mathbf{d}$
9. $5\mathbf{a} - 3\mathbf{b} + 2\mathbf{c}$
10. $4\mathbf{d} + 2\mathbf{a} - 4\mathbf{e}$
11. $4\mathbf{b} - \mathbf{e} - 3\mathbf{c}$
12. $\mathbf{c} - 3\mathbf{d} + 2\mathbf{e}$

Worked Example:

Given that $\mathbf{a} = \begin{pmatrix} 2 \\ -3 \\ 4 \end{pmatrix}$ and $\mathbf{b} = \begin{pmatrix} -3 \\ -2 \\ 5 \end{pmatrix}$, calculate the resultant vector of $2\mathbf{a} + 3\mathbf{b}$.

Solution:

$$2\mathbf{a} - 3\mathbf{b} = 2\begin{pmatrix} 2 \\ -3 \\ 4 \end{pmatrix} - 3\begin{pmatrix} -3 \\ -2 \\ 5 \end{pmatrix} = \begin{pmatrix} 4 \\ -6 \\ 8 \end{pmatrix} - \begin{pmatrix} -9 \\ -6 \\ 15 \end{pmatrix} = \begin{pmatrix} -5 \\ 0 \\ 23 \end{pmatrix}$$

NB: $\begin{pmatrix} 4 \\ -6 \\ 8 \end{pmatrix} - \begin{pmatrix} -9 \\ -6 \\ 15 \end{pmatrix} = \begin{pmatrix} 4 \\ -6 \\ 8 \end{pmatrix} + \begin{pmatrix} 9 \\ 6 \\ -15 \end{pmatrix}$

Exercise 14.1B

$\mathbf{s} = \begin{pmatrix} 5 \\ 2 \\ 1 \end{pmatrix}$ $\quad \mathbf{t} = \begin{pmatrix} 3 \\ 8 \\ 0 \end{pmatrix}$ $\quad \mathbf{u} = \begin{pmatrix} -2 \\ 4 \\ -3 \end{pmatrix}$ $\quad \mathbf{v} = \begin{pmatrix} 5 \\ -7 \\ 6 \end{pmatrix}$ $\quad \mathbf{w} = \begin{pmatrix} -11 \\ -2 \\ -12 \end{pmatrix}$

Using the vectors above, find the resultant vector of each of the following. Express your answer in component form:

1. $\mathbf{s} + \mathbf{t}$
2. $\mathbf{t} + \mathbf{u}$
3. $\mathbf{v} - \mathbf{w}$
4. $\mathbf{w} - \mathbf{t}$
5. $2\mathbf{v} + \mathbf{s}$
6. $3\mathbf{v} - 2\mathbf{u}$
7. $4\mathbf{w} + 2\mathbf{s}$
8. $3\mathbf{t} - 2\mathbf{u}$
9. $2\mathbf{v} - \mathbf{s}$
10. $3\mathbf{v} + 2\mathbf{u}$
11. $4\mathbf{t} - \mathbf{w} - 3\mathbf{u}$
12. $\mathbf{v} - 3\mathbf{w} + 2\mathbf{s}$

14.2 Using Position Vectors

National 5 Skills

Position vectors are vectors that are always fixed at one end. In mathematics, a **position vector** is a vector from the origin to a point on a coordinate axis,

e.g. the position vector of coordinate $A(2, 4, 5)$ is $\mathbf{a} = \begin{pmatrix} 2 \\ 4 \\ 5 \end{pmatrix}$.

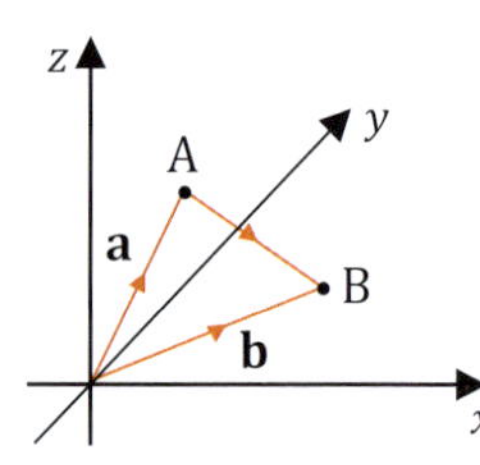

Position vectors are used to find the vector which joins two coordinates. If we know the coordinates of points A and B (as in the diagram), to find the vector joining the points A and B, ($\overrightarrow{AB}$), we need to go from point A to point B using the vectors we know, **i.e.** the position vectors.

Therefore, $\overrightarrow{AB} = -\mathbf{a} + \mathbf{b}$ or, more commonly, $\overrightarrow{AB} = \mathbf{b} - \mathbf{a}$.

Worked Examples:

For each of the coordinates $A(5, -3)$, $B(-2, 1)$ and $C(9, 0)$, find the following vectors:

(a) $\overrightarrow{AB}$

$= \mathbf{b} - \mathbf{a}$

$= \begin{pmatrix} -2 \\ 1 \end{pmatrix} - \begin{pmatrix} 5 \\ -3 \end{pmatrix}$

$= \begin{pmatrix} -7 \\ 4 \end{pmatrix}$

(b) $\overrightarrow{AC}$

$= \mathbf{c} - \mathbf{a}$

$= \begin{pmatrix} 9 \\ 0 \end{pmatrix} - \begin{pmatrix} 5 \\ -3 \end{pmatrix}$

$= \begin{pmatrix} 4 \\ 3 \end{pmatrix}$

(c) $2\overrightarrow{BC}$

$= 2(\mathbf{c} - \mathbf{b})$

$= 2\left(\begin{pmatrix} 9 \\ 0 \end{pmatrix} - \begin{pmatrix} -2 \\ 1 \end{pmatrix}\right)$

$= 2\left(\begin{pmatrix} 11 \\ -1 \end{pmatrix}\right)$

$= \begin{pmatrix} 22 \\ -2 \end{pmatrix}$

Exercise 14.2A

A(6, 2) B(4, 5) C(−3, 0) D(7, −5) E(5, −11) F(0, 12)

Using the coordinates above, find the vector specified in each of the following. Express your answer in component form:

1. $\overrightarrow{AB}$
2. $\overrightarrow{AC}$
3. $\overrightarrow{BD}$
4. $\overrightarrow{CE}$
5. $2\overrightarrow{ED}$
6. $5\overrightarrow{FC}$
7. $-\overrightarrow{DE}$
8. $4\overrightarrow{CF}$
9. $\overrightarrow{AB}+\overrightarrow{FE}$
10. $2\overrightarrow{DF}-3\overrightarrow{BF}$
11. $2\overrightarrow{CF}+5\overrightarrow{CB}$
12. $5\overrightarrow{FA}-5\overrightarrow{AF}$

Worked Examples:

For each of the points A(1, −4, 8), B(0, 7, −6) and C(5, 12, 0) find: **(a)** $\overrightarrow{AB}$ and **(b)** $\overrightarrow{BC}$

Solutions:

(a) $\overrightarrow{AB}$

$= \mathbf{b}-\mathbf{a}$

$= \begin{pmatrix} 0 \\ 7 \\ -6 \end{pmatrix} - \begin{pmatrix} 1 \\ -4 \\ 8 \end{pmatrix}$

$= \begin{pmatrix} -1 \\ 11 \\ -14 \end{pmatrix}$

(b) $\overrightarrow{BC}$

$= \mathbf{c}-\mathbf{b}$

$= \begin{pmatrix} 5 \\ 12 \\ 0 \end{pmatrix} - \begin{pmatrix} 0 \\ 7 \\ -6 \end{pmatrix}$

$= \begin{pmatrix} 5 \\ 5 \\ 6 \end{pmatrix}$

Exercise 14.2B

A(3, 2, 1) B(−4, 9, 13) C(6, −3, −7) D(0, 9, 0) E(4, −12, −17)

Using the coordinates above, find the vector specified in each of the following. Express your answer in component form:

1. $\overrightarrow{AB}$
2. $\overrightarrow{AC}$
3. $\overrightarrow{CD}$
4. $\overrightarrow{BE}$
5. $2\overrightarrow{ED}$
6. $5\overrightarrow{DC}$
7. $-\overrightarrow{DE}$
8. $4\overrightarrow{CE}$
9. $\overrightarrow{AB}+\overrightarrow{EB}$
10. $3\overrightarrow{CA}-2\overrightarrow{EA}$
11. $\overrightarrow{DB}+3\overrightarrow{BD}$
12. $4\overrightarrow{BA}-3\overrightarrow{AE}$

14.3 Magnitude of Vectors

National 5 Skills

The **magnitude** of a vector is the length or size of the vector. The notation for magnitude is two vertical bars, **e.g.** the magnitude of $\mathbf{u}$ is $|\mathbf{u}|$. To calculate the magnitude of a vector, we use the following formula:

$|\mathbf{u}| = \sqrt{x^2+y^2}$ or in three dimensions: $|\mathbf{u}| = \sqrt{x^2+y^2+z^2}$

NB: This is effectively Pythagoras' Theorem in one line, like the distance formula.

Worked Examples:

1. Find $|\mathbf{u}|$, the magnitude of vector $\mathbf{u} = \begin{pmatrix} 2 \\ -3 \\ 6 \end{pmatrix}$

$|\mathbf{u}| = \sqrt{x^2 + y^2 + z^2}$

$|\mathbf{u}| = \sqrt{2^2 + (-3)^2 + 6^2}$

$|\mathbf{u}| = \sqrt{49}$

$|\mathbf{u}| = 7$

NB: $|\overrightarrow{AB}| = |\overrightarrow{BA}|$ and $|\mathbf{u}| = |-\mathbf{u}|$ but $|\mathbf{u}| \neq -|\mathbf{u}|$

2. Given that $A(5, 4, -7)$ and $B(3, -8, 2)$, find $|\overrightarrow{AB}|$, the magnitude of the vector joining points A and B.

$\overrightarrow{AB} = \mathbf{b} - \mathbf{a}$

$\overrightarrow{AB} = \begin{pmatrix} 3 \\ -8 \\ 2 \end{pmatrix} - \begin{pmatrix} 5 \\ 4 \\ -7 \end{pmatrix}$

$\overrightarrow{AB} = \begin{pmatrix} -2 \\ -12 \\ 9 \end{pmatrix}$

$|\overrightarrow{AB}| = \sqrt{x^2 + y^2 + z^2}$

$|\overrightarrow{AB}| = \sqrt{(-2)^2 + (-12)^2 + 9^2}$

$|\overrightarrow{AB}| = 15.1$ (1 d.p)

Exercise 14.3

1. Calculate the magnitude of the following vectors:

(a) $\mathbf{a} = \begin{pmatrix} 3 \\ -4 \end{pmatrix}$ (b) $\mathbf{b} = \begin{pmatrix} 12 \\ -5 \end{pmatrix}$ (c) $\mathbf{c} = \begin{pmatrix} 8 \\ -15 \end{pmatrix}$ (d) $\mathbf{d} = \begin{pmatrix} -7 \\ 24 \end{pmatrix}$

(e) $\mathbf{t} = \begin{pmatrix} -2 \\ 4 \\ 4 \end{pmatrix}$ (f) $\mathbf{u} = \begin{pmatrix} 4 \\ -6 \\ -12 \end{pmatrix}$ (g) $\mathbf{v} = \begin{pmatrix} 16 \\ -14 \\ -13 \end{pmatrix}$ (h) $\mathbf{w} = \begin{pmatrix} -12 \\ 35 \\ 0 \end{pmatrix}$

2. Using the coordinates below, find the magnitude of the vector in each of the following. Give your answer correct to 1 decimal place:

$A(3, 7, 2)$ $B(4, 5, 6)$ $C(3, 0, -5)$ $D(11, -2, 9)$ $E(14, -3, 0)$

(a) $|\overrightarrow{AB}|$ (b) $|\overrightarrow{AC}|$ (c) $|\overrightarrow{AD}|$ (d) $|\overrightarrow{AE}|$

(e) $|\overrightarrow{BC}|$ (f) $|\overrightarrow{DB}|$ (g) $|\overrightarrow{DA}|$ (h) $|\overrightarrow{CE}|$

3. Given the vectors: $\mathbf{p} = \begin{pmatrix} 1 \\ 0 \\ 7 \end{pmatrix}$, $\mathbf{q} = \begin{pmatrix} -3 \\ 4 \\ -5 \end{pmatrix}$ and $\mathbf{r} = \begin{pmatrix} 9 \\ -11 \\ -2 \end{pmatrix}$, calculate each of the following. Give your answer correct to 1 decimal place:

(a) $|\boldsymbol{p} + \boldsymbol{q}|$ (b) $|\boldsymbol{p} + \boldsymbol{r}|$ (c) $|\boldsymbol{q} - \boldsymbol{r}|$ (d) $|\boldsymbol{p} - \boldsymbol{r}|$

(e) $|5\boldsymbol{q} + 2\boldsymbol{r}|$ (f) $|2\boldsymbol{r} + 2\boldsymbol{q}|$ (g) $|4\boldsymbol{p} + 3\boldsymbol{r} - \boldsymbol{q}|$ (h) $|2\boldsymbol{p} + 3\boldsymbol{q} - \boldsymbol{r}|$

(i) $|5\boldsymbol{q} - 2\boldsymbol{r}|$ (j) $|-2\boldsymbol{r} - 2\boldsymbol{q}|$ (k) $|4\boldsymbol{p} + 3\boldsymbol{r} + \boldsymbol{q}|$ (l) $|\boldsymbol{r} - \boldsymbol{p}|$

14.4 Calculating and Using Unit Vectors

A **unit vector** is a vector with a magnitude of 1 unit. For every vector, there is a parallel unit vector. To calculate a unit vector of a vector, calculate the magnitude of the vector and divide each component by the magnitude.

Worked Example:

Calculate $\mathbf{u}$, the unit vector of vector $\mathbf{v} = \begin{pmatrix} -8 \\ -1 \\ 4 \end{pmatrix}$.

Solution:

$$|\mathbf{v}| = \sqrt{x^2 + y^2 + z^2}$$

$$|\mathbf{v}| = \sqrt{(-8)^2 + (-1)^2 + 4^2}$$

$$|\mathbf{v}| = \sqrt{81}$$

$$|\mathbf{v}| = 9$$

$$\mathbf{u} = \frac{1}{9}\begin{pmatrix} -8 \\ -1 \\ 4 \end{pmatrix}$$

$$\mathbf{u} = \begin{pmatrix} -{}^{8}/_{9} \\ -{}^{1}/_{9} \\ {}^{4}/_{9} \end{pmatrix}$$

Exercise 14.4

Calculate the unit vector $\mathbf{u}$ of the following vectors:

1. $\mathbf{a} = \begin{pmatrix} -2 \\ 1 \\ 2 \end{pmatrix}$
2. $\mathbf{b} = \begin{pmatrix} 9 \\ -2 \\ -6 \end{pmatrix}$
3. $\mathbf{c} = \begin{pmatrix} -4 \\ 12 \\ -3 \end{pmatrix}$
4. $\mathbf{d} = \begin{pmatrix} -2 \\ 4 \\ -2 \end{pmatrix}$
5. $\mathbf{e} = \begin{pmatrix} -12 \\ -9 \\ 8 \end{pmatrix}$
6. $\mathbf{f} = \begin{pmatrix} 11 \\ -2 \\ 10 \end{pmatrix}$
7. $\mathbf{g} = \begin{pmatrix} 4 \\ 1 \\ -8 \end{pmatrix}$
8. $\mathbf{h} = \begin{pmatrix} 15 \\ -6 \\ 10 \end{pmatrix}$
9. $\mathbf{l} = \begin{pmatrix} 12 \\ 20 \\ 9 \end{pmatrix}$
10. $\mathbf{m} = \begin{pmatrix} 4 \\ -20 \\ 5 \end{pmatrix}$
11. $\mathbf{n} = \begin{pmatrix} 14 \\ 5 \\ -2 \end{pmatrix}$
12. $\mathbf{p} = \begin{pmatrix} 15 \\ -16 \\ 12 \end{pmatrix}$

14.5 Working with Unit Vectors

A standardised way of writing vectors is using the unit vectors $\mathbf{i}$, $\mathbf{j}$ and $\mathbf{k}$, where each is the unit vector in the x, y and z direction respectively. These are denoted as:

$$\mathbf{i} = \begin{pmatrix} 1 \\ 0 \\ 0 \end{pmatrix} \qquad \mathbf{j} = \begin{pmatrix} 0 \\ 1 \\ 0 \end{pmatrix} \qquad \mathbf{k} = \begin{pmatrix} 0 \\ 0 \\ 1 \end{pmatrix}$$

For example, for vector $\mathbf{v}$, we can express the vector in either component form or unit vector form,

i.e. $\mathbf{v} = \begin{pmatrix} 4 \\ 3 \\ -7 \end{pmatrix} = 4\mathbf{i} + 3\mathbf{j} - 7\mathbf{k}$.

When working with vectors that are written in terms of $\mathbf{i}$, $\mathbf{j}$ and $\mathbf{k}$, it is useful to write them in component form.

Exercise 14.5

1. Express each of the following vectors in terms of $\mathbf{i}$, $\mathbf{j}$ and $\mathbf{k}$:

(a) $\mathbf{a} = \begin{pmatrix} -2 \\ 4 \\ 4 \end{pmatrix}$ (b) $\mathbf{b} = \begin{pmatrix} 4 \\ -6 \\ -12 \end{pmatrix}$ (c) $\mathbf{c} = \begin{pmatrix} 16 \\ -14 \\ -13 \end{pmatrix}$ (d) $\mathbf{d} = \begin{pmatrix} -12 \\ 35 \\ 0 \end{pmatrix}$

(e) $\mathbf{e} = \begin{pmatrix} 0 \\ -1 \\ 3 \end{pmatrix}$ (f) $\mathbf{f} = \begin{pmatrix} 5 \\ 0 \\ -9 \end{pmatrix}$ (g) $\mathbf{g} = \begin{pmatrix} 0 \\ -2 \\ 0 \end{pmatrix}$ (h) $\mathbf{h} = \begin{pmatrix} 5 \\ -12 \\ 18 \end{pmatrix}$

2. Vectors $\mathbf{a}$ and $\mathbf{b}$ are such that $\mathbf{a} = 5\mathbf{i} + 2\mathbf{j} - 7\mathbf{k}$ and $\mathbf{b} = 6\mathbf{i} + 4\mathbf{j} - 3\mathbf{k}$. Find $|3\mathbf{a} - \mathbf{b}|$.

3. Vectors $\mathbf{c}$ and $\mathbf{d}$ are such that $\mathbf{c} = 9\mathbf{i} - 6\mathbf{k}$ and $\mathbf{d} = 5\mathbf{i} + \mathbf{j} - 9\mathbf{k}$. Find $|\mathbf{c} - \mathbf{d}|$.

4. Vectors $\mathbf{e}$ and $\mathbf{f}$ are such that $\mathbf{e} = 2\mathbf{i} - 4\mathbf{j} + 7\mathbf{k}$ and $\mathbf{f} = 2\mathbf{i} + 2\mathbf{j} + a\mathbf{k}$ and $|2\mathbf{e} - \mathbf{f}| = 11$. Find the value of a.

5. Vectors $\mathbf{g}$ and $\mathbf{h}$ are such that $\mathbf{g} = a\mathbf{i} - 4\mathbf{j} + 2\mathbf{k}$ and $\mathbf{h} = \mathbf{i} + 2\mathbf{j} + 3\mathbf{k}$ and $|\mathbf{g} - 2\mathbf{h}| = 9$. Find the value of a.

14.6 Collinearity

Collinearity is when three or more points lie on the same line in two- or three-dimensional space. We have already encountered collinearity in two dimensions when studying the straight line (see **section 1.5**). In three dimensions, we prove that three points are collinear by showing two pieces of information about any two vectors joining two pairs of the points.

1. The vector joining one pair of points is a scalar multiple of the vector joining a different pair (this shows that the vectors are going in the same direction, **i.e.** they are parallel).
2. The two vectors share a common point.

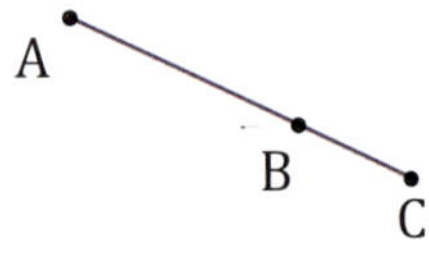

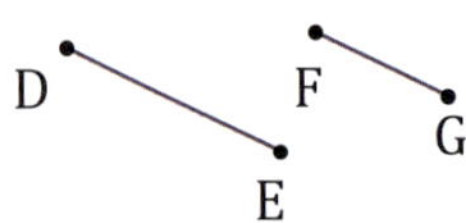

$p\overrightarrow{AB} = q\overrightarrow{BC}$ so the vectors are **parallel**. Point B is common, ∴ points A, B and C **are** collinear.

$p\overrightarrow{DE} = q\overrightarrow{FG}$, but these vectors do not share a common point, ∴ points are **not** collinear.

$p\overrightarrow{HJ} \neq q\overrightarrow{JK}$, ∴ points H, J and K are **not** collinear.

Worked Examples:

1. Show that $A(4, 1, -2)$, $B(7, 7, -5)$ and $C(11, 15, -9)$ are collinear.

Solution:

$\overrightarrow{AB} = \mathbf{b} - \mathbf{a}$

$\overrightarrow{AB} = \begin{pmatrix} 7 \\ 7 \\ -5 \end{pmatrix} - \begin{pmatrix} 4 \\ 1 \\ -2 \end{pmatrix}$

$\overrightarrow{BC} = \mathbf{c} - \mathbf{b}$

$\overrightarrow{BC} = \begin{pmatrix} 11 \\ 15 \\ -9 \end{pmatrix} - \begin{pmatrix} 7 \\ 7 \\ -5 \end{pmatrix}$

$$\overrightarrow{AB} = \begin{pmatrix} 3 \\ 6 \\ -3 \end{pmatrix} \qquad \overrightarrow{BC} = \begin{pmatrix} 4 \\ 8 \\ -4 \end{pmatrix}$$

$$\overrightarrow{AB} = 3\begin{pmatrix} 1 \\ 2 \\ -1 \end{pmatrix} \qquad \overrightarrow{BC} = 4\begin{pmatrix} 1 \\ 2 \\ -1 \end{pmatrix}$$

NB: the ratio of $\overrightarrow{AB}:\overrightarrow{BC}$ is $3:4$, $\therefore 4\overrightarrow{AB} = 3\overrightarrow{BC}$.

$4\overrightarrow{AB} = 3\overrightarrow{BC} \Rightarrow$ vectors are parallel. Point B is common, $\therefore$ points A, B and C are collinear.

2. Points $D(7,-3,1)$, $E(9,-2,0)$ and $F(k,0,-2)$ are collinear. Determine the value of k.

Solution: For collinearity $\overrightarrow{DE} = n\overrightarrow{EF}$

$\overrightarrow{DE} = \mathbf{e} - \mathbf{d}$ $\qquad$ $\overrightarrow{EF} = \mathbf{f} - \mathbf{e}$

$$\overrightarrow{DE} = \begin{pmatrix} 9 \\ -2 \\ 0 \end{pmatrix} - \begin{pmatrix} 7 \\ -3 \\ 1 \end{pmatrix} \qquad \overrightarrow{EF} = \begin{pmatrix} k \\ 0 \\ -2 \end{pmatrix} - \begin{pmatrix} 9 \\ -2 \\ 0 \end{pmatrix}$$

$$\overrightarrow{DE} = \begin{pmatrix} 2 \\ 1 \\ -1 \end{pmatrix} \qquad \overrightarrow{EF} = \begin{pmatrix} k-9 \\ 2 \\ -2 \end{pmatrix} = 2\overrightarrow{DE} = \begin{pmatrix} 4 \\ 2 \\ -2 \end{pmatrix}$$

$k - 9 = 4$

$\therefore k = 13$

Exercise 14.6

1. Determine whether each of the following groups of points are collinear:

(a) $A(3,-2,3)$, $B(4,-1,2)$ and $C(6,1,0)$.

(b) $D(5,-3,0)$, $E(3,1,-2)$ and $F(2,3,-3)$.

(c) $G(1,-2,6)$, $H(3,3,5)$ and $I(5,8,5)$.

(d) $J(-2,0,10)$, $K(0,5,-7)$ and $L(6,20,2)$.

(e) $M(-5,1,-8)$, $N(-1,-3,-2)$ and $P(-5,-9,7)$.

(f) $Q(-3,2,-3)$, $R(-6,5,9)$ and $S(-7,6,13)$.

(g) $T(6,2,4)$, $U(4,4,0)$ and $V(1,7,-6)$.

(h) $W(-10,2,9)$, $X(-4,5,2)$ and $Y(4,9,-10)$.

(i) $A(3,0,-15)$, $B(17,-7,6)$ and $C(21,-9,12)$.

(j) $D(-1,5,-15)$, $E(17,20,-6)$ and $F(47,45,9)$.

2. The following groups of points are collinear. Determine the value of k:

(a) $A(2,1,3)$, $B(7,4,0)$ and $C(k,7,-3)$.

(b) $D(-4,5,2)$, $E(-2,9,-4)$ and $F(-1,k,-7)$.

(c) $G(-1,-5,9)$, $H(1,-1,3)$ and $I(4,5,k)$.

(d) $J(-10,2,-6)$, $K(-8,-4,-2)$ and $L(-5,k,4)$.

(e) $M(12,22,-3)$, $N(15,k,3)$ and $P(17,-3,7)$.

(f) $Q(8,15,-11)$, $R(k,27,-5)$ and $S(23,35,-1)$.

(g) $T(k,1,28)$, $U(14,13,16)$ and $V(10,16,13)$.

(h) $W(7,-4,k)$, $X(25,-1,9)$ and $Y(37,1,-5)$.

(i) $A(15,2,29)$, $B(-6,9,k)$ and $C(-12,11,-34)$.

(j) $D(34,15,2)$, $E(22,19,-10)$ and $F(19,20,k)$.

14.7 Determining the Coordinates of an internal Point of Division

If a point divides a line segment in a given ratio, we can calculate the coordinates of the point using a variety of different methods.

Worked Example:

Points A and B are $(-2, 5, 4)$ and $(8, 10, 19)$ respectively. Point P divides AB in the ratio $2:3$. Find the coordinates of P.

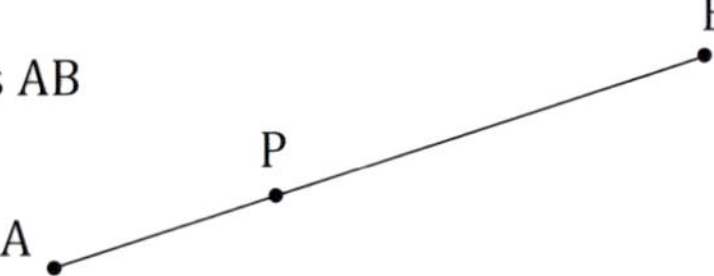

Solution:

As P divides AB in the ratio $2:3$, P is $\frac{2}{2+3} = \frac{2}{5}$ of the distance in x, y and z along the line from A.

Step 1: Determine the difference in x, y and z between coordinates A and B.

AB difference in x: $\Delta x = 8 - (-2) = 10$

AB difference in y: $\Delta y = 10 - 5 = 5$

AB difference in z: $\Delta z = 19 - 4 = 15$

A 2 P 3 B

$(-2, 5, 4)$ $(8, 10, 19)$

-2 $\Delta x = 10$ 8

5 $\Delta y = 5$ 10

4 $\Delta z = 15$ 19

Step 2: Multiply the difference by $\frac{2}{5}$.

$x = 10 \times \frac{2}{5} = 4$

$y = 5 \times \frac{2}{5} = 2$

$z = 15 \times \frac{2}{5} = 6$

Step 3: Add the answers to coordinate A.

$P = (-2 + 4, 5 + 2, 4 + 6) = (2, 7, 10)$

NB: Alternatively, we could calculate $3/5$ of the difference and take it away from coordinate B.

Exercise 14.7

1. In each of the following questions, point P divides AB in the given ratio. Find the coordinates of P:

(a) $A(3, 1, 4)$, $B(9, 4, 13)$ in ratio $2:1$.

(b) $A(5, 2, 6)$, $B(13, 18, 2)$ in ratio $3:1$.

(c) $A(3, 4, -2)$, $B(23, -6, 3)$ in ratio $3:2$.

(d) $A(-1, 5, 8)$, $B(14, -10, -2)$ in ratio $3:2$.

(e) $A(6, 2, -7)$, $B(-2, -10, 5)$ in ratio $1:3$.

(f) $A(-14, 1, -8)$, $B(16, 11, 7)$ in ratio $2:3$.

(g) $A(22, 15, -3)$, $B(2, -20, 7)$ in ratio $4:1$.

(h) $A(46, 18, 2)$, $B(16, 0, 5)$ in ratio $2:1$.

(i) $A(32, -12, 7)$, $B(-10, 24, 25)$ in ratio $5:1$.

(j) $A(3, -17, 6)$, $B(8, -2, 41)$ in ratio $2:3$.

(k) $A(6, 1, -11)$, $B(20, -13, 31)$ in ratio $4:3$.

(l) $A(41, 22, -37)$, $B(27, 1, -2)$ in ratio $3:4$.

2. In each of the following questions, point P divides AB in the given ratio. Find the coordinates of B:

(a) $A(-18, 6, 2)$, $P(-14, 12, 6)$ in ratio $2:1$.

(b) $A(2, 11, -5)$, $P(4, 3, 1)$ in ratio $2:3$.

(c) $A(10, -5, 3)$, $P(19, 7, 6)$ in ratio $3:1$.

(d) $A(-11, 10, 35)$, $P(-2, 22, 38)$ in ratio $3:2$.

(e) $A(64, -2, -41)$, $P(44, 10, -25)$ in ratio $2:5$.

(f) $A(3, 102, 34)$, $P(23, 87, 24)$ in ratio $5:1$.

(g) $A(17, -19, 23)$, $P(5, 1, 31)$ in ratio $4:3$.

(h) $A(82, -54, 76)$, $P(102, -69, 96)$ in ratio $5:2$.

14.8 Determining the Ratio of Division of a Line Segment

If we have three collinear points, we can calculate the ratio in which the middle point divides the line segment.

Worked Example:

Points A, B and C are $(16, -5, 2)$, $(28, 1, -4)$ and $(32, 3, -6)$ respectively. The points are collinear. Find the ratio in which B divides AC.

Solution:

To find the ratio, determine the distance between A and B, and B and C in either x, y or z.

Step 1: Determine the difference in x.

AB difference in x: $\Delta x = 28 - 16 = 12$

BC difference in x: $\Delta x = 32 - 28 = 4$

Step 2: State and simplify the ratio.

$\text{AB}:\text{BC} \rightarrow 12:4 \rightarrow 3:1$

$\therefore$ B divides AC in the ratio $3:1$.

NB: It does not matter which of the coordinates we choose, provided the same coordinate is used for both AB and BC.

Exercise 14.8

1. Points A, B and C are collinear. State the ratio in which B divides AC:

(a) $A(-8, 3, 4)$, $B(0, 7, 0)$ and $C(4, 9, -2)$.

(b) $A(5, -1, 6)$, $B(9, -3, 9)$ and $C(21, -9, 18)$.

(c) $A(-11, 3, -1)$, $B(-7, 9, -3)$ and $C(-1, 18, -6)$.

(d) $A(25, 4, -2)$, $B(9, 8, -4)$ and $C(1, 10, -5)$.

(e) $A(-20, 7, 1)$, $B(-2, -2, 7)$ and $C(10, -8, 11)$.

(f) $A(7, 54, 18)$, $B(19, 10, -2)$ and $C(22, -1, -7)$.

(g) $A(20, -1, 24)$, $B(17, 1, 21)$ and $C(2, 11, 6)$.

(h) $A(86, 64, -15)$, $B(62, 44, -5)$ and $C(2, -6, 20)$.

(i) $A(-8, 17, 35)$, $B(19, 11, 44)$ and $C(37, 7, 50)$.

(j) $A(67, 35, 2)$, $B(55, 21, 8)$ and $C(37, 0, 17)$.

(k) $A(27, 15, 91)$, $B(3, 7, 31)$ and $C(-15, 1, -14)$.

(l) $A(102, -2, -12)$, $B(70, 14, 8)$ and $C(30, 34, 33)$.

2. Points A, B and C are collinear. (i) State the ratio in which B divides AC, (ii) determine the value of k:

(a) $A(4, 7, 1)$, $B(14, k, 5)$ and $C(19, -2, 7)$.

(b) $A(12, -4, 18)$, $B(27, -13, k)$ and $C(32, -16, 6)$.

(c) $A(-16, 5, k)$, $B(-20, 9, 16)$ and $C(-26, 15, 7)$.

(d) $A(-27, 4, 11)$, $B(-9, 10, 2)$ and $C(-3, k, -1)$.

(e) $A(k, -16, 4)$, $B(18, 2, -20)$ and $C(24, 14, -36)$.

(f) $A(53, -21, 22)$, $B(61, k, 12)$ and $C(81, 28, -13)$.

14.9 The Scalar Product

We cannot multiply two vectors together, as a vector consists of both a magnitude and a direction. We can, however, find a scalar value called the scalar product. The **scalar product** or **dot product** of two vectors is a scalar value which results from the sum of the product of the x, y and z components of each vector, or from the product of the two magnitudes and the cosine of the angle less than $180°$ between the vectors.

The scalar product is widely used in mathematics, but for Higher Mathematics, it is used primarily to find the angle between two vectors (see **section 14.11**).

For vectors $\mathbf{a} = \begin{pmatrix} x_a \\ y_a \\ z_a \end{pmatrix}$ and $\mathbf{b} = \begin{pmatrix} x_b \\ y_b \\ z_b \end{pmatrix}$, the scalar product is $\mathbf{a} \cdot \mathbf{b} = x_a x_b + y_a y_b + z_a z_b$

Worked Example:

Two vectors are given by $\mathbf{a} = 5\mathbf{i} + 2\mathbf{j} - 7\mathbf{k}$ and $\mathbf{b} = 6\mathbf{i} + 4\mathbf{j} - 3\mathbf{k}$. Find the value of $\mathbf{a} \cdot \mathbf{b}$.

Solution:

$\mathbf{a} \cdot \mathbf{b} = x_a x_b + y_a y_b + z_a z_b = 5 \times 6 + 2 \times 4 + (-7) \times (-3) = 30 + 8 + 21 = 59$

NB: When vectors meet at $90°$, the scalar product is zero.

Exercise 14.9A

1. Calculate the scalar product for each pair of vectors:

(a) $\mathbf{a} = 6\mathbf{i} + 2\mathbf{j} + \mathbf{k}$ and $\mathbf{b} = \mathbf{i} - 2\mathbf{j} + 3\mathbf{k}$.

(b) $\mathbf{c} = 4\mathbf{i} + 3\mathbf{k}$ and $\mathbf{d} = 2\mathbf{i} + 2\mathbf{j} - 7\mathbf{k}$.

(c) $\mathbf{e} = 12\mathbf{i} - 2\mathbf{j} - 3\mathbf{k}$ and $\mathbf{f} = 3\mathbf{i} + 5\mathbf{j} - \mathbf{k}$.

(d) $\mathbf{g} = 7\mathbf{i} + \mathbf{j} - \mathbf{k}$ and $\mathbf{h} = 2\mathbf{i} - 3\mathbf{j} + 11\mathbf{k}$.

(e) $\mathbf{m} = 22\mathbf{i} + 3\mathbf{j}$ and $\mathbf{n} = \mathbf{i} - 3\mathbf{k}$.

(f) $\mathbf{p} = 18\mathbf{i} + 2\mathbf{j} + 2\mathbf{k}$ and $\mathbf{q} = \mathbf{i} - 6\mathbf{j} - 3\mathbf{k}$.

(g) $\mathbf{r} = 5\mathbf{i} - 4\mathbf{j} - 2\mathbf{k}$ and $\mathbf{s} = 3\mathbf{i} + 4\mathbf{j} - \mathbf{k}$.

(h) $\mathbf{t} = 6\mathbf{j} - 2\mathbf{k}$ and $\mathbf{v} = 3\mathbf{i} + 2\mathbf{j}$.

2. Calculate the scalar product for each pair of vectors:

(a) $\mathbf{a} = \begin{pmatrix} 1 \\ -1 \\ 2 \end{pmatrix}$ and $\mathbf{b} = \begin{pmatrix} 4 \\ 3 \\ 5 \end{pmatrix}$

(b) $\mathbf{c} = \begin{pmatrix} 7 \\ 5 \\ -4 \end{pmatrix}$ and $\mathbf{d} = \begin{pmatrix} 2 \\ -6 \\ 2 \end{pmatrix}$

(c) $\mathbf{e} = \begin{pmatrix} 11 \\ -7 \\ 10 \end{pmatrix}$ and $\mathbf{f} = \begin{pmatrix} 1 \\ 0 \\ -8 \end{pmatrix}$

(d) $\mathbf{g} = \begin{pmatrix} 5 \\ 5 \\ 0 \end{pmatrix}$ and $\mathbf{h} = \begin{pmatrix} 8 \\ -12 \\ 2 \end{pmatrix}$

(e) $\mathbf{m} = \begin{pmatrix} 21 \\ 18 \\ 3 \end{pmatrix}$ and $\mathbf{n} = \begin{pmatrix} 2 \\ -3 \\ 4 \end{pmatrix}$

(f) $\mathbf{p} = \begin{pmatrix} 36 \\ 5 \\ 15 \end{pmatrix}$ and $\mathbf{q} = \begin{pmatrix} 2 \\ -8 \\ -2 \end{pmatrix}$

3.

(a) Calculate $\overrightarrow{BA} \cdot \overrightarrow{BC}$ from $A(1, -3, 2)$, $B(6, 4, 3)$ and $C(4, 11, 5)$.

(b) Calculate $\overrightarrow{DC} \cdot \overrightarrow{DE}$ from $C(2, -3, -10)$, $D(5, 2, 3)$ and $E(4, 3, 7)$.

(c) Calculate $\overrightarrow{FE} \cdot \overrightarrow{FG}$ from $E(3, 19, -3)$, $F(2, 0, 2)$ and $G(6, 4, -2)$.

(d) Calculate $\overrightarrow{LK} \cdot \overrightarrow{LM}$ from $K(9, -4, 3)$, $L(6, -5, 8)$ and $M(2, 11, 9)$.

(e) Calculate $\overrightarrow{PN} \cdot \overrightarrow{PQ}$ from $N(0, 2, 12)$, $P(9, 4, -7)$ and $Q(5, 11, -8)$.

(f) Calculate $\overrightarrow{SR} \cdot \overrightarrow{ST}$ from $R(8, 0, 1)$, $S(10, -5, 2)$ and $T(6, 0, 35)$.

4. Show that vectors $\mathbf{r} = 11\mathbf{i} - 5\mathbf{j} + 3\mathbf{k}$ and $\mathbf{s} = 3\mathbf{i} + 6\mathbf{j} - \mathbf{k}$ are perpendicular.

5. Show that vectors $\mathbf{t} = 3\mathbf{i} - 8\mathbf{j} + 7\mathbf{k}$ and $\mathbf{v} = -5\mathbf{i} + 6\mathbf{j} + 9\mathbf{k}$ are perpendicular.

6. Vectors $\mathbf{v}$ and $\mathbf{w}$ are such that $\mathbf{v} = 4\mathbf{i} + 3\mathbf{j} + 2\mathbf{k}$ and $\mathbf{w} = -9\mathbf{i} + a\mathbf{j} + 6\mathbf{k}$. If $\mathbf{v} \cdot \mathbf{w} = 0$, determine the value of a.

7. Vectors $\mathbf{r} = 7\mathbf{i} + 3\mathbf{k}$ and $\mathbf{s} = 2\mathbf{i} + a\mathbf{k}$ are perpendicular. Determine the value of a.

8. Vectors $\mathbf{c} = 9\mathbf{i} + \mathbf{j} + a\mathbf{k}$ and $\mathbf{d} = 3\mathbf{i} - 8\mathbf{j} + 2\mathbf{k}$ are perpendicular. Determine the value of a.

9. A, B and C are the coordinates $(2, 11, -7)$, $(8, -4, 3)$ and $(6, a, 4)$ respectively. $\overrightarrow{BA} \cdot \overrightarrow{BC} = 2$. Find the value of a.

10. P, Q and R are the coordinates $(9, 3, a)$, $(2, -10, 5)$ and $(7, -7, -2)$ respectively. $\overrightarrow{QP} \cdot \overrightarrow{QR} = 11$. Find the value of a.

11. D, E and F are the coordinates $(-5, 2, -6)$, $(2, a, -7)$ and $(3, 3, -6)$ respectively. $\overrightarrow{ED} \cdot \overrightarrow{EF} = 0$. Find the value(s) of a.

12. L, M and N are the coordinates $(18, a, 6)$, $(3, 16, 2)$ and $(1, 7, 23)$ respectively. $\overrightarrow{ML}$ is perpendicular to $\overrightarrow{MN}$. Find the value of a.

We can also calculate the scalar product from the magnitude of the two vectors and the angle (less than 180°) between them. For vectors **a** and **b**, the scalar product is $\mathbf{a} \cdot \mathbf{b} = |\mathbf{a}||\mathbf{b}| \cos\theta$

NB: When identifying the angle between the two vectors, the vectors must either **both** point **away** from the vertex or **both** point **towards** the vertex.

Worked Example:

Given that $|\mathbf{a}| = 10$ and $\mathbf{b} = 5\mathbf{i} + 2\mathbf{j} - 4\mathbf{k}$. Find the value of $\mathbf{a} \cdot \mathbf{b}$.

Solution: Find the magnitude of **b** and substitute into the formula.

$|\mathbf{b}| = \sqrt{5^2 + 2^2 + (-4)^2} = \sqrt{45} = 3\sqrt{5}$

$\mathbf{a} \cdot \mathbf{b} = |\mathbf{a}||\mathbf{b}| \cos\theta = 10 \times 3\sqrt{5} \times \cos 120 = 30\sqrt{5} \times \left(-\frac{1}{2}\right) = -15\sqrt{5}$

Exercise 14.9B

1. Calculate the scalar product (a calculator may be used for (e) and (f)):

(a)

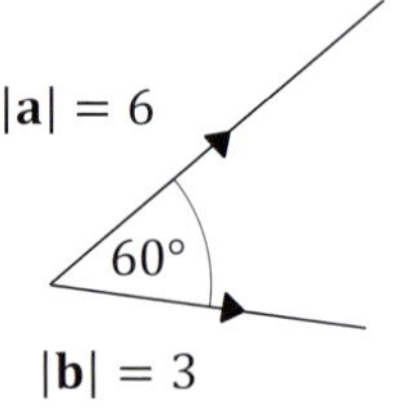

(b)

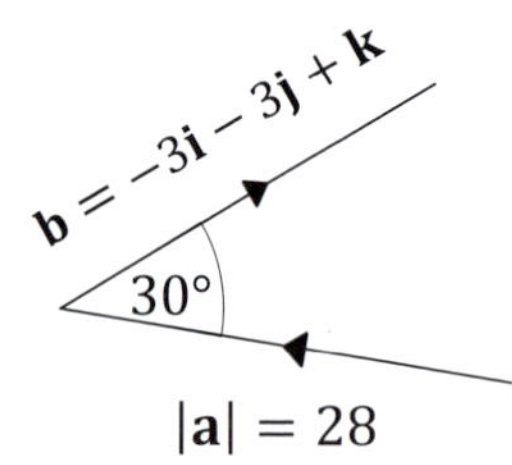

(c)

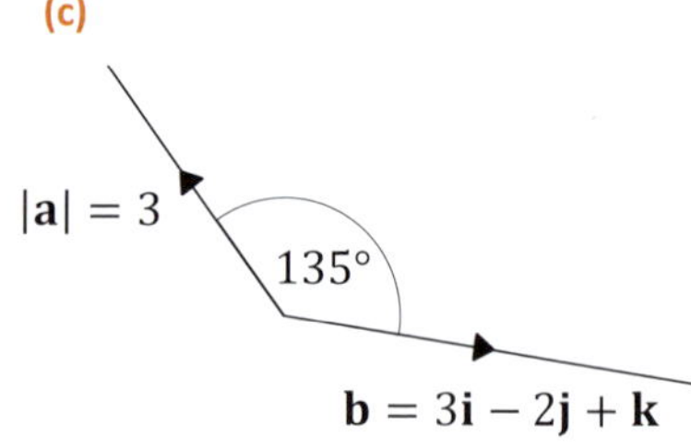

(d)

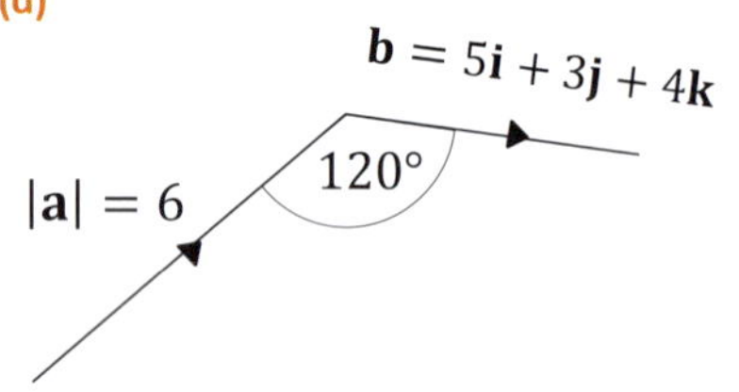

(e)

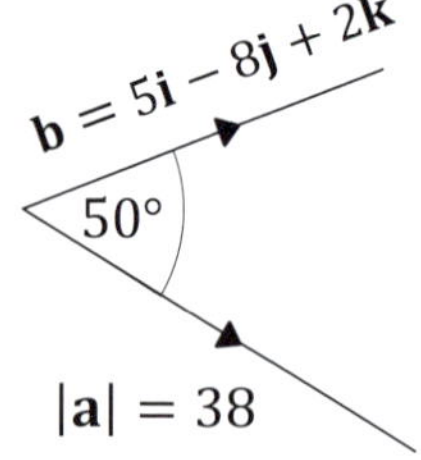

(f)

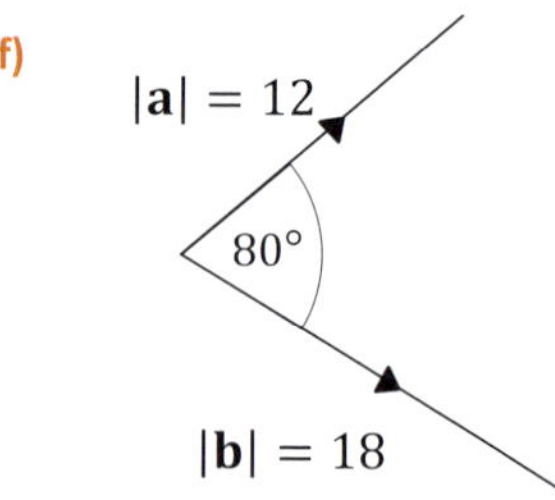

14.10 Finding the Angle Between Two Vectors

To calculate the angle between two vectors, the two vectors must either **both** point **away** from the vertex or **both** point **towads** the vertex.

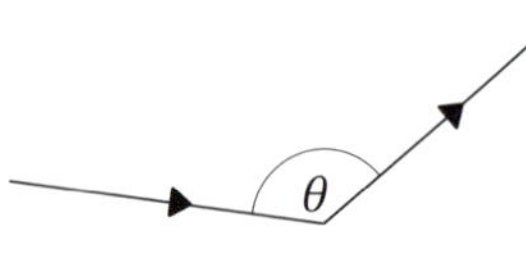

Incorrect - vectors end to end

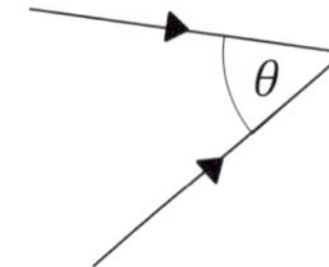

Correct - vectors point towards vertex

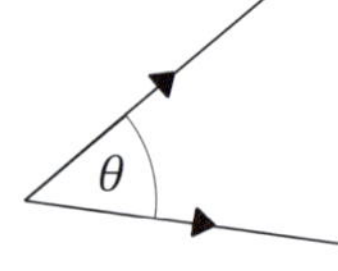

Correct - vectors point away from vertex

To calculate the angle between two vectors, we can rearrange the formula for the scalar product:

$$\cos\theta = \frac{\mathbf{a} \, . \, \mathbf{b}}{|\mathbf{a}||\mathbf{b}|}$$

Worked Examples:

1. Two vectors are given by $\mathbf{v} = 3\mathbf{i} - 4\mathbf{j} + 5\mathbf{k}$ and $\mathbf{w} = 6\mathbf{i} + 3\mathbf{j} - 3\mathbf{k}$. Calculate the angle between the two vectors.

Solution:

Step 1: Calculate the scalar product.

$\mathbf{v} \, . \, \mathbf{w} = x_v x_w + y_v y_w + z_v z_w = 3 \times 6 + (-4) \times 3 + 5 \times (-3) = 18 - 12 - 15 = -9$

Step 2: Calculate the magnitude of each vector (leave in root form).

$|\mathbf{v}| = \sqrt{x^2 + y^2 + z^2}$ $\quad |\mathbf{w}| = \sqrt{x^2 + y^2 + z^2}$

$|\mathbf{v}| = \sqrt{3^2 + (-4)^2 + 5^2}$ $\quad |\mathbf{w}| = \sqrt{6^2 + 3^2 + (-3)^2}$

$|\mathbf{v}| = \sqrt{50} = 5\sqrt{2}$ $\quad |\mathbf{w}| = \sqrt{54} = 3\sqrt{6}$

Step 3: Substitute into the formula

$$\cos\theta = \frac{\mathbf{v}\,.\,\mathbf{w}}{|\mathbf{v}||\mathbf{w}|} = \frac{-9}{5\sqrt{2} \times 3\sqrt{6}}$$

$$\theta = \cos^{-1}\left(\frac{-9}{5\sqrt{2} \times 3\sqrt{6}}\right)$$

$\theta = 100.0°$ (1 d.p.)

2. Points P, Q and R are $(3, 0, 7)$, $(5, 1, -10)$ and $(3, 5, 4)$ respectively. Calculate angle PQR.

Solution:

Step 1: Express $\overrightarrow{QP}$ and $\overrightarrow{QR}$ in component form.

$\overrightarrow{QP} = \mathbf{p} - \mathbf{q}$

$$\overrightarrow{QP} = \begin{pmatrix} 3 \\ 0 \\ 7 \end{pmatrix} - \begin{pmatrix} 5 \\ 1 \\ -10 \end{pmatrix} = \begin{pmatrix} -2 \\ -1 \\ 17 \end{pmatrix}$$

$\overrightarrow{QR} = \mathbf{r} - \mathbf{q}$

$$\overrightarrow{QR} = \begin{pmatrix} 3 \\ 5 \\ 4 \end{pmatrix} - \begin{pmatrix} 5 \\ 1 \\ -10 \end{pmatrix} = \begin{pmatrix} -2 \\ 4 \\ 14 \end{pmatrix}$$

Step 2: Calculate the scalar product.

$$\overrightarrow{QP}\,.\,\overrightarrow{QR} = x_Q x_R + y_Q y_R + z_Q z_R = (-2) \times (-2) + (-1) \times 4 + 17 \times 14 = 4 - 4 + 238 = 238$$

Step 3: Calculate the magnitude of each vector (leave in root form).

$$|\overrightarrow{QP}| = \sqrt{x^2 + y^2 + z^2}$$

$$|\overrightarrow{QP}| = \sqrt{(-2)^2 + (-1)^2 + 17^2}$$

$$|\overrightarrow{QP}| = \sqrt{294}$$

$$|\overrightarrow{QP}| = \sqrt{x^2 + y^2 + z^2}$$

$$|\overrightarrow{QP}| = \sqrt{(-2)^2 + 4^2 + 14^2}$$

$$|\overrightarrow{QP}| = \sqrt{216}$$

Step 4: Substitute into the formula

$$\cos\theta = \frac{\overrightarrow{QP}\,.\,\overrightarrow{QR}}{|\overrightarrow{QP}||\overrightarrow{QR}|} = \frac{238}{7\sqrt{6} \times 6\sqrt{6}}$$

$$\theta = \cos^{-1}\left(\frac{238}{7\sqrt{6} \times 6\sqrt{6}}\right)$$

$\theta = 19.2°$ (1 d.p.)

Exercise 14.10

1. Calculate the angle between each pair of vectors:

(a) $\mathbf{a} = 3\mathbf{i} + \mathbf{j} + \mathbf{k}$ and $\mathbf{b} = 2\mathbf{i} + \mathbf{j} - 2\mathbf{k}$.

(b) $\mathbf{c} = -2\mathbf{i} + \mathbf{j} - \mathbf{k}$ and $\mathbf{d} = \mathbf{j} - \mathbf{k}$.

(c) $\mathbf{e} = 9\mathbf{i} - 4\mathbf{j} + 2\mathbf{k}$ and $\mathbf{f} = 7\mathbf{i} + 8\mathbf{j} - 2\mathbf{k}$.

(d) $\mathbf{g} = 9\mathbf{i} + 14\mathbf{k}$ and $\mathbf{h} = 7\mathbf{i} + 8\mathbf{j} + 5\mathbf{k}$.

(e) $\mathbf{m} = 6\mathbf{i} - 2\mathbf{j} + 7\mathbf{k}$ and $\mathbf{n} = 2\mathbf{i} - 5\mathbf{j} + 13\mathbf{k}$.

(f) $\mathbf{p} = 2\mathbf{i} + 4\mathbf{j} - 5\mathbf{k}$ and $\mathbf{q} = 4\mathbf{i} + 4\mathbf{j} - 8\mathbf{k}$.

2. Calculate the angle between each pair of vectors:

(a) $\mathbf{a} = 2\mathbf{i} + \mathbf{j} + \mathbf{k}$ and $\mathbf{b} = -1\mathbf{i} + 2\mathbf{j} - 2\mathbf{k}$.

(b) $\mathbf{c} = 2\mathbf{i} - 2\mathbf{j} + \mathbf{k}$ and $\mathbf{d} = -2\mathbf{i} - \mathbf{j} - 4\mathbf{k}$.

(c) $\mathbf{e} = 3\mathbf{i} - 2\mathbf{j} + 2\mathbf{k}$ and $\mathbf{f} = -\mathbf{i} - \mathbf{j} - 3\mathbf{k}$.

(d) $\mathbf{g} = \mathbf{i} - 6\mathbf{j} + 2\mathbf{k}$ and $\mathbf{h} = \mathbf{i} + 3\mathbf{j} + 2\mathbf{k}$.

(e) $\mathbf{m} = -\mathbf{i} - 5\mathbf{j}$ and $\mathbf{n} = -\mathbf{i} + 4\mathbf{j} + 2\mathbf{k}$.

(f) $\mathbf{p} = -\mathbf{i} + 4\mathbf{j} + 3\mathbf{k}$ and $\mathbf{q} = -\mathbf{i} - 5\mathbf{j} - 3\mathbf{k}$.

3. Given the points A, B and C, calculate the size of angle ABC:

(a) $A(2, 0, 5)$, $B(0, 0, 0)$ and $C(6, 9, 1)$.

(b) $A(4, 3, 6)$, $B(1, 0, 1)$ and $C(7, 2, 5)$.

(c) $A(7, -2, 2)$, $B(0, 0, 0)$ and $C(7, 7, 12)$.

(d) $A(15, -4, 5)$, $B(0, 1, 0)$ and $C(11, -2, 8)$.

4. Given the points P, Q and R, calculate the size of angle PQR:

(a) $P(11, 5, -16)$, $Q(21, -2, 4)$ and $R(-5, 6, 3)$.

(b) $P(-1, 14, -7)$, $Q(3, 8, 3)$ and $R(13, 9, -8)$.

(c) $P(15, 7, 10)$, $Q(12, 3, 4)$ and $R(14, 0, 5)$.

(d) $P(13, 2, 0)$, $Q(2, 7, -3)$ and $R(5, 13, -4)$.

5. Given the points S, T and U, calculate the size of angle STU:

(a) $S(6,12, -2)$, $T(1, -4, 3)$ and $U(2, 6, 9)$.

(b) $S(14, -10, -6)$, $T(9, -8, -4)$ and $U(3, 5, 0)$.

(c) $S(9, 17, 8)$, $T(10, -13, 5)$ and $U(6, -5, 3)$.

(d) $S(18, 59, 34)$, $T(22, 35, -12)$ and $U(-17, -22, 8)$.

14.11 Properties of the Scalar Product

The **scalar product** has several properties that we need to know for Higher Mathematics:

$\mathbf{a}\,.\,\mathbf{b} = \mathbf{b}\,.\,\mathbf{a}$ — The commutative law applies to vectors.

$\mathbf{a}\,.\,(\mathbf{b} + \mathbf{c}) = \mathbf{a}\,.\,\mathbf{b} + \mathbf{a}\,.\,\mathbf{c}$ — The distributive law also applies to vectors.

$\mathbf{a}\,.\,\mathbf{a} = |\mathbf{a}|^2$ — Equal vectors (since $\cos\theta = 1$ then $\mathbf{a}\,.\,\mathbf{a} = |\mathbf{a}||\mathbf{a}|\cos\theta = |\mathbf{a}|^2$).

$\mathbf{a}\,.\,\mathbf{b} = 0$ — Perpendicular vectors.

NB: It is helpful to memorise these properties.

Worked Examples:

1. For the vectors in the diagram opposite $|\mathbf{a}| = 5$, $|\mathbf{b}| = 4$ and $|\mathbf{c}| = 3$. Evaluate $\mathbf{a}\,.\,(\mathbf{b} + \mathbf{c})$.

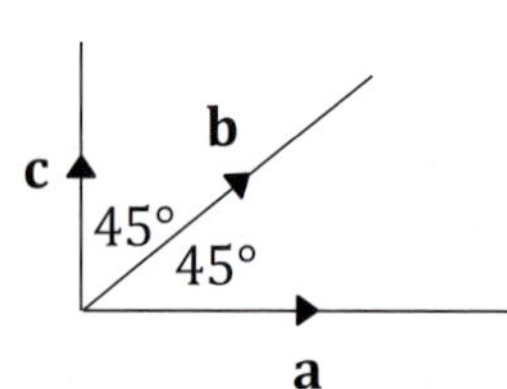

Solution:

$$\mathbf{a}\,.\,(\mathbf{b} + \mathbf{c}) = \mathbf{a}\,.\,\mathbf{b} + \mathbf{a}\,.\,\mathbf{c} = |\mathbf{a}||\mathbf{b}|\cos\theta_b + 0 = 5 \times 4 \times \tfrac{1}{\sqrt{2}} = \tfrac{20}{\sqrt{2}} = 10\sqrt{2}$$

2. For the vectors $\mathbf{e} = 2\mathbf{i} - 6\mathbf{j} + 3\mathbf{k}$ and $\mathbf{f} = -\mathbf{i} - \mathbf{j} - 3\mathbf{k}$, evaluate $\mathbf{e} \cdot (\mathbf{e} + \mathbf{f})$.

Solution:

$$\mathbf{e} \cdot (\mathbf{e} + \mathbf{f}) = \mathbf{e} \cdot \mathbf{e} + \mathbf{e} \cdot \mathbf{f} = |\mathbf{e}|^2 + \mathbf{e} \cdot \mathbf{f} = (2^2 + (-6)^2 + 3^2) + (-2 + 6 - 9) = 49 - 5 = 44$$

Exercise 14.11

1. Evaluate $\mathbf{a} \cdot (\mathbf{a} + \mathbf{b})$ for each pair of vectors:

(a)

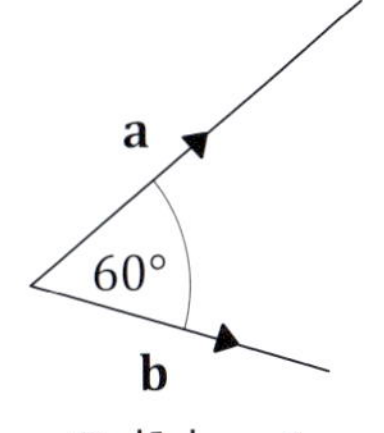

$|\mathbf{a}| = 7$, $|\mathbf{b}| = 4$

(b)

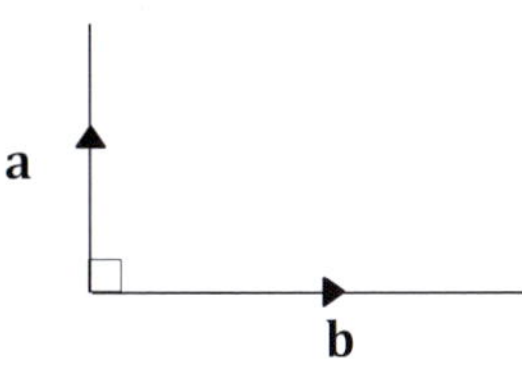

$|\mathbf{a}| = 5$, $|\mathbf{b}| = 8$

(c)

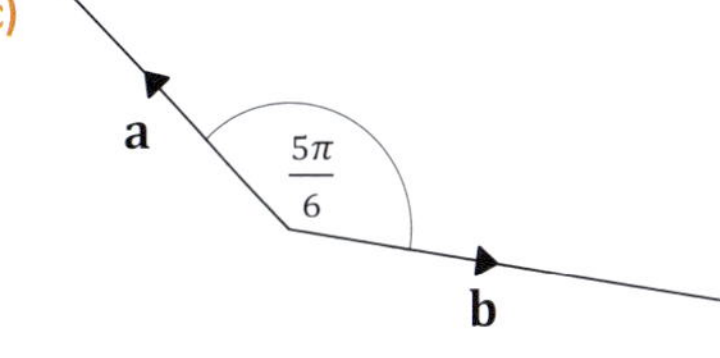

$|\mathbf{a}| = 8$, $|\mathbf{b}| = 7\sqrt{3}$

(d)

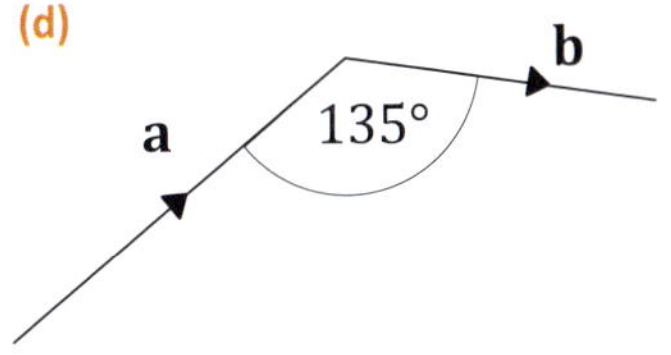

$|\mathbf{a}| = 9\sqrt{2}$, $|\mathbf{b}| = 12$

(e)

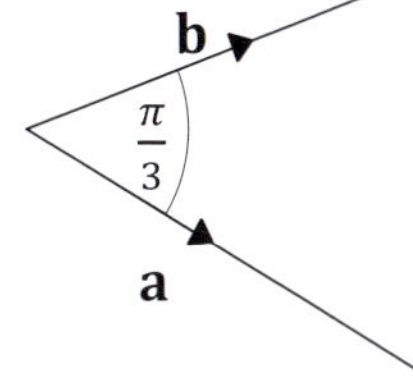

$|\mathbf{a}| = 15$, $|\mathbf{b}| = 12$

(f)

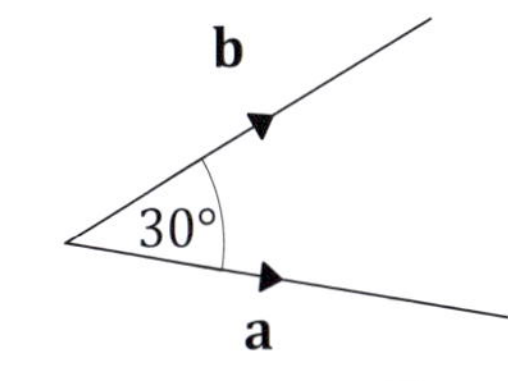

$|\mathbf{a}| = |\mathbf{b}|$, $|\mathbf{b}| = 4\sqrt{3}$

2. Evaluate:

(a)

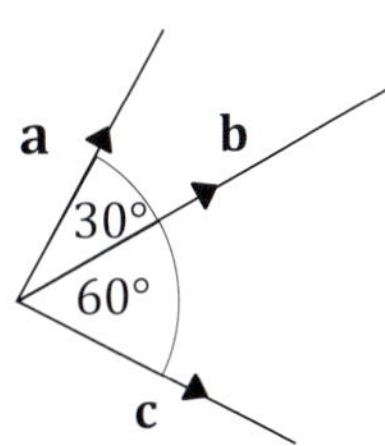

$|\mathbf{a}| = 2\sqrt{3}$, $|\mathbf{b}| = 5$, $|\mathbf{c}| = 4$

(i) $\mathbf{a} \cdot (\mathbf{b} + \mathbf{c})$

(ii) $\mathbf{a} \cdot (\mathbf{a} + \mathbf{b} + \mathbf{c})$

(ii) $(\mathbf{a} + \mathbf{b}) \cdot (\mathbf{a} + \mathbf{b})$

(b)

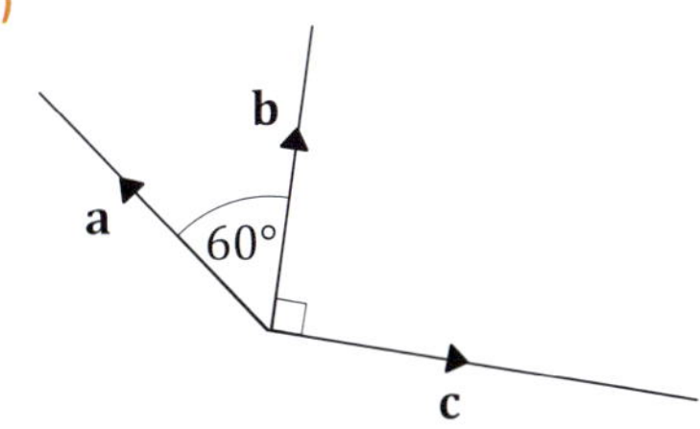

$|\mathbf{a}| = 2\sqrt{3}$, $|\mathbf{b}| = 5$, $|\mathbf{c}| = 4$

(i) $\mathbf{a} \cdot (\mathbf{b} + \mathbf{c})$

(ii) $\mathbf{b} \cdot (\mathbf{b} + \mathbf{a} + \mathbf{c})$

(ii) $\mathbf{c} \cdot (\mathbf{b} + \mathbf{c})$

(c)

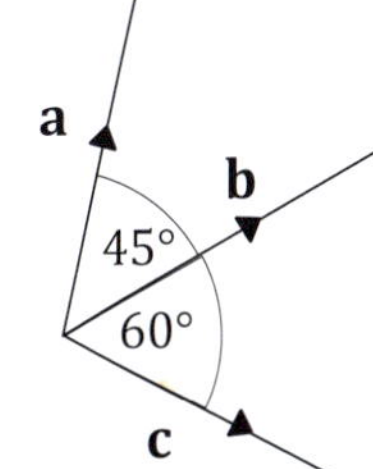

$|\mathbf{a}| = 3\sqrt{2}$, $|\mathbf{b}| = 4$, $|\mathbf{c}| = 2\sqrt{3}$

(i) $\mathbf{b} \cdot (\mathbf{a} + \mathbf{c})$

(ii) $\mathbf{b} \cdot (\mathbf{b} + 2\mathbf{a} + \mathbf{c})$

(ii) $(\mathbf{c} + \mathbf{b}) \cdot (\mathbf{b} + \mathbf{c})$

14.12 Vector Pathways

National 5 Skills

A **vector pathway** is a description of the pathway from the beginning to the end of the vector. Vector pathways can be described either in terms of their components or by combinations of known vectors.

In the diagram, the pathway from S to U, which we call vector $\overrightarrow{SU}$ may be described in three ways:

$$\overrightarrow{SU} = \overrightarrow{ST} + \overrightarrow{TU} = \mathbf{a} + \mathbf{b}$$

Each of these vectors above represent the same journey, each starts at S and ends at U.

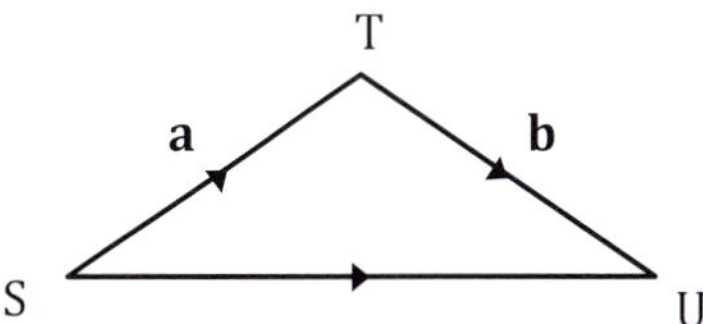

Worked Example:

NB: A vector pathway can only be described by combinations of known vectors.

In the diagram shown, $\overrightarrow{SV}$ and $\overrightarrow{VU}$ are represented by vectors $\mathbf{a}$ and $\mathbf{b}$ respectively.
Express the following vectors in terms of $\mathbf{a}$ and $\mathbf{b}$:

(a) $\overrightarrow{SU}$ (b) $\overrightarrow{UT}$ (c) $\overrightarrow{VT}$

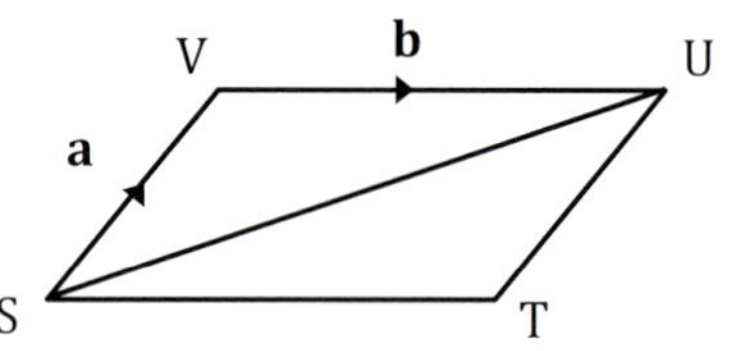

Solution:

(a) $\overrightarrow{SU} = \overrightarrow{SV} + \overrightarrow{VU} = \mathbf{a} + \mathbf{b}$
(b) $\overrightarrow{UT} = -\overrightarrow{SV} = -\mathbf{a}$
(c) $\overrightarrow{VT} = \overrightarrow{VU} + \overrightarrow{UT} = \overrightarrow{VU} - \overrightarrow{SV} = \mathbf{b} - \mathbf{a}$

Exercise 14.12A

1. In the diagram, CDEFGH is a regular hexagon.

   Express the following vectors in terms of $\mathbf{a}$ and $\mathbf{b}$:

   (a) $\overrightarrow{FE}$ (b) $\overrightarrow{GC}$ (c) $\overrightarrow{DG}$ (d) $\overrightarrow{FC}$

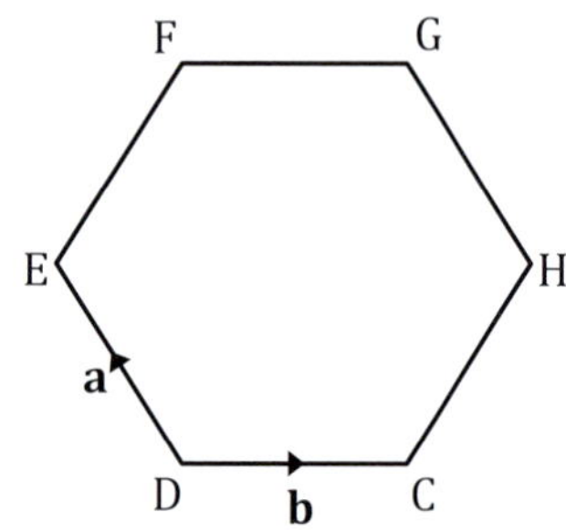

2. In the diagram, PQRSTU is a regular hexagon.

   Express the following vectors in terms of $\mathbf{a}$ and $\mathbf{b}$:

   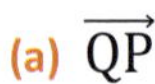
   (a) $\overrightarrow{QP}$ (b) $\overrightarrow{RU}$ (c) $\overrightarrow{PT}$ (d) $\overrightarrow{RS}$

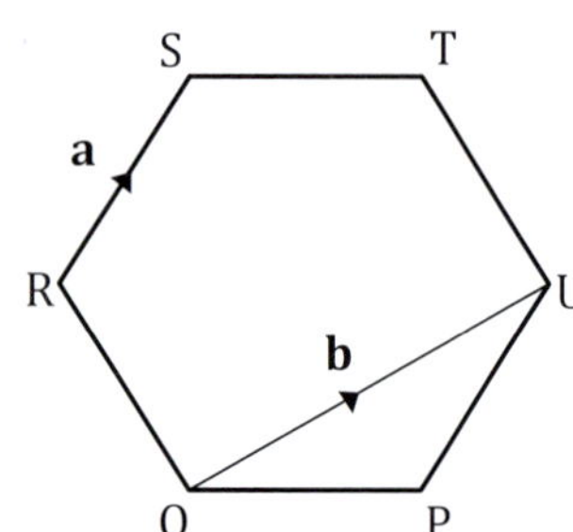

3. In the diagram, OABCDE is a regular hexagon with centre M.

   Vectors $\mathbf{a}$ and $\mathbf{b}$ are represented by $\overrightarrow{OA}$ and $\overrightarrow{OB}$ respectively.

   Express the following vectors in terms of $\mathbf{a}$ and $\mathbf{b}$:

   (a) $\overrightarrow{CD}$ (b) $\overrightarrow{BC}$ (c) $\overrightarrow{OM}$ (d) $\overrightarrow{DO}$

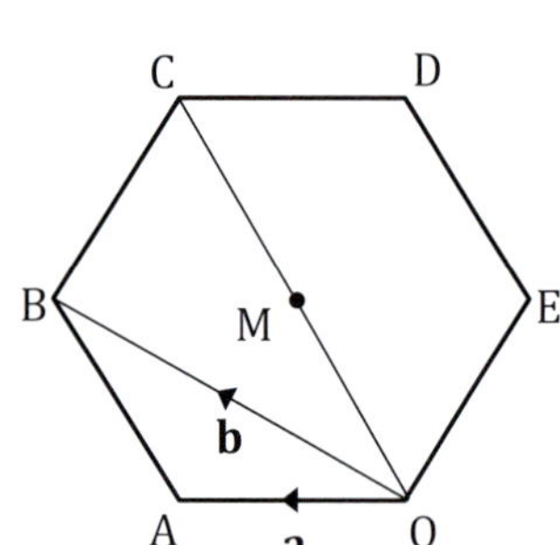

4. In the diagram, ABCD is a rectangle. E divides AC in the ratio 2:1.
   Express the following vectors in terms of $\mathbf{a}$ and $\mathbf{b}$:

   (a) $\overrightarrow{AD}$ (b) $\overrightarrow{AE}$ (c) $\overrightarrow{EC}$ (d) $\overrightarrow{BE}$

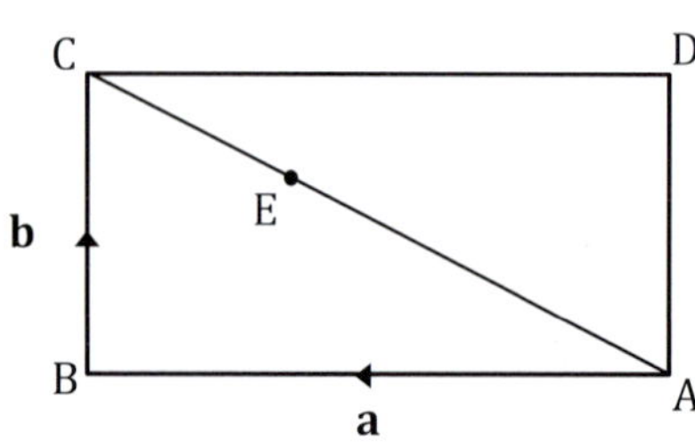

5. In the diagram, ABCD is a parallelogram. E divides AC in the ratio 1:3. Express the following vectors in terms of **a** and **b**:

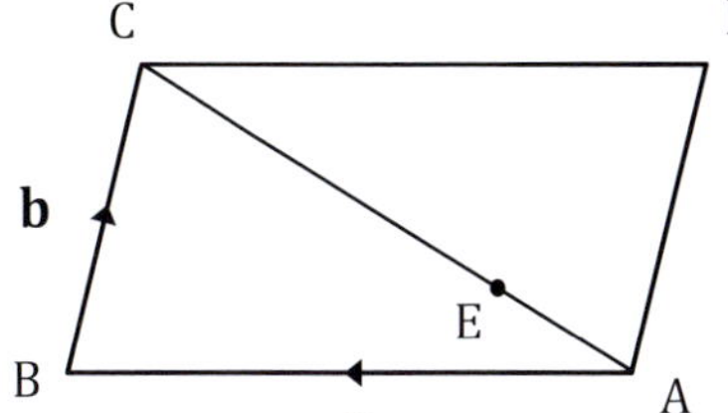

(a) $\overrightarrow{AC}$ (b) $\overrightarrow{AE}$ (c) $\overrightarrow{DE}$ (d) $\overrightarrow{EB}$

6. In the diagram, $\overrightarrow{BC} = 2\overrightarrow{AE}$ and $\overrightarrow{AB} = 2\overrightarrow{CD}$. F divides BD in the ratio 2:3. Express the following vectors in terms of **a** and **b**:

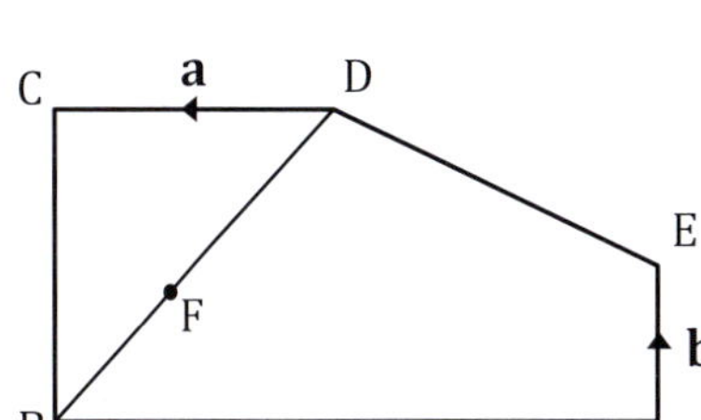

(a) $\overrightarrow{DB}$ (b) $\overrightarrow{FA}$ (c) $\overrightarrow{DE}$ (d) $\overrightarrow{EF}$

Higher Skills

In Higher Mathematics, we also need to use **vector pathways** in **three dimensions**. As with two dimensional pathways, this is a description of the pathway from the beginning to the end of the vector. These vector pathways can also be described either in terms of their components or by combinations of known vectors.

Worked Example:

In the diagram, ABCDEFGH is a cuboid. J divides BH in the ratio 1:2.
Express the following vectors in terms of **p**, **q** and **r**:

(a) $\overrightarrow{AG}$ **(b)** $\overrightarrow{HB}$ **(c)** $\overrightarrow{JH}$

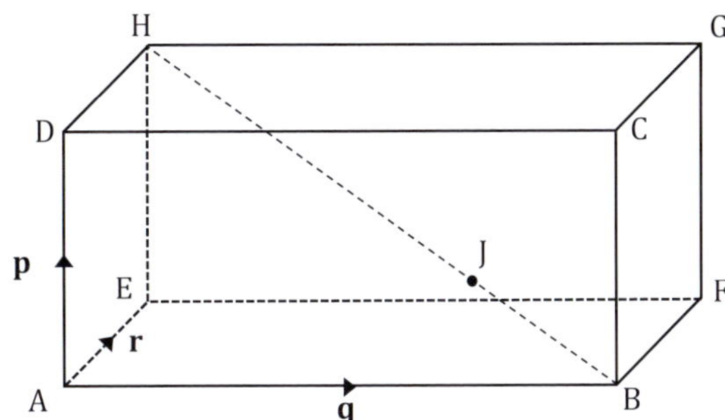

NB: $\overrightarrow{AE} = \overrightarrow{DH} = \overrightarrow{CG} = \overrightarrow{BF} = \mathbf{r}$
$\overrightarrow{AD} = \overrightarrow{EH} = \overrightarrow{BC} = \overrightarrow{FG} = \mathbf{p}$
$\overrightarrow{AB} = \overrightarrow{EF} = \overrightarrow{DC} = \overrightarrow{HG} = \mathbf{q}$

Solution:

(a) $\overrightarrow{AG} = \overrightarrow{AB} + \overrightarrow{AE} + \overrightarrow{AD} = \mathbf{q} + \mathbf{r} + \mathbf{p}$

(b) $\overrightarrow{HB} = -\overrightarrow{AE} - \overrightarrow{AD} + \overrightarrow{AB} = -\mathbf{r} - \mathbf{p} + \mathbf{q}$

(c) $\overrightarrow{JH} = \frac{2}{3}\overrightarrow{BH} = -\frac{2}{3}\overrightarrow{HB} = \frac{2}{3}\mathbf{r} + \frac{2}{3}\mathbf{p} - \frac{2}{3}\mathbf{q}$

Exercise 14.12B

1. In the diagram, ABCDEFGH is a cuboid. J divides BH in the ratio 1:3. Express the following vectors in terms of **p**, **q** and **r**:

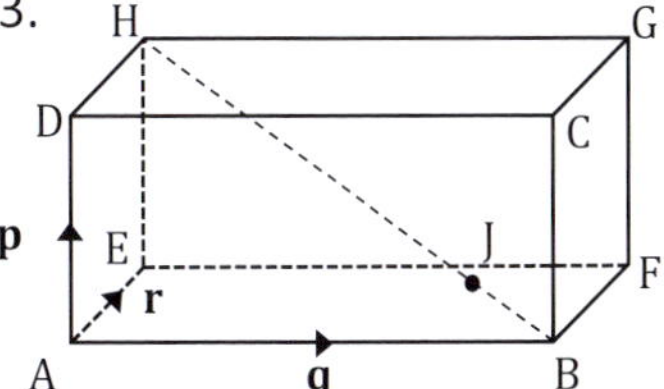

(a) $\overrightarrow{HE}$ (b) $\overrightarrow{FH}$ (c) $\overrightarrow{GJ}$ (d) $\overrightarrow{JE}$

2. In the diagram, ABCDEFGH is a cuboid. J divides BE in the ratio 1:2. Express the following vectors in terms of **p**, **q** and **r**:

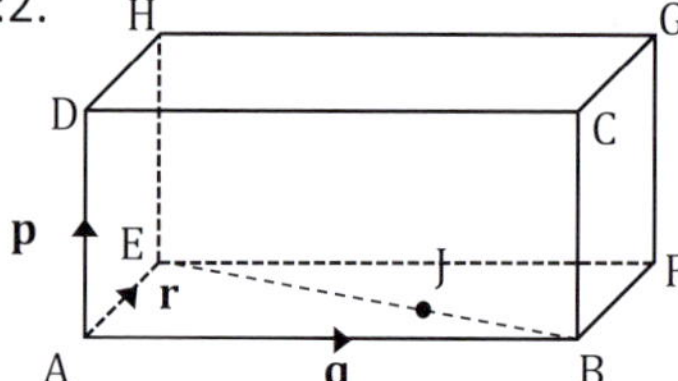

(a) $\overrightarrow{AJ}$ (b) $\overrightarrow{JH}$ (c) $\overrightarrow{GJ}$ (d) $\overrightarrow{EJ}$

3. In the diagram, ABCDEFGH is a cuboid. M is the midpoint of BE. Express the following vectors in terms of **p**, **q** and **r**:

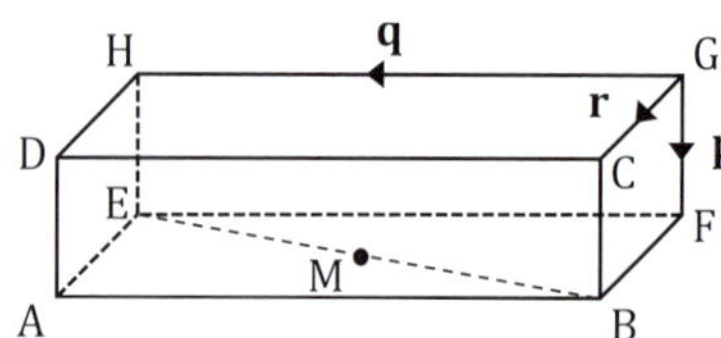

(a) $\overrightarrow{AM}$ (b) $\overrightarrow{MH}$ (c) $\overrightarrow{GM}$ (d) $\overrightarrow{EM}$

4. In the diagram, ABCDEF is a triangular prism. $AF = BF$. M is the midpoint of BE. Express the following vectors in terms of **p**, **q** and **r**:

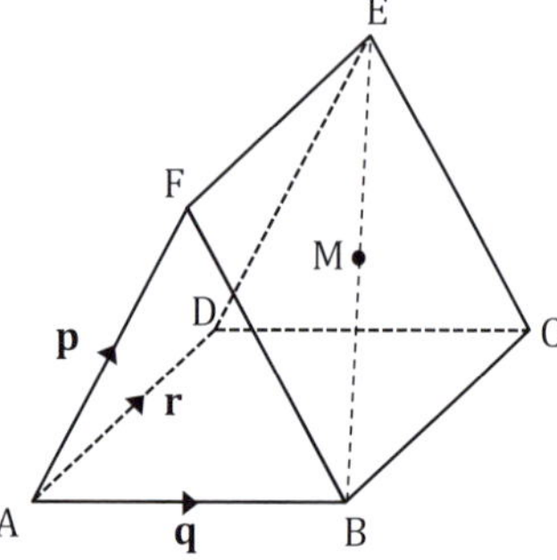

(a) $\overrightarrow{AE}$ (b) $\overrightarrow{DF}$ (c) $\overrightarrow{BE}$ (d) $\overrightarrow{EM}$

5. In the diagram, ABCDEF is a triangular prism. $AF = BF$. J divides FC in the ratio 3: 1. Express the following vectors in terms of **p**, **q** and **r**:

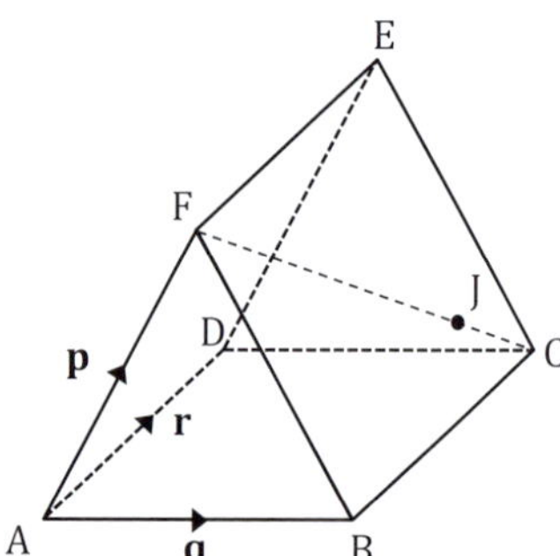

(a) $\overrightarrow{EC}$ (b) $\overrightarrow{FJ}$ (c) $\overrightarrow{CJ}$ (d) $\overrightarrow{JA}$

6. In the diagram, ABCDE is a square based pyramid. F divides EC in the ratio 2: 1. Express the following vectors in terms of **p**, **q** and **r**:

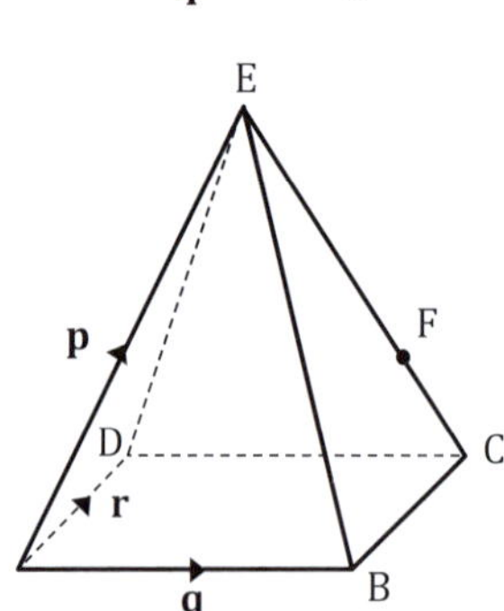

(a) $\overrightarrow{EB}$ (b) $\overrightarrow{FA}$ (c) $\overrightarrow{EF}$ (d) $\overrightarrow{FB}$

7. In the diagram, ABCDE is a square based pyramid. G is the midpoint of the pyramid. F divides EG in the ratio 2: 1. Express the following vectors in terms of **p**, **q** and **r**:

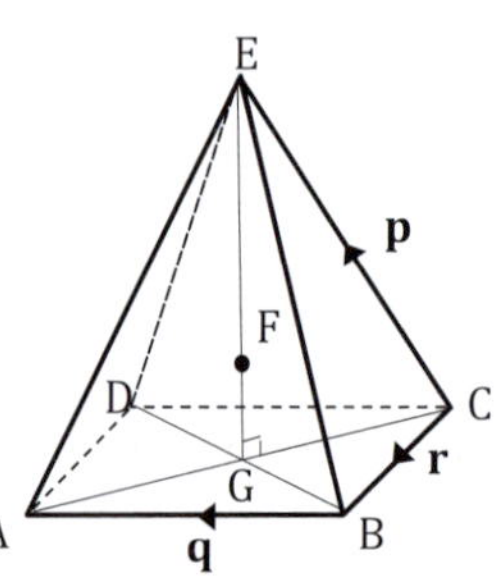

(a) $\overrightarrow{GC}$ (b) $\overrightarrow{FD}$ (c) $\overrightarrow{EG}$ (d) $\overrightarrow{FE}$

Vector pathways are also used when calculating components of vectors, angles between vectors and the scalar product.

Worked Example:

In triangle ABC, $\overrightarrow{AB} = -\mathbf{i} + \mathbf{j} + 2\mathbf{k}$ and $\overrightarrow{BC} = -\mathbf{i} + 3\mathbf{j}$. M is the midpoint of AC.

(a) Express $\overrightarrow{AM}$ in terms of $\mathbf{i}$, $\mathbf{j}$ and $\mathbf{k}$.

(b) Calculate angle BAM.

Solution:

(a) $\overrightarrow{AM} = \frac{1}{2}\left(\overrightarrow{AB} + \overrightarrow{BC}\right) = \frac{1}{2}\left(\begin{pmatrix} -1 \\ 1 \\ 2 \end{pmatrix} + \begin{pmatrix} -1 \\ 3 \\ 0 \end{pmatrix}\right) = \frac{1}{2}\begin{pmatrix} -2 \\ 4 \\ 2 \end{pmatrix} = \begin{pmatrix} -1 \\ 2 \\ 1 \end{pmatrix}$

(b) **Step 1:** Calculate the scalar product.

$\overrightarrow{AM}.\overrightarrow{AB} = \overrightarrow{AM}_1\overrightarrow{AB}_1 + \overrightarrow{AM}_2\overrightarrow{AB}_2 + \overrightarrow{AM}_3\overrightarrow{AB}_3 = (-1) \times (-1) + 2 \times 1 + 1 \times 2 = 1 + 2 + 2 = 5$

Step 2: Calculate the magnitude of each vector (leave in root form).

$|\overrightarrow{AM}| = \sqrt{x^2 + y^2 + z^2}$ $\quad |\overrightarrow{AB}| = \sqrt{x^2 + y^2 + z^2}$

$|\overrightarrow{AM}| = \sqrt{(-1)^2 + 2^2 + 1^2}$ $\quad |\overrightarrow{AB}| = \sqrt{(-1)^2 + 1^2 + 2^2}$

$|\overrightarrow{AM}| = \sqrt{6}$ $\quad |\overrightarrow{AB}| = \sqrt{6}$

Step 3: Substitute into formula

$\cos\theta = \dfrac{\overrightarrow{AM}.\overrightarrow{AB}}{|\overrightarrow{AM}||\overrightarrow{AB}|} = \dfrac{5}{\sqrt{6} \times \sqrt{6}}$

NB: If introducing θ, ensure that the diagram is labelled with θ.

$\theta = \cos^{-1}\left(\frac{5}{6}\right)$

$\theta = 33.6°$ (1 d.p.)

Exercise 14.12C

1. In triangle ABC, $\overrightarrow{AB} = -3\mathbf{i} + 5\mathbf{j} + 3\mathbf{k}$ and $\overrightarrow{BC} = -\mathbf{i} + 3\mathbf{j} - 4\mathbf{k}$.

   (a) Express $\overrightarrow{AC}$ in terms of $\mathbf{i}$, $\mathbf{j}$ and $\mathbf{k}$.

   (b) Calculate angle BAC.

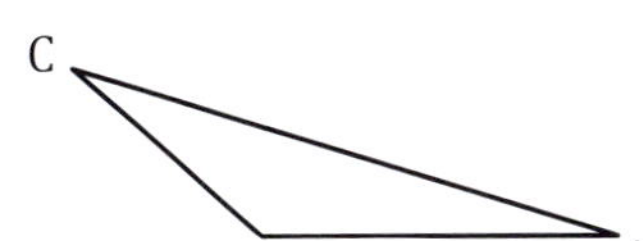

2. The square-based pyramid OABCD is shown. E divides BD in the ratio 1: 2. $\overrightarrow{OD} = 3\mathbf{i} + 3\mathbf{j} + 9\mathbf{k}$.

   (a) Express $\overrightarrow{BA}$ in terms of $\mathbf{i}$, $\mathbf{j}$ and $\mathbf{k}$.

   (b) Express $\overrightarrow{BE}$ in terms of $\mathbf{i}$, $\mathbf{j}$ and $\mathbf{k}$.

   (c) Calculate angle ABE.

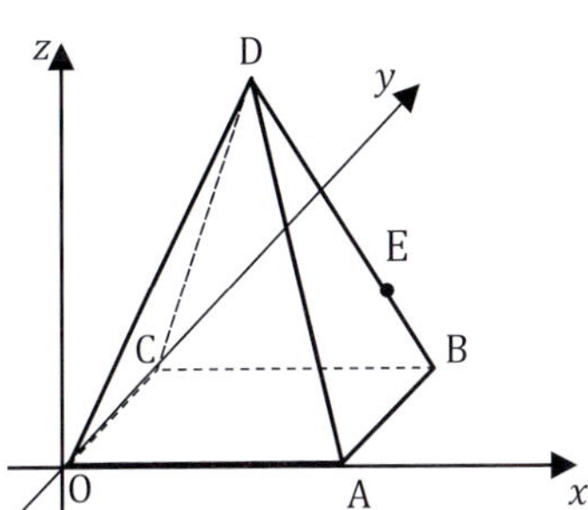

3. In triangle ABC, $\overrightarrow{AB} = 4\mathbf{i} + 8\mathbf{j} + 4\mathbf{k}$ and $\overrightarrow{BC} = -2\mathbf{i} - 2\mathbf{j} - 2\mathbf{k}$. M is the midpoint of AC.

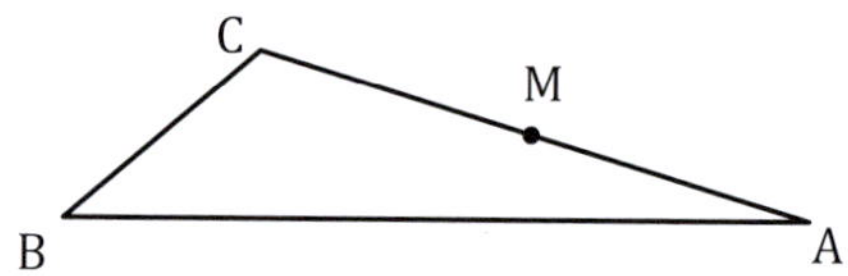

(a) Express $\overrightarrow{AM}$ in terms of $\mathbf{i}$, $\mathbf{j}$ and $\mathbf{k}$.

(b) Calculate angle BAM.

4. The square-based pyramid OABCD is shown. M is the midpoint of AD. $\overrightarrow{OM} = 6\mathbf{i} + 6\mathbf{j} + 4\mathbf{k}$.

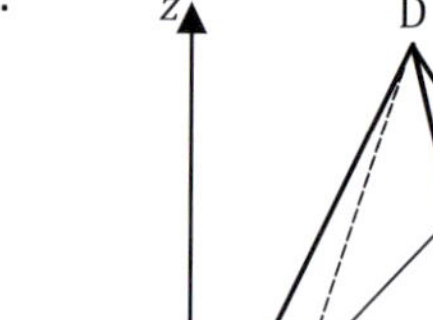
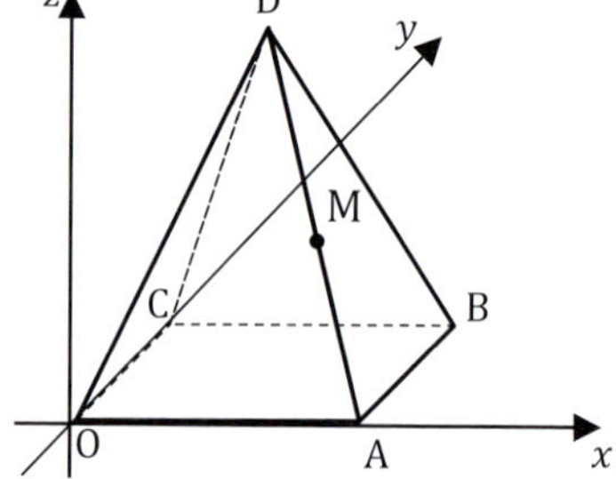

(a) Express $\overrightarrow{AB}$ in terms of $\mathbf{i}$, $\mathbf{j}$ and $\mathbf{k}$.

(b) Express $\overrightarrow{AM}$ in terms of $\mathbf{i}$, $\mathbf{j}$ and $\mathbf{k}$.

(c) Calculate angle MAB.

5. The square-based pyramid OABCD is shown. M is the midpoint of AB and E divides BD in the ratio $1:3$. The coordinates of D are $(14, 14, 36)$.

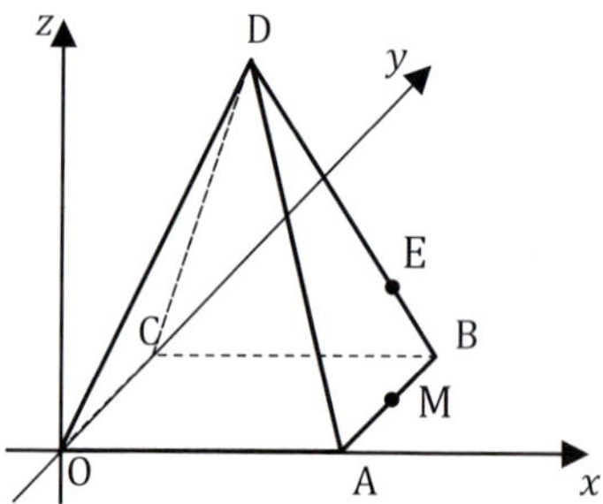

(a) State the coordinates of E and M.

(b) Calculate $\overrightarrow{ED}.\overrightarrow{EM}$.

(c) Calculate angle DEM.

6. In the diagram $\overrightarrow{CA} = -6\mathbf{i} - 7\mathbf{j} + 2\mathbf{k}$ and $\overrightarrow{AB} = 8\mathbf{i} + 12\mathbf{j}$.

(a) Express $\overrightarrow{CB}$ in terms of $\mathbf{i}$, $\mathbf{j}$ and $\mathbf{k}$.

D divides AB in the ratio $1:3$.

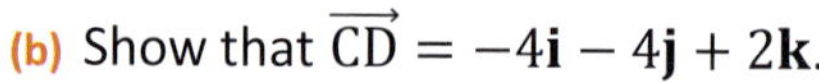

(b) Show that $\overrightarrow{CD} = -4\mathbf{i} - 4\mathbf{j} + 2\mathbf{k}$.

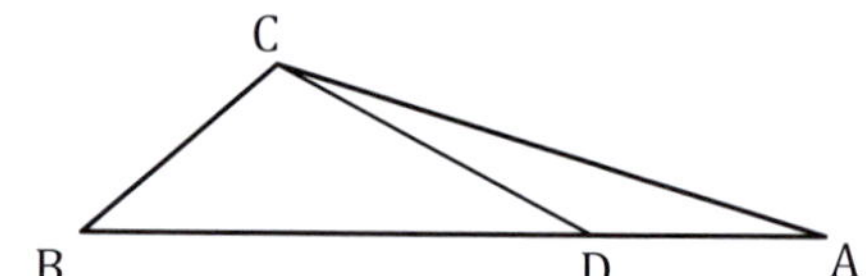

(c) Hence, calculate angle BCD.

7. The diagram shows an isosceles trapezium and an equilateral triangle. Vectors $\mathbf{p}$, $\mathbf{q}$ and $\mathbf{r}$ are shown in the diagram. $|\mathbf{p}| = 4$ and Angle ABC $= 90°$.

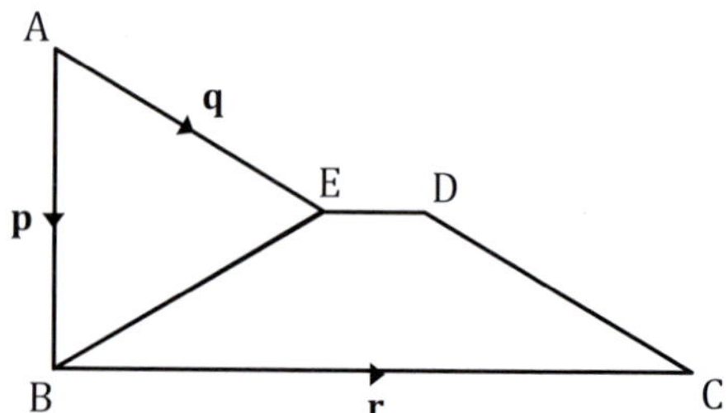

(a) Evaluate $\mathbf{p}\,.\,(\mathbf{p} + \mathbf{q} + \mathbf{r})$.

(b) Express $\overrightarrow{ED}$ in terms of $\mathbf{p}$, $\mathbf{q}$ and $\mathbf{r}$.

14.13 Review

Exercise 14.13

14.4 Calculate the unit vector $\mathbf{u}$ to the following vectors:

(a) $\mathbf{b} = \begin{pmatrix} 4 \\ -3 \\ 0 \end{pmatrix}$ (b) $\mathbf{b} = \begin{pmatrix} 6 \\ -7 \\ -6 \end{pmatrix}$ (c) $\mathbf{b} = \begin{pmatrix} 4 \\ -5 \\ -8 \end{pmatrix}$

14.5 (a) Vectors $\mathbf{c}$ and $\mathbf{d}$ are such that $\mathbf{c} = 5\mathbf{i} - 2\mathbf{k}$ and $\mathbf{d} = 3\mathbf{i} + 4\mathbf{j} - \mathbf{k}$. Find $|\mathbf{c} - \mathbf{d}|$.

(b) Vectors $\mathbf{e}$ and $\mathbf{f}$ are such that $\mathbf{e} = 3\mathbf{i} - 2\mathbf{j} - 3\mathbf{k}$ and $\mathbf{f} = 4\mathbf{i} + a\mathbf{j} + \mathbf{k}$ and $|\mathbf{e} + \mathbf{f}| = 9$. Find the value of a.

14.6 (a) Determine whether the points $\mathrm{A}(3, -5, -9)$, $\mathrm{B}(1, -2, 7)$ and $\mathrm{C}(-5, 7, 1)$ are collinear.

(b) Determine whether the points $\mathrm{D}(3, -2, 11)$, $\mathrm{E}(7, -8, 17)$ and $\mathrm{F}(13, -16, 26)$ are collinear.

(c) The points $\mathrm{G}(-3, 5, -2)$, $\mathrm{H}(3, -4, 7)$ and $\mathrm{J}(11, -16, k)$ are collinear. Determine the value of k.

14.7 (a) Point P divides the points $\mathrm{A}(7, -2, -11)$ and $\mathrm{B}(-8, 18, -1)$ in the ratio $3:2$. Find the coordinates of P.

(b) Point P divides AB in the ratio $4:1$. The coordinates of points A and P are $(-13, 8, -2)$ and $(-5, -4, 18)$ respectively. Find the coordinates of B.

14.8 (a) Points $\mathrm{A}(22, -11, 4)$, $\mathrm{B}(16, 4, 13)$ and $\mathrm{C}(8, 24, 25)$ are collinear. Find the ratio in which B divides AC.

(b) Points $\mathrm{D}(35, 13, 8)$, $\mathrm{E}(23, 4, 17)$ and $\mathrm{F}(k, -2, 23)$ are collinear. Determine the value of k.

14.9 (a) Calculate the scalar product of:

(i) $\mathbf{a} = 3\mathbf{i} - 2\mathbf{j} + \mathbf{k}$ and $\mathbf{b} = \mathbf{i} - 2\mathbf{j} + 3\mathbf{k}$. (ii) $\mathbf{c} = \begin{pmatrix} -6 \\ 3 \\ -11 \end{pmatrix}$ and $\mathbf{d} = \begin{pmatrix} 4 \\ -2 \\ -1 \end{pmatrix}$.

(b) Calculate $\overrightarrow{\mathrm{BA}} \cdot \overrightarrow{\mathrm{BC}}$ from $\mathrm{A}(4, 1, 2)$, $\mathrm{B}(-2, 3, 2)$ and $\mathrm{C}(3, 5, 4)$.

(c) Show that vectors $\mathbf{t} = 8\mathbf{i} + 2\mathbf{j}$ and $\mathbf{v} = 3\mathbf{i} - 12\mathbf{j} + 6\mathbf{k}$ are perpendicular.

(d) P, Q and R are the coordinates $(4, -1, a)$, $(3, -4, 2)$ and $(2, 11, -20)$ respectively. $\overrightarrow{\mathrm{QP}}$ is perpendicular to $\overrightarrow{\mathrm{QR}}$. Find the value of a.

(e) Calculate the scalar product.

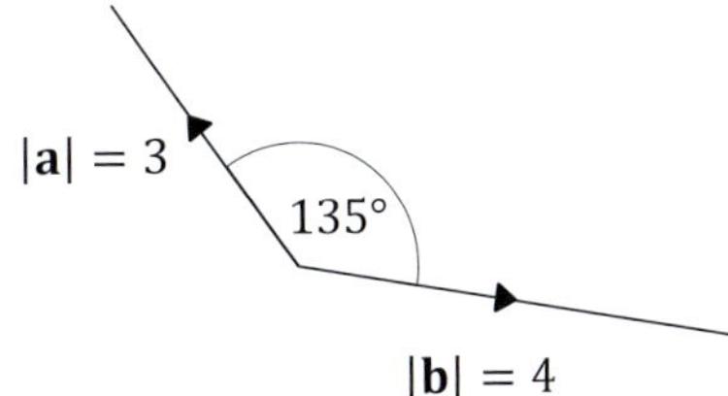

14.10 (a) Calculate the angle between the vectors $\mathbf{a} = 3\mathbf{i} - 3\mathbf{j} + \mathbf{k}$ and $\mathbf{b} = \mathbf{i} - 9\mathbf{j} - 8\mathbf{k}$.

(b) P, Q and R are the coordinates $(4, -1, 4)$, $(-3, 2, -1)$ and $(4, -3, -6)$ respectively. Calculate the size of angle PQR.

14.11 In the diagram $|\mathbf{a}| = \sqrt{3}$, $|\mathbf{b}| = 3$, $|\mathbf{c}| = 4$, evaluate:

(a) $\mathbf{a} \,.\, (\mathbf{b} + \mathbf{c})$

(b) $\mathbf{a} \,.\, (\mathbf{a} + \mathbf{b} + \mathbf{c})$

(c) $(\mathbf{a} + \mathbf{b}) \,.\, (\mathbf{a} + \mathbf{b})$

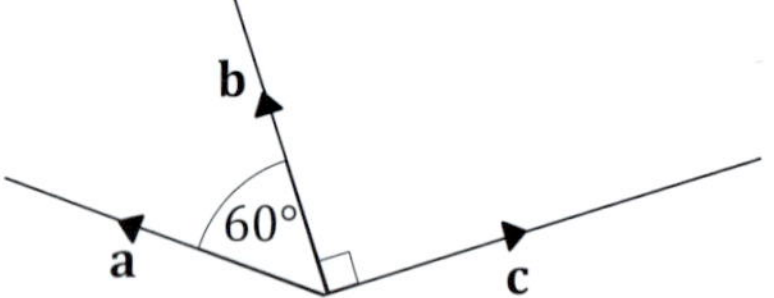

14.12 In the diagram, ABCDEF is a triangular prism. AB = BF = FA. M is the midpoint of CD. G divides EM in the ratio 1: 3.

Express the following vectors in terms of $\mathbf{p}$, $\mathbf{q}$ and $\mathbf{r}$:

(a) $\overrightarrow{AE}$ (b) $\overrightarrow{BM}$ (c) $\overrightarrow{GA}$ (d) $\overrightarrow{FM}$

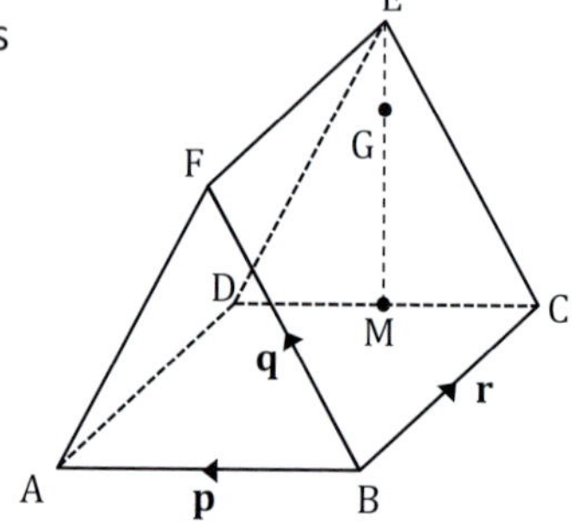

Chapter 15
Logarithmic & Exponential Functions

Logarithmic & Exponential Functions

Exponential Functions

An **exponential function** is a function in which the **variable** is the **exponent** or the power of the function. For example, the function $y = 2^x$ is an exponential function.

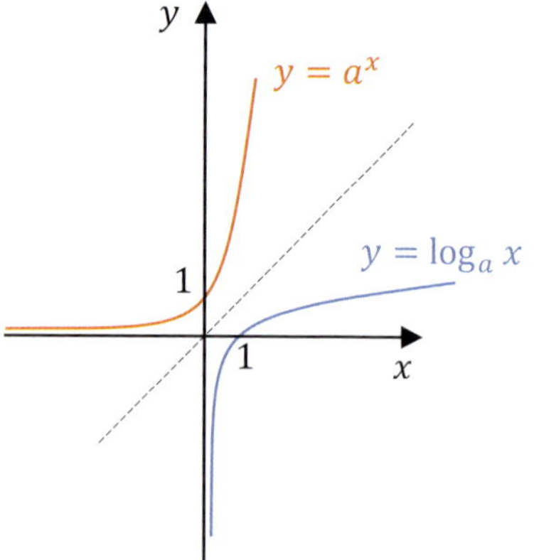

In general: $y = a^x$, where a is the base and x is the exponent. With an exponential function of this form, $y > 0$ for every value of x, and the graph always intersects the y-axis at $(0, 1)$. These values change with related graphs (**see section 15.2**).

Logarithmic Functions

A **logarithmic function** is the inverse of an exponential function. The logarithm of a number determines the value of the exponent of a base. For example, if we know $42 = 2^x$, we can use logarithms with a base of 2 to determine the value of x.

In general, for the graph of $y = \log_a x$, where a is the base, $x > 0$ for every value of y, and the graph always intersects the x-axis at $(1, 0)$. These values change with related graphs (**see section 15.3**).

Extra Info

The Exponential Function

This is a special exponential function, denoted e^x or $\exp x$. The base e is an irrational number, approximately 2.71828... It is known as **Euler's Number**, after the mathematician, Leonard Euler, and may be defined by:

$$e^x = \lim_{n \to \infty} \left(1 + \frac{x}{n}\right)^n$$

This function is present in any problems involving growth or decay, where the value grows in proportion to its current value. It has many important uses in mathematics; at Higher Mathematics, our study of the exponential function will be limited to growth and decay (see **section 15.7**).

Another important feature of the exponential function is that the function is equivalent to its derivative, **i.e.** if $f(x) = e^x, f'(x) = e^x$. This means that the measure of the slope of the function is its value.

The Natural Log Function

This logarithmic function denoted $\ln x$ or $\log_e x$ is the inverse of the exponential function, e^x (see **section 15.7**).

15.1 Using Logarithms and Exponentials

Logarithmic and exponential functions are inverse functions. If we have an exponential function $y = a^x$ – to write this in logarithmic form, then $x = \log_a y$. We can use this fact to calculate unknown values within a logarithmic or exponential equation or expression.

Worked Examples:

1. Express the following in logarithmic form:

(a) $c^d = e$	(b) $17^2 = 289$	(c) $8^3 = 512$
$\log_c e = d$	$\log_{17} 289 = 2$	$\log_8 512 = 3$

2. Express the following in exponential form:

(a) $\log_s t = v$

$s^v = t$

(b) $\log_9 81 = 2$

$9^2 = 81$

(c) $\log_7 343 = 3$

$7^3 = 343$

Exercise 15.1A

1. Express each of the following in logarithmic form:

(a) $a^b = c$ (b) $a^x = y$ (c) $6^3 = 216$ (d) $15^2 = 225$ (e) $17^2 = 289$ (f) $9^2 = 81$

(g) $10^3 = 1000$ (h) $11^3 = 1331$ (i) $4^5 = 1024$ (j) $8^0 = 1$ (k) $9^1 = 9$ (l) $12^0 = 1$

2. Express each of the following in exponential form:

(a) $\log_a x = y$ (b) $\log_a b = c$ (c) $\log_2 32 = 5$ (d) $\log_6 36 = 2$

(e) $\log_5 125 = 3$ (f) $\log_4 2 = \frac{1}{2}$ (g) $\log_5 1 = 0$ (h) $\log_4 4 = 1$

(i) $\log_9 3 = \frac{1}{2}$ (j) $\log_8 4 = \frac{2}{3}$ (k) $\log_2 2 = 1$ (l) $\log_{17} 1 = 0$

To evaluate logarithmic or exponential equations or expressions, it is often easiest to consider the exponential form. The laws of indices will be helpful.

Worked Examples:

1. Find the value of a.

(a) $2^a = 16$

$2^a = 16 = 2^4$

$a = 4$

(b) $4^a = \frac{1}{16}$

$4^a = \frac{1}{16} = \frac{1}{4^2} = 4^{-2}$

$a = -2$

(c) $100^a = \frac{1}{10}$

$100^a = \frac{1}{10} = \frac{1}{\sqrt{100}} = 100^{-\frac{1}{2}}$

$a = -\frac{1}{2}$

2. Evaluate:

(a) $\log_8 64$

$8^x = 64 = 8^2$

$x = 2$

(b) $\log_{64} 8$

$64^x = 8 = \sqrt{64} = 64^{\frac{1}{2}}$

$x = \frac{1}{2}$

(c) $\log_{64}\left(\frac{1}{4}\right)$

$64^x = \frac{1}{4} = \frac{1}{\sqrt[3]{64}} = 64^{-\frac{1}{3}}$

$x = -\frac{1}{3}$

Exercise 15.1B

1. Find the value of a in each of the following equations:

(a) $3^a = 9$ (b) $2^a = 16$ (c) $4^a = 64$ (d) $5^a = 125$ (e) $3^a = 81$ (f) $7^a = 1$

(g) $10^a = 1000$ (h) $8^a = 64$ (i) $4^a = 256$ (j) $6^a = 216$ (k) $3^a = 27$ (l) $4^a = 4$

2. Find the value of a in each of the following equations:

(a) $10^a = 1$ (b) $12^a = 1$ (c) $4^a = 2$ (d) $8^a = 2$ (e) $25^a = 5$ (f) $16^a = 4$

(g) $4^a = \frac{1}{4}$ (h) $2^a = \frac{1}{8}$ (i) $4^a = \frac{1}{16}$ (j) $9^a = \frac{1}{81}$ (k) $6^a = \frac{1}{36}$ (l) $2^a = \frac{1}{16}$

(m) $4^a = \frac{1}{2}$ (n) $16^a = \frac{1}{4}$ (o) $25^a = \frac{1}{5}$ (p) $36^a = \frac{1}{6}$ (q) $9^a = \frac{1}{3}$ (r) $16^a = \frac{1}{2}$

3. Evaluate:

(a) $\log_2 4$ (b) $\log_5 5$ (c) $\log_4 16$ (d) $\log_6 1$ (e) $\log_2 2$ (f) $\log_3 27$

(g) $\log_2 1$ (h) $\log_4 64$ (i) $\log_7 7$ (j) $\log_5 125$ (k) $\log_2 16$ (l) $\log_4 256$

(m) $\log_3 3$ (n) $\log_9 1$ (o) $\log_8 8$ (p) $\log_{16} 1$ (q) $\log_{10} 10$ (r) $\log_7 343$

4. Evaluate:

(a) $\log_{10} 10{,}000$ (b) $\log_{12} 1$ (c) $\log_9 3$ (d) $\log_8 2$ (e) $\log_{16} 2$ (f) $\log_{125} 5$

(g) $\log_{10}\left(\frac{1}{10}\right)$ (h) $\log_8\left(\frac{1}{2}\right)$ (i) $\log_{16}\left(\frac{1}{4}\right)$ (j) $\log_{25}\left(\frac{1}{5}\right)$ (k) $\log_{100} 10$ (l) $\log_9\left(\frac{1}{3}\right)$

We can use a calculator to calculate the answer to a logarithmic expression or an exponential equation. The logarithm button on your calculator should look like this [log■□].

Worked Examples:

1. Evaluate $\log_2 5$. Give your answer correct to two decimal places.

Solution: Use the log button to input the base and argument.

$\log_2 5 = 0.430 \ldots = 0.43$ (2 d.p.)

2. Given the expression $7^a = 22$, calculate the value of a. Give your answer correct to two decimal places.

Solution: Write in logarithmic form with a base of 7.

$a = \log_7 22 = 1.588 \ldots = 1.59$ (2 d.p.)

Exercise 15.1C

1. Evaluate. Give your answer correct to two decimal places:

(a) $\log_3 7$ (b) $\log_5 12$ (c) $\log_4 6$ (d) $\log_7 2$ (e) $\log_{12} 2$ (f) $\log_3 11$

(g) $\log_5 11$ (h) $\log_{15} 4$ (i) $\log_6 3$ (j) $\log_{17} 52$ (k) $\log_8 9$ (l) $\log_9 2$

(m) $\log_{10} 8$ (n) $\log_{18} 6$ (o) $\log_{12} 9$ (p) $\log_5\left(\frac{1}{2}\right)$ (q) $\log_{10} 3$ (r) $\log_{10} 2$

2. Find the value of x in each of the following equations. Give your answer correct to two decimal places:

(a) $10^x = 3$ (b) $3^x = 5$ (c) $4^x = 7$ (d) $6^x = 12$ (e) $5^x = 18$ (f) $6^x = 2$

(g) $11^x = 5$ (h) $3^x = 10$ (i) $4^x = 20$ (j) $50^x = 3$ (k) $6^x = 18$ (l) $5^x = 2$

(m) $4^x = 1$ (n) $13^x = \frac{1}{3}$ (o) $10^x = \frac{1}{3}$ (p) $15^x = \frac{1}{2}$ (q) $5^x = \frac{2}{3}$ (r) $9^x = \frac{1}{4}$

15.2 Finding the Equation of a Function from its Graph

To determine the equation of the graph of an exponential function, substitute the information from the graph into the equation.

Worked Examples:

1. The function f is of the form $f(x) = a^x$. The graph of $y = f(x)$ is shown.
   (a) Write down the equation of the graph.
   (b) State the range of f.

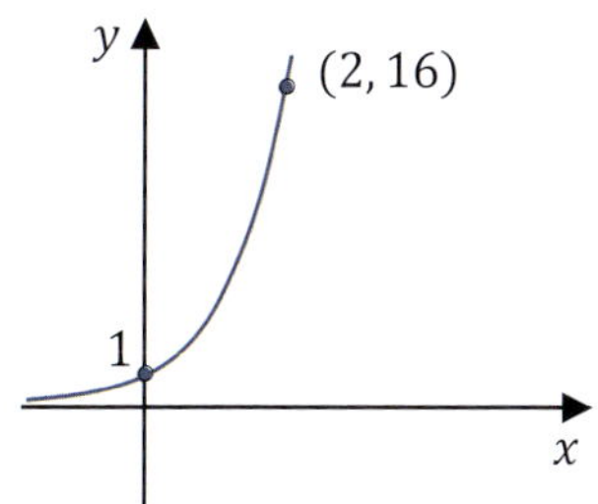

Solution:

(a) Substitute the coordinate $(2, 16)$

$a^2 = 16$
$a = 4 \quad \therefore \boldsymbol{y = 4^x}$

(b) Range, $\boldsymbol{f(x) > 0}$.

NB: A function of the form $f(x) = a^x$ will always intersect the y-axis at the point $(0, 1)$.

2. The function f is of the form $f(x) = ba^x$. The graph of $y = f(x)$ is shown.
   (a) Write down the equation of the graph.
   (b) State the range of f.

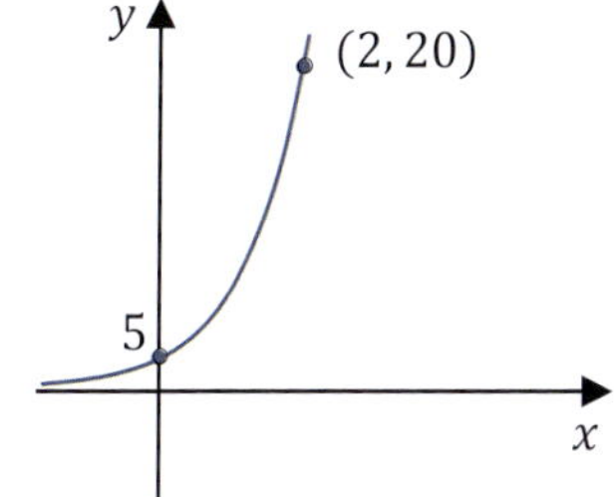

Solution:

(a) Substitute the coordinate $(0, 5)$

$5 = ba^0$
$5 = b \quad \therefore y = 5a^x$

Then substitute the coordinate $(2, 20)$

$20 = 5a^2$
$4 = a^2$
$a = 2 \quad \therefore \boldsymbol{y = 5(2)^x}$

(b) Range, $\boldsymbol{f(x) > 0}$.

NB: The range of any exponential function will always be $f(x) > 0$, unless the graph is of the form $y = -f(x)$ or $y = f(x) \pm b$.

Exercise 15.2A

1. Each function f is of the form $f(x) = a^x$. The graph of $y = f(x)$ is shown.
   (i) Write down the equation of each graph and (ii) state the range of f:

(a)

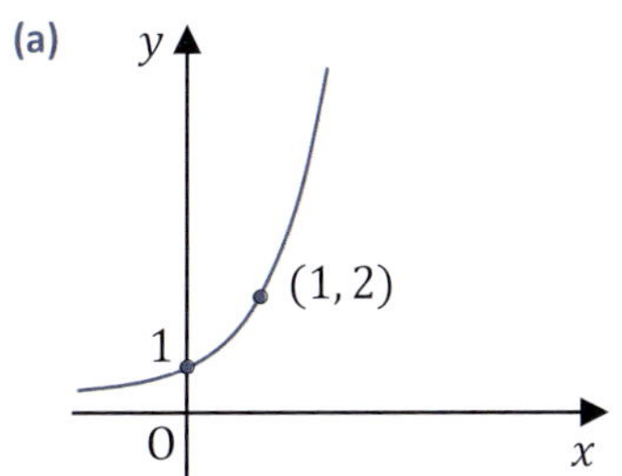

(b)

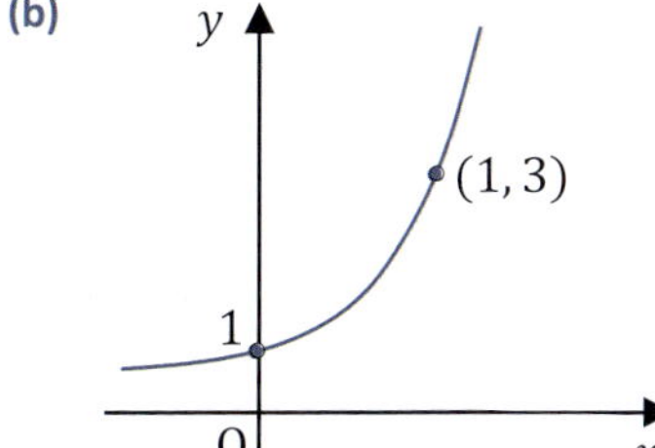

(c)

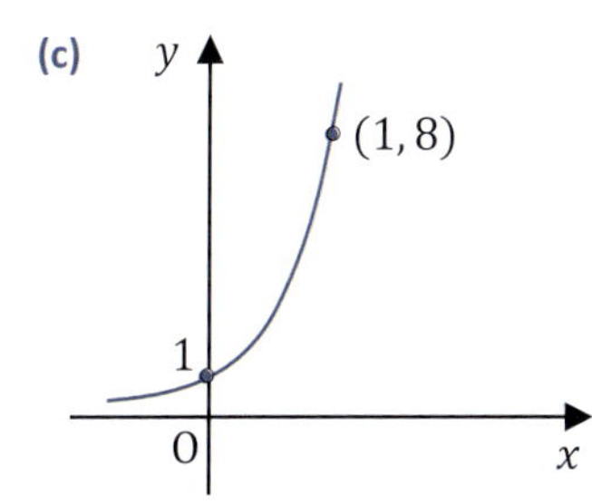

(d)

(e)

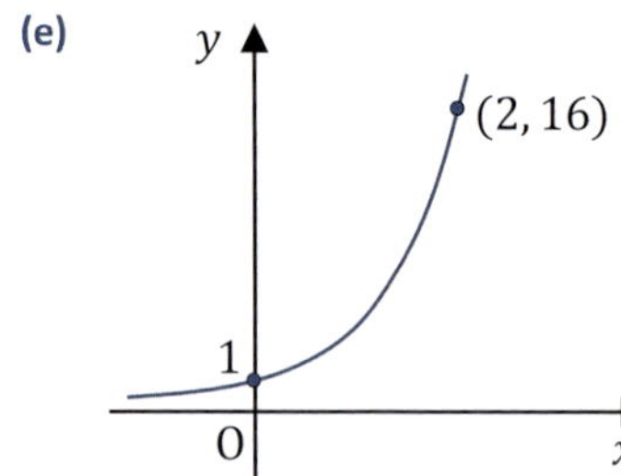

(f)

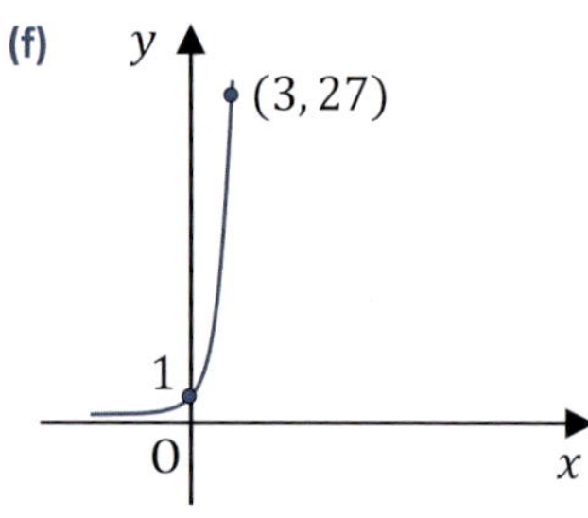

2. Each function f is of the form $f(x) = a^x$ or $f(x) = a^{-x}$. The graph of $y = f(x)$ is shown.
(i) Write down the equation of each graph and (ii) state the range of f:

(a)

(b)

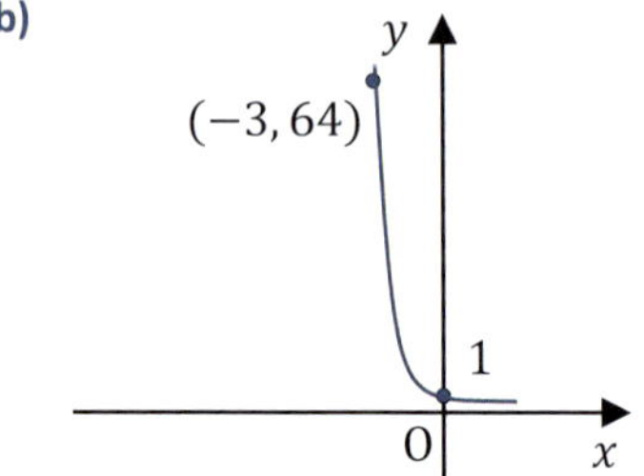

(c)

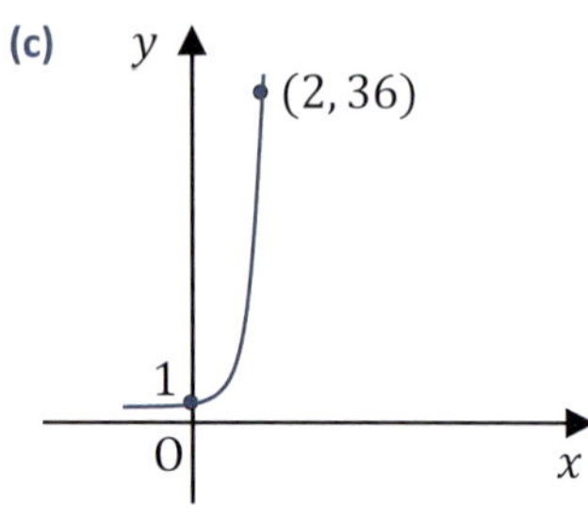

(d)

(e)

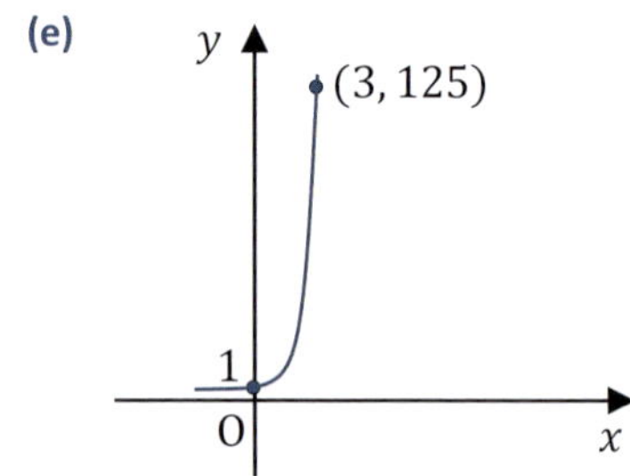

(f)

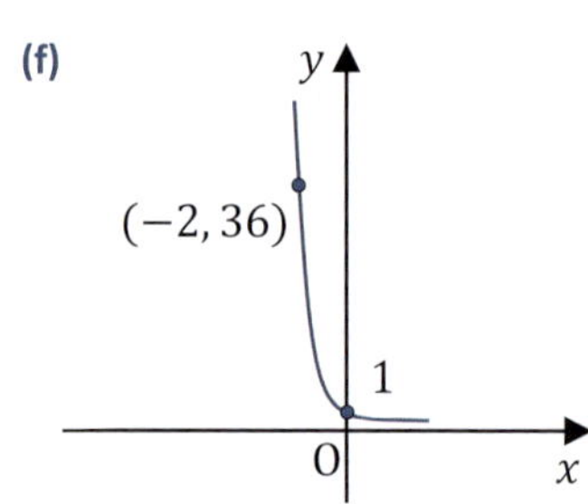

3. The function f is of the form $f(x) = ba^x$. The graph of $y = f(x)$ is shown.
(i) Write down the equation of each graph and (ii) state the range of f:

(a)

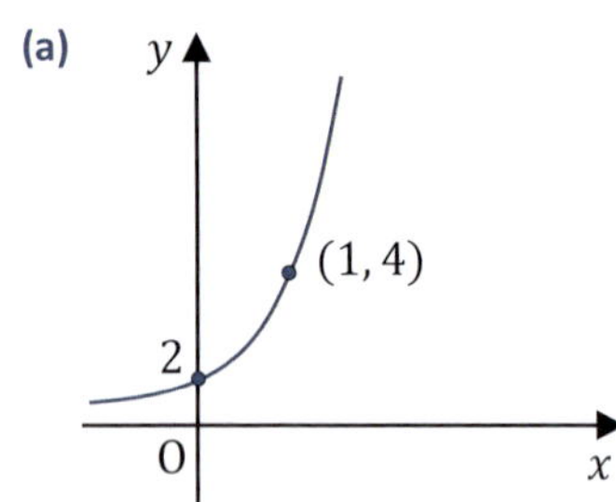

(b)

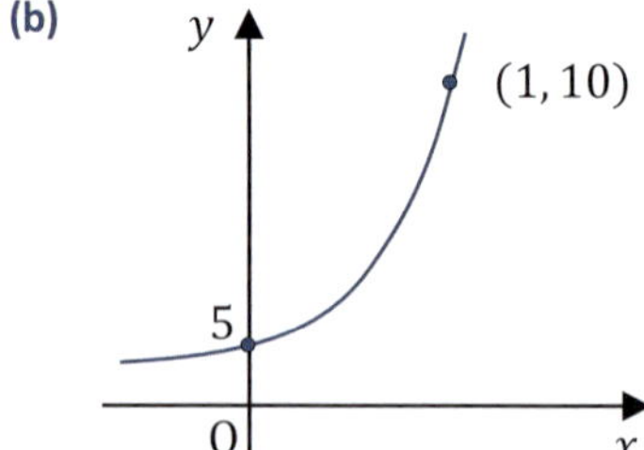

(c)

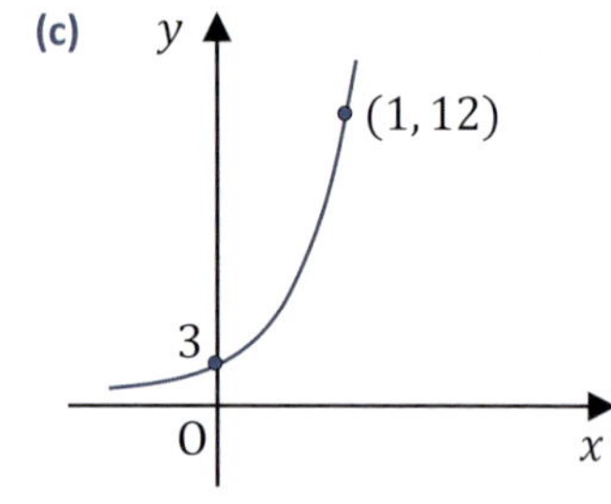

(d)

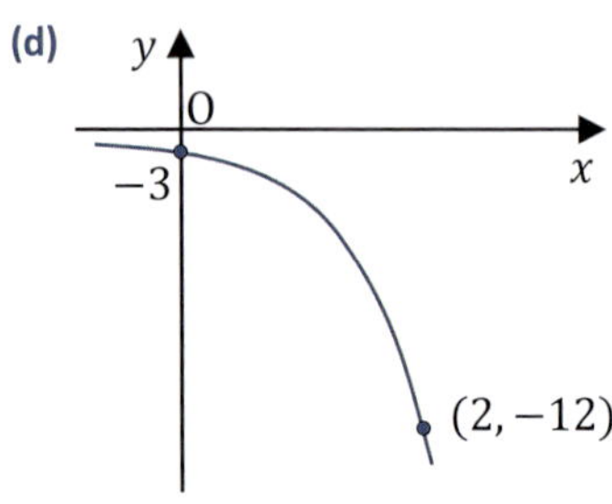

(e)

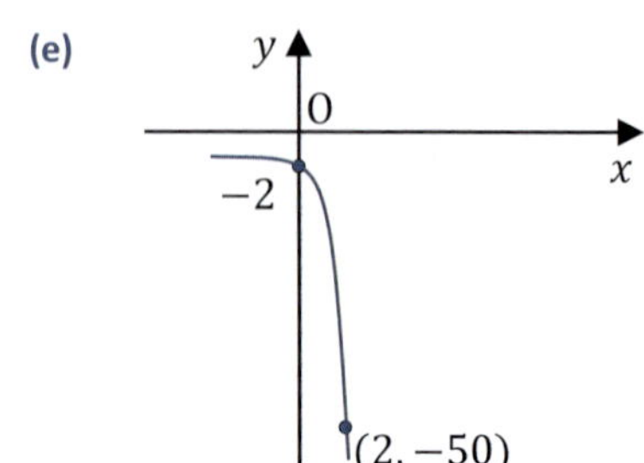

(f)

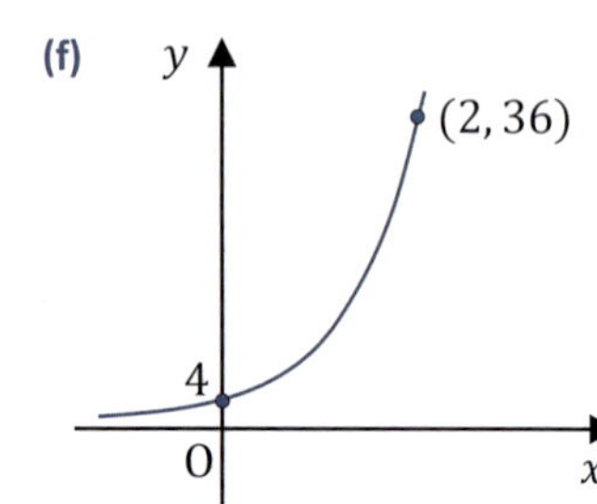

4. The function f is of the form $f(x) = a^x \pm b$. The graph of $y = f(x)$ is shown.
   (i) Write down the equation of each graph and **(ii)** state the range of f:

(a)
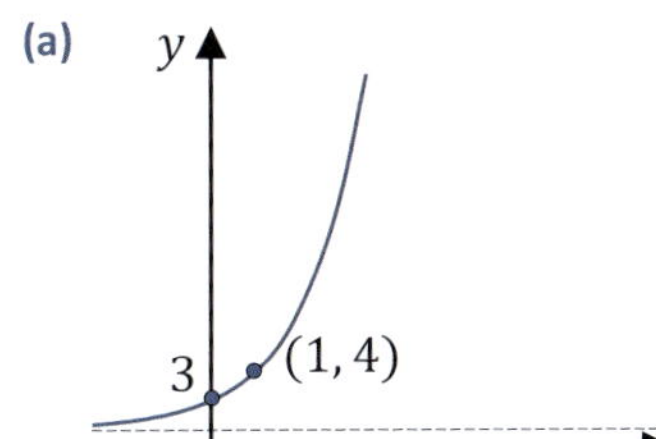

(b)
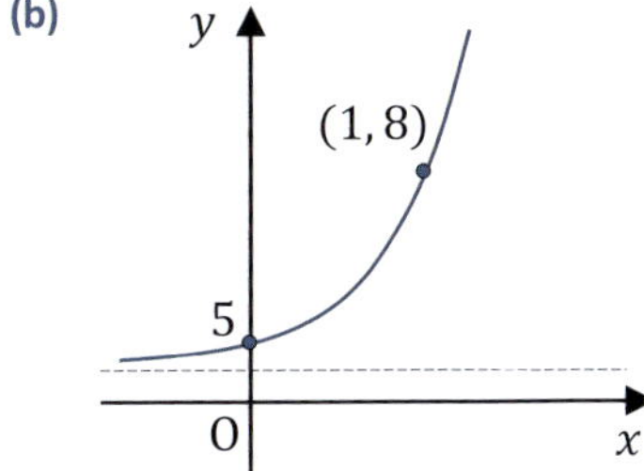

(c)
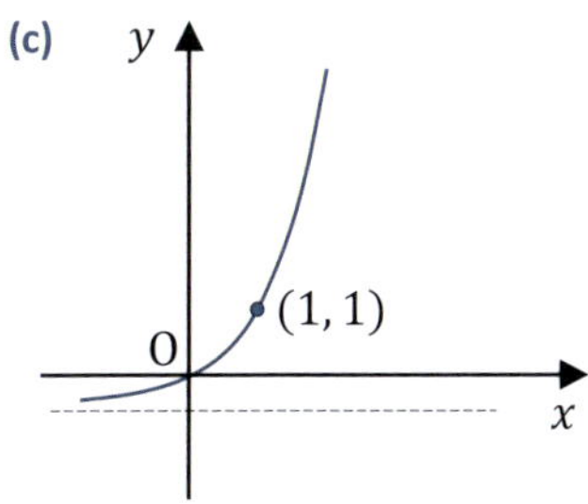

(d)
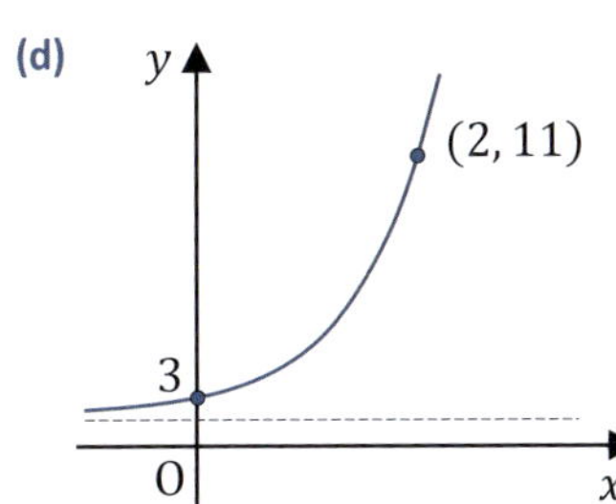

(e)
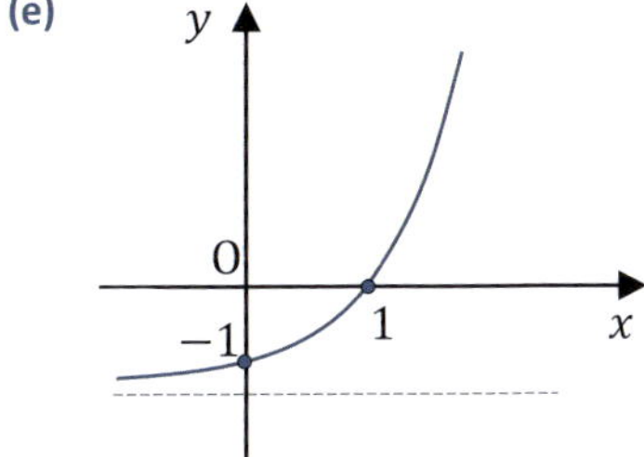

(f)
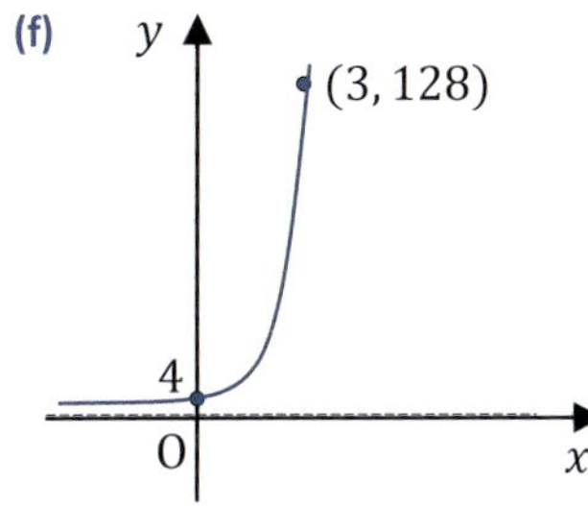

To determine the equation of the graph of a logarithmic function, substitute the information from the graph into the equation.

Worked Examples:

1. The function f is of the form $f(x) = \log_a x$. The graph of $y = f(x)$ is shown.
   (a) Write down the equation of the graph.
   (b) State the domain of f.

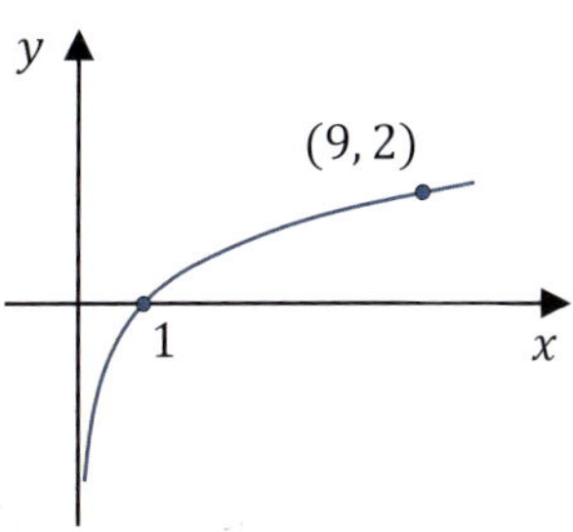

Solution:

(a) Substitute the coordinate $(9, 2)$

$\log_a 9 = 2$
$a^2 = 9$
$a = 3 \quad \therefore \boldsymbol{y = \log_3 x}$

(b) Domain, $\boldsymbol{x > 0}$.

NB: A function of the form $f(x) = \log_a x$ will always intersect the x-axis at the point $(1, 0)$ and its domain is always $x > 0$.

2. The function f is of the form $f(x) = \log_a(x - b)$. The graph of $y = f(x)$ is shown.
   (a) Write down the equation of the graph.
   (b) State the domain of f.

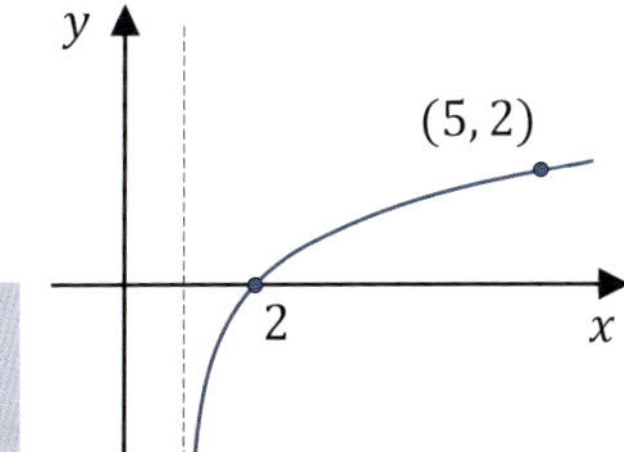

Solution:

(a) Substitute the coordinate $(2, 0)$

NB: The graph has moved to the right, so the form is $y = \log_a(x - b)$.

$\log_a(2 - b) = 0$
$a^0 = 1 = 2 - b$
$b = 1 \quad \therefore y = \log_a(x - 1)$

Then substitute the coordinate $(5, 2)$

$\log_a(5 - 1) = 2$
$a^2 = 4$
$a = 2 \quad \therefore \boldsymbol{y = \log_2(x - 1)}$

(b) Domain, $x - 1 > 0 \therefore \boldsymbol{x > 1}$.

Exercise 15.2B

1. The function f is of the form $f(x) = \log_a x$. The graph of $y = f(x)$ is shown.
   (i) Write down the equation of each graph and **(ii)** state the domain of f:

(a)

$(3, 1)$

(b)

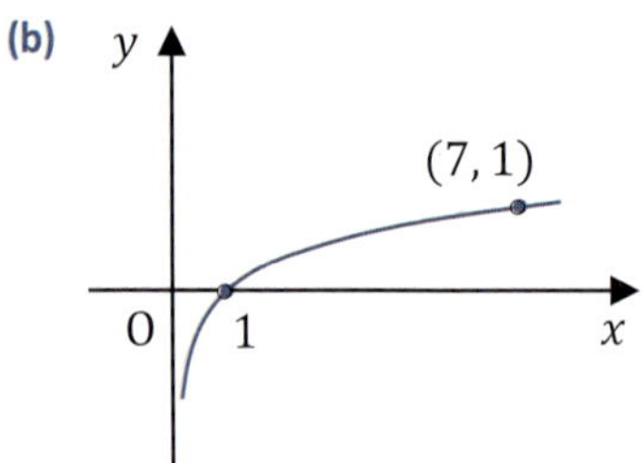

(c)

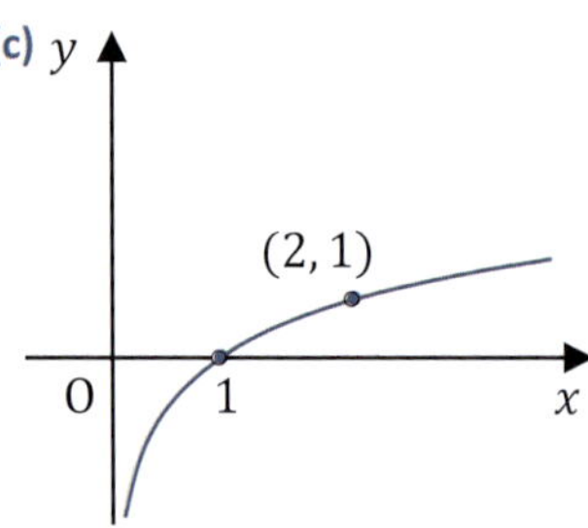

(d)

$(4, 2)$

(e)

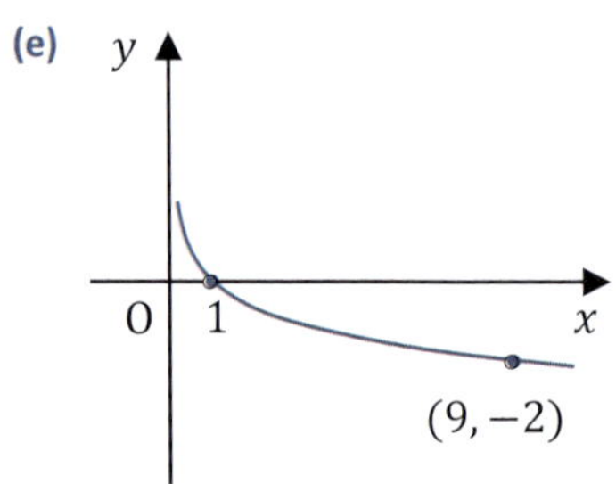

(f)

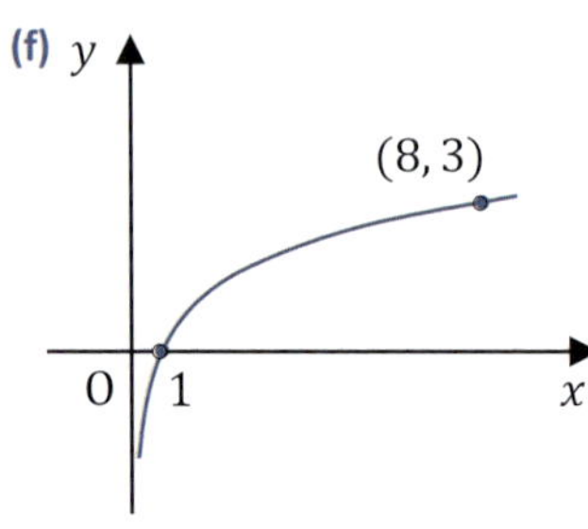

(g)

$(16, -2)$

(h)

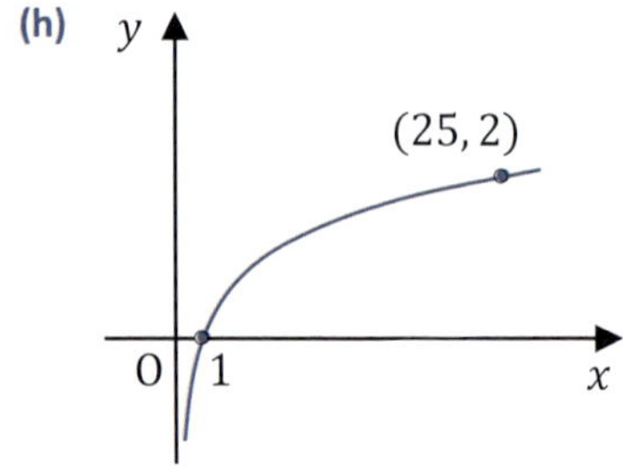

(i)

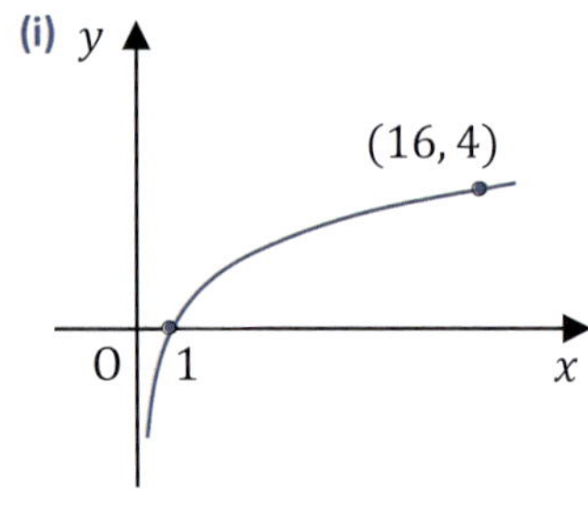

(j)

$(27, 3)$

(k)

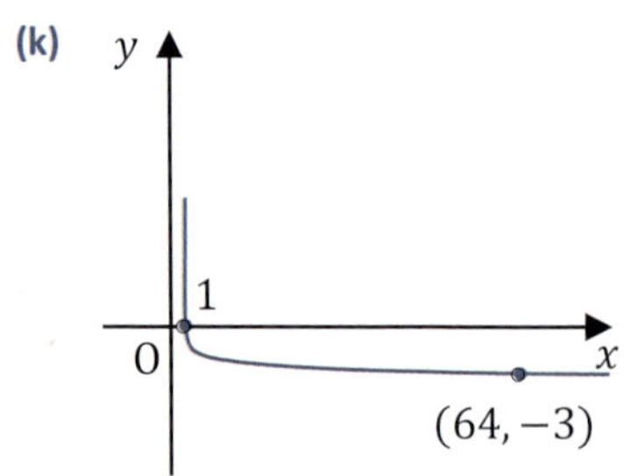

(l)

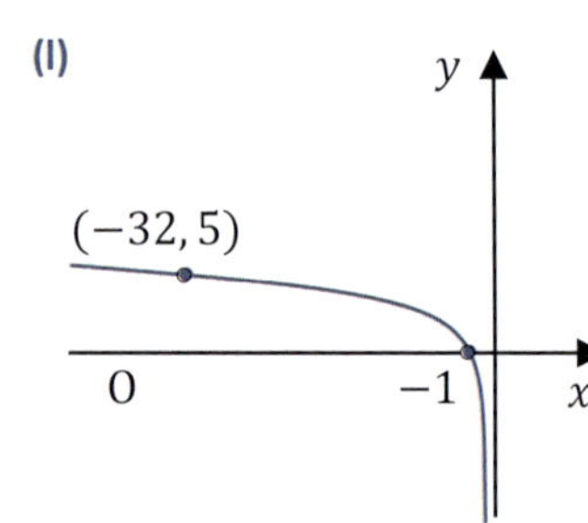

2. The function f is of the form $f(x) = \log_a(x - b)$. The graph of $y = f(x)$ is shown.
   (i) Write down the equation of each graph and **(ii)** state the domain of f:

(a)

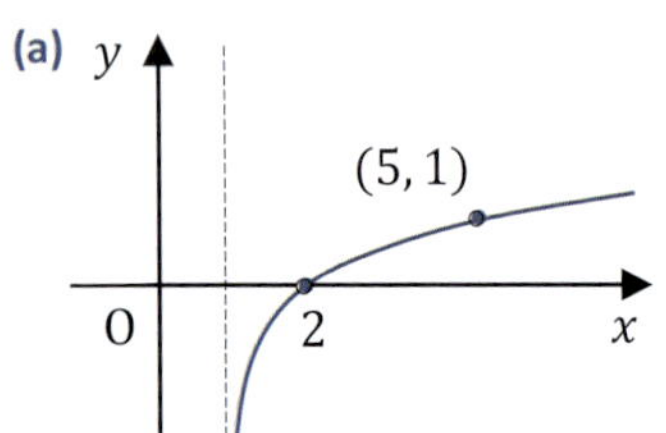

(b)

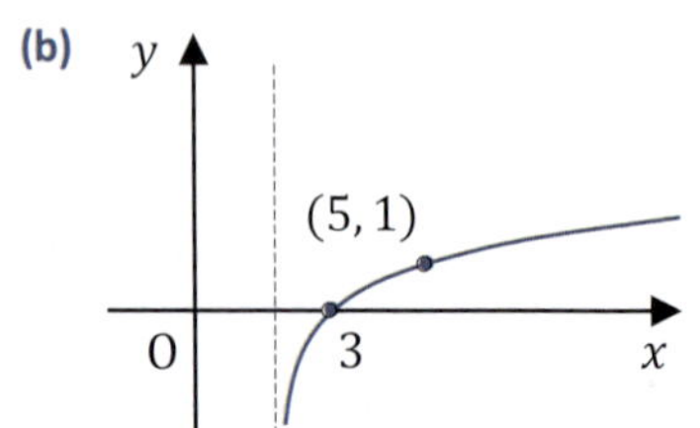

(c)

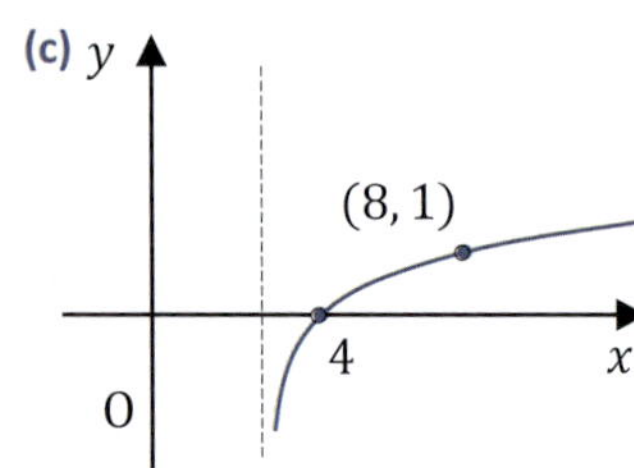

(d) y, $(10, 1)$, 0, 4, x

(e) y, $(7, 1)$, 0, 2, x

(f)

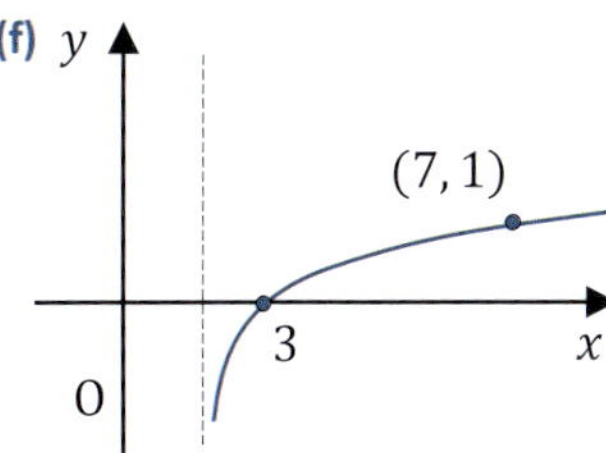

3. The function f is of the form $f(x) = \log_a(x + b)$. The graph of $y = f(x)$ is shown.
(i) Write down the equation of each graph and (ii) state the domain of f:

(a)

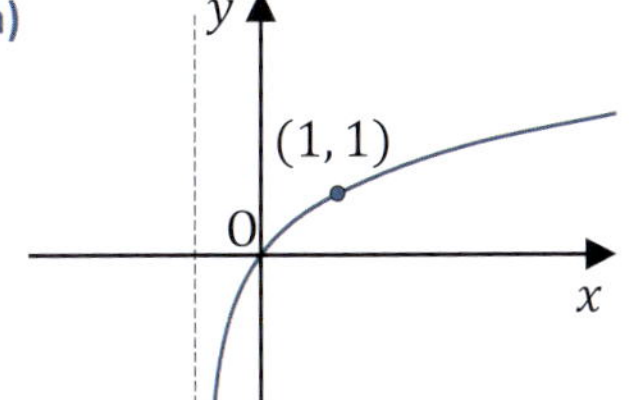

(b)

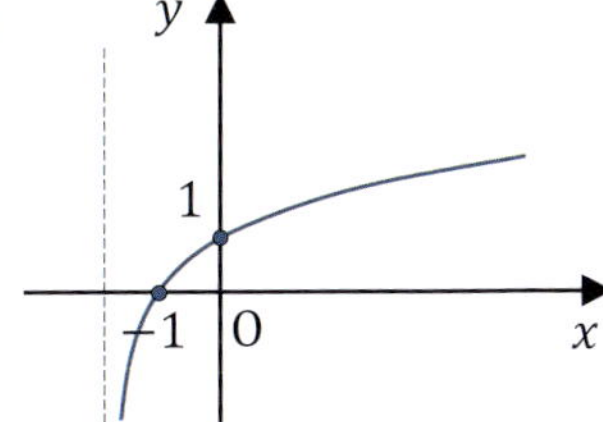

(c)

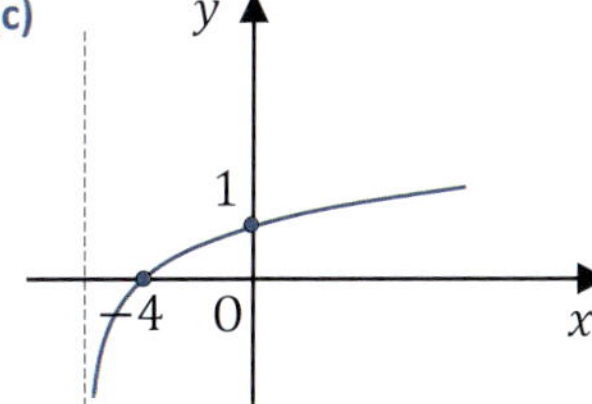

(d)

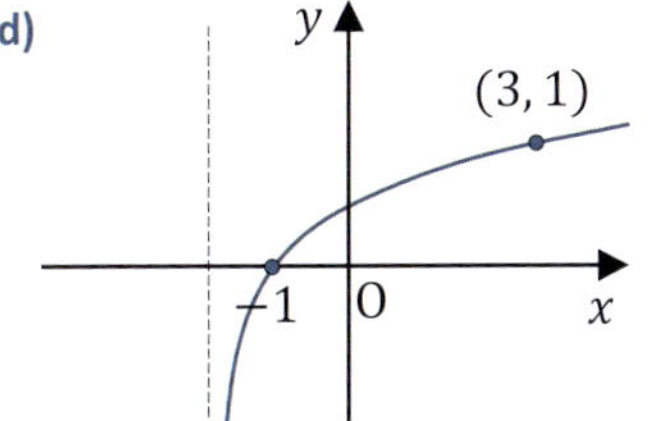

(e)

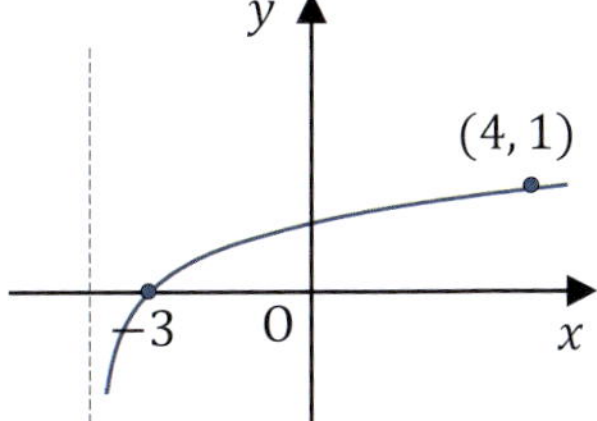

(f)

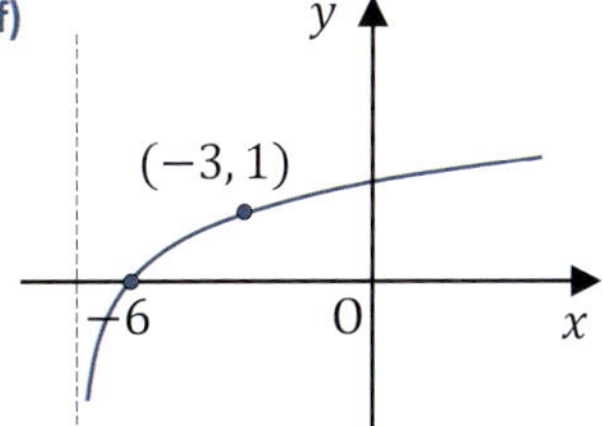

15.3 Sketching a Graph From its Equation

To sketch the graph of an exponential function from its equation, two coordinates are needed: the coordinate when $x = 0$ and the coordinate when $x = 1$.

Worked Example:

Sketch and annotate the graph of $y = f(x)$ when $f(x) = 3^x$.

Solution:

When $x = 0$, $f(0) = 3^0 = 1$, $\therefore (0, 1)$.

When $x = 1$, $f(1) = 3^1 = 3$, $\therefore (1, 3)$.

Now sketch an exponential graph marking the coordinates of the points.

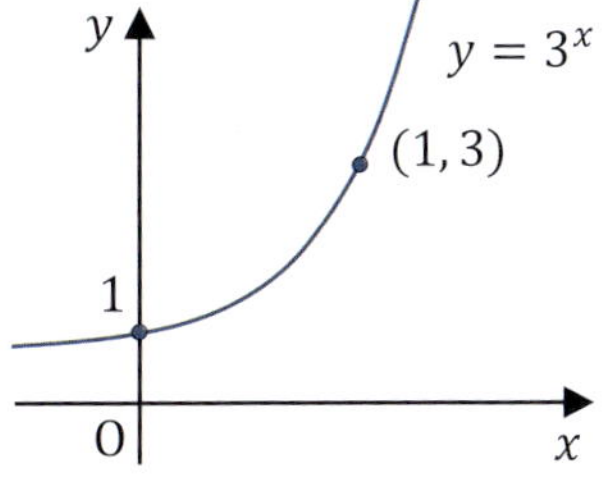

Exercise 15.3A

Sketch and annotate the graph of $y = f(x)$ for the given functions:

1. $f(x) = 2^x$
2. $f(x) = 4^x$
3. $f(x) = 7^x$
4. $f(x) = a^x$
5. $f(x) = 5^x$
6. $f(x) = 6^x$
7. $f(x) = 10^x$
8. $f(x) = b^x$
9. $f(x) = 8^x$
10. $f(x) = 0.5^x$
11. $f(x) = 0.8^x$
12. $f(x) = c^x$

To sketch the graph of a logarithmic function from its equation, two coordinates are needed: the coordinate when $y = 0$ and the coordinate when $y = 1$.

Worked Example:

Sketch and annotate the graph of $y = f(x)$ when $f(x) = \log_5 x$.

Solution:

When $y = 0$, $\log_5 x = 0$

$x = 1, \therefore (1, 0)$

When $y = 1$, $\log_5 x = 1$

$x = 5, \therefore (5, 1)$

Now sketch an exponential graph marking the coordinates of the points.

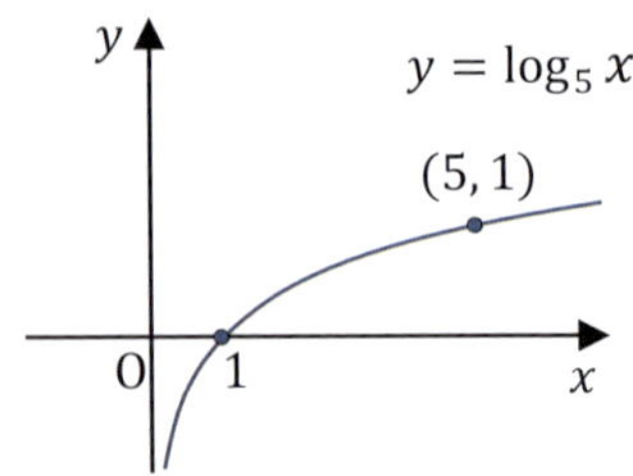

Exercise 15.3B

Sketch and annotate the graph of $y = f(x)$ for the given functions:

1. $f(x) = \log_2 x$
2. $f(x) = \log_4 x$
3. $f(x) = \log_7 x$
4. $f(x) = \log_a x$
5. $f(x) = \log_5 x$
6. $f(x) = \log_6 x$
7. $f(x) = \log_{10} x$
8. $f(x) = \log_b x$
9. $f(x) = \log_8 x$
10. $f(x) = \log_{0.5} x$
11. $f(x) = \log_{0.8} x$
12. $f(x) = \log_c x$

15.4 Sketching the Inverse Function

The inverse function of an exponential function is a logarithmic function with the same base, **i.e.** the inverse of a^x is $\log_a x$ and vice versa.

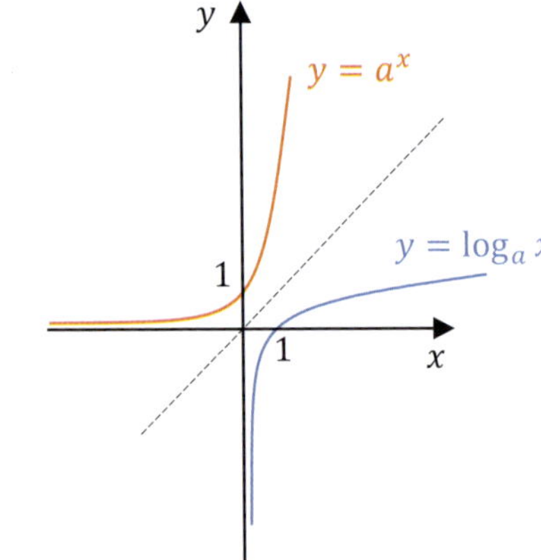

The graph of an inverse function is reflected in the line $y = x$. To sketch the graph of an inverse function:

Step 1: Sketch the graph of the function.
Step 2: Sketch the line $y = x$.
Step 3: Sketch the inverse graph as a reflection of the original function; remember to annotate the image of each coordinate.

NB: When sketching the inverse function, rotate the page so that the line $y = x$ is vertical, this will make reflecting the original easier.

Worked Example:

Sketch and annotate the graph of $y = f^{-1}(x)$ when $f(x) = 2^x$.

Solution:

Step 1: When $x = 0$, $f(0) = 2^0 = 1, \therefore (0, 1)$.

When $x = 1$, $f(1) = 2^1 = 2, \therefore (1, 2)$.

Now sketch an exponential graph marking the coordinates of the points.

Step 2: Sketch the line $y = x$ using a ruler.

Step 3: Turn your page 45° and sketch the reflection of $y = f(x)$.

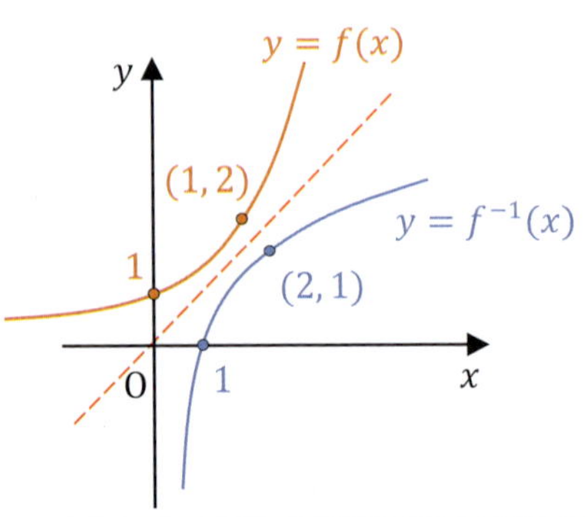

Exercise 15.4

Sketch and annotate the graph of $y = f^{-1}(x)$ for the given functions:

1. $f(x) = \log_4 x$
2. $f(x) = 2^x$
3. $f(x) = \log_a x$
4. $f(x) = b^x$
5. $f(x) = \log_6 x$
6. $f(x) = 5^x$
7. $f(x) = \log_{10} x$
8. $f(x) = 0.4^x$
9. $f(x) = \log_{0.2} 2x$
10. $f(x) = 0.1^{2x}$
11. $f(x) = \log_c 2x$
12. $f(x) = d^{2x}$

15.5 Sketching Related Graphs

The graph transformations of logarithmic and exponential functions follow the same principles as the functions we have already seen in **chapter 5**. Below is a recap of the transformations.

For the function $f(x) = a^x$:

$f(x) + b = a^x + b$	Graph moves up by b.
$f(x \pm b) = a^{x \pm b}$	Graph moves left $(+)$ and right $(-)$ by b.
$kf(x) = ka^x$	When $k > 1$ or $k < -1$, the graph is **stretched vertically** from the x-axis.
	When $-1 < k < 1$, the graph is **squashed vertically** towards the x-axis.
$f(kx) = a^{kx}$	When $k > 1$ or $k < -1$, the graph is **squashed horizontally** towards the y-axis.
	When $-1 < k < 1$, the graph is **stretched horizontally** away from the y-axis.
$-f(x) = -a^x$	Graph reflected in x-axis.
$f(-x) = a^{-x}$	Graph reflected in y-axis.

Worked Example:

For the function $f(x) = 4^x$, the diagram shows the graph of $y = f(x)$.

Sketch the graph of $y = f(x - 2) + 1$.

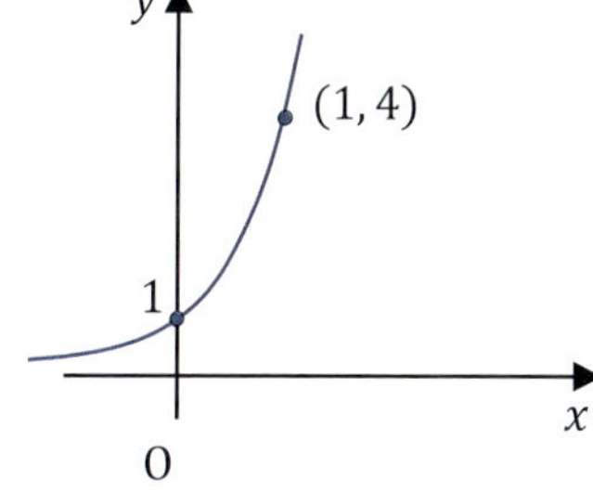

Solution:

- Sketch the original graph lightly on the axes.
- Calculate each new coordinate.

  For each coordinate $(x + 2, y + 1)$

  $(0, 1) \rightarrow (2, 2)$

  $(1, 4) \rightarrow (3, 5)$
- Add a horizontal line (asymptote) at $y = 1$.
- Sketch the transformed graph.

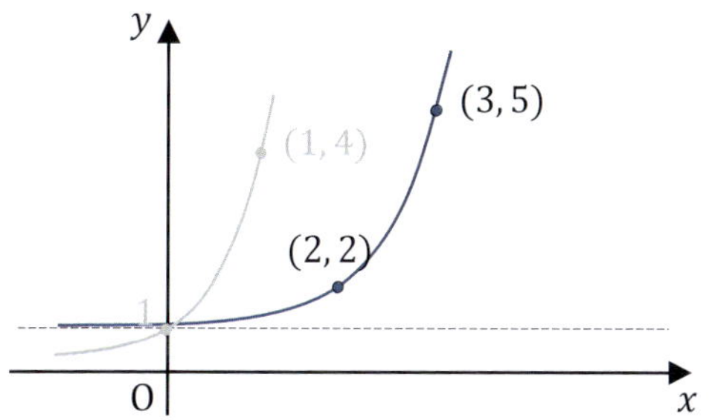

NB: The horizontal line (asymptote) is the value the function will approach as x is large and negative.

Exercise 15.5A

In each of the following diagrams the graph of $y = f(x)$ is shown. Sketch the graph with the given transformation:

1.

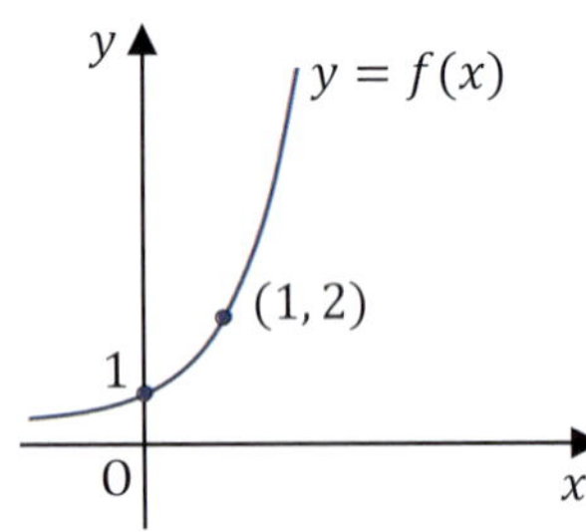

$f(x) = 2^x$
Sketch $y = f(x) + 1$

2.

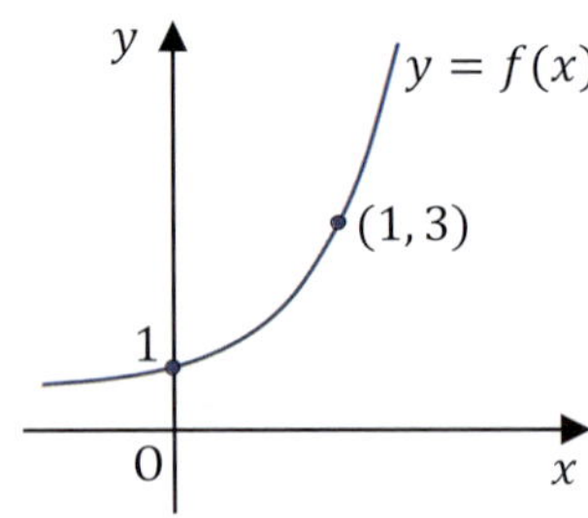

$f(x) = 3^x$
Sketch $y = f(x) - 2$

3.

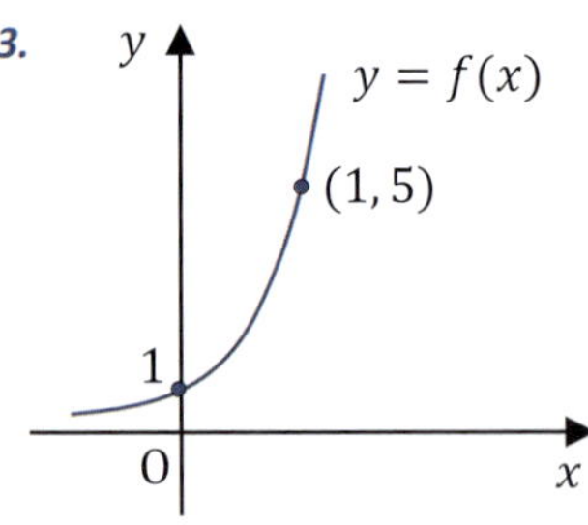

$f(x) = 5^x$
Sketch $y = f(x - 2) + 1$

4.

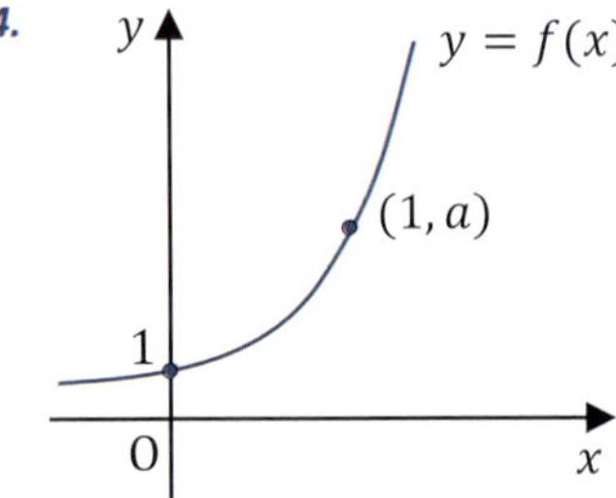

$f(x) = a^x$
Sketch $y = f(x + 1) - 2$

5.

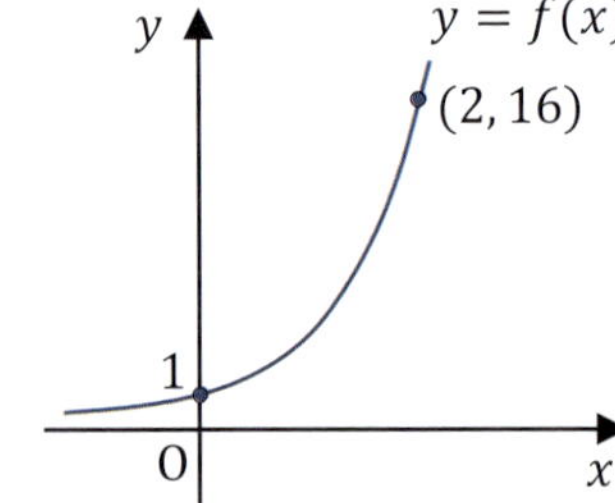

$f(x) = 4^x$
Sketch $y = 1 - f(x)$

6.

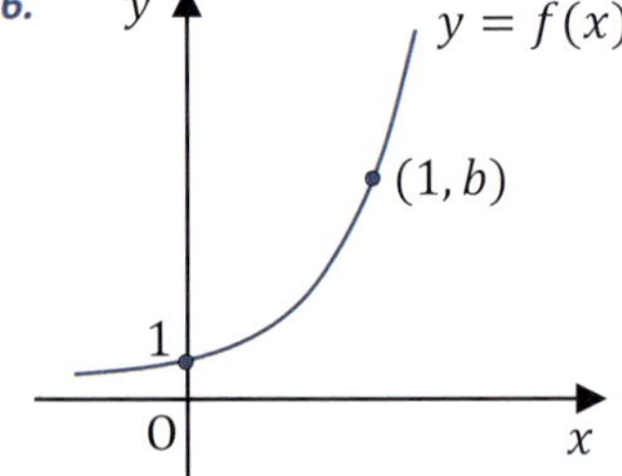

$f(x) = b^x$
Sketch $y = 2 - f(x)$

7.

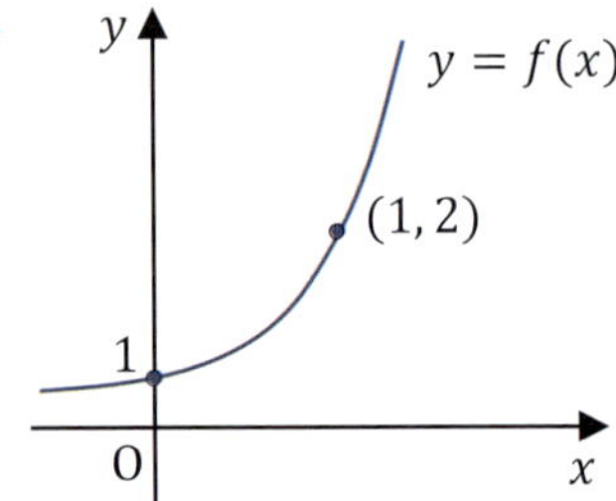

$f(x) = 2^x$
Sketch $y = f(-x)$

8.

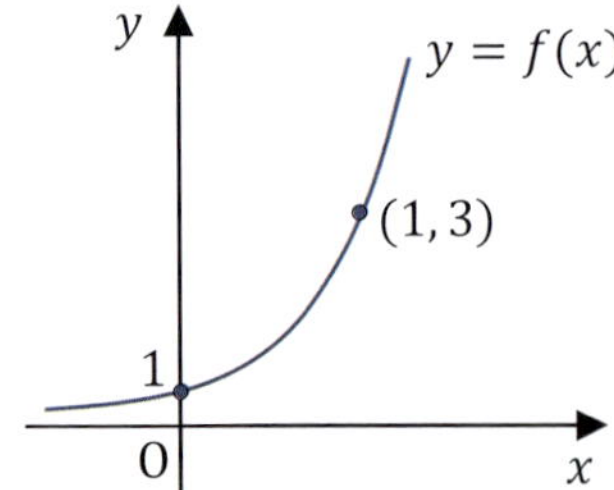

$f(x) = 3^x$
Sketch $y = 2f(x) + 1$

9.

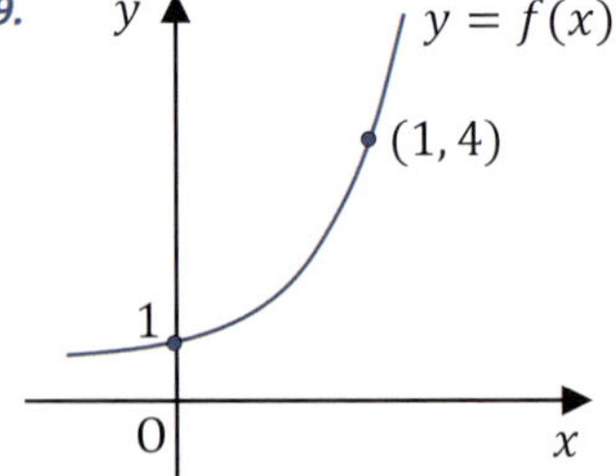

$f(x) = 4^x$
Sketch $y = 1 - 2f(-x)$

10.

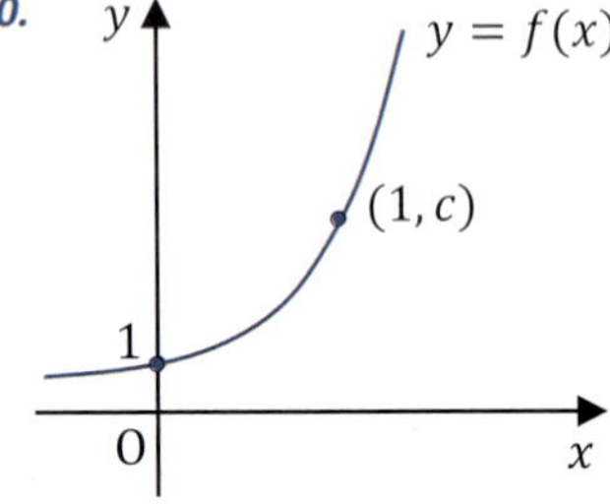

$f(x) = c^x$
Sketch $y = 2 - f(2x)$

11.

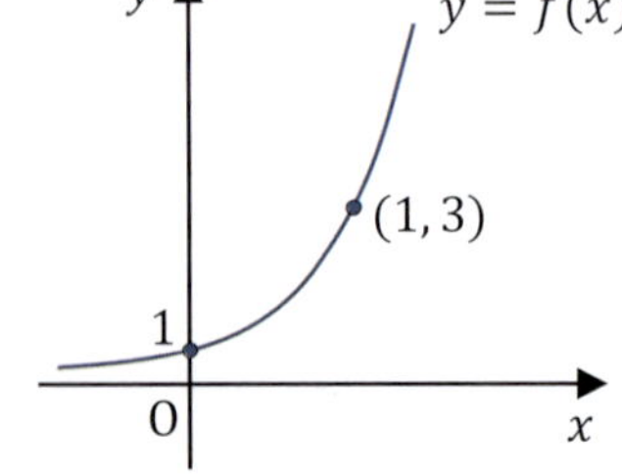

$f(x) = 3^x$
Sketch $y = 4 - f(x + 3)$

12.

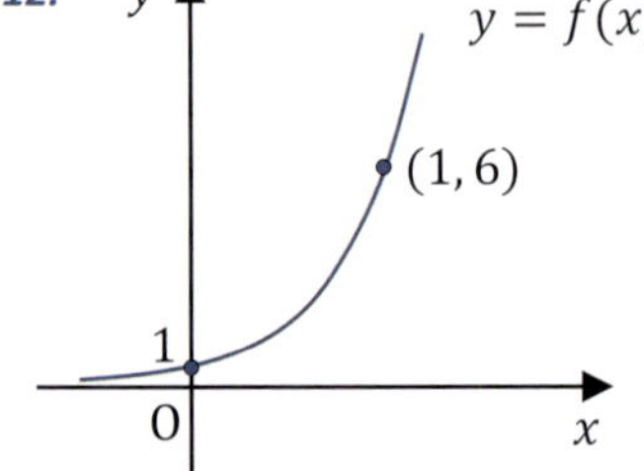

$f(x) = 6^x$
Sketch $y = 2 - \frac{1}{2}f(-x)$

For the function $f(x) = \log_a x$:

$f(x) + b = \log_a x + b$	Graph moves up by b.
$f(x \pm b) = \log_a(x \pm b)$	Graph moves left $(+)$ and right $(-)$ by b.
$kf(x) = k\log_a x$	When $k > 1$ or $k < -1$, the graph is **stretched vertically** from the x-axis.
	When $-1 < k < 1$, the graph is **squashed vertically** towards the x-axis.
$f(kx) = \log_a kx$	When $k > 1$ or $k < -1$, the graph is **squashed horizontally** towards the y-axis.
	When $-1 < k < 1$, the graph is **stretched horizontally** away from the y-axis.
$-f(x) = -\log_a x$	Graph reflected in x-axis.
$f(-x) = \log_a -x$	Graph reflected in y-axis.

Worked Example:

For the function $f(x) = \log_2 x$, the diagram shows the graph of $y = f(x)$.

Sketch the graph of $y = 1 - f(x + 3)$.

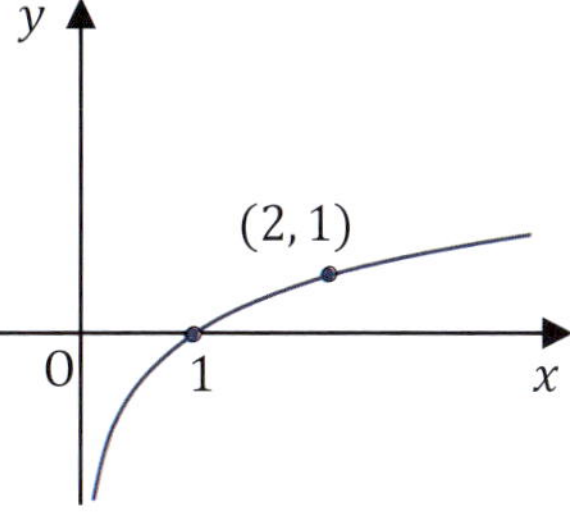

Solution:

- Sketch the original graph lightly on the axes.
- Calculate each new coordinate.

  For each coordinate $(x - 3, 1 - y)$

  $(1, 0) \rightarrow (-2, 1)$

  $(2, 1) \rightarrow (-1, 0)$
- Add a vertical line (asymptote) at $x = -3$.
- Sketch the transformed graph.

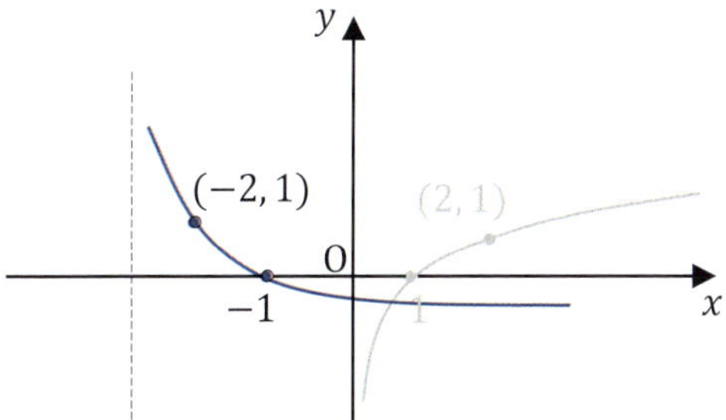

NB: The vertical line (asymptote) is the value the function will approach as y is large and positive.

Exercise 15.5B

In each of the following diagrams the graph of $y = f(x)$ is shown. Sketch the graph with the given transformation:

1.

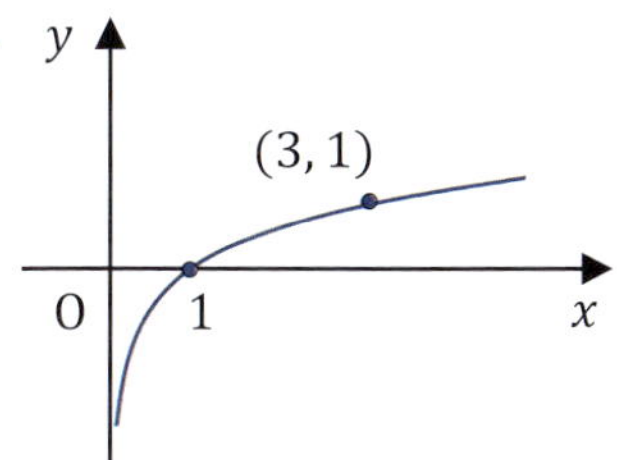

$f(x) = \log_3 x$

Sketch $y = f(x) + 1$

2.

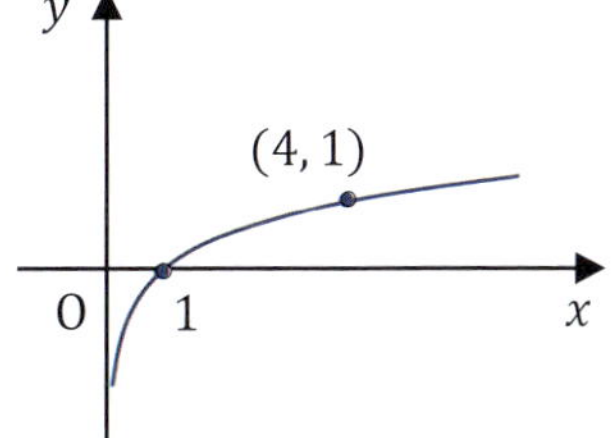

$f(x) = \log_4 x$

Sketch $y = f(x) - 2$

3.

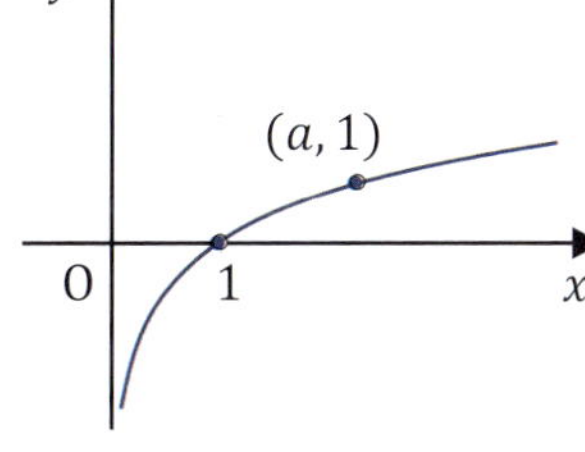

$f(x) = \log_a x$

Sketch $y = f(x - 2) + 1$

4.

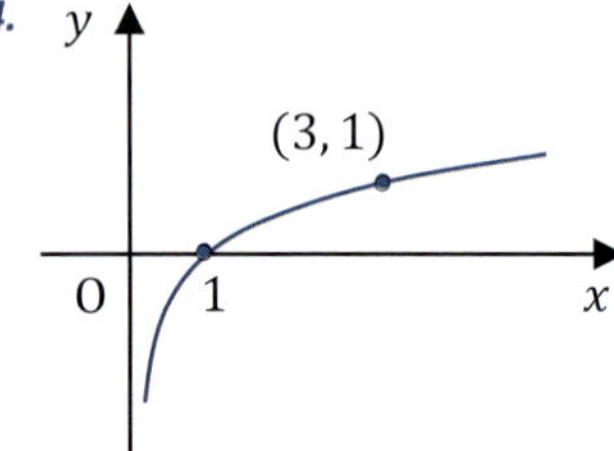

$f(x) = \log_5 x$

Sketch $y = f(x) + 2$

5.

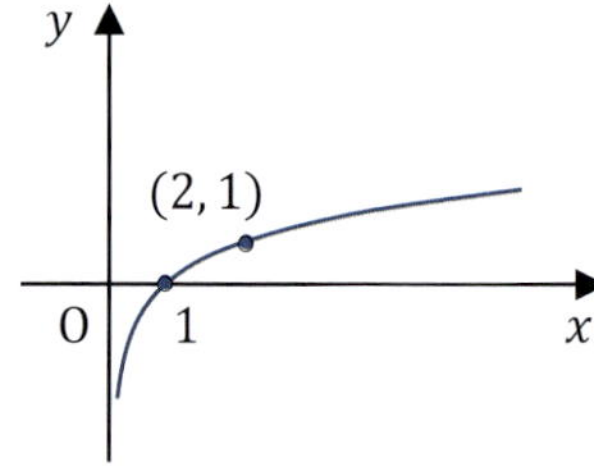

$f(x) = \log_2 x$

Sketch $y = 2 - f(x)$

6.

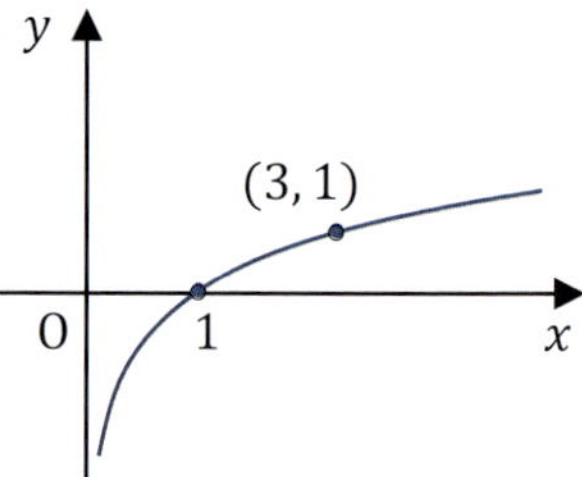

$f(x) = \log_3 x$

Sketch $y = -3f(x)$

7.

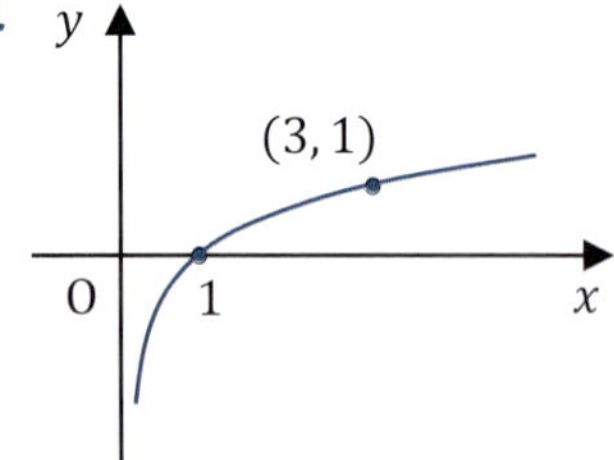

$f(x) = \log_3 x$

Sketch $y = f(2x)$

8.

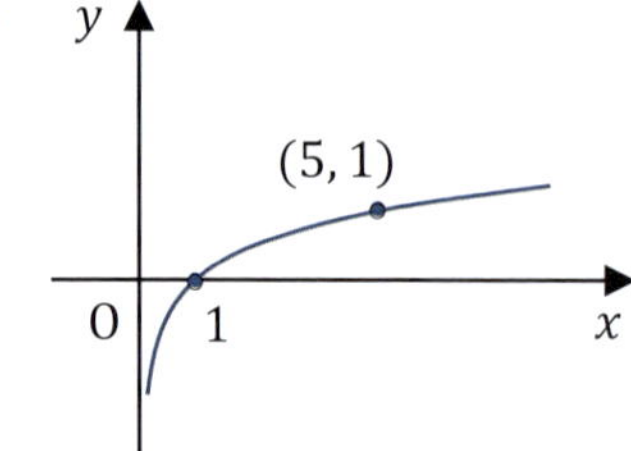

$f(x) = \log_5 x$

Sketch $y = 2f(x) - 2$

9.

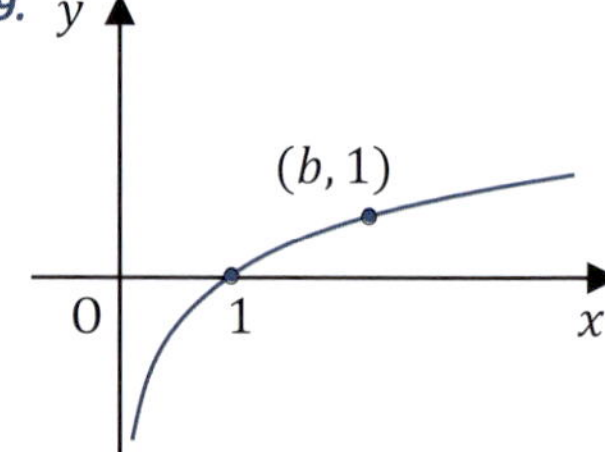

$f(x) = \log_b x$

Sketch $y = f(-x) + 1$

10.

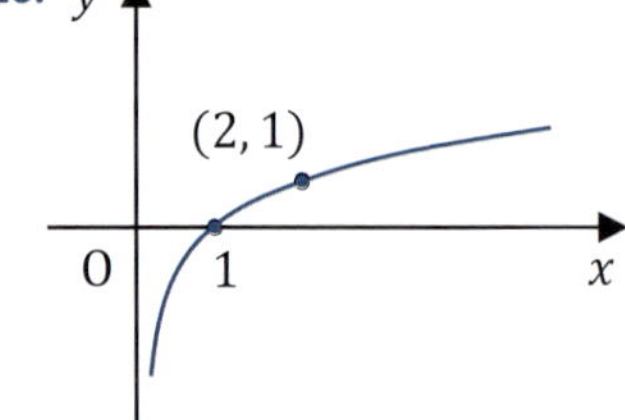

$f(x) = \log_2 x$

Sketch $y = 3 - 2f(x)$

11.

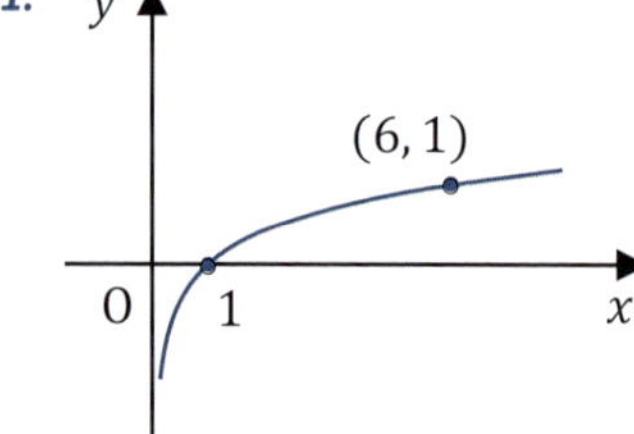

$f(x) = \log_6 x$

Sketch $y = 3f(-2x)$

12.

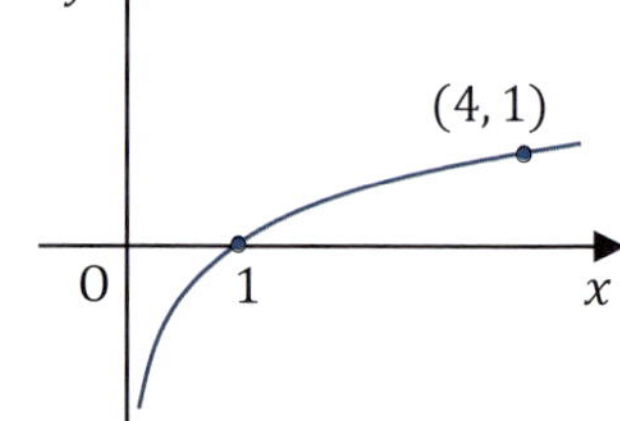

$f(x) = \log_4 x$

Sketch $y = 1 - f(x + 2)$

15.6 Evaluating Expressions Using the Laws of Logarithms

The Laws of Logarithms

There are five laws when using logarithms that are useful for evaluating expressions and solving equations. These laws should be memorised. They are directly related to the laws of indices (exponents), which may help in memorisation.

The First Law:

When two logarithms of the same base are added, the argument is multiplied.

$$\log_a b + \log_a c = \log_a bc$$

This is related to $a^{b+c} = a^b \times a^c$.

The Second Law:

When two logarithms of the same base are subtracted, the argument is divided.

$$\log_a b - \log_a c = \log_a \frac{b}{c}$$

This is related to $a^{b-c} = a^b \div a^c$.

The Third Law:

When the argument of a logarithm is raised to a power, this is equivalent to multiplying the logarithm by the power.

$$\log_a b^c = c \log_a b$$

This is related to $(a^b)^c = a^{bc}$.

The Fourth Law:

When the argument of a logarithms is 1, the answer is zero.

$$\log_a 1 = 0$$

This is related to $a^0 = 1$.

The Fifth Law:

When the argument is the same as the base, the answer is one.

$$\log_a a = 1$$

This is related to $a^1 = a$.

Worked Examples:

Evaluate:

1. $\log_{10} 4 + \log_{10} 25$
2. $\log_6 108 - \log_6 3$
3. $\log_3 3 + 2\log_3 6 - \log_3 4$

Solutions:

1. $\log_{10} 4 + \log_{10} 25$

$= \log_{10}(4 \times 25)$

$= \log_{10} 100$

$= 2$

2. $\log_6 108 - \log_6 3$

$= \log_6 \left(\frac{108}{3}\right)$

$= \log_6 36$

$= 2$

3. $\log_3 3 + 2\log_3 6 - \log_3 4$

$= 1 + \log_3 \left(\frac{6^2}{4}\right)$

$= 1 + \log_3 \left(\frac{36}{4}\right)$

$= 1 + \log_3 9$

$= 3$

Exercise 15.6

1. Evaluate:

(a) $\log_4 8 + \log_4 2$ (b) $\log_{10} 5 + \log_{10} 20$ (c) $\log_2 8 + \log_2 4$

(d) $\log_6 12 + \log_6 3$ (e) $\log_8 32 + \log_8 2$ (f) $\log_4 8 + \log_4 32$

2. Evaluate:

(a) $\log_3 36 - \log_3 4$ (b) $\log_5 50 - \log_5 2$ (c) $\log_{10} 300 - \log_{10} 3$

(d) $\log_4 320 - \log_4 5$ (e) $\log_3 162 - \log_3 6$ (f) $\log_7 147 - \log_7 3$

3. Evaluate:

(a) $\log_2 8^3$ (b) $\log_3 27^4$ (c) $\log_5 125^6$

(d) $\log_4 16^3$ (e) $\log_2 32^6$ (f) $\log_3 81^5$

4. Evaluate:

(a) $\log_3 12 + \log_3 3 - \log_3 4$ (b) $\log_5 10 + \log_5 10 - \log_5 4$ (c) $3\log_4 2 + \log_4 2$

(d) $2\log_6 3 + \log_6 4$ (e) $4\log_8 2 + \log_8 2$ (f) $\log_6 9 + \frac{1}{2}\log_6 16$

(g) $2\log_6 3 + \log_6 8 - \log_6 2$ (h) $\log_8 256 - \frac{1}{2}\log_8 16$ (i) $\log_5 5 + \log_5 20 - \frac{1}{3}\log_5 64$

5. Evaluate:

(a) $\log_2 24 - \frac{1}{2}\log_2 9$ (b) $\log_3 36 + \log_3 2 - \frac{1}{2}\log_3 64$ (c) $2\log_{10} 5 + \frac{1}{2}\log_{10} 16$

(d) $\frac{1}{2}\log_4 36 + 3\log_4 2 - \log_4 3$ (e) $\log_5 1.5 + 2\log_5 10 - \log_5 2$ (f) $3\log_4 4 + \log_4 2 - 3\log_4 2$

15.7 Solving Logarithmic Equations Using the Laws of Logarithms

The laws of logarithms can also be used to solve logarithmic equations. It should be noted that there is often more than one way to solve each equation.

Worked Examples:

Solve:

1. $\log_3 12 + \log_3 x = \log_3 36$

$$\log_3 12x = \log_3 36$$
$$12x = 36$$
$$x = 3$$

2. $\text{Log}_5 x - \log_5 25 = \log_2 2$

$$\log_5\left(\frac{x}{25}\right) = 1$$
$$\frac{x}{25} = 5$$
$$x = 125$$

3. $\text{Log}_3(x+1) + \log_3 6 = 2$

$$\log_3(6x+6) = \log_3 9$$
$$6x + 6 = 9$$
$$x = \frac{1}{2}$$

Exercise 15.7A

1. Solve:

(a) $\log_4 8 + \log_4 x = \log_4 24$ (b) $\log_3 x - \log_3 5 = \log_3 2$ (c) $\log_2 11 + \log_2 x = \log_2 33$

(d) $\log_5 21 - \log_5 x = \log_5 3$ (e) $2\log_3 4 + \log_3 x = \log_3 4$ (f) $3\log_{10} 3 - \log_{10} x = \log_{10} 9$

2. Solve:

(a) $\log_3 2 + \log_3 x = \log_2 16$ (b) $\log_5 x - \log_5 5 = \log_3 27$ (c) $2\log_3 4 + \log_3 x = \log_2 16$

(d) $3\log_6 2 - \log_6 x = \log_{16} 4$ (e) $\log_7 x - 2\log_7 2 = \log_3 1$ (f) $4\log_8 2 + \log_8 x = \log_2 2$

3. Solve:

(a) $\log_5 3 + \log_5(x-2) = \log_5 9$

(b) $\log_2 6 + \log_2(2x-1) = \log_2 4$

(c) $\log_3(4x+2) + \log_3 3 = \log_3 12$

(d) $\log_4(3x-1) + \log_4 2 = \log_4 22$

(e) $\log_7(2x+1) - \log_7 3 = \log_7 5$

(f) $\log_{10}(2-3x) + \log_{10} 3 = \log_{10} 21$

(g) $\log_5 14 - \log_5(3x+2) = \log_2 4$

(h) $\log_6 5 - \log_6(4x+1) = \log_6 6$

(i) $\log_5(x+1) + \log_5 4 = 2\log_{81} 3$

(j) $\log_9 5 - \log_9(2x-1) = \log_4 64$

Worked Examples:

Solve:

1. $\log_3 x + \log_3(x+2) = 1$

$$\log_3(x^2+2x) = \log_3 3$$
$$x^2+2x = 3$$
$$x^2+2x-3 = 0$$
$$(x+3)(x-1) = 0$$
$$\cancel{x=-3}, x = 1$$

2. $\log_3(x-1) + \log_3(x+5) = 3$

$$\log_3(x-1)(x+5) = \log_3 27$$
$$(x-1)(x+5) = 27$$
$$x^2+4x-5-27 = 0$$
$$x^2+4x-32 = 0$$
$$(x+8)(x-4) = 0$$
$$\cancel{x=-8},\ x = 4$$

In both examples, one of the solutions has been discarded, this is because the logarithm of a negative value does not exist. In general, if we have $\log_a(x \pm b)$, $x \pm b > 0$. In example 2, when $x = -8$, the bracket of both $\log_3(x-1)$ and $\log_3(x+5)$ would be negative.

Exercise 15.7B

1. Solve, where x is a real number:

(a) $\log_4 x + \log_4(x-3) = 1$

(b) $\log_3(x+2) + \log_3 x = 1$

(c) $\log_2 x + \log_2(x-1) = 1$

(d) $\log_5(x+1)^2 - \log_5 x = \log_5 4$

(e) $2\log_3(x+2) - \log_3 x = 2$

(f) $\log_2(x-3) + \log_2 x = 2$

(g) $\frac{1}{2}\log_2(x^2+12x+36) + \log_2 x = 4$

(h) $\log_3(x-7) + \log_3(x+7) = 2$

2. Solve, where x is a real number:

(a) $\log_2(x+4) + \log_2(x-2) = 4$

(b) $\log_3(x-5) + \log_3(x+3) = 2$

(c) $\log_2(x-5) + \log_2(x+2) = 3$

(d) $\log_6(x^2-1) - \log_6(x+1) = 2$

(e) $\log_2(x+3) + \log_2(x+3) = 4$

(f) $\log_4(x+8) + \log_4(x+2) = \log_2 4$

(g) $\log_5(x^2-9) - 3 = \log_5(x+3)$

(h) $\log_4(x+7) + \log_4(x+1) = 2$

Worked Examples:

1. Solve $\log_a 9 + \log_a 3 = 27$ where a is a real number:

Solutions:

$$\log_a 9 + \log_a 3 = 3$$

$$\log_a 3^2 + \log_a 3 = 3$$

$$2\log_a 3 + \log_a 3 = 3$$

$$3\log_a 3 = 3$$

$$\log_a 3 = 1$$

$$a^1 = 3, \qquad \therefore a = 3$$

2. Solve $\log_2 x + \log_4 x = 3$

$$\log_2 x + \log_4 x = 3$$

$$\log_2 x + \log_2 x^{\frac{1}{2}} = 3$$

$$\log_2 x + \frac{1}{2}\log_2 x = 3$$

$$\frac{3}{2}\log_2 x = 3$$

$$\log_2 x = 2$$

$$x = 4$$

Exercise 15.7C

1. Solve, where a is a real number:

(a) $\log_a 8 + \log_a 2 = 2$

(b) $\log_a 72 - \log_a 2 = 2$

(c) $2\log_a 8 - \log_a 2 = 5$

(d) $\log_a 20 - \log_a 50 = 3$

(e) $3\log_a 4 - \log_a 16 = \frac{1}{2}$

(f) $\log_a 375 - \log_a 3 = 3$

(g) $3\log_a 10 - \log_a 40 = 2$

(h) $\log_a 144 - \frac{1}{2}\log_a 16 = \frac{1}{2}$

(i) $\log_a 225 - 2\log_a 5 = \frac{3}{2}$

2. Solve:

(a) $\log_3 x + \log_9 x = 3$

(b) $\log_4 x - \log_{16} x = 1$

(c) $\log_2 x + \log_4 x = 3$

(d) $\log_4 x + \log_{64} x = 6$

(e) $\log_5 x - \log_{125} x = 2$

(f) $2\log_3 x - \log_{27} x = 5$

15.8 Exponential Growth and Decay

Exponential growth or decay are processes that take place over time, in which the rate of change of the function, **i.e.** the derivative of the function, is proportional to the current value. These functions appear in many different spheres, including the natural world, science, computing science and finance.

Examples of exponential growth could be the increase of a financial investment, the spread of a virus, the sales of a new toy or gadget or the 'going viral' of video, post, news article or meme on the internet.

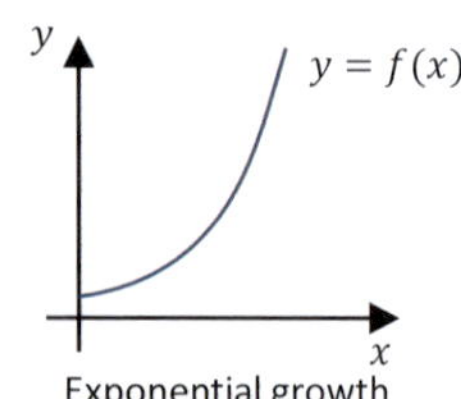

Exponential growth

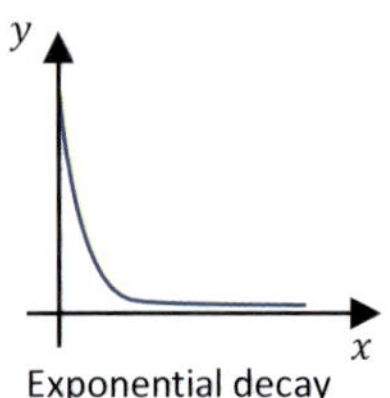

Exponential decay

Examples of exponential decay include many types of chemical reactions and the decay of radioactive materials.

When working with exponential growth and decay, we will primarily use the exponential function (e^x or $\exp x$) and the natural log function ($\ln x$ or $\log_e x$).

Worked Examples:

1. Evaluate $A(x) = 4e^{2x}$ when $x = 0$.

Solution: Substitute $x = 0$ into function.

$A(0) = 4e^0$

$A(0) = 4(1)$

$A(0) = 4$

2. Evaluate $A(x) = 12e^{-0.3x}$ when $x = 4$. Give your answer to two decimal places.

Solution: Substitute $x = 4$ into function.

$A(4) = 12e^{-0.3(4)}$

$A(4) = 3.61$ (2 d.p.)

Exercise 15.8A

1. Evaluate $A(x)$ when $x = 0$:

(a) $A(x) = 3e^x$
(b) $A(x) = 5e^x$
(c) $A(x) = 20e^{3x}$
(d) $A(x) = 4e^{12x}$

(e) $A(x) = 6e^{1.2x}$
(f) $A(x) = 19e^{-2.3x}$
(g) $A(x) = 11e^{-0.3x}$
(h) $A(x) = 100e^{-0.45x}$

(i) $A(x) = 50e^{-1.2x}$
(j) $A(x) = \frac{2}{3}e^{0.5x}$
(k) $A(x) = \frac{1}{4}e^{0.43x}$
(l) $A(x) = 8.4e^{-0.9x}$

2. Evaluate $A(x)$ given the following information:

(a) $A(x) = 4e^x$, when $x = 2$
(b) $A(x) = 10e^x$, when $x = 6$

(c) $A(x) = 8e^{2x}$, when $x = 3$
(d) $A(x) = 0.5e^{5x}$, when $x = 0.1$

(e) $A(x) = 4e^{1.5x}$, when $x = 2$
(f) $A(x) = 6e^{0.5x}$, when $x = 4$

(g) $A(x) = 20e^{-0.4x}$, when $x = 5$
(h) $A(x) = 100e^{-0.4x}$, when $x = 3$

Worked Examples:

3. Solve the following equations. Give your answer to two decimal places.

(a) $e^x = 27$
(b) $\frac{1}{2}e^{3x} = 6$

Solution: Put the equations into natural log form and solve with a calculator.

(a) $e^x = 27$

$\ln e^x = \ln 27$

$x = \ln 27$

$x = 3.30$ (2 d.p.)

(b) $\frac{1}{2}e^{3x} = 6$

$e^{3x} = 12$

$\ln e^{3x} = \ln 12$

$3x = \ln 12$

$3x = 2.48 \ldots$

$x = 0.83$ (2 d.p.)

NB: $\ln e^x = \log_e e^x = x$

Exercise 15.8B

1. Solve. Give your answer to two decimal places:

(a) $e^x = 10$ (b) $e^x = 8$ (c) $e^x = 14$ (d) $e^x = 200$

(e) $2e^x = 1$ (f) $8e^x = 6$ (g) $5e^x = 20$ (h) $2e^x = 5$

(i) $\frac{1}{2}e^x = 18$ (j) $\frac{1}{2}e^x = 50$ (k) $\frac{1}{2}e^x = 102$ (l) $\frac{1}{2}e^x = 962$

2. Solve. Give your answer to two decimal places:

(a) $3e^{2x} = 6$ (b) $4e^{5x} = 20$ (c) $6e^{4x} = 24$ (d) $7e^{3x} = 63$

(e) $2e^{0.4x} = 3$ (f) $40e^{0.5x} = 12$ (g) $280e^{-0.5x} = 20$ (h) $60e^{-0.3x} = 4000$

(i) $\frac{1}{2}e^{-0.64x} = 8000$ (j) $\frac{1}{4}e^{-0.58x} = 2080$ (k) $\frac{2}{3}e^{-0.75x} = 2100$ (l) $\frac{3}{2}e^{-0.89x} = 50{,}000$

Worked Examples:

1. The growth of a certain strain of bacteria, t hours after initial observation, is given by $B(t) = 6000e^{0.21t}$.

(a) Calculate the number of bacteria present at the beginning of the observation.

(b) How long would it take for the number of bacteria to double?

Solution:

(a) At the beginning of any exponential growth or decay problem, $t = 0$.

$B(0) = 6000e^{0.21(0)} = 6000$ bacteria

(b) For the bacteria to double $B(t) = 12{,}000$.

$$6000e^{0.21t} = 12{,}000$$
$$e^{0.21t} = 2$$
$$\ln e^{0.21t} = \ln 2$$
$$0.21t = \ln 2$$
$$t = \frac{\ln 2}{0.21}$$
$$t = 3.30 \text{ hours (2 d.p.)}$$

NB: In this type of question, doubling will always produce a value of 2 as this is 200% of the initial value, so the first line in part **(b)** is unnecessary.

2. The amount of radioactive substance in a sample of contaminated soil after t years is given by the equation $A(t) = A_0e^{-0.003t}$ where A_0 is the initial amount.

(a) After 40 years there was 78 grams of radiation in the sample. Calculate the amount of substance in the soil during initial observations.

(b) Calculate the half-life of the substance.

Solution:

(a) Substitute $t = 40$ and $A(t) = 78{,}000$

$78{,}000 = A_0e^{-0.003(40)}$

$78 = A_0(0.886\ldots)$

$A_0 = 87.94$ grams

(b) For the radioactive substance to decay to half its weight, $A(t)/A_0 = 0.5$.

$$e^{-0.003t} = 0.5$$

$$\ln e^{-0.003t} = \ln 0.5$$

$$e^{-0.003t} = \ln 0.5$$

$$-0.003t = -0.69\ldots$$

$$t = \frac{-0.69\ldots}{-0.003} = 231 \text{ years (3 s.f.)}$$

NB: As in example 1, a half-life will produce a value of 0.5 as this is 50% of the initial value.

Exercise 15.8C

1. The following functions show the exponential decay of a given value. Calculate the value of t required for each value to halve:

(a) $A(t) = 2e^{-0.03t}$ (b) $A(t) = 20e^{-0.04t}$ (c) $A(t) = 64e^{-0.001t}$ (d) $A(t) = 580e^{-0.069t}$

(e) $A(t) = 1.7e^{-0.058t}$ (f) $A(t) = 6.9e^{-0.0023t}$ (g) $A(t) = 576e^{-0.00401t}$ (h) $A(t) = 6980e^{-0.0033t}$

2. The following functions show the exponential growth of a given value. Calculate the value of t required for each value to double:

(a) $A(t) = 8e^{0.02t}$ (b) $A(t) = 15e^{0.4t}$ (c) $A(t) = 100e^{0.003t}$ (d) $A(t) = 65e^{0.005t}$

(e) $A(t) = 1.5e^{0.0043t}$ (f) $A(t) = 8.76e^{0.0065t}$ (g) $A(t) = 9.74e^{0.00038t}$ (h) $A(t) = 43{,}000e^{0.0041t}$

Exercise 15.8D

1. The growth of a certain strain of bacteria, t hours after initial observation, is given by $B(t) = 2800e^{0.14t}$.

   (a) Calculate the number of bacteria present at the beginning of the observation.

   (b) How long would it take for the number of bacteria to double?

2. The spread of a virus, t days after initial infection, is given by $A(t) = 8e^{0.2t}$.

   (a) Calculate the initial number of infections.

   (b) How long would it take for the number of infections to double?

3. The number of views of a viral video on the internet, t hours after it was first uploaded, can be modelled by the equation $V(t) = 56e^{0.23t}$.

   (a) Calculate the number of views when the video was first uploaded.

   (b) How long would it take for the number of views to treble?

4. The amount of a radioactive substance after t years is given by the equation $A(t) = 196e^{-0.042t}$.

   (a) Calculate the amount of radioactive substance at the beginning of observation.

   (b) Calculate the half-life of the radioactive substance.

5. The population P of a certain insect after t days is given by the equation, $P(t) = 32e^{0.081t}$.

(a) Calculate the population of insects at the beginning of the observation.

(b) How long would it take for the population to double?

6. The sales S of a new phone, t days after launch, is given by the equation $S(t) = S_0e^{0.67t}$.

(a) If 15,300 phones were sold on the second day after launch, how many were sold when the phone was launched?

(b) At this rate, how long would it take to sell 500,000 phones?

7. The number of views of an internet meme, t hours after it was posted online, is given by the equation, $A(t) = 42e^{kt}$.

(a) After 3 hours there are 6000 views. Find the value of k to two significant figures.

(b) At this rate, how long would it take to reach 1 million views?

8. The amount of chemical waste in a sample of contaminated river water after t days is given by the equation, $A(t) = A_0e^{-kt}$.

(a) After 28 days the amount of contaminant had reduced by half. Find the value of k to two significant figures.

(b) It is predicted that after 100 days, there will be less than 10% of the waste remaining in the water. Is this prediction correct? Justify your answer.

9. The amount of a radioactive substance R, after t years, is given by the equation, $R(t) = R_0e^{-kt}$.

(a) After 1.5 years half of the substance remains. Find the value of k to two significant figures.

(b) After 4 years there is 8 grams. Find the initial amount of radioactive substance.

10. The population P of an invasive weed in a conservation area, after t years, is modelled by the equation, $P(t) = 16e^{0.091t}$.

(a) Calculate the population of weeds at the beginning of the observation.

(b) At this rate, if left to grow, how long would it take for the population to reach 1000?

11. The sales of a new game on an app store, t days after launch, is given by the equation, $S(t) = S_0e^{0.14t}$.

(a) If 200,000 games were sold on the fifth day after launch, how many were sold when the game was launched?

(b) At this rate, how long would it take to sell 1 million games?

12. The number of views of an internet post, t hours after it was first posted online, is given by the equation, $A(t) = 17e^{kt}$.

(a) After 5 hours there are 11,000 views. Find the value of k to two significant figures.

(b) At this rate, how long would it take to reach 2 million views?

13. The amount of chemical waste in a sample of contaminated soil after t days is given by the equation, $A(t) = A_0e^{-kt}$.

(a) After 15 days the amount of contaminant had reduced by half. Find the value of k to two significant figures.

(b) It is predicted that, after 50 days, there will be less than 10% of the waste remaining in the soil. Is this prediction correct? Justify your answer.

15.9 Log-Linear & Log-Log Graphs (Experimental Data)

We have already studied the graphs of exponential functions. These graphs and graphs of other functions involving powers are not always useful in practical applications, as one of the variables can have very large values when compared with the other. A way to avoid this, is to use logarithms to produce a straight-line relationship with either the **$\log y$** and **x**, or **$\log y$** and **$\log x$**. With a straight-line relationship, it can be much simpler to estimate values and make predictions than when using an exponential graph.

In Higher Mathematics, we are primarily concerned with using the straight-line graph to identify the unknown values in an exponential function, or a function involving a power. A function of the form, **$y = ka^x$**, will take the form, **$\log y = x\log a + \log k$**.

This can be derived by taking logs of both sides of $y = ka^x$.

$$y = ka^x$$
$$\log y = \log ka^x$$
$$\log y = \log k + \log a^x$$
$$\log y = \log k + x\log a$$

We already know that a straight-line relationship takes the form, $y = mx + c$, so with a straight-line graph in the form, $\log y = x\log a + \log k$, we could say $Y = \log y$, $m = \log a$ and the c is the Y-intercept. We can then use this information to calculate the unknown values.

Worked Example:

Two variables x and y are related by the equation, $y = ka^x$. When $\log y$ is plotted against x, a straight line passing through the points $(0, 2)$ and $(3, 11)$ is obtained.

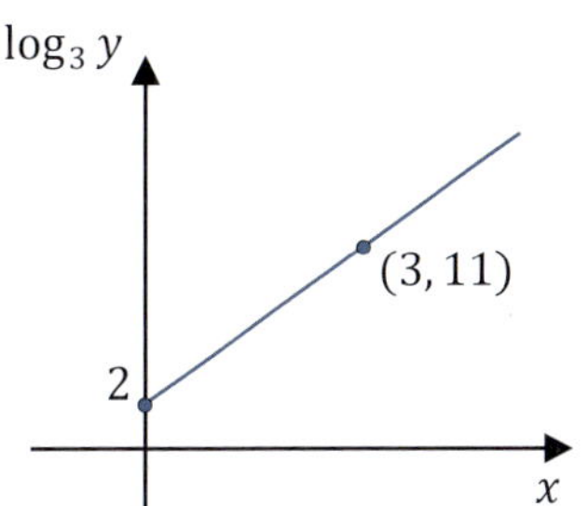

Find the values of k and a.

Solution:

Step 1: Express $y = ka^x$ in logarithmic form.

$\log_3 y = x \log_3 a + \log_3 k$

Step 2: Determine k.

$\log_3 k = 2 \therefore k = 9$

Step 3: Determine m. This can be done using the gradient formula with the two coordinates or by substitution of $\log_3 k$ and the other coordinate.

$$11 = 3\log_3 a + 2$$
$$9 = 3\log_3 a$$
$$3 = \log_3 a$$
$$a = 27$$

NB: If there is no Y-intercept given, then the values can be found by substitution and simultaneous equations, or by using the gradient formula to calculate $\log a$ then substitution.

$\therefore k = 9, a = 27$ and $y = 27(3)^x$

Exercise 15.9A

Two variables x and y are related by the equation $y = ka^x$. The graph in each of the following is a straight line. Find the values of k and a:

1.
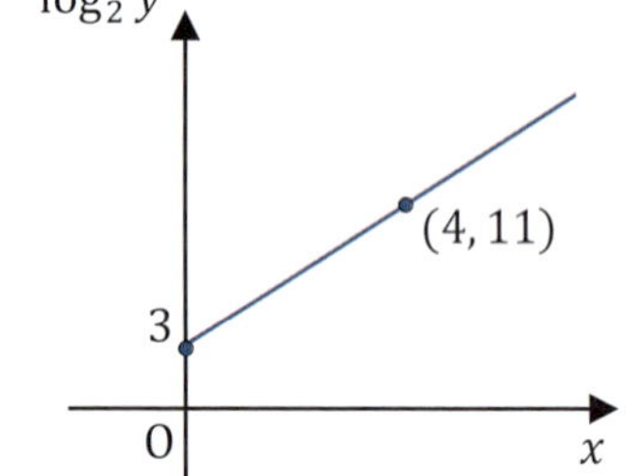

2.
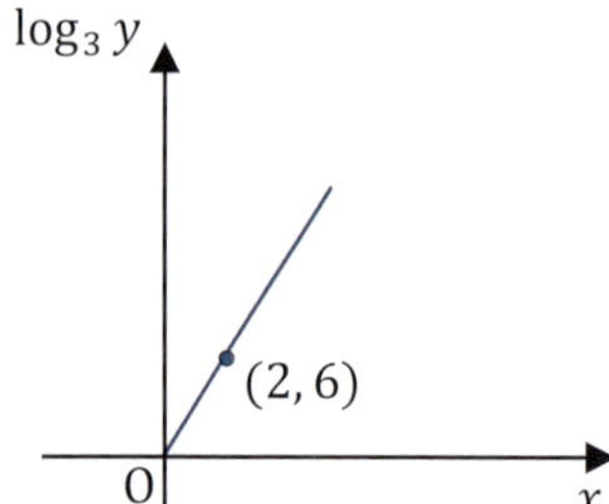

3.
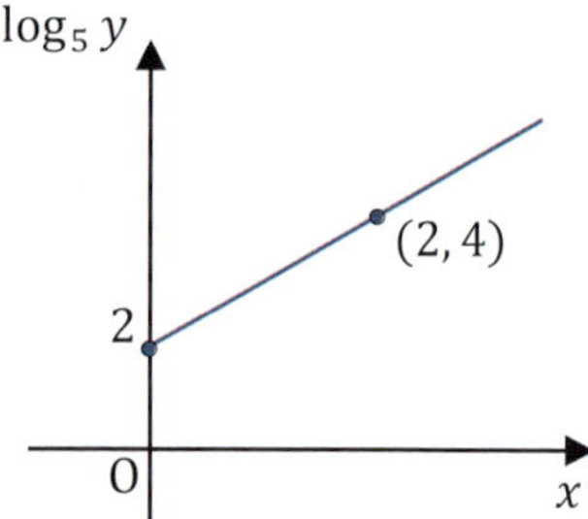

4.
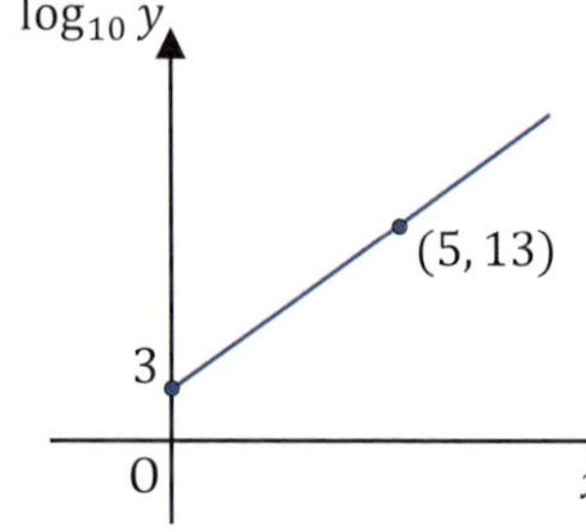

5.
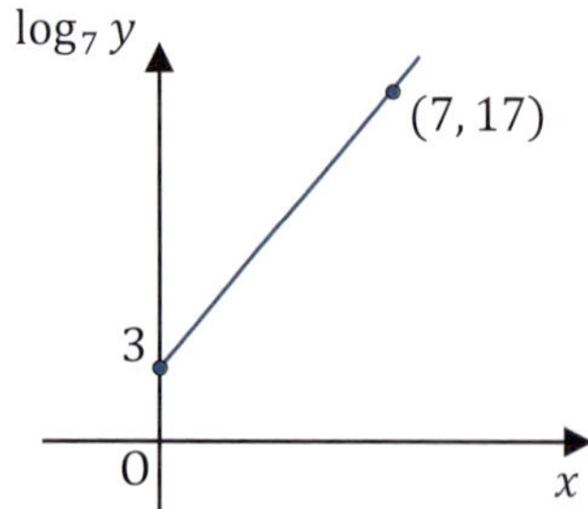

6.
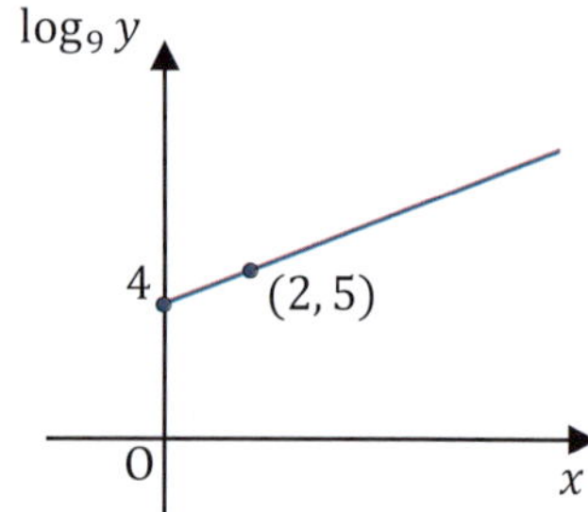

7.
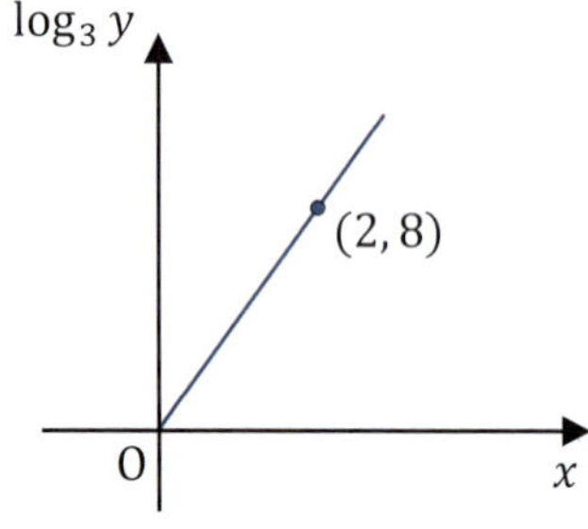

8.
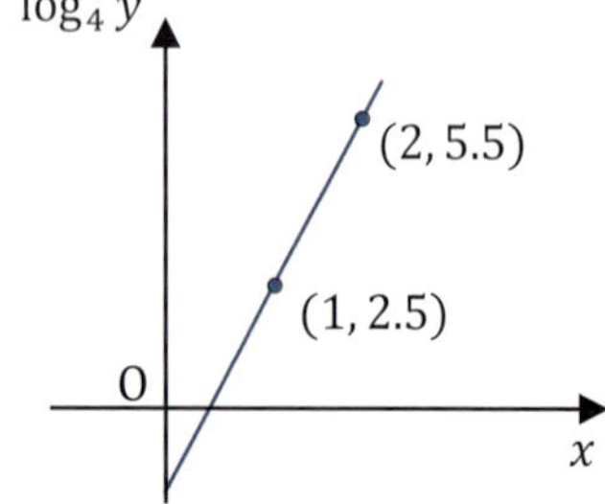

9.
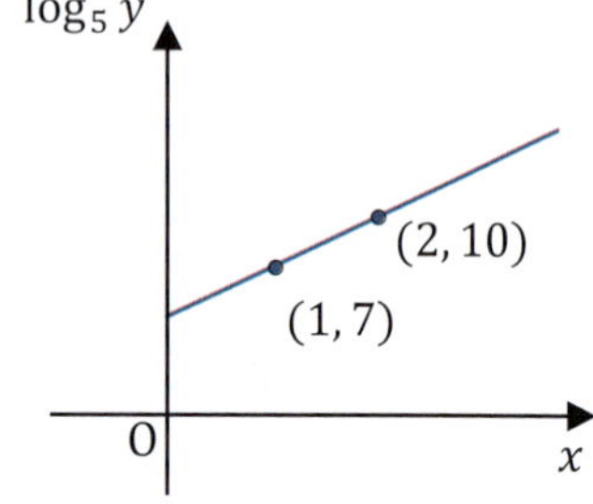

We can also express functions that involve non-variable powers in the form $\boldsymbol{y = kx^n}$ as straight-line relationships. These will take the form $\boldsymbol{\log y = n \log x + \log k}$.

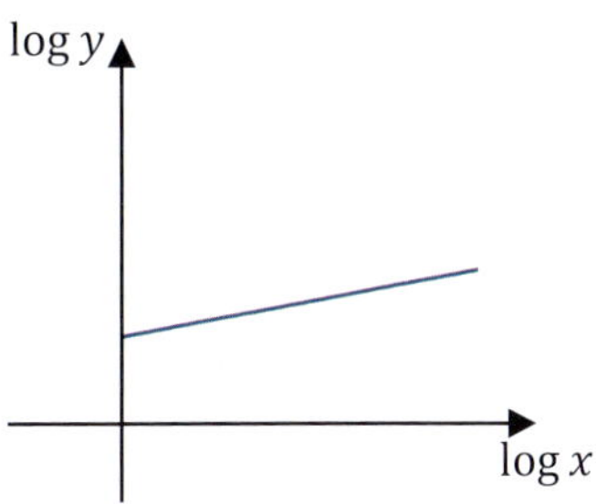

We can derive by taking logs of both sides of $y = kx^n$.

$$y = kx^n$$
$$\log y = \log kx^n$$
$$\log y = \log k + \log x^n$$
$$\log y = \log k + n \log x$$

As before, the equation of a straight-line takes the form, $\boldsymbol{y = mx + c}$, so with a straight-line graph in form $\boldsymbol{\log y = n \log x + \log k}$, where $\boldsymbol{Y = \log y}$, $\boldsymbol{n = m}$ and $\boldsymbol{c = \log k}$.

Worked Example:

Two variables x and y are related by the equation $y = kx^n$. When $\log y$ is plotted against $\log x$, a straight line passing through the points $(0, 2)$ and $(3, 11)$ is obtained.

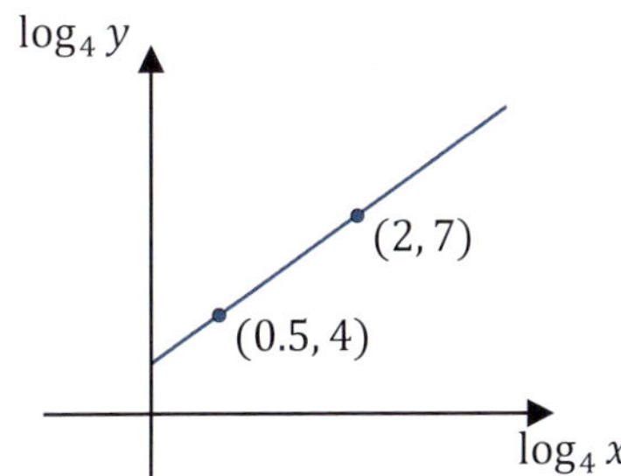

Find the values of k and n.

Solution:

Step 1: Express $y = kx^n$ in logarithmic form.

$\log_4 y = n \log_4 x + \log_4 k$

Step 2: Either use the same method as before, calculating m, or substitute the coordinates and solve simultaneously.

	$7 = 2m + \log_4 k$	**(A)**	Substitute $m = 2$ into **(A)**
	$4 = 0.5m + \log_4 k$	**(B)**	$7 = 4 + \log_4 k$
(A) – (B)	$3 = 1.5m$		$3 = \log_4 k$
	$\therefore m = 2$		$k = 4^3 = 64$

$\therefore k = 64, m = 2$ and $y = 64x^2$

Exercise 15.9B

Two variables x and y are related by the equation $y = kx^n$. The graph in each of the following is a straight line. Find the values of k and n:

1. 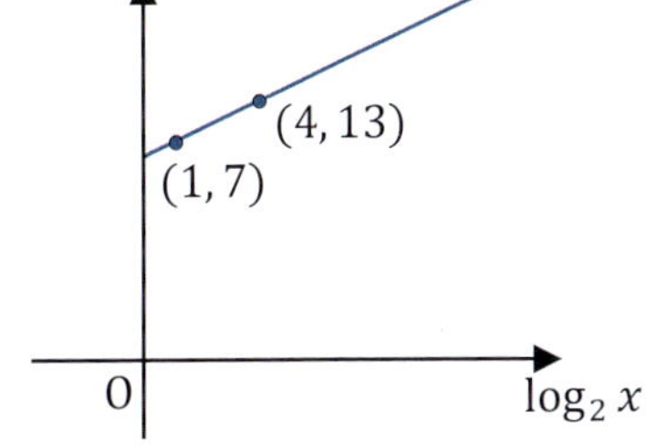

2. 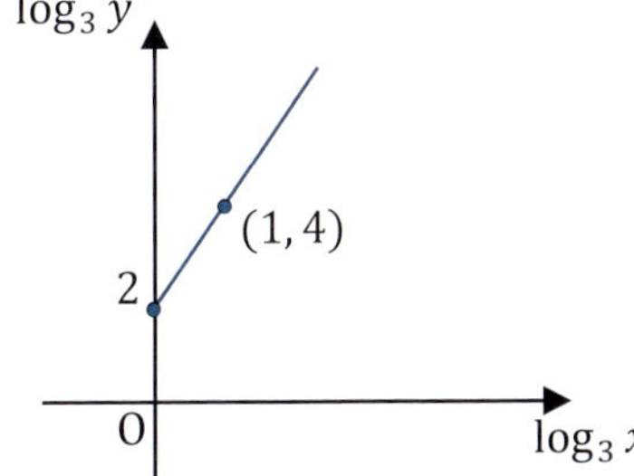

3. 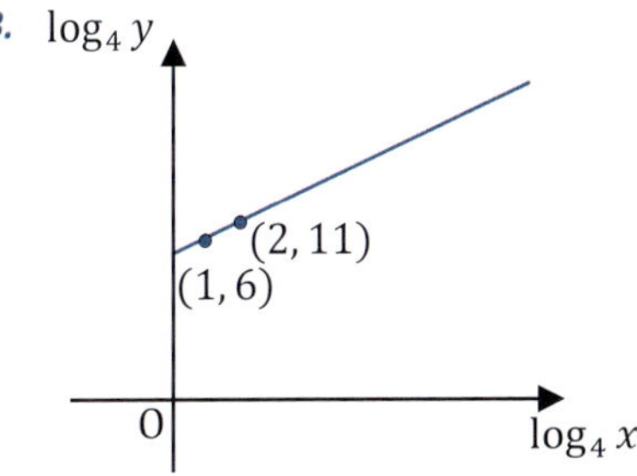

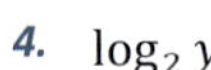

4.

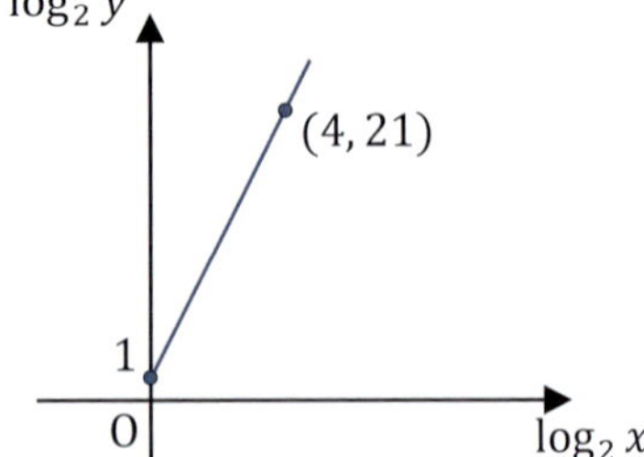

5.

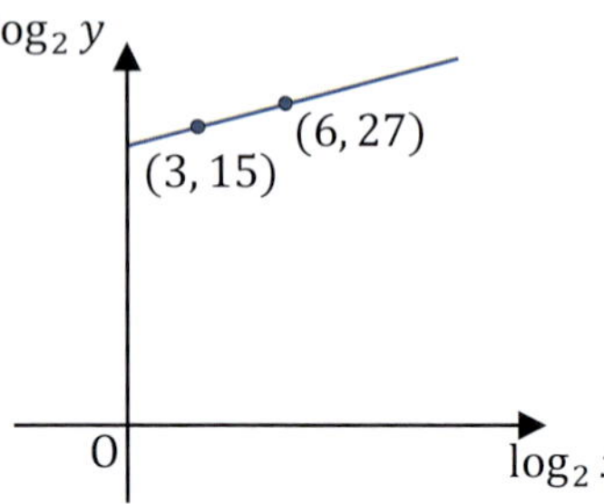

6.

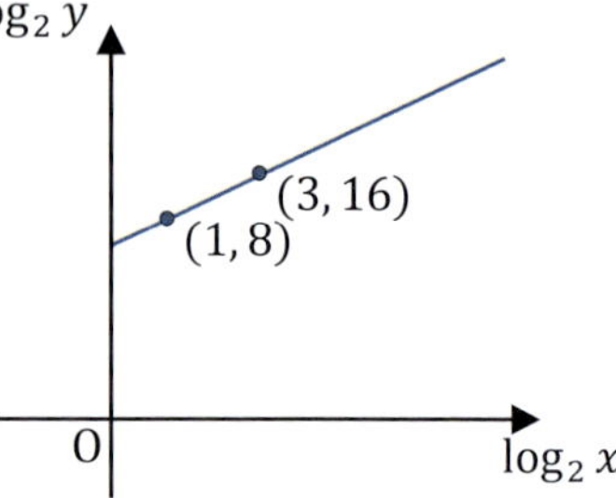

7.

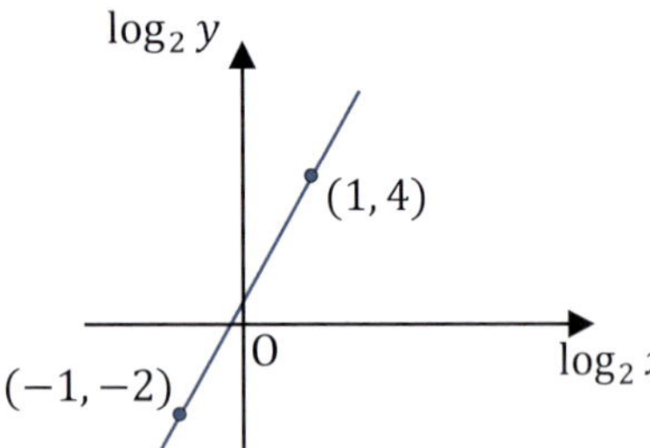

8.

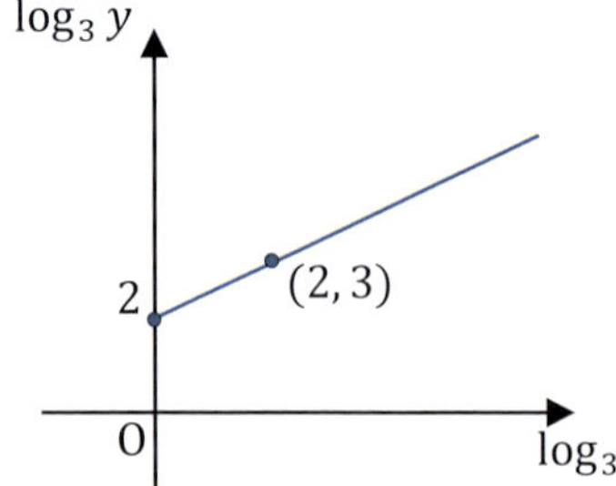

9.

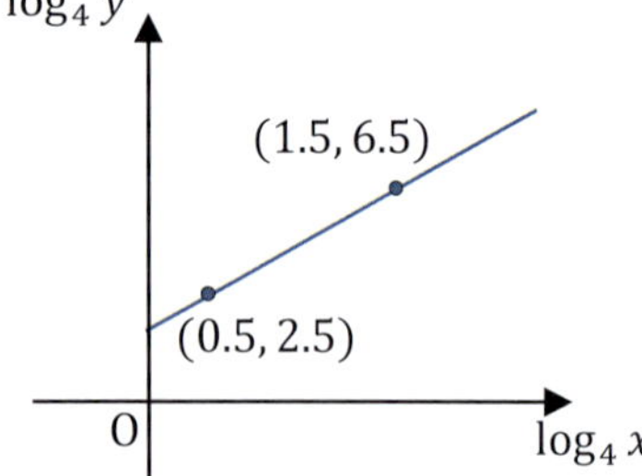

15.10 Review

Exercise 15.10

15.1

(a) Find: **(i)** $3^a = 9$ **(ii)** $2^a = \frac{1}{8}$ **(iii)** $a^3 = \frac{1}{64}$

(b) Evaluate: **(i)** $\log_5 1$ **(ii)** $\log_4 15$ **(iii)** $\log_3\left(\frac{1}{27}\right)$

15.2 The function f is of the form given. The graph of $y = f(x)$ is shown.
For each question, write down the equation of f:

(a)

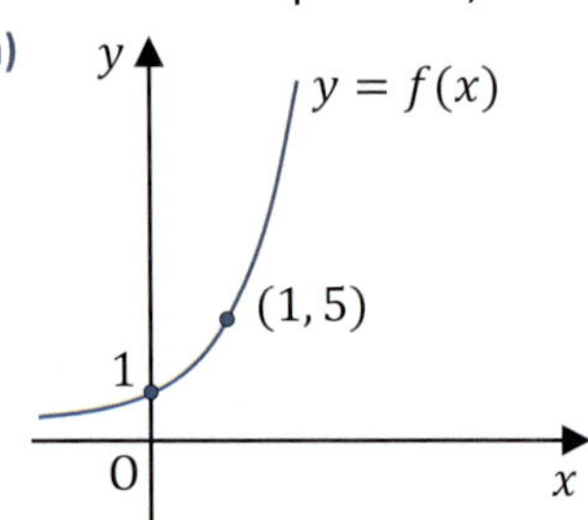

$f(x) = a^x$

(b)

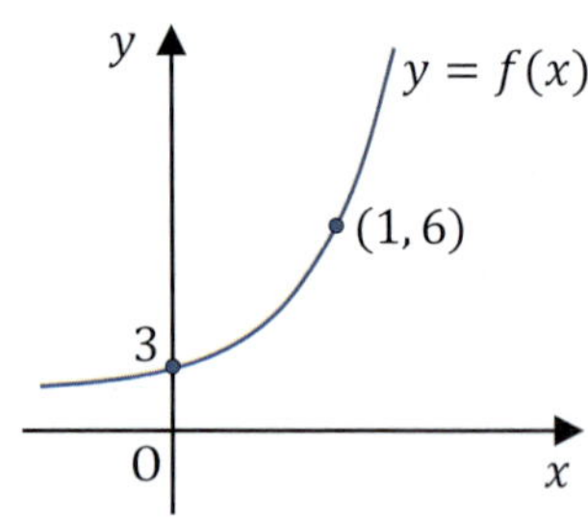

$f(x) = a^x \pm b$

(c)

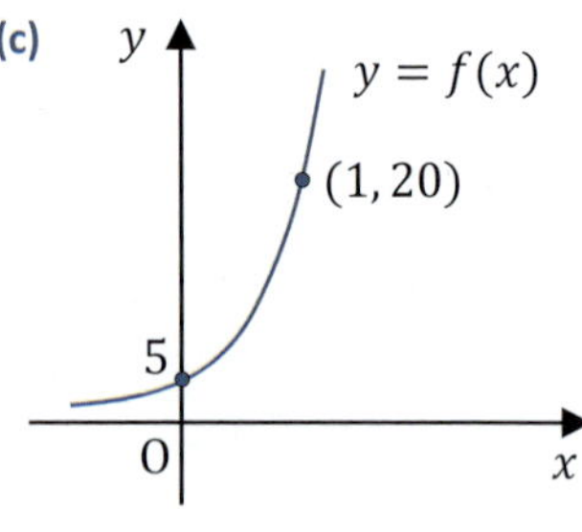

$f(x) = ba^x$

(d) y (4, 2) 0 1 x

$f(x) = \log_a x$

(e)

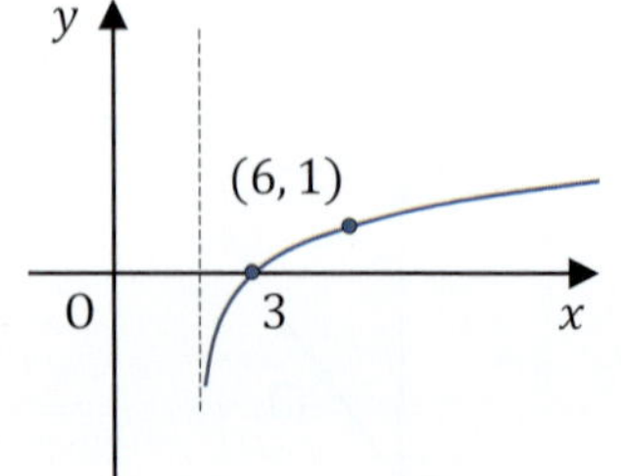

$f(x) = \log_a(x - b)$

(f)

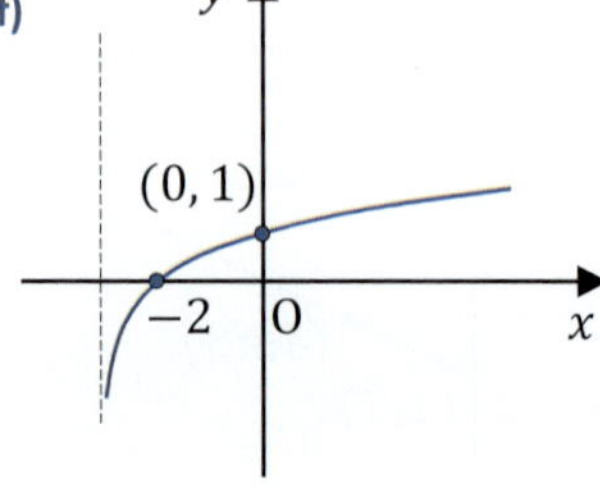

$f(x) = \log_a(x + b)$

15.3 Sketch and annotate the graph of $y = f(x)$ for the given functions:

(a) $f(x) = 8^x$ **(b)** $f(x) = 0.5^x$ **(c)** $f(x) = \log_6 x$ **(d)** $f(x) = \log_{10} x$

15.4 Sketch and annotate the graph of $y = f^{-1}(x)$ for the given functions:

(a) $f(x) = 6^x$ **(b)** $f(x) = 3^x$ **(c)** $f(x) = \log_5 x$ **(d)** $f(x) = \log_4 2x$

15.5 In each of the following diagrams the graph of $y = f(x)$ is shown.

Sketch the graph with the given transformation:

(a)

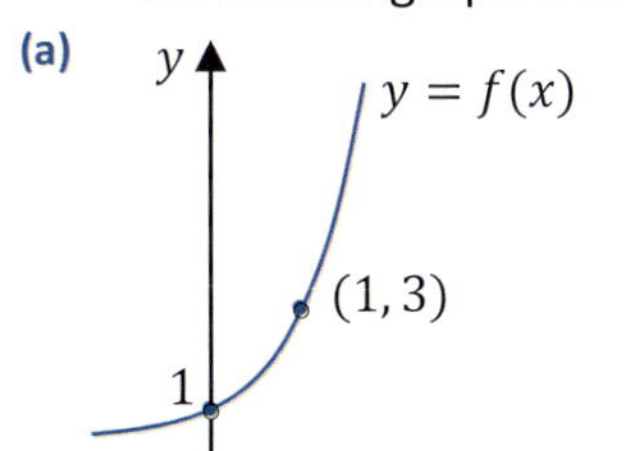

$f(x) = 3^x$

Sketch $y = f(x) - 2$

(b)

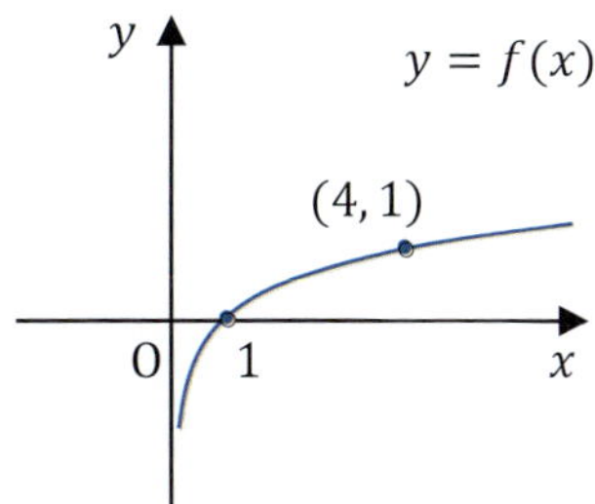

$f(x) = \log_4 x$

Sketch $y = f(x-1) + 2$

(c)

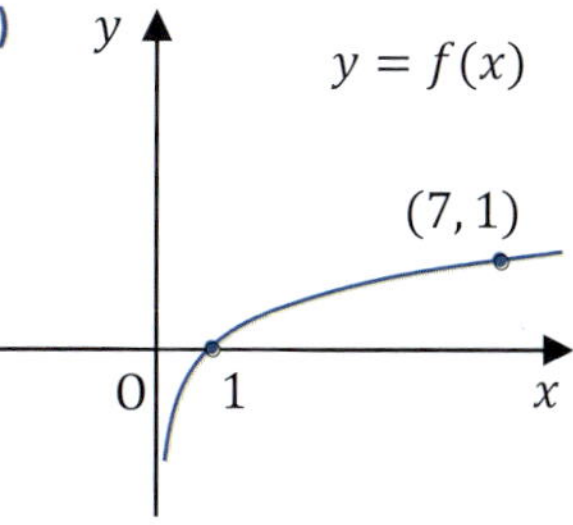

$f(x) = \log_7 x$

Sketch $y = 3 - f(x+1)$

15.6 Evaluate:

(a) $\log_2 32 - \log_2 16$ **(b)** $\log_4 48 + \log_4 2 - \log_4 6$ **(c)** $2\log_5 100 + \frac{1}{2}\log_5 16$

15.7 Solve:

(a) $\log_4 3 + \log_4 x = \log_4 24$ **(b)** $\log_2 4 - \log_2(x+2) = 2$

(c) $\log_3 x + \log_3(x+2) = 1$ **(d)** $4\log_a 3 - \log_a 9 = \frac{1}{2}$

15.8 The number of views of a viral video on the internet t hours after it was first uploaded can be modelled by the equation $V(t) = 44e^{0.32t}$.

(a) Calculate the number of views when the video was first uploaded.

(b) How long would it take for the number of views to reach 1 million?

15.9 Two variables x and y are related by the equation $y = ka^x$. When $\log y$ is plotted against x, a straight line passing through the points $(0, 1)$ and $(4, 13)$ is obtained.

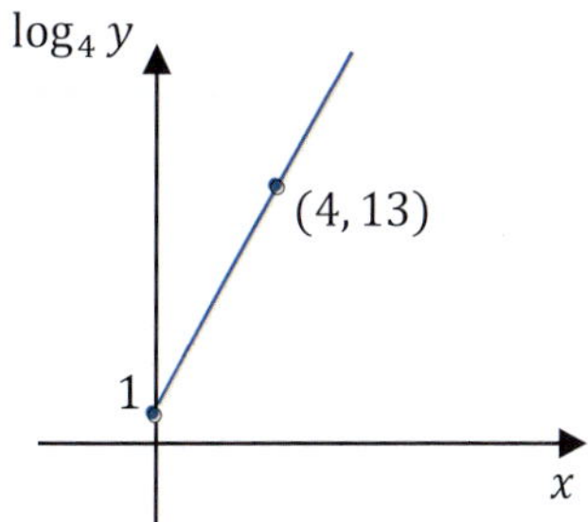

Find the values of k and a.

Chapter 16
Whole Course Revision

Whole Course Revision

This chapter focuses on preparation for the examination. All the skills in this chapter are Higher skills. There are two main sections covered in this chapter: Basic Skills (**16.1-16.4**) and Integrated & Reasoning Skills (**16.5**).

Most of the Higher Mathematics examination is given over to the demonstration of basic skills, so it is vital for all learners to be competent in this section.

Integrated Skills questions require a combination of skills from different topics. These questions are typically more difficult than basic skills. Reasoning Skills questions require careful reading and reasoning. These are possibly the most challenging of all the questions and may also contain a number of different skills in each question.

How to use this section

Each question number corresponds to the section of the book that the question is taken from. This is to help you as you revise and to target specific areas in need of improvement.

Step 1: Work through one exercise at a time and mark each exercise carefully.

Step 2: Take note of the section numbers of the questions that you have not answered correctly.

Step 3: Go to each section that you have answered incorrectly and practice these individual skills further.

Step 4: Use the Higher Mathematics Checklist (available to download from www.zetamaths.com), to check off each section where you are confident and identify the sections where you are in need of further practice.

16.1 Algebraic Skills Revision

Exercise 16.1A – Quadratic Functions and Graphs

2.4-5 Solve the following quadratic equations:

(a) $x^2 - 6 = 4x - x^2$ (b) $x^2 - 8 = 10 + 3x - 2x^2$ (c) $x^2 - 42 = 86 - x^2$

(d) $3x^2 + 8x = 1 - x^2$ (e) $3x^2 - 4x + 3 = 3x - x^2$ (f) $x^2 + 4x = 3x^2 - 11$

2.6 Express the following in the form $a(x+b)^2 + c$:

(a) $x^2 - 9x + 14$ (b) $8 + 7x - x^2$ (c) $4x^2 - 12x + 14$

2.7 Solve the following quadratic equations:

(a) $x^2 - 4x - 3 = 0$ (b) $x^2 - 4x - 20 = 0$ (c) $4x^2 - 16x + 3 = 0$

2.10 Solve the following quadratic inequations:

(a) $x^2 - 5x - 36 > 0$ (b) $x^2 - 4x - 21 < 0$ (c) $4x^2 - 15x \geq 4$

2.12 (a) The equation $2x^2 - 2kx + 3k = 0$ has two real distinct roots.
Determine the range of values for k.

(b) The equation $x^2 + (k+1)x + k = 0$ has equal roots.
Determine the of value(s) for k.

(c) The equation $x^2 + 4x - kx + 7 - k = 0$ has no real roots.
Determine the range of values for k.

2.13 In each of the following, show the line is a tangent to the curve and find the point of contact:

(a) $y = 5 - 3x$ and $y = x^2 + 5x + 21$ (b) $y = 6x + 4$ and $y = x^2 + 13$

2.14 In each of the following, determine whether the line and the curve intersect (justify your answer):

(a) $y = x - 2$ and $y = x^2 + x + 8$ (b) $y = 2x + 4$ and $y = x^2 + 3x - 8$

2.15 In each of the following, find the points of intersection between the line and the curve:

(a) $y = x - 5$ and $y = x^2 + 2x - 25$ (b) $y = 2x + 10$ and $y = x^2 - 14$

2.16 In each of the following, find the points of intersection between the two curves:

(a) $y = x^2 + 9x + 15$ and $y = 2x^2 + 3x - 1$ (b) $y = x^2 - 13$ and $y = 2x^2 - 6x - 8$

Exercise 16.1B – Functions

4.1A The following functions are defined on $\mathbb{R}$, the set of real numbers. State any restrictions on their domains:

(a) $f(x) = \dfrac{4}{x-2}$ (b) $f(x) = \dfrac{5x}{5-x^2}$ (c) $f(x) = \dfrac{4x-8}{x^2-2x-3}$

(d) $f(x) = \sqrt{8+x}$ (e) $f(x) = \sqrt{x^2-9}$ (f) $f(x) = \sqrt{5-2x}$

4.1B (a) A function f is defined by $f(x) = x^3 + 6$. The domain of f is $0 \leq x \leq 10, x \in \mathbb{R}$. State the range of the function.

(b) A function g is defined by $g(x) = 3x^3 - 2$. The domain of g is $0 \leq x \leq 5, x \in \mathbb{R}$. State the range of the function.

(c) A function h is defined by $h(x) = 6x^2 + 11$. The domain of f is $0 \leq x \leq 5, x \in \mathbb{R}$. State the range of the function.

4.3A (a) Functions f and g are defined on a suitable domain by $f(x) = x^3 + 4$ and $g(x) = 2x - 7$. Find an expression for $h(x)$ where $h(x) = g\big(f(x)\big)$.

(b) Functions f and g are defined on a suitable domain by $f(x) = 3x^2 - 9$ and $g(x) = 4x + 1$. Find an expression for $h(x)$ where $h(x) = g\big(f(x)\big)$.

(c) Functions f and g are defined on a suitable domain by $f(x) = \dfrac{3}{x-5}$ and $g(x) = \dfrac{2}{x-3}$. Find an expression for $h(x)$ where $h(x) = g\big(f(x)\big)$.

4.3B (a) Functions f and g are defined on suitable domain by $f(x) = 3x^2 - 1$ and $g(x) = 2x + 6$. Evaluate $g\big(f(-3)\big)$.

(b) Functions f and g are defined on suitable domain by $f(x) = 3x^3 - 12$ and $g(x) = 2x + 3$. Evaluate $f\big(g(-2)\big)$.

4.4 For each of the following, the function f is defined by $f(x)$, where $x \in \mathbb{R}$.
Determine an expression for $f^{-1}(x)$:

(a) $f(x) = \frac{5}{2}x - 4$ (b) $f(x) = \frac{4x - 8}{5}$ (c) $f(x) = \frac{2x^3 - 5}{6}$

Exercise 16.1C – Graphs of Functions

1. In each of the following diagrams the graph of $y = f(x)$ is shown. Sketch the graph with the given transformation:

(a)

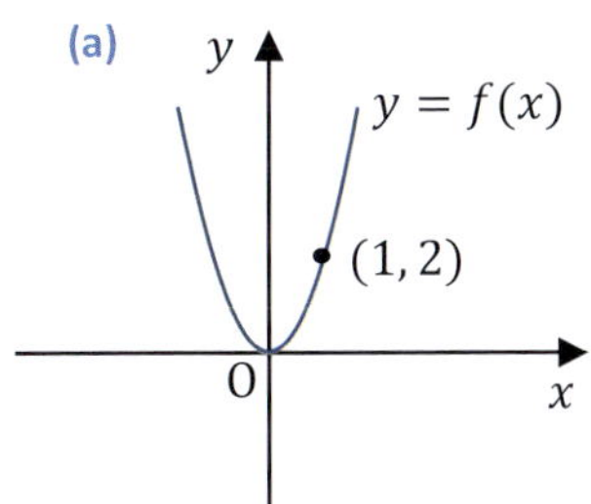

Sketch $y = f(x - 2) + 1$

(b)

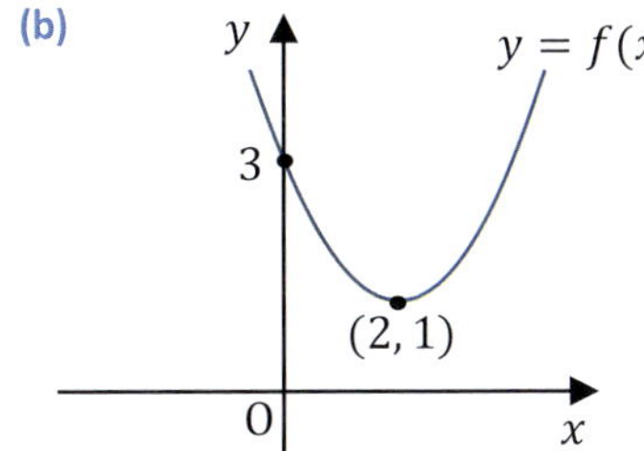

Sketch $y = 1 - 2f(x)$

(c)

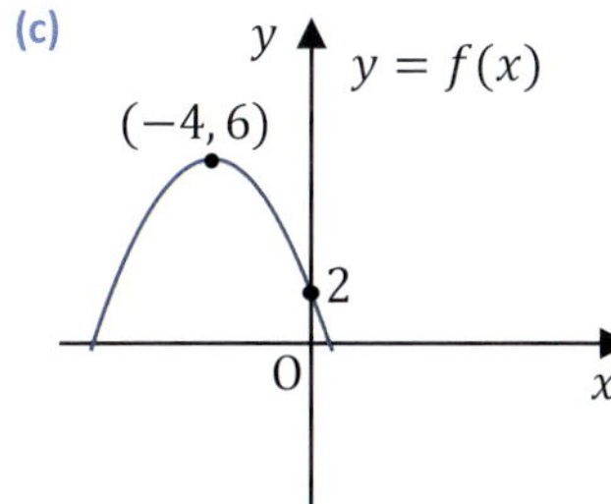

Sketch $y = \frac{1}{2}f(-2x)$

2. In each of the following diagrams the graph of $y = f(x)$ is shown. Sketch the graph with the given transformation:

(a)

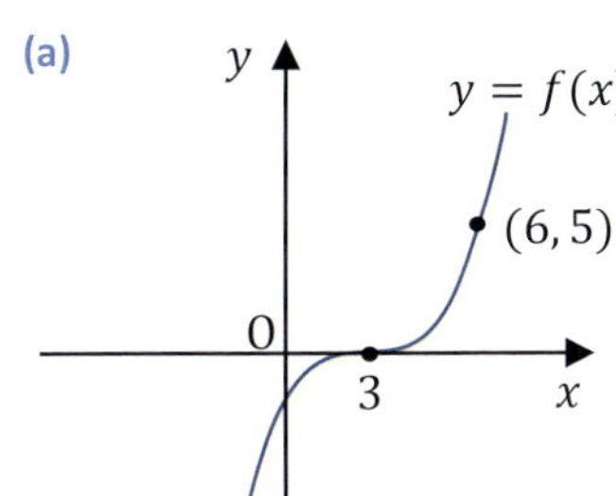

Sketch $y = f(x + 2) - 1$

(b)

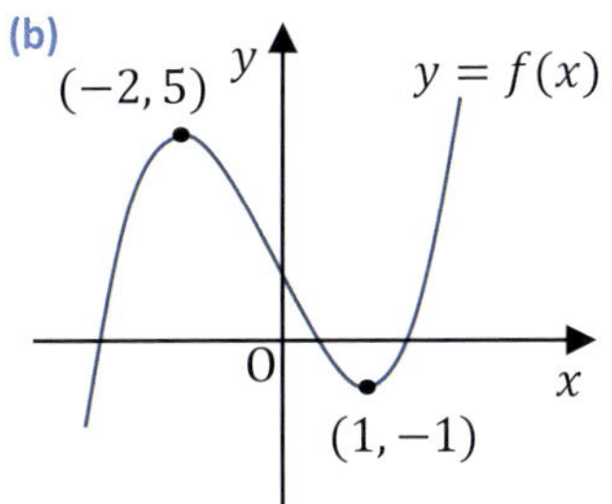

Sketch $y = 2 - f(x)$

(c)

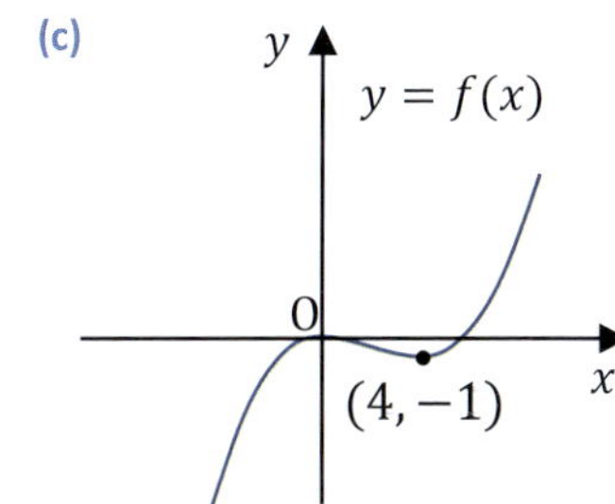

Sketch $y = 3f\left(\frac{1}{2}x\right)$

3. In each of the following diagrams the graph of $y = f(x)$ is shown. Sketch the graph with the given transformation:

(a)

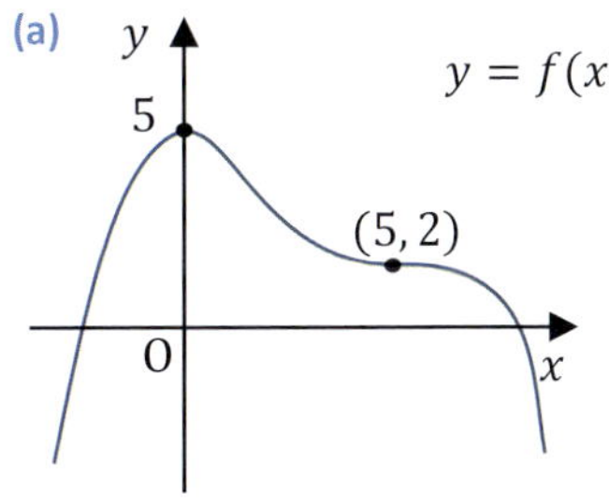

Sketch $y = f(x - 2) + 2$

(b)

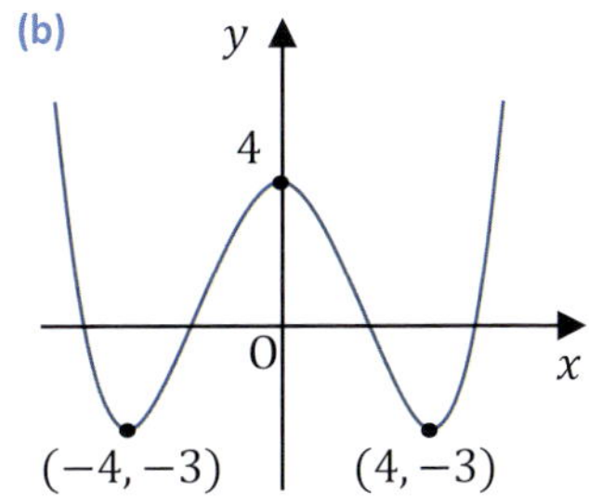

Sketch $y = 3 - 2f(x)$

(c)

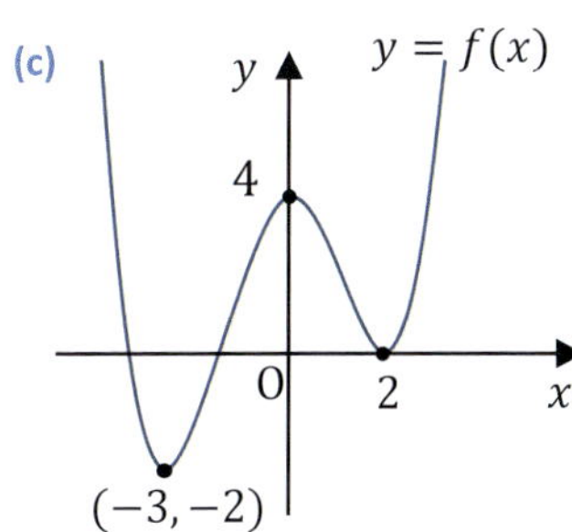

Sketch $y = 3f(-x)$

Exercise 16.1D – Recurrence Relations

6.1 For each of the following recurrence relations, calculate the value of u_4.

(a) $u_{n+1} = 2.6u_n + 30,\ u_0 = 82$ (b) $u_{n+1} = 0.5u_n - 90,\ u_0 = 3500$ (c) $u_{n+1} = 6u_n + 41, u_0 = 8$

6.2 The first three terms of the recurrence relation defined by $u_{n+1} = au_n + b$ are given in the following questions. Find the values of a and b:

(a) $32, 68, 140$ (b) $38, 68, 113$ (c) $28, 128, 628$

6.3A In each of the following recurrence relations, state whether the sequence has a limit as $n \to \infty$. Give a reason for your answer.

(a) $u_{n+1} = 5u_n + 13$ (b) $u_{n+1} = 0.35u_n - 12$ (c) $u_{n+1} = -0.8u_n + 8$

6.3B In each of the following recurrence relations, for what range of values of k does each sequence have a limit?

(a) $u_{n+1} = (k-2)u_n + 12$ (b) $u_{n+1} = (3-k)u_n - 9$ (c) $u_{n+1} = (2k-6)u_n + 4$

6.4 Calculate the limit of each of the following recurrence relations:

(a) $u_{n+1} = 0.3u_n + 70$ (b) $u_{n+1} = 0.7u_n + 450$ (c) $u_{n+1} = \frac{3}{5}u_n + 60$

6.5A A person takes out an £18,000 loan for a car with an interest rate of 5.8% per annum. Each year he pays back £4300. How much does he owe after four years of payments?

6.5B A forester sprays 500 litres of insecticide on an area of freshly planted trees. Each week 17% of the insecticide is lost to rain and evaporation, so the forester sprays a further 35 litres of insecticide.

(a) How much insecticide will there be after 7 weeks?

In order for the trees to survive in the long term, they need to retain 200 litres of the insecticide.

(b) Will the trees survive? Give a reason for your answer.

Exercise 16.1E - Polynomials

7.1 (a) Show that $(x-3)$ is a factor of $x^3 - 2x^2 - 5x + 6$.

(b) Show that $(x+2)$ is a factor of $x^3 + 3x^2 - 4x - 12$.

(c) Fully factorise: (i) $x^3 + 2x^2 - 11x - 12$ (ii) $x^3 + 2x^2 - 13x + 10$

7.2 Solve:

(a) $x^3 + x^2 - 9x - 9 = 0$ (b) $x^3 + 3x^2 - 9x - 27 = 0$ (c) $x^3 - 8x^2 + 11x + 20 = 0$

7.3 Find the remainder when:

(a) $x^3 - 8x^2 + 7$ is divided by $(x-3)$. (b) $x^3 - 4x^2 + 3x - 6$ is divided by $(x-2)$.

7.4. In each of the following, determine the values of a and b:

(a) For the polynomial $x^3 + 2x^2 + ax + b$, $(x + 1)$ is a factor and the remainder is 4 when the polynomial is divided by $(x + 2)$.

(b) For the polynomial $x^3 - x^2 + ax + b$, $(x + 2)$ is a factor and the remainder is 10 when the polynomial is divided by $(x - 3)$.

7.5 Find the coordinates of the points of intersection of the graphs with equations $y = f(x)$ and $y = g(x)$:

(a) $f(x) = x^3 + 6x^2 + 4x - 11$
$g(x) = 5x - 5$

(b) $f(x) = x^3 - x^2 + x + 3$
$g(x) = x^2 + 5x - 5$

(c) $f(x) = 2x^3 - x$
$g(x) = x^3 + 4x^2 - 4$

7.6 In each of the diagrams the graph of $y = f(x)$ is shown. Determine the equation of the function $f(x)$:

(a)

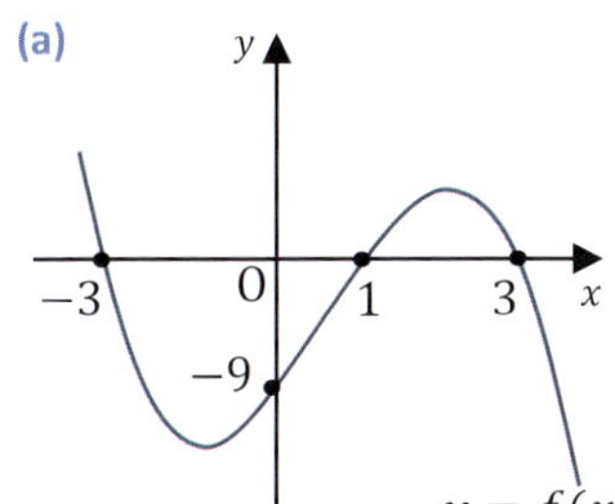

(b)

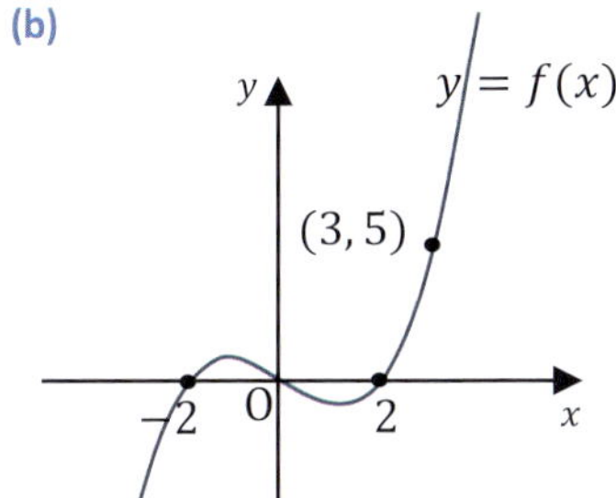

(c)

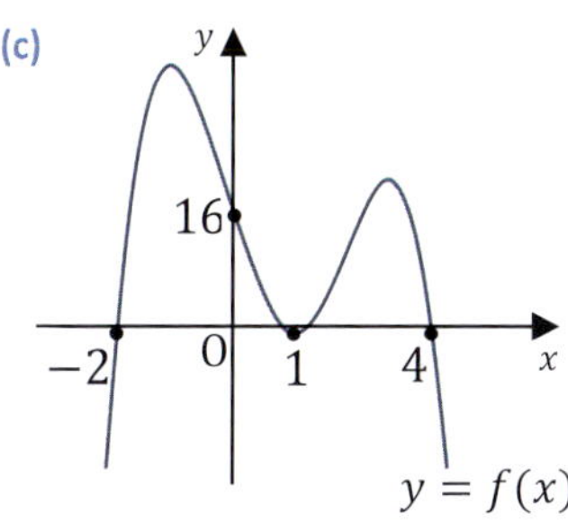

Exercise 16.1F – Logarithmic & Exponential Functions

15.1

(a) Find: (i) $4^a = 16$ (ii) $2^a = \frac{1}{16}$ (iii) $a^3 = \frac{1}{27}$

(b) Evaluate: (i) $\log_4 1$ (ii) $\log_5 125$ (iii) $\log_2\left(\frac{1}{32}\right)$

15.2A The function f is of the form given. The graph of $y = f(x)$ is shown.
Write down the equation of each f:

(a)

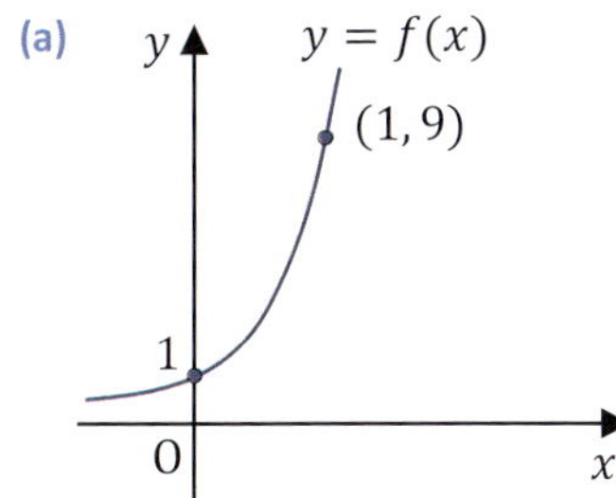

$f(x) = a^x$

(b)

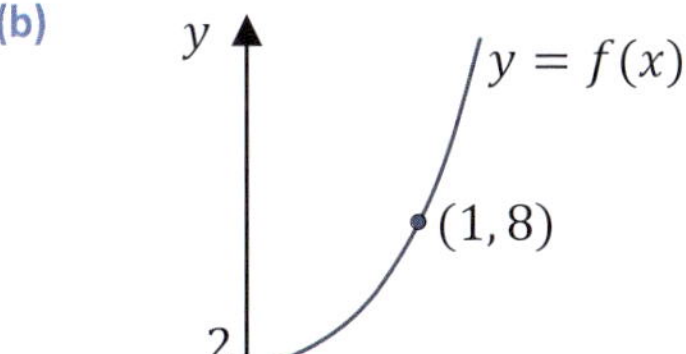

$f(x) = a^x \pm b$

(c)

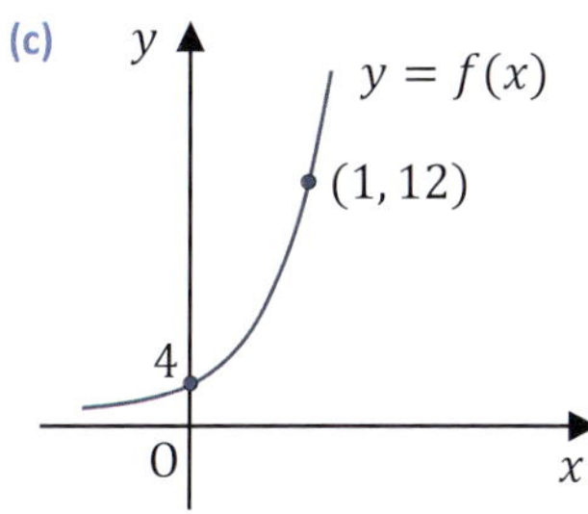

$f(x) = ba^x$

(d)

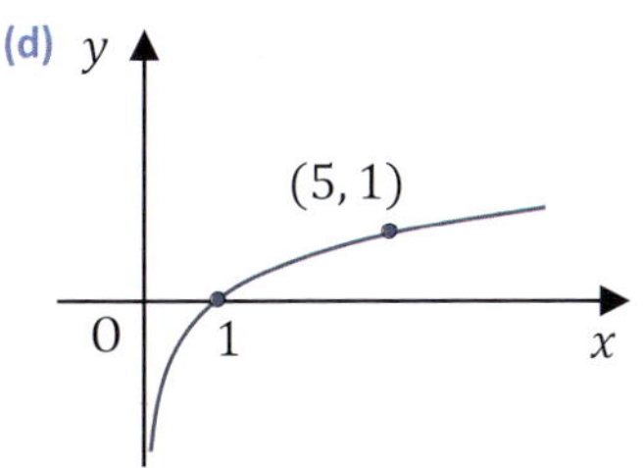

$f(x) = \log_a x$

(e) y (4, 1) 0 2 x

$f(x) = \log_a(x - b)$

(f) y (0, 1) −3 0 x

$f(x) = \log_a(x + b)$

15.3 Sketch and annotate the graph of $y = f(x)$ for the given functions:

(a) $f(x) = 7^x$ (b) $f(x) = 0.4^x$ (c) $f(x) = \log_5 x$ (d) $f(x) = \log_8 x$

15.4 Sketch and annotate the graph of $y = f^{-1}(x)$ for the given functions:

(a) $f(x) = 4^x$ (b) $f(x) = 2^x$ (c) $f(x) = \log_3 x$ (d) $f(x) = \log_4 2x$

15.5 In each of the following diagrams the graph of $y = f(x)$ is shown.
Sketch the graph with the given transformation:

(a)

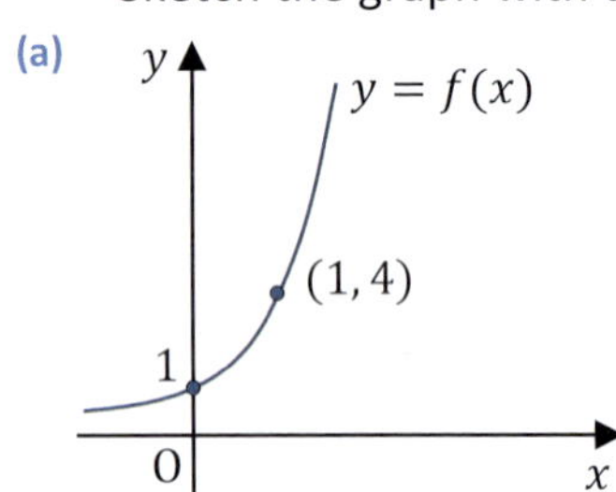

$f(x) = 4^x$
Sketch $y = f(x) - 1$

(b)

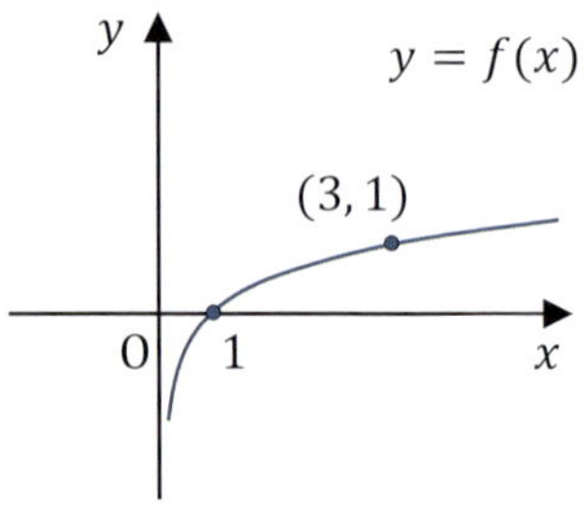

$f(x) = \log_3 x$
Sketch $y = f(x - 1) + 2$

(c)

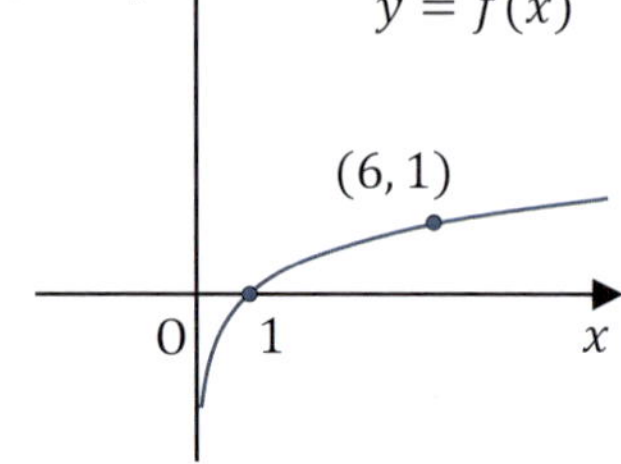

$f(x) = \log_6 x$
Sketch $y = 2 - f(x + 1)$

15.6 Evaluate:

(a) $\log_4 50 - \log_4 25$ (b) $\log_3 15 + \log_3 3 - \log_3 5$ (c) $2\log_{10} 5 + \frac{1}{2}\log_{10} 16$

15.7 Solve:

(a) $\log_6 2 + \log_6 3x = \log_6 24$ (b) $\log_2(2x - 6) - \log_2 3 = 4$

(c) $\log_4 x + \log_4(x - 3) = 1$ (d) $3\log_a 4 - \log_a 2 = \frac{5}{2}$

15.8 The spread of a virus t days after initial infection is given by, $A(t) = 14e^{0.21t}$.

(a) Calculate the initial number of cases.

(b) How long would it take for the number of cases to double?

15.9 Two variables x and y are related by the equation $y = ka^x$. When $\log y$ is plotted against x, a straight line passing through the points $(3, 11)$ and $(5, 16)$ is obtained.

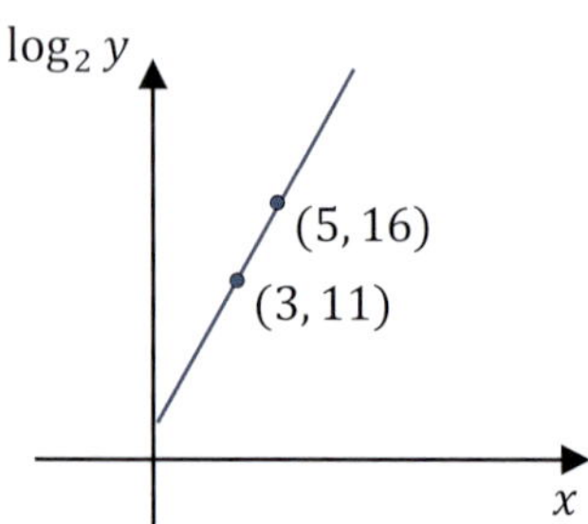

Find the values of k and a.

16.2 Geometric Skills Revision

Exercise 16.2A – The Straight Line

1.1 Find the equation of the line joining the following points:

(a) $(1, 2)$ and $(-2, 0)$ (b) $(4, 8)$ and $(-3, 29)$ (c) $(2, -4)$ and $(3, 0)$

1.2 Find the midpoint of the line joining the following points:

(a) $\mathrm{A}(8, -3)$ and $\mathrm{B}(12, -7)$ (b) $\mathrm{C}(3, 8)$ and $\mathrm{D}(-7, 10)$ (c) $\mathrm{E}(2, 15)$ and $\mathrm{F}(-2, -3)$

1.3 Find the gradient of a line perpendicular to the line joining each of the following points:

(a) $\mathrm{A}(4, -1)$ and $\mathrm{B}(3, 6)$ (b) $\mathrm{C}(-2, 3)$ and $\mathrm{D}(0, 2)$ (c) $\mathrm{E}(8, -7)$ and $\mathrm{F}(12, 11)$

1.4 (a) A line, l, has the equation $y - x - 6 = 0$. Calculate the angle that the line makes with the positive direction of the x-axis.

(b) Find the equation of the line in the diagram opposite.

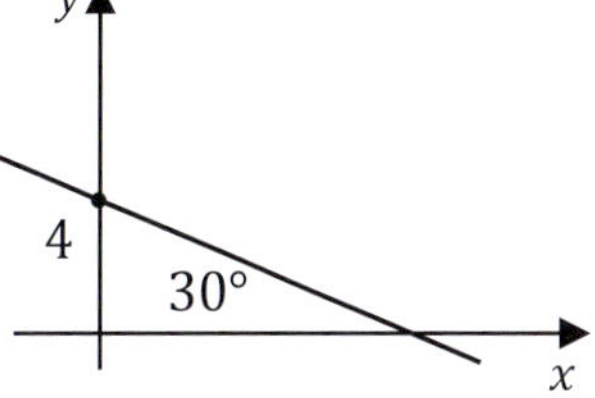

1.5 Determine whether the following sets of points are collinear:

(a) $\mathrm{A}(3, 4)$, $\mathrm{B}(12, 5)$ and $\mathrm{C}(15, 9)$ (b) $\mathrm{D}(-9, 7)$, $\mathrm{E}(-5, 6)$ and $\mathrm{F}(3, 4)$

1.6 (a) Find the equation of the line which intersects the y-axis at $y = 4$ and is perpendicular to the line with the equation $5x + 2y - 10 = 0$.

(b) Find the equation of the line which passes through $(3, -20)$ and the midpoint of the line joining points $\mathrm{A}(-2, 8)$ and $\mathrm{B}(6, 12)$.

1.7 Find the point of intersection of each of the following lines:

(a) $x + 3y = 5$
$y = 2x - 3$

(b) $y = 2x - 15$
$y = 9 - 4x$

(c) $4x + 2y = 12$
$3x - 4y = -13$

1.8 Find the equation of the perpendicular bisector of the line joining each pair of points:

(a) $\mathrm{A}(1, 9)$ and $\mathrm{B}(5, 17)$ (b) $\mathrm{C}(3, -2)$ and $\mathrm{D}(7, -4)$ (c) $\mathrm{E}(-6, 2)$ and $\mathrm{F}(0, 12)$

1.9 Sketch the triangle and find the equation of the median from C in each of the following sets of points:

(a) $\mathrm{A}(-4, 12)$, $\mathrm{B}(2, 8)$, $\mathrm{C}(5, 16)$ (b) $\mathrm{D}(-5, 10)$, $\mathrm{C}(7, -4)$, $\mathrm{E}(-1, 8)$

1.10 Sketch the triangle and find the equation of the altitude from A in each of the following sets of points:

(a) $\mathrm{A}(10, 11)$, $\mathrm{B}(3, 7)$, $\mathrm{C}(12, 6)$ (b) $\mathrm{A}(1, 8)$, $\mathrm{D}(-4, -3)$, $\mathrm{E}(11, 9)$

Exercise 16.2B – The Circle

2.1 Find the distance between the following points:

(a) $(-2, -1)$ and $(3, 11)$ (b) $(-11, 3)$ and $(3, -8)$ (c) $(-4, 1)$ and $(11, -19)$

2.2 Find the equation of the following circles. In each question, AB is a radius or diameter. Give your answer in standard (centre-radius) form:

(a)

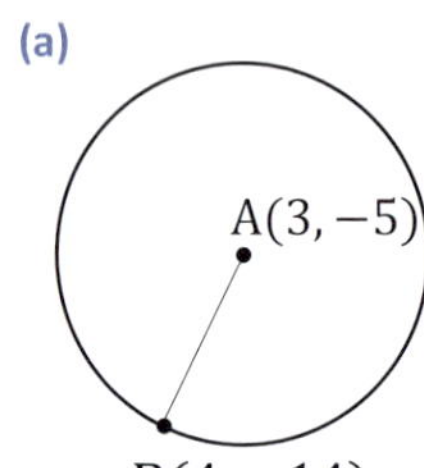

(b)

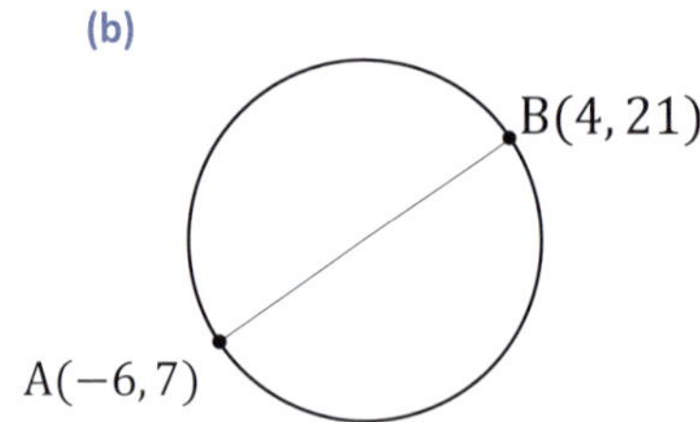

(c)

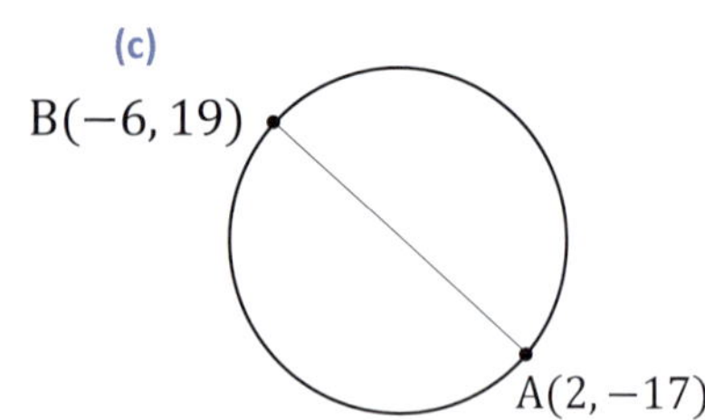

2.3 Find the centre and radius of the circles with the following equations:

(a) $x^2 + y^2 = 36$ (b) $(x - 2)^2 + (y + 7)^2 = 45$

(c) $x^2 + y^2 - 6x + 8y - 39 = 0$ (d) $x^2 + y^2 - 12y - 48 = 0$

2.4 Determine where the following points lie in relation to the given circles (justify your answer):

(a) $(4, -7)$ and $(x - 3)^2 + (y + 2)^2 = 28$ (b) $(-2.5, 1)$ and $x^2 + y^2 - 5x + 9y - 3 = 0$

2.5 Determine the nature of intersection between the following lines and circles:

(a) $y = 4x + 15$ and $(x + 3)^2 + (y + 2)^2 = 50$ (b) $y = x + 6$ and $x^2 + y^2 + 4x + 8y - 12 = 0$

2.6 (a) Find the coordinates of the points of intersection of the following lines and circles:

(i) $y = \frac{1}{2}x - 2$ and $(x - 5)^2 + (y + 2)^2 = 25$ (ii) $y = -x - 5$ and $x^2 + y^2 - 4x + 6y - 45 = 0$

(b) Show that the line with equation $4x + 3y - 35 = 0$ is a tangent to the circle with the equation $x^2 + y^2 + 20x - 125 = 0$ and find the coordinates of the point of contact.

2.7 Find the equation of the tangent to the circle with the following equations at the given points:

(a) $(x + 5)^2 + (y - 7)^2 = 32$ and $(-1, 11)$ (b) $x^2 + y^2 - 8x + 6y - 137 = 0$ and $(13, -12)$

2.8 In the following pairs of equation, determine whether circles intersect at two points, touch internally/externally or do not intersect:

(a) $(x - 5)^2 + (y + 5)^2 = 100$ and $x^2 + y^2 - 4x + 10y - 140 = 0$

(b) $(x + 13)^2 + (y - 7)^2 = 48$ and $x^2 + y^2 + 8x + 6y - 14 = 0$

2.9 In each of the following questions, the line going through the centres is parallel with the x-axis. Determine the equation of the circle with centre P.

(a) The circle with centre A has equation
$x^2 + y^2 - 10x - 12y + 45 = 0$.
The centre of circle P is $(12, 6)$.

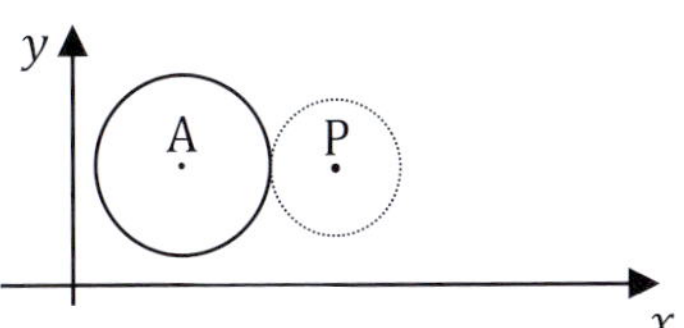

(b) The coordinates of point A are $(8, 4)$.

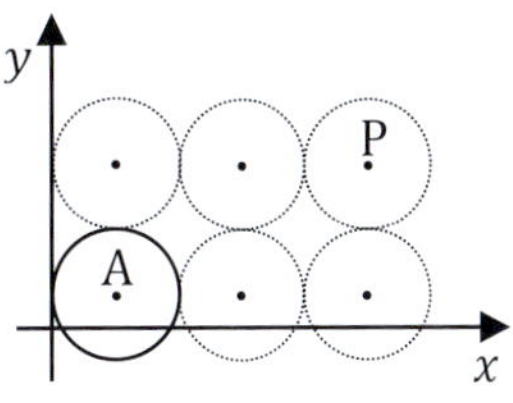

Exercise 16.2C – Vectors

14.4 Calculate the unit vector $\mathbf{u}$ of the following vectors:

(a) $\mathbf{a} = \begin{pmatrix} 6 \\ 0 \\ -8 \end{pmatrix}$ (b) $\mathbf{b} = \begin{pmatrix} -8 \\ 9 \\ -12 \end{pmatrix}$ (c) $\mathbf{c} = \begin{pmatrix} 14 \\ -2 \\ 5 \end{pmatrix}$

14.5 (a) Vectors $\mathbf{e}$ and $\mathbf{f}$ are such that $\mathbf{e} = 2\mathbf{i} - 2\mathbf{j} + 4\mathbf{k}$ and $\mathbf{f} = 3\mathbf{i} - 8\mathbf{j} + 2\mathbf{k}$. Find $|\mathbf{e} - 2\mathbf{f}|$.

(b) Vectors $\mathbf{g}$ and $\mathbf{h}$ are such that $\mathbf{g} = \mathbf{i} + a\mathbf{j} + 5\mathbf{k}$ and $\mathbf{h} = 2\mathbf{i} - \mathbf{j} + \mathbf{k}$ and $|\mathbf{g} + \mathbf{h}| = 7$.
Find the value(s) of a.

14.6 (a) Show that the points $A(-3, -10, 5)$, $B(-1, -13, 9)$ and $C(5, -22, 21)$ are collinear.

(b) Determine whether the points $D(7, -2, 12)$, $E(-1, 2, 25)$ and $F(-13, 8, 47)$ are collinear.

(c) The points $G(-11, 16, 2)$, $H(-17, 25, -13)$ and $J(-21, 31, k)$ are collinear.
Determine the value of k.

14.7 (a) Point P divides the points $A(5, -8, 3)$ and $B(-1, 1, -12)$ in the ratio $2:1$.
Find the coordinates of P.

(b) Point P divides the points A and B in the ratio $4:1$. The coordinates of A and P are $(-3, 12, -5)$ and $(-9, 16, 1)$ respectively. Find the coordinates of B.

14.8 (a) Points $A(-15, 2, 14)$, $B(-9, -7, 11)$ and $C(-5, -13, 9)$ are collinear.
State the ratio in which B divides AC.

(b) Points $D(23, 18, -3)$, $E(17, 14, 5)$ and $F(k, 12, 9)$ are collinear.
Determine the value of k.

14.9 (a) Calculate the scalar product of:

(i) $\mathbf{a} = 5\mathbf{i} - 2\mathbf{j} + \mathbf{k}$ and $\mathbf{b} = 2\mathbf{i} - 3\mathbf{j} + 4\mathbf{k}$. (ii) $\mathbf{c} = \begin{pmatrix} 11 \\ 3 \\ -8 \end{pmatrix}$ and $\mathbf{d} = \begin{pmatrix} -5 \\ 4 \\ -6 \end{pmatrix}$.

(b) Calculate $\overrightarrow{BA} \cdot \overrightarrow{BC}$ from $A(2, -9, 3)$, $B(4, 1, -2)$ and $C(3, 4, 5)$.

(c) Show that vectors $\mathbf{t} = -3\mathbf{i} - \mathbf{j} - 11\mathbf{k}$ and $\mathbf{v} = -2\mathbf{i} - 5\mathbf{j} + \mathbf{k}$ are perpendicular.

(d) P, Q and R are the coordinates $(-2, 7, a)$, $(3, -2, 5)$ and $(1, -4, 1)$ respectively. $\overrightarrow{QP}$ is perpendicular to $\overrightarrow{QR}$. Find the value of a.

(e) Calculate the scalar product.

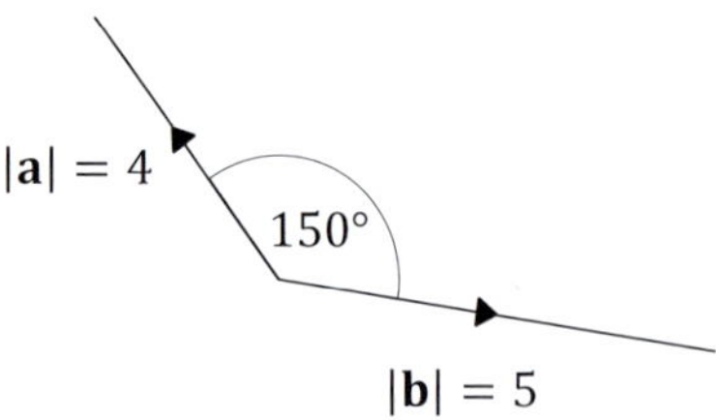

14.10 (a) Calculate the angle between the vectors $\mathbf{a} = 2\mathbf{j} + 7\mathbf{k}$ and $\mathbf{b} = -3\mathbf{i} - 7\mathbf{j} + 5\mathbf{k}$.

(b) P, Q and R are the coordinates $(-6, 2, -11)$, $(5, 6, 3)$ and $(1, -4, 1)$ respectively. Calculate the size of angle PQR.

14.11 In the diagram $|\mathbf{a}| = \sqrt{2}$, $|\mathbf{b}| = 2$, $|\mathbf{c}| = 3$. Evaluate:

(a) $\mathbf{a} \,.\, (\mathbf{b} + \mathbf{c})$

(b) $\mathbf{a} \,.\, (\mathbf{a} + \mathbf{b} + \mathbf{c})$

(c) $(\mathbf{a} + \mathbf{b}) \,.\, (\mathbf{a} + \mathbf{b})$

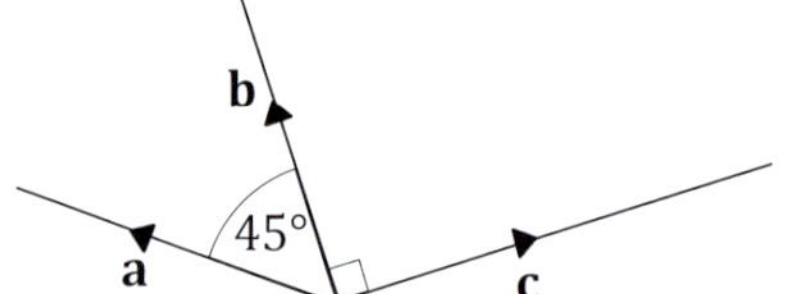

14.12 In the diagram, ABCDEF is a triangular prism. AB = BF = FA. M is the midpoint of CD. G divides EM in the ratio 1: 2.

Express the following vectors in terms of $\mathbf{p}$, $\mathbf{q}$ and $\mathbf{r}$:

(a) $\overrightarrow{BE}$ (b) $\overrightarrow{AM}$ (c) $\overrightarrow{AG}$ (d) $\overrightarrow{GM}$

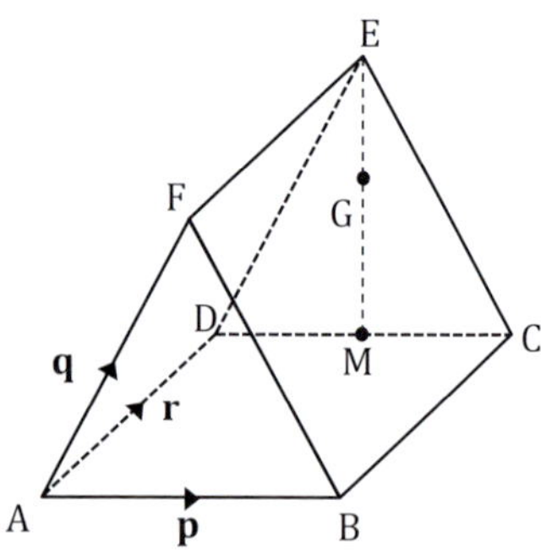

16.3 Trigonometric Skills Revision

Exercise 16.3A – Trigonometric Functions

8.1 State the equation of each of the following trigonometric functions:

(a)

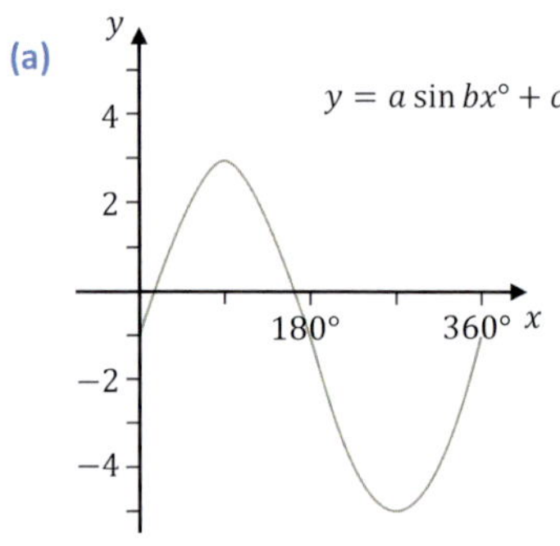

(b)

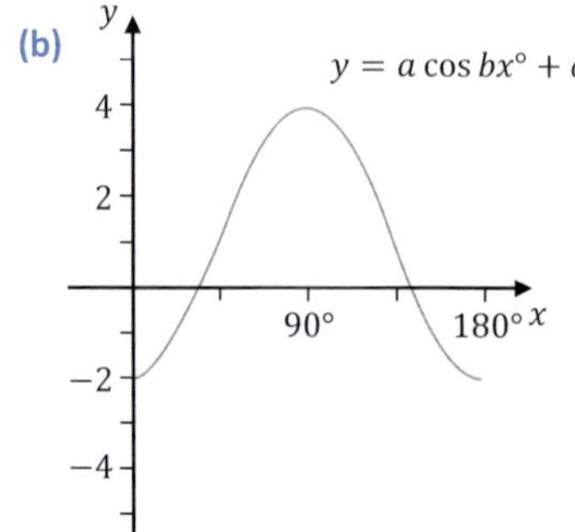

(c)

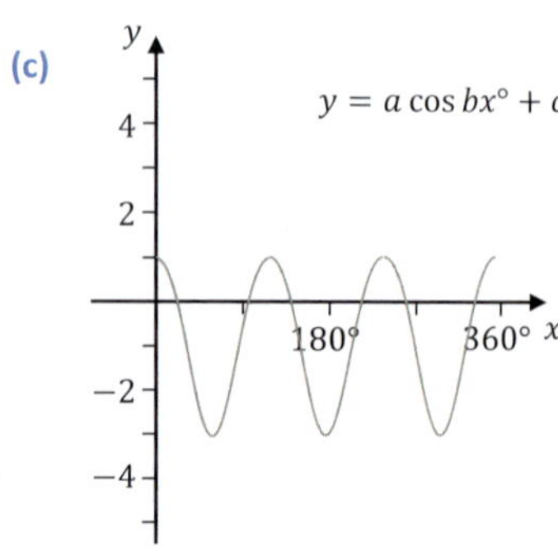

(d)

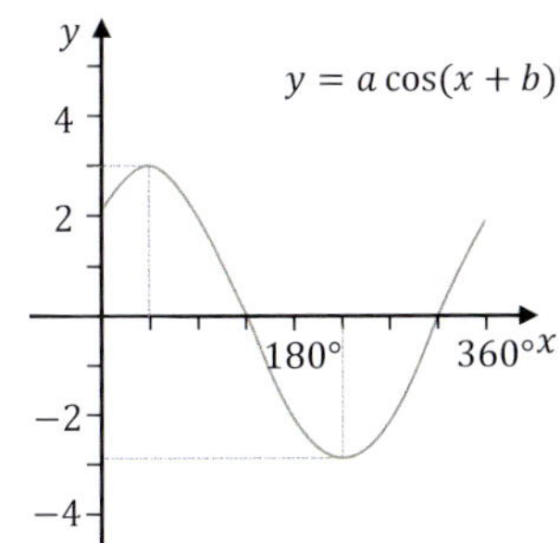

(e)

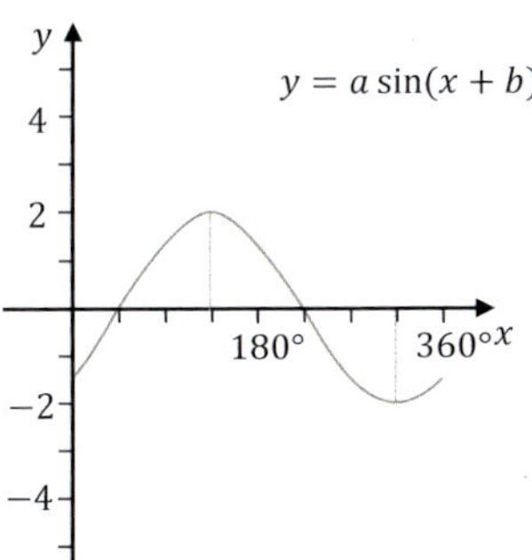

(f)

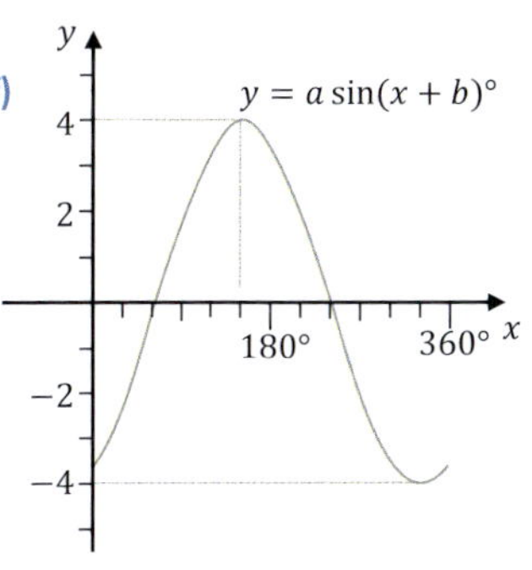

8.2 Solve the following equations for $0 \leq x \leq 360$. Give your answer correct to 1 decimal place:

(a) $2\tan x° + 3 = 4$ (b) $2\sin x° + 5 = 3$ (c) $2\sin 2x° + 2 = 3$

(d) $\cos 3x° + 1 = 2$ (e) $6\cos(x - 10)° + 6 = 3$ (f) $3\sin(x + 20)° + 5 = 6$

8.3 Without using a calculator, find the exact value of:

(a) $\sin 60°$ (b) $\cos 30°$ (c) $\tan 315°$ (d) $\sin 300°$

(e) $\cos 240°$ (f) $\cos 315°$ (g) $\tan 240°$ (h) $\sin 150°$

8.4 Solve the following equations for $0 \leq x \leq 360$:

(a) $\sin x° + 2 = 3$ (b) $3\cos x° + 4 = 2$ (c) $2\cos 2x° - \sqrt{2} = 0$

(d) $2\sin 2x° - \sqrt{3} = 0$ (e) $2\tan(x - 15)° + 5 = 3$ (f) $2\cos(x + 20)° + \sqrt{3} = 0$

8.5 Solve the following equations for $0 \leq x \leq 2\pi$. Give your answer correct to 1 decimal place:

(a) $2\tan x - 1 = 5$ (b) $3\sin x + 2 = 1$ (c) $2\sin 2x + 2 = 3$

(d) $4\sin 2x - 3 = 0$ (e) $2\cos(x - 0.45) + 1 = 0$ (f) $3\sin(x + 0.2) + 5 = 4$

8.6 Find the points of intersection between the line and the trigonometric graph in the range $0 \leq x \leq 2\pi$. Give your answer correct to 1 decimal place:

(a)

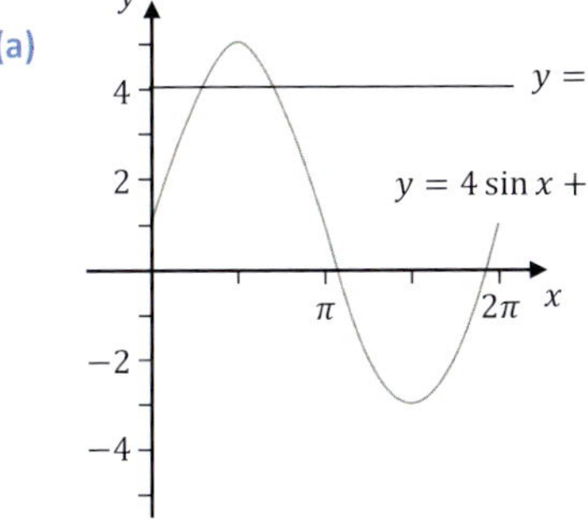

(b)

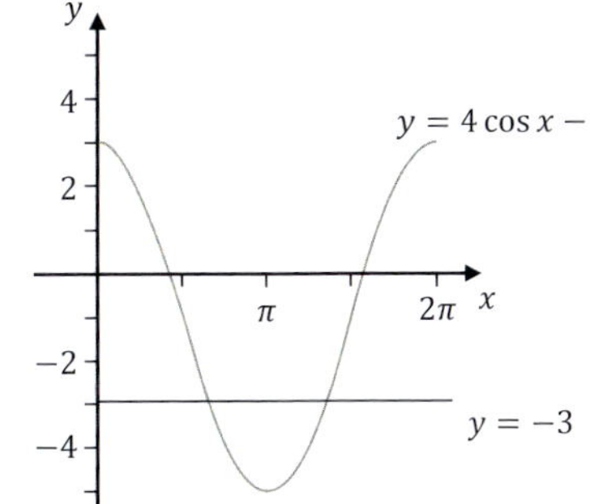

(c)

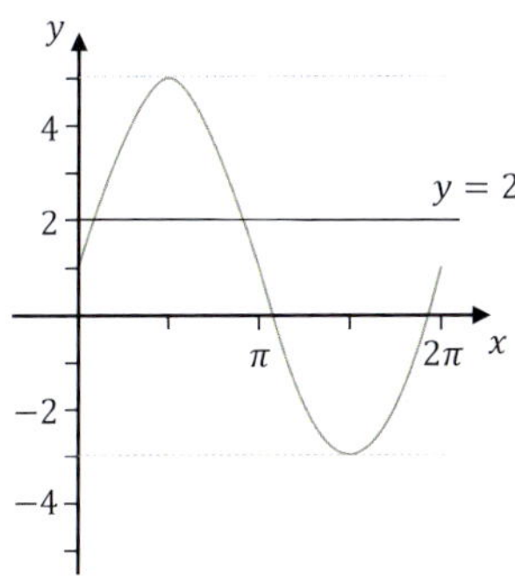

Exercise 16.3B – Addition Formulae

9.1 Use the addition formulae to expand and evaluate each of the following:

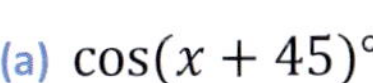
(a) $\cos(x + 45)°$ (b) $\sin\left(x + \frac{\pi}{6}\right)$ (c) $\sin\left(x - \frac{2\pi}{3}\right)$

9.2 Given $0 \leq a \leq \frac{\pi}{2}$ and $0 \leq b \leq \frac{\pi}{2}$, find an exact value for each of the following:

(a) $\cos(a + b)$, if $\sin a = \frac{5}{13}$ and $\cos b = \frac{1}{2}$

(b) $\sin(a + b)$, if $\sin a = \frac{3}{5}$ and $\cos b = \frac{3}{\sqrt{13}}$

9.3 Given $0 \leq x \leq 90$, find the exact value of:

(a) $\cos 2x$, if $\sin x = \frac{3}{\sqrt{7}}$

(b) $\sin 2x$, if $\cos x = \frac{1}{\sqrt{10}}$

(c) $\cos 2x$, if $\tan x = \frac{2}{5}$

9.4 Show:

(a) $2 \sin x \cos^2 x = 2 \sin x - 2 \sin^3 x$

(b) $\cos 2x + \sin^2 x = \cos^2 x$

9.5 Solve the following equations for $0 \leq x \leq 2\pi$:

(a) $\sin 2x = \cos x$

(b) $2\cos 2x - 10 \cos x + 8 = 0$

Exercise 16.3C – The Wave Function

10.1 Write the following expressions in the required form:

(a) $2 \cos x° + 3\sin x°$ in the form $k \cos(x - \alpha)°$ where $k > 0$ and $0 < x < 360$.

(b) $3 \sin x + \sqrt{5} \cos x$ in the form $k \sin(x + \alpha)$ where $k > 0$ and $0 < x < 2\pi$.

(c) $5 \cos x + 2 \sin x$ in the form $k \cos(x + \alpha)$ where $k > 0$ and $0 < x < 2\pi$.

(d) $4 \cos x° - 5 \sin x°$ in the form $k \sin(x - \alpha)°$ where $k > 0$ and $0 < x < 360$.

10.2 Solve each of the following by first expressing them in the form $k \sin(x \pm \alpha)$ or $k \cos(x \pm \alpha)$, where $k > 0$ and $0 \leq x \leq 2\pi$:

(a) $3 \cos x - \sqrt{3} \sin x = 1$

(b) $3 \cos x - 4 \sin x = \sqrt{2}$

(c) $\sqrt{5} \cos x + 3 \sin x = 1$

(d) (i) Express $2 \cos x° + \sin x°$ in the form $k \cos(x - \alpha)°, k > 0$ and $0 < x < 360$.
(ii) Hence solve $2 \cos x° + \sin x° = 1$.

(e) (i) Express $3 \sin x° + \cos x°$ in the form $k \sin(x + \alpha)°, k > 0$ and $0 < x < 360$.
(ii) Hence solve $3 \sin x° + \cos x° = 2$.

(f) (i) Express $3 \cos x + 3 \sin x$ in the form $k \cos(x + \alpha), k > 0$ and $0 < x < 2\pi$.
(ii) Hence solve $3 \cos 2x + 3 \sin 2x = 2$.

(g) (i) Express $\sqrt{5} \cos x + 2 \sin x$ in the form $k \sin(x - \alpha), k > 0$ and $0 < x < 2\pi$.
(ii) Hence solve $\sqrt{5} \cos 3x° + 2 \sin 3x° = 3$.

10.3 Answer each of the following:

(a) (i) Express $\cos x° + 2 \sin x°$ in the form $k \cos(x - \alpha)°, k > 0$ and $0 < x < 360$.
(ii) Hence sketch $y = \cos x° + 2 \sin x°$.

(b) (i) Express $4 \sin x° + \sqrt{2} \cos x°$ in the form $k \sin(x + \alpha)°, k > 0$ and $0 < x < 360$.
(ii) Hence sketch $y = 4 \sin x° + \sqrt{2} \sin x°$.

(c) (i) Express $\sqrt{5}\sin x° + \cos x°$ in the form $k\sin(x - \alpha)°$, $k > 0$ and $0 < x < 360$.

(ii) Hence sketch $y = \sqrt{5}\sin x° + \cos x° - 1$.

(d) (i) Express $\sqrt{2}\sin x° + \cos x°$ in the form $k\cos(x + \alpha)°$, $k > 0$ and $0 < x < 360$.

(ii) Hence sketch $y = 1 - \sqrt{2}\sin x° - \cos x°$.

10.4 Answer each of the following:

(a) (i) Express $4\cos x° - 2\sin x°$ in the form $k\cos(x + \alpha)°$, $k > 0$ and $0 \le x \le 360$.

(ii) Hence, state the maximum value of the function $y = 4\cos x° - 2\sin x° - 3$.

(iii) The x-coordinate for which it occurs, where $0 \le x \le 360$.

(b) (i) Express $5\cos x - 3\sin x$ in the form $k\sin(x + \alpha)$, $k > 0$ and $0 \le x \le 2\pi$.

(ii) Hence, state the minimum value of the function $y = 10\cos x - 6\sin x + 3$.

(iii) The x-coordinate for which it occurs, where $0 \le x \le 2\pi$.

16.4 Calculus Skills Revision

Exercise 16.4A – Differentiation

11.2 Differentiate each of the following functions:

(a) $f(x) = 8x^{\frac{3}{4}}$ (b) $y = 2x^3 - 6x^2 - 7$ (c) $f(x) = \dfrac{5}{\sqrt[3]{x}}$

11.3 Differentiate each of the following functions:

(a) $f(x) = x^3(\sqrt{x} - 3x)$ (b) $y = \dfrac{4x^3 + 6x^2 + 2x}{2x^5}$ (c) $y = \dfrac{8x^2 - 2x + 1}{\sqrt{x}}$

11.4 (a) Given that $f(x) = 3\sqrt{x^3} + x^3$, find $f'(4)$.

(b) Find the gradient of the tangent to the curve $y = 2x^3 - x^2 + 4$ when $x = -2$.

(c) A function f is defined on a suitable domain by $f(x) = \dfrac{3x^3 + 2}{\sqrt{x}}$. Calculate the rate of change of f when $x = 9$.

11.5 Find the equation of the tangent to the curve $y = 4x^3 - 3x^2 + 5x + 2$ at the point where $x = -1$.

11.6 (a) A function f is defined on a suitable domain by $f(x) = x + \dfrac{4}{x}$. Show that the function is strictly increasing at the point where $x = -3$.

(b) A function f is defined on a suitable domain by $f(x) = x^3 - 3x^2 - 4$. Determine the range of values for which f is strictly increasing.

(c) A function f is defined on a suitable domain by $f(x) = 2x^3 - 9x^2 - 3$. Determine the range of values for which f is strictly decreasing.

(d) Given that $f(x) = \frac{1}{3}x^3 - 2x^2 + 11x$. Explain why the curve $y = f(x)$ is increasing for all values of x.

11.7 Find the stationary points on the curve with equation $y = x^3 - 6x^2 - 15x + 2$ and determine their nature.

11.8 Sketch the graph of the curve with equation $y = \frac{1}{3}x^3 - 9x$.

11.9 The roof of a new house is in the shape of a triangular prism. The volume of the roof space is 108 cubic metres. The roof must be covered in roofing felt before tiling, including both ends.

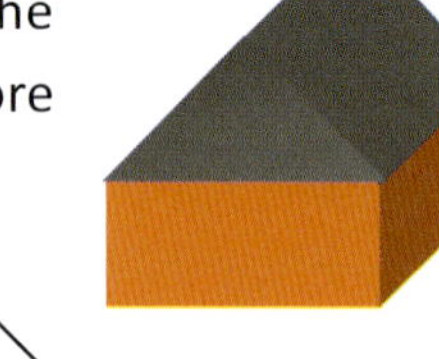

The cross-section of the roof is a right-angled, isosceles triangle of sides x and the length of the prism is l.

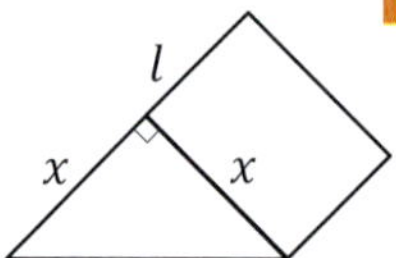

(a) Show that the surface area of the roof $A\ m^2$ requiring felt, is given by $A(x) = x^2 + \dfrac{432}{x}$.

(b) Find the value of x which minimises the surface area.

11.10 A function f is defined on the domain $1 \leq x \leq 5$ by $f(x) = x^3 - 12x + 5$. Determine the maximum and minimum values of f.

11.11 The diagram shows the graph of $y = f(x)$, with stationary points at $(-3, 11)$ and $(1, 0)$.

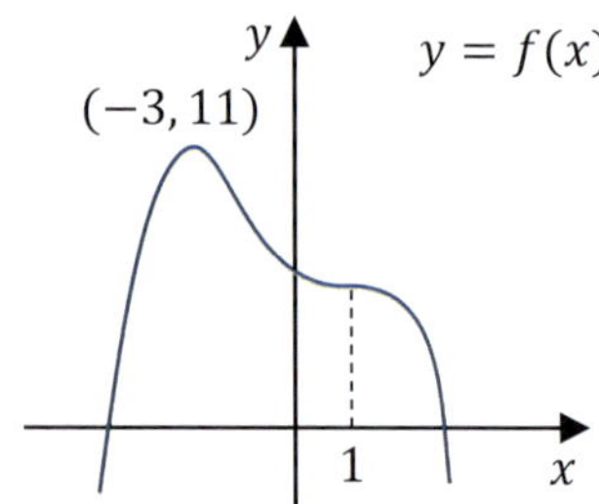

Sketch the graph of $y = f'(x)$.

Exercise 16.4B – Integration

12.1 Find:

(a) $\int 5x^2\,dx$ (b) $\int (x^2 + 3x - 1)\,dx$ (c) $\int 6x^{\frac{1}{2}}\,dx$

12.2 Find:

(a) $\int \frac{1}{\sqrt{x}}\,dx$ (b) $\int \left(x + \frac{1}{x}\right)^2 dx$ (c) $\int 2x\left(\sqrt{x} + \frac{1}{\sqrt{x}}\right) dx$

12.3

(a) Evaluate:

(i) $\int_1^3 \frac{2}{x^3}\,dx$ (ii) $\int_{-1}^4 (x^2 - 5x + 2)\,dx$ (iii) $\int_0^9 \frac{x^2 + 2x}{\sqrt{x}}\,dx$

(b) Find the value of a in each of the following questions:

(i) $\int_a^5 (2x - 3)\,dx = 12$ (ii) $\int_{-1}^a 3x^2\,dx = 126$ (iii) $\int_1^a \frac{7}{\sqrt{x}}\,dx = 28$

12.4 Calculate the shaded area:

(a)

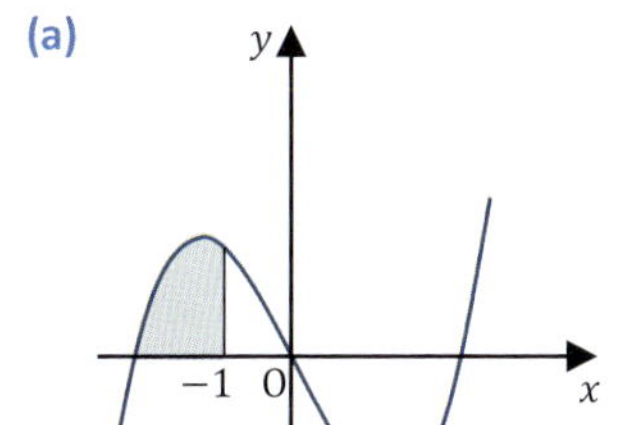

(b)

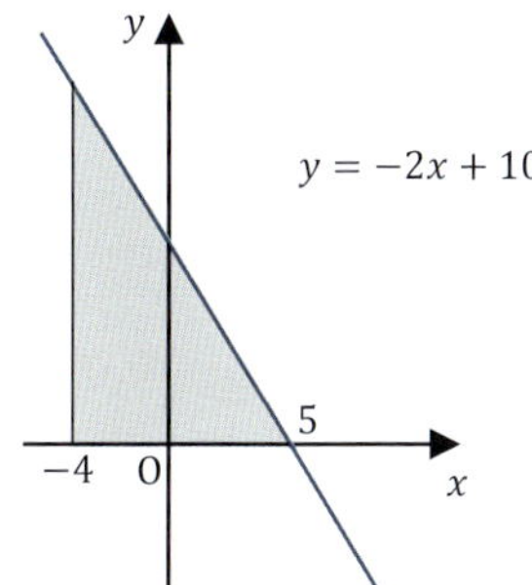

(c)

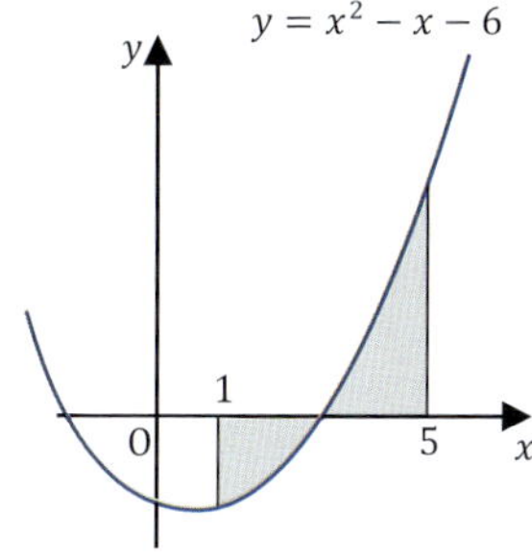

12.5 Calculate the shaded area:

(a)

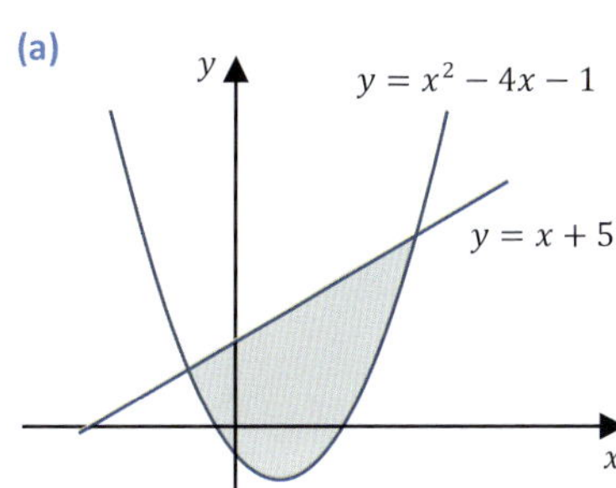

(b)

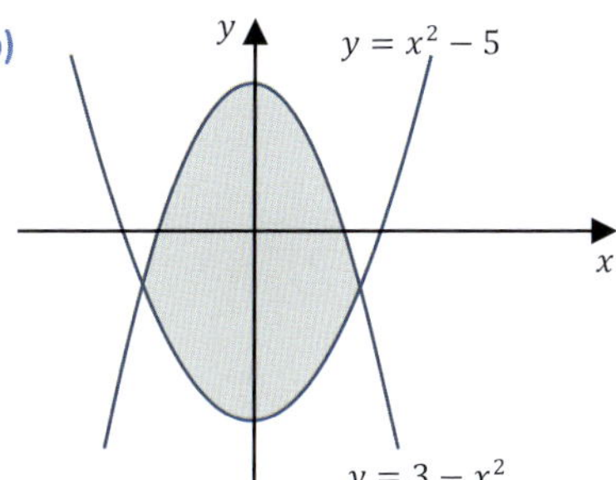

(c)

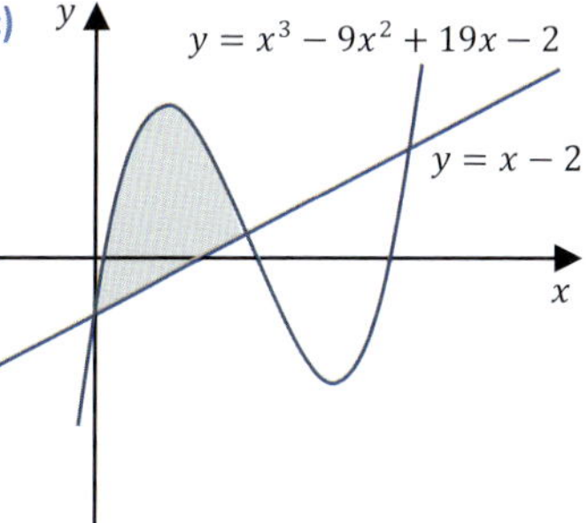

12.6 The rate of change of the volume, V litres of an object with respect to time, t hours, is given by $\frac{dV}{dt} = 18\sqrt{t} + 5t$. The volume of the object after 4 hours is 56 litres. Calculate the volume of the object after 8 hours.

Exercise 16.4C – Further Calculus

13.1A Find the derivative:

(a) $f(x) = (3x + 5)^3$ (b) $y = (x^2 - 2)^4$ (c) $f(x) = (3x + 4)^{-2}$

(d) $f(x) = (x^2 - x)^3$ (e) $y = (x^3 + 2x)^{-\frac{1}{2}}$ (f) $f(x) = \frac{1}{2}(x^3 - 2x)^4$

13.1B Differentiate:

(a) $f(x) = \frac{2}{(2x + 1)^3}$ (b) $f(x) = \frac{1}{(4x - 2)^{\frac{1}{2}}}$ (c) $f(x) = \frac{3}{\sqrt[3]{(x^2 + 2x)}}$

13.1C Evaluate:

(a) $f'(-2)$, when $f(x) = (x^2 - 5)^3$.

(b) $g'(5)$, when $g(x) = (4x + 3)^{-2}$.

(c) $g'(-1)$, when $g(x) = \dfrac{3}{(3x - 2)^3}$.

(d) $h'(4)$, when $h(x) = \dfrac{2}{\sqrt{x^3 - 5}}$.

(e) Calculate the rate of change of $f(x) = (x^2 - 5x)^3$ when $x = -2$.

(f) Calculate the gradient of the tangent to the curve $y = \sqrt{x^3 + 2}$ when $x = 2$.

13.2B Differentiate:

(a) $y = 4\cos 3x$

(b) $f(x) = 2\sin 2x + \cos 2x$

(c) $f(x) = 5 - 3\sin 2x$

(d) $y = \sin(2x^2 + 1)$

(e) $f(x) = \cos(x^3 - 1)$

(f) $f(x) = -\cos(5x^2 + 8)$

13.2C Differentiate:

(a) $f(x) = 5\sin^2 x$

(b) $y = 2\cos^3 x$

(c) $f(x) = \cos^2 x + \sin^3 x$

13.2D Evaluate:

(a) $f'(\ 3\ )$, when $f(x) = 4\cos 3x$.

(b) $f'\left(\frac{\pi}{3}\right)$, when $f(x) = 2\sin^2 x$.

(c) $f'\left(\frac{\pi}{6}\right)$, when $f(x) = 2\sin\left(2x + \frac{\pi}{3}\right)$.

(d) $f'\left(\frac{\pi}{4}\right)$, when $2\cos(2x - 1)$.

13.3A Find:

(a) $\int (3x - 5)^3\, dx$

(b) $\int 3(4x + 2)^{\frac{1}{2}}\, dx$

(c) $\int 4(7 - 2x)^5\, dx$

(d) $\int 8(2x + 4)^{-2}\, dx$

(e) $\int 2(3x + 5)^{-\frac{1}{2}}\, dx$

(f) $\int 9(2 - 3x)^{-\frac{2}{3}}\, dx$

13.3B Find:

(a) $\int \dfrac{1}{(3x + 2)^3}\, dx$

(b) $\int \dfrac{3}{\sqrt[3]{(2x - 2)}}\, dx$

(c) $\int \dfrac{4}{\sqrt{(2x - 5)^3}}\, dx$

13.3C Evaluate:

(a) $\int_0^1 (2x + 6)^2\, dx$

(b) $\int_0^5 (3 - 4x)^2\, dx$

(c) $\int_1^6 \dfrac{1}{(5x - 3)^2}\, dx$

(d) $\int_{-3}^0 \dfrac{3}{(4x - 2)^2}\, dx$

(e) $\int_0^3 \dfrac{2}{(3x - 4)^3}\, dx$

(f) $\int_0^2 \dfrac{1}{\sqrt{5 - 2x}}\, dx$

13.4A Find:

(a) $\int \sin 2x\, dx$

(b) $\int 3\cos 2x\, dx$

(c) $\int 1 - 2\sin 2x\, dx$

(d) $\int \cos\left(2x - \frac{\pi}{6}\right) dx$

(e) $\int 2\sin\left(3x - \frac{\pi}{4}\right) dx$

(f) $\int 1 + \sin(2x - 0.6\ )\, dx$

13.4C Evaluate:

(a) $\int_{-1}^{0} \sin 3x \, dx$ (b) $\int_{0}^{\pi/3} 3\cos(2x+2) \, dx$ (c) $\int_{0.1}^{3\pi/8} \frac{1}{4}\sin\left(3x - \frac{\pi}{8}\right) dx$

16.5 Reasoning & Integrated Skills Revision

This section contains questions that are a combination of skills from different topics, more difficult questions from a given topic, questions within a context, or a combination of all three.

By the time you have reached this section you will already have covered all the basic skills. This section is by no means exhaustive, but is simply a start, to equip and enable you to approach more challenging questions with the correct method.

Some questions can be very straightforward in what they ask you to do, and the difficulty is in the mathematical manipulation of a function, etc. Other questions can be more difficult to access – this may be because they are written in an unfamiliar way, or the question is included in a real-life context. If the question is in a context, this context should be appropriate for the question, but this may not always be the case. Regardless, it is important not to be confused by, or distracted by a given context, but instead, to see past the context to the mathematics that lies behind it.

When beginning a question of this type, or indeed any question, the following steps may be useful:

Step 1: Glance at the diagram (if there is one) and the given information and, before reading the question, consider what kind of question it may be. It may be one of any number of questions or topics.

Step 2: Read the question *carefully*, identifying the **key words** and **phrases** that are relevant to the mathematics.

Step 3: Answer the question. It is always good practice in Higher Mathematics to re-read the question once you have reached an answer – to ensure you have answered what was asked.

NB: In this section some of the context questions have an intentionally obscure context.

Exercise 16.5A

1. The diagram opposite shows a right-angled triangle:

   (a) Calculate the exact value of $\sin 2a$.

   (b) Calculate the exact value of $\sin 3a$.

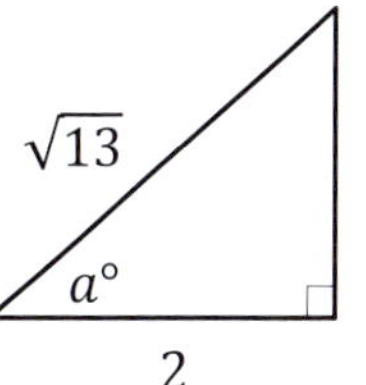

2. A sequence is defined by the recurrence relation $u_{n+1} = ku_n - 2$, with $u_0 = 4$.

   (a) Show that $u_2 = 4k^2 - 2k - 2$.

   (b) For what range of values of k is $u_2 > u_0$?

3. For a function defined on a suitable domain, it is known that:

$$f'(x) = 6x^2 - 2x + 1$$

$$f(-1) = 5\,.$$

   Express $f(x)$ in terms of x.

4. Calculate the range of values of c for which the equation $x^2 + y^2 + 16x - 4y + c = 0$ represents a circle.

5. The diagram opposite shows a rectangle with sides of length $(x + 5)$ centimetres and $(x - 2)$ centimetres.

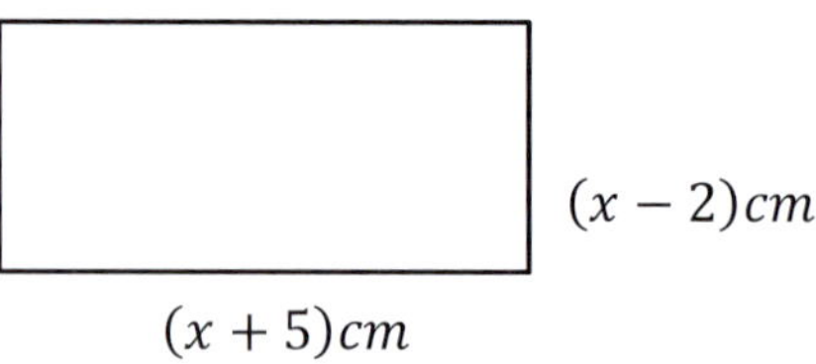

If the area of the rectangle is less than $18\ cm^2$, determine the range of values of x.

6. Functions f and g are defined on suitable domains by $f(x) = x^2 - 4x + 25$ and $g(x) = 2x + 3$.

(a) Given $h(x) = f(g(x))$, show that $h(x) = 4x^2 + 4x + 22$.

(b) Express $h(x)$ in the form $p(x + q)^2 + r$.

(c) Sketch the graph of $y = h(x) - 10$.

7. Triangle ABC is isosceles, as shown in the diagram below.

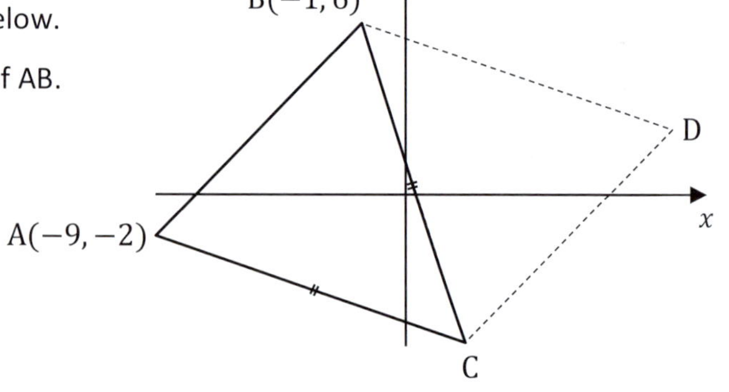

(a) Find the equation of the perpendicular bisector of AB.

The gradient of AC is $-\frac{1}{3}$.

(b) Find the coordinates of C.

ABCD is a parallelogram.

(c) Find the coordinates of D.

8. The diagram opposite shows the graph of $y = f(x)$.

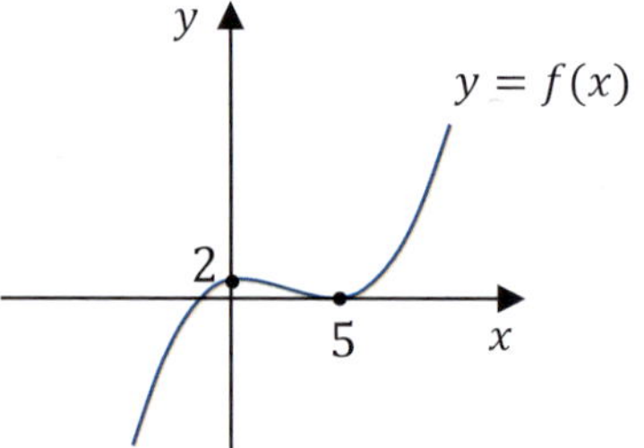

(a) Sketch the graph of $y = 2 - f(x - 1)$.

(b) On a separate diagram, sketch the graph of $y = f'(x)$.

9. In the diagram below $\overrightarrow{AB} = 12\mathbf{i} - 4\mathbf{j} + 28\mathbf{k}$ and $\overrightarrow{AC} = -3\mathbf{i} - 12\mathbf{j} + 9\mathbf{k}$.

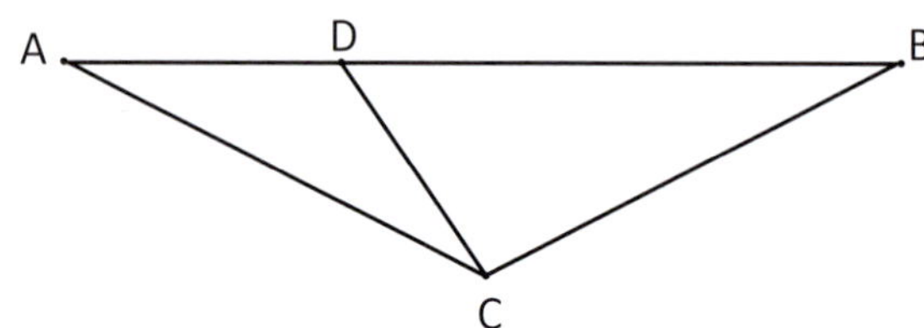

Point D divides AB in the ratio 1:3. Express $\overrightarrow{DC}$ in component form.

Exercise 16.5B

1. A farmer is constructing a grain barn and wants to cover the roof with rubber membrane. The area to be covered is in the shape of a half-cylinder. The curved surface and the semi-circular ends of the half-cylinder are to be covered. The volume of the half cylinder is 900 cubic metres.

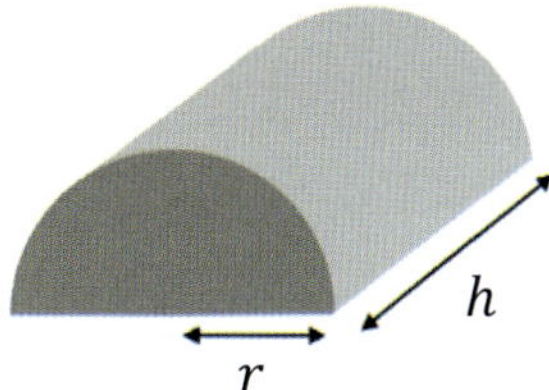

(a) Show that the surface area of membrane needed to cover the grain barn is given by:

$$A = \pi r^2 + \frac{1800}{r}$$

(b) Determine the value of r which minimises the amount of membrane needed.

2. Three circles are drawn with centres that are collinear. Circle C_1 has equation $x^2 + y^2 + 12x - 2y - 188 = 0$. The centre of circle C_2 is $(14, 16)$.

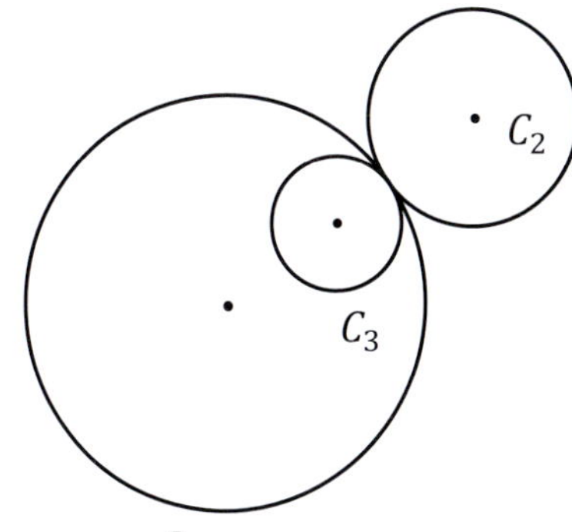

(a) Determine the radius of C_2.

C_3 touches C_1 internally and divides the line joining the centres of C_1 and C_2 in the ratio $2:3$.

(b) Determine the equation of C_3.

3. A slug and a snail climb up a 1 metre wall. The slug climbs 20 centimetres every hour and stops for a break. During the break, the slug slides $\frac{1}{5}$ of the way back down. This can be modelled by the recurrence relation $u_{n+1} = \frac{4}{5}u_n + 20$.

(a) Calculate the height of the slug after 3 hours.

The snail climbs 40 centimetres every hour and stops for a break. During the break, the snail slides $\frac{1}{3}$ of the way back down.

(b) Write a recurrence relation to represent the snail's journey.

(c) Will either the snail or the slug reach the top? Give a reason for your answer.

4. The value V pounds of a new cryptocurrency coin over time t months can be modelled by the equation $V(t) = 0.0008e^{1.4t}$.

(a) Calculate the value of the currency when it was launched.

(b) How long did the currency take to double in value?

5. The diagram opposite shows a curve with equation $y = f(x)$, where $f(x) = k(x + a)^2(x + b)$.

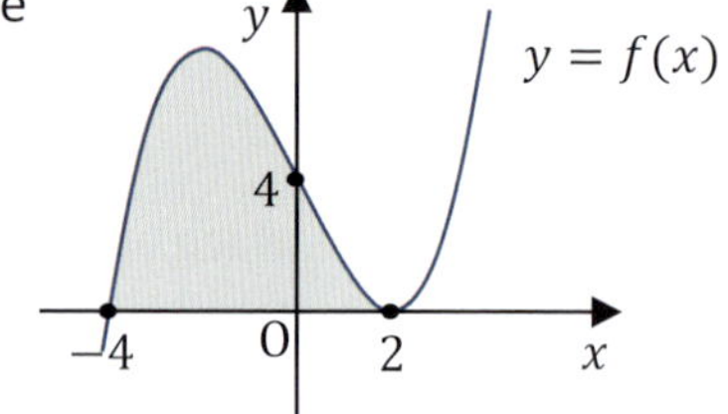

(a) Find the values of a, b and k.

(b) Calculate the shaded area

6. An investor buys cryptocurrency during a bull run. The value V thousands of pounds of the currency can be modelled over time, t months, by the function, $V(t) = (t + 1)(t - 4)^2$.

(a) Calculate the initial investment.

The investor kept his money in the investment for four months.

(b) How much is the investment worth in the fourth month?

(c) When was the investment worth the most and what was the maximum amount that the investment was worth?

7. A carpenter wants to build a storage container out of wood in the shape of a square-based cuboid with no lid. The container should have a volume of 13.5 litres. The carpenter wants to line the inside of the box with lining paper. He wants to use as little paper as possible to line the box.

Calculate the minimum area of paper he will need. Justify your answer.

8. A circle has the equation $x^2 + y^2 - 8x - 4y - 80 = 0$. Point $(c, -2)$ lies on the circle. Give two possible values for c.

Answers

Chapter 1

Exercise 1.1

1.

(a) $y = 3x - 11$ (b) $y = -2x + 18$ (c) $y = -4x + 26$
(d) $y = -2x - 4$ (e) $y = -4x - 18$ (f) $y = 3x - 2$
(g) $y = \frac{1}{2}x - 9$ (h) $y = -\frac{5}{2}x - \frac{3}{2}$ (i) $x = -4$

2.

(a) $4x - y - 6 = 0$ (b) $4x - y - 18 = 0$
(c) $x - y + 8 = 0$ (d) $x - 2y + 3 = 0$
(e) $y = -5$ (f) $3x + 4y + 14 = 0$
(g) $4x - 7y + 45 = 0$ (h) $3x - 17y - 155 = 0$
(i) $8x + 3y = 0$

3.

(a) $y = -2x + 12$ (b) $4y = -x + 6$ (c) $10y = 3x + 107$
(d) $y = -3x + 3$ (e) $5y = x - 29$ (f) $5y = 6x - 40$
(g) $3y = 4x - 11$ (h) $3y = -5x + 11$ (i) $4y = 3x - 24$
(j) $3y = 5x + 15$ (k) $y = -3$ (l) $2y = -3x + 3$
(m) $x = 5$ (n) $2y = -x - 8$ (o) $3y = -x$
(p) $5y = 9x + 9$ (q) $4y = -7x + 51$ (r) $y = 7$

Exercise 1.2

1.

(a) $(7, 4)$ (b) $(1, 7)$ (c) $(-5, 7)$
(d) $(2, -3)$ (e) $(-4, 7)$ (f) $(-7, 17)$
(g) $(-6, -1)$ (h) $(2, -2)$ (i) $(1, -6)$
(j) $\left(9, -\frac{3}{2}\right)$ (k) $\left(\frac{3}{2}, -\frac{13}{2}\right)$ (l) $\left(\frac{17}{2}, -\frac{9}{2}\right)$

2. $y = -x - 2$ 3. $y = -2x + 16$
4. $(2, 7)$ 5. $C(15, 4), D(-1, -12)$
6. $\left(-3, \frac{21}{2}\right)$ 7. $(-9, 2)$
8. $y = 2x + 9$ 9. $8y = 9x - 16$

Exercise 1.3A

1.

(a) $m = -1/3$ (b) $m = -2$ (c) $m = 1/5$
(d) $m = 2$ (e) $m = -1/8$ (f) $m = -1/2$
(g) $m = -1/9$ (h) $m = 1/5$ (i) $m = -4/5$
(j) $m = 2/3$ (k) $m = -3/4$ (l) $m = 7/16$

Exercise 1.3B

1. $m = 1/8$ 2. $m = 2/3$
3. $m = 0$ 4. $m = -7/4$
5. $m\ is\ undefined$ 6. $proof: m_{LM} \times m = -1$
7. $proof: m_{NP} \times m = -1$ 8. $proof: m_{QR} \times m_{ST} = -1$
9. $proof: m_{UV} \times m_{WX} = -1$
10. $perpendicular, m_{AB} \times m_{CD} = -1$
11. $not\ perpendicular, m_{EF} \times m_{GH} \neq -1$
12. $perpendicular, m_{JK} \times m_{LM} = -1$
13. $d = -14$ 14. $e = 6$
15. $f = -2$

Exercise 1.4A

1.

(a) $m = 1$ (b) $m = \sqrt{3}$ (c) $m = 1/\sqrt{3}$
(d) $m = -1/\sqrt{3}$ (e) $m = -\sqrt{3}$ (f) $m = -1$

2. $\theta = 135°$ 3. $\theta = 150°$ 4. $\theta = 120°$
5. $\theta = 45°$ 6. $\theta = 60°$ 7. $\theta = 150°$
8. $\theta = 120°$

Exercise 1.4B

1.

(a) $m = 0.7$ (b) $m = 3.1$ (c) $m = 5.7$
(d) $m = 0.2$ (e) $m = -1.4$ (f) $m = -0.07$
(g) $m = -0.5$ (h) $m = 0.2$ (i) $m = -3.5$
(j) $m = 0.05$ (k) $m = -0.02$ (l) $m\ is\ undefined$

2. $\theta = 63.4°$ 3. $\theta = 53.1°$ 4. $\theta = 161.6°$
5. $\theta = 158.2°$ 6. $\theta = 50.2°$ 7. $\theta = 128.7°$

Exercise 1.5

1.

(a) *proof* (b) *proof* (c) *proof*
(d) *proof* (e) *proof* (f) *proof*
(g) *proof* (h) *proof*

2.

(a) *not collinear* (b) *collinear* (c) *not collinear*
(d) *not collinear* (e) *collinear* (f) *not collinear*
(g) *collinear* (h) *not collinear*

3. $x = 20$ 4. $x = 2/3$
5. $y = -7$ 6. $y = 2$

Exercise 1.6

1. $y = \frac{4}{3}x + 1$ 2. $y = 2x - 4$
3. $x + 3y - 13 = 0$ 4. $3x - 2y - 24 = 0$
5. $2x + 3y + 9 = 0$ 6. $7x + 11y - 72 = 0$
7. $x + y - 10 = 0$

8.

(a) $\sqrt{3}y = x - 3$ (b) $x + y - 7 = 0$
(c) $x + \sqrt{3}y - 11\sqrt{3} + 12 = 0$

Exercise 1.7

1. $(2, 2)$ 2. $(4, -2)$ 3. $(-3, 1)$ 4. $(2, -8)$
5. $(5, 1)$ 6. $(6, 2)$ 7. $(-1, -4)$ 8. $(5, 3)$
9. $(-13, -16)$ 10. $(12, -5)$ 11. $(2, 9)$ 12. $(-5, 3)$
13. $(0.5, 3)$ 14. $(4, 1)$ 15. $(-1, 3)$ 16. $(11, -3)$
17. $(8, -13)$ 18. $(6, -0.5)$ 19. $(0.25, -8)$ 20. $(5, -4)$
21. $(5, -0.5)$ 22. $(-1, 10)$ 19. $(1/3, -7)$ 20. $(2, -1)$

Exercise 1.8

1.

(a) $3y = -x + 11$ (b) $y = -2x - 7$ (c) $y = -5x - 16$
(d) $y = 5x + 9$ (e) $y = -5x + 9$ (f) $y = -3x - 15$
(g) $4y = -9x + 22$ (h) $8y = 9x - 34$ (i) $y = -5x + 12$
(j) $y = -3x + 18$ (k) $2y = 8x + 9$ (l) $x = 8$

2.

(a) $3x + 2y - 31 = 0$ **(b)** $2x - 4y + 4 = 0$
(c) $2x + 8y - 53 = 0$ **(d)** $x - y + 2 = 0$
(e) $y = -2$ **(f)** $3x - 2y + 47 = 0$
(g) $2x + 3y - 24 = 0$ **(h)** $3x - 2y - 14 = 0$
(i) $5x + 4y - 18 = 0$ **(j)** $5x + 3y - 26 = 0$
(k) $7x - 3y + 36 = 0$ **(l)** $3x - 4y - 68 = 0$

3.

(a) $(-2, 6)$ **(b)** $(5, 3)$ **(c)** $(7, 17)$
(d) $(10, -4)$ **(e)** $(-8, -14)$ **(f)** $(-9, 3)$

Exercise 1.9

1.

(a) $y = -2x + 6$ **(b)** $9y = -14x - 48$
(c) $y = 2x + 3$ **(d)** $y = 6x - 34$
(e) $y = 6x - 2$ **(f)** $3y = x + 30$

2.

(a) $4x + y + 17 = 0$ **(b)** $5x - 3y + 7 = 0$
(c) $3x - 2y + 2 = 0$ **(d)** $3x + 2y - 5 = 0$
(e) $3x - 13y + 53 = 0$ **(f)** $2x + 5y - 20 = 0$

3.

(a) $(-2, 4)$ **(b)** $(8, 6)$ **(c)** $(-3, 0)$
(d) $(15, 7)$ **(e)** $(8, -5)$ **(f)** $(2, 4)$

Exercise 1.10

1.

(a) $y = 2x + 4$ **(b)** $3y = -x - 2$
(c) $y = -3x + 7$ **(d)** $y = -5x + 35$
(e) $2y = 3x - 8$ **(f)** $3y = 2x + 25$

2.

(a) $3x - 4y + 25 = 0$ **(b)** $4x - 3y - 2 = 0$
(c) $5x + 2y - 56 = 0$ **(d)** $x + 4y + 7 = 0$
(e) $2x + 3y + 9 = 0$ **(f)** $2x - 5y - 33 = 0$

3.

(a) $(5, 6)$ **(b)** $(3, -4)$ **(c)** $(-3, -3)$
(d) $(7/2, 13/2)$ **(e)** $(-1, 7)$ **(f)** $(-2, -2)$

Exercise 1.11A

1.1

(a) $3x - 4y + 1 = 0$ **(b)** $2x + y - 18 = 0$
(c) $4x + y - 26 = 0$

1.2 (a) $(7, 4)$ **(b)** $(1, 7)$ **(c)** $(0, 7)$

1.3 (a) $m = -\frac{1}{3}$ **(b)** $m = -2$ **(c)** $m = -\frac{1}{5}$

1.4 (a) $\theta = 315°$ **(b)** $y = -x + 6$

1.5 (a) *not collinear* **(b)** *collinear*

1.6 (a) $2x + 3y + 9 = 0$ **(b)** $x + y - 10 = 0$

1.7 (a) $(2, 2)$ **(b)** $(4, -2)$ **(c)** $(-3, 1)$

1.8 (a) $x + 3y - 11 = 0$ **(b)** $8x - 2y + 9 = 0$
(c) $5x + y + 16 = 0$

1.9 (a) $2x + y - 6 = 0$ **(b)** $14x + 9y + 48 = 0$

1.10 (a) $x + 3y - 41 = 0$ **(b)** $x + 2y - 19 = 0$

Exercise 1.11B

1. **(a)** $y = -2x - 2$ **(b)** $y = -1$ **(c)** $\left(-\frac{1}{2}, -1\right)$

2. **(a)** $y = -\frac{11}{2}x + 9$ **(b)** $4y = 3x + 11$ **(c)** $\left(1, \frac{7}{2}\right)$

3. **(a)** $y = -\frac{1}{2}x - \frac{1}{2}$ **(b)** $y = \frac{1}{2}x - \frac{11}{2}$ **(c)** $(5, -3)$

4. $3x - y + 32 = 0$

5. **(a)** $y = -\frac{4}{3}x + 21$ **(b)** $(4, -1)$
(c) $A(-4, -7), B(-10, 1)$

6. $y = 15$ **7.** $d = 12$ **8.** $a = -\frac{5}{2}$ **9.** $(27, -9)$

10. **(a)** $y = -x - 2$ **(b)** $(5, -7)$ **(c)** $x - 5y - 8 = 0$

Chapter 2

Exercise 2.1

1. $y = 2x^2$ **2.** $y = 4(x - 3)^2$
3. $y = 3(x + 2)^2$ **4.** $y = 2(x - 3)^2 + 3$
5. $y = 2x^2 + 5$ **6.** $y = 3(x + 3)^2 + 4$
7. $y = -4x^2$ **8.** $y = 2(x + 4)^2 + 3$
9. $y = -2(x + 5)^2 - 2$ **10.** $y = \frac{1}{2}x^2$
11. $y = 2x^2 + 3$ **12.** $y = 2(x + 2)^2$
13. $y = -2x^2 - 5$ **14.** $y = \frac{1}{2}(x - 4)^2 + 2$
15. $y = 3(x + 2)^2 + 4$ **16.** $y = -\frac{1}{2}(x + 4)^2 - 3$
17. $y = -\frac{1}{3}x^2 - 4$ **18.** $y = \frac{2}{3}(x + 3)^2 + 4$

Exercise 2.2

1. $y = 2(x - 1)(x - 3)$ **2.** $y = \frac{1}{2}(x + 3)(x - 4)$
3. $y = -3(x + 1)(x - 3)$ **4.** $y = 2(x + 2)(x - 5)$
5. $y = -2(x + 6)(x - 2)$ **6.** $y = 3(x + 5)(x + 1)$
7. $y = 3x(x - 4)$ **8.** $y = -5x(x + 6)$
9. $y = \frac{1}{3}(x + 7)(x - 3)$ **10.** $y = \frac{1}{4}(x + 4)(x - 6)$
11. $y = -\frac{1}{4}(x + 6)(x - 6)$ **12.** $y = \frac{1}{8}(x + 8)^2$

Exercise 2.3

1.

(a) $x = 0, x = 5$ **(b)** $x = 0, x = 1$ **(c)** $x = 0, x = -9$
(d) $x = 0, x = 6$ **(e)** $x = 0, x = -2$ **(f)** $x = 0, x = -\frac{4}{3}$
(g) $x = 0, x = \frac{7}{4}$ **(h)** $x = 0, x = -\frac{9}{5}$ **(i)** $x = 0, x = \frac{5}{6}$

2.

(a) $x = -1, x = 1$ **(b)** $x = -5, x = 5$ **(c)** $x = -3, x = 3$

(d) $x=-5, x=5$ (e) $x=-5, x=5$ (f) $x=-2, x=2$

(g) $x=-2, x=2$ (h) $x=-\frac{1}{2}, x=\frac{1}{2}$ (i) $x=-\frac{1}{3}, x=\frac{1}{3}$

3.

(a) $x=-4, x=-1$ (b) $x=3, x=4$ (c) $x=-2, x=7$

(d) $x=1, x=9$ (e) $x=-2, x=4$ (f) $x=-3$ *twice*

(g) $x=-\frac{3}{2}, x=1$ (h) $x=-3, x=-\frac{1}{3}$ (i) $x=-\frac{3}{5}, x=2$

4.

(a) $x=0, x=\frac{3}{2}$ (b) $x=-1, x=1$ (c) $x=-3, x=5$

(d) $x=-\frac{1}{2}, x=\frac{1}{2}$ (e) $x=0, x=16$ (f) $x=-3, x=-1$

(g) $x=-1, x=1$ (h) $x=-3, x=3$ (i) $x=0, x=\frac{1}{2}$

(j) $x=-4, x=9$ (k) $x=-3, x=3$ (l) $x=-12, x=1$

(m) $x=1, x=\frac{5}{2}$ (n) $x=0, x=\frac{11}{9}$ (o) $x=-2, x=-\frac{2}{3}$

(p) $x=0, x=4$ (q) $x=-\frac{1}{4}, x=\frac{1}{4}$ (r) $x=-\frac{1}{\sqrt{2}}, x=\frac{1}{\sqrt{2}}$

(s) $x=-\frac{3}{4}, x=2$ (t) $x=-\frac{3}{4}, x=\frac{5}{2}$ (u) $x=0, x=\frac{2}{3}$

Exercise 2.4

1. $x=0, x=6$ 2. $x=-1, x=1$ 3. $x=-1, x=4$
4. $x=0, x=2$ 5. $x=-1, x=6$ 6. $x=-3, x=\frac{2}{3}$
7. $x=-2, x=\frac{4}{5}$ 8. $x=-\frac{3}{4}, x=\frac{1}{2}$ 9. $x=0, x=\frac{7}{37}$
10. $x=-3, x=3$ 11. $x=-3, x=\frac{5}{6}$ 12. $x=-3, x=4$
13. $x=-3$ *twice* 14. $x=-3, x=5$ 15. $x=-\frac{15}{2}, x=1$
16. $x=-\frac{5}{2}, x=2$ 17. $x=-\frac{4}{3}, x=3$ 18. $x=-2, x=4$

Exercise 2.5

1. $x=-4.65, x=0.65$ 2. $x=-1.14, x=6.14$
3. $x=-6.16, x=0.16$ 4. $x=-0.41, x=2.41$
5. $x=0.58, x=10.42$ 6. $x=-1.24, x=3.24$
7. $x=-0.70, x=2.37$ 8. $x=-5.35, x=-0.65$
9. $x=-0.14, x=2.47$ 10. $x=-0.47, x=3.22$
11. $x=-0.78, x=0.16$ 12. $x=-4.19, x=1.19$
13. $x=-2.52, x=-0.08$ 14. $x=-0.72, x=9.72$
15. $x=-3.87, x=3.87$ 16. $x=1.55, x=6.45$
17. $x=-9.11, x=0.11$ 18. $x=-3.48, x=0.48$
19. $x=-2.20, x=0.53$ 20. $x=0.13, x=14.87$
21. $x=-0.56, x=12.56$

Exercise 2.6A

1. $(x+1)^2+2$ 2. $(x+4)^2-23$ 3. $(x-5)^2-16$
4. $(x+3)^2-5$ 5. $(x-2)^2+8$ 6. $(x+4)^2-28$
7. $(x-1)^2+6$ 8. $(x+10)^2-74$ 9. $(x-2)^2+1$
10. $(x+3)^2+6$ 11. $(x-7)^2-64$ 12. $(x+6)^2-47$
13. $(x-6)^2-27$ 14. $(x+9)^2-31$ 15. $(x-2)^2-23$

Exercise 2.6B

1. $\left(x+\frac{1}{2}\right)^2+\frac{7}{4}$ 2. $\left(x+\frac{3}{2}\right)^2+\frac{3}{4}$ 3. $\left(x+\frac{5}{2}\right)^2+\frac{23}{4}$
4. $\left(x-\frac{3}{2}\right)^2+\frac{35}{4}$ 5. $\left(x-\frac{7}{2}\right)^2+\frac{39}{4}$ 6. $\left(x-\frac{11}{2}\right)^2-\frac{21}{4}$
7. $\left(x+\frac{5}{2}\right)^2+\frac{11}{4}$ 8. $\left(x+\frac{11}{2}\right)^2-\frac{49}{4}$ 9. $\left(x+\frac{13}{2}\right)^2+\frac{11}{4}$
10. $\left(x+\frac{1}{2}\right)^2+\frac{43}{4}$ 11. $\left(x+\frac{9}{2}\right)^2-\frac{57}{4}$ 12. $\left(x-\frac{15}{2}\right)^2-\frac{125}{4}$
13. $\left(x+\frac{9}{2}\right)^2-\frac{141}{4}$ 14. $\left(x+\frac{13}{2}\right)^2-\frac{73}{4}$ 15. $\left(x+\frac{9}{2}\right)^2-\frac{101}{4}$

Exercise 2.6C

1. $-(x+1)^2+3$ 2. $-(x+2)^2+5$
3. $-(x-4)^2+21$ 4. $-\left(x+\frac{3}{2}\right)^2+\frac{17}{4}$
5. $-\left(x-\frac{5}{2}\right)^2+\frac{41}{4}$ 6. $-\left(x+\frac{7}{2}\right)^2+\frac{61}{4}$
7. $-\left(x-\frac{5}{2}\right)^2+\frac{61}{4}$ 8. $-\left(x+\frac{5}{2}\right)^2+\frac{69}{4}$
9. $-(x-3)^2+11$ 10. $-(x-5)^2+35$
11. $-\left(x+\frac{13}{2}\right)^2+\frac{205}{4}$ 12. $-\left(x-\frac{11}{2}\right)^2+\frac{209}{4}$
13. $-\left(x+\frac{5}{2}\right)^2+\frac{73}{4}$ 14. $-(x-12)^2+159$
15. $-\left(x+\frac{15}{2}\right)^2+\frac{297}{4}$

Exercise 2.6D

1. $2(x+1)^2+5$ 2. $3(x-1)^2+6$
3. $5(x+1)^2+7$ 4. $2(x-2)^2-3$
5. $5(x+3)^2-50$ 6. $4(x-2)^2-27$
7. $3\left(x-\frac{3}{2}\right)^2+\frac{17}{4}$ 8. $6\left(x+\frac{1}{2}\right)^2+\frac{7}{2}$
9. $7\left(x+\frac{3}{2}\right)^2-\frac{163}{4}$ 10. $-2\left(x+\frac{3}{2}\right)^2+\frac{15}{2}$
11. $-2\left(x-\frac{5}{2}\right)^2+\frac{47}{2}$ 12. $4\left(x-\frac{3}{2}\right)^2$
13. $3\left(x-\frac{1}{2}\right)^2+\frac{53}{4}$ 14. $4\left(x-\frac{5}{2}\right)^2-12$
15. $-2\left(x+\frac{5}{4}\right)^2+\frac{105}{8}$

Exercise 2.7

1. $x=-2, x=4$ 2. $x=1, x=5$
3. $x=1, x=9$ 4. $x=-6, x=4$
5. $x=-2, x=6$ 6. $x=-3, x=11$
7. $x=1-\sqrt{13}, x=1+\sqrt{13}$ 8. $x=-2-\sqrt{7}, x=-2+\sqrt{7}$
9. $x=3-\sqrt{11}, x=3+\sqrt{11}$ 10. $x=2-\sqrt{11}, x=2+\sqrt{11}$
11. $x=-3-3\sqrt{2}, x=-3+3\sqrt{2}$
12. $x=4-\sqrt{17}, x=4+\sqrt{17}$
13. $x=\frac{-4-3\sqrt{2}}{2}, x=\frac{-4+3\sqrt{2}}{2}$
14. $x=\frac{6-\sqrt{30}}{3}, x=\frac{6+\sqrt{30}}{3}$
15. $x=\frac{4-\sqrt{22}}{3}, x=\frac{4+\sqrt{22}}{3}$
16. $x=\frac{-10-\sqrt{95}}{5}, x=\frac{-10+\sqrt{95}}{5}$
17. $x=\frac{6-\sqrt{42}}{2}, x=\frac{6+\sqrt{42}}{2}$
18. $x=\frac{-3-2\sqrt{3}}{2}, x=\frac{-3+2\sqrt{3}}{2}$
19. $x=-3-2\sqrt{5}, x=-3+2\sqrt{5}$
20. $x=\frac{5-\sqrt{21}}{2}, x=\frac{5+\sqrt{21}}{2}$
21. $x=\frac{-7-\sqrt{61}}{2}, x=\frac{-7+\sqrt{61}}{2}$
22. $x=\frac{3-\sqrt{7}}{2}, x=\frac{3+\sqrt{7}}{2}$
23. $x=\frac{-9-\sqrt{93}}{6}, x=\frac{-9+\sqrt{93}}{6}$

24. $x = \frac{-15-\sqrt{185}}{10}, x = \frac{-15+\sqrt{185}}{10}$

Exercise 2.8

1.

(a)

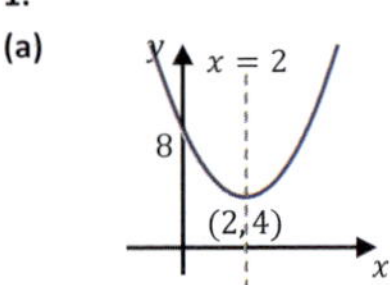

(b)

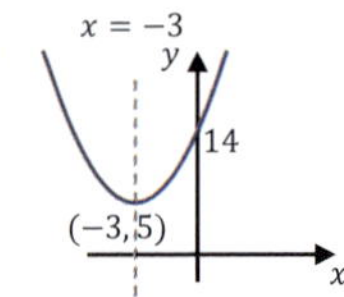

(c)

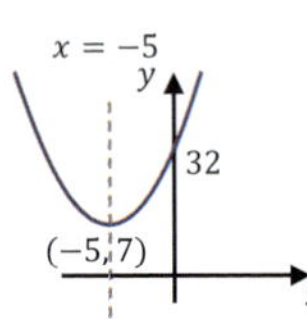

(d)

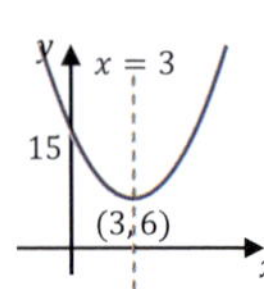

(e)

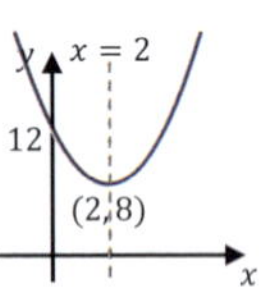

(f)

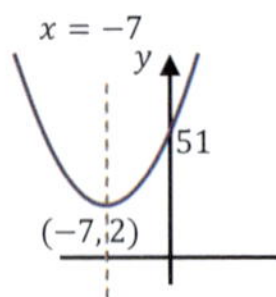

2.

(a)

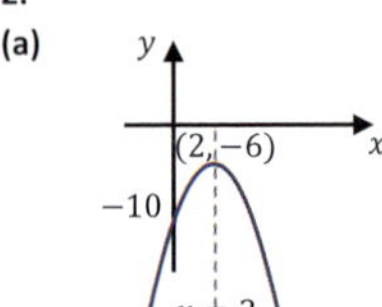

(b)

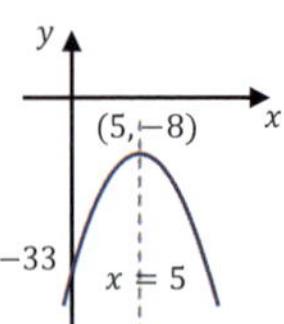

(c)

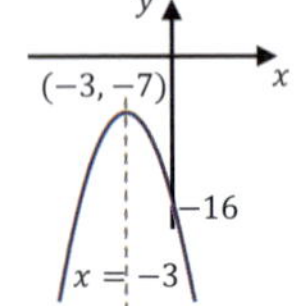

(d)

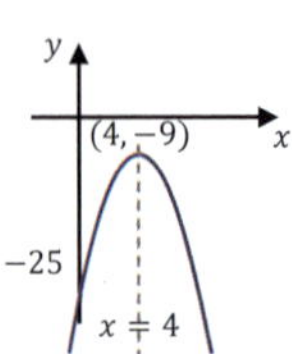

(e)

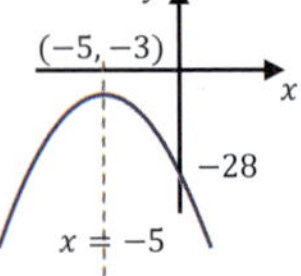

(f)

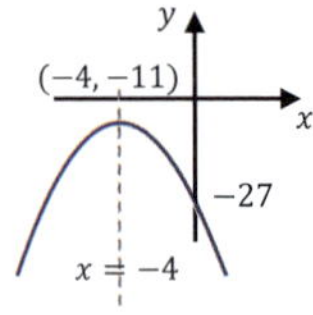

3.

(a)

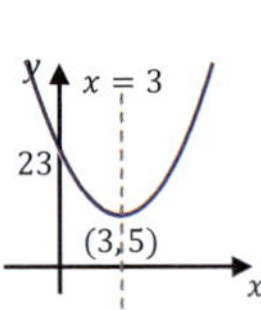

(b)

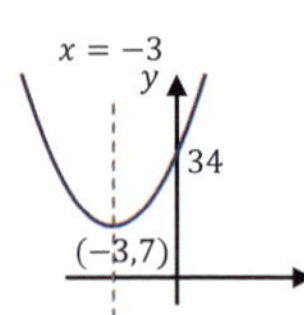

(c)

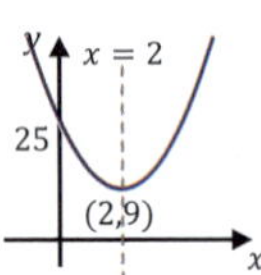

(d)

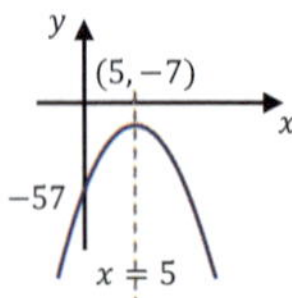

(e)

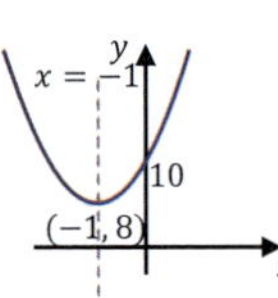

(f)

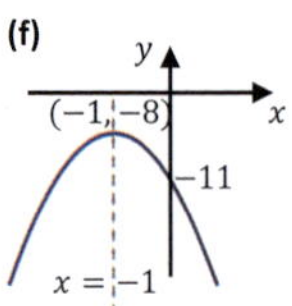

(g)

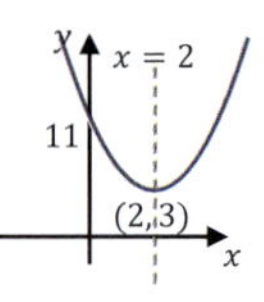

(h)

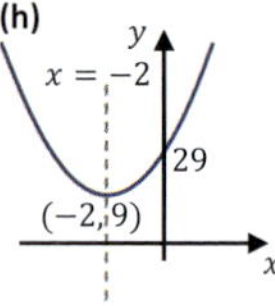

(i)

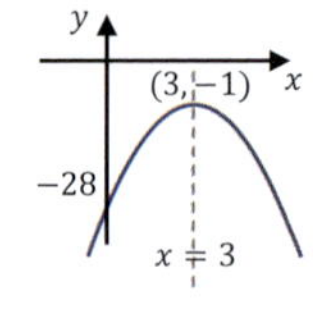

Exercise 2.9

1.

(a)

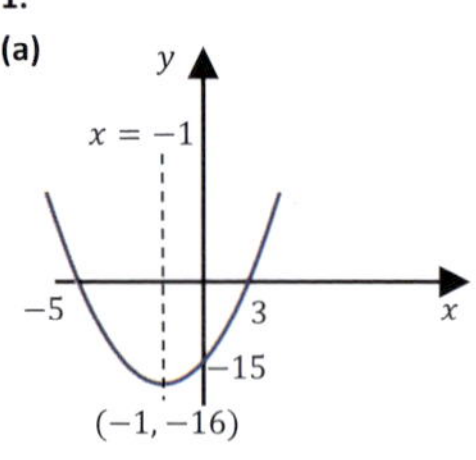

(b)

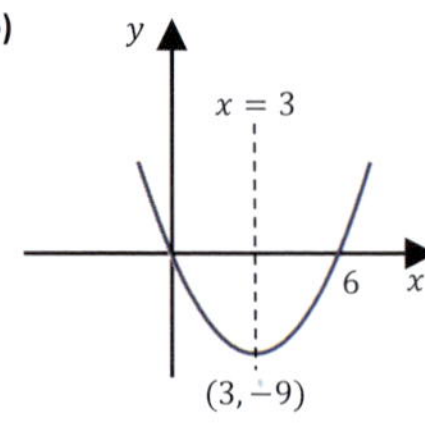

(c)

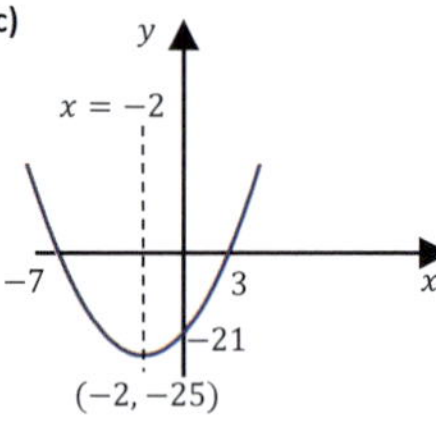

(d)

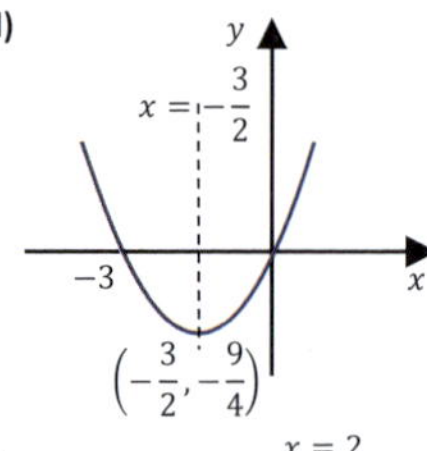

(e)

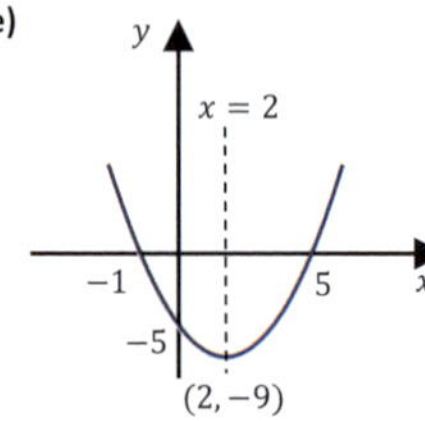

(f)

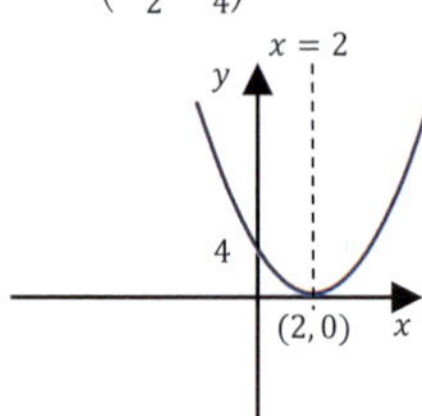

(g)

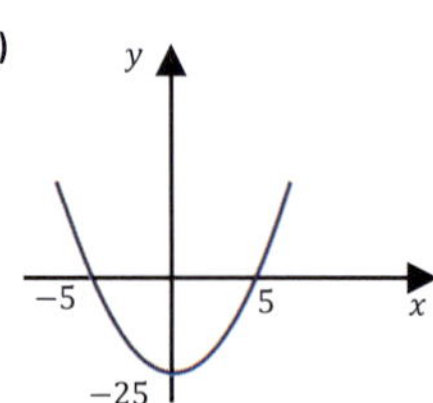

(h)

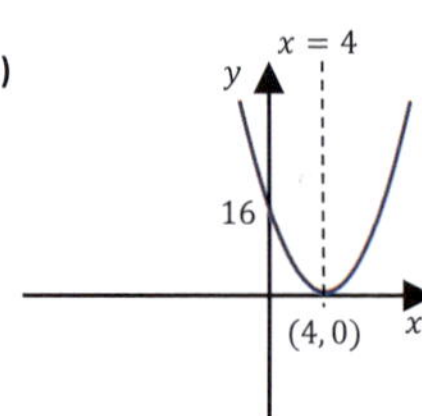

(i)

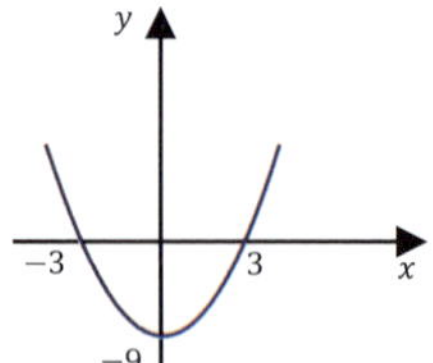

2.

(a)

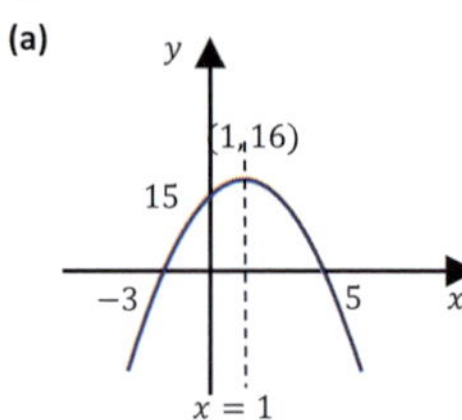

(b)

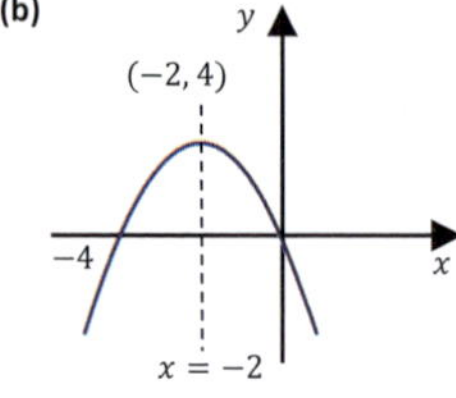

(c)

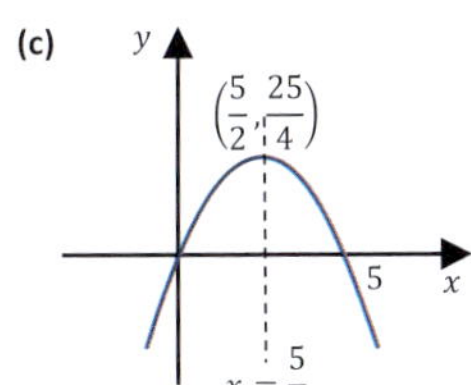

(d)

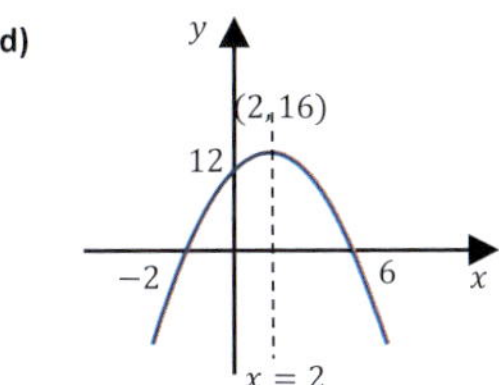

(e)

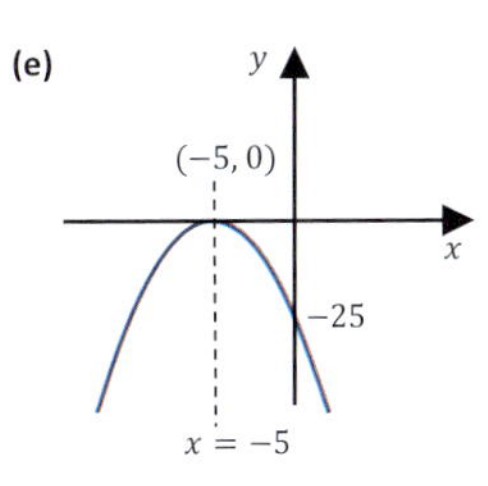

(f)

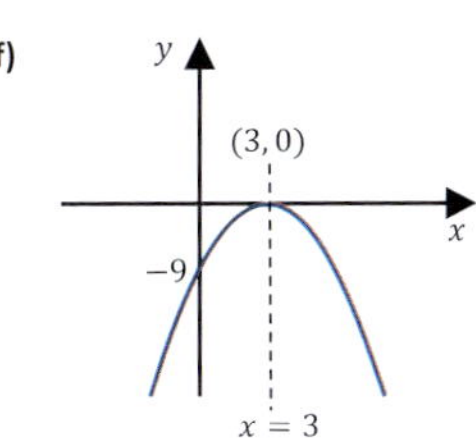

3.

(a)

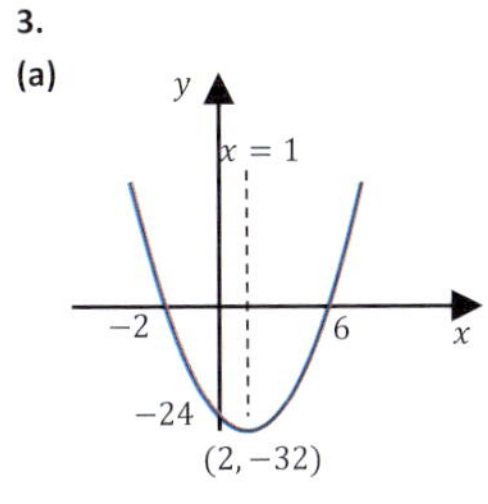

(b)

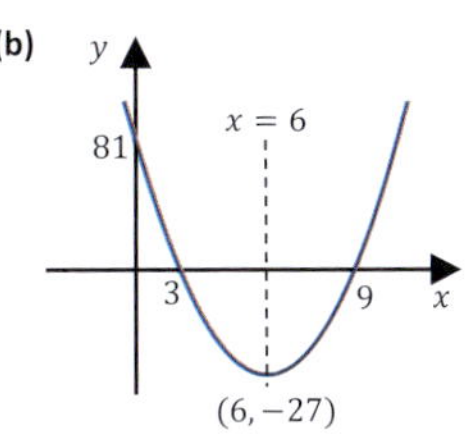

(c)

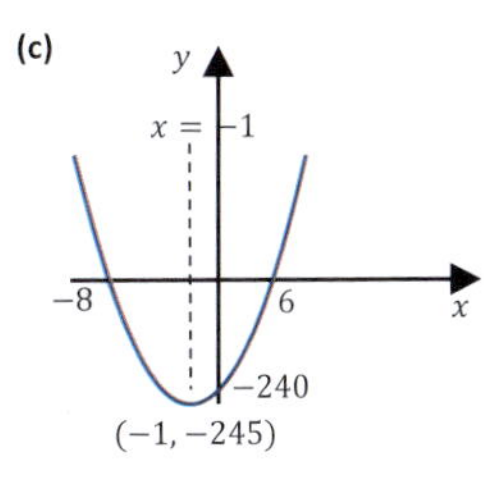

(d)

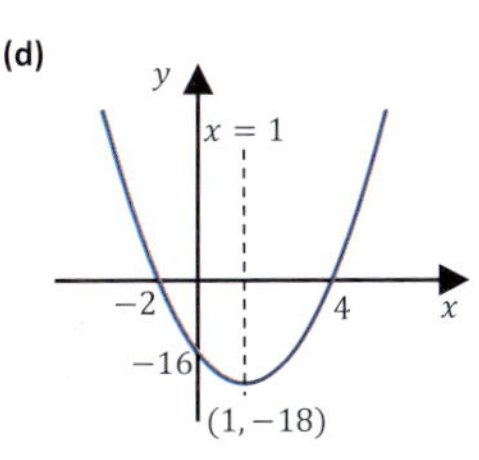

(e)

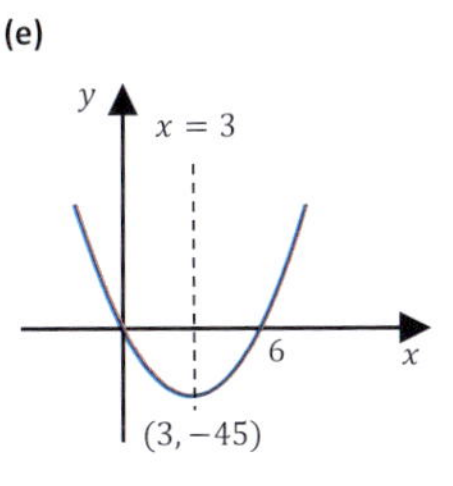

(f)

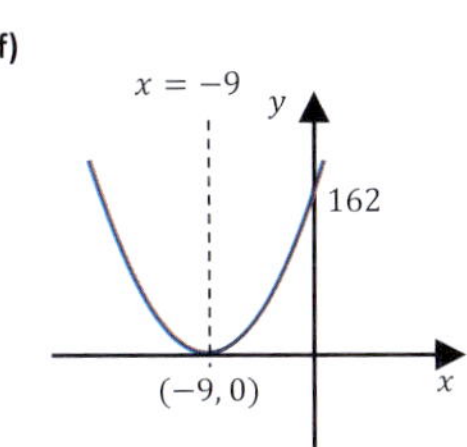

(g)

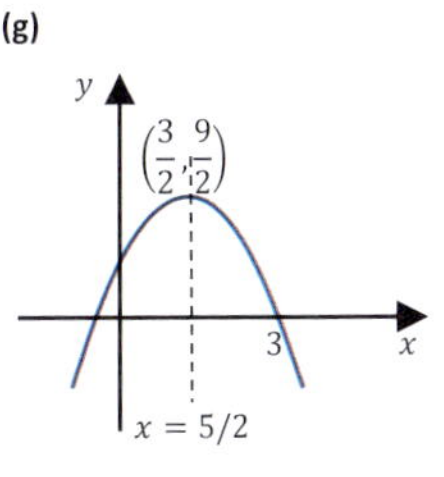

(h)

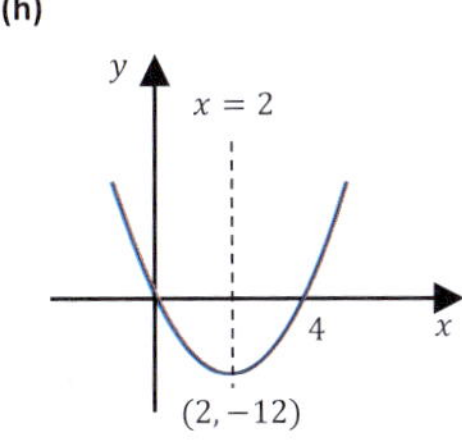

(i)

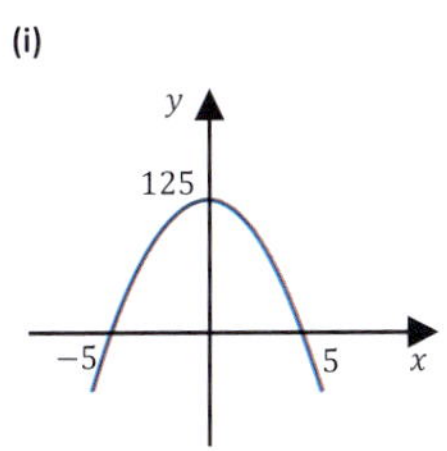

Exercise 2.10

1. $0 < x < 3$ **2.** $0 < x < 2$ **3.** $x < -5, x > 5$
4. $x \leq -3, x \geq 3$ **5.** $1 \leq x \leq 2$ **6.** $x < -2, x > 3$
7. $-3 < x < -2$ **8.** $x < -6, x > -2$ **9.** $-5 \leq x \leq 3$
10. $-8 < x < 1$ **11.** $x \leq 3, x \geq 6$ **12.** $-7 < x < -2$
13. $x < -8, x > 1$ **14.** $1 \leq x \leq 4$ **15.** $-5 \leq x \leq 5$
16. $x \leq -4, x \geq 5$ **17.** $-4 < x < 3$ **18.** $-1 \leq x \leq 1$
19. $x < -9, x > 6$ **20.** $x \leq -\frac{1}{2}, x \geq \frac{2}{3}$ **21.** $-\frac{1}{3} \leq x \leq 4$

Exercise 2.11

1. $b^2 - 4ac > 0$, ∴ there are two real and distinct roots.
2. $b^2 - 4ac < 0$, ∴ there are no real roots.
3. $b^2 - 4ac = 0$, ∴ there are two real and equal roots.
4. $b^2 - 4ac > 0$, ∴ there are two real and distinct roots.
5. $b^2 - 4ac = 0$, ∴ there are two real and equal roots.
6. $b^2 - 4ac < 0$, ∴ there are no real roots.
7. $b^2 - 4ac = 0$, ∴ there are two real and equal roots.
8. $b^2 - 4ac < 0$, ∴ there are no real roots.
9. $b^2 - 4ac > 0$, ∴ there are two real and distinct roots.
10. $b^2 - 4ac > 0$, ∴ there are two real and distinct roots.
11. $b^2 - 4ac < 0$, ∴ there are no real roots.
12. $b^2 - 4ac > 0$, ∴ there are two real and distinct roots.

Exercise 2.12

1.

(a) $k = 4$ (b) $k = 4, k = -4$ (c) $k = 0, k = 4$
(d) $k = -2\ k = 2$ (e) $k = -6, k = 2$ (f) $k = 16$
(g) $k = 0, k = -4$ (h) $k = -3, k = 1$ (i) $k = 0, k = 6$

2.

(a) $k > 4$ (b) $-10 < k < 10$ (c) $-8 < k < 8$
(d) $1 < k < 9$ (e) $-2 < k < 6$ (f) $-4 < k < 8$
(g) $-3 < k < 1$ (h) $-4 < k < 0$ (i) $0 < k < 6$

3.

(a) $k < 1$ (b) $k < -10, k > 10$ (c) $k < -8, k > 8$
(d) $k < 2, k > 22$ (e) $k < -\frac{4}{5}, k > 0$ (f) $k < 1, k > 25$
(g) $k < -2, k > 6$ (h) $k \neq 2$ (i) $k \leq -8, k \geq 0$

Exercise 2.13

All questions are proofs.

Exercise 2.14

1. $b^2 - 4ac > 0$, ∴ there are two points of intersection.
2. $b^2 - 4ac < 0$, ∴ the line and curve do not intersect.
3. $b^2 - 4ac > 0$, ∴ there are two points of intersection.
4. $b^2 - 4ac < 0$, ∴ the line and curve do not intersect.
5. $b^2 - 4ac = 0$, ∴ the line is a tangent to the curve.
6. $b^2 - 4ac > 0$, ∴ there are two points of intersection.
7. $b^2 - 4ac = 0$, ∴ the line is a tangent to the curve.
8. $b^2 - 4ac > 0$, ∴ there are two points of intersection.
9. $b^2 - 4ac < 0$, ∴ the line and curve do not intersect.
10. $b^2 - 4ac > 0$, ∴ there are two points of intersection.
11. $b^2 - 4ac > 0$, ∴ there are two points of intersection.
12. $b^2 - 4ac < 0$, ∴ the line and curve do not intersect.

Exercise 2.15

1.

(a) $(-2,1),(5,15)$ (b) $(4,21),(1,9)$ (c) $(3,6),(4,4)$
(d) $(-7,40),(2,-5)$ (e) $(-4,2),(4,26)$ (f) $(-3,16),(3,16)$
(g) $(-9,-35),(0,1)$ (h) $(1,18),(9,98)$ (i) $(0,1),(2,17)$
(j) $(-3,2),(3,14)$

2.

(a) Proof, $(1,4)$ (b) Proof, $(3,9)$ (c) Proof, $(2,2)$
(d) Proof, $(2,3)$ (e) Proof, $(-5,-13)$ (f) Proof, $(-4,-11)$

Exercise 2.16

1. $(-3,-9),(3,-9)$
2. $(2,-11),(3,-6)$
3. $(-1,-8),(4,12)$
4. $(1,4),(4,4)$
5. $(-2,16),(9,192)$
6. $(-2,-8),(2,0)$
7. $(-3,16),(3,16)$
8. $(0,5),(-8,53)$
9. $(-5,90),(-2,27)$
10. $(-2,9),(6,-15)$

Exercise 2.17A

2.4-5

(a) $x=-2, x=7$ (b) $x=-3, x=4$
(c) $x=-6, x=6$ (d) $x=\frac{1-\sqrt{3}}{2}, x=\frac{1+\sqrt{3}}{2}$
(e) $x=-\frac{1}{2}, x=2$ (f) $x=\frac{2-\sqrt{22}}{2}, x=\frac{2+\sqrt{22}}{2}$

2.6

(a) $\left(x-\frac{5}{2}\right)^2+\frac{3}{4}$ (b) $-\left(x-\frac{3}{2}\right)^2+\frac{29}{4}$
(c) $3\left(x+\frac{3}{2}\right)^2+\frac{53}{4}$

2.7

(a) $x=2-\sqrt{19}, x=2+\sqrt{19}$
(b) $x=-4-2\sqrt{3}, x=-4+2\sqrt{3}$
(c) $x=\frac{5-\sqrt{15}}{2}, x=\frac{5+\sqrt{15}}{2}$

2.10

(a) $x<-4, x>7$ (b) $-3<x<1$ (c) $x\leq-\frac{1}{3}, x\geq5$

2.12

(a) $k<-2, k>6$ (b) $k=-5, k=3$ (c) $-3<k<0$

2.13

(a) $(-3,10)$ (b) $(2,11)$

2.14

(a) $b^2-4ac<0$, ∴ the line and curve do not intersect.
(b) $b^2-4ac>0$, ∴ there are two points of intersection.

2.15

(a) $(-1,-3),(7,37)$ (b) $(-4,-3),(6,17)$

2.16

(a) $(-4,0),(7,110)$ (b) $(2,-9),(3,-4)$

Chapter 3

Exercise 3.1

1. 5
2. 13
3. 17
4. 10
5. 25
6. 25
7. $2\sqrt{29}$
8. $2\sqrt{41}$
9. $2\sqrt{5}$
10. $2\sqrt{17}$
11. $3\sqrt{29}$
12. $\sqrt{53}$
13. $2\sqrt{10}$
14. $\sqrt{205}$
15. $\sqrt{146}$

Exercise 3.2

1.

(a) $x^2+y^2-8x-2y-8=0$
(b) $x^2+y^2+6x-4y-36=0$
(c) $x^2+y^2+12x-10y+45=0$
(d) $x^2+y^2-18x-22y+138=0$
(e) $x^2+y^2-10x+18y+70=0$
(f) $x^2+y^2-9=0$
(g) $x^2+y^2-12x-4y+34=0$
(h) $x^2+y^2+14x-6y+37=0$
(i) $x^2+y^2-18y+33=0$
(j) $x^2+y^2-6x+16y+28=0$
(k) $x^2+y^2+14x-437=0$
(l) $x^2+y^2-24x-4y+49=0$

2.

(a) $(x+4)^2+(y-6)^2=20$ (b) $(x-5)^2+(y+12)^2=34$
(c) $(x+9)^2+(y-4)^2=49$ (d) $(x-11)^2+(y-4)^2=68$
(e) $(x-22)^2+(y-14)^2=40$ (f) $(x+5)^2+(y-13)^2=37$
(g) $(x-9)^2+(y-7)^2=125$ (h) $x^2+(y-9)^2=117$
(i) $(x-5)^2+y^2=153$

3.

(a) $(x+2)^2+(y+1)^2=100$ (b) $(x-7)^2+(y-6)^2=404$
(c) $(x-15)^2+y^2=45$ (d) $x^2+(y+19)^2=80$
(e) $(x-5)^2+(y-11)^2=200$ (f) $x^2+y^2=65$
(g) $(x-5)^2+(y-11)^2=90$ (h) $(x+22)^2+(y-5)^2=121$
(i) $(x+12)^2+(y-7)^2=153$

Exercise 3.3

1.

(a) $Centre: (0,0), Radius=5$
(b) $Centre: (5,3), Radius=8$
(c) $Centre: (-12,1), Radius=1$
(d) $Centre: (0,32), Radius=5\sqrt{3}$
(e) $Centre: (-9,-7), Radius=2\sqrt{17}$
(f) $Centre: (-15,0), Radius=6\sqrt{3}$
(g) $Centre: (21,-9), Radius=8\sqrt{3}$
(h) $Centre: (0,0), Radius=7\sqrt{5}$
(i) $Centre: (2,13), Radius=6\sqrt{7}$
(j) $Centre: (-17,0), Radius=17$
(k) $Centre: (-56,-19), Radius=9\sqrt{3}$
(l) $Centre: (0,10), Radius=6\sqrt{5}$

2.

(a) $Centre: (6,-3), Radius=8$
(b) $Centre: (12,-5), Radius=12$
(c) $Centre: (-2,7), Radius=7$

(d) $Centre: (5,4), Radius = 2\sqrt{3}$
(e) $Centre: (12,-3), Radius = 5\sqrt{2}$
(f) $Centre: (1,-7), Radius = 2\sqrt{7}$
(g) $Centre: (-15,-2), Radius = 5\sqrt{7}$
(h) $Centre: (-2,-12), Radius = 3\sqrt{11}$
(i) $Centre: (0,13), Radius = 3\sqrt{7}$
(j) $Centre: (7,-1), Radius = 5\sqrt{13}$
(k) $Centre: (8,-4), Radius = 16$
(l) $Centre: (11,0), Radius = 12\sqrt{3}$

3.
(a) circle (b) not a circle (c) circle
(d) circle (e) not a circle (f) not a circle
(g) circle (h) circle (i) circle
(j) not a circle (k) not a circle (l) not a circle

Exercise 3.4

1.
(a) outwith (b) within (c) within
(d) on (e) within (f) outwith
(g) within (h) on (i) within
(j) outwith (k) within (l) on

2.
(a) outwith (b) within (c) on
(d) on (e) outwith (f) on
(g) within (h) within (i) outwith
(j) on (k) within (l) outwith

Exercise 3.5

1.
(a) no points of intersection between the line and the circle
(b) two points of intersection between the line and the circle
(c) no points of intersection between the line and the circle
(d) line is a tangent to the circle
(e) no points of intersection between the line and the circle
(f) line is a tangent to the circle
(g) no points of intersection between the line and the circle
(h) two points of intersection between the line and the circle

2.
(a) no points of intersection between the line and the circle
(b) two points of intersection between the line and the circle
(c) two points of intersection between the line and the circle
(d) line is a tangent to the circle
(e) line is a tangent to the circle
(f) two points of intersection between the line and the circle
(g) no points of intersection between the line and the circle
(h) line is a tangent to the circle

Exercise 3.6

1.
(a) $(8,6)$ and $(-6,-8)$ (b) $(3,-6)$ and $(6,3)$
(c) $(-3,-1)$ and $(1,11)$ (d) $(-6,3)$ and $(-6,7)$
(e) $(-2,-2)$ twice (f) $(-11,10)$ and $(-6,5)$
(g) $(-24,2)$ and $(3,11)$ (h) $(9,7)$ twice

2.
(a) $(-8,-2)$ and $(2,8)$ (b) $(0,8)$ and $(1,-1)$
(c) $(13,-11)$ and $(-3,-3)$ (d) $(4,-4)$ twice
(e) $(5,2)$ twice (f) $(2,4)$ and $(8,10)$
(g) $(5,0)$ and $(-10,-5)$ (h) $(19,-9)$ and $(-3,-9)$

3. proof, point of contact $(1,1)$
4. proof, point of contact $(-1,2)$
5. proof, point of contact $(-3,-7)$
6. proof, point of contact $(-2,-4)$
7. proof, point of contact $(6,1)$
8. proof, point of contact $(-9,10)$

Exercise 3.7

1.
(a) $y = 2x - 9$ (b) $x + y - 9 = 0$ (c) $2x - y + 8 = 0$
(d) $3x - y + 33 = 0$ (e) $y = -x$ (f) $2x - y - 7 = 0$
(g) $2x - 3y + 8 = 0$ (h) $x - 2y + 27 = 0$

2.
(a) $2x - y + 3 = 0$ (b) $y = 9$
(c) $3x - 2y - 7 = 0$ (d) $x - 4y + 13 = 0$
(e) $x - 3y + 5 = 0$ (f) $x + 5y - 15 = 0$
(g) $2x + 3y + 14 = 0$ (h) $2x + 5y - 21 = 0$

3. $x - 3y + 15 = 0$ **4.** $2x + 3y + 5 = 0$
5. $(0, 6.5)$ **6.** $2x + 3y - 16 = 0$

Exercise 3.8

1.
(a) circles touch externally (b) circles intersect
(c) circles do not intersect (d) circles touch internally
(e) circles touch externally (f) circles intersect
(g) circles do not intersect (h) circles do not intersect

2.
(a) circles do not intersect (b) circles do not intersect
(c) circles intersect (d) circles touch externally

3.
(a) proof (b) $(2,2)$ and $(11,-7)$

4. 3 units

Exercise 3.9A

1.
(a) $(x - 34)^2 + (y - 6)^2 = 36$ (b) $(x - 28)^2 + (y - 11)^2 = 16$
(c) $(x - 5)^2 + (y - 15)^2 = 25$ (d) $(x - 3)^2 + (y - 12)^2 = 9$
(e) $(x - 17)^2 + (y - 5)^2 = 16$ (f) $(x - 19)^2 + (y - 11)^2 = 16$

2.
(a) $(x - 10)^2 + (y - 16)^2 = 16$ (b) $(x - 5)^2 + (y - 6)^2 = 9$

Exercise 3.9B

1.
(a) $(x - 20)^2 + (y - 7)^2 = 164$ (b) $(x + 13)^2 + (y - 6)^2 = 153$
(c) $(x + 4)^2 + (y - 2)^2 = 45$ (d) $(x - 18)^2 + (y + 1)^2 = 90$

2. $(x - 8)^2 + (y - 15)^2 = 13$

3. $(x-23)^2+(y+15)^2=52$
4. $(x-4)^2+(y+2)^2=144$
5. $(x+9)^2+(y+5)^2=10$
6. $(x-4)^2+(y-9)^2=500$

Exercise 3.10A

2.1

(a) $3\sqrt{2}$ (b) 13 (c) $2\sqrt{34}$

2.2

(a) $(x-8)^2+(y+7)^2=61$ (b) $(x-4)^2+(y-16)^2=65$
(c) $x^2+y^2=125$

2.3

(a) $Centre: (0,0), Radius = 12$
(b) $Centre: (-9,1), Radius = 3\sqrt{7}$
(c) $Centre: (-8,4), Radius = 3\sqrt{11}$
(d) $Centre: (1,-3), Radius = 5\sqrt{2}$

2.4

(a) outside the circle (b) on the circle

2.5

(a) two points of intersection between the line and the circle
(b) no points of intersection between the line and the circle

2.6

(a) (i) $(4,2)$ and $(10,0)$ (ii) $(-4,0)$ and $(-2,2)$

(b) proof, point of contact $(5,1)$

2.7

(a) $x+y=10$ (b) $x+2y=6$

2.8

(a) circles touch externally (b) circles do not intersect

2.9

(a) $(x-28)^2+(y-5)^2=25$ (b) $(x-30)^2+(y-18)^2=36$

Exercise 3.10B

1. proof 2. $p<9$

3. (a) $(1,2)$ and $(7,-4)$ (b) $(x+3)^2+(y+8)^2=116$

4. (a) 10 (b) $(x-27)^2+(y-25)^2=25$

5. $(x-4)^2+(y+5)^2=20$

Chapter 4

Exercise 4.1A

1.

(a) $x\neq 0$ (b) $x\neq 1$ (c) $x\neq -\frac{2}{5}$
(d) $x\neq \frac{3}{2}$ (e) $x\neq \pm 1$ (f) $x\neq -2,0$
(g) $x\neq 2$ (h) $x\neq \pm 3$ (i) $x\neq -3$
(j) $x\neq 3$ (k) $x\neq 1$ (l) $x\neq -2$
(m) $x\neq 0$ (n) $x\neq -3,\frac{1}{2}$ (o) $x\neq -5$

2.

(a) $x\geq 0$ (b) $x\geq 3$ (c) $x\leq 5$
(d) $x\leq 7$ (e) $x\geq 5$ (f) $x\leq 2$
(g) $x\leq -3, x\geq 3$ (h) $x\leq -2, x\geq 2$ (i) $x\leq -\sqrt{10}, x\geq \sqrt{10}$
(j) $-4\leq x\leq 4$ (k) $0\leq x\leq 1$ (l) $x\leq 0, x\geq 1$
(m) $x<-2, x>2$ (n) $0<x<2$ (o) $x<-1, x>2$

Exercise 4.1B

1.

(a) $f(x)\geq 1$ (b) $f(x)\leq 14$ (c) $f(x)\geq -9$
(d) $f(x)\geq 2$ (e) $f(x)\leq 5$ (f) $f(x)\geq -12$
(g) $f(x)\geq -3$ (h) $f(x)\geq -7$ (i) $f(x)\geq \frac{27}{4}$
(j) $f(x)\leq 17$ (k) $f(x)\leq \frac{33}{4}$ (l) $f(x)\geq \frac{13}{2}$

2.

(a) $1\leq f(x)\leq 26$ (b) $-1\leq f(x)\leq 53$
(c) $-14<f(x)<2$ (d) $-18\leq f(x)\leq 352$
(e) $2<f(x)\leq 1002$ (f) $-2\leq f(x)\leq 30$
(g) $34\leq f(x)\leq 1007$ (h) $-21\leq f(x)\leq 4$
(i) $-2999\leq f(x)<1$ (j) $-4012\leq f(x)\leq -8$
(k) $-9\leq f(x)\leq 5$ (l) $-10\leq f(x)\leq 5$

Exercise 4.2

1.

(a) 4 (b) 11 (c) 5 (d) 28
(e) -15 (f) 5 (g) 25 (h) -52
(i) 109 (j) 1 (k) 137 (l) -5

2.

(a) 108 (b) $\frac{4}{3}$ (c) -7 (d) 37
(e) 4 (f) -12 (g) -32 (h) $-\frac{1}{2}$
(i) -431 (j) 500 (k) 676 (l) -25

3.

(a) 6 (b) 9 (c) 8 (d) -11
(e) 3 (f) $\frac{1}{2}$ (g) -8 (h) 2
(i) 3 (j) -1 (k) -3 (l) 6

Exercise 4.3A

1.

(a) $6x$ (b) $6x-8$ (c) $29-12x$
(d) $14-12x$ (e) $14-8x$ (f) $34-8x$
(g) $2-8x$ (h) $22-8x$ (i) $4x+6$
(j) $9x-4$ (k) $4x-18$ (l) $16x-30$

2.

(a) $5x^2+4$ (b) $25x^2-10x+2$ (c) $10x^2+19$
(d) $50x^2-20x+6$ (e) $4x^4+16x^2+17$ (f) $2x^4+4x^2+6$
(g) $\frac{1}{4x^2+9}$ (h) $\frac{1}{2x^2+3}$ (i) $\frac{1}{10x-1}$
(j) x^4+2x^2+2 (k) $25x-6$ (l) $8x^4+32x^2+36$

3.

(a) $\sin 4x$ (b) $\cos 4x$ (c) $\sin(x+3)$
(d) $\cos(x+3)$ (e) $4\sin x$ (f) $4x+12$

(g) $16x$ (h) $x+6$ (i) $\sin x+3$
(j) $4\cos x$ (k) $\cos x+3$ (l) $64x$

4.
(a) $\frac{x+2}{4x+9}$ (b) $\frac{5x+20}{2x+7}$ (c) $\frac{x+4}{-2x-5}$
(d) $\frac{x+4}{4x+17}$ (e) $\frac{2-x}{9-2x}$ (f) $\frac{2-x}{2x+11}$
(g) $\frac{2-x}{13-4x}$ (h) $\frac{10-5x}{-2x-1}$ (i) $\frac{5x+10}{2x+3}$
(j) $\frac{x+2}{-2x-1}$ (k) $\frac{x+2}{2x+5}$ (l) $\frac{3x+2}{6x-3}$

Exercise 4.3B

1.
(a) 23 (b) 2 (c) 49
(d) 35 (e) 1 (f) 8
(g) -1 (h) $\frac{5}{3}$ (i) $\frac{5}{9}$
(j) 8 (k) $-\frac{5}{6}$ (l) -9
(m) 168 (n) $1/3$ (o) $\frac{5}{11}$
(p) 15

2.
(a) -30 (b) -3 (c) 16
(d) 4 (e) 100 (f) $\frac{1}{11}$
(g) 1 (h) -240 (i) -6
(j) -6 (k) $-\frac{1}{4}$ (l) 4
(m) -33 (n) $\frac{5}{36}$ (o) $-\frac{1}{11}$
(p) $\frac{2}{11}$

Exercise 4.4

1.
(a) $\frac{x-7}{4}$ (b) $\frac{x+9}{5}$ (c) $\frac{8-x}{2}$
(d) $\frac{x+20}{7}$ (e) $2x+4$ (f) $3x-27$
(g) $\frac{5x+2}{3}$ (h) $\frac{4x+40}{3}$ (i) $5-7x$
(j) $\frac{12x-6}{5}$ (k) $\frac{9x+5}{3}$ (l) $\frac{3x-3}{11}$
(m) $\frac{5x+3}{4}$ (n) $\frac{12-5x}{2}$ (o) $\frac{12x-8}{7}$
(p) $\frac{9-2x}{2}$

2.
(a) $\sqrt[3]{x}$ (b) $\sqrt[3]{x-1}$ (c) $\sqrt[3]{3-x}$
(d) $\sqrt[3]{\frac{x-5}{4}}$ (e) $\sqrt[5]{\frac{x}{2}}$ (f) $\sqrt[3]{\frac{x+7}{5}}$
(g) $\sqrt[5]{\frac{x-1}{3}}$ (h) $\sqrt[3]{\frac{4-x}{3}}$ (i) $\sqrt[3]{\frac{4x+5}{2}}$
(j) $\sqrt[5]{3x-6}$ (k) $\sqrt[3]{\frac{12x+2}{3}}$ (l) $\sqrt[5]{6x+11}$

3.
(a) $\sqrt[3]{\frac{x-1}{3}}$ (b) $f\left(f^{-1}(x)\right)=x$

4.
(a) $\frac{x+7}{4}$ (b) $f^{-1}\left(f(x)\right)=x$

Exercise 4.5A

4.1A.
(a) $x\neq 3$ (b) $x\neq \pm\sqrt{2}$ (c) $x\neq 2,-1$
(d) $x\geq -6$ (e) $x\leq -2, x\geq 2$ (f) $x\leq \frac{4}{3}$

4.1B.
(a) $2\leq x\leq 1002$ (b) $-5\leq x\leq 245$ (c) $9\leq x\leq 184$

4.3A.
(a) $2x^3+3$ (b) $9x^2-13$ (c) $\frac{3x-9}{7-x}$

4.3B.
(a) 106 (b) -1543

4.4.
(a) $\frac{3x+9}{4}$ (b) $\frac{7x+6}{5}$ (c) $\left(\frac{5x+7}{2}\right)^{1/3}$

Exercise 4.5B

1.
(a) $\frac{5}{\sqrt{3-x}}$ (b) $x\geq 3$

2.
(a) $4\sin 2x$ (b) $2\sqrt{3}$

3.
(a) $(x+5)^3$ (b) $-4\leq x\leq 0$

4.
(a) *proof* (b) $(x+4)^2+4$

5.
(a) 55 (b) $-5\leq x\leq 55$

6.
(a) $\sqrt{x-6}$ (b) $x=6$

Chapter 5

Exercise 5.1

1.
(a)
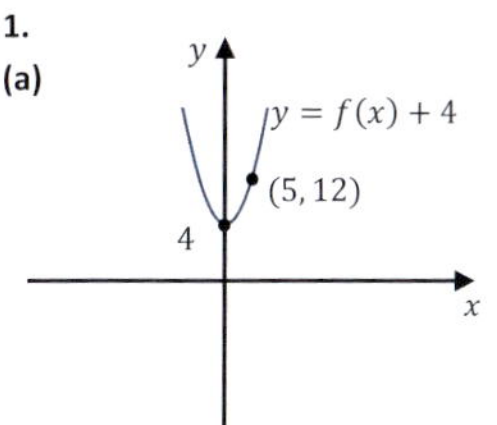

(b)
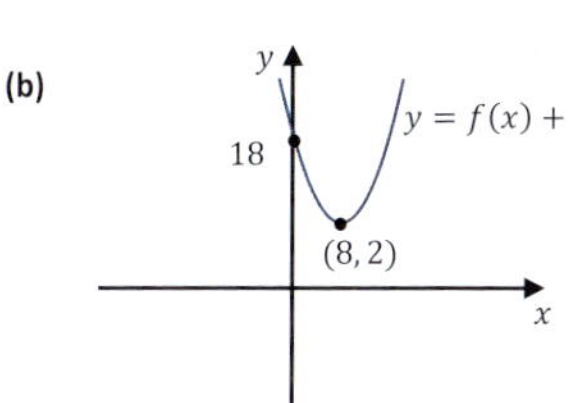

(c)
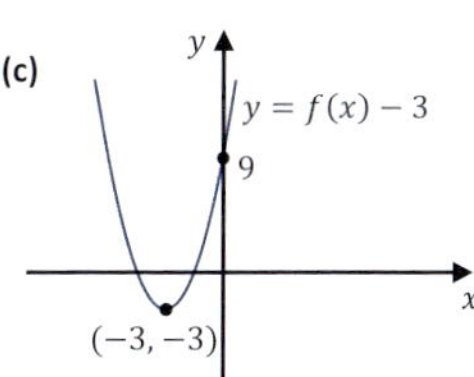

(d)
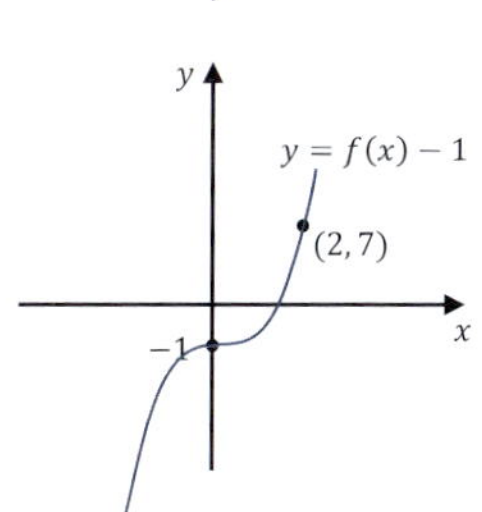

(e)

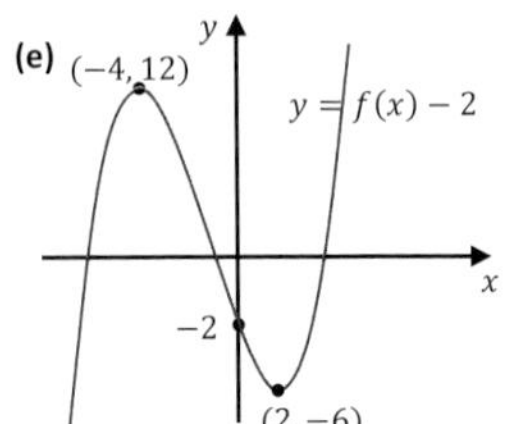

(f)

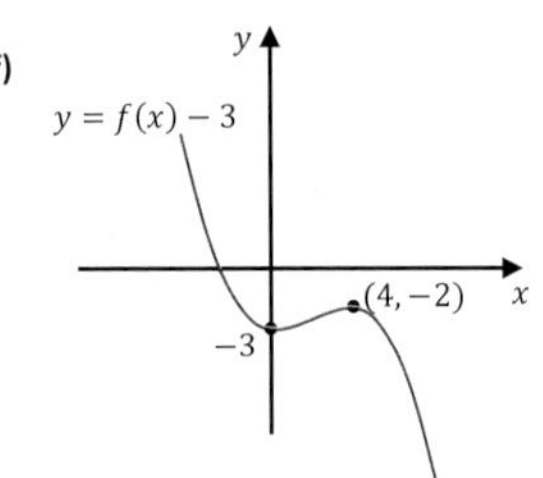

(g)

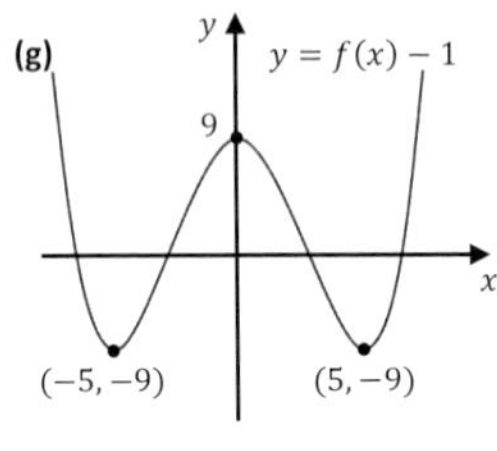

(h)

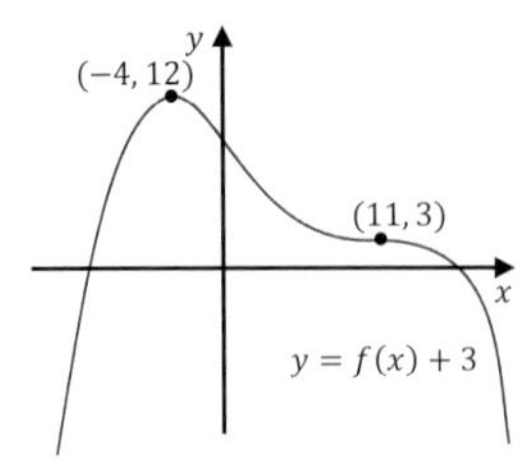

(e)

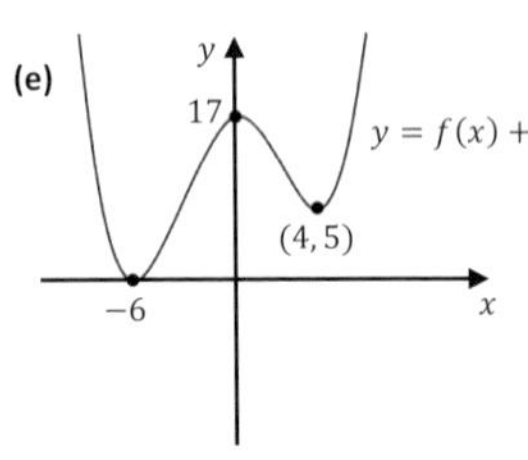

Exercise 5.2

1.

(a)

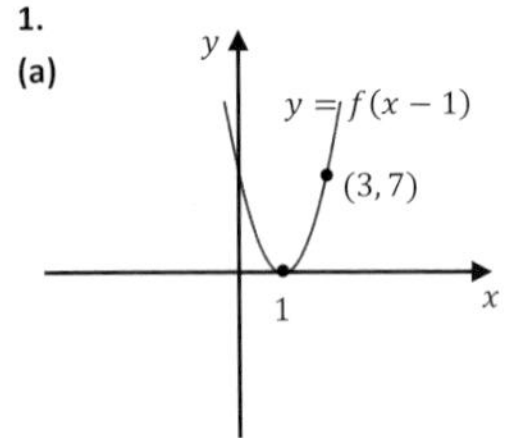

(b)

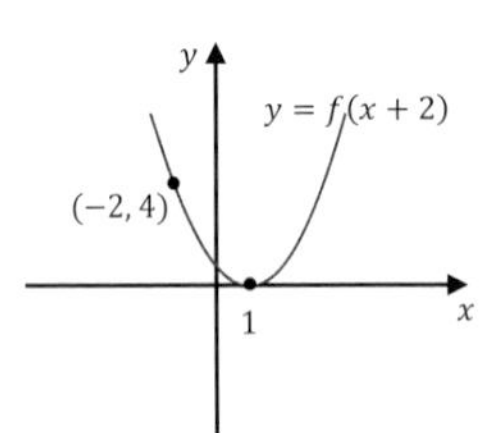

(c)

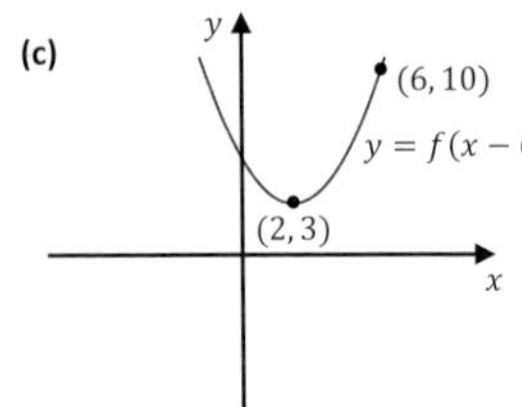

(d)

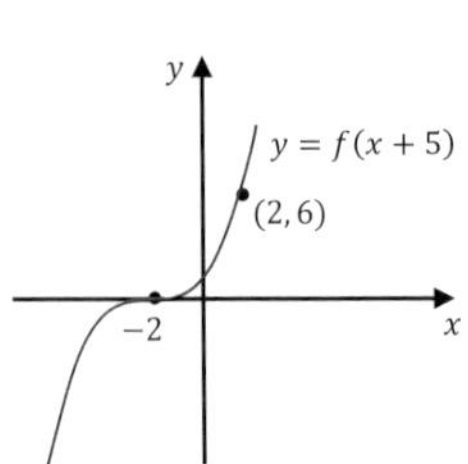

(e)

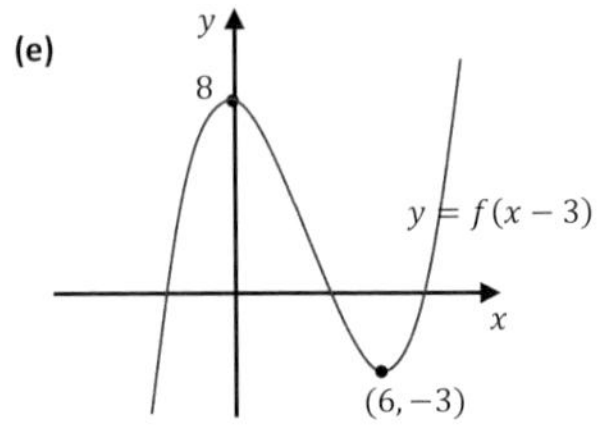

(f)

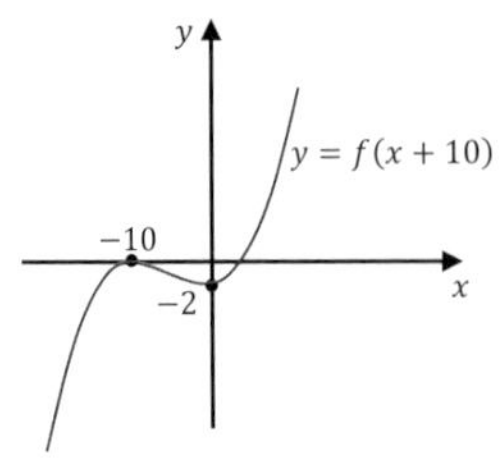

(g)

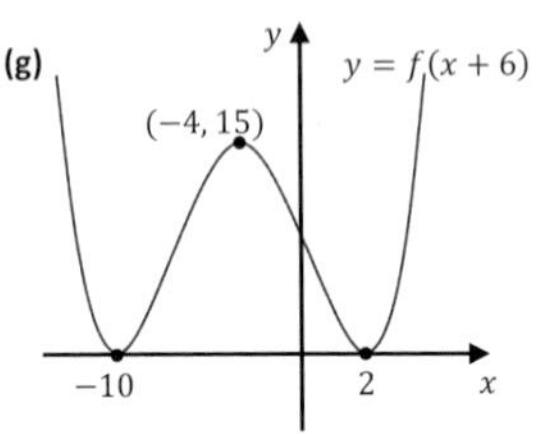

(h)

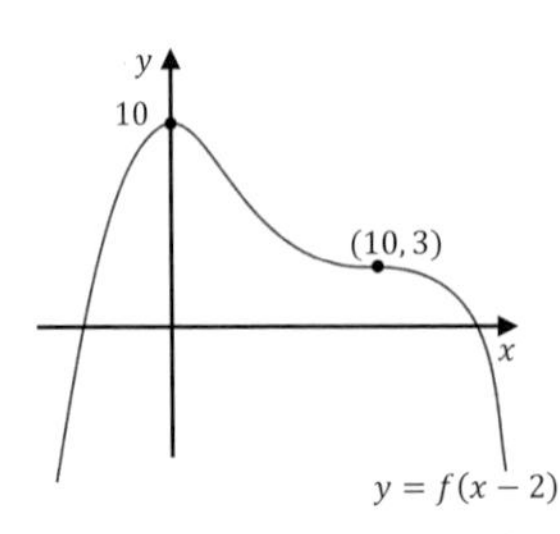

(e)

y
(5, 9)
y = f(x) + 5
9
x
(−1, −7)

Exercise 5.3

1.

(a)

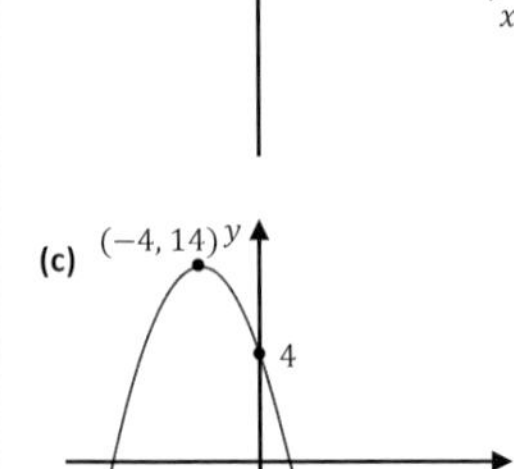

(b)

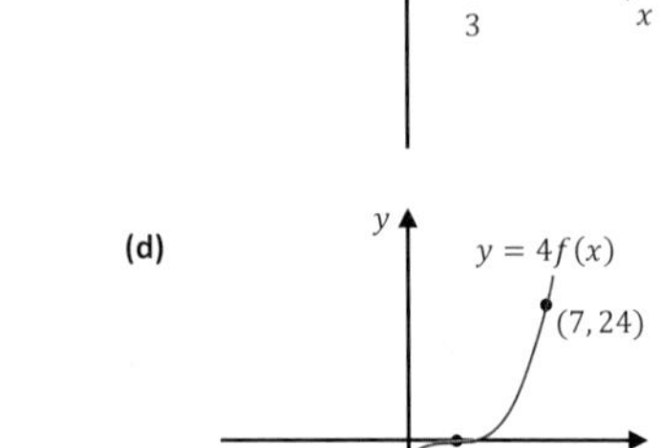

(c)

(−4, 14) y
4
y = 2f(x)
x

(d)

y
y = 4f(x)
(7, 24)
3
x

(e)

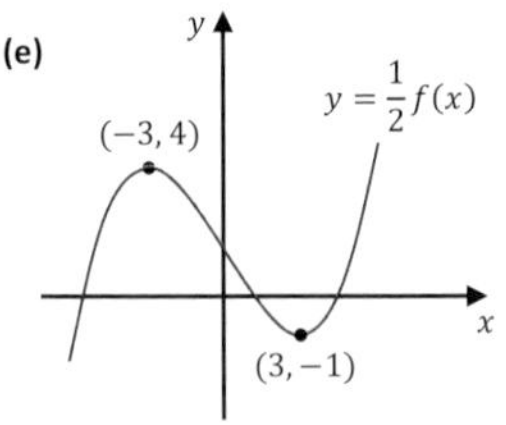

(f)

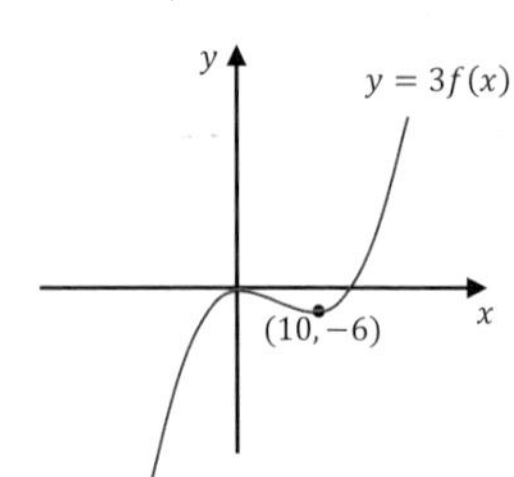

(g)

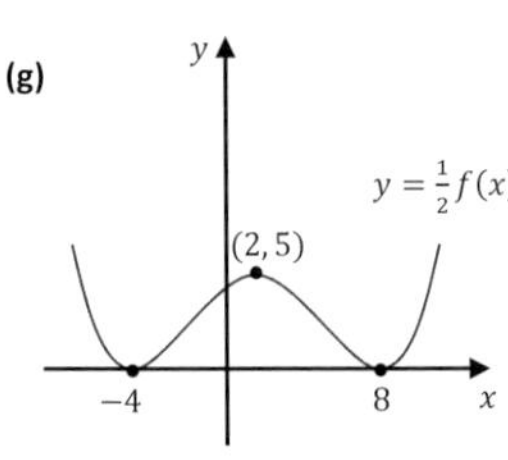

(h)

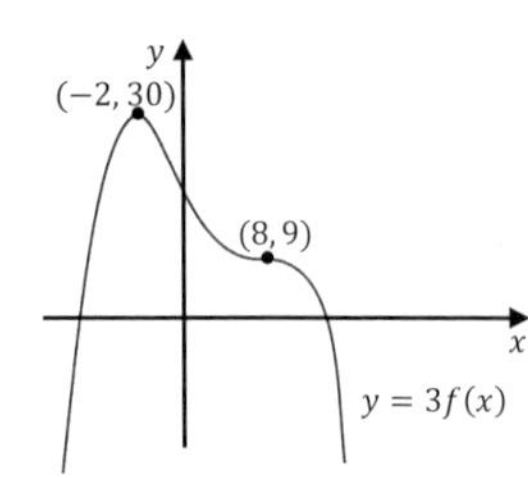

(e)

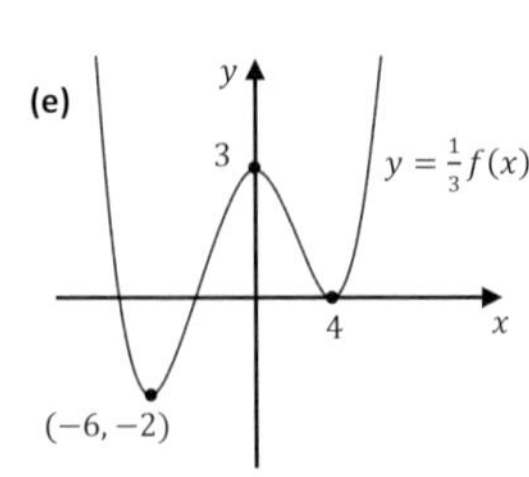

2.

(a)

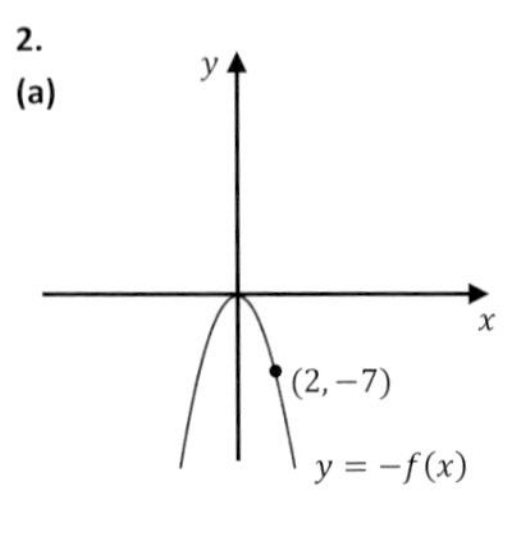

(b)

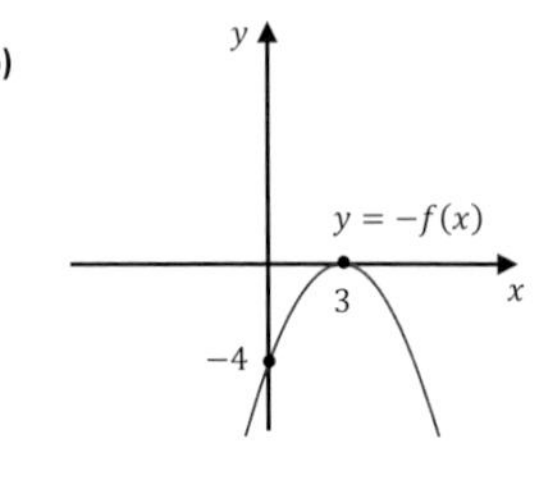

(c)

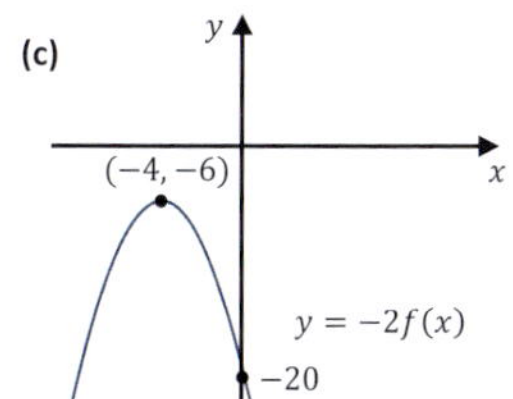

(d)

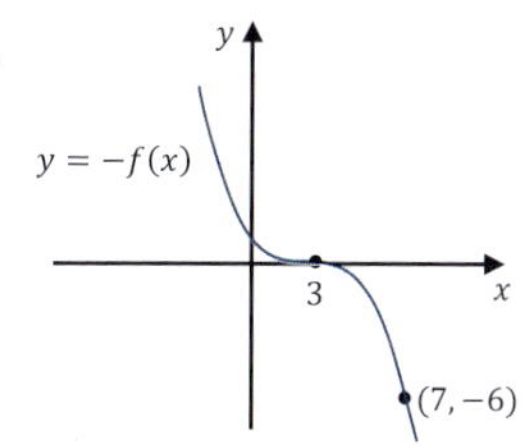

(e)

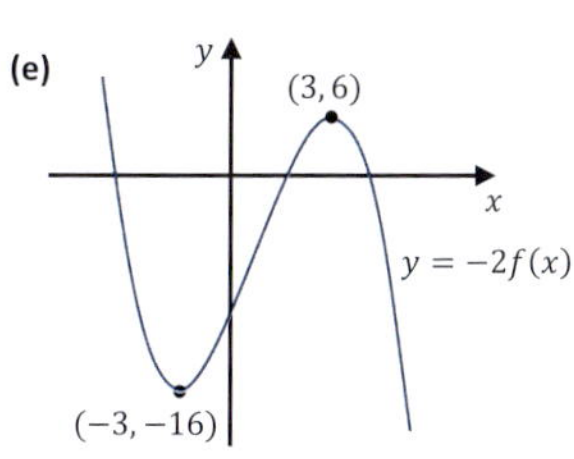

(f)

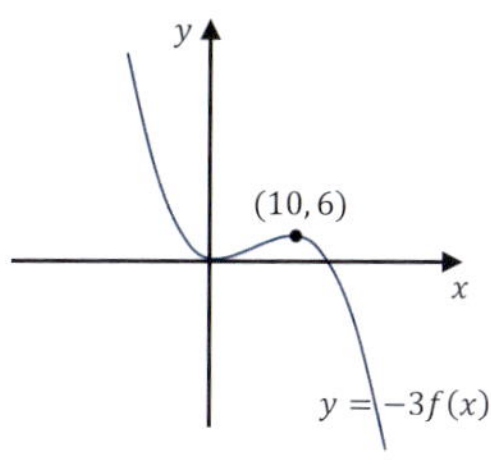

(g)

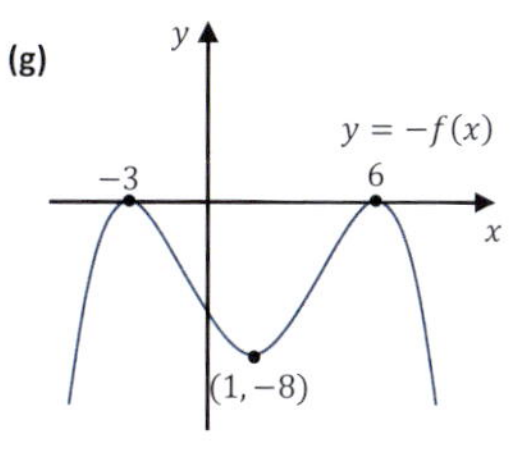

(h)

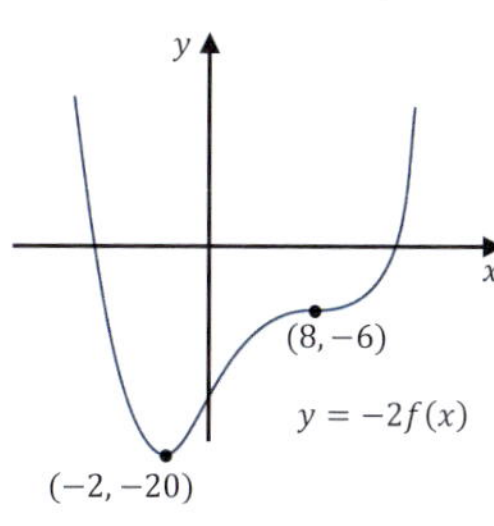

(i)

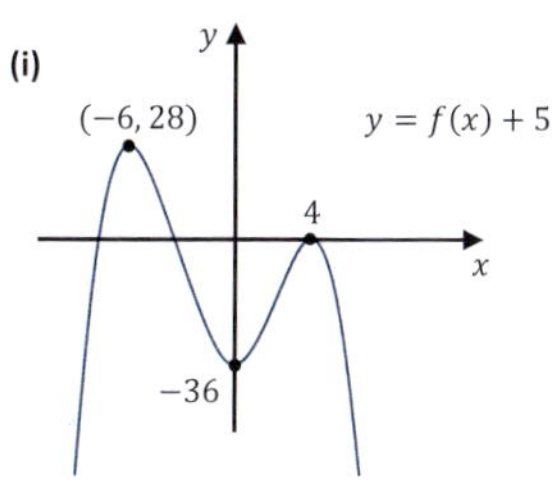

Exercise 5.4

1.

(a)

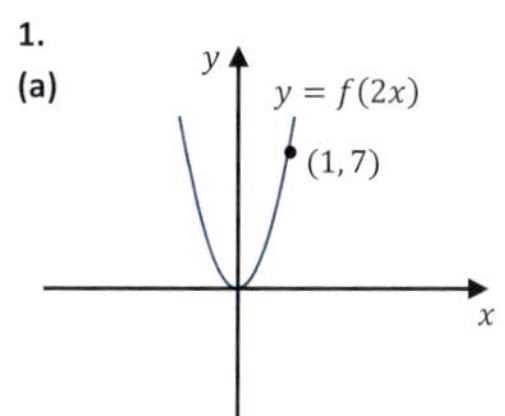

(b)

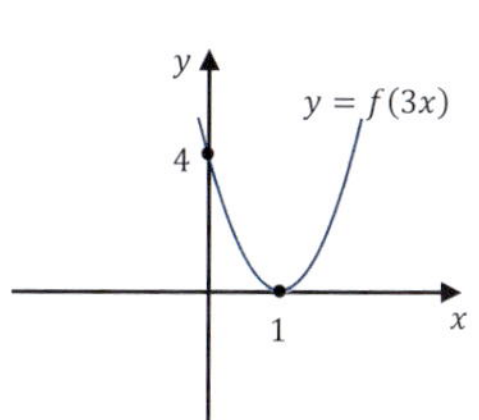

(c)

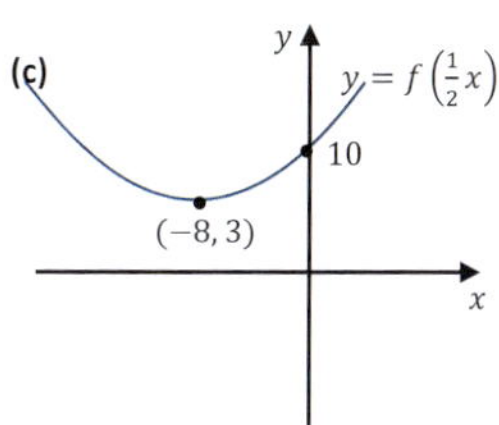

(d)

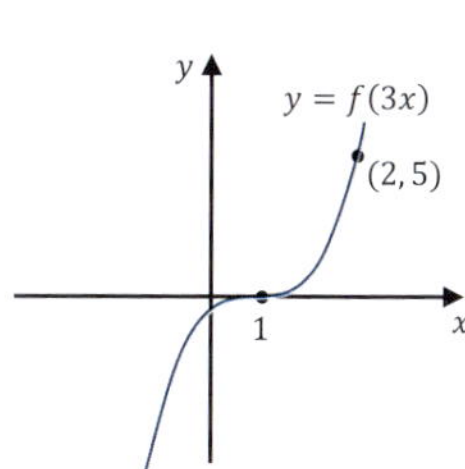

(e)

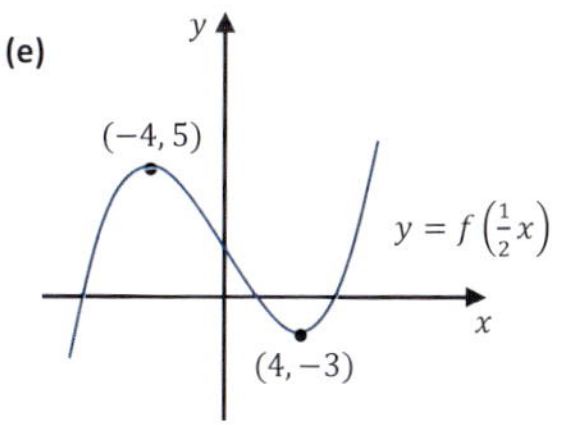

(f)

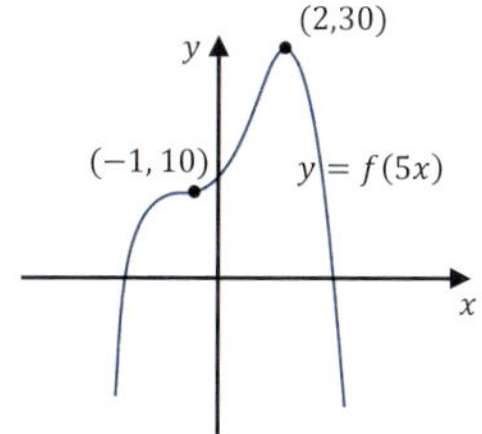

2.

(a)

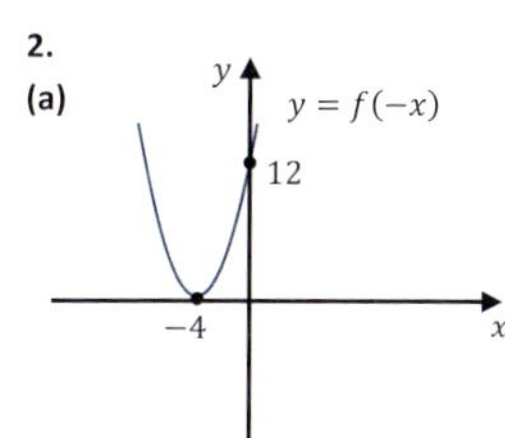

(b)

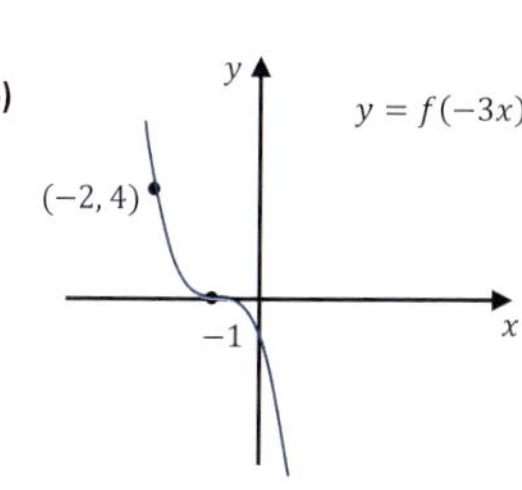

(c)

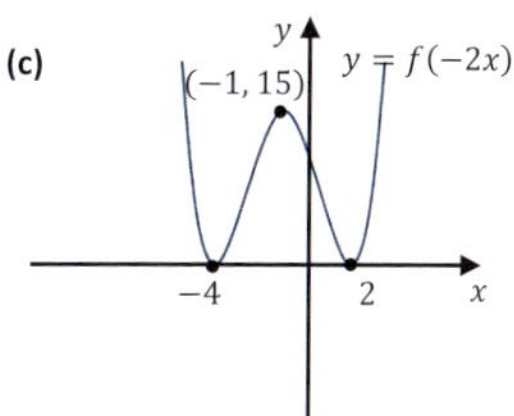

(d)

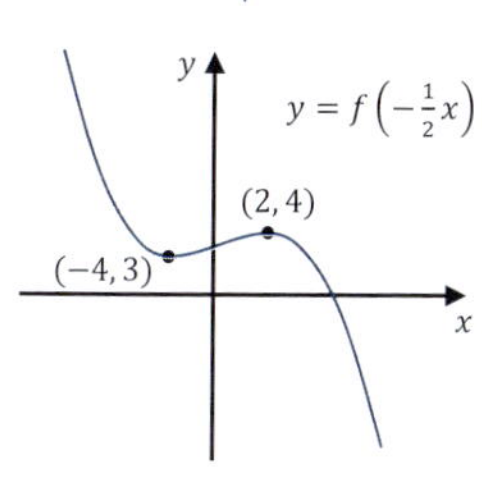

(e)

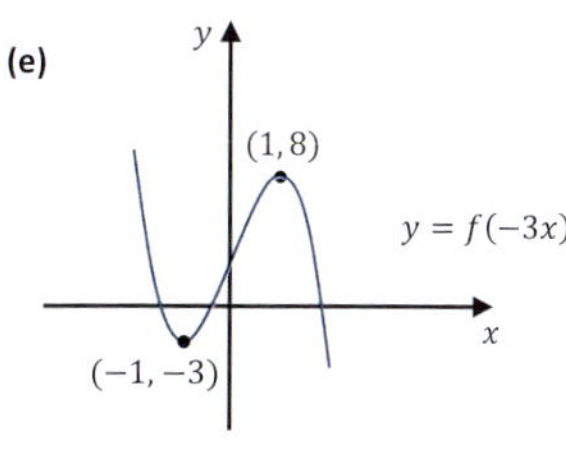

(f)

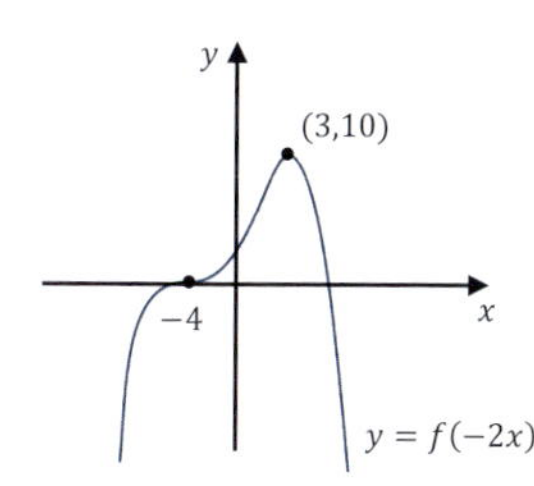

Exercise 5.5

1.

(a)

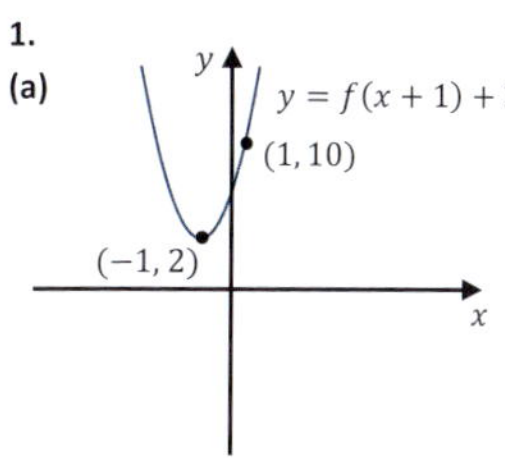

(b)

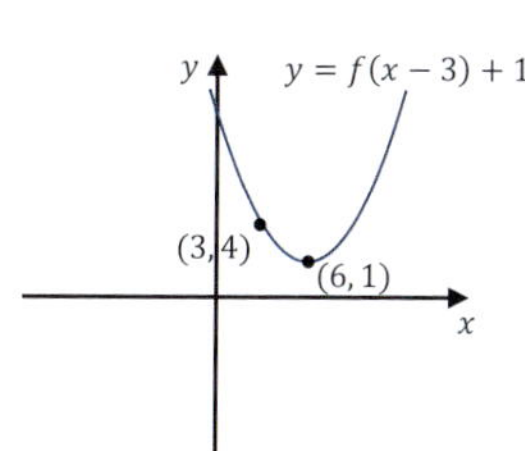

(c)

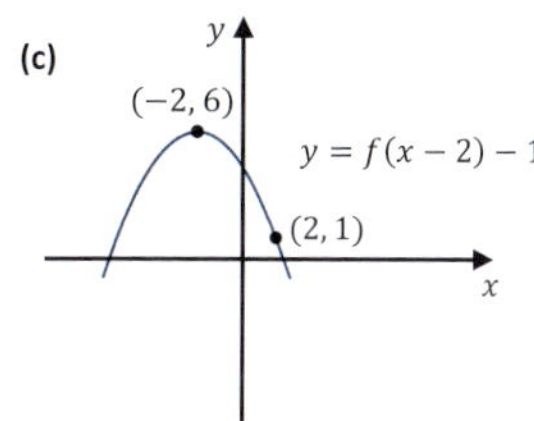

(d)

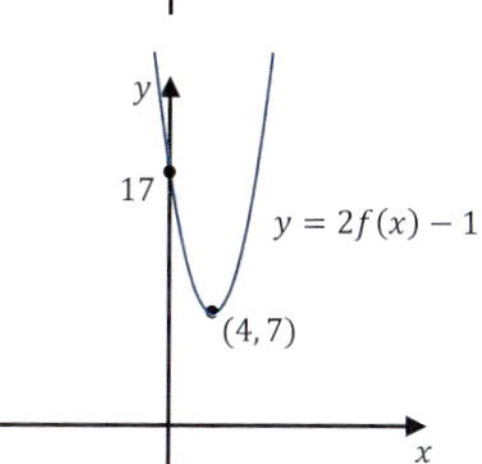

(e)

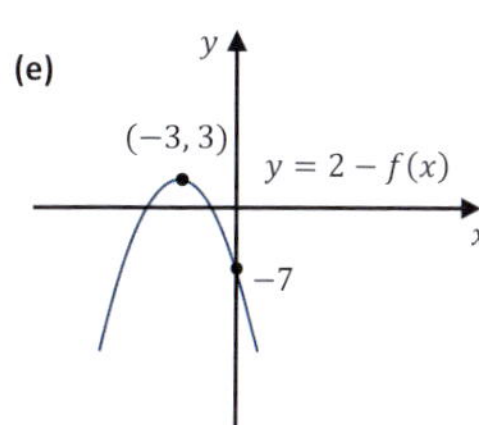

(f)

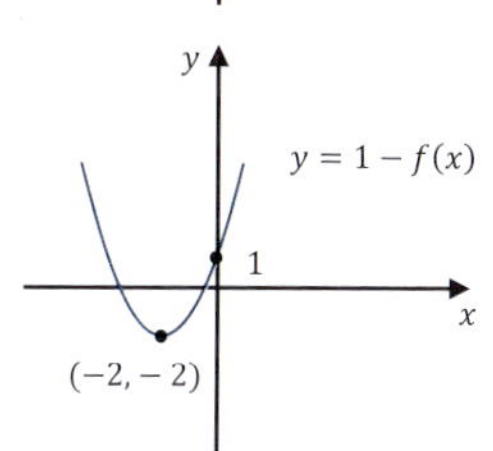

(g)

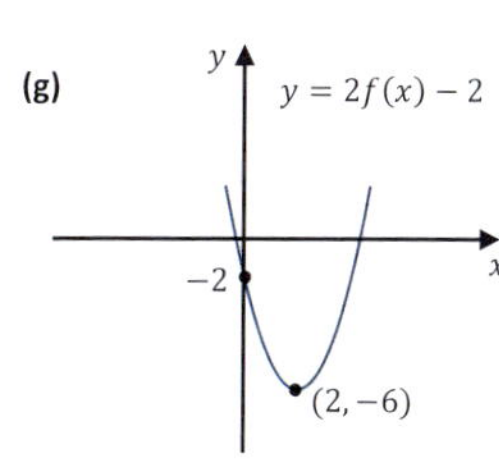

(h)

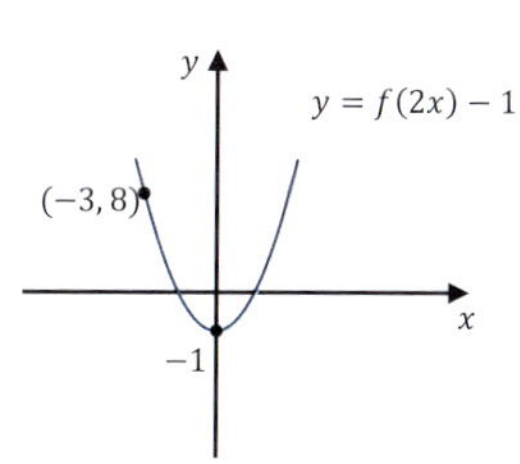

(i)

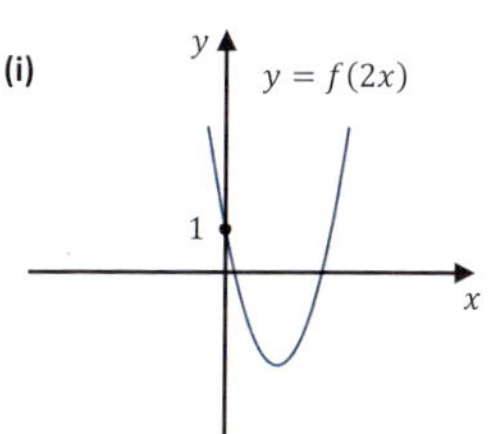

2.

(a)

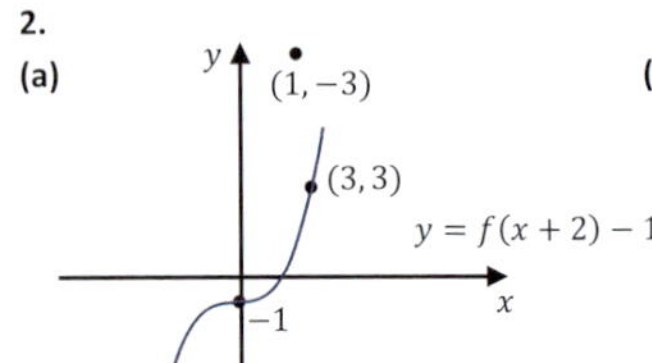

(b)

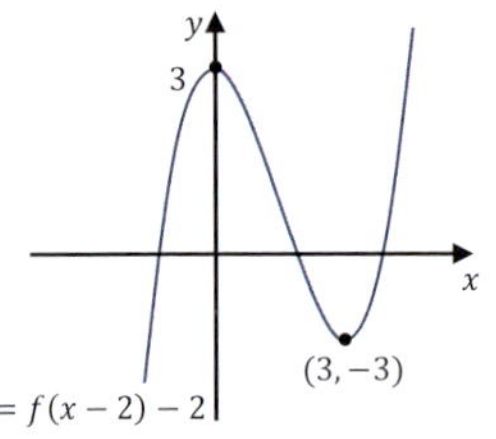

(c)

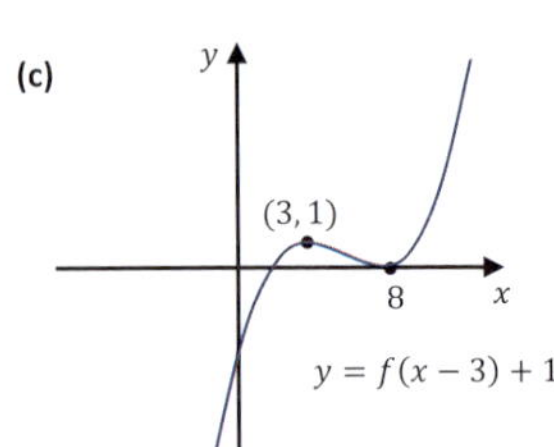

(d)

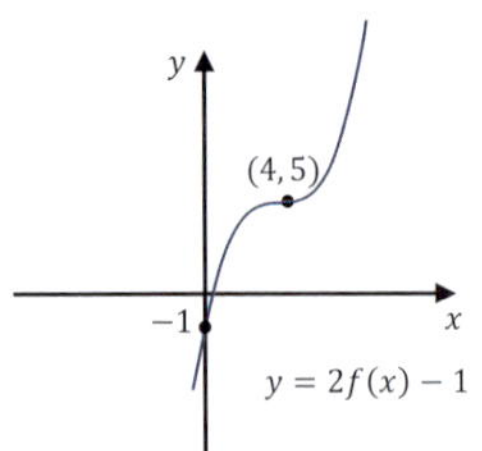

(e)

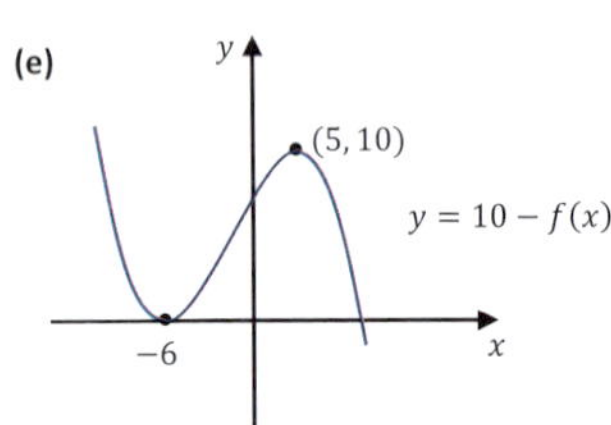

(f)

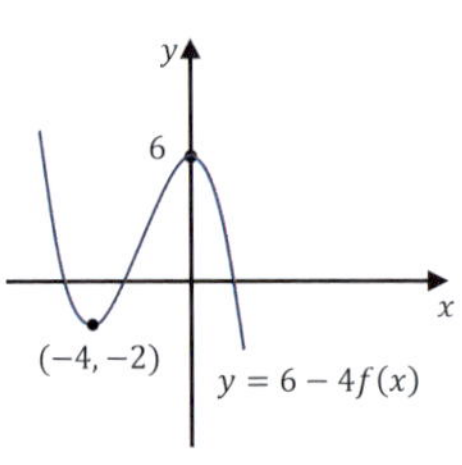

(g)

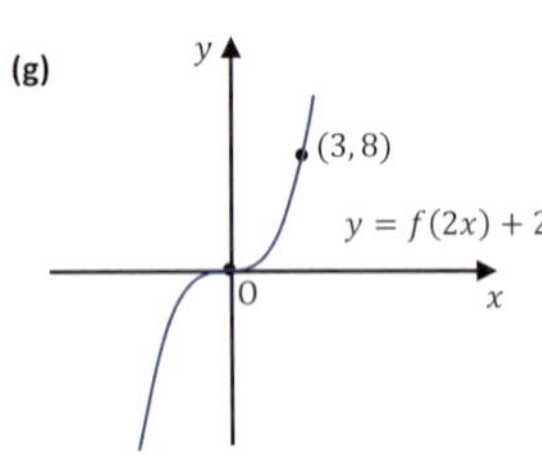

(h)

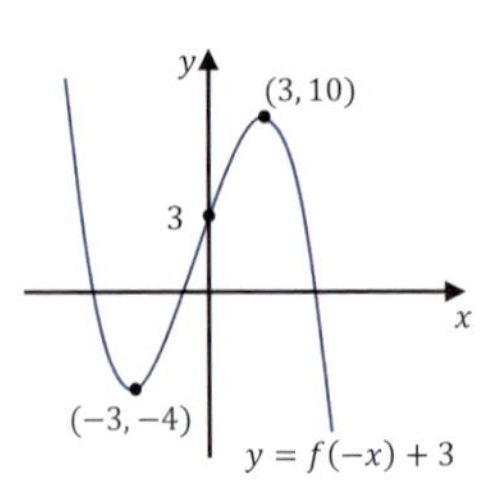

(i)

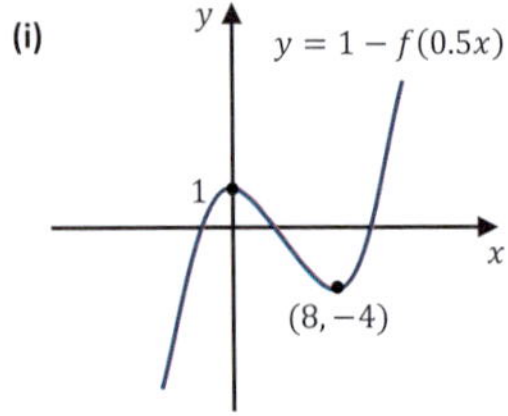

3.

(a)

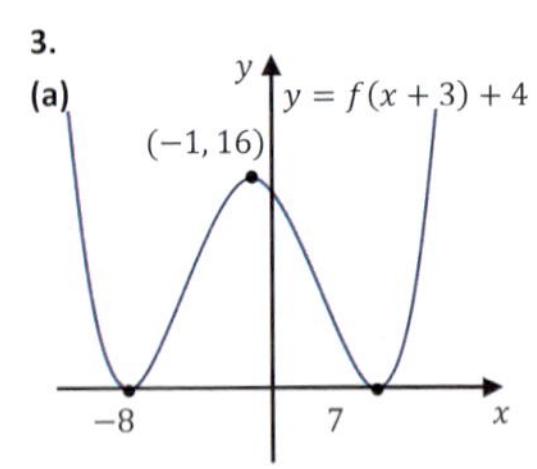

(b)

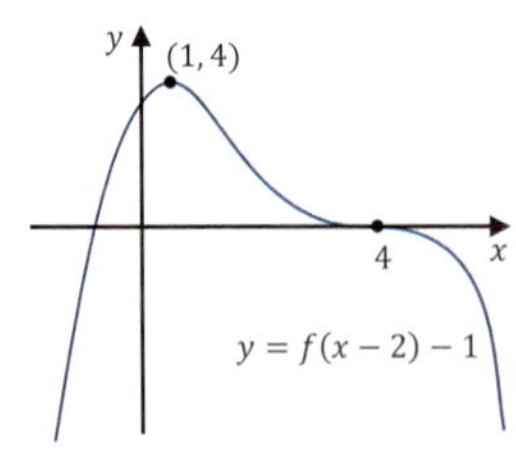

(c)

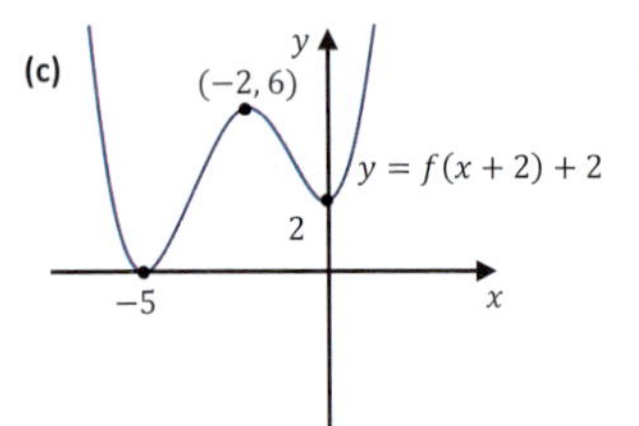

(d)

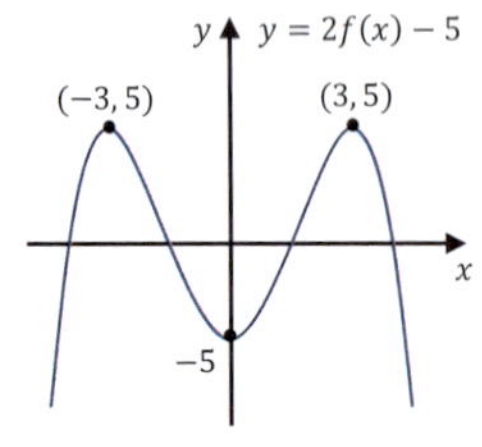

(e)

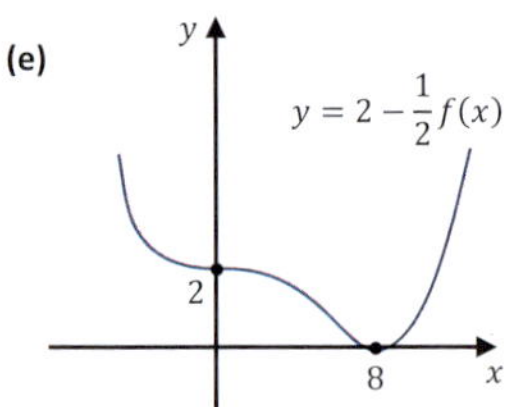

(f)

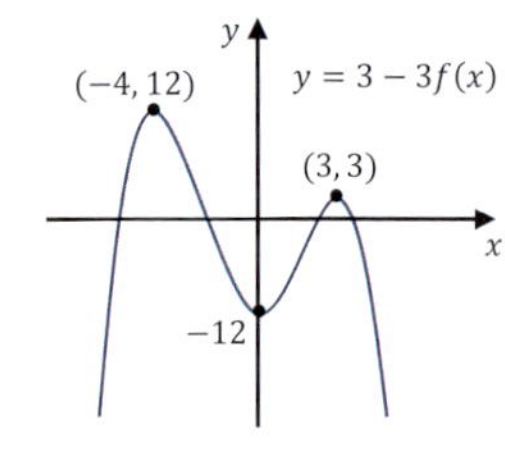

(g)

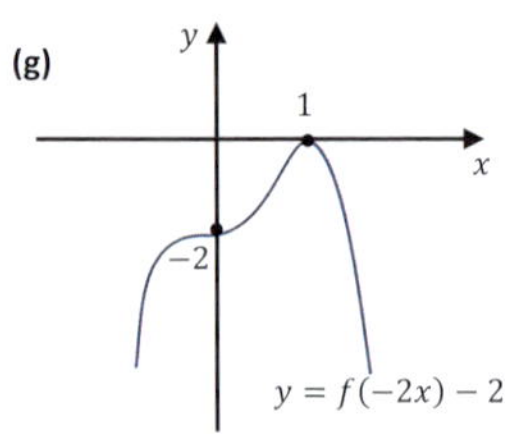

(h)

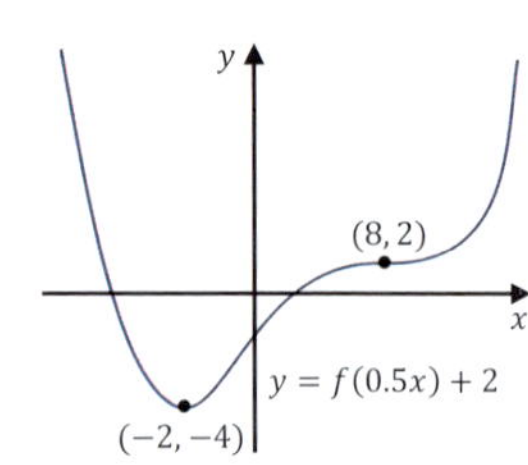

(i)

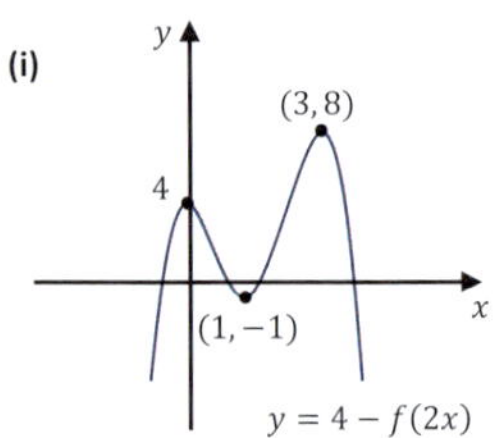

Chapter 6

Exercise 6.1

1.

(a) $u1 = 30, u2 = 63, u3 = 112.5$

(b) $u1 = 0, u2 = -3, u3 = -4.5$

(c) $u1 = 23, u2 = 74, u3 = 227$

(d) $u1 = 20, u2 = 40, u3 = 90$

(e) $u1 = 25, u2 = 73, u3 = 217$

(f) $u1 = 26, u2 = 70, u3 = 158$

(g) $u1 = 32, u2 = 36, u3 = 38$

(h) $u1 = 58, u2 = 163, u3 = 425.5$

(i) $u1 = 100, u2 = 380, u3 = 1500$

2.

(a) $u1 = 30, u2 = 63, u3 = 112.5, u4 = 186.75, u5 = 298.125$

(b) $u1 = 0, u2 = -3, u3 = -4.5, u4 = -5.25, u5 = -5.625$

(c) $u1 = 23, u2 = 74, u3 = 227, u4 = 686, u5 = 2063$

(d) $u1 = 20, u2 = 40, u3 = 90, u4 = 215, u5 = 527.5$

(e) $u1 = 25, u2 = 73, u3 = 217, u4 = 649, u5 = 1945$

(f) $u1 = 26, u2 = 70, u3 = 158, u4 = 334, u5 = 686$

(g) $u1 = 32, u2 = 36, u3 = 38, u4 = 39, u5 = 39.5$

(h) $u1 = 58, u2 = 163, u3 = 425.5, u4 = 1081.75,$
$u5 = 2722.375$

(i) $u1 = 100, u2 = 380, u3 = 1500, u4 = 5980, u5 = 23900$

3.

(a) $u1 = -26, u2 = 72, u3 = -124, u4 = 268, u5 = -516$

(b) $u1 = 6.2, u2 = -1.76, u3 = -3.352, u4 = -3.6704,$
$u5 = -3.73408$

(c) $u1 = -20.2, u2 = 33.28, u3 = -41.592, u4 = 63.2288,$
$u5 = -83.52032$

(d) $u1 = 34.2, u2 = 8.68, u3 = -1.528, u4 = -5.6112,$

$u5 = -7.24448$

(e) $u1 = -40.5, u2 = 76.05, u3 = -168.705, u4 = 345.2805,$
$u5 = -734.08905$

(f) $u1 = -32, u2 = -146, u3 = -488, u4 = -1514,$
$u5 = -4592$

(g) $u1 = 7.8, u2 = 8.22, u3 = 8.178, u4 = 8.1822,$
$u5 = 8.18178$

(h) $u1 = -9.2, u2 = 21.04, u3 = -15.248, u4 = 28.2976,$
$u5 = -23.95712$

(i) $u1 = 6, u2 = -7.2, u3 = -11.16, u4 = -12.348,$
$u5 = -12.7044$

Exercise 6.2

1.

(a) $a = 2, b = 3$ (b) $a = 3, b = -1$ (c) $a = 2, b = -4$
(d) $a = 1, b = -5$ (e) $a = 4, b = 5$ (f) $a = -2, b = 18$
(g) $a = 5, b = -3$ (h) $a = 0.5, b = 7$ (i) $a = 1.5, b = -9$
(j) $a = -0.5, b = 3$ (k) $a = 2, b = -3$ (l) $a = 1.5, b = -4$

2.

(a) $a = 0.6, b = -12$ (b) $a = 0.5, b = 8$ (c) $a = 1.3, b = 6$
(d) $a = 2.1, b = -4$ (e) $a = 3, b = 1.5$ (f) $a = -1.2, b = 2$
(g) $a = 3, b = -2$ (h) $a = 2, b = 3$ (i) $a = 1.1, b = -5$
(j) $a = 2, b = -1.2$ (k) $a = 1.2, b = 12$ (l) $a = -0.8, b = 15$

Exercise 6.3

1.

(a) No, $1.5 > 1$ (b) Yes, $-1 < 0.5 < 1$
(c) No, $3 > 1$ (d) Yes, $-1 < -\frac{1}{3} < 1$
(e) Yes, $-1 < \frac{1}{4} < 1$ (f) No, $1.2 > 1$
(g) No, $\frac{5}{4} > 1$ (h) Yes, $-1 < -\frac{3}{5} < 1$
(i) Yes, $-1 < \frac{5}{7} < 1$ (j) Yes, $-1 < -\frac{2}{3} < 1$
(k) No, $-\frac{7}{6} < -1$ (l) No, $4 < -1$

2.

(a) $2 < k < 4$ (b) $-10 < k < -8$ (c) $4 < k < 6$
(d) $3 < k < 5$ (e) $-\frac{1}{2} < k < \frac{3}{2}$ (f) $4 < k < 6$
(g) $0 < k < 2$ (h) $1 < k < 3$ (i) $-\frac{1}{4} < k < \frac{7}{4}$
(j) $1 < k < 2$ (k) $-\frac{3}{5} < k < -\frac{1}{5}$ (l) $\frac{3}{2} < k < 2$

Exercise 6.4

1.

(a) $L = 22.5$ (b) $L = 30$ (c) $L = 280$
(d) $L = -90$ (e) $L = 37\frac{1}{3}$ (f) $L = 300$
(g) $L = 600$ (h) $L = -15$ (i) $L = -175$
(j) $L = 1350$ (k) $L = -3600$ (l) $L = 25{,}000$

2.

(a) $L = 1050$ (b) $L = 228.57$ (c) $L = 233.33$
(d) $L = -1750$ (e) $L = -1770.83$ (f) $L = 540$
(g) $L = 342.86$ (h) $L = -129.73$ (i) $L = -346.15$
(j) $L = 171.05$ (k) $L = -139.71$ (l) $L = 103.61$

Exercise 6.5A

1. £6725.81 2. £26 352.03 3. 2231 sheep
4. 2297 sheep 5. £136,823.61 6. 93 cm
7. £5121.39 8. £194,540.20 9. 14.07 mg
10. 6.76 mg

Exercise 6.5B

1.

(a) 3764 people
(b) yes, the lowest the population will reach is 1294 people

2.

(a) 16.66 mg
(b) yes, the dosage is safe as the limit is 16.67mg and $16.67 < 17$

3.

(a) 15,161 people (b) 4166 people

4.

(a) 6.69 mg
(b) no, as the limit is 4.29 mg/L and $4.29 < 6$

5.

(a) 6.5 mg
(b) No, the vaccine falls below 6mg as $(6.67 - 2) < 6$

6.

(a) 5.5 litres
(b) yes, as the limit is 5.4 litres and $5.4 > 4$

7.

(a) £225,915
(b) the amount of interest being added each month is more than his repayment

8.

(a) 292 rats
(b) 227 rats, as this is the limit as $n \to \infty$

9.

(a) 80 gorillas (b) 9 years

10.

(a) 5,438,707 people (b) 77,000 immigrants per year

Exercise 6.6A

6.1

(a) $u_4 = 3791.97$ (b) $u_4 = 25$ (c) $u_4 = 20{,}987$

6.2

(a) $a = 3, b = 2$ (b) $a = 2.5, b = 12$ (c) $a = 3, b = -16$

6.3A

(a) No, $7 > 1$ (b) Yes, $-1 < 0.1 < 1$
(c) Yes, $-1 < -0.9 < 1$

6.3B

(a) $2 < k < 4$ (b) $4 < k < 6$ (c) $\frac{4}{3} < k < 2$

6.4

(a) $L = 250$ (b) $L = 1000$ (c) $L = 280$

6.5A £8192.47

6.5B

(a) 244 Litres

(b) No, the trees will not survive as the limit is 195.7 and $195.7 < 200$.

Exercise 6.6B

1.

(a) $a = 0.8, b = 16$ (b) 80 tigers

2.

(a) (b) $-1 < a < 1$, as $a = 0.4$

(c) 233.3

3. $a = -2$ **4.** $a = -\frac{5}{9}$ **5.** $b = 21.3$

6.

(a) $a = 2, b = 6$ (b) $u_4 = 162$

7.

(a) $a = 1.5, b = 24$ (b) $u_4 = 181.5$

(c) $a > 1$, as $a = 1.5$

8.

(a) $a = 0.8, b = 20$ (b) $u_4 = 125.6$

(c) $-1 < a < 1$, as $a = 0.8$

9.

(a) *proof* (b) $k < -1, k > 5$

10.

(a) *proof* (b) $k < -1, k > 3$

11.

(a) *proof* (b) $k < -1, k > 4$

12. $m = -13.7$

13.

(a) 1815 sheep

(b) 510 sheep, as this is how many are lost each year

14.

(a) £163,047.83

(b) The monthly interest is greater than the repayments.

Chapter 7

Exercise 7.1A

2.

(a) (ii) $(x-1)(x-4)(x+3)$ (b) (ii) $(x-3)(x-5)(x+4)$

(c) (ii) $(x+2)(x-3)(x+7)$ (d) (ii) $(x-4)(x-3)(x+2)$

(e) (ii) $(x-6)(x+2)(x-3)$ (f) (ii) $(x+9)(x-6)(x-3)$

(g) (ii) $(x-7)(x-3)(x-3)$ (h) (ii) $(x-8)(x-2)(x+2)$

Exercise 7.1B

1.

(a) $(x-2)(x-1)(x+1)$ (b) $(x-4)(x-3)(x+2)$

(c) $(x-3)(x-1)(x+2)$ (d) $(x-2)(x-2)(x+2)$

(e) $(x-3)(x-1)(x+1)$ (f) $(x-5)(x-3)(x-1)$

2.

(a) $(x+3)(x-3)(x+1)$ (b) $(x-2)(x+1)(x+1)$

(c) $(x^2+3)(x+3)(x-3)$ (d) $(x+2)(x+2)(x-4)$

(e) $(x+2)(x+2)(x-1)$ (f) $(x-2)(x+3)(x+6)$

3.

(a) $(x-2)(x-1)(x+1)(x+3)$

(b) $(x-2)(x-1)(x+1)(x+2)$

(c) $(x-2)(x-2)(x+1)(x+3)$

(d) $(x-4)(x-1)(x+1)(x+4)$

(e) $(x-1)(x-1)(x-1)(x+2)$

(f) $(x-3)(x-3)(x+3)(x+3)$

4.

(a) $(2x+1)(x-3)(x+1)$ (b) $(2x+3)(x-3)(x-1)$

(c) $(3x-1)(x-2)(x-1)$ (d) $(3x+2)(x-1)(x-1)$

(e) $(3x+4)(x-2)(x-1)$ (f) $(5x+1)(x-3)(x+1)$

5.

(a) $(x+1)(x^2-3)$ (b) $(x-4)(x^3-2)$

(c) $(x+2)(x-1)(x^2+2)$

Exercise 7.2

1.

(a) $x = -1, x = 2, x = 3$ (b) $x = -3, x = -1, x = 1$

(c) $x = -4, x = -1, x = 2$ (d) $x = -3, x = 2$ *twice*

(e) $x = -4, x = -2, x = 1$ (f) $x = 1, x = 2$ *twice*

2.

(a) $x = -1$ *twice*, $x = 2$ (b) $x = -6, x = -3, x = 2$

(c) $x = -2, x = -1, x = 3$ (d) $x = -2$ *twice*, $x = 4$

(e) $x = -3, x = -1, x = 4$ (f) $x = -1, x = 2$ *twice*

3.

(a) $x = -3, x = -1, x = 2$ *twice*

(b) $x = -3, x = -1, x = 2, x = 3$

(c) $x = -1$ *twice*, $x = 1, x = 3$

(d) $x = -2, x = -1, x = 1, x = 2$

(e) $x = -3, x = -2, x = 1, x = 2$

(f) $x = -5, x = -1, x = 2, x = 4$

4.

(a) $x = \frac{1}{3}, x = 1, x = 2$ (b) $x = -3, x = -1, x = \frac{1}{2}$

(c) $x = -2, x = 1, x = \frac{5}{2}$ (d) $x = \frac{2}{3}, x = 2, x = 3$

(e) $x = -\frac{3}{2}, x = 1, x = 2$ (f) $x = -4, x = \frac{1}{5}, x = 3$

5.

(a) $x = 2$ (b) $x = -3$ (c) $x = 2$

Exercise 7.3

1.

(a) 63 (b) -41 (c) 64

(d) -39 (e) 49 (f) 57

(g) -184 (h) 60 (i) -366

(j) 347

Exercise 7.4

1.
(a) $a = 3$ (b) $a = -5$ (c) $a = -3$
(d) $a = -11$ (e) $a = 4$ (f) $a = -5$

2.
(a) $a = -7$ (b) $a = 4$ (c) $a = 6$
(d) $a = -7$ (e) $a = -9$ (f) $a = 3$

3.
(a) $a = 5, b = 2$ (b) $a = 1, b = -6$
(c) $a = -11, b = 12$ (d) $a = -13, b = -10$
(e) $a = -13, b = 6$ (f) $a = 7, b = -15$
(g) $a = -7, b = 7$ (h) $a = 13, b = -6$
(i) $a = 30, b = -8$ (j) $a = -10, b = 3$

Exercise 7.5

1.
(a) $(3, 15), (-2, 5)$ (b) $(-1, 5), (6, 19)$
(c) $(3, 17), (4, 25)$ (d) $(-2, -10), (4, 68)$
(e) $(-4, 85), (4, 109)$ (f) $\left(-\frac{1}{2}, \frac{3}{4}\right)$

2.
(a) $(-1, -5), (1, 5), (3, 47)$ (b) $(-2, 0), (-1, 1), (2, 28)$
(c) $(-1, 2)$ *twice*, $(3, 46)$ (d) $(-5, -33), (-1, -5), (4, 120)$
(e) $(-3, 130)$ *twice*, $(-4, 184)$ (f) $(-2, 17), (1, 5), (9, 589)$

3.
(a) $(-3, -29), (1, -1), (4, 125)$ (b) $(-4, -167), (2, 1), (3, 36)$
(c) $(1, -2), (-3, -14), (0.5, -4.375)$

Exercise 7.6

1.
(a) $f(x) = \frac{1}{2}(x + 5)(x - 4)$ (b) $f(x) = \frac{1}{2}(x + 2)(x - 6)$
(c) $f(x) = 3(x - 1)(x - 5)$ (d) $f(x) = 4(x + 2)^2$
(e) $f(x) = -\frac{1}{2}(x + 2)(x - 7)$ (f) $f(x) = -3(x - 3)^2$

2.
(a) $f(x) = 2(x + 3)(x - 1)(x - 2)$
(b) $f(x) = 3(x + 1)(x - 1)(x - 2)$
(c) $f(x) = \frac{1}{6}(x + 3)(x - 2)^2$
(d) $f(x) = \frac{1}{4}(x - 2)^3$
(e) $f(x) = 3x(x + 1)(x - 1)$
(f) $f(x) = -2x(x + 2)(x - 3)$

3.
(a) $f(x) = 2(x + 2)(x + 1)(x - 1)(x - 2)$
(b) $f(x) = \frac{4}{3}(x + 1)^2(x - 3)^2$
(c) $f(x) = \frac{1}{8}(x + 4)(x + 2)(x - 3)^2$
(d) $f(x) = \frac{1}{9}(x + 5)(x + 3)(x - 1)(x - 3)$
(e) $f(x) = -\frac{1}{4}(x + 2)(x - 2)^3$
(f) $f(x) = \frac{1}{2}x^3(x - 5)$

Exercise 7.7

7.1 (b) (i) $(x - 5)(x - 2)(x + 2)$
(ii) $(x - 3)(x + 1)(x + 5)$

7.2
(a) $x = -1, x = 3, x = 4$ (b) $x = -2$ *twice*, $x = 4$
(c) $x = -2, x = 1, x = 6$

7.3
(a) -42 (b) -36

7.4
(a) $a = -10, b = 8$ (b) $a = -7, b = 10$

7.5
(a) $(-4, -17), (-2, -11), (1, -2)$
(b) $(-1, -9)$ *twice*, $(2, 27)$
(c) $(-1, -3), (2, 18), (3, 57)$

7.6
(a) $f(x) = -\frac{1}{3}(x + 2)(x - 1)(x - 3)$
(b) $f(x) = 2x(x - 2)(x + 2)$
(c) $f(x) = -\frac{1}{4}(x + 3)(x - 2)^2(x - 6)$

Chapter 8

Exercise 8.1A

1. $y = 2 \sin x°$ 2. $y = 5 \cos x°$ 3. $y = 3 \sin 2x°$
4. $y = 3 \cos 4x°$ 5. $y = -8 \sin 4x°$ 6. $y = 4 \sin 3x°$
7. $y = 3 \sin \frac{1}{2}x°$ 8. $y = -0.4 \cos x°$ 9. $y = 7 \cos 4x°$

Exercise 8.1B

1. $y = 3 \sin x° - 1$ 2. $y = 3 \cos x° - 1$
3. $y = 3 \sin 2x° + 1$ 4. $y = -3 \sin 2x° + 1$
5. $y = -3 \cos x° - 2$ 6. $y = -2 \sin 3x° + 2$
7. $y = \sin 4x° - 2$ 8. $y = 2 \cos 4x° - 2$
9. $y = -4 \cos 2x° + 1$

Exercise 8.1C

1. $y = 2 \sin(x + 45)°$ 2. $y = 2 \cos (x - 90)°$
3. $y = 3 \sin (x - 45)°$ 4. $y = 4 \sin(x - 90)°$
5. $y = 3 \cos (x + 45)°$ 6. $y = 2 \sin (x - 45)°$
7. $y = 4 \sin (x + 30)°$ 8. $y = 3 \cos (x - 60)°$
9. $y = 5 \sin (x - 60)°$

Exercise 8.2A

1.
(a) $x = 70.5°, 289.5°$ (b) $x = 30°, 150°$
(c) $x = 26.6°, 206.6°$ (d) $x = 60°, 300°$
(e) $x = 45°, 315°$ (f) $x = 45°, 225°$
(g) $x = 14.5°, 165.5°$ (h) $x = 48.2°, 311.8°$
(i) $x = 36.9°, 143.1°$

2.
(a) $x = 225°, 315°$ (b) $x = 150°, 210°$
(c) $x = 135°, 315°$ (d) $x = 210°, 330°$
(e) $x = 131.8°, 228.2°$ (f) $x = 104.0°, 284.0°$
(g) $x = 108.4°, 288.4°$ (h) $x = 120°, 240°$
(i) $x = 221.8°, 318.2°$

3.
(a) $x = 66.4°, 293.6°$ (b) $x = 120°, 240°$
(c) $x = 63.4°, 243.4°$ (d) $x = 56.4°, 123.6°$

(e) $x = 191.5°, 348.5°$
(f) $x = 150°, 330°$
(g) $x = 166.0°, 346.0°$
(h) $x = 109.5°, 250.5°$
(i) $x = 30°, 150°$

Exercise 8.2B

1.

(a) $x = 15°, 75°, 195°, 255°$
(b) $x = 35.3°, 144.7°, 215.3°, 324.7°$
(c) $x = 15°, 75°, 135°, 195°, 255°, 315°$
(d) $x = 52.2°, 127.8°, 232.2°, 307.8°$
(e) $x = 73.9°, 106.1°, 193.9°, 226.1°, 313.9°, 346.1°$
(f) $x = 39.3°, 129.3°, 219.3°, 309.3°$

2.

(a) $x = 60°, 120°, 240°, 300°$
(b) $x = 30°, 150°, 270°$
(c) $x = 23.5°, 96.5°, 143.5°, 216.5°, 263.51°, 336.5°$
(d) $x = 27.4°, 62.6°, 117.4°, 152.6°, 207.4°, 242.6°, 297.4°, 332.6°$
(e) $x = 70°, 110°, 190°, 230°, 310°, 350°$
(f) $x = 8.9°, 68.9°, 128.9°, 188.9°, 248.9°, 308.9°$

Exercise 8.2C

1.

(a) $x = 73.1°, 326.9°$
(b) $x = 49.5°, 190.5°$
(c) $x = 86.6°, 266.6°$
(d) $x = 96.6°, 276.6°$
(e) $x = 41.4°, 268.6°$
(f) $x = 259.4°, 350.6°$

2.

(a) $x = 48.5°, 251.5°$
(b) $x = 5.5°, 214.5°$
(c) $x = 51.9°, 231.9°$
(d) $x = 146.0°, 326.0°$
(e) $x = 64.6°, 225.4°$
(f) $x = 55.3°, 194.7°$

Exercise 8.3

1.

(a) $\frac{1}{\sqrt{2}}$
(b) $\frac{1}{2}$
(c) 1
(d) $\frac{\sqrt{3}}{2}$
(e) 0
(f) 1
(g) $\sqrt{3}$
(h) 1
(i) 0
(j) -1
(k) $\frac{1}{\sqrt{3}}$
(l) 0
(m) 0
(n) 1
(o) 0
(p) -1

2.

(a) $-\frac{\sqrt{3}}{2}$
(b) $\frac{1}{2}$
(c) $\frac{1}{\sqrt{2}}$
(d) $-\frac{\sqrt{3}}{2}$
(e) $-\frac{1}{2}$
(f) 1
(g) $-\frac{1}{2}$
(h) $\frac{\sqrt{3}}{2}$
(i) $-\frac{1}{\sqrt{2}}$
(j) $-\frac{\sqrt{3}}{2}$
(k) -1
(l) -1
(m) $-\sqrt{3}$
(n) $-\frac{\sqrt{3}}{2}$
(o) $\frac{1}{2}$
(p) $-\frac{1}{\sqrt{2}}$

Exercise 8.4

1.

(a) $x = 30°, 150°$
(b) $x = 30°, 330°$
(c) $x = 30°, 210°$
(d) $x = 60°, 240°$
(e) $x = 45°, 315°$
(f) $x = 45°, 225°$
(g) $x = 135°, 315°$
(h) $x = 240°, 300°$
(i) $x = 135°, 225°$

2.

(a) $x = 22.5°, 67.5°, 202.5°, 247.5°$
(b) $x = 67.5°, 112.5°, 247.5°, 292.5°$
(c) $x = 30°, 120°, 210°, 300°$
(d) $x = 105°, 165°, 285°, 345°$
(e) $x = 30°, 150°, 210°, 330°$
(f) $x = 40°, 100°, 160°, 220°, 280°, 340°$
(g) $x = 75°, 105°, 195°, 225°, 315°, 345°$
(h) $x = 15°, 105°, 135°, 225°, 255°, 345°$
(i) $x = 75°, 165°, 255°, 345°$

3.

(a) $x = 70°, 160°$
(b) $x = 125°, 215°$
(c) $x = 65°, 245°$
(d) $x = 165°, 345°$
(e) $x = 205°, 295°$
(f) $x = 45°, 345°$
(g) $x = 90°, 150°$
(h) $x = 140°, 200°$
(i) $x = 105°, 285°$

Exercise 8.5A

1.

(a) $x = \frac{\pi}{6}, \frac{5\pi}{6}$
(b) $x = \frac{\pi}{6}, \frac{11\pi}{6}$
(c) $x = \frac{\pi}{3}, \frac{4\pi}{3}$
(d) $x = \frac{\pi}{6}, \frac{7\pi}{6}$
(e) $x = \frac{\pi}{4}, \frac{7\pi}{4}$
(f) $x = \frac{\pi}{4}, \frac{5\pi}{4}$
(g) $x = \frac{3\pi}{4}, \frac{7\pi}{4}$
(h) $x = \frac{4\pi}{3}, \frac{5\pi}{3}$
(i) $x = \frac{3\pi}{4}, \frac{5\pi}{4}$

2.

(a) $x = \frac{\pi}{8}, \frac{3\pi}{8}, \frac{9\pi}{8}, \frac{11\pi}{8}$
(b) $x = \frac{3\pi}{8}, \frac{5\pi}{8}, \frac{11\pi}{8}, \frac{13\pi}{8}$
(c) $x = \frac{\pi}{6}, \frac{2\pi}{3}, \frac{7\pi}{6}, \frac{5\pi}{3}$
(d) $x = \frac{7\pi}{12}, \frac{11\pi}{12}, \frac{19\pi}{12}, \frac{23\pi}{12}$
(e) $x = \frac{\pi}{6}, \frac{5\pi}{6}, \frac{7\pi}{6}, \frac{11\pi}{6}$
(f) $x = \frac{2\pi}{9}, \frac{5\pi}{9}, \frac{8\pi}{9}, \frac{11\pi}{9}, \frac{14\pi}{9}, \frac{17\pi}{9}$
(g) $x = \frac{5\pi}{12}, \frac{7\pi}{12}, \frac{13\pi}{12}, \frac{5\pi}{4}, \frac{7\pi}{4}, \frac{23\pi}{12}$
(h) $x = \frac{\pi}{12}, \frac{7\pi}{12}, \frac{3\pi}{4}, \frac{5\pi}{4}, \frac{17\pi}{12}, \frac{23\pi}{12}$
(i) $x = \frac{\pi}{12}, \frac{7\pi}{12}, \frac{13\pi}{12}, \frac{19\pi}{12}$

3.

(a) $x = \frac{5\pi}{12}, \frac{11\pi}{12}$
(b) $x = \frac{11\pi}{12}, \frac{17\pi}{12}$
(c) $x = \frac{7\pi}{12}, \frac{23\pi}{12}$
(d) $x = \pi, \frac{5\pi}{3}$
(e) $x = \pi, \frac{3\pi}{2}$
(f) $x = \frac{\pi}{12}, \frac{5\pi}{12}$
(g) $x = \frac{5\pi}{6}, \frac{3\pi}{2}$
(h) $x = \frac{13\pi}{12}, \frac{19\pi}{12}$
(i) $x = \frac{3\pi}{2}, \frac{11\pi}{6}$

Exercise 8.5B

1.

(a) $x = 0.17, 2.97$
(b) $x = 0.84, 5.44$
(c) $x = 1.33, 4.47$
(d) $x = 1.37, 4.51$
(e) $x = 0.80, 5.49$
(f) $x = 0.46, 3.61$
(g) $x = 3.79, 5.64$
(h) $x = 3.87, 5.55$
(i) $x = 1.82, 4.46$

2.

(a) $x = 1.16, 5.12$
(b) $x = 3.48, 5.94$
(c) $x = 0.88, 4.02$
(d) $x = 0.49, 1.08, 3.63, 4.22$
(e) $x = 2.30, 3.98$
(f) $x = 1.26, 2.83, 4.40, 5.98$
(g) $x = 1.28, 2.85, 4.42, 5.99$
(h) $x = 1.29, 1.85, 3.38, 3.95, 5.48, 6.04$
(i) $x = 0.58, 2.56, 3.72, 5.70$

3.

(a) $x = 0.82, 2.73$
(b) $x = 2.66, 4.23$
(c) $x = 1.84, 4.99$
(d) $x = 1.18, 4.33$
(e) $x = 3.21, 5.42$
(f) $x = 1.06, 5.43$
(g) $x = 1.73, 3.95$
(h) $x = 0.64, 3.10$
(i) $x = 0.42, 5.26$

Exercise 8.6

1.

(a) $x = (30°, 2), (150°, 2)$
(b) $x = (70.5°, 1), (289.5°, 1)$
(c) $x = (203.6°, -2), (336.4°, -2)$
(d) $x = (75.5°, 1), (284.5°, 1)$
(e) $x = (110.9°, -2), (159.1°, -2)$
(f) $x = (42.3°, -3), (77.7°, -3)$
(g) $x = (30°, 3), (150°, 3)$
(h) $x = (90°, -2), (270°, -2)$
(i) $x = (20.9°, 1), (69.1°, 1)$

2.

(a) $x = (0.3, 1), (2.9, 1)$
(b) $x = (2.3, -2), (4.0, -2)$
(c) $x = (0.3, 1), (2.8, 1)$
(d) $x = (0.3, 2), (2.9, 2)$
(e) $x = (2.1, -3), (4.2, -3)$
(f) $x = (1.6, 3)$
(g) $x = (3.9, 1), (5.6, 1)$
(h) $x = (2.1, -3), (4.2, -3)$
(i) $x = (3.5, -2), (5.9, -2)$

Exercise 8.7

8.1

(a) $y = 3\sin x - 1$
(b) $y = -4\cos x$
(c) $y = 2\cos 4x + 2$
(d) $y = 2\cos(x - 45°)$
(e) $y = 4\sin(x - 45°)$
(f) $y = 3\sin(x - 60°)$

8.2

(a) $x = 33.7°, 213.7°$
(b) $x = 210°, 330°$
(c) $x = 60°, 120°, 240°, 300°$
(d) $x = 105°, 165°, 285°, 345°$
(e) $x = 130°, 250°$
(f) $x = 179.5°, 320.5°$

8.3

(a) $\frac{1}{\sqrt{2}}$
(b) $\frac{1}{2}$
(c) -1
(d) $-\frac{\sqrt{3}}{2}$
(e) 0
(f) $-\frac{1}{\sqrt{2}}$
(g) -1
(h) -1

8.4

(a) $x = 45°, 225°$
(b) $x = 210°, 330°$
(c) $x = 15°, 165°, 195°, 345°$
(d) $x = 15°, 75°, 195°, 255°$
(e) $x = 130°, 250°$
(f) $x = 215°, 275°$

8.5A

(a) $x = \frac{\pi}{4}, \frac{3\pi}{4}$
(b) $x = \frac{\pi}{4}, \frac{5\pi}{4}$
(c) $x = \frac{\pi}{9}, \frac{5\pi}{9}$

8.5B

(a) $x = 1.1, 4.2$
(b) $x = 3.4, 6.0$
(c) $x = \frac{\pi}{3}, \frac{2\pi}{3}, \frac{4\pi}{3}, \frac{5\pi}{3}$
(d) $x = 0.4, 1.2, 3.5, 4.3$
(e) $x = 2.3, 4.4$
(f) $x = 3.6, 5.0$

8.6

(a) $(4.0, -2), (5.4, -2)$
(b) $(1.8, -2), (4.5, -2)$
(c) $\left(\frac{\pi}{6}, 3\right), \left(\frac{5\pi}{6}, 3\right)$

Chapter 9

Exercise 9.1A

1.

(a) $\cos\alpha\cos\beta - \sin\alpha\sin\beta$
(b) $\cos\alpha\cos\beta + \sin\alpha\sin\beta$
(c) $\cos a\cos b - \sin a\sin b$
(d) $\cos a\cos b + \sin a\sin b$
(e) $\cos\theta\cos q + \sin\theta\sin q$
(f) $\cos 2b\cos c - \sin 2b\sin c$
(g) $\cos 4b\cos 2c + \sin 4b\sin 2c$
(h) $\cos^2 a - \sin^2 a$

2.

(a) $2\cos^2 a - 1$ or $1 - 2\sin^2 a$
(b) $2\cos^2 a - 1$ or $1 - 2\sin^2 a$

3.

(a) $\sin\alpha\cos\beta + \cos\alpha\sin\beta$
(b) $\sin\alpha\cos\beta - \cos\alpha\sin\beta$
(c) $\sin a\cos b + \cos a\sin b$
(d) $\sin a\cos b - \cos a\sin b$
(e) $\sin\theta\cos\phi - \cos\theta\sin\phi$
(f) $\sin 3b\cos c + \cos 3b\sin c$
(g) $\sin 2b\cos 3c - \cos 2b\sin 3c$
(h) $2\sin a\cos a$

Exercise 9.1B

1.

(a) $\frac{1}{\sqrt{2}}\cos x° - \frac{1}{\sqrt{2}}\sin x°$
(b) $\frac{1}{2}\sin x° + \frac{\sqrt{3}}{2}\cos x°$
(c) $\frac{\sqrt{3}}{2}\cos x° + \frac{1}{2}\sin x°$
(d) $\frac{1}{\sqrt{2}}\sin x° + \frac{1}{\sqrt{2}}\cos x°$
(e) $-\cos x°$
(f) $-\sin x°$
(g) $\frac{\sqrt{3}}{2}\sin x° - \frac{1}{2}\cos x°$
(h) $\frac{1}{\sqrt{2}}\cos x° + \frac{1}{\sqrt{2}}\sin x°$
(i) $\frac{1}{2}\cos x° + \frac{\sqrt{3}}{2}\sin x°$
(j) $\frac{1}{2}\sin x° + \frac{\sqrt{3}}{2}\cos x°$
(k) $\sin x°$
(l) $\cos x°$

2.

(a) $-\frac{\cos x°}{\sin x°}$
(b) $-\frac{\cos x°}{\sin x°}$

3.

(a) $\frac{1}{2}\cos x - \frac{\sqrt{3}}{2}\sin x$
(b) $\frac{\sqrt{3}}{2}\sin x - \frac{1}{2}\cos x$
(c) $\sin x$
(d) $\frac{1}{2}\sin x + \frac{\sqrt{3}}{2}\cos x$
(e) $\frac{1}{\sqrt{2}}\sin x - \frac{1}{\sqrt{2}}\cos x$
(f) $\frac{\sqrt{3}}{2}\cos x - \frac{1}{2}\sin x$
(g) $-\cos x$
(h) $\frac{1}{\sqrt{2}}\cos x + \frac{1}{\sqrt{2}}\sin x$

Exercise 9.2

1.

(a) $\frac{4}{5}\cos x - \frac{3}{5}\sin x$
(b) $\frac{3}{\sqrt{10}}\sin x + \frac{1}{\sqrt{10}}\cos x$
(c) $\frac{3}{5}\cos x + \frac{4}{5}\sin x$
(d) $\frac{5}{13}\cos x + \frac{12}{13}\sin x$
(e) $\frac{\sqrt{5}}{3}\sin x - \frac{2}{3}\cos x$
(f) $\frac{12}{13}\cos x - \frac{5}{13}\sin x$
(g) $\frac{\sqrt{7}}{\sqrt{11}}\cos x - \frac{2}{\sqrt{11}}\sin x$
(h) $\frac{2}{\sqrt{10}}\sin x + \frac{\sqrt{3}}{\sqrt{5}}\cos x$
(i) $\frac{8}{17}\cos x + \frac{15}{17}\sin x$

2.

(a) $-\frac{16}{65}$ (b) $\frac{63}{65}$ (c) $\frac{1}{5\sqrt{2}}$

(d) $\frac{77}{85}$ (e) $\frac{10-12\sqrt{5}}{39}$ (f) $\frac{75+8\sqrt{11}}{102}$

(g) $\frac{1-4\sqrt{2}}{3\sqrt{5}}$ (h) $\frac{18}{5\sqrt{13}}$

3.

(a) $\cos(a+b)=\frac{1}{\sqrt{10}}$ (b) $\sin(a+b)=\frac{3}{\sqrt{10}}$

4.

(a) $\cos(a+b)=\frac{9}{5\sqrt{10}}$ (b) $\sin(a+b)=\frac{13}{5\sqrt{10}}$

5.

(a) $\cos(b-a)=\frac{3}{\sqrt{10}}$ (b) $\sin(b-a)=\frac{1}{\sqrt{10}}$

6.

(a) $\frac{1-\sqrt{3}}{2\sqrt{2}}$ (b) $\frac{\sqrt{3}-1}{2\sqrt{2}}$ (c) $\frac{1+\sqrt{3}}{2\sqrt{2}}$

(d) $\frac{1+\sqrt{3}}{2\sqrt{2}}$ (e) $-\frac{1}{2}$ (f) $\frac{1+\sqrt{3}}{2\sqrt{2}}$

(g) $\frac{\sqrt{3}-1}{2\sqrt{2}}$ (h) $\frac{\sqrt{3}-1}{2\sqrt{2}}$ (i) $\frac{1-\sqrt{3}}{2\sqrt{2}}$

(j) $\frac{1+\sqrt{3}}{2\sqrt{2}}$ (k) $\frac{1+\sqrt{3}}{2\sqrt{2}}$ (l) $\frac{1+\sqrt{3}}{2\sqrt{2}}$

7.

(a) $\frac{\sqrt{3}-1}{2\sqrt{2}}$ (b) $-\frac{1+\sqrt{3}}{2\sqrt{2}}$ (c) $\frac{1+\sqrt{3}}{2\sqrt{2}}$

(d) $-\frac{1+\sqrt{3}}{2\sqrt{2}}$ (e) $\frac{1-\sqrt{3}}{2\sqrt{2}}$ (f) $-\frac{1+\sqrt{3}}{2\sqrt{2}}$

(g) $\frac{1-\sqrt{3}}{2\sqrt{2}}$ (h) $\frac{1-\sqrt{3}}{2\sqrt{2}}$

Exercise 9.3

1.

(a) $\frac{7}{25}$ (b) $\frac{120}{169}$ (c) $-\frac{7}{18}$

(d) $\frac{240}{289}$ (e) $\frac{17}{49}$ (f) $\frac{9\sqrt{19}}{50}$

(g) $\frac{5}{13}$ (h) $\frac{\sqrt{15}}{8}$ (i) $\frac{161}{289}$

2.

(a) (i) $\frac{24}{25}$ (ii) $\frac{7}{25}$ (b) (i) $\frac{40}{41}$ (ii) $\frac{9}{41}$

(c) (i) $\frac{20}{29}$ (ii) $\frac{21}{29}$ (d) (i) $\frac{4}{5}$ (ii) $-\frac{3}{5}$

(e) (i) $\frac{4\sqrt{5}}{9}$ (ii) $\frac{1}{9}$ (f) (i) $\frac{15}{17}$ (ii) $\frac{8}{17}$

(g) (i) $\frac{18\sqrt{19}}{100}$ (ii) $\frac{31}{50}$ (h) (i) $\frac{12}{13}$ (ii) $\frac{5}{13}$

(i) (i) $\frac{4\sqrt{21}}{25}$ (ii) $\frac{17}{25}$

3.

(a) (i) $\frac{24}{25}$ (ii) $\frac{7}{25}$ (b) (i) $\frac{240}{289}$ (ii) $-\frac{161}{289}$

(c) (i) $\frac{240}{289}$ (ii) $\frac{161}{289}$ (d) (i) $\frac{24}{25}$ (ii) $\frac{7}{25}$

(e) (i) $\frac{840}{841}$ (ii) $\frac{41}{841}$ (f) (i) $\frac{120}{169}$ (ii) $-\frac{119}{169}$

4.

(a) $\sin 2\theta=\frac{3\sqrt{7}}{8}$ (b) $\cos 2\theta=-\frac{1}{8}$ (c) $\tan 2\theta=-3\sqrt{7}$

5.

(a) $\sin 2\theta=\frac{4}{5}$ (b) $\cos 2\theta=-\frac{3}{5}$ (c) $\tan 2\theta=-\frac{4}{3}$

6.

(a) $\sin 2\theta=\frac{12}{13}$ (b) $\cos 2\theta=\frac{5}{13}$ (c) $\tan 2\theta=\frac{12}{5}$

7.

(a) $\sin 2\theta=\frac{2}{5}$ (b) $\sin 4\theta=\frac{4\sqrt{21}}{25}$

8.

(a) $\cos 2\theta=\frac{4}{5}$ (b) $\cos 3\theta=\frac{9}{5\sqrt{10}}$

Exercise 9.4

All questions are proofs.

Exercise 9.5A

1.

(a) $x=90°, 120°, 330°$ (b) $x=60°, 180°, 300°$

(c) $x=30°, 90°, 150°$

2.

(a) $x=\frac{3\pi}{2},\frac{7\pi}{6},\frac{11\pi}{6}$ (b) $x=\frac{2\pi}{3},\pi,\frac{4\pi}{3}$ (c) $x=\frac{\pi}{6},\frac{5\pi}{6},\frac{7\pi}{6},\frac{11\pi}{6}$

3.

(a) $x=0°, 60°, 180°, 300°, 360°$

(b) $x=90°, 210°, 270°, 330°$

(c) $x=30°, 90°, 150°, 270°$

4.

(a) $x=0,\frac{\pi}{6},\pi\ \frac{11\pi}{6},2\pi$ (b) $x=\frac{\pi}{4},\frac{\pi}{2},\frac{3\pi}{4},\frac{3\pi}{2}$

(c) $x=\frac{\pi}{3},\frac{\pi}{2},\frac{2\pi}{3},\frac{3\pi}{2}$

5.

(a) $x=60°, 180°, 300°$ (b) $x=120°, 180°, 240°$

(c) $x=30°, 150°, 270°$

6.

(a) $x=\frac{7\pi}{6},\frac{11\pi}{6}$ (b) $x=\pi$ (c) $x=0,\frac{2\pi}{3},\frac{4\pi}{3},2\pi$

7.

(a) $x=0°, 60°, 120°\ 180°, 240°, 300°, 360°$

(b) $x=0°, 45°, 180°, 225°, 360°$

(c) $x=45°, 90°, 225°, 270°$

Exercise 9.5B

1.

(a) $x=180°$ (b) $x=245.3°, 294.7°$

(c) $x=180°$

2.

(a) $x = 1.91, 4.37$ (b) $x = 0.85,\ 2.29, \frac{3\pi}{2}$

(c) $x = 0, 1.32, 4.97, 2\pi$

Exercise 9.6A

9.1

(a) $\frac{1}{\sqrt{2}}(\sin x + \cos x)$ (b) $\frac{\sqrt{3}}{2}\cos x - \frac{1}{2}\sin x$

(c) $\frac{1}{2}\sin x + \frac{\sqrt{3}}{2}\cos x$

9.2

(a) $\cos(a+b) = \frac{6-4\sqrt{5}}{15}$

(b) $\sin(a+b) = \frac{27}{13\sqrt{10}}$

9.3

(a) $\cos 2x = -\frac{3}{5}$ (b) $\sin 2x = \frac{15}{17}$ (c) $\cos 2x = \frac{5}{13}$

9.4

All questions are proofs

9.5

(a) $x = \frac{\pi}{3}, \frac{\pi}{2}, \frac{2\pi}{3}, \frac{3\pi}{2}$ (b) $x = \frac{\pi}{3}, \frac{5\pi}{3}$

Exercise 9.6B

1.

(a) $\sin 2x = \frac{20}{29}$ (b) $\cos 2x = \frac{21}{29}$

2.

(a) $\sin 2x = \frac{5}{13}$ (b) $\sin x = \frac{1}{\sqrt{26}}$

3.

(a) (i) $\sin 2\theta = \frac{120}{169}$ (ii) $\cos 2\theta = -\frac{119}{169}$ (b) $\tan 2\theta = -\frac{120}{119}$

4.

(a) $\cos\left(x - \frac{\pi}{4}\right)$ (b) $\cos 2x$ (c) $\frac{3}{5}$

5.

(a) $\sin 2\theta = \frac{4}{5}$ (b) $\cos 2\theta = \frac{3}{5}$

6.

(a) $\sin(a+b) = \frac{32\sqrt{41}}{205}$

(b) $\cos(a+b) = \frac{1}{5\sqrt{41}}$

7.

(a) $\sin\left(x + \frac{\pi}{6}\right)$ (b) $\frac{\sqrt{3}}{2}\sin x + \frac{1}{2}\cos x$

8.

(a) $\cos(a+b) = \frac{7}{\sqrt{65}}$ (b) $\sin(a+b) = \frac{4}{\sqrt{65}}$

(b) $\sin 2a = \frac{3}{5}$

9.

(a) $\cos(b-a) = \frac{19}{5\sqrt{17}}$ (b) $\sin(b-a) = \frac{8}{\sqrt{17}}$

(b) $\cos 2a = \frac{15}{17}$

10.

(a) $\sin 2\theta = \frac{3}{5}$ (b) $\cos 2\theta = \frac{4}{5}$ (b) $\cos\theta = \frac{3}{\sqrt{10}}$

11.

(a) $f(g(x)) = \cos\left(x + \frac{\pi}{4}\right)$ (b) $h(g(x)) = 2x + \frac{\pi}{2}$

(b) $f(h(g(x))) = -\frac{3}{5}$

Chapter 10

Exercise 10.1A

1.

(a) $2\cos(x - 60)°$ (b) $\sqrt{7}\cos(x + 40.9)°$

(c) $\sqrt{29}\sin(x + 21.8)°$ (d) $\sqrt{5}\cos(x + 26.6)°$

(e) $\sqrt{5}\sin(x + 63.4)°$ (f) $\sqrt{29}\cos(x + 21.8)°$

(g) $\sqrt{13}\sin(x + 33.7)°$ (h) $\sqrt{17}\sin(x - 75.96)°$

2.

(a) $2\cos(x - 1.05)$ (b) $\sqrt{5}\sin(x + 0.46)$

(c) $\sqrt{17}\cos(x + 0.24)$ (d) $\sqrt{34}\sin(x - 1.03)$

(e) $\sqrt{13}\sin(x - 0.98)$ (f) $\sqrt{6}\cos(x - 0.62)$

(g) $5\sin(x + 0.93)$ (h) $5\cos(x - 0.64)$

Exercise 10.1B

1.

(a) $\sqrt{3}\ \cos(x - 305.3)°$ (b) $2\sqrt{3}\cos(x + 30)°$

(c) $\sqrt{29}\sin(x + 291.8)°$ (d) $\sqrt{5}\sin(x + 333.4)°$

(e) $\sqrt{5}\sin(x - 296.6)°$ (f) $\sqrt{29}\cos(x + 21.8)°$

(g) $\sqrt{13}\sin(x + 33.7)°$ (h) $\sqrt{17}\sin(x - 76.0)°$

2.

(a) $\sqrt{11}\cos(x - 2.01)$ (b) $\sqrt{5}\cos(x + 5.18)$

(c) $\sqrt{13}\sin(x + 2.16)$ (d) $\sqrt{17}\sin(x + 2.90)$

(e) $\sqrt{20}\sin(x + 2.03)$ (f) $\sqrt{10}\cos(x + 4.39)$

(g) $\sqrt{29}\sin(x + 1.19)$ (h) $\sqrt{13}\sin(x - 3.73)$

Exercise 10.2

1.

(a) $x = 44.5°, 185.5°$ (b) $x = 44.7°, 295.3°$

(c) $x = 110°$ (d) $x = 63.2°, 326.8°$

(e) $x = 16.9°, 123.1°$ (f) $x = 84.7°, 305.3°$

2.

(a) $x = 47.2°, 262.3°$ (b) $x = 90°, 323.1°$

(c) $x = 129.0°, 349.1°$ (d) $x = 61.9°, 270°$

(e) $x = 45°, 168.7°, 225°, 348.7°$

(f) $x = 13.6°, 67.0°, 133.6°, 187.0°, 253.6°, 307.0°$

3.

(a) $x = 1.31, 6.02$ (b) $x = 4.45, 6.02$ (c) $x = 1.28, 3.38$

(d) $x = 0.71, 4.90$ (e) $x = 0.29, 4.41$ (f) $x = 1.61, 2.65$

4.

(a) $x = 0.53, 4.52$ **(b)** $x = 0.14, 3.93$ **(c)** $x = 2.62, 6.14$

(d) $x = 1.01, 2.78$ **(e)** $x = 0.97, 2.81, 4.11, 5.95$

(f) $x = 0.17, 0.76, 1.74, 2.33, 3.31, 3.90, 4.88, 5.47$

Exercise 10.3

1.

(a)

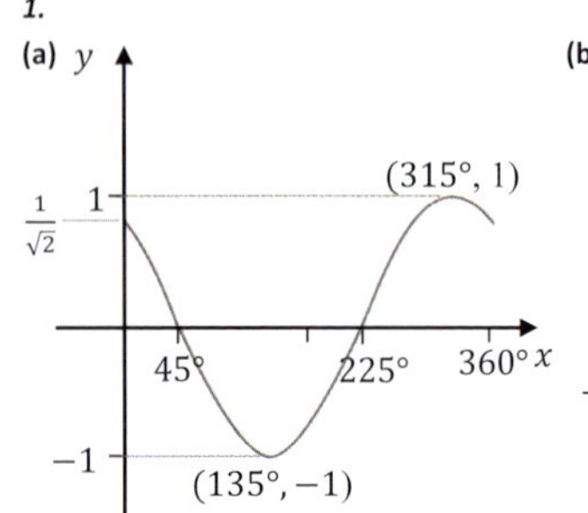

(b)

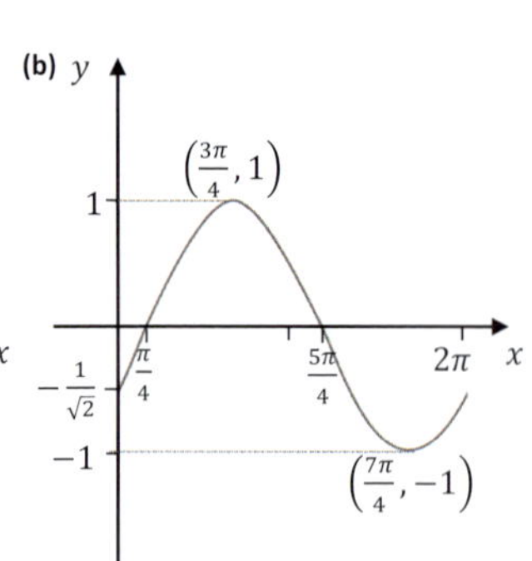

(c)

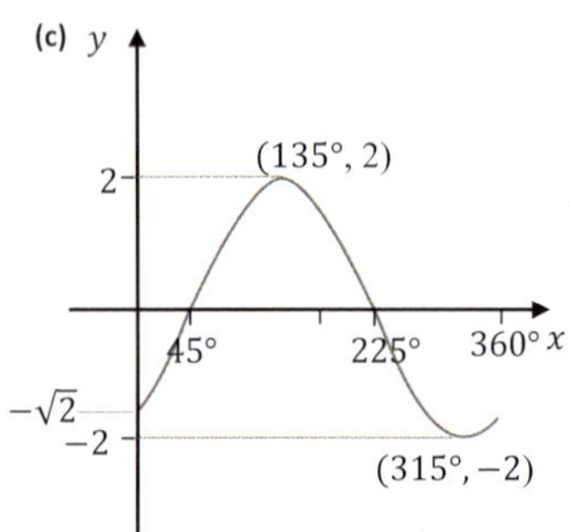

(d)

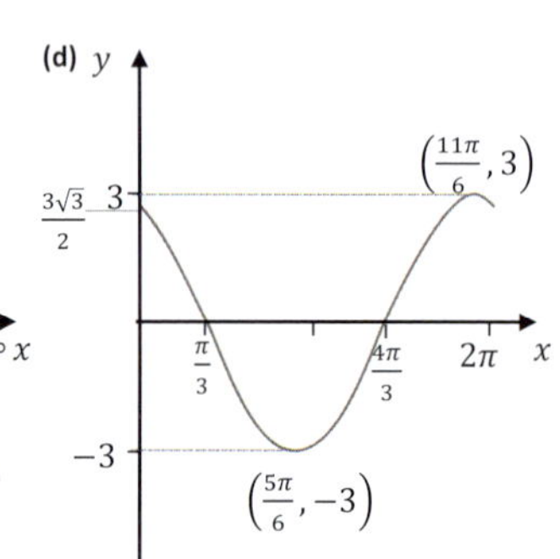

(e)

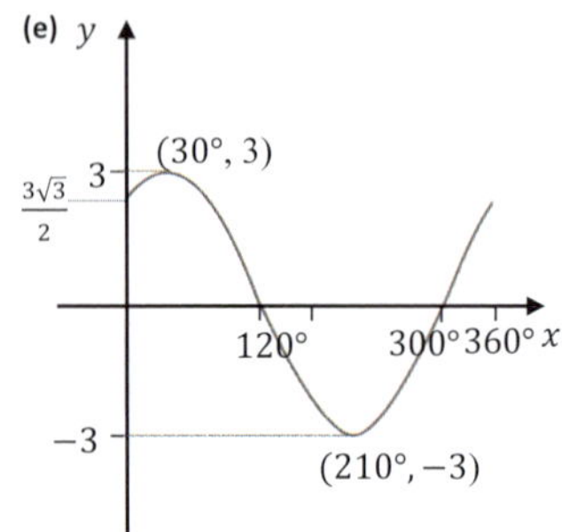

(f)

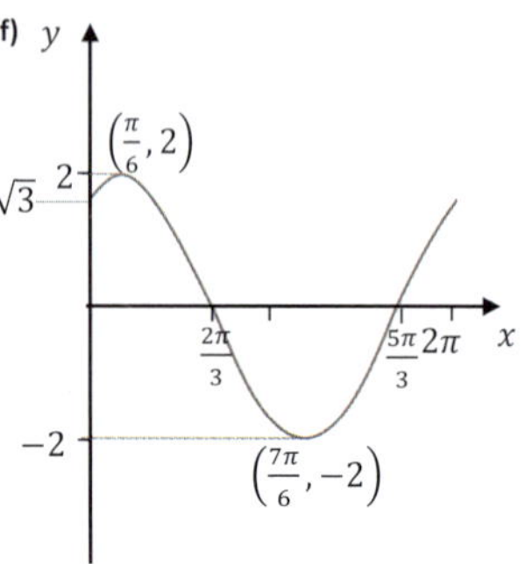

(g)

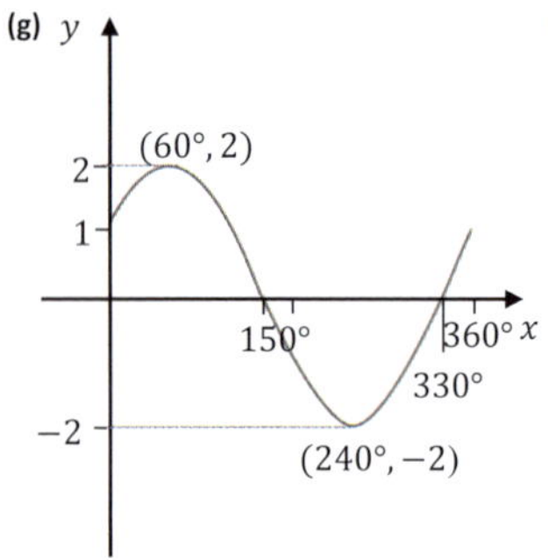

(h)

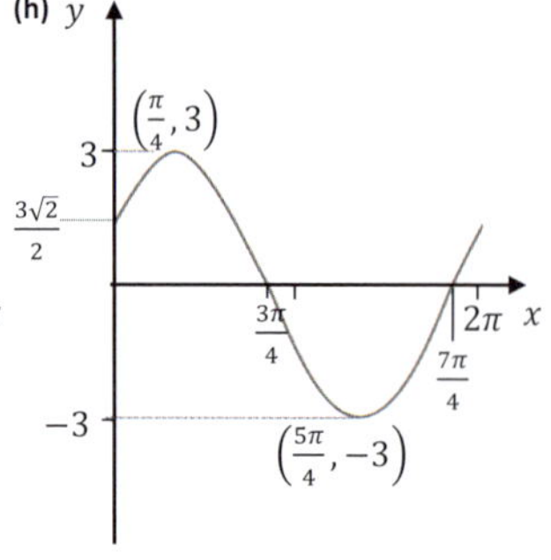

(i)

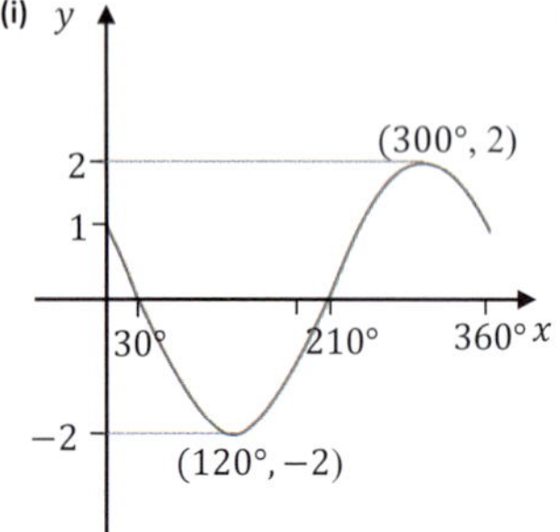

(j)

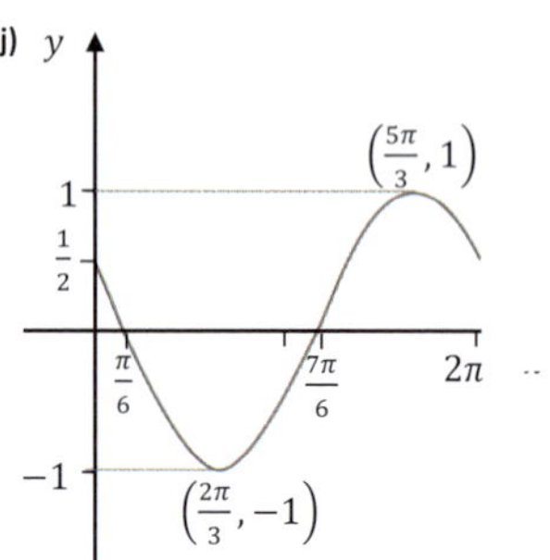

(k) **(l)**

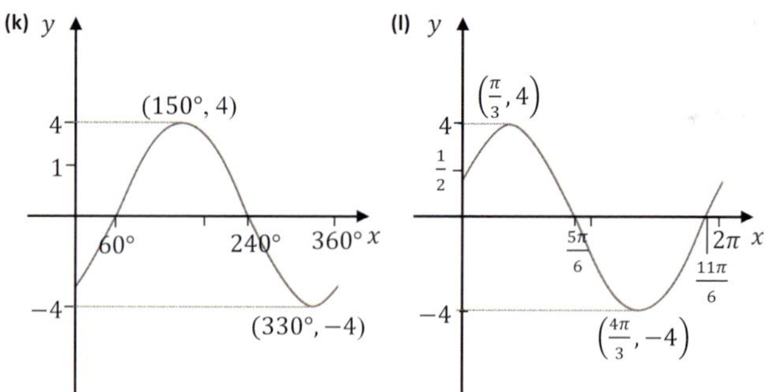

2.

(a) **(b)**

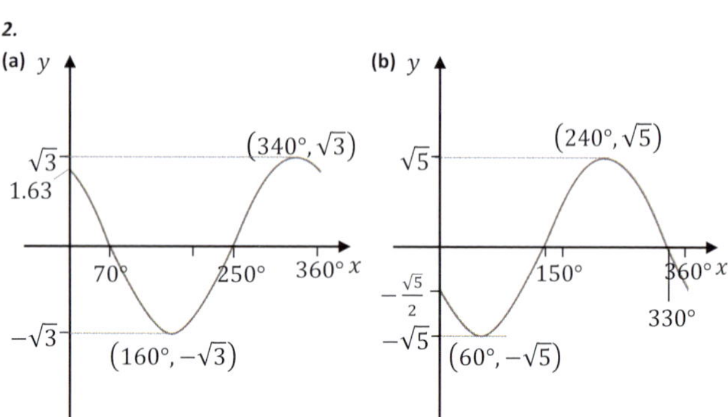

(c) **(d)**

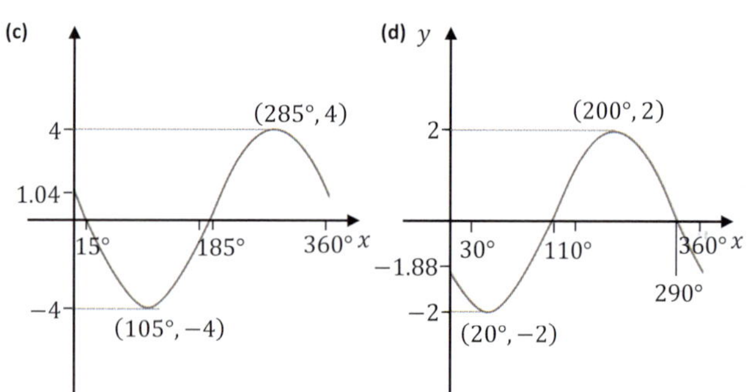

(e) **(f)**

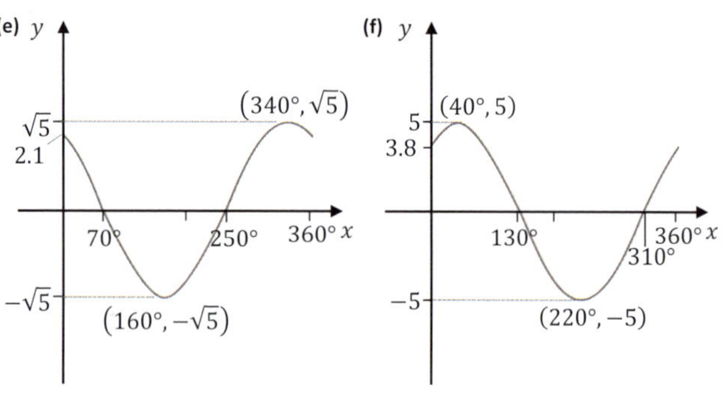

3.

(a) (i) $\sqrt{6}\cos(x + 35.3)°$ **(b) (i)** $3\sqrt{3}\sin(x + 344.2)°$

(ii) **(ii)**

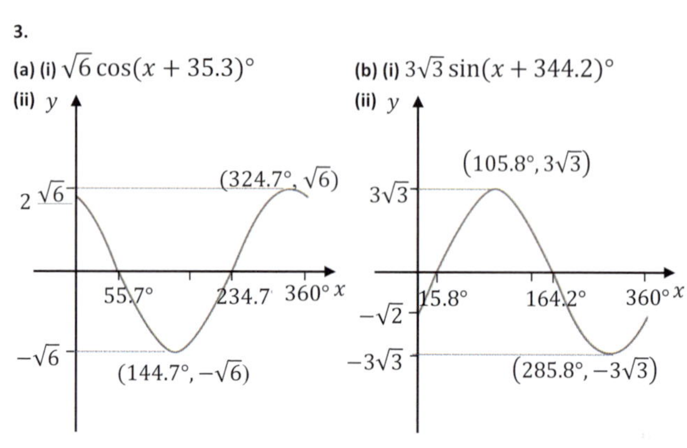

(c) (i) $\sqrt{13}\cos(x+236.3)°$

(ii)

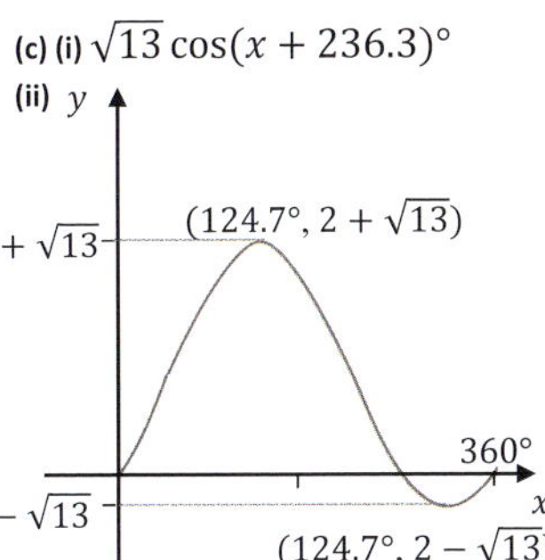

(d) (i) $\sqrt{6}\sin(x+35.3)°$

(ii)

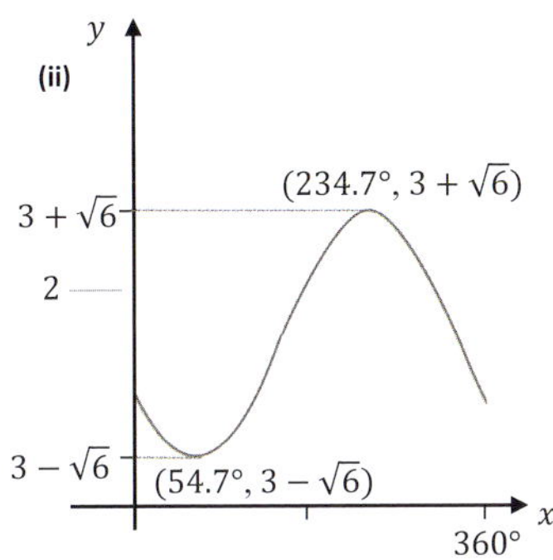

Exercise 10.4

1.

(a) (i) $max = 3$ **(ii)** $x = 135°$

(b) (i) $max = 7$ **(ii)** $x = \frac{5\pi}{6}$

(c) (i) $max = 5$ **(ii)** $x = 70°$

(d) (i) $max = 4$ **(ii)** $x = \frac{5\pi}{4}$

(e) (i) $max = 5$ **(ii)** $x = 315°$

(f) (i) $max = 2$ **(ii)** $x = 345°$

(g) (i) $max = 2$ **(ii)** $x = 3.44$

(h) (i) $max = 6$ **(ii)** $x = 5.78$

2.

(a) (i) $\sqrt{6}\ \cos(x+35.3)°$ **(ii)** $max = \sqrt{6}$ **(iii)** $x = 324.7°$

(b) (i) $\sqrt{34}\ \sin(x-1.03)$ **(ii)** $min = -\sqrt{34}$ **(iii)** $x = 5.74$

(c) (i) $\sqrt{34}\ \cos(x-5.25)$ **(ii)** $min = -3\sqrt{34}$ **(iii)** $x = 2.11$

(d) (i) $\sqrt{29}\ \sin(x+338.2)°$ **(ii)** $max = 2\sqrt{29}$ **(iii)** $x = 111.8°$

(e) (i) $\sqrt{13}\ \cos(x+236.3)°$ **(ii)** $min = 3-\sqrt{13}$ **(iii)** $x = 303.7°$

(f) (i) $\sqrt{3}\ \sin(x-3.76)$ **(ii)** $max = \sqrt{3}-4$ **(iii)** $x = 5.33$

(g) (i) $\sqrt{34}\ \sin(x+329.0)°$ **(ii)** $max = 2\sqrt{34}+1$ **(iii)** $x = 121°$

(h) (i) $\sqrt{10}\sin(x-3.46)$ **(ii)** $max = 3\sqrt{10}-4$ **(iii)** $x = 5.03$

Exercise 10.5

10.1

(a) $\sqrt{5}\ \cos(x-26.6)°$ **(b)** $\sqrt{7}\sin(x+0.71)$

(c) $2\sqrt{5}\cos(x+5.82)$ **(d)** $\sqrt{34}\sin(x-211.0)°$

10.2

(a) $x = 0.53, 4.52$

(b) $x = 0.14, 3.93$

(c) $x = 2.62, 6.14$

(d) (i) $\sqrt{10}\cos(x-18.4)°$ **(ii)** $x = 69.2°, 327.7°$

(e) (i) $\sqrt{5}\sin(x+26.6)°$ **(ii)** $x = 126.9°$

(f) (i) $2\sqrt{2}\cos\left(x+\frac{7\pi}{4}\right)$ **(ii)** $x = 0.92, 2.00, 4.06, 5.14$

(g) (i) $3\sin(x-5.44)$ **(ii)** $x = 0.73, 2.82, 4.92$

10.3

(a) (i) $2\cos(x-30)°$

(ii)

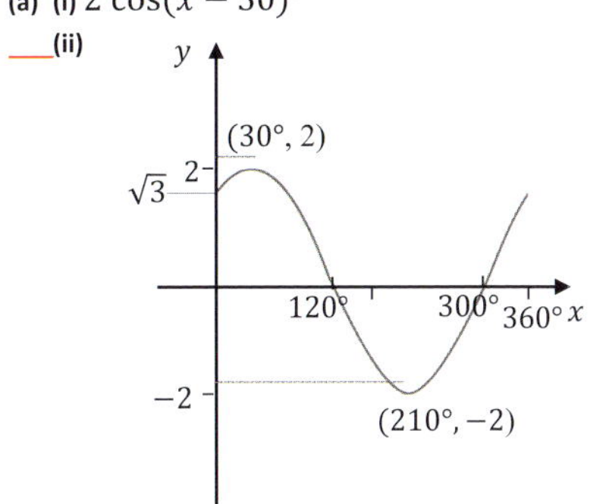

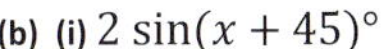

(b) (i) $2\sin(x+45)°$

(ii)

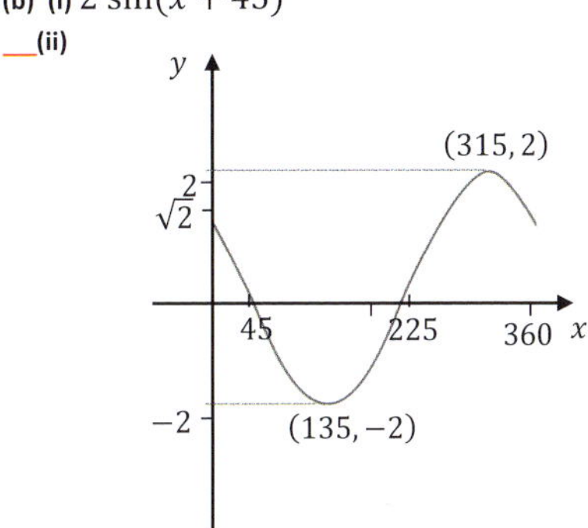

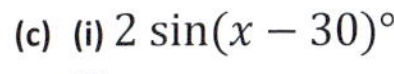

(c) (i) $2\sin(x-30)°$

(ii)

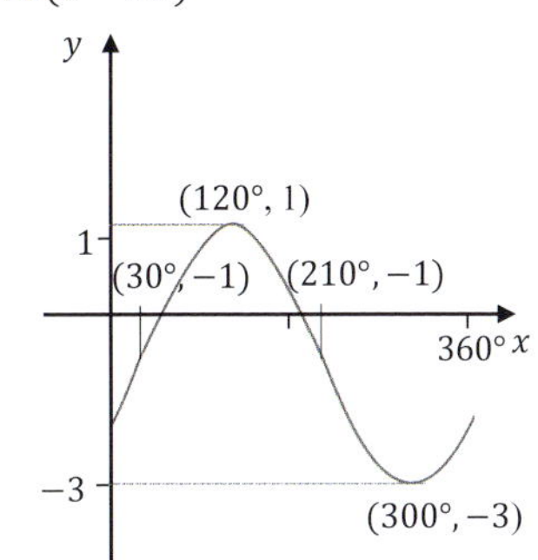

(d) (i) $2\cos(x+60)°$

(ii)

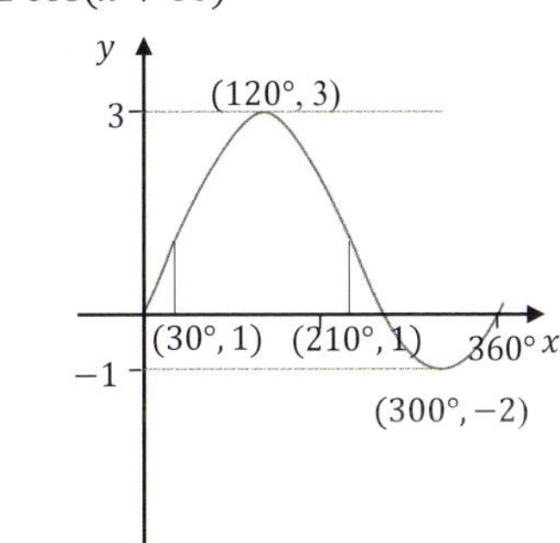

10.4

(a) (i) $\sqrt{34}\cos(x+31.0)°$ **(ii)** $max = \sqrt{34}-2$ **(iii)** $x = 329.0°$

(b) (i) $\sqrt{13}\sin(x+2.16)$ **(ii)** $min = 3-2\sqrt{13}$ **(iii)** $x = 2.56$

Chapter 11

Exercise 11.1

1.

(a) $2x^{-1}$ (b) $\frac{1}{2}x^{-1}$ (c) $2x^{-2}$ (d) $4x^{-3}$

(e) $\frac{1}{4}x^{-5}$ (f) $6x^{-2}$ (g) $\frac{1}{3}x^{-6}$ (h) $\frac{2}{3}x^{-1}$

(i) $\frac{3}{5}x^{-4}$ (j) $5x^{-2}$ (k) $\frac{1}{12}x^{-3}$ (l) $\frac{7}{3}x^{-4}$

2.

(a) $x^{\frac{1}{3}}$ (b) $x^{\frac{3}{4}}$ (c) $x^{\frac{3}{2}}$ (d) $x^{\frac{4}{3}}$

(e) $3x^{\frac{5}{2}}$ (f) $4x^{\frac{2}{3}}$ (g) $2x^{-\frac{3}{2}}$ (h) $x^{-\frac{5}{3}}$

(i) $5x^{-\frac{3}{4}}$ (j) $\frac{1}{4}x^{-\frac{2}{3}}$ (k) $\frac{3}{4}x^{-\frac{5}{2}}$ (l) $\frac{11}{5}x^{-\frac{3}{4}}$

3.

(a) $\frac{1}{x^3}$ (b) $\frac{1}{x^4}$ (c) $\frac{2}{x^3}$ (d) $\frac{1}{2x^5}$

(e) $\frac{2}{3x^3}$ (f) $\frac{3}{4x^5}$ (g) $\sqrt[5]{x^3}$ (h) $\sqrt{x^3}$

(i) $\sqrt[4]{x^3}$ (j) $\sqrt[3]{x^4}$ (k) $3\sqrt{x}$ (l) $2\sqrt[3]{x^2}$

(m) $\frac{3}{\sqrt[4]{x}}$ (n) $\frac{2}{\sqrt[5]{x^3}}$ (o) $\frac{1}{2\sqrt[3]{x^2}}$ (p) $\frac{1}{2\sqrt[3]{x}}$

(q) $\frac{3}{2\sqrt[3]{x^2}}$ (r) $\frac{2}{3\sqrt[3]{x^4}}$

Exercise 11.2A

1.

(a) $2x$ (b) $3x^2$ (c) 1 (d) $4x^3$

(e) $7x^6$ (f) $5x^4$ (g) $6x^5$ (h) $9x^8$

(i) $-2x^{-3}$ (j) $-4x^{-5}$ (k) $-6x^{-7}$ (l) $-3x^{-4}$

(m) $4x$ (n) $6x$ (o) $6x^2$ (p) $12x^3$

(q) $12x^2$ (r) 5 (s) $-3x^{-2}$ (t) $-4x^{-3}$

2.

(a) $9x^2$ (b) $28x^6$ (c) 2 (d) $-6x^{-3}$

(e) $-12x^{-4}$ (f) $35x^4$ (g) $-5x^{-2}$ (h) $24x^5$

3.

(a) $\frac{1}{2\sqrt{x}}$ (b) $\frac{1}{3\sqrt[3]{x^2}}$ (c) $\frac{2}{3\sqrt[3]{x}}$ (d) $-\frac{2}{3\sqrt[3]{x}}$

(e) $\frac{1}{\sqrt{x}}$ (f) $\frac{3}{\sqrt[4]{x}}$ (g) $-\frac{2}{\sqrt[3]{x^4}}$ (h) $\frac{10}{\sqrt[6]{x}}$

(i) $\frac{1}{4\sqrt{x}}$ (j) $\frac{1}{4\sqrt[3]{x^2}}$ (k) $\frac{1}{\sqrt[3]{x}}$ (l) $-\frac{1}{12\sqrt[3]{x^5}}$

Exercise 11.2B

1.

(a) $2x+1$ (b) $4x-4$ (c) $2x-9$

(d) $3x^2-4x$ (e) $3x^2-6$ (f) $8x-18$

(g) $2x-1$ (h) $3x^2-2x+6$ (i) $3x^2+2x+3$

(j) $-12x-3x^2$ (k) $4x^3+9x^2-2$ (l) $12x^3-23$

2.

(a) $4x^3-\frac{1}{x^2}$ (b) $3x^2+\frac{3}{x^2}$ (c) $5x^4+\frac{6}{x^4}$

(d) $7x^6+\frac{10}{x^3}$ (e) $-\frac{3}{x^4}+\frac{6}{x^2}$ (f) $\frac{2}{3\sqrt[3]{x}}+\frac{2}{x^3}$

(g) $-\frac{1}{\sqrt[3]{x^4}}-\frac{1}{3\sqrt{x}}$ (h) $-\frac{8}{3\sqrt[3]{x^5}}-\frac{1}{4\sqrt{x}}$ (i) $\frac{3}{\sqrt[4]{x}}-\frac{3}{16\sqrt[4]{x^5}}$

Exercise 11.3A

1.

(a) $\frac{1}{3\sqrt[3]{x^2}}$ (b) $\frac{3}{2}\sqrt{x}$ (c) $\frac{5}{4}\sqrt[4]{x}$ (d) $\frac{6}{\sqrt[5]{x^2}}$

(e) $-\frac{2}{x^2}$ (f) $\frac{-2}{x^3}$ (g) $\frac{-1}{x^3}$ (h) $\frac{-12}{x^4}$

(i) $\frac{-4}{3x^2}$ (j) $\frac{-12}{x^5}$ (h) $\frac{-1}{2\sqrt{x^3}}$ (i) $\frac{-4}{3\sqrt[3]{x^5}}$

Exercise 11.3B

1.

(a) $2x+1$ (b) $8x-8$ (c) $9x^2-3$

(d) $2x-6$ (e) $6x^2+1$ (f) $6x-\frac{2}{x^3}$

(g) $\frac{5}{2}\sqrt{x^3}-4x$ (h) $\frac{7}{2}\sqrt{x^5}-4x^3$ (i) $\frac{7}{6}\sqrt[6]{x}-\frac{4}{3\sqrt[3]{x}}$

(j) $\frac{-1}{2\sqrt{x^3}}+\frac{2}{3\sqrt[3]{x^5}}$ (k) $\frac{-3}{2\sqrt{x^5}}+\frac{15}{2\sqrt{x^7}}$ (l) $\frac{5}{4}\sqrt[4]{x}-\frac{21}{4}\sqrt[4]{x^3}$

(m) $3x^2+\frac{1}{2\sqrt{x}}$ (n) $\frac{3}{2}\sqrt{x}-\frac{3}{2\sqrt{x}}$ (o) $2x$

2.

(a) 1 (b) 1 (c) $4-2x$

(d) $10x+6$ (e) $-\frac{2}{x^2}-\frac{4}{x^3}$ (f) $-\frac{4}{x^3}+\frac{3}{x^4}$

(g) $-\frac{1}{x^2}+3$ (h) $10x-\frac{6}{x^3}$ (i) $-\frac{2}{3x^2}$

(j) $-\frac{4}{x^3}+\frac{15}{2x^4}$ (k) $-\frac{3}{2x^2}+\frac{1}{x^3}+\frac{6}{x^5}$ (l) $-\frac{1}{3x^2}+\frac{10}{3x^3}-\frac{1}{x^4}$

(m) $\frac{3}{2}\sqrt{x}-\frac{3}{2\sqrt{x}}$ (n) $\frac{9}{4}\sqrt{x}+\frac{5}{4\sqrt{x}}$ (o) $\frac{2}{3}\sqrt[3]{x^2}-\frac{1}{5\sqrt[3]{x^4}}$

(p) $\frac{3}{8}\sqrt{x}-\frac{1}{4\sqrt{x}}+\frac{1}{8\sqrt{x^3}}$

Exercise 11.4A

1.

(a) 2 (b) -4 (c) $\frac{244}{9}$ (d) 205

(e) $\frac{3}{8}$ (f) $\frac{191}{4}$ (g) $\frac{19}{2}$ (h) $\frac{-193}{12}$

(i) $\frac{43}{4}$ (j) $\frac{3}{2}$ (k) $\frac{19}{16}$ (l) $\frac{289}{54}$

2.

(a) -4 (b) 0 (c) 124 (d) -48

(e) $-\frac{7}{4}$ (f) $\frac{9}{2}$ (g) $\frac{11}{9}$ (h) $\frac{37}{9}$

(i) $\frac{65}{8}$ (j) $\frac{5}{64}$ (k) $\frac{1}{2}$ (l) $\frac{5}{64}$

3.

(a) 3 (b) -2 (c) 4 (d) 79

(e) 1 (f) $\frac{-119}{10}$ (g) $\frac{3}{2}$ (h) $\frac{8}{27}$

(i) $\frac{17}{16}$ (j) $\frac{973}{54}$ (k) $\frac{317}{16}$ (l) $-\frac{5}{2}$

Exercise 11.4B

1. $2\ ms^{-1}$ **2.** $-4\ litres\ per\ second$

3. $6\ ms^{-1}$ **4.** 36 **5.** $-\frac{1}{144}$

6. $\frac{1}{2\sqrt{10}}$ **7.** $\frac{2}{5}ms^{-2}$ **8.** $-\frac{2}{343}$

9. $\frac{50{,}429}{343}$ **8.** 563

Exercise 11.5

1.

(a) $y=3x-16$ (b) $y=-7x-1$ (c) $y=3x-10$

(d) $y=6x-1$ (e) $y=-6x+25$ (f) $y=9x-43$

2.

(a) $y = 9x - 15$ (b) $y = 6x - 5$ (c) $y = 8x + 10$
(d) $y = 4$ (e) $y = 7x - 13$ (f) $y = -8x$
(g) $y = -5$ (h) $y = 20x + 132$

3.

(a) $2x + 3y + 12 = 0$ (b) $y = 3x - 8$
(c) $6y = x + 27$ (d) $17x - 4y - 8 = 0$
(e) $x + 2y - 12 = 0$ (f) $7x - 18y - 45 = 0$

Exercise 11.6

1. *Proof* 2. *Proof*

3.

(a) $x > -1$ (b) $x > 2$ (c) $x < 1$
(d) $x < -1, x > 1$ (e) $0 < x < 2$ (f) $x < 0, x > 2$
(g) $x < -3, x > 5$ (h) $x \neq -1$ (i) $-1 < x < 3$
(j) $x < -3, x > 7$ (k) $-2 < x < 0$ (l) $x < -4, x > 0$

4.

(a) $x < 3$ (b) $x < 2$ (c) $x > 0$
(d) $0 < x < 4$ (e) $x < 0, x > 4$ (f) $-5 < x < -1$
(g) $-3 < x < 5$ (h) $-1 < x < 5$ (i) $x < -6, x > 4$
(j) $-1 < x < 1$ (k) $x < -2, x > 0$ (l) $0 < x < 2$

5. $f'(x) > 0\ \forall x$ 6. $f'(x) < 0\ \forall x$

Exercise 11.7

1.

(a) Min. T.P. at $(-1, 1)$
(b) Min. T.P. at $(2, -3)$
(c) Max. T.P. at $(3, 20)$
(d) Rising point of inflection at $(1, -1)$
(e) Falling point of inflection at $(2, 7)$
(f) Max. T.P. at $\left(-\frac{2}{3}, \frac{4}{27}\right)$ and Min. T.P. at $(0, 0)$
(g) Max. T.P. at $(-3, 85)$ and Min. T.P. at $(5, -171)$
(h) Min. T.P. at $(-6, -35)$ and Max. T.P. at $(0, 1)$
(i) Rising point of inflection at $\left(\frac{1}{3}, -\frac{218}{27}\right)$
(j) Max. T.P. at $(-3, 117)$ and Min. T.P. at $(7, -383)$
(k) Max. T.P. at $(0, 1)$ and Min. T.P. at $(-2, -1/3)$
(l) Falling point of inflection at $(4, -10/3)$

2.

(a) Min. T.P. at $(-2, -10)$ and Rising point of inflection at $(0, 6)$
(b) Min. T.P. at $(-3, -27)$ and Rising point of inflection at $(0, 0)$
(c) Min. T.P. at $(-1, -1/4)$ and $(1, -1/4)$. Max. T.P. at $(0, 0)$
(d) Max. T.P. at $(-1, 10)$ and $(1, 10)$. Min. T.P. at $(0, 9)$
(e) Max. T.P. at $(-2, 16)$ and $(2, 16)$. Min. T.P. at $(0, 0)$
(f) Min. T.P. at $(3, -33)$ and falling point of inflection at $(0, -6)$

3.

(a) Min. T.P. at $(2, 4)$ and Max. T.P. at $(-2, -4)$
(b) Min. T.P. at $(1/4, 8)$ and Max. T.P. at $(-1/4, -8)$
(c) Min. T.P. at $(4, 16)$ and Max. T.P. at $(-4, -16)$

Exercise 11.8

1.

(a)

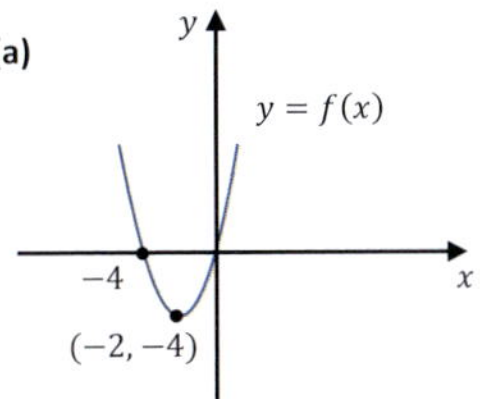

(b)

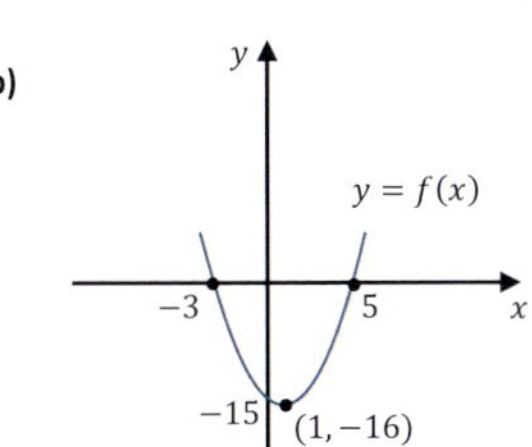

(c)

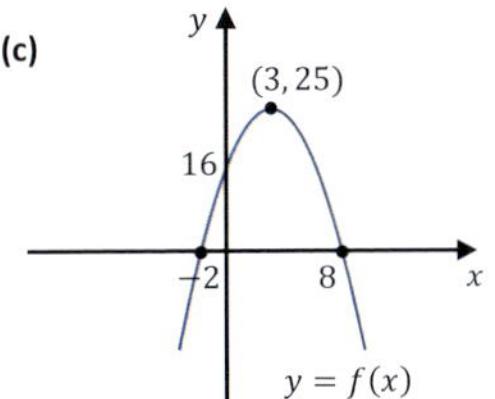

(d)

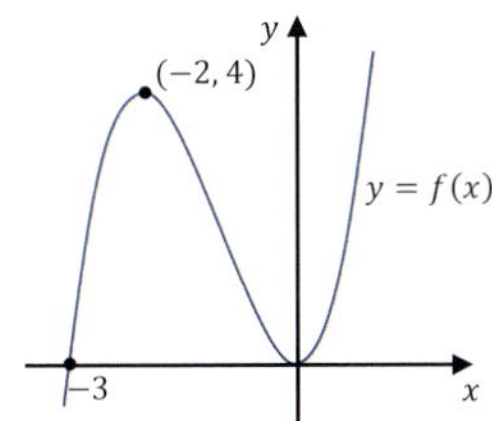

(e)

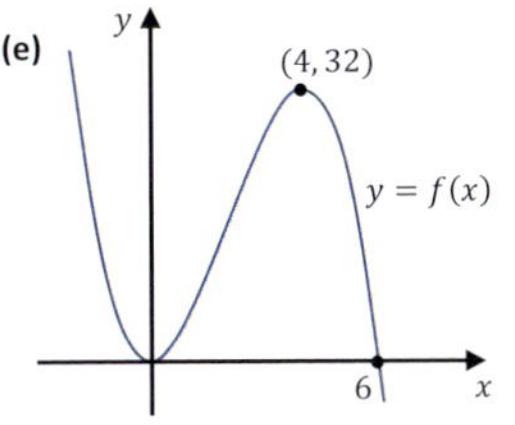

(f)

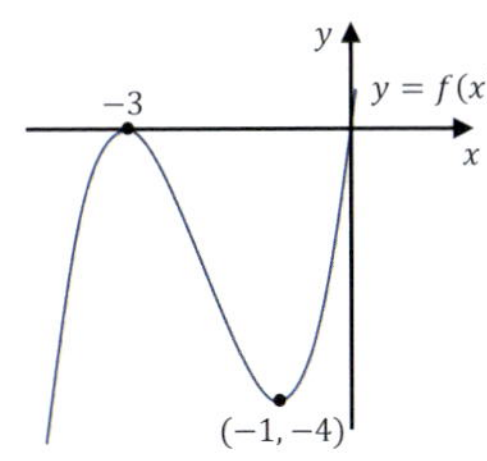

2.

(a)

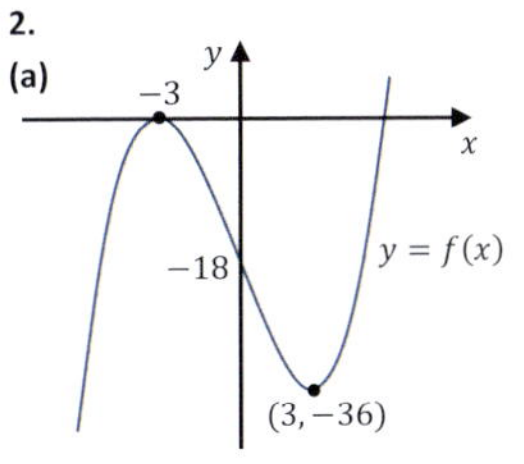

(b)

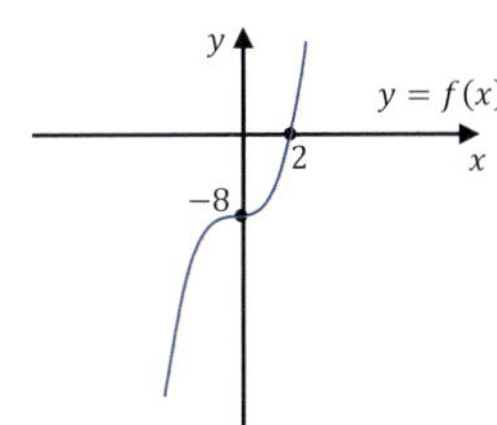

(c)

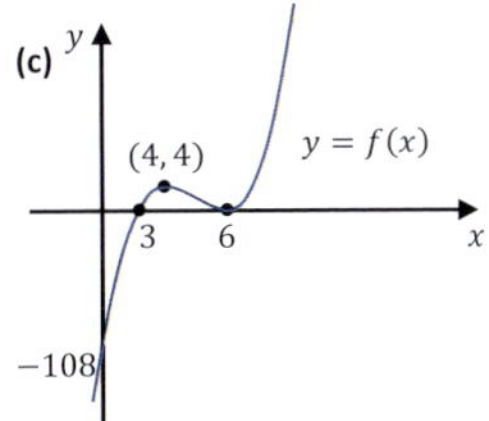

(d)

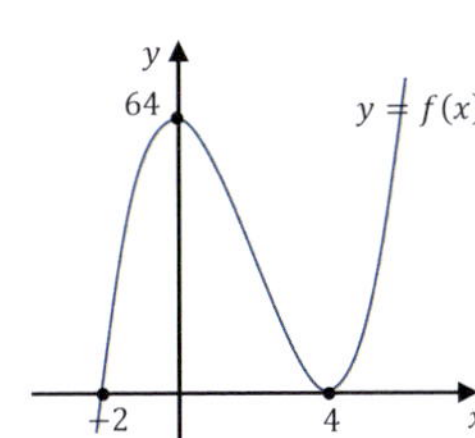

(e)

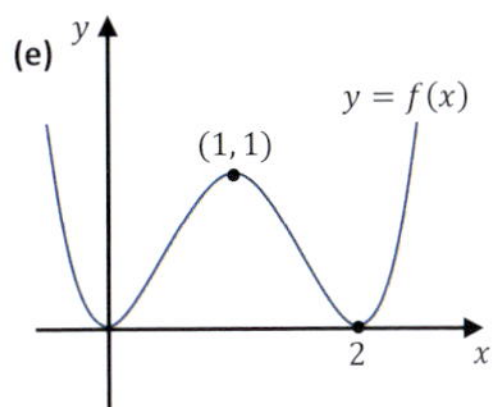

(f)

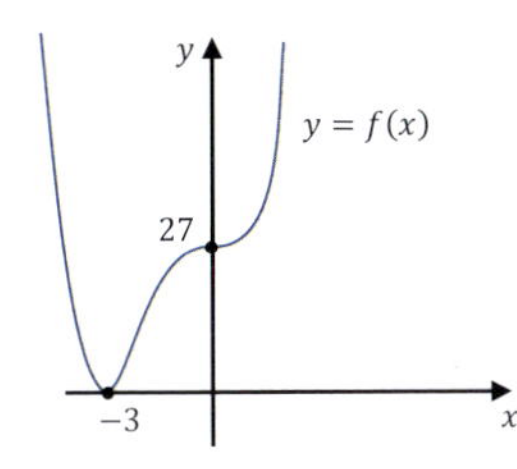

Exercise 11.9A

1.

(a) $x = 4$, Area $= 64\ units^2$
(b) $x = 4$, Area $= 128\ units^2$
(c) $x = 32$, Area $= 16{,}384\ units^2$
(d) $x = 6$, Area $= 1932\ units^2$
(e) $x = 6$, Area $= 432\ units^2$
(f) $x = 3$, Area $= 69\ units^2$

2.

(a) $x = 3$, Surface area $= 12\ units^2$

(b) $x = 3$, Surface area $= 30\ units^2$

(c) $x = 4$, Surface area $= 56\ units^2$

(d) $x = 7$, Surface area $= 112\ units^2$

(e) $x = 9$, Surface area $= 198\ units^2$

(f) $x = 4$, Surface area $= 120\ units^2$

3.

(a) $x = 2$, Surface area $= 24\ units^2$

(b) $x = 3$, Surface area $= 81\ units^2$

(c) $x = 6$, Surface area $= 108\ units^2$

(d) $x = 7$, Surface area $= 294\ units^2$

(e) $x = 11$, Surface area $= 1089\ units^2$

(f) $x = 10$, Surface area $= 1200\ units^2$

Exercise 11.9B

1. **(b)** $x = 4$, Area $= 50\ cm^2$
2. **(b)** $l = 33.75\ m$,
3. **(b)** $r = 1.563cm$
4. **(b)** $x = 2\sqrt{2}\ cm$, Area $= 16\ cm^2$
5. **(b)** $x = \sqrt{2}\ cm$, Area $= 5.657\ cm^2$
6. **(b)** $x = 70\ cm$, Area $= 14{,}700cm^2$
7. **(b)** $b = 333\frac{1}{3}m$
8. **(b)** $r = 6.0cm$
9. **(b)** $x = 8\ cm$, Area $= 192cm^2$
10. **(b)** $x = 3\sqrt{2}\ m$, Area $= 36m^2$
11. **(b)** $x = 2\sqrt{2}\ m$, Area $= 45.255m^2$

Exercise 11.10

1.

(a) Max -5 when $x = 1$, Min -9 when $x = 3$

(b) Max -5 when $x = 3$, Min -9 when $x = 1$

(c) Max 9 when $x = -2$, Min -7 when $x = 2$

(d) Max 25 when $x = 2$, Min -11 when $x = -4$

2.

(a) Max 27 when $x = 3$, Min 8.85 when $x = \frac{2}{3}$

(b) Max 5 when $x = 1$, Min -11 when $x = 3$

(c) Max 128 when $x = 5$, Min -34 when $x = 2$

(d) Max 7 when $x = 0$, Min -121 when $x = -4$

(e) Max 11 when $x = 3$, Min -14 when $x = 2$

(f) Max 7 when $x = -1$, Min -25 when $x = 3$

(g) Max 144 when $x = 7$, Min -128 when $x = 5$

(h) Max 4 when $x = 0$, Min -132.7 when $x = \frac{9}{2}$

Exercise 11.11

1.

(a)

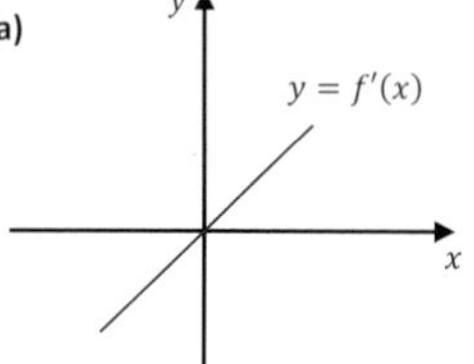

(b)

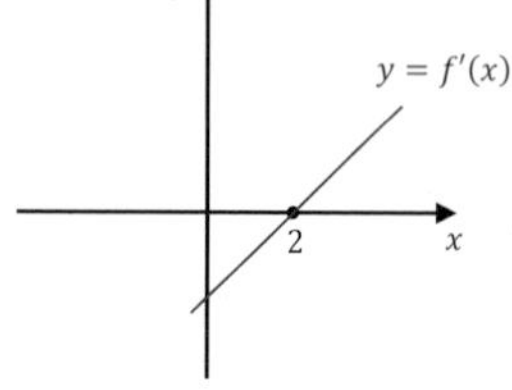

(c)

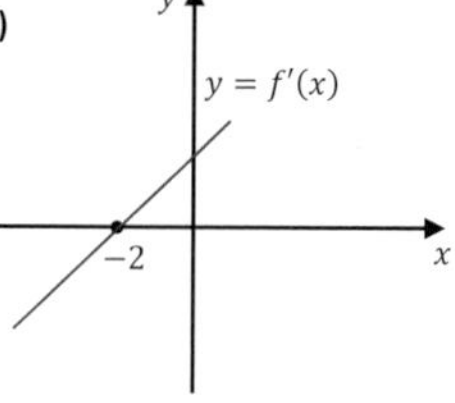

(d)

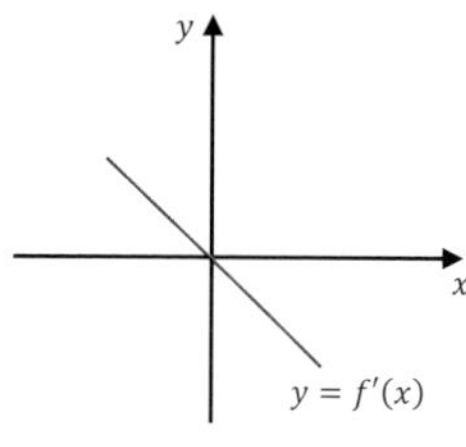

(e)

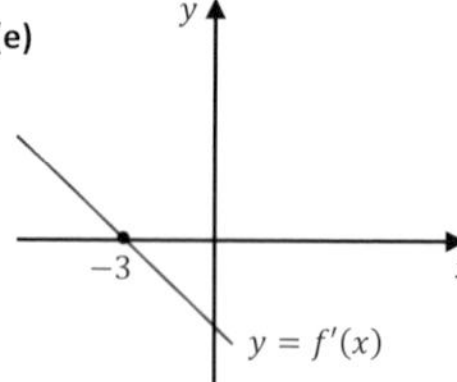

(f)

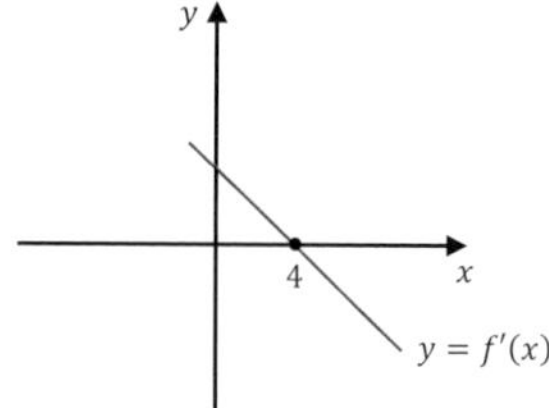

2.

(a)

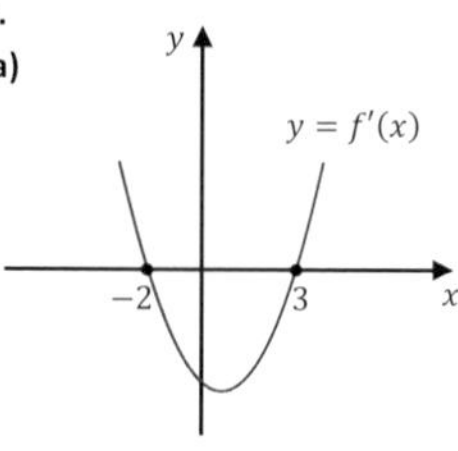

(b)

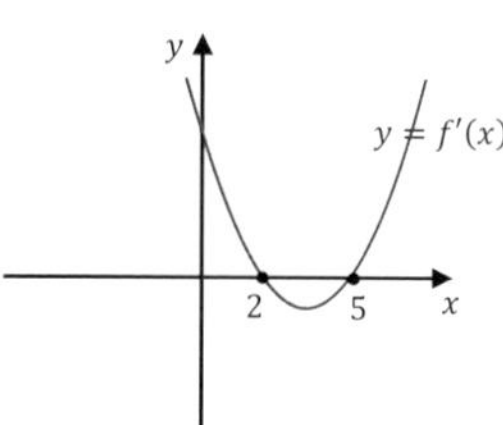

(c)

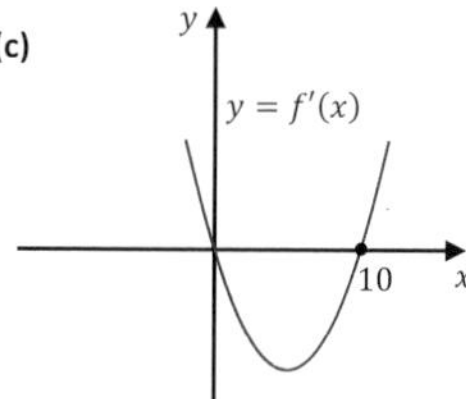

(d)

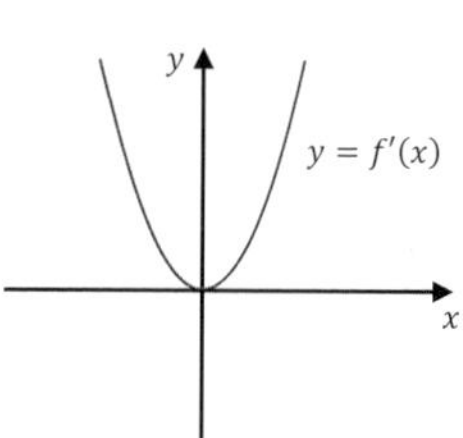

(e)

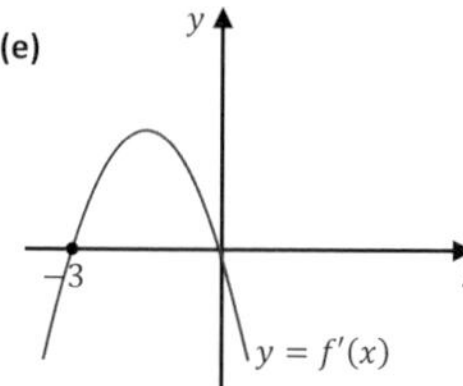

(f)

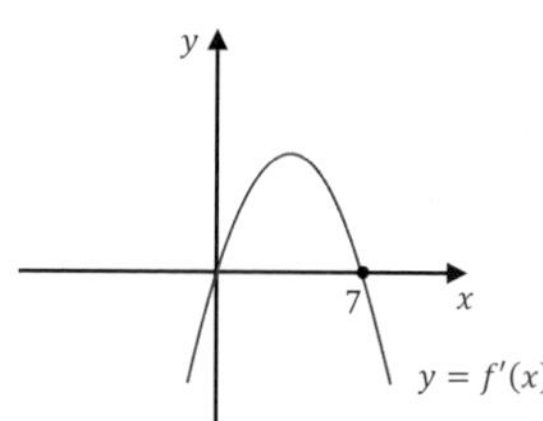

(g)

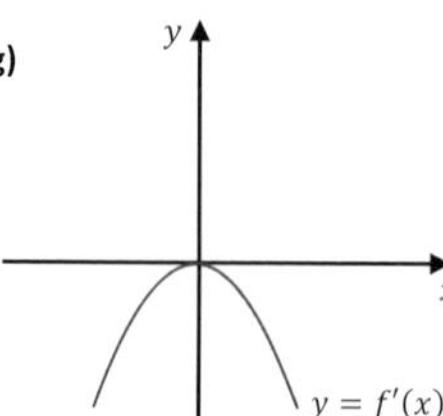

(h)

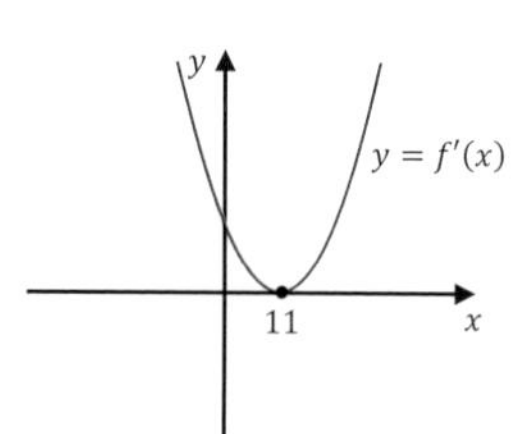

(i)

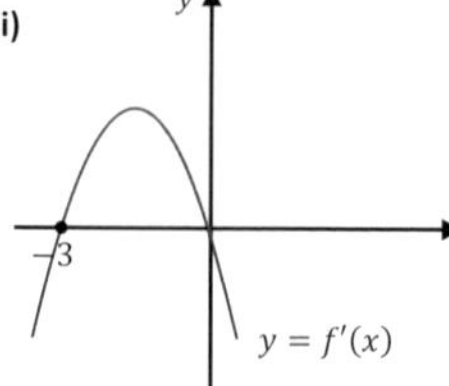

3.

(a)

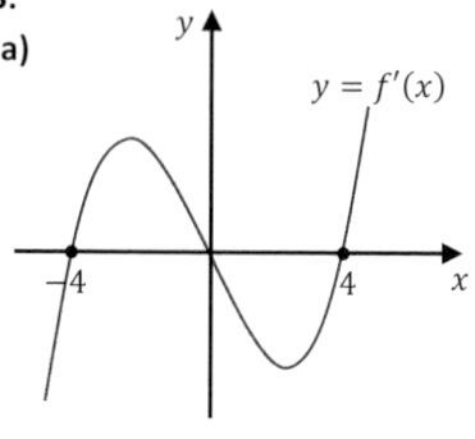

(b)

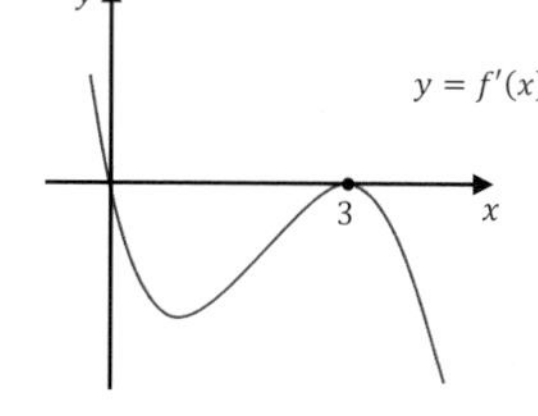

(c)
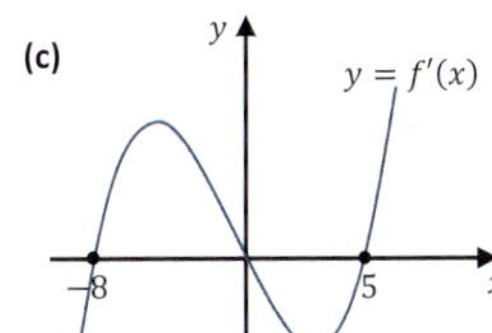

(d)
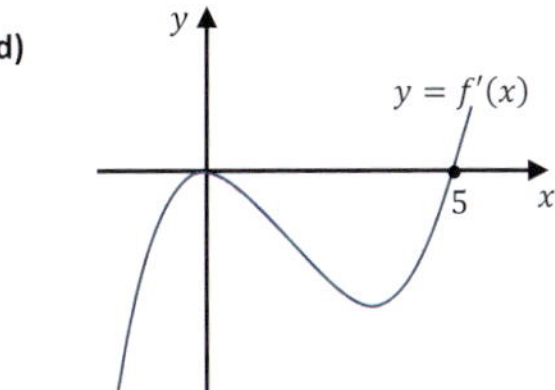

(e)
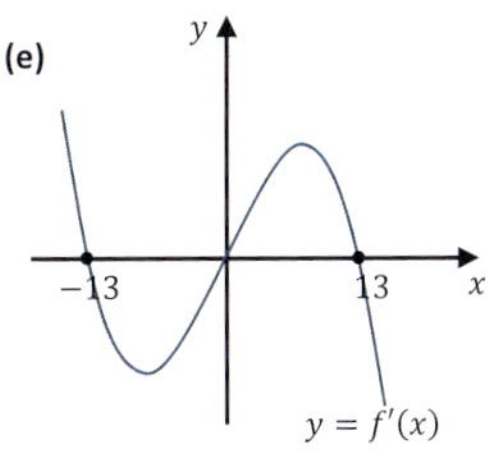

(f)
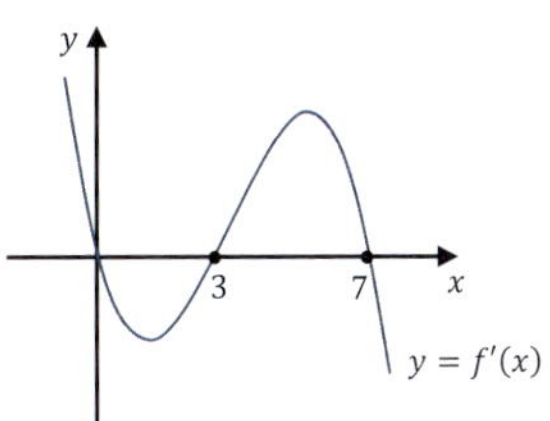

(g)
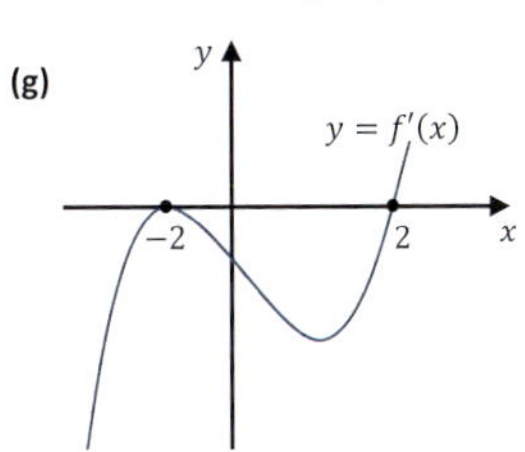

(h)
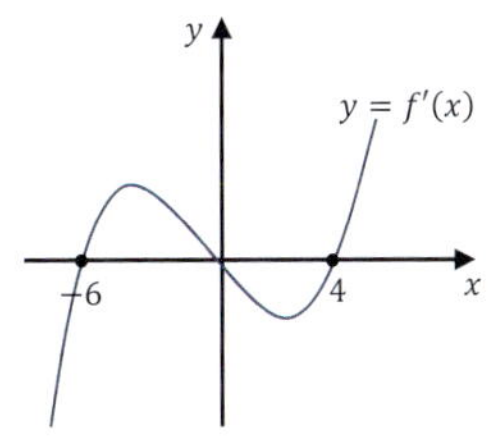

(i)
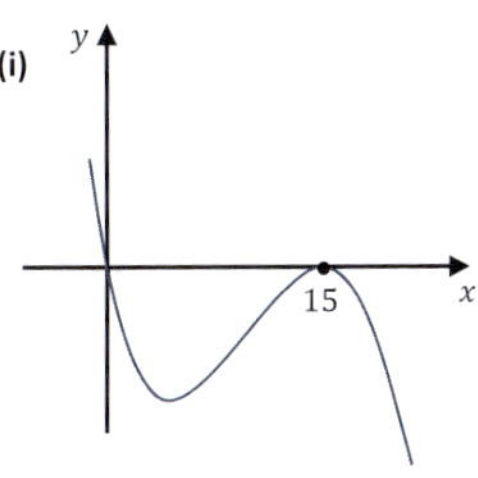

Exercise 11.12

11.2

(a) $\frac{6}{\sqrt[5]{x^2}}$ (b) $8x - 18$ (c) $-\frac{3}{2\sqrt{x^3}}$

11.3

(a) $\frac{5}{2}\sqrt{x^3} - 3x^2$ (b) $-\frac{5}{2x^2} + \frac{1}{x^3} + \frac{8}{x^5}$ (c) $\frac{3}{8}\sqrt{x} + \frac{1}{4\sqrt{x}} + \frac{1}{8\sqrt{x^3}}$

11.4

(a) -18 (b) 10 (c) $\frac{45}{16}$

11.5 $y = x + 10$

11.6

(a) $proof$ (b) $0 < x < 2$ (c) $x < -2, x > 0$

(c) $3(x-2)^2 + 7 > 0, \therefore f'(x) > 0\ \forall x, \Rightarrow$ function is always increasing.

11.7 Max. T.P. at $(0, 18)$ and Min. T.P. at $(4, -14)$

11.8

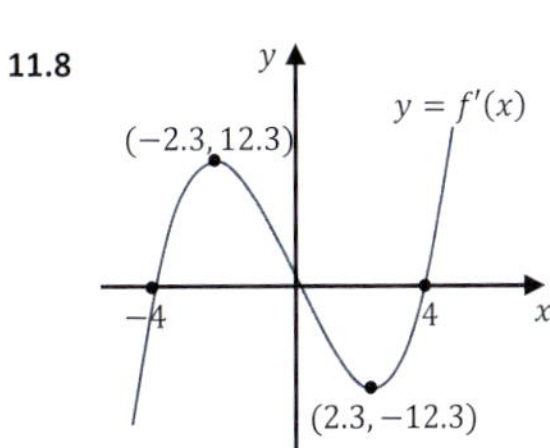

11.9 $r = 2.942$

11.10 Max -1.5 when $x = 1$, Min -35.9 when $x = 5.3$

11.11

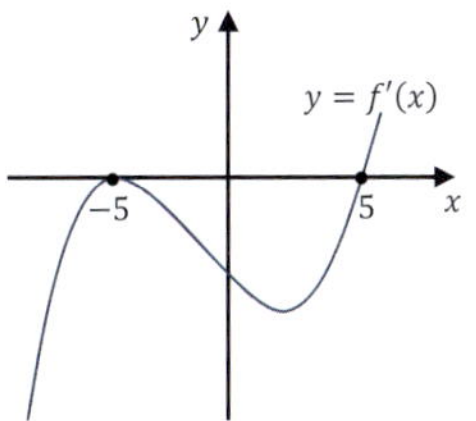

Chapter 12

Exercise 12.1A

1.

(a) $\frac{x^2}{2} + C$ (b) $x^2 + C$ (c) $5x + C$

(d) $8x + C$ (e) $\frac{x^3}{3} + C$ (f) $\frac{x^4}{4} + C$

(g) $\frac{x^7}{7} + C$ (h) $\frac{x^5}{5} + C$ (i) $-\frac{3}{x} + C$

(j) $-\frac{2}{x^2} + C$ (k) $-\frac{10}{x} + C$ (l) $-\frac{3}{4x^4} + C$

(m) $\frac{4x^3}{3} + C$ (n) $-\frac{5}{4x^4} + C$ (o) $\frac{3x^8}{8} + C$

(p) $-\frac{3}{4x^8} + C$

2.

(a) $\frac{2x^{\frac{3}{2}}}{3} + C$ (b) $\frac{4x^{\frac{3}{2}}}{3} + C$ (c) $\frac{15x^{\frac{4}{3}}}{4} + C$

(d) $\frac{32x^{\frac{5}{4}}}{5} + C$ (e) $\frac{3x^{\frac{2}{3}}}{2} + C$ (f) $8x^{\frac{1}{2}} + C$

(g) $\frac{6x^{\frac{5}{3}}}{5} + C$ (h) $\frac{24x^{\frac{7}{4}}}{7} + C$ (i) $\frac{9x^{\frac{5}{3}}}{5} + C$

(j) $-\frac{8}{x^{\frac{1}{2}}} + C$ (k) $\frac{3x^{\frac{7}{4}}}{7} + C$ (l) $\frac{32x^{\frac{3}{4}}}{3} + C$

(m) $\frac{3x^{\frac{1}{3}}}{4} + C$ (n) $6x^{\frac{5}{6}} + C$ (o) $\frac{6x^{\frac{1}{3}}}{5} + C$

(p) $\frac{4x^{\frac{3}{4}}}{9} + C$

Exercise 12.1B

1.

(a) $\frac{x^3}{3} + 2x + C$ (b) $\frac{x^4}{4} + \frac{x^2}{2} + C$

(c) $\frac{2x^3}{3} + \frac{3x^2}{2} + C$ (d) $\frac{4x^3}{3} + x^2 - x + C$

(e) $\frac{5x^3}{3} - \frac{x^2}{2} + 3x + C$ (f) $\frac{x^3}{3} - \frac{7x^2}{2} - 4x + C$

(g) $8x - \frac{3x^2}{2} + \frac{x^3}{3} + C$ (h) $\frac{x^4}{4} + \frac{x^3}{3} - 6x + C$

(i) $\frac{x^4}{2} + 2x^3 - 2x^2 + C$ (j) $\frac{x^5}{5} + \frac{x^4}{2} + C$

(k) $x + \frac{x^2}{2} + \frac{x^5}{5} + C$ (l) $\frac{x^4}{2} - \frac{5x^2}{2} + x + C$

2.

(a) $-\frac{1}{x} + 5x + C$ (b) $-\frac{1}{3x^3} + \frac{3x^2}{2} + C$

(c) $\frac{5x^4}{4} - \frac{x^2}{2} + C$ (d) $\frac{8x^{\frac{3}{2}}}{3} - \frac{1}{2x^2} + C$

(e) $\frac{x^3}{3} - \frac{2x^{\frac{3}{2}}}{3} + 7x + C$ (f) $2x^{\frac{1}{2}} - \frac{x^2}{8} + x + C$

(g) $12x^{\frac{2}{3}} + \frac{4x^3}{3} + C$ (h) $\frac{x^4}{4} + \frac{x^3}{6} - 6x + C$

(i) $\frac{x^4}{2} + \frac{5}{3}x^3 + 3x + C$ (j) $\frac{x^2}{6} + \frac{2}{x} + 5x + C$

(k) $-\frac{1}{4x^2} + \frac{4x^{\frac{3}{4}}}{3} + C$ (l) $\frac{4x^{\frac{5}{2}}}{5} - \frac{5x^2}{4} + 4x^{\frac{1}{4}} + C$

Exercise 12.2A

1.

(a) $-\frac{1}{x}+C$ (b) $-\frac{2}{x}+C$ (c) $-\frac{1}{2x^2}+C$

(d) $-\frac{1}{3x^3}+C$ (e) $-\frac{2}{x^2}+C$ (f) $-\frac{1}{4x^2}+C$

(g) $-\frac{1}{5x^3}+C$ (h) $-\frac{3}{14x^4}+C$ (i) $\frac{3\sqrt[3]{x^4}}{4}+C$

(j) $\frac{2\sqrt{x^3}}{3}+C$ (k) $\frac{2\sqrt{x^5}}{5}+C$ (l) $\frac{3\sqrt[3]{x^5}}{5}+C$

(m) $3\sqrt[3]{x^2}+C$ (n) $-\frac{10}{\sqrt{x}}+C$ (o) $-\frac{1}{\sqrt{x^3}}+C$

(p) $\frac{5\sqrt[5]{x^2}}{3}+C$

Exercise 12.2B

1.

(a) $\frac{x^3}{3}+x^2+C$ (b) $\frac{x^4}{4}+\frac{2x^3}{3}+C$

(c) $\frac{2x^5}{5}+x^2+C$ (d) $\frac{x^3}{3}+\frac{3x^2}{2}+2x+C$

(e) $\frac{x^3}{3}+3x^2+9x+C$ (f) $\frac{x^4}{4}+\frac{x^2}{2}-\frac{4x^3}{3}-4x+C$

(g) $\frac{2\sqrt{x^7}}{7}-\frac{2x^3}{3}+C$ (h) $x^3+4x-\frac{1}{x}+C$

(i) $\frac{2\sqrt{x^9}}{9}-\frac{x^5}{5}+C$ (j) $\frac{x^4}{4}+\frac{2\sqrt{x^3}}{3}+C$

(k) $\frac{x^3}{3}+\frac{4\sqrt{x^5}}{5}+\frac{x^2}{2}+C$ (l) $\frac{2\sqrt{x^5}}{5}-2\sqrt{x^3}+C$

(m) $\frac{x^3}{3}+4x+C$ (n) $\frac{x^2}{2}+4\sqrt{x}-\frac{1}{x}+C$

(o) $\frac{6\sqrt[6]{x^{11}}}{11}-\frac{9\sqrt[3]{x^7}}{7}+C$

2.

(a) $\frac{x^2}{2}+2x+C$ (b) $\frac{x^2}{2}-3x+C$

(c) $2x^2-\frac{x^3}{3}+C$ (d) $-\frac{2}{x}-\frac{1}{x^2}+C$

(e) $-\frac{4}{x}+\frac{3}{x^2}+C$ (f) $\frac{5x^3}{3}-\frac{3}{x}+C$

(g) $-\frac{3}{2x}+\frac{1}{4x^2}+\frac{3}{8x^4}+C$ (h) $-\frac{5}{3x}-\frac{1}{6x^2}-\frac{1}{9x^3}+C$

(i) $\frac{2\sqrt{x^5}}{5}-2\sqrt{x^3}+C$ (j) $\frac{2\sqrt{x^5}}{5}+10\sqrt{x}+C$

(k) $\frac{3\sqrt{x^5}}{5}+\frac{5\sqrt{x^3}}{3}+C$ (l) $\frac{\sqrt{x^5}}{10}+\frac{\sqrt{x^3}}{3}-\frac{\sqrt{x}}{2}+C$

Exercise 12.3A

1.

(a) $\frac{3}{2}$ (b) 39 (c) 14 (d) $\frac{35}{3}$

(e) -12 (f) $\frac{104}{3}$ (g) $-\frac{65}{2}$ (h) 20

(i) $\frac{1}{2}$ (j) $\frac{10\sqrt{5}}{3}$ (k) 1 (l) 468

(m) $\frac{296}{3}$ (n) $\frac{4}{27}$ (o) 30 (p) 477

2.

(a) $-\frac{4}{3}$ (b) 12 (c) $\frac{665}{6}$

(d) 10 (e) 24 (f) $-\frac{34}{3}$

3.

(a) $\frac{425}{3}$ (b) $\frac{1859}{6}$ (c) $\frac{3006}{5}$

(d) $-\frac{187}{7}$ (e) $\frac{69}{2}$ (f) $18\sqrt{3}-\frac{2188}{45}$

4.

(a) $-\frac{15}{2}$ (b) $-\frac{41}{900}$ (c) $-\frac{8}{5}$

(d) $\frac{188}{81}$ (e) 8 (f) $\frac{25}{54}$

Exercise 12.3B

1.

(a) $a=4$ (b) $a=7$ (c) $a=-6$

(d) $a=2$ (e) $a=4$ (f) $a=3$

(g) $a=-6$ (h) $a=-3$

2.

(a) $a=8$ (b) $a=-4$ (c) $a=-2, a=-1$

(d) $a=-\frac{3}{2}, a=5$ (e) $a=4$ (f) $a=7$

3.

(a) $a=1$ (b) $a=9$ (c) $a=25$

Exercise 12.4A

1.

(a) $\frac{9}{2}\ units^2$ (b) $\frac{117}{4}\ units^2$ (c) $25\ units^2$

(d) $\frac{25}{2}\ units^2$ (e) $\frac{11}{6}\ units^2$ (f) $\frac{5}{3}\ units^2$

Exercise 12.4B

1.

(a) $8\ units^2$ (b) $\frac{125}{6}\ units^2$ (c) $2\ units^2$

(d) $\frac{63}{4}\ units^2$ (e) $\frac{58}{3}\ units^2$ (f) $\frac{28}{3}\ units^2$

Exercise 12.4C

1.

(a) $4\ units^2$ (b) $34\ units^2$ (c) $26\ units^2$

(d) $169\ units^2$ (e) $\frac{82}{5}\ units^2$ (f) $\frac{195}{2}\ units^2$

2.

(a) $\frac{184}{3}\ units^2$ (b) $\frac{662}{3}\ units^2$ (c) $\frac{568}{3}\ units^2$

(d) $\frac{1289}{6}\ units^2$ (e) $\frac{233}{6}\ units^2$ (f) $\frac{61}{6}\ units^2$

3.

(a) $\frac{1}{2}\ units^2$ (b) $\frac{253}{12}\ units^2$ (c) $8\ units^2$

(d) $92\ units^2$ (e) $\frac{569}{12}\ units^2$ (f) $\frac{3}{2}\ units^2$

Exercise 12.5A

1.

(a) $36\ units^2$ (b) $\frac{9}{2}\ units^2$ (c) $\frac{125}{6}\ units^2$

(d) $\frac{343}{6}\ units^2$ (e) $\frac{64}{3}\ units^2$ (f) $\frac{99}{4}\ units^2$

(g) $32\ units^2$ (h) $\frac{32}{3}\ units^2$ (i) $\frac{343}{6}\ units^2$

Exercise 12.5B

1.

(a) $\frac{343}{6}\ units^2$ (b) $\frac{32}{3}\ units^2$ (c) $\frac{256}{3}\ units^2$

(d) $\frac{125}{6}\ units^2$ (e) $36\ units^2$ (f) $\frac{9}{2}\ units^2$

2.

(a) $\frac{64}{3}\ units^2$ (b) $\frac{9}{2}\ units^2$ (c) $\frac{125}{2}\ units^2$

(d) $\frac{125}{6}\ units^2$ (e) $\frac{64}{3}\ units^2$ (f) $\frac{243}{2}\ units^2$

Exercise 12.5C

1.

(a) $\frac{99}{4}\ units^2$ (b) $\frac{27}{4}\ units^2$ (c) $\frac{63}{4}\ units^2$

(d) $4\ units^2$ (e) $\frac{99}{4}\ units^2$ (f) $8\ units^2$

2.

(a) $\frac{63}{4}units^2$ (b) $\frac{2401}{12}\ units^2$ (c) $\frac{45}{4}units^2$

(d) $\frac{28}{3}\ units^2$ (e) $\frac{2187}{4}\ units^2$ (f) $\frac{937}{12}\ units^2$

Exercise 12.6

1.

(a) $y = 2x^2 - 2x + 8$ (b) $y = 9x - 3x^2 + 9$

(c) $y = x^3 + 3x^2 + 6$ (d) $y = \frac{x^3}{3} + x^2 + 12$

(e) $y = 2x^3 + 6x^2 + 2x + 10$ (f) $y = x - x^4 + 159$

(g) $y = x^3 + x^2 - 5x + 13$ (h) $y = 3x^3 + 4x^2 - 4x + 28$

2.

(a) $f(x) = \frac{3x^2}{2} + 5x - 24$ (b) $f(x) = -x^2 + 9x + 17$

(c) $f(x) = x^3 - 5x + 20$ (d) $f(x) = 2x^3 - \frac{x^2}{2} + \frac{21}{2}$

(e) $f(x) = \frac{x^3}{3} + 9x - 21$ (f) $f(x) = \frac{2x^{\frac{3}{2}}}{3} - 2x + 25$

(g) $f(x) = x^2 + 5x - 30$ (h) $f(x) = \frac{x^2}{2} - 2x^{\frac{3}{2}} + 28$

(i) $f(x) = 4x^{\frac{3}{2}} + 16x^{\frac{1}{2}} - 44$ (j) $f(x) = 6x^{\frac{3}{2}} - 12x^{\frac{1}{2}} - 291$

3. $y = 4x^2 + \frac{4}{x} - 10$ **4.** $y = 77\ metres$

5. $V = 1192\ litres$ **6.** $y = 3x^2 + \frac{10}{x} + 2$

7. $y = 263\ ms^{-1}$

Exercise 12.7

12.1.

(a) $x^3 + C$ (b) $\frac{x^3}{3} - \frac{x^2}{2} + 3x + C$ (c) $6x^{\frac{3}{2}} + C$

12.2.

(a) $4\sqrt{x} + C$ (b) $\frac{x^3}{3} + 4x - \frac{4}{x} + C$ (c) $\frac{4x^{\frac{5}{2}}}{5} - \frac{4x^{\frac{3}{2}}}{3} + C$

12.3.

(a)

(i) $\frac{15}{8}$ (ii) 40 (iii) $-\frac{8}{5}$

(b)

(i) $a = -6$ (ii) $a = -4$ (iii) $a = 25$

12.4.

(a) $\frac{495}{4}units^2$ (b) $64\ units^2$ (c) $\frac{136}{3}units^2$

12.5.

(a) $\frac{256}{3}units^2$ (b) $72\ units^2$ (c) $4\ units^2$

12.6 $V = 96\sqrt{2} + 178\ litres$

Chapter 13

Exercise 13.1A

1.

(a) $f'(x) = 6(2x-1)^2$ (b) $\frac{dy}{dx} = 21(3x+2)^6$

(c) $f'(x) = 18(6x+5)^2$ (d) $\frac{dy}{dx} = 45(9x-2)^4$

(e) $f'(x) = 60(4x+5)^4$ (f) $\frac{dy}{dx} = 48(6x-11)^3$

(g) $\frac{dy}{dx} = 36(2x+3)^2$ (h) $f'(x) = 150(6x-1)^4$

(i) $f'(x) = 180(3x+11)^9$

2.

(a) $\frac{dy}{dx} = 6x(x^2+1)^2$ (b) $f'(x) = 24x^2(2x^3+5)^3$

(c) $f'(x) = 42x(3x^2-10)^6$ (d) $f'(x) = 48x^2(4x^3+1)^3$

(e) $g'(x) = 48x^3(x^4+5)^5$ (f) $\frac{dy}{dx} = 140x(2x^2-7)^6$

(g) $f'(x) = 405x^4(3x^5+5)^2$ (h) $\frac{dy}{dx} = 360x^5(3x^6-2)^4$

(i) $h'(x) = 1080x^8(2x^9+15)^9$

3.

(a) $f'(x) = 3(2x+1)(x^2+x)^2$

(b) $\frac{dy}{dx} = 3(3x^2-1)(x^3-x)^2$

(c) $f'(x) = 10(2x-4)(x^2-4x)^4$

(d) $\frac{dy}{dx} = 18(3x^2+1)(x^3+x)^5$

(e) $g'(x) = 15(2-2x)(2x-x^2)^2$

(f) $\frac{dy}{dx} = 28(10x-3x^2)(5x^2-x^3)^6$

(g) $h'(x) = 10(4x^3-4x)(x^4-2x^2)^4$

(h) $\frac{dy}{dx} = 3(6x^2-4x^3)(2x^3-x^4)^2$

(i) $k'(x) = 18(12x^3+2)(3x^4+2x)^8$

4.

(a) $f'(x) = -\frac{4x}{(x^2+2)^3}$ (b) $f'(x) = -\frac{9x^2}{(x^3-2)^4}$

(c) $g'(x) = -\frac{12x}{(x^2+4)^4}$ (d) $f'(x) = -\frac{24x^2}{(x^3+1)^5}$

(e) $\frac{dy}{dx} = -\frac{40}{(2x-3)^5}$ (f) $f'(x) = \frac{84x^2}{(6-x^3)^8}$

(g) $h'(x) = -\frac{12(2x-2)}{(x^2-2x)^5}$ (h) $f'(x) = -\frac{6(3x^2-3)}{(x^3-3x)^4}$

(i) $g'(x) = -\frac{6(2x+5)}{(x^2+5x)^3}$

5.

(a) $f'(x) = \frac{2}{\sqrt{4x+2}}$ (b) $g'(x) = \frac{1}{\sqrt{2x-2}}$

(c) $f'(x) = 3x\sqrt{x^2+4}$ (d) $f'(x) = -\frac{2x}{\sqrt{(2x^2+1)^3}}$

(e) $\frac{dy}{dx} = -\frac{3}{\sqrt{(2x-3)^5}}$ (f) $h'(x) = \frac{16x}{3\sqrt[3]{x^2+2}}$

(g) $f'(x) = -\frac{2(2x+1)}{\sqrt[3]{(x^2+x)^5}}$ (h) $f'(x) = -\frac{2(4x-1)}{\sqrt{(2x^2-x)^3}}$

(i) $g'(x) = -\frac{4(12x^2+1)}{3\sqrt[3]{(4x^3+x)^5}}$

Exercise 13.1B

1.

(a) $f'(x) = -\frac{24}{(3x+2)^3}$ (b) $f'(x) = -\frac{60}{(5x+2)^4}$

(c) $f'(x) = \frac{90}{(4-2x)^6}$ (d) $g'(x) = -\frac{6(2x+2)}{(x^2+2x)^3}$

(e) $f'(x) = -\frac{15(6x^2+1)}{(2x^3+x)^4}$

(f) $h'(x) = \frac{21(2x-5)}{(5x-x^2)^4}$

(g) $f'(x) = -\frac{8}{\sqrt{(4x+3)^3}}$

(h) $k'(x) = -\frac{40}{3\sqrt[3]{(5x-2)^5}}$

(i) $f'(x) = \frac{6(x-2)}{\sqrt{(4x-x^2)^5}}$

2.

(a) $f'(x) = -\frac{2}{\sqrt{(x+2)^3}}$

(b) $f'(x) = -\frac{6}{\sqrt{(4x+2)^3}}$

(c) $g'(x) = \frac{15}{2\sqrt{(7-3x)^3}}$

(d) $f'(x) = -\frac{x}{\sqrt{(x^2+2)^3}}$

(e) $h'(x) = -\frac{5(2x+1)}{2\sqrt{(x^2+x)^3}}$

(f) $f'(x) = -\frac{4x+1}{\sqrt{(2x^2+x)^3}}$

(g) $k'(x) = -\frac{9x}{\sqrt{(x^2+2)^5}}$

(h) $g'(x) = \frac{-7(3x^2-5)}{3\sqrt[3]{(x^3-5x)^4}}$

(i) $f'(x) = -\frac{9(2x+2)}{2\sqrt{(x^2+2x)^5}}$

Exercise 13.1C

1.

(a) $f'(2) = 768$

(b) $g'(-1) = -3{,}456$

(c) $h'(1) = 21$

(d) $f'(-2) = 4000$

(e) $g'(-2) = -20{,}736$

(f) $h'(3) = 158{,}760$

2.

(a) $f'(-1) = -\frac{9}{8}$

(b) $g'(1) = -\frac{10}{729}$

(c) $h'(3) = -\frac{4}{5625}$

(d) $f'(-2) = -16$

(e) $g'(2) = -\frac{3}{4}$

(f) $h'(4) = \frac{4}{\sqrt{7}}$

3.

(a) $f'(2) = -\frac{3}{256}$

(b) $g'(1) = -\frac{3}{8}$

(c) $h'(2) = -12$

(d) $f'(-1) = -24$

(e) $g'(-3) = \frac{9}{4}$

(f) $h'(2) = -\frac{4}{9}$

4.

(a) $f'(2) = 108$

(b) $f'(-1) = -72$

(c) $f'(3) = -\frac{3}{128}$

(d) $f'(1) = 0$

(e) $f'(-2) = \frac{3}{256}$

(f) $f'(4) = -\frac{1}{5\sqrt{5}}$ or $-\frac{\sqrt{5}}{25}$

5.

(a) $f'(2) = 972$

(b) $f'(-2) = -2{,}904$

(c) $f'(-2) = \frac{3}{343}$

(d) $f'(1) = 9$

(e) $f'(3) = -\frac{5}{2{,}916}$

(f) $f'(-3) = \frac{3}{10\sqrt{10}}$ or $\frac{3\sqrt{10}}{1000}$

Exercise 13.2A

1.

(a) $f'(x) = 4\cos x$

(b) $\frac{dy}{dx} = -2\sin x$

(c) $f'(x) = 6\cos x$

(d) $\frac{dy}{dx} = -10\sin x$

(e) $f'(x) = -7\sin x$

(f) $\frac{dy}{dx} = 8\cos x$

2.

(a) $\frac{dy}{dx} = \cos x - \sin x$

(b) $f'(x) = -\sin x - \cos x$

(c) $\frac{dy}{dx} = 2\cos x - 3\sin x$

(d) $\frac{dy}{dx} = \cos x - 4\sin x$

(e) $f'(x) = 2\cos x + 4\sin x$

(f) $f'(x) = -9\sin x - 2\cos x$

Exercise 13.2B

1.

(a) $f'(x) = 3\cos 3x$

(b) $\frac{dy}{dx} = -2\sin 2x$

(c) $f'(x) = 5\cos 5x$

(d) $\frac{dy}{dx} = -4\sin 4x$

(e) $f'(x) = -6\sin 3x$

(f) $\frac{dy}{dx} = 8\cos 4x$

2.

(a) $\frac{dy}{dx} = -15\sin 5x$

(b) $f'(x) = 4\sin 2x$

(c) $f'(x) = -4\cos 2x$

(d) $\frac{dy}{dx} = 2\cos 2x - 15\sin 5x$

(e) $f'(x) = 8\cos 4x + 6\sin 2x$

(f) $f'(x) = -\sin x - 15\cos 5x$

(g) $\frac{dy}{dx} = 12\cos 2x - 3\sin 3x$

(h) $f'(x) = 10\sin 2x - 3\sin 3x$

(i) $f'(x) = -\sin x - 6\cos 2x$

3.

(a) $\frac{dy}{dx} = -2\sin(2x-3)$

(b) $f'(x) = 4\cos(4x+2)$

(c) $f'(x) = -5\sin(5x+1)$

(d) $\frac{dy}{dx} = \cos\left(x + \frac{\pi}{3}\right)$

(e) $f'(x) = -3\sin\left(3x - \frac{\pi}{3}\right)$

(f) $f'(x) = 2\cos\left(2x + \frac{3\pi}{2}\right)$

(g) $\frac{dy}{dx} = 2x\cos(x^2+1)$

(h) $f'(x) = -4x\sin(2x^2-2)$

(i) $f'(x) = 6x\sin(3x^2-2)$

Exercise 13.2C

1.

(a) $f'(x) = 3\sin^2 x\cos x$

(b) $\frac{dy}{dx} = -2\cos x\sin x$

(c) $f'(x) = 5\sin^4 x\cos x$

(d) $\frac{dy}{dx} = -7\cos^6 x\sin x$

(e) $f'(x) = -4\cos^3 x\sin x$

(f) $\frac{dy}{dx} = 6\sin^5 x\cos x$

2.

(a) $f'(x) = 10\sin x\cos x$

(b) $\frac{dy}{dx} = -18\cos^2 x\sin x$

(c) $f'(x) = 44\sin^3 x\cos x$

(d) $\frac{dy}{dx} = -12\cos^3 x\sin x$

(e) $f'(x) = 16\sin x\cos x$

(f) $\frac{dy}{dx} = 24\sin^3 x\cos x$

3.

(a) $f'(x) = 4\sin x\cos x$

(b) $\frac{dy}{dx} = -2\sin x\cos x - 4\cos 2x$

(c) $f'(x) = -3\cos^2 x\sin x + 3\sin^2 x\cos x$

(d) $\frac{dy}{dx} = 12\cos 3x + 2\sin x\cos x$

(e) $f'(x) = 15\sin^2 x\cos x + 2\sin x\cos x$

(f) $\frac{dy}{dx} = 5\sin^4 x\cos x - 21\sin 3x$

Exercise 13.2D

1.

(a) $f'\left(\frac{\pi}{6}\right) = -\sqrt{3}$

(b) $f'\left(\frac{\pi}{3}\right) = -3$

(c) $f'\left(\frac{\pi}{4}\right) = -8$

(d) $f'\left(\frac{\pi}{4}\right) = -6$

(e) $f'\left(\frac{3\pi}{4}\right) = 1$

(f) $f'\left(\frac{\pi}{6}\right) = \frac{\sqrt{3}}{2}$

(g) $f'\left(\frac{\pi}{3}\right) = 3$

(h) $f'\left(\frac{5\pi}{6}\right) = -\frac{45}{8}$

2.

(a) $f'\left(\frac{\pi}{6}\right) = 1$

(b) $f'\left(\frac{\pi}{3}\right) = 0$

(c) $f'\left(\frac{\pi}{3}\right) = \frac{15\sqrt{3}}{2}$

(d) $f'\left(\frac{5\pi}{6}\right) = 0$

(e) $f'\left(\frac{\pi}{4}\right) = -1$

(f) $f'\left(\frac{2\pi}{3}\right) = -\frac{\sqrt{3}}{2}$

(g) $f'\left(\frac{\pi}{6}\right) = -\frac{9}{4}$ (h) $f'\left(\frac{5\pi}{6}\right) = -\frac{9\sqrt{3}}{8}$

Exercise 13.3A

1.

(a) $\frac{(x+2)^3}{3} + C$ (b) $\frac{(4x+3)^3}{12} + C$ (c) $\frac{(5x-2)^4}{20} + C$

(d) $\frac{(5x+1)^5}{5} + C$ (e) $\frac{(3x-3)^4}{6} + C$ (f) $\frac{3(7x+1)^7}{49} + C$

(g) $-\frac{(3-x)^6}{3} + C$ (h) $-\frac{(1-3x)^8}{12} + C$ (i) $-\frac{8(5-x)^5}{5} + C$

(j) $\frac{(2x+4)^3}{12} + C$ (k) $\frac{(3x-2)^4}{48} + C$ (l) $-\frac{(5-4x)^4}{32} + C$

(m) $\frac{(4x+7)^6}{72} + C$ (n) $\frac{3(5x-3)^4}{20} + C$ (o) $\frac{(7x+1)^6}{21} + C$

(p) $-\frac{(3-x)^6}{9} + C$ (q) $-\frac{(4-5x)^3}{20} + C$ (r) $-\frac{4(1-5x)^3}{75} + C$

2.

(a) $-\frac{1}{4(2x+4)^2} + C$ (b) $-\frac{1}{4x-8} + C$ (c) $\frac{1}{4(1-4x)^2} + C$

(d) $-\frac{5}{9(3x+5)^3} + C$ (e) $-\frac{1}{7(7x-2)^2} + C$ (f) $-\frac{1}{3(3x-2)^4} + C$

(g) $-\frac{1}{10(5x-3)} + C$ (h) $-\frac{1}{24(3x-2)^4} + C$ (i) $-\frac{1}{36(4x-1)^6} + C$

3.

(a) $\frac{\sqrt{(4x-3)^3}}{6} + C$ (b) $\frac{3\sqrt[3]{(2x+2)^4}}{8} + C$ (c) $\frac{8\sqrt{3x+5}}{3} + C$

(d) $3\sqrt[3]{(3x-1)^2} + C$ (e) $\frac{3\sqrt[3]{(5x-4)^5}}{5} + C$ (f) $\frac{21\sqrt[3]{(4x+1)^2}}{8} + C$

(g) $\sqrt[3]{4+2x} + C$ (h) $\sqrt[4]{3x+2} + C$ (i) $\frac{\sqrt[5]{(5x+1)^4}}{8} + C$

Exercise 13.3B

1.

(a) $-\frac{1}{2x+1} + C$ (b) $-\frac{1}{3(5x-2)^3} + C$ (c) $-\frac{1}{(2x-1)^2} + C$

(d) $-\frac{1}{3x+2} + C$ (e) $-\frac{1}{4(x-2)^4} + C$ (f) $\frac{2}{(9-2x)^2} + C$

(g) $3\sqrt{2x+4} + C$ (h) $-\frac{9\sqrt[3]{(1-x)^2}}{2} + C$ (i) $\frac{9\sqrt[3]{4x+7}}{2} + C$

2.

(a) $2\sqrt{x+2} + C$ (b) $\frac{4\sqrt{3x+2}}{3} + C$ (c) $\frac{8\sqrt{3x-2}}{3} + C$

(d) $\sqrt{4x+5} + C$ (e) $-\frac{9\sqrt[3]{(5-2x)^2}}{2} + C$ (f) $-\frac{2\sqrt{6-5x}}{5} + C$

(g) $-\frac{18}{7\sqrt{7x+2}} + C$ (h) $-\frac{3\sqrt[3]{6-4x}}{2} + C$ (i) $-\frac{6}{5\sqrt{5x+9}} + C$

Exercise 13.3C

1.

(a) 84 (b) $-\frac{795}{4}$ (c) $\frac{5632}{5}$

(d) -810 (e) $\frac{341}{5}$ (f) $\frac{25,493}{40,000}$

2.

(a) $\frac{4}{9}$ (b) $\frac{2}{39}$ (c) $-\frac{8}{49}$

(d) $\frac{11}{1568}$ (e) $\frac{26}{81}$ (f) $-\frac{14}{169}$

3.

(a) $\frac{1}{24}$ (b) $\frac{2}{225}$ (c) $\frac{2}{15}$

(d) 2 (e) 4 (f) 2

(g) 2 (h) 24 (i) -18

Exercise 13.4A

1.

(a) $-\frac{1}{3}\cos 3x + C$ (b) $\frac{1}{2}\sin 2x + C$ (c) $-\frac{1}{5}\cos 5x + C$

(d) $\frac{1}{7}\sin 7x + C$ (e) $3\sin\left(\frac{x}{3}\right) + C$ (f) $-2\cos\left(\frac{1}{2}x\right) + C$

2.

(a) $\frac{3}{2}\sin 2x + C$ (b) $-\frac{4}{3}\cos 3x + C$ (c) $-\cos 2x + C$

(d) $2\sin 2x + C$ (e) $-\frac{5}{6}\cos 6x + C$ (f) $\frac{3}{5}\sin 5x + C$

3.

(a) $\frac{1}{2}\sin(2x-2) + C$ (b) $-\frac{1}{3}\cos(3x-2) + C$

(c) $-\frac{1}{4}\cos(4x+1) + C$ (d) $\frac{1}{3}\sin\left(3x - \frac{\pi}{3}\right) + C$

(e) $-\frac{1}{2}\cos(2x-1) + C$ (f) $\frac{1}{2}\sin\left(2x + \frac{\pi}{6}\right) + C$

4.

(a) $\frac{3}{2}\sin(2x-2) + C$ (b) $-\cos(2x+1) + C$

(c) $-\frac{1}{9}\cos(3x+1) + C$ (d) $\frac{1}{6}\sin\left(3x - \frac{\pi}{3}\right) + C$

(e) $-\cos(2x-1) + C$ (f) $\frac{2}{5}\sin\left(2x - \frac{\pi}{3}\right) + C$

Exercise 13.4B

1.

(a) $\frac{1}{4}\sin 2x + \frac{x}{2} + C$ (b) $x - \frac{1}{2}\sin 2x + C$

(c) $\frac{3x}{2} - \frac{3}{4}\sin 2x + C$ (d) $x + C$

(e) $-\frac{1}{2}\cos 2x + C$ (f) $-\frac{1}{2}\cos 4x + C$

Exercise 13.4C

1.

(a) $\frac{1}{2}$ (b) $\frac{1}{2}$ (c) $\frac{1}{2}$ (d) $\frac{1}{2}$

(e) 1.327 (f) 0.699 (g) 1.592 (h) 1.189

2.

(a) 0.460 (b) 0.383 (c) 0.499

(d) 1.025 (e) 1.673 (f) 1.236

Exercise 13.5A

13.1A

(a) $f'(x) = 6(2x-3)^2$ (b) $\frac{dy}{dx} = 10x(x^2+9)^4$

(c) $f'(x) = -\frac{18}{(6x+5)^4}$

(d) $f'(x) = 6(3x^2-1)(x^3-x)^2$

(e) $\frac{dy}{dx} = -\frac{6x^2+1}{2\sqrt{(2x^3-x)^3}}$

(f) $f'(x) = 2(2x^3+4x)^3(6x^2+4)$

13.1B

(a) $f'(x) = -\frac{63}{(7x+3)^4}$ (b) $f'(x) = -\frac{5}{3\sqrt[3]{(5x-2)^4}}$

(c) $f'(x) = -\frac{5(1-2x)}{3\sqrt[3]{(x-x^2)^4}}$

13.1C

(a) $f'(3) = 2,178$ (b) $g'(-2) = \frac{5}{108}$

(c) $g'(-1) = -\frac{9}{4}$ (d) $h'(2) = -\frac{120}{\sqrt{12,167}}$

(e) $f'(-1) = 0$ (f) $m = \frac{3\sqrt{10}}{5}$

13.2B

(a) $\frac{dy}{dx} = -15\sin 5x$ (b) $f'(x) = 6\sin 2x - 4\cos 2x$

(c) $f'(x) = -4\cos 2x$ (d) $\frac{dy}{dx} = 2x\cos(x^2+1)$

(e) $f'(x) = -4x\sin(2x^2-2)$ (f) $f'(x) = 6x\sin(3x^2-2)$

13.2C

(a) $f'(x) = 8\sin x\cos x$ (b) $\frac{dy}{dx} = -12\sin x\cos^3 x$

(c) $f'(x) = 3\cos x\sin^2 x - 3\sin x\cos^2 x$

13.2D

(a) $f'(2) = 10.88$ (b) $f'\left(\frac{\pi}{6}\right) = \frac{3\sqrt{3}}{2}$

(c) $f'\left(\frac{\pi}{3}\right) = 0$ (d) $f'\left(\frac{\pi}{4}\right) = -5.86$

13.3A

(a) $\frac{(2x-3)^4}{8} + C$ (b) $\frac{8\sqrt{(5x+2)^3}}{15} + C$ (c) $-\frac{4(7-3x)^5}{15} + C$

(d) $-\frac{6}{5(5x-3)} + C$ (e) $\frac{5\sqrt{4x+1}}{2} + C$ (f) $-3\sqrt[3]{5-4x} + C$

13.3B

(a) $-\frac{1}{6(6x+2)^2} + C$ (b) $\sqrt[3]{(3x-2)^2} + C$ (c) $-\frac{6}{5\sqrt{5x-1}} + C$

13.3C

(a) 13 (b) $\frac{158}{3}$ (c) $\frac{1}{90}$

(d) $\frac{1}{6}$ (e) $\frac{40}{8281}$ (f) $\frac{2}{3}$

13.4A

(a) $-\frac{1}{3}\cos 3x + C$ (b) $\frac{2}{5}\sin 5x + C$

(c) $x + \frac{3}{2}\cos 2x + C$ (d) $\frac{1}{3}\sin\left(3x - \frac{\pi}{3}\right) + C$

(e) $-2\cos\left(2x - \frac{\pi}{2}\right) + C$ (f) $x - \frac{1}{5}\cos(5x - 1.2) + C$

13.4B

(a) $\frac{x}{2} - \frac{1}{4}\sin 2x + C$ (b) $\frac{x}{2} + \frac{1}{4}\sin 2x + C$

(c) $-\frac{1}{4}\cos 2x + C$

13.4C

(a) -0.708 (b) 1.730 (c) 0.330

Exercise 13.5B

1. $x \le \frac{3}{2}$ 2. $f'\left(\frac{\pi}{6}\right) = 7$

3.

(a) $k = \sqrt{13}, a = 1.0$ (b) $b = 2.23$

4. $y = -\frac{5}{2}\cos 2x + \frac{5}{4}$ 5. $f'(1.2) = -3.32$

6. $a = \frac{3\pi}{8}$

7.

(a) $f(x) = 3\cos 2x - 1$ (b) $g(x) = -4\cos 2x - 1$

(c) $\left(\frac{\pi}{4}, -1\right), \left(\frac{3\pi}{4}, -1\right)$ (d) $7\ units^2$

8. $-\sqrt{5} < x < \sqrt{5}$ 9. $f'\left(\frac{\pi}{3}\right) = -6 - 3\sqrt{3}$

10. $y = \frac{3}{2}\sin\left(2x - \frac{\pi}{6}\right) - \frac{3\sqrt{3}}{4}$ 11. $f'(0.4) = -3.50$

12. $a = \frac{4\pi}{9}$

13.

(a) $f(x) = 3\cos 2x - 1$ (b) $g(x) = 3\sin 2x - 1$

(c) $\left(\frac{\pi}{8}, \frac{3\sqrt{2}-2}{2}\right), \left(\frac{5\pi}{8}, -\frac{3\sqrt{2}+2}{2}\right)$ (d) $3\sqrt{2}\ units^2$

Chapter 14

Exercise 14.1A

1. $\begin{pmatrix}7\\6\end{pmatrix}$ 2. $\begin{pmatrix}3\\7\end{pmatrix}$ 3. $\begin{pmatrix}-4\\1\end{pmatrix}$ 4. $\begin{pmatrix}3\\-8\end{pmatrix}$

5. $\begin{pmatrix}13\\10\end{pmatrix}$ 6. $\begin{pmatrix}-11\\5\end{pmatrix}$ 7. $\begin{pmatrix}-20\\12\end{pmatrix}$ 8. $\begin{pmatrix}-7\\25\end{pmatrix}$

9. $\begin{pmatrix}-19\\4\end{pmatrix}$ 10. $\begin{pmatrix}14\\-28\end{pmatrix}$ 11. $\begin{pmatrix}37\\7\end{pmatrix}$ 12. $\begin{pmatrix}-8\\27\end{pmatrix}$

Exercise 14.1B

1. $\begin{pmatrix}8\\10\\1\end{pmatrix}$ 2. $\begin{pmatrix}1\\12\\-3\end{pmatrix}$ 3. $\begin{pmatrix}16\\-5\\18\end{pmatrix}$ 4. $\begin{pmatrix}-14\\-10\\-12\end{pmatrix}$

5. $\begin{pmatrix}15\\-12\\13\end{pmatrix}$ 6. $\begin{pmatrix}19\\-29\\24\end{pmatrix}$ 7. $\begin{pmatrix}-34\\-4\\-46\end{pmatrix}$ 8. $\begin{pmatrix}13\\16\\6\end{pmatrix}$

9. $\begin{pmatrix}5\\-16\\11\end{pmatrix}$ 10. $\begin{pmatrix}11\\-13\\12\end{pmatrix}$ 11. $\begin{pmatrix}29\\22\\21\end{pmatrix}$ 12. $\begin{pmatrix}48\\3\\44\end{pmatrix}$

Exercise 14.2A

1. $\begin{pmatrix}-2\\3\end{pmatrix}$ 2. $\begin{pmatrix}-9\\-2\end{pmatrix}$ 3. $\begin{pmatrix}3\\-10\end{pmatrix}$ 4. $\begin{pmatrix}8\\-11\end{pmatrix}$

5. $\begin{pmatrix}4\\12\end{pmatrix}$ 6. $\begin{pmatrix}-15\\-60\end{pmatrix}$ 7. $\begin{pmatrix}2\\6\end{pmatrix}$ 8. $\begin{pmatrix}12\\48\end{pmatrix}$

9. $\begin{pmatrix}3\\-20\end{pmatrix}$ 10. $\begin{pmatrix}-2\\13\end{pmatrix}$ 11. $\begin{pmatrix}41\\49\end{pmatrix}$ 12. $\begin{pmatrix}60\\-100\end{pmatrix}$

Exercise 14.2B

1. $\begin{pmatrix}-7\\7\\12\end{pmatrix}$ 2. $\begin{pmatrix}3\\-5\\-8\end{pmatrix}$ 3. $\begin{pmatrix}-6\\12\\7\end{pmatrix}$ 4. $\begin{pmatrix}8\\-21\\-30\end{pmatrix}$

5. $\begin{pmatrix}-8\\42\\34\end{pmatrix}$ 6. $\begin{pmatrix}30\\-60\\-35\end{pmatrix}$ 7. $\begin{pmatrix}-4\\21\\17\end{pmatrix}$ 8. $\begin{pmatrix}-8\\-36\\-40\end{pmatrix}$

9. $\begin{pmatrix}-15\\28\\42\end{pmatrix}$ 10. $\begin{pmatrix}-7\\-13\\-12\end{pmatrix}$ 11. $\begin{pmatrix}8\\0\\-26\end{pmatrix}$ 12. $\begin{pmatrix}25\\14\\6\end{pmatrix}$

Exercise 14.3

1.

(a) 5 (b) 13 (c) 17 (d) 25

(e) 6 (f) 14 (g) 24.9 (h) 37

2.

(a) 4.6 (b) 9.9 (c) 13.9 (d) 15

(e) 12.1 (f) 10.3 (g) 13.9 (h) 12.4

3.

(a) 4.9 (b) 15.7 (c) 19.4 (d) 16.3

(e) 29.2 (f) 23.2 (g) 57.0 (h) 28.0

(i) 57.4 (j) 23.2 (k) 48.5 (l) 16.3

Exercise 14.4

1. $\begin{pmatrix} -\frac{2}{3} \\ \frac{1}{3} \\ \frac{2}{3} \end{pmatrix}$ 2. $\begin{pmatrix} \frac{9}{11} \\ -\frac{2}{11} \\ -\frac{6}{11} \end{pmatrix}$ 3. $\begin{pmatrix} -\frac{4}{13} \\ \frac{12}{13} \\ -\frac{3}{13} \end{pmatrix}$ 4. $\begin{pmatrix} -\frac{1}{\sqrt{6}} \\ \frac{2}{\sqrt{6}} \\ -\frac{1}{\sqrt{6}} \end{pmatrix}$

5. $\begin{pmatrix} -\frac{12}{17} \\ -\frac{9}{17} \\ \frac{8}{17} \end{pmatrix}$ 6. $\begin{pmatrix} \frac{11}{15} \\ \frac{-2}{15} \\ \frac{2}{3} \end{pmatrix}$ 7. $\begin{pmatrix} \frac{4}{9} \\ \frac{1}{9} \\ -\frac{8}{9} \end{pmatrix}$ 8. $\begin{pmatrix} \frac{15}{19} \\ -\frac{6}{19} \\ \frac{10}{19} \end{pmatrix}$

9. $\begin{pmatrix} \frac{12}{25} \\ \frac{4}{5} \\ \frac{9}{25} \end{pmatrix}$ 10. $\begin{pmatrix} \frac{4}{21} \\ -\frac{20}{21} \\ \frac{5}{21} \end{pmatrix}$ 11. $\begin{pmatrix} \frac{14}{15} \\ \frac{1}{3} \\ -\frac{2}{15} \end{pmatrix}$ 12. $\begin{pmatrix} \frac{3}{5} \\ -\frac{16}{25} \\ \frac{12}{25} \end{pmatrix}$

Exercise 14.5

1.
(a) $\mathbf{a} = -2\mathbf{i} + 4\mathbf{j} + 4\mathbf{k}$ (b) $\mathbf{b} = 4\mathbf{i} - 6\mathbf{j} - 12\mathbf{k}$
(c) $\mathbf{c} = 16\mathbf{i} - 14\mathbf{j} - 13\mathbf{k}$ (d) $\mathbf{d} = -12\mathbf{i} + 35\mathbf{j}$
(e) $\mathbf{e} = -\mathbf{j} + 3\mathbf{k}$ (f) $\mathbf{f} = 5\mathbf{i} - 9\mathbf{k}$
(g) $\mathbf{g} = -2\mathbf{j}$ (h) $\mathbf{h} = 5\mathbf{i} - 12\mathbf{j} + 18\mathbf{k}$

2. $|3\mathbf{a} - \mathbf{b}| = 20.2$ 3. $|\mathbf{c} - \mathbf{d}| = 5.1$

4. $a = 14 \pm \sqrt{17}$ 5. $a = 1, a = 3$

Exercise 14.6

1.
(a) A, B and C are collinear. (b) D, E and F are collinear.
(c) G, H and I are **not** collinear. (d) J, K and L are **not** collinear.
(e) M, N and P are **not** collinear. (f) Q, R and S are collinear.
(g) T, U and V are collinear. (h) W, X and Y are **not** collinear.
(i) A, B and C are collinear. (j) D, E and F are collinear.

2.
(a) $k = 12$ (b) $k = 11$ (c) $k = -6$ (d) $k = -13$
(e) $k = 7$ (f) $k = 17$ (g) $k = 30$ (h) $k = 30$
(i) $k = -20$ (j) $k = -13$

Exercise 14.7

1.
(a) P(7, 3, 10) (b) P(11, 14, 3) (c) P(15, −2, 1)
(d) P(8, −4, 2) (e) P(4, −1, −4) (f) P(−2, 5, −2)
(g) P(6, −13, 5) (h) P(26, 6, 4) (i) P(−3, 18, 22)
(j) P(5, −11, 20) (k) P(14, −7, 13) (l) P(35, 13, −22)

2.
(a) B(−12, 15, 8) (b) B(7, −9, 10) (c) B(22, 11, 7)
(d) B(4, 30, 40) (e) B(−6, 40, 15) (f) B(27, 84, 22)
(g) B(−4, 16, 37) (h) B(110, −75, 104)

Exercise 14.8

1.
(a) 2: 1 (b) 1: 3 (c) 2: 3 (d) 2: 1
(e) 3: 2 (f) 4: 1 (g) 1: 5 (h) 2: 5
(i) 3: 2 (j) 2: 3 (k) 4: 3 (l) 4: 5

2.
(a) (i) 2: 1 (ii) $k = 1$ (b) (i) 3: 1 (ii) $k = 9$ (c) (i) 2: 3 (ii) $k = 22$
(d) (i) 3: 1 (ii) $k = 12$ (e) (i) 3: 2 (ii) $k = 9$ (f) (i) 2: 5 (ii) $k = -7$

Exercise 14.9A

1.
(a) 5 (b) −13 (c) 29 (d) 0
(e) 22 (f) 0 (g) 1 (h) 12

2.
(a) 11 (b) −24 (c) −69 (d) −20
(e) 0 (f) 2

3.
(a) −41 (b) −54 (c) 100 (d) −1
(e) 3 (f) 0

4. Proof 5. Proof 6. 8 7. 14/3
8. −19/2 9. −4 10. 14 11. 0, 5
12. 22

Exercise 14.9B

1.
(a) $\mathbf{a} \cdot \mathbf{b} = 9$ (b) $\mathbf{a} \cdot \mathbf{b} = 14\sqrt{57}$ (c) $\mathbf{a} \cdot \mathbf{b} = -3\sqrt{7}$
(d) $\mathbf{a} \cdot \mathbf{b} = -15\sqrt{2}$ (e) $\mathbf{a} \cdot \mathbf{b} = 235.6$ (f) $\mathbf{a} \cdot \mathbf{b} = 37.5$

Exercise 14.10

1.
(a) $\theta = 59.8°$ (b) $\theta = 54.7°$ (c) $\theta = 75.6°$
(d) $\theta = 47.1°$ (e) $\theta = 31.7°$ (f) $\theta = 13.2°$

2.
(a) $\theta = 105.8°$ (b) $\theta = 115.9°$ (c) $\theta = 120.8°$
(d) $\theta = 122.9°$ (e) $\theta = 144.4°$ (f) $\theta = 158.2°$

3.
(a) $\theta = 73.1°$ (b) $\theta = 26.3°$ (c) $\theta = 59.8°$
(d) $\theta = 17.7°$

4.
(a) $\theta = 58.2°$ (b) $\theta = 65.6°$ (c) $\theta = 90°$
(d) $\theta = 90°$

5.
(a) $\theta = 48.8°$ (b) $\theta = 138.5°$ (c) $\theta = 30.6°$
(d) $\theta = 94.5°$

Exercise 14.11

1.
(a) 63 (b) 25 (c) −20
(d) 270 (e) 315 (f) $48 + 24\sqrt{3}$

2.
(a) (i) 15 (ii) 27 (iii) 67
(b) (i) $5\sqrt{3} - 12$ (ii) $25 + 5\sqrt{3}$ (iii) 16
(c) (i) $12 + 4\sqrt{3}$ (ii) $40 + 4\sqrt{3}$ (iii) $28 + 8\sqrt{3}$

Exercise 14.12A

1.
(a) $\overrightarrow{FE} = -\mathbf{a} - \mathbf{b}$ (b) $\overrightarrow{GC} = -2\mathbf{a} - \mathbf{b}$
(c) $\overrightarrow{DG} = 2\mathbf{a} + 2\mathbf{b}$ (d) $\overrightarrow{FC} = -2\mathbf{a}$

2.
(a) $\overrightarrow{QP} = \mathbf{b} - \mathbf{a}$ (b) $\overrightarrow{RU} = 2\mathbf{b} - 2\mathbf{a}$
(c) $\overrightarrow{PT} = 3\mathbf{a} - \mathbf{b}$ (d) $\overrightarrow{RS} = \mathbf{a}$

3.
(a) $\overrightarrow{CD} = -\mathbf{a}$ (b) $\overrightarrow{BC} = \mathbf{b} - 2\mathbf{a}$
(c) $\overrightarrow{OM} = \mathbf{b} - \mathbf{a}$ (d) $\overrightarrow{DO} = 3\mathbf{a} - 2\mathbf{b}$

4.
(a) $\overrightarrow{AD} = \mathbf{b}$ (b) $\overrightarrow{AE} = \frac{2}{3}(\mathbf{a} + \mathbf{b})$
(c) $\overrightarrow{EC} = \frac{1}{3}(\mathbf{a} + \mathbf{b})$ (d) $\overrightarrow{BE} = \frac{2}{3}\mathbf{b} - \frac{1}{3}\mathbf{a}$

5.
(a) $\overrightarrow{AC} = \mathbf{a} + \mathbf{b}$ (b) $\overrightarrow{AE} = \frac{1}{4}(\mathbf{a} + \mathbf{b})$
(c) $\overrightarrow{DE} = \frac{1}{4}\mathbf{a} - \frac{3}{4}\mathbf{b}$ (d) $\overrightarrow{EB} = \frac{3}{4}\mathbf{a} - \frac{1}{4}\mathbf{b}$

6.
(a) $\overrightarrow{DB} = \mathbf{a} - 2\mathbf{b}$ (b) $\overrightarrow{FA} = -\frac{8}{5}\mathbf{a} - \frac{4}{5}\mathbf{b}$
(c) $\overrightarrow{DE} = -\mathbf{a} - \mathbf{b}$ (d) $\overrightarrow{EF} = \frac{8}{5}\mathbf{a} - \frac{1}{5}\mathbf{b}$

Exercise 14.12B

1.
(a) $\overrightarrow{HE} = -\mathbf{p}$ (b) $\overrightarrow{FH} = \mathbf{p} - \mathbf{q}$
(c) $\overrightarrow{GJ} = -\frac{3}{4}\mathbf{p} - \frac{1}{4}\mathbf{q} - \frac{3}{4}\mathbf{r}$ (d) $\overrightarrow{JE} = \frac{3}{4}\mathbf{r} - \frac{1}{4}\mathbf{p} - \frac{3}{4}\mathbf{q}$

2.
(a) $\overrightarrow{AJ} = \frac{2}{3}\mathbf{q} + \frac{1}{3}\mathbf{r}$ (b) $\overrightarrow{JH} = \mathbf{p} - \frac{2}{3}\mathbf{q} + \frac{2}{3}\mathbf{r}$
(c) $\overrightarrow{GJ} = -\mathbf{p} - \frac{2}{3}\mathbf{r} - \frac{1}{3}\mathbf{q}$ (d) $\overrightarrow{EJ} = \frac{2}{3}(\mathbf{q} - \mathbf{r})$

3.
(a) $\overrightarrow{AM} = -\frac{1}{2}\mathbf{q} - \frac{1}{2}\mathbf{r}$ (b) $\overrightarrow{MH} = \frac{1}{2}\mathbf{q} - \frac{1}{2}\mathbf{r} - \mathbf{p}$
(c) $\overrightarrow{GM} = \mathbf{p} + \frac{1}{2}\mathbf{q} + \frac{1}{2}\mathbf{r}$ (d) $\overrightarrow{EM} = \frac{1}{2}(\mathbf{r} - \mathbf{q})$

4.
(a) $\overrightarrow{AE} = \mathbf{p} + \mathbf{r}$ (b) $\overrightarrow{DF} = \mathbf{p} - \mathbf{r}$
(c) $\overrightarrow{BE} = \mathbf{p} + \mathbf{r} - \mathbf{q}$ (d) $\overrightarrow{EM} = \frac{1}{2}(\mathbf{q} - \mathbf{r} - \mathbf{p})$

5.
(a) $\overrightarrow{EC} = \mathbf{q} - \mathbf{p}$ (b) $\overrightarrow{FJ} = \frac{3}{4}(\mathbf{q} - \mathbf{p} + \mathbf{r})$
(c) $\overrightarrow{CJ} = \frac{1}{4}(\mathbf{p} - \mathbf{q} - \mathbf{r})$ (d) $\overrightarrow{JA} = -\frac{1}{4}\mathbf{p} - \frac{3}{4}\mathbf{q} - \frac{3}{4}\mathbf{r}$

6.
(a) $\overrightarrow{EB} = \mathbf{q} - \mathbf{p}$ (b) $\overrightarrow{FA} = -\frac{1}{3}\mathbf{p} - \frac{2}{3}\mathbf{q} - \frac{2}{3}\mathbf{r}$
(c) $\overrightarrow{EF} = \frac{2}{3}(\mathbf{q} + \mathbf{r} - \mathbf{p})$ (d) $\overrightarrow{FB} = \frac{1}{3}\mathbf{q} - \frac{2}{3}\mathbf{r} - \frac{1}{3}\mathbf{p}$

7.
(a) $\overrightarrow{GC} = \frac{1}{2}(-\mathbf{q} - \mathbf{r})$ (b) $\overrightarrow{FD} = -\frac{1}{3}\mathbf{p} + \frac{2}{3}\mathbf{q} - \frac{1}{3}\mathbf{r}$
(c) $\overrightarrow{EG} = \frac{1}{2}\mathbf{q} + \frac{1}{2}\mathbf{r} - \mathbf{p}$ (d) $\overrightarrow{FE} = \frac{2}{3}\mathbf{p} - \frac{1}{3}\mathbf{q} - \frac{1}{3}\mathbf{r}$

Exercise 14.12C

1.
(a) $\overrightarrow{AC} = -4\mathbf{i} + 8\mathbf{j} - \mathbf{k}$ (b) $\angle BAC = 33.9°$

2.
(a) $\overrightarrow{BA} = -6\mathbf{j}$ (b) $\overrightarrow{BE} = -\mathbf{i} - \mathbf{j} + 3\mathbf{k}$
(c) $\angle ABE = 72.5°$

3.
(a) $\overrightarrow{AM} = \mathbf{i} + 3\mathbf{j} + \mathbf{k}$ (b) $\angle BAM = 10.0°$

4.
(a) $\overrightarrow{AB} = 8\mathbf{j}$ (b) $\overrightarrow{AM} = -2\mathbf{i} + 6\mathbf{j} + 4\mathbf{k}$
(c) $\angle MAB = 36.7°$

5.
(a) $E = \left(\frac{49}{2}, \frac{49}{2}, 9\right), M = (28,14,0)$
(b) $\overrightarrow{ED} \cdot \overrightarrow{EM} = -\frac{339}{2}$ (c) $\angle DEM = 112.7°$

6.
(a) $\overrightarrow{CB} = 2\mathbf{i} + 5\mathbf{j} + 2\mathbf{k}$ (b) Proof
(c) $\angle BCD = 134.1°$

7.
(a) 24 (b) $\overrightarrow{ED} = \mathbf{p} - 2\mathbf{q} + \mathbf{r}$

Exercise 14.13

14.4
(a) $\begin{pmatrix} \frac{4}{5} \\ -\frac{3}{5} \\ 0 \end{pmatrix}$ (b) $\begin{pmatrix} \frac{6}{11} \\ -\frac{7}{11} \\ -\frac{6}{11} \end{pmatrix}$ (b) $\begin{pmatrix} \frac{4}{\sqrt{105}} \\ -\frac{5}{\sqrt{105}} \\ -\frac{8}{\sqrt{105}} \end{pmatrix}$

14.5
(a) $|\boldsymbol{c} - \boldsymbol{d}| = \sqrt{21}$ (b) $a = 2 \pm 2\sqrt{7}$

14.6
(a) A, B and C are **not** collinear.
(b) D, E and F are **not** collinear.
(c) $k = 19$

14.7
(a) $P = (-2, 10, -5)$ (b) $B = (-3, -7, 23)$

14.8
(a) 3: 4 (b) $k = 15$

14.9
(a) (i) $\mathbf{a} \cdot \mathbf{b} = 10$ (ii) $\mathbf{c} \cdot \mathbf{d} = -19$
(b) $\overrightarrow{BA} \cdot \overrightarrow{BC} = 26$ (c) Proof (d) $a = 4$
(e) $\mathbf{a} \cdot \mathbf{b} = -6\sqrt{2}$

14.10
(a) 65.3° (b) 64.5°

14.11
(a) $\mathbf{a} \cdot (\mathbf{b} + \mathbf{c}) = \frac{3\sqrt{3}}{2} - 6$ (b) $\mathbf{a} \cdot (\mathbf{a} + \mathbf{b} + \mathbf{c}) = \frac{3\sqrt{3}}{2} - 3$
(c) $(\mathbf{a} + \mathbf{b}) \cdot (\mathbf{a} + \mathbf{b}) = 12 + 3\sqrt{3}$

14.12
(a) $\overrightarrow{AE} = \mathbf{q} + \mathbf{r} - \mathbf{p}$ (b) $\overrightarrow{BM} = \frac{1}{2}\mathbf{p} + \mathbf{r}$
(c) $\overrightarrow{GA} = \frac{7}{8}\mathbf{p} - \frac{3}{4}\mathbf{q} - \mathbf{r}$ (d) $\overrightarrow{FM} = \mathbf{r} - \frac{1}{4}\mathbf{q} + \frac{1}{8}\mathbf{p}$

Chapter 15

Exercise 15.1A

1.

(a) $log_a c = b$ (b) $log_a y = x$ (c) $log_6 216 = 3$
(d) $log_{15} 225 = 2$ (e) $log_{17} 289 = 2$ (f) $log_9 81 = 2$
(g) $log_{10} 1000 = 3$ (h) $log_{11} 1331 = 3$ (i) $log_4 1024 = 5$
(j) $log_8 1 = 0$ (k) $log_9 9 = 1$ (l) $log_{12} 1 = 0$

2.

(a) $a^y = x$ (b) $a^c = b$ (c) $2^5 = 32$ (d) $6^2 = 36$
(e) $5^3 = 125$ (f) $4^{1/2} = 2$ (g) $5^0 = 1$ (h) $4^1 = 4$
(i) $9^{1/2} = 3$ (j) $8^{2/3} = 4$ (k) $2^1 = 2$ (l) $17^0 = 1$

Exercise 15.1B

1.

(a) $a = 2$ (b) $a = 4$ (c) $a = 3$ (d) $a = 3$
(e) $a = 4$ (f) $a = 0$ (g) $a = 3$ (h) $a = 2$
(i) $a = 4$ (j) $a = 3$ (k) $a = 3$ (l) $a = 1$

2.

(a) $a = 0$ (b) $a = 0$ (c) $a = \frac{1}{2}$ (d) $a = \frac{1}{3}$
(e) $a = \frac{1}{2}$ (f) $a = \frac{1}{2}$ (g) $a = -1$ (h) $a = -3$
(i) $a = -2$ (j) $a = -2$ (k) $a = -2$ (l) $a = -4$
(m) $a = -\frac{1}{2}$ (n) $a = -\frac{1}{2}$ (o) $a = -\frac{1}{2}$ (p) $a = -\frac{1}{2}$
(q) $a = -\frac{1}{2}$ (r) $a = -\frac{1}{4}$

3.

(a) $x = 2$ (b) $x = 1$ (c) $x = 2$ (d) $x = 0$
(e) $x = 1$ (f) $x = 3$ (g) $x = 0$ (h) $x = 3$
(i) $x = 1$ (j) $x = 3$ (k) $x = 4$ (l) $x = 4$
(m) $x = 1$ (n) $x = 0$ (o) $x = 1$ (p) $x = 0$
(q) $x = 1$ (r) $x = 3$

4.

(a) $x = 4$ (b) $x = 0$ (c) $x = \frac{1}{2}$ (d) $x = \frac{1}{3}$
(e) $x = \frac{1}{4}$ (f) $x = \frac{1}{3}$ (g) $x = -1$ (h) $x = -\frac{1}{3}$
(i) $x = -\frac{1}{2}$ (j) $x = -\frac{1}{2}$ (k) $x = \frac{1}{2}$ (l) $x = -\frac{1}{2}$

Exercise 15.1C

1.

(a) 1.77 (b) 1.54 (c) 1.29 (d) 0.36
(e) 0.28 (f) 2.18 (g) 1.49 (h) 0.51
(i) 0.61 (j) 1.39 (k) 1.06 (l) 0.32
(m) 0.90 (n) 0.62 (o) 0.88 (p) -0.43
(q) 0.48 (r) 0.30

2.

(a) $x = 0.48$ (b) $x = 1.46$ (c) $x = 1.40$
(d) $x = 1.39$ (e) $x = 1.80$ (f) $x = 0.39$
(g) $x = 0.67$ (h) $x = 2.10$ (i) $x = 2.16$
(j) $x = 0.28$ (k) $x = 1.61$ (l) $x = 0.43$
(m) $x = 0$ (n) $x = -0.43$ (o) $x = -0.48$
(p) $x = -0.26$ (q) $x = -0.25$ (r) $x = -0.63$

Exercise 15.2A

1.

(a) (i) $f(x) = 2^x$ (ii) $f(x) > 0$
(b) (i) $f(x) = 3^x$ (ii) $f(x) > 0$
(c) (i) $f(x) = 8^x$ (ii) $f(x) > 0$
(d) (i) $f(x) = 2^x$ (ii) $f(x) > 0$
(e) (i) $f(x) = 4^x$ (ii) $f(x) > 0$
(f) (i) $f(x) = 3^x$ (ii) $f(x) > 0$

2.

(a) (i) $f(x) = 2^x$ (ii) $f(x) > 0$
(b) (i) $f(x) = 4^{-x}$ (ii) $f(x) > 0$
(c) (i) $f(x) = 6^x$ (ii) $f(x) > 0$
(d) (i) $f(x) = 2^{-x}$ (ii) $f(x) > 0$
(e) (i) $f(x) = 5^x$ (ii) $f(x) > 0$
(f) (i) $f(x) = 6^{-x}$ (ii) $f(x) > 0$

3.

(a) (i) $f(x) = 2(2)^x$ (ii) $f(x) > 0$
(b) (i) $f(x) = 5(2)^x$ (ii) $f(x) > 0$
(c) (i) $f(x) = 3(4)^x$ (ii) $f(x) > 0$
(d) (i) $f(x) = -3(2)^x$ (ii) $f(x) < 0$
(e) (i) $f(x) = -2(5)^x$ (ii) $f(x) < 0$
(f) (i) $f(x) = 4(3)^x$ (ii) $f(x) > 0$

4.

(a) (i) $f(x) = 2^x + 2$ (ii) $f(x) > 2$
(b) (i) $f(x) = 4^x + 4$ (ii) $f(x) > 4$
(c) (i) $f(x) = 2^x - 1$ (ii) $f(x) > -1$
(d) (i) $f(x) = 3^x + 2$ (ii) $f(x) > 2$
(e) (i) $f(x) = 2^x - 2$ (ii) $f(x) > -2$
(f) (i) $f(x) = 5^x + 3$ (ii) $f(x) > 3$

Exercise 15.2B

1.

(a) (i) $f(x) = log_3 x$ (ii) $x > 0$
(b) (i) $f(x) = log_7 x$ (ii) $x > 0$
(c) (i) $f(x) = log_2 x$ (ii) $x > 0$
(d) (i) $f(x) = log_2 x$ (ii) $x > 0$
(e) (i) $f(x) = -log_3 x$ (ii) $x > 0$
(f) (i) $f(x) = log_2 x$ (ii) $x > 0$
(g) (i) $f(x) = -log_4 x$ (ii) $x > 0$
(h) (i) $f(x) = log_5 x$ (ii) $x > 0$
(i) (i) $f(x) = log_2 x$ (ii) $x > 0$
(j) (i) $f(x) = log_3 x$ (ii) $x > 0$
(k) (i) $f(x) = -log_4 x$ (ii) $x > 0$
(l) (i) $f(x) = log_2(-x)$ (ii) $x < 0$

2.

(a) (i) $f(x) = log_4(x - 1)$ (ii) $x > 1$
(b) (i) $f(x) = log_3(x - 2)$ (ii) $x > 2$
(c) (i) $f(x) = log_5(x - 3)$ (ii) $x > 3$
(d) (i) $f(x) = log_7(x - 3)$ (ii) $x > 3$
(e) (i) $f(x) = log_6(x - 1)$ (ii) $x > 1$
(f) (i) $f(x) = log_5(x - 2)$ (ii) $x > 2$

3.

(a) (i) $f(x) = log_2(x + 1)$ (ii) $x > -1$
(b) (i) $f(x) = log_2(x + 2)$ (ii) $x > -2$

(c) (i) $f(x) = log_5(x+5)$ (ii) $x > -5$

(d) (i) $f(x) = log_5(x+2)$ (ii) $x > -2$

(e) (i) $f(x) = log_8(x+4)$ (ii) $x > -4$

(f) (i) $f(x) = log_4(x+7)$ (ii) $x > -7$

Exercise 15.3A

1.

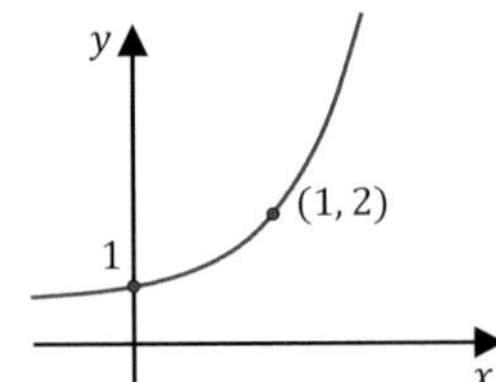

2.

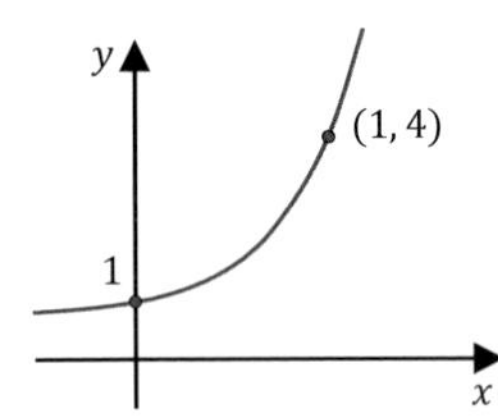

3.

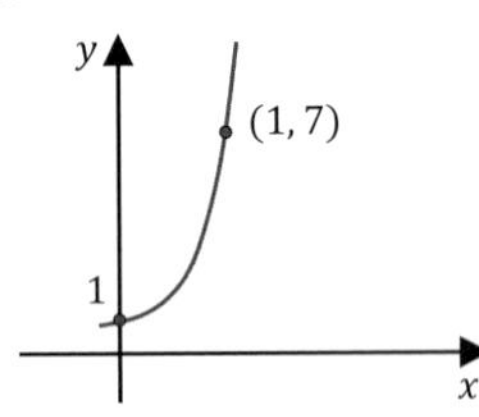

4.

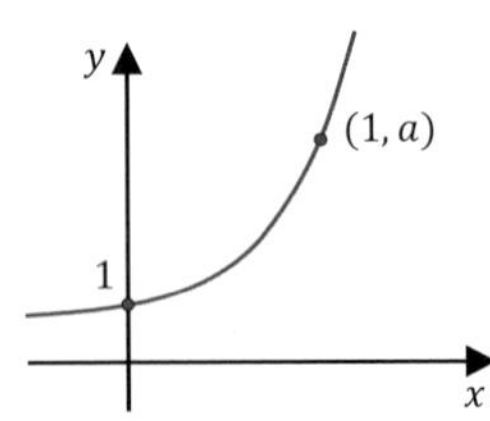

5.

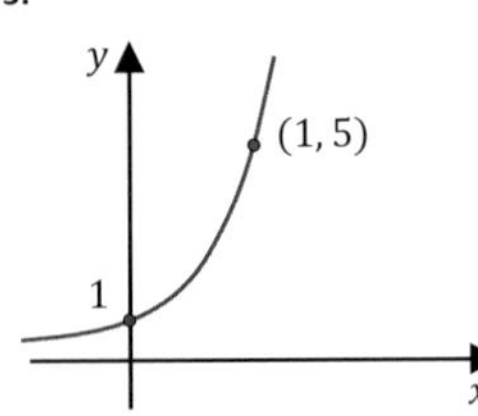

6.

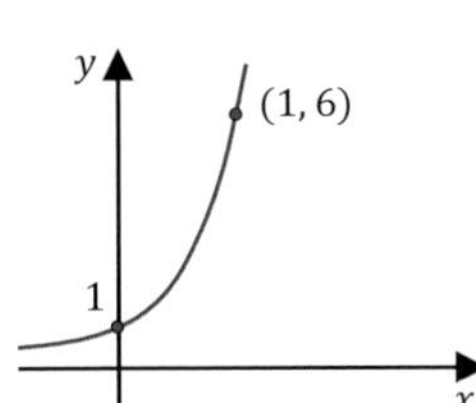

7.

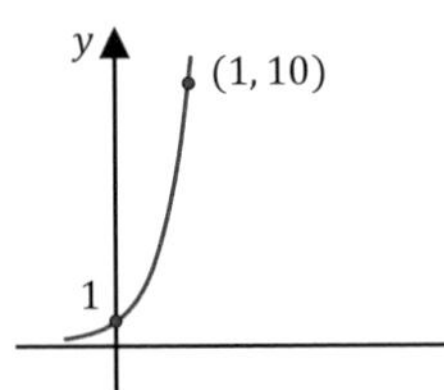

8.

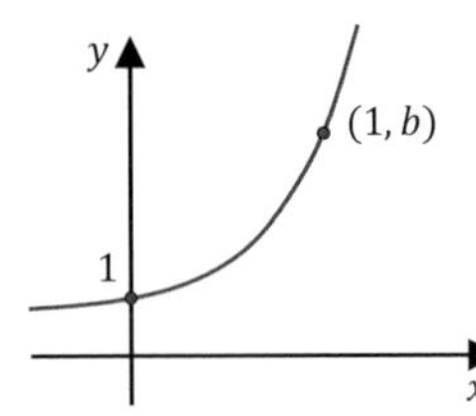

9.

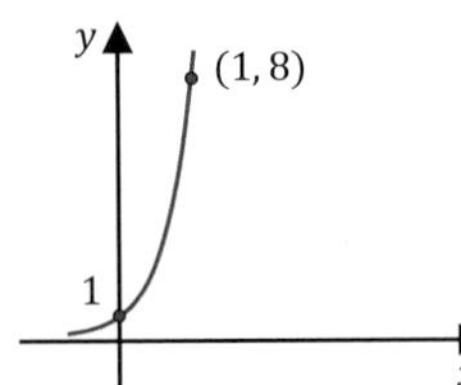

10.

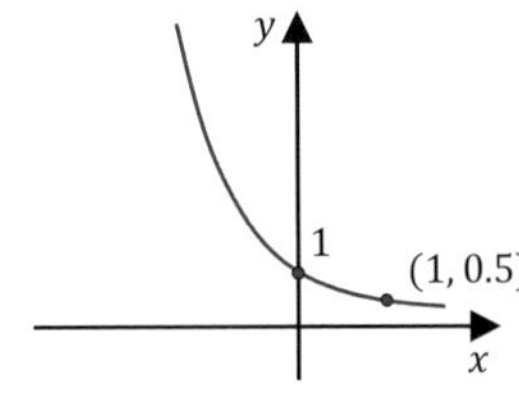

11.

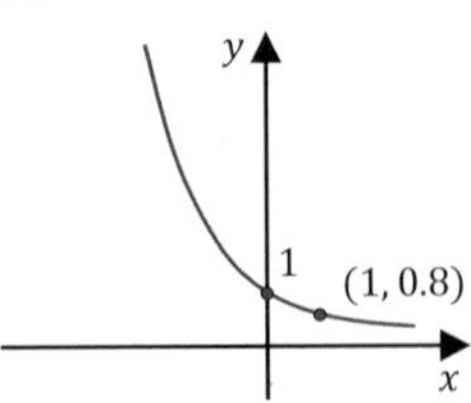

12.

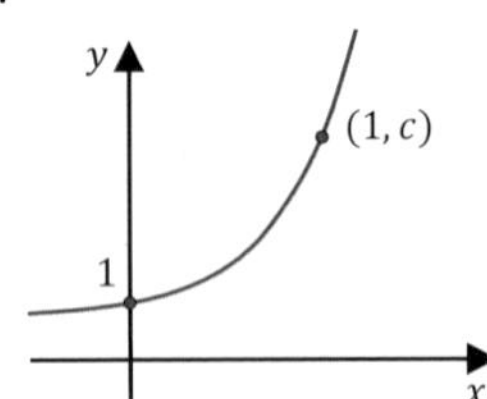

Exercise 15.3B

1.

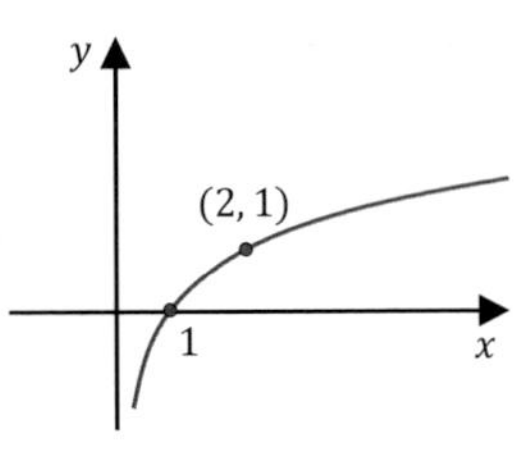

2.

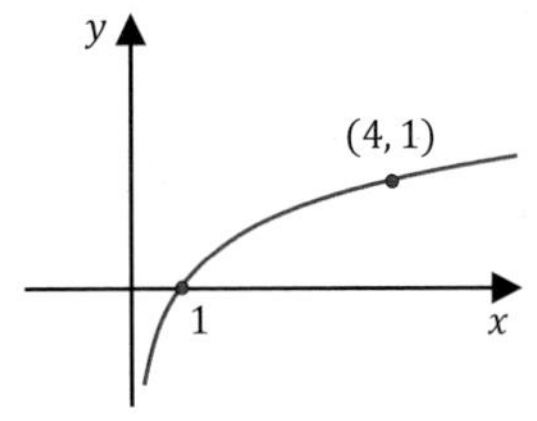

3.

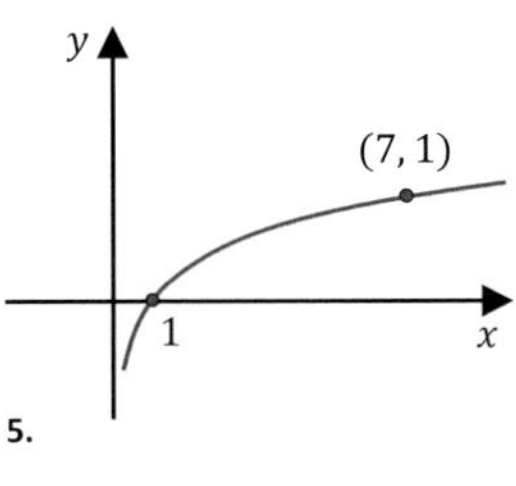

4.

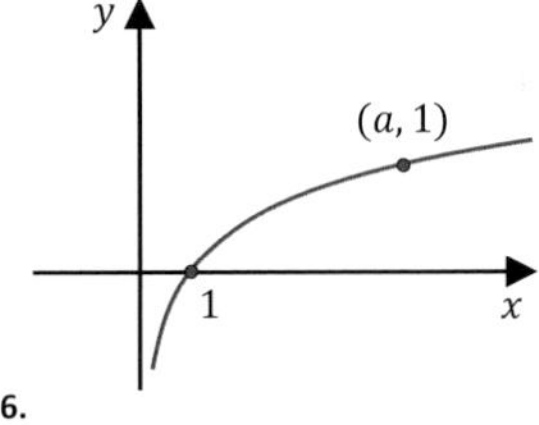

5.

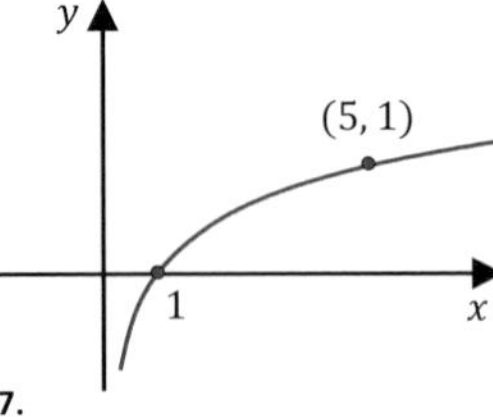

6.

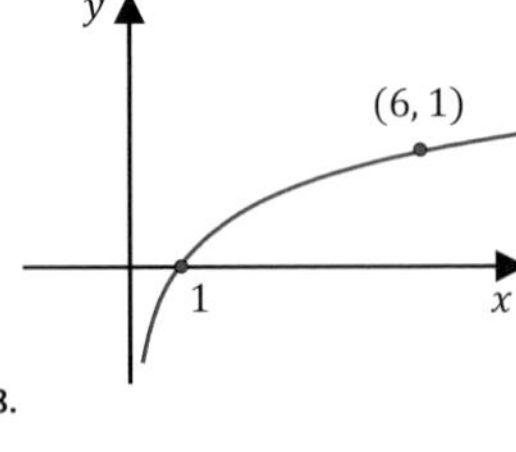

7.

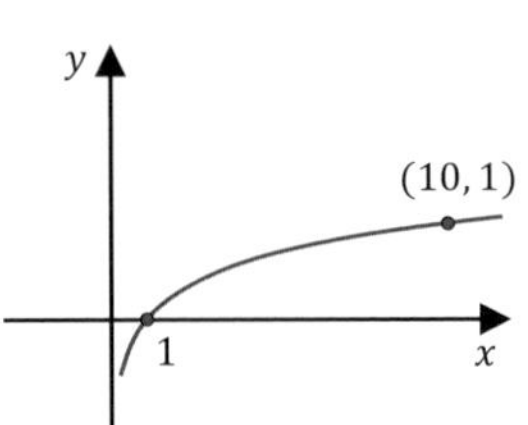

8.

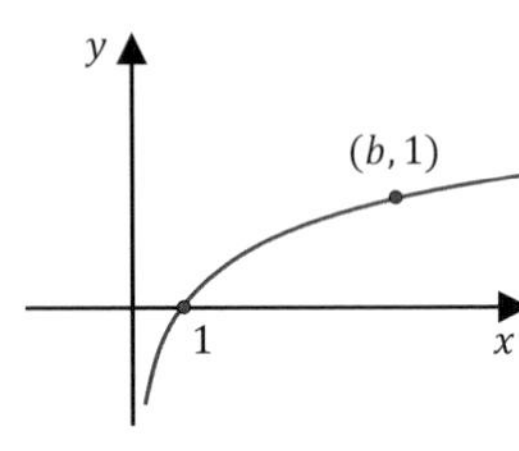

9.

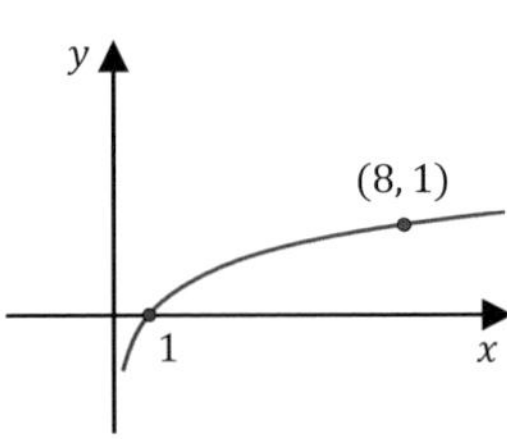

10.

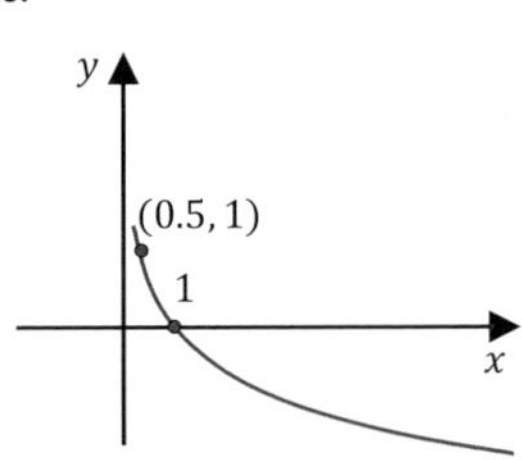

11.

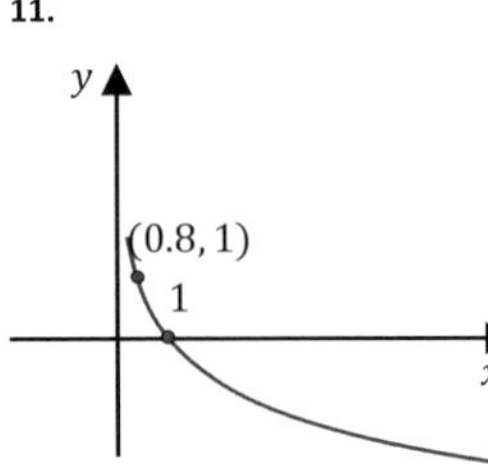

12.

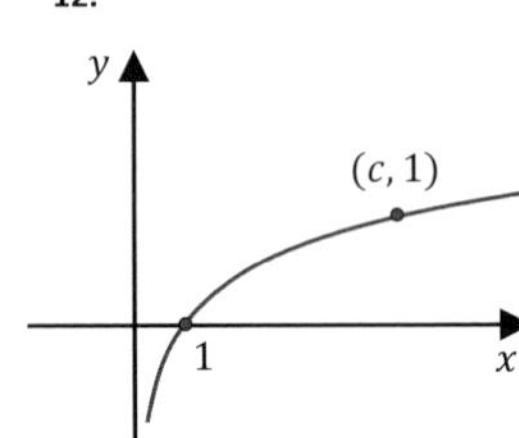

Exercise 15.4

1.

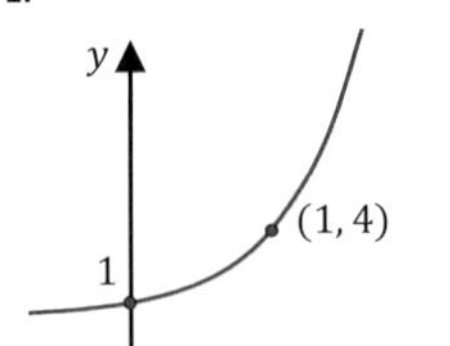

2.

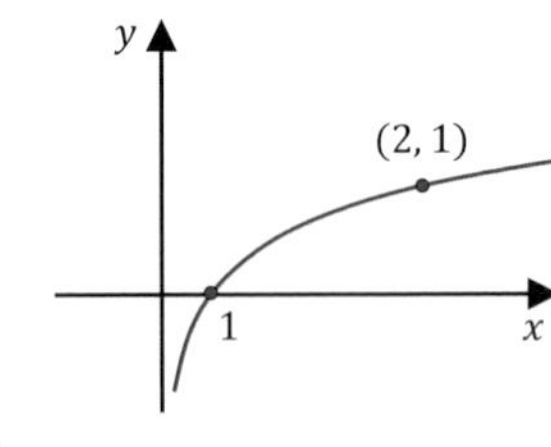

3.

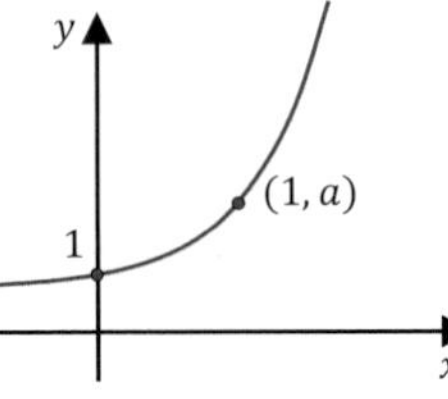

4.

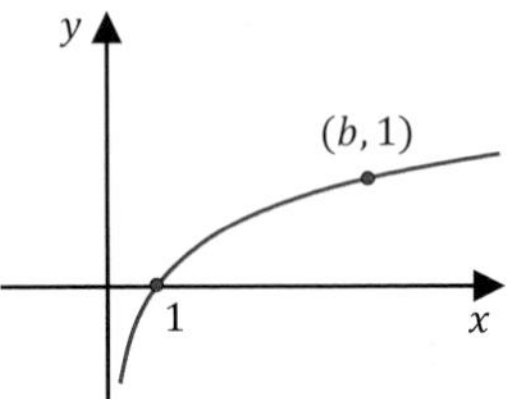

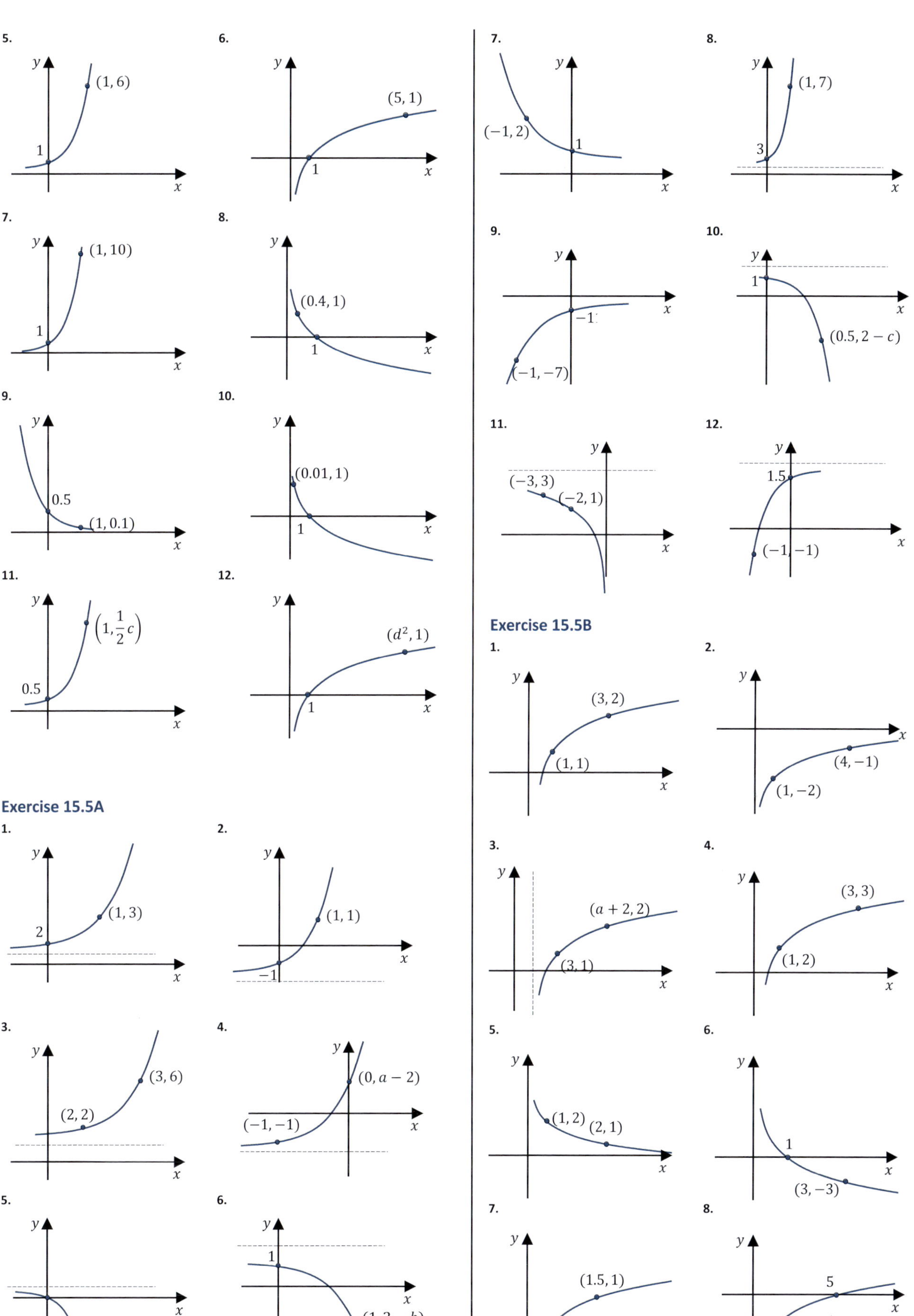

5.
(1, 6)
1
6.
(5, 1)
1
7.
(1, 10)
1
8.
(0.4, 1)
1
9.
0.5
(1, 0.1)
10.
(0.01, 1)
1
11.
$\left(1, \frac{1}{2}c\right)$
0.5
12.
$(d^2, 1)$
1
Exercise 15.5A
1.
(1, 3)
2
2.
(1, 1)
−1
3.
(3, 6)
(2, 2)
4.
(0, a − 2)
(−1, −1)
5.
(2, −15)
6.
1
(1, 2 − b)
7.
(−1, 2)
1
8.
(1, 7)
3
9.
−1
(−1, −7)
10.
1
(0.5, 2 − c)
11.
(−3, 3)
(−2, 1)
12.
1.5
(−1, −1)
Exercise 15.5B
1.
(3, 2)
(1, 1)
2.
(4, −1)
(1, −2)
3.
(a + 2, 2)
(3, 1)
4.
(3, 3)
(1, 2)
5.
(1, 2)
(2, 1)
6.
1
(3, −3)
7.
(1.5, 1)
0.5
8.
5
(1, −2)

9.

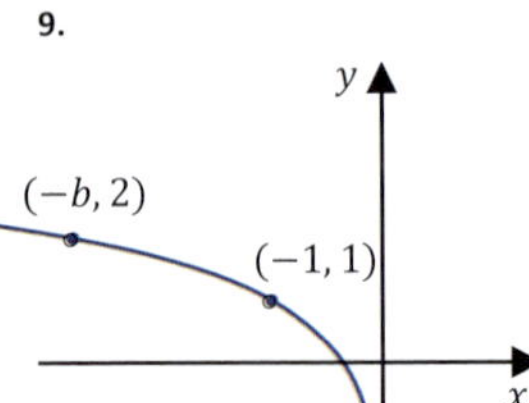

10.

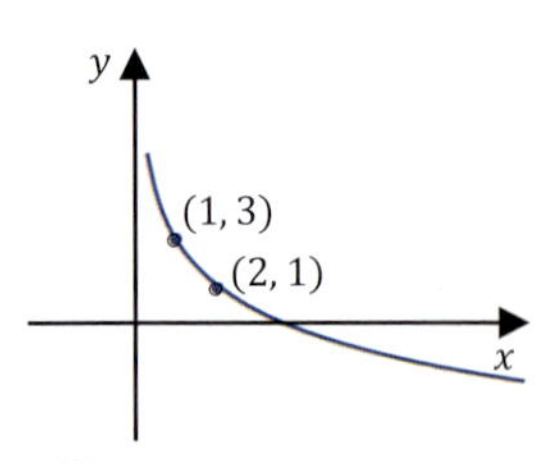

11.

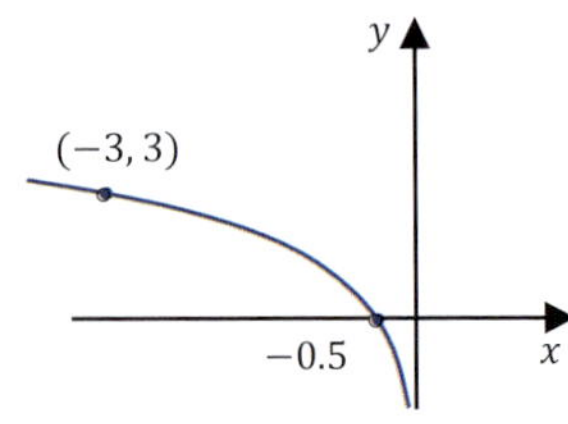

12.

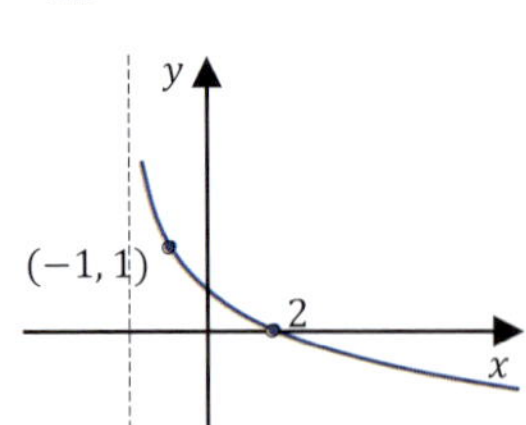

Exercise 15.6

1.

(a) 2 (b) 2 (c) 5
(d) 2 (e) 2 (f) 4

2.

(a) 2 (b) 2 (c) 2
(d) 3 (e) 3 (f) 2

3.

(a) 9 (b) 12 (c) 18
(d) 6 (e) 30 (f) 20

4.

(a) 2 (b) 2 (c) 2
(d) 2 (e) $\frac{5}{3}$ (f) 2
(g) 2 (h) 2 (i) 2

5.

(a) 3 (b) 2 (c) 2
(d) 2 (e) 2.68 (f) 2

Exercise 15.7A

1.

(a) $x = 3$ (b) $x = 10$ (c) $x = 3$
(d) $x = 7$ (e) $x = \frac{1}{4}$ (f) $x = 3$

2.

(a) $x = \frac{81}{2}$ (b) $x = 625$ (c) $x = \frac{81}{16}$
(d) $x = 3.27$ (e) $x = 4$ (f) $x = \frac{1}{2}$

3.

(a) $x = 5$ (b) $x = \frac{5}{6}$ (c) $x = \frac{1}{2}$
(d) $x = 4$ (e) $x = 7$ (f) $x = -\frac{5}{3}$
(g) $x = -\frac{12}{25}$ (h) $x = -\frac{1}{24}$ (i) $x = -0.44$
(j) $x = \frac{367}{729}$

Exercise 15.7B

1.

(a) $x = 4$ (b) $x = 1$ (c) $x = 2$
(d) $x = 1$ *twice* (e) $x = 1,4$ (f) $x = 4$
(g) $x = 2$ (h) $x = \sqrt{58}$

2.

(a) $x = 4$ (b) $x = 6$ (c) $x = 6$
(d) $x = 37$ (e) $x = 1$ (f) $x = 0$
(g) $x = 128$ (h) $x = 1$

Exercise 15.7C

1.

(a) $a = 4$ (b) $a = 6$ (c) $a = 2$
(d) $a = 0.74$ (e) $a = 16$ (f) $a = 5$
(g) $a = 5$ (h) $a = 1296$ (i) $a = 4.33$

2.

(a) $x = 9$ (b) $x = 16$ (c) $x = 4$
(d) $x = 512$ (e) $x = 125$ (f) $x = 27$

Exercise 15.8A

1.

(a) $A(x) = 3$ (b) $A(x) = 5$ (c) $A(x) = 20$
(d) $A(x) = 4$ (e) $A(x) = 6$ (f) $A(x) = 19$
(g) $A(x) = 11$ (h) $A(x) = 100$ (i) $A(x) = 50$
(j) $A(x) = \frac{2}{3}$ (k) $A(x) = \frac{1}{4}$ (l) $A(x) = 8.4$

2.

(a) $A(x) = 29.56$ (b) $A(x) = 4034.29$ (c) $A(x) = 3227.43$
(d) $A(x) = 0.82$ (e) $A(x) = 80.34$ (f) $A(x) = 44.33$
(g) $A(x) = 2.71$ (h) $A(x) = 30.12$

Exercise 15.8B

1.

(a) $x = 2.30$ (b) $x = 2.08$ (c) $x = 2.64$
(d) $x = 5.30$ (e) $x = -0.69$ (f) $x = -0.29$
(g) $x = 1.39$ (h) $x = 0.92$ (i) $x = 3.58$
(j) $x = 4.61$ (k) $x = 5.32$ (l) $x = 7.56$

2.

(a) $x = 0.35$ (b) $x = 0.32$ (c) $x = 0.35$
(d) $x = 0.73$ (e) $x = 1.01$ (f) $x = -2.41$
(g) $x = 5.28$ (h) $x = -14.00$ (i) $x = -15.13$
(j) $x = -15.56$ (k) $x = -10.74$ (l) $x = -11.70$

Exercise 15.8C

1.

(a) $t = 23.10$ (b) $t = 17.33$ (c) $t = 693.15$
(d) $t = 10.05$ (e) $t = 11.95$ (f) $t = 301.37$
(g) $t = 172.85$ (h) $t = 210.04$

2.

(a) $t = 34.66$ (b) $t = 1.73$ (c) $t = 231.05$
(d) $t = 138.63$ (e) $t = 161.20$ (f) $t = 106.64$
(g) $t = 1824.07$ (h) $t = 169.06$

Exercise 15.8D

1. (a) $B(0) = 2800$ (b) $t = 4.95$ *hours*

2. (a) $A(0) = 8$ (b) $t = 3.47\ days$
3. (a) $V(0) = 56$ (b) $t = 4.78\ hours$
4. (a) $A(0) = 196$ (b) $t = 16.50\ years$
5. (a) $P(0) = 32$ (b) $t = 8.56\ days$
6. (a) $S_0 = 4006$ (b) $t = 8\ days$
7. (a) $k = 1.7$ (b) $t = 5.93\ hours$
8. (a) $k = 0.025$ (b) $Correct$, there is 8.2%.
9. (a) $k = 0.46$ (b) $R_0 = 50.37g$
10. (a) $P(0) = 16$ (b) $t = 45.44\ years$
11. (a) $S_0 = 99{,}317$ (b) $t = 17\ days$
12. (a) $k = 1.3$ (b) $t = 9\ hours$
13. (a) $k = 0.046$ (b) $incorrect$

Exercise 15.9A

1. $a = 4, k = 8$
2. $a = 27, k = 1$
3. $a = 5, k = 25$
4. $a = 100, k = 1000$
5. $a = 49, k = 343$
6. $a = 3, k = 6561$
7. $a = 81, k = 1$
8. $a = 64, k = 0.5$
9. $a = 125, k = 625$

Exercise 15.9B

1. $k = 32, n = 2$
2. $k = 9, n = 2$
3. $k = 4, n = 5$
4. $k = 2, n = 5$
5. $k = 8, n = 4$
6. $k = 16, n = 3$
7. $k = 2, n = 3$
8. $k = 9, n = 1/2$
9. $k = 2, n = 4$

Exercise 15.10

15.1.

(a) (i) $a = 2$ (ii) $a = -3$ (iii) $a = \frac{1}{4}$

(b) (i) 0 (ii) 1.95 (iii) -3

15.2.

(a) $f(x) = 5^x$ (b) $f(x) = 4^x + 2$ (c) $f(x) = 5(4)^x$

(d)) $f(x) = log_2 x$ (e) $f(x) = log_4(x-2)$

(f) $f(x) = log_3(x+3)$

15.3.

(a)

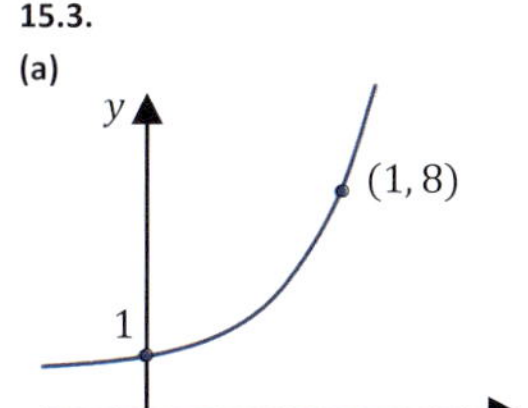

(b)

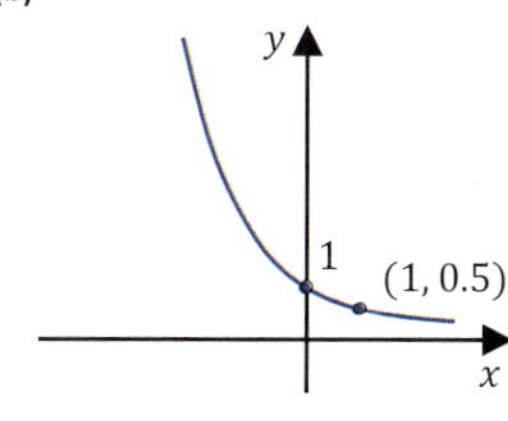

(c)

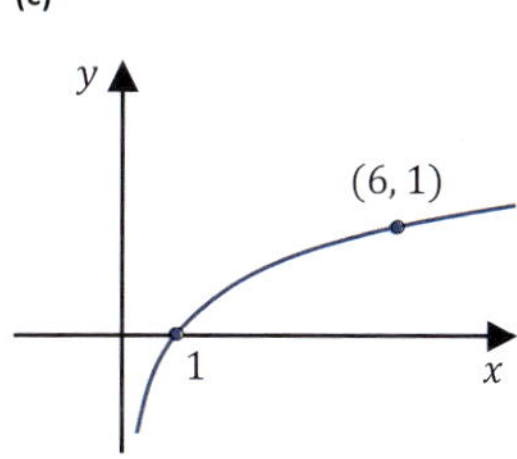

(d)

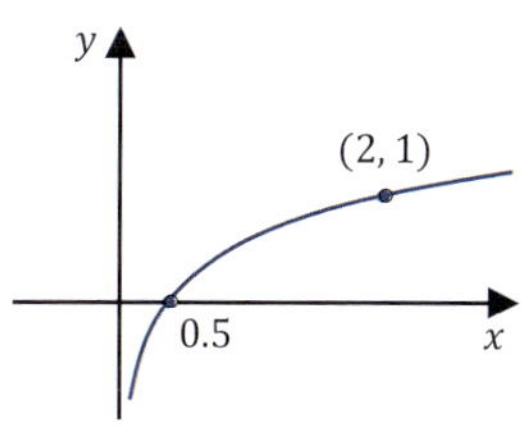

15.4.

(a)

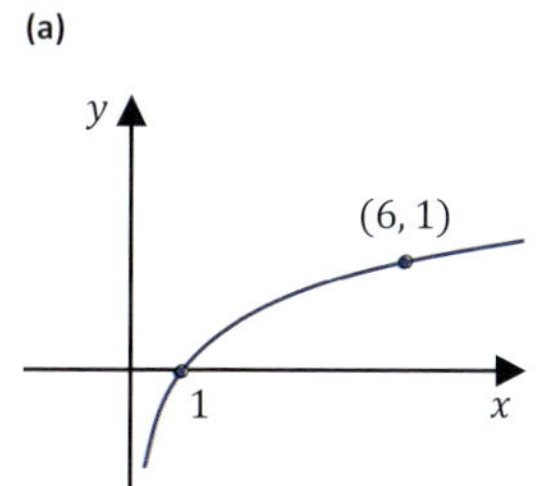

(b)

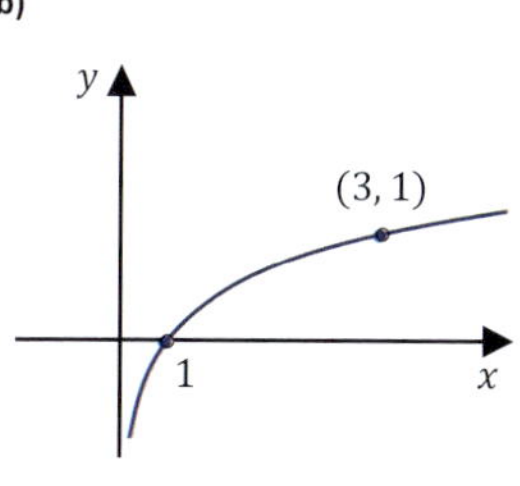

(c)

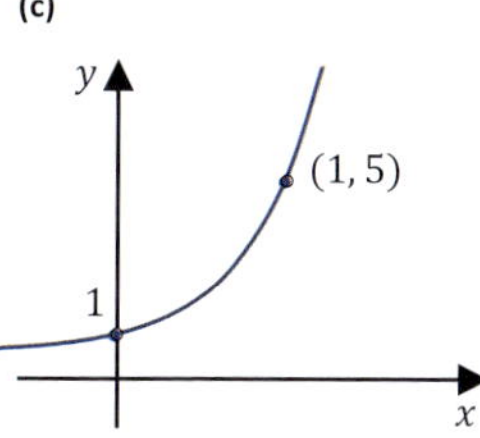

(d)

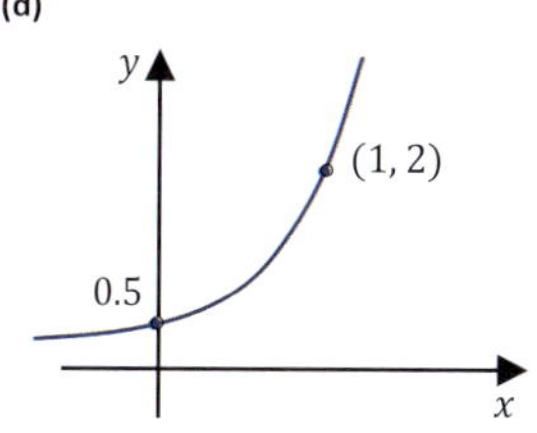

15.5

(a)

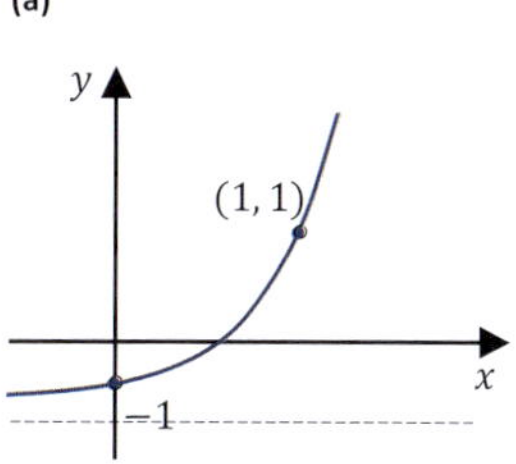

(b)

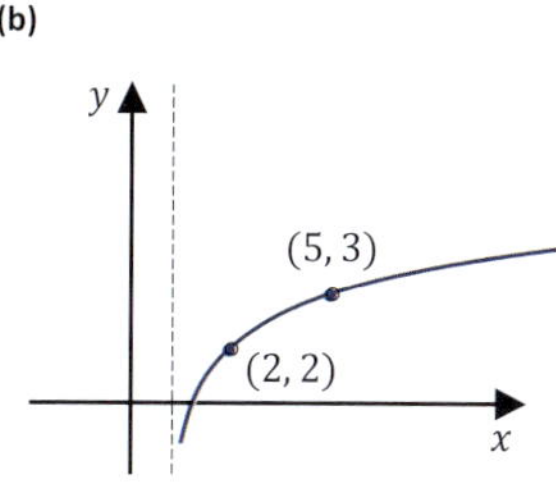

(c)

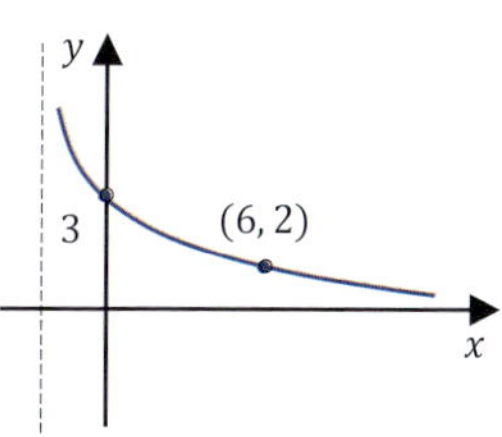

15.6.

(a) 1 (b) 2 (c) 6.58

15.7.

(a) $x = 8$ (b) $x = -1$ (c) $x = 1$

(d) $a = 81$

15.8.

(a) $V(0) = 44$ (b) $t = 31.35\ hours$

15.9.

$a = 64, k = 4$

Chapter 16

Exercise 16.1A

2.4-5

(a) $x = -1, x = 3$ (b) $x = -2, x = 3$

(c) $x = -8, x = 8$ (d) $x = \frac{-2-\sqrt{5}}{2}, x = \frac{-2+\sqrt{5}}{2}$

(e) $x = \frac{3}{4}, x = 1$ (f) $x = \frac{2-\sqrt{26}}{2}, x = \frac{2+\sqrt{26}}{2}$

2.6

(a) $\left(x+\frac{9}{2}\right)^2-\frac{25}{4}$ (b) $-\left(x-\frac{7}{2}\right)^2+\frac{81}{4}$ (c) $4\left(x-\frac{3}{2}\right)^2+5$

2.7

(a) $x=2-\sqrt{7}, x=2+\sqrt{7}$ (b) $x=2-2\sqrt{6}, x=2+2\sqrt{6}$

(c) $x=\frac{4-\sqrt{13}}{2}, x=\frac{4+\sqrt{13}}{2}$

2.10

(a) $x<-4, x>9$ (b) $-3<x<7$ (c) $x\leq-\frac{1}{4}, x\geq 4$

2.12

(a) $k<0, k>6$ (b) $k=1$ (c) $-2<k<6$

2.13

(a) $(-4,17)$ (b) $(3,22)$

2.14

(a) $b^2-4ac<0$, $\therefore$ the line and curve do not intersect.

(b) $b^2-4ac>0$, $\therefore$ there are two points of intersection.

2.15

(a) $(-5,-10), (4,-1)$ (b) $(-4,2), (6,22)$

2.16

(a) $(-2,1), (8,151)$ (b) $(1,-12), (5,12)$

Exercise 16.1B

4.1A.

(a) $x\neq 2$ (b) $x\neq\pm\sqrt{5}$ (c) $x\neq 3,-1$

(d) $x\geq-8$ (e) $x\leq-3, x\geq 3$ (f) $x\leq\frac{5}{2}$

4.1B.

(a) $6\leq x\leq 1006$ (b) $-2\leq x\leq 373$ (c) $11\leq x\leq 161$

4.3A.

(a) $2x^3+1$ (b) $12x^2-35$ (c) $\frac{2x-10}{18-3x}$

4.3B.

(a) 58 (b) -15

4.4.

(a) $\frac{2x+8}{5}$ (b) $\frac{5x+8}{4}$ (c) $\left(\frac{6x+5}{2}\right)^{1/3}$

Exercise 16.1C

1.

(a)

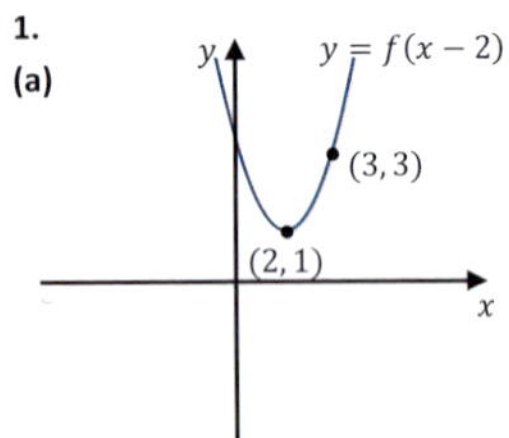

(b)

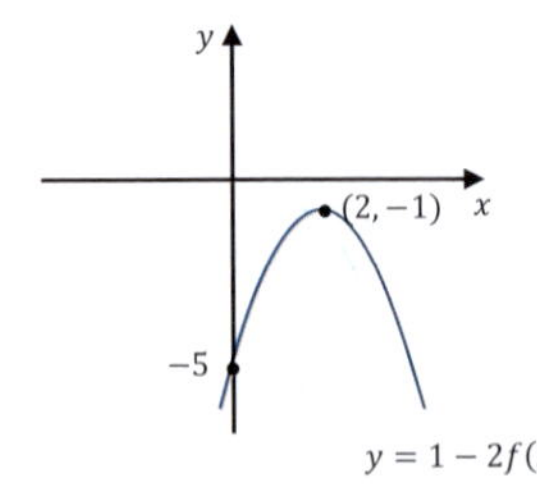

(c)

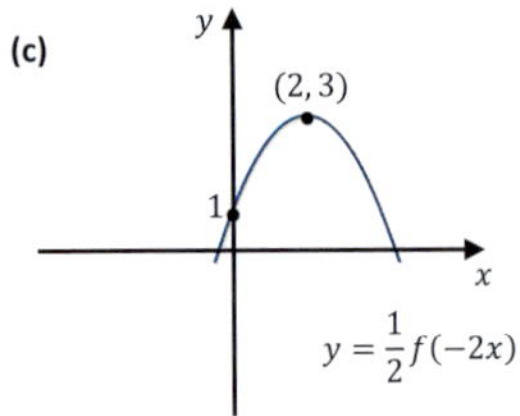

2.

(a)

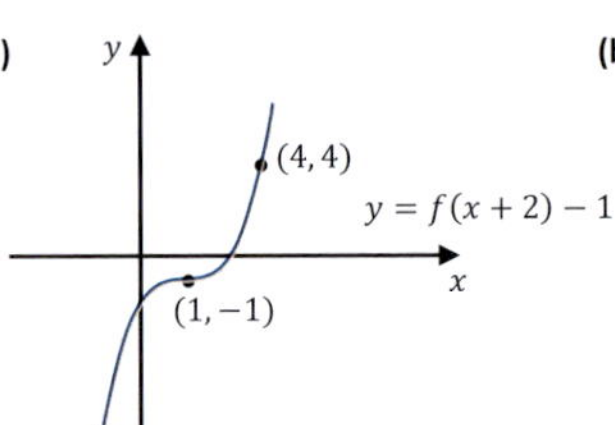

(b)

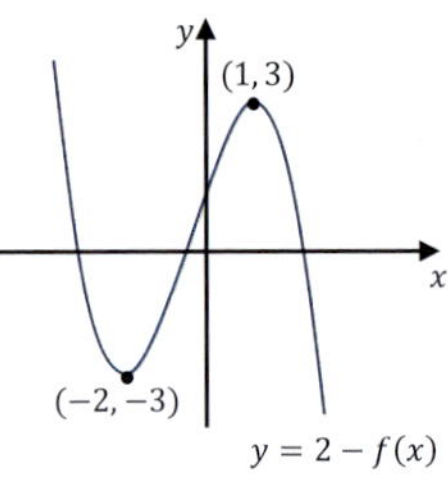

(c)

y
$y=3f\left(\frac{1}{2}x\right)$
x
(8, −3)

3.

(a)

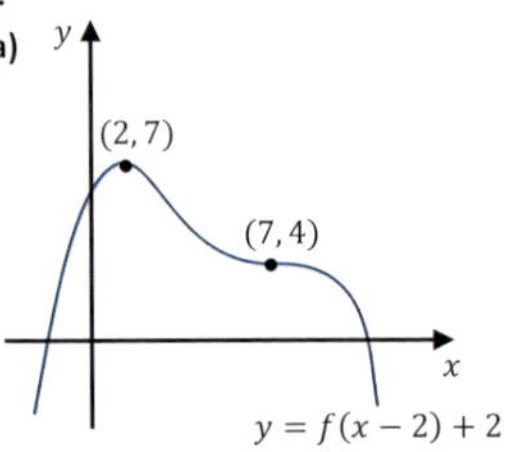

(b)

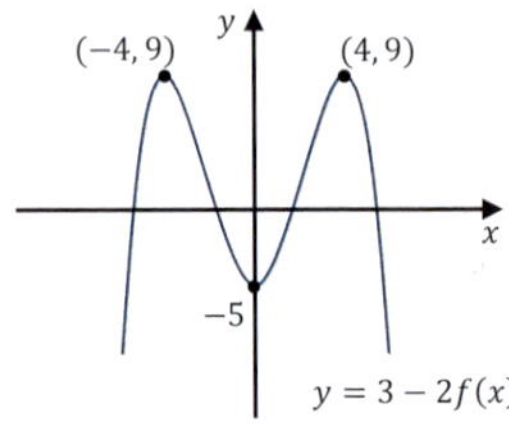

(c)

y
12
$y=f(x+2)+2$
−2
x
(3, −6)

Exercise 16.1D

6.1

(a) $u_4=4585.28$ (b) $u_4=50$ (c) $u_4=20{,}987$

6.2

(a) $a=2, b=4$ (b) $a=1.5, b=11$ (c) $a=5, b=-12$

6.3A

(a) No, $5>1$ (b) Yes, $-1<0.35<1$

(c) Yes, $-1<-0.8<1$

6.3B

(a) $1<k<3$ (b) $2<k<4$ (c) $\frac{5}{2}<k<\frac{7}{2}$

6.4

(a) $L=100$ (b) $L=1500$ (c) $L=150$

6.5A £3798.46

6.5B

(a) 286 Litres

(b) Yes, the trees will survive as the limit is 205.9 and $205.9>200$.

Exercise 16.1E

7.1

(a) $(x-3)(x-1)(x+2)$ (b) $(x-2)(x+2)(x+3)$

(c) (i) $(x-3)(x+1)(x+4)$ (ii) $(x-2)(x-1)(x+5)$

7.2

(a) $x = -3, x = -1, x = 3$ **(b)** $x = -3\ twice, x = 3$

(c) $x = -1, x = 4, x = 5$

7.3

(a) -38 **(b)** -8

7.4

(a) $a = -5, b = -6$ **(b)** $a = -4, b = 4$

7.5

(a) $(-1, -10), (-6, -35), (1, 0)$

(b) $(-2, -11), (2, 9)$

(c) $(-1, -1), (1, 1), (4, 124)$

7.6

(a) $f(x) = -(x+3)(x-1)(x-3)$

(b) $f(x) = \frac{1}{3}x(x-2)(x+2)$

(c) $f(x) = -2(x+2)(x-1)^2(x-4)$

Exercise 16.1F

15.1.

(a) (i) $a = 2$ **(ii)** $a = -4$ **(iii)** $a = \frac{1}{3}$

(b) (i) 0 **(ii)** 3 **(iii)** -5

15.2.

(a) $f(x) = 9^x$ **(b)** $f(x) = 7^x + 1$ **(c)** $f(x) = 4(3)^x$

(d) $f(x) = log_5 x$ **(e)** $f(x) = log_3(x-1)$

(f) $f(x) = log_4(x+4)$

15.3.

(a)

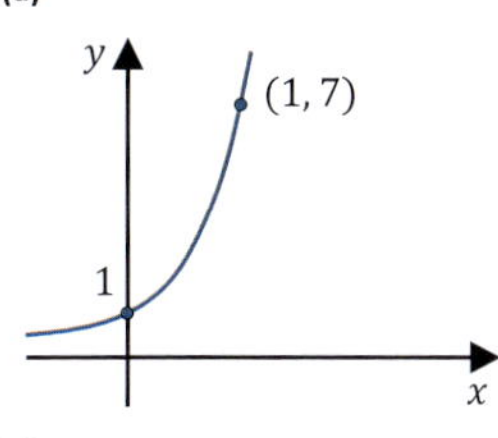

(b)

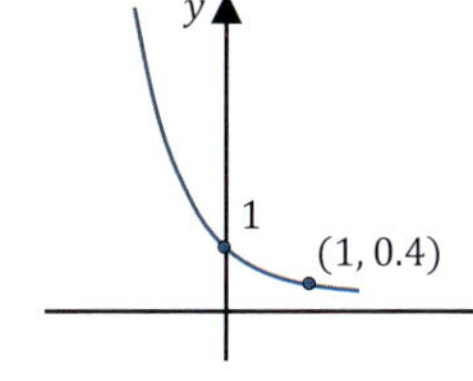

(c)

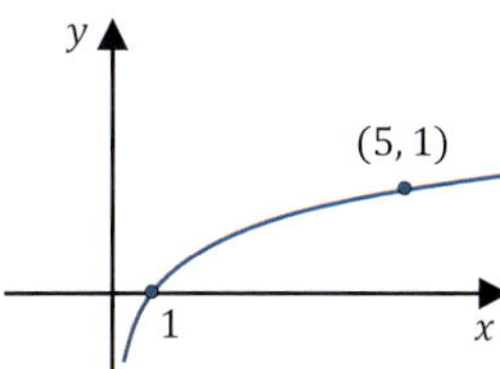

(d)

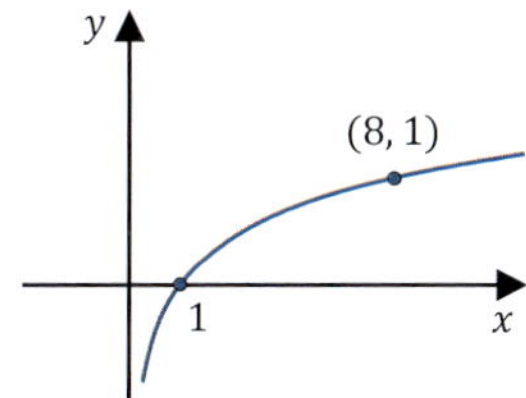

15.4

(a)

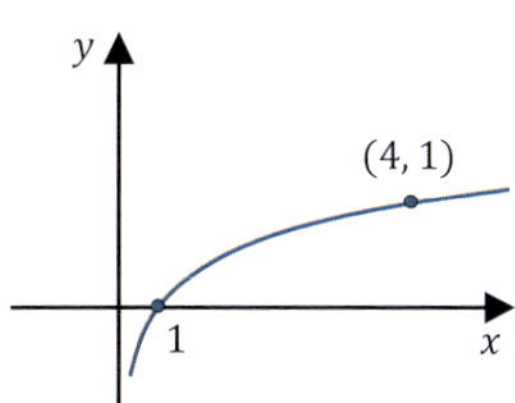

(b)

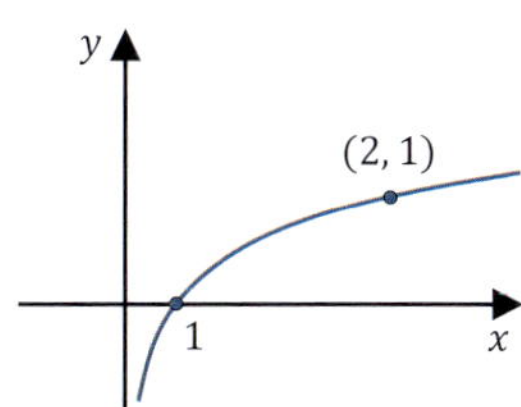

(c)

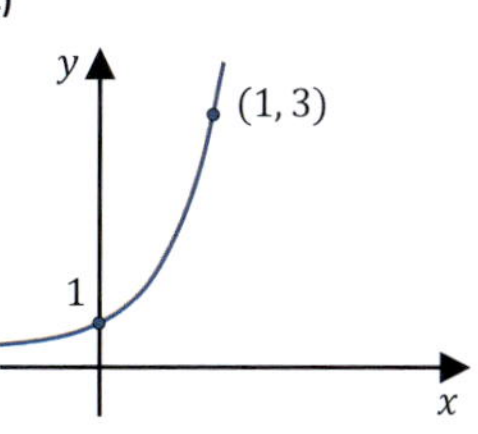

(d)

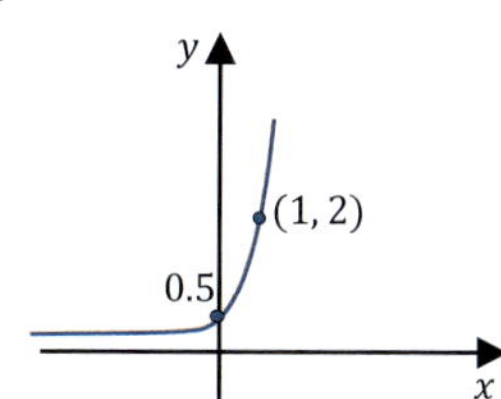

15.5

(a)

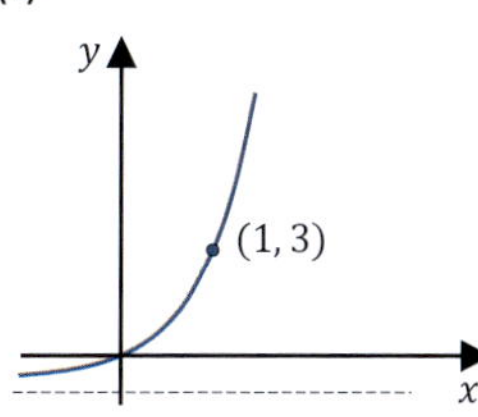

(b)

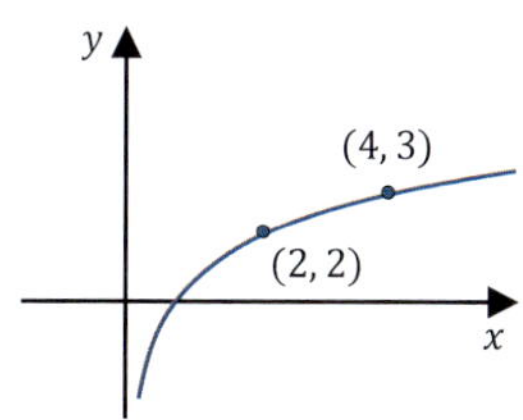

(c)

15.6.

(a) $\frac{1}{2}$ **(b)** 2 **(c)** 2

15.7.

(a) $x = 4$ **(b)** $x = 27$ **(c)** $x = 4$

(d) $a = 4$

15.8. (a) $A(0) = 14$ **(b)** $t = 3.3\ days$

15.9. $a = 4\sqrt{2}, k = 8\sqrt{2}$

Exercise 16.2A

1.1

(a) $2x - 3y + 4 = 0$ **(b)** $3x + y - 20 = 0$

(c) $4x - y - 12 = 0$

1.2 (a) $(10, -5)$ **(b)** $(-2, 9)$ **(c)** $(0, 6)$

1.3 (a) $m = \frac{1}{7}$ **(b)** $m = 2$ **(c)** $m = -\frac{2}{9}$

1.4 (a) $\theta = 45°$ **(b)** $y = -\frac{1}{\sqrt{3}}x + 4$

1.5 (a) *not collinear* **(b)** *collinear*

1.6 (a) $2x - 5y + 20 = 0$ **(b)** $y = -30x + 70$

1.7 (a) $(2, 1)$ **(b)** $(4, -7)$ **(c)** $(1, 4)$

1.8 (a) $x + 2y - 29 = 0$ **(b)** $2x - y - 13 = 0$

(c) $3x + 5y - 26 = 0$

1.9 (a) $x - y + 11 = 0$ **(b)** $3x + 10y - 51 = 0$

1.10(a) $9x - y - 79 = 0$ **(b)** $5x + 4y - 37 = 0$

Exercise 16.2B

2.1

(a) 13 **(b)** $\sqrt{317}$ **(c)** 25

2.2

(a) $(x-3)^2 + (y+5)^2 = 82$ **(b)** $(x+1)^2 + (y-14)^2 = 74$

(c) $(x+2)^2 + (y-1)^2 = 340$

2.3

(a) $Centre: (0,0), Radius = 6$

(b) $Centre: (2,-7), Radius = 3\sqrt{5}$

(c) $Centre: (3,-4), Radius = 8$

(d) $Centre: (0,6), Radius = 2\sqrt{21}$

2.4

(a) inside the circle **(b)** outside the circle

2.5

(a) two points of intersection between the line and the circle

(b) one point of intersection between the line and the circle

2.6

(a) (i) $(0,-2)$ and $(8,2)$ **(ii)** $(5,-10)$ and $(-5,0)$

(b) proof, point of contact $(2,9)$

2.7

(a) $y = 10 - x$ **(b)** $y = x - 25$

2.8

(a) circles touch internally **(b)** circles do not intersect

2.9

(a) $(x-12)^2 + (y-6)^2 = 9$ **(b)** $(x-40)^2 + (y-20)^2 = 64$

Exercise 16.2C

14.4

(a) $\boldsymbol{u} = \begin{pmatrix} \frac{3}{5} \\ 0 \\ -\frac{4}{5} \end{pmatrix}$ **(b)** $\boldsymbol{u} = \begin{pmatrix} -\frac{8}{17} \\ \frac{9}{17} \\ -\frac{12}{17} \end{pmatrix}$ **(c)** $\boldsymbol{u} = \begin{pmatrix} \frac{14}{15} \\ -\frac{2}{15} \\ \frac{1}{3} \end{pmatrix}$

14.5

(a) $2\sqrt{53}$ **(b)** $a = -1, a = 3$

14.6

(a) Proof **(b)** Points are **not** collinear **(c)** $k = -23$

14.7

(a) $P = (1,-2,-7)$ **(b)** $B = \left(-\frac{21}{2}, 17, \frac{5}{2}\right)$

14.8

(a) $3:2$ **(b)** $k = 14$

14.9

(a) (i) 20 **(ii)** 5 **(b)** 7

(c) Proof **(d)** $a = 3$ **(e)** $-10\sqrt{3}$

14.10

(a) $71.5°$ **(b)** $55.9°$

14.11

(a) -1 **(b)** 1 **(c)** 10

14.12

(a) $\overrightarrow{BE} = \boldsymbol{q} + \boldsymbol{r} - \boldsymbol{p}$ **(b)** $\overrightarrow{AM} = \boldsymbol{r} + \frac{1}{2}\boldsymbol{p}$

(c) $\overrightarrow{AG} = \frac{1}{6}\boldsymbol{p} + \frac{2}{3}\boldsymbol{q} + \boldsymbol{r}$ **(d)** $\overrightarrow{GM} = \frac{1}{3}\boldsymbol{p} - \frac{2}{3}\boldsymbol{q}$

Exercise 16.3A

8.1

(a) $y = 4\sin x - 1$ **(b)** $y = -3\cos 2x + 1$

(c) $y = 2\cos 3x - 1$ **(d)** $y = 3\cos(x - 45°)$

(e) $y = 2\sin(x - 45°)$ **(f)** $y = 4\sin(x - 60°)$

8.2

(a) $x = 26.6°, 206.6°$

(b) $x = 270°$

(c) $x = 15°, 75°, 195°, 255°$

(d) $x = 0°, 120°, 240°, 360°$

(e) $x = 130°, 250°$

(f) $x = 140.5°, 359.5°$

8.3

(a) $\frac{\sqrt{3}}{2}$ **(b)** $\frac{\sqrt{3}}{2}$ **(c)** -1 **(d)** $-\frac{\sqrt{3}}{2}$

(e) $-\frac{1}{2}$ **(f)** $\frac{\sqrt{2}}{2}$ **(g)** $\sqrt{3}$ **(h)** $\frac{1}{2}$

8.4

(a) $x = 90°$

(b) $x = 131.8°, 228.2°$

(c) $x = 22.5°, 157.5°, 202.5°, 337.5°$

(d) $x = 30°, 60°, 210°, 240°$

(e) $x = 330°, 150°$

(f) $x = 130°, 190°$

8.5

(a) $x = 1.2, 4.4$ **(b)** $x = 3.5, 5.9$

(c) $x = \frac{\pi}{12}, \frac{5\pi}{12}, \frac{13\pi}{12}, \frac{17\pi}{12}$ **(d)** $x = 0.4, 1.1, 3.6, 4.3$

(e) $x = 2.5, 4.6$ **(f)** $x = 3.3, 5.7$

8.6

(a) $(0.8, 4), (2.3, 4)$ **(b)** $\left(\frac{2\pi}{3}, -3\right), \left(\frac{4\pi}{3}, -3\right)$

(c) $(0.3, 2), (2.9, 2)$

Exercise 16.3B

9.1

(a) $\frac{1}{\sqrt{2}}(\cos x - \sin x)$ **(b)** $\frac{\sqrt{3}}{2}\sin x + \frac{1}{2}\cos x$

(c) $-\frac{1}{2}\sin x - \frac{\sqrt{3}}{2}\cos x$

9.2

(a) $\cos(a+b) = \frac{12-5\sqrt{3}}{26}$ **(b)** $\sin(a+b) = \frac{17}{5\sqrt{13}}$

9.3

(a) $\cos 2x = -\frac{11}{7}$ (b) $\sin 2x = \frac{3}{5}$ (c) $\cos 2x = \frac{21}{29}$

9.4

All questions are proofs

9.5

(a) $x = \frac{\pi}{6}, \frac{\pi}{2}, \frac{5\pi}{6}, \frac{3\pi}{2}$ (b) $x = 0, 2\pi$

Exercise 16.3C

10.1

(a) $\sqrt{13}\cos(x - 56.3)°$ (b) $\sqrt{14}\sin(x + 0.64)$

(c) $\sqrt{29}\cos(x + 5.90)$ (d) $\sqrt{41}\sin(x - 38.7)°$

10.2

(a) $x = 0.75, 4.48$ (b) $x = 0.36, 4.07$ (c) $x = 2.23, 5.91$

(d) (i) $\sqrt{5}\cos(x - 26.6)°$ (ii) $x = 90.0°, 323.2°$

(e) (i) $\sqrt{10}\sin(x + 18.4)°$ (ii) $x = 20.8°, 122.4°$

(f) (i) $3\sqrt{2}\cos\left(x + \frac{7\pi}{4}\right)$ (ii) $x = 0.93, 2.99, 4.07, 6.13$

(g) (i) $3\sin(x - 5.44)$ (ii) $x = 0.24, 2.34, 4.43$

10.3

(a) (i) $\sqrt{5}\cos(x - 63.43)°$

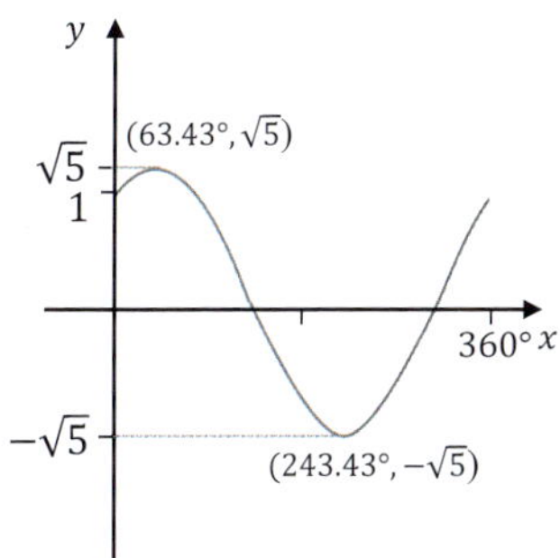

(b) (i) $\sqrt{18}\sin(x + 19.47)°$

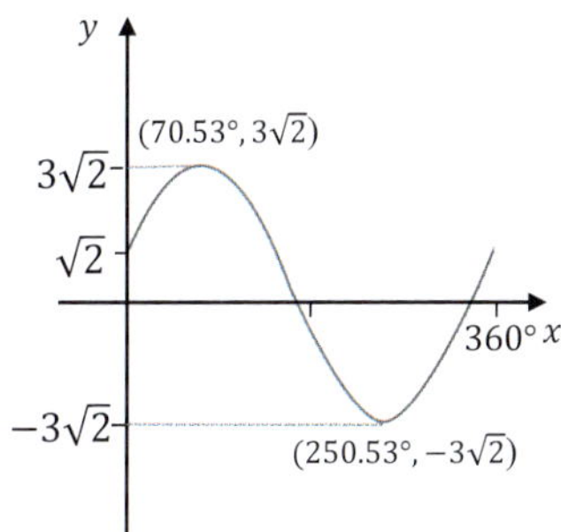

(c) (i) $\sqrt{6}\sin(x - 335.91)°$

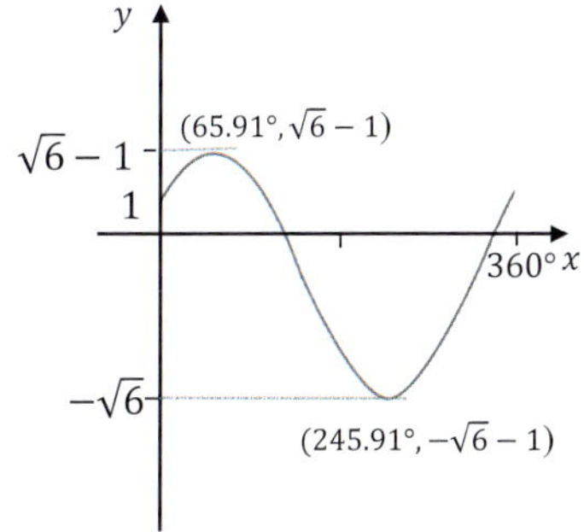

(d) (i) $\sqrt{3}\cos(x + 305.26)°$

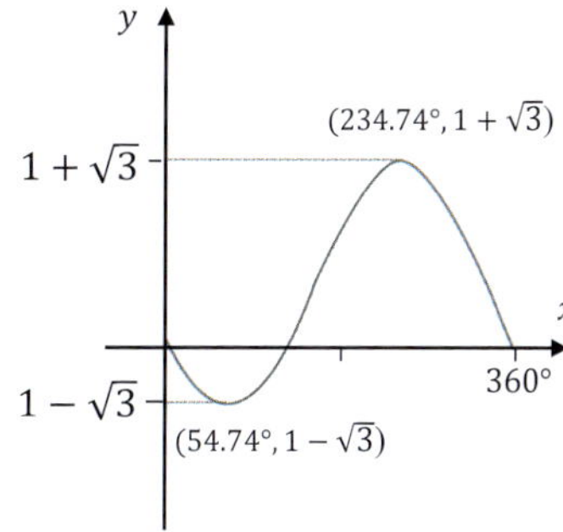

10.4

(a) (i) $2\sqrt{5}\cos(x + 26.6)°$ (ii) $max = 2\sqrt{5} - 3$ (iii) $x = 333.4°$

(b) (i) $\sqrt{34}\sin(x + 5.25)$ (ii) $min = 3 - 2\sqrt{34}$ (iii) $x = 2.60$

Exercise 16.4A

11.2

(a) $\frac{6}{\sqrt[4]{x}}$ (b) $6x^2 - 12x$ (c) $-\frac{5}{3\sqrt[3]{x^4}}$

11.3

(a) $\frac{7\sqrt{x^5}}{2} - 12x^3$ (b) $-\frac{4}{x^3} - \frac{9}{x^4} - \frac{4}{x^5}$ (c) $12\sqrt{x} - \frac{1}{\sqrt{x}} - \frac{1}{2\sqrt{x^3}}$

11.4

(a) 57 (b) 28 (c) $\frac{10{,}933}{54}$

11.5 $y = 23x + 13$

11.6

(a) $proof$ (b) $x < 0$ or $2 < x$ (c) $0 < x < 3$

(c) $x^2 - 4x + 11 > 0, \therefore f'(x) > 0\ \forall x, \Rightarrow$ function is always increasing.

11.7 Max. T.P. at $(-1, 10)$ and Min. T.P. at $(5, -98)$

11.8

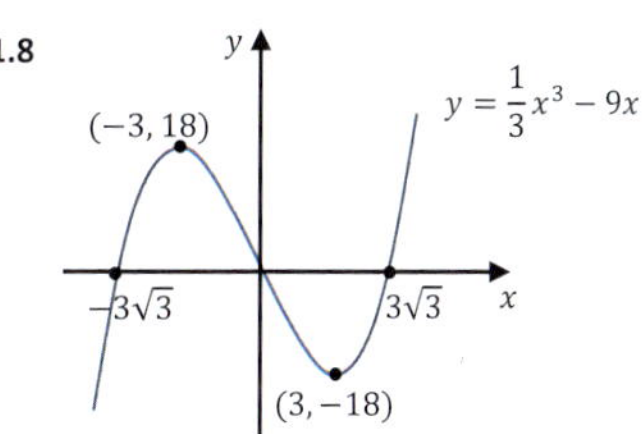

11.9

(a) $proof$ (b) $x = 6$

11.10 Max 70 when $x = 5$, Min -11 when $x = 2$

11.11

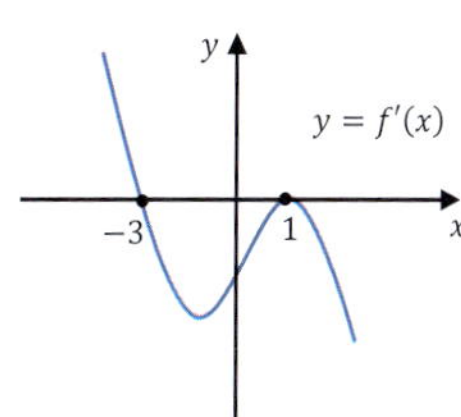

Exercise 16.4B

12.1

(a) $\frac{5x^3}{3}+C$ (b) $\frac{x^3}{3}+\frac{3x^2}{2}-x+C$ (c) $4\sqrt{x^3}+C$

12.2

(a) $2\sqrt{x}+C$ (b) $\frac{x^3}{3}+2x-\frac{1}{x}+C$ (c) $\frac{4\sqrt{x^5}}{5}+\frac{4\sqrt{x^3}}{3}+C$

12.3

(a)

(i) $\frac{8}{9}$ (ii) $-\frac{35}{6}$ (iii) $\frac{666}{5}$

(b)

(i) $a=1, a=2$ (ii) $a=5$ (iii) $a=9$

12.4

(a) $\frac{58}{3}\,units^2$ (b) $81\,units^2$ (c) $20\,units^2$

12.5

(a) $\frac{275}{6}\,units^2$ (b) $\frac{64}{3}\,units^2$ (c) $\frac{81}{4}\,units^2$

12.6

(a) $351.5\ litres$

Exercise 16.4C

13.1A

(a) $9(3x+5)^2$ (b) $8x(x^2-2)^3$

(c) $-6(3x+4)^{-3}$ (d) $3(2x-1)(x^2-x)^2$

(e) $-\frac{3x^2+2}{2\sqrt{(x^3+2x)^3}}$ (f) $2(3x^2-2)(x^3-2x)^3$

13.1B

(a) $-\frac{12}{(2x+1)^4}$ (b) $-\frac{2}{\sqrt{(4x-2)^3}}$ (c) $-\frac{2x+2}{\sqrt[3]{(x^2+2x)^4}}$

13.1C

(a) -12 (b) $-\frac{8}{12{,}167}$

(c) $-\frac{27}{625}$ (d) $-\frac{32}{\sqrt{205{,}379}}$

(e) $-5{,}292$ (f) $\frac{3\sqrt{10}}{5}$

13.2B

(a) $-12\sin 3x$ (b) $4\cos 2x-2\sin 2x$

(c) $-6\cos 2x$ (d) $4x\cos(2x^2+1)$

(e) $-3x^2\sin(x^3-1)$ (f) $10x\sin(5x^2+8)$

13.2C

(a) $10\sin x\cos x$ (b) $-6\cos^2 x\sin x$

(c) $-2\sin x\cos x+3\sin^2 x\cos x$

13.2D

(a) -4.95 (b) $\sqrt{3}$

(c) -2 (d) -2.43

13.3A

(a) $\frac{(3x-5)^4}{12}+C$ (b) $\frac{\sqrt{(4x+2)^3}}{2}+C$

(c) $-\frac{(7-2x)^6}{3}+C$ (d) $-\frac{2}{x+2}+C$

(e) $\frac{4\sqrt{3x+5}}{3}+C$ (f) $-9\sqrt[3]{2-3x}+C$

13.3B

(a) $-\frac{1}{6(3x+2)^2}+C$ (b) $\frac{9\sqrt[3]{(2x-2)^2}}{4}+C$ (c) $-\frac{4}{\sqrt{2x-5}}+C$

13.3C

(a) $\frac{148}{3}$ (b) $\frac{1{,}235}{3}$

(c) $\frac{5}{54}$ (d) $\frac{9}{28}$

(e) $\frac{3}{400}$ (f) $\sqrt{5}-1$

13.4A

(a) $-\frac{1}{2}\cos 2x+C$ (b) $\frac{3}{2}\sin 2x+C$

(c) $x+\cos 2x+C$ (d) $\frac{1}{2}\sin\left(2x-\frac{\pi}{6}\right)+C$

(e) $-\frac{2}{3}\cos\left(3x-\frac{\pi}{4}\right)+C$ (f) $x-\frac{1}{2}\cos(2x-0.6)+C$

13.4C

(a) -0.66 (b) -2.59 (c) 0.17

Exercise 16.5A

1.

(a) $\frac{12}{13}$ (b) $\frac{9\sqrt{13}}{169}$

2. (a) proof (b) $k<-1\ or\ k>\frac{3}{2}$

3. $f(x)=2x^3-x^2+x+9$

4. $c<68$

5. $2<x<4$

6. (a) proof (b) $4\left(x+\frac{1}{2}\right)^2+21$

(c)

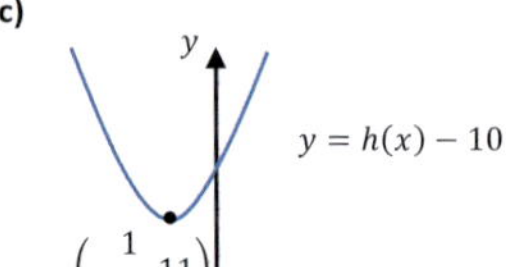

7.

(a) $y=-x-3$ (b) $C=(3,-6)$ (c) $D=(11,2)$

8.

(a)

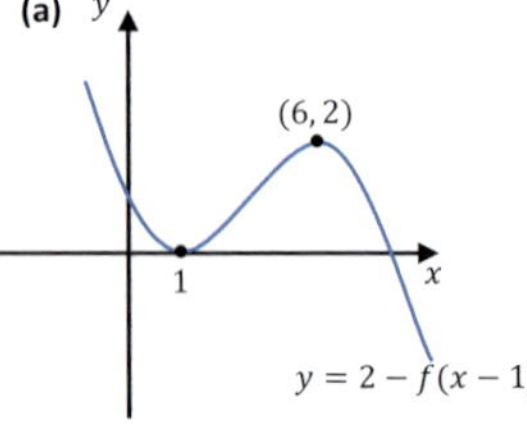

(b)

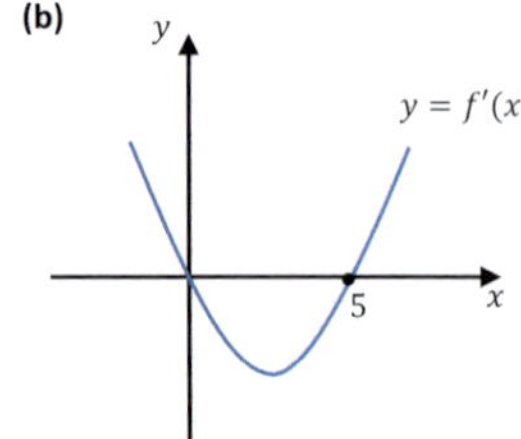

9. $\overrightarrow{DC}=\begin{pmatrix}-6\\-11\\2\end{pmatrix}$

Exercise 16.5B

1.

(a) proof (b) $r = 6.59$

2.

(a) 10 (b) $(x-2)^2 + (y-7)^2 = 25$

3.

(a) $48.8cm$ (b) $u_{n+1} = \frac{2}{3}u_n + 40$

(c) The slug and the snail will both reach the top.

4.

(a) $£0.0008$ (b) $0.50\ months$

5.

(a) $a = -2, b = 4, k = \frac{1}{4}$ (b) $27\ units^2$

6.

(a) $£16{,}000$ (b) $£0$

(c) Within the 4-month period, the investment reaches a maximum of £18,519 when $t = \frac{2}{3}$

7. $27{,}000cm^2$

8. $c = 4 + 2\sqrt{21}, c = 4 - 2\sqrt{21}$